CW00505368

BIG EASY REA

BRITAIN

Contents

15th edition June 2019

© AA Media Limited 2019

Original edition printed 1991.

Cartography: All cartography in this atlas edited, designed and produced by the Mapping Services Department of AA Publishing (A05685).

This atlas contains Ordnance Survey data © Crown copyright and database right 2019.

Contains public sector information licensed under the Open Government Licence v3.0

Distances and journey times contains data available from openstreetmap.org © under the Open Database License found at opendatacommons.org

Publisher's Notes: Published by AA Publishing (a trading name of AA Media Limited, whose registered office is Fanum House, Basing View, Basingstoke, Hampshire RG21 4EA, UK. Registered number 06112600).

ISBN: 978 0 7495 8127 5 (spiral bound)
ISBN: 978 0 7495 8126 8 (paperback)

A CIP catalogue record for this book is available from The British Library.

Disclaimer: The contents of this atlas are believed to be correct at the time of the latest revision, it will not contain any subsequent amended, new or temporary information including diversions and traffic control or enforcement systems. The publishers cannot be held responsible or liable for any loss or damage occasioned to any person acting or refraining from action as a result of any use or reliance on material in this atlas, nor for any errors, omissions or changes in such material. This does not affect your statutory rights.

The publishers would welcome information to correct any errors or omissions and to keep this atlas up to date. Please write to the Atlas Editor, AA Publishing, The Automobile Association, Fanum House, Basing View, Basingstoke, Hampshire RG21 4EA, UK.
E-mail: *roadatlasfeedback@theaa.com*

Acknowledgements: AA Publishing would like to thank the following for information used in the creation of this atlas:
Cadw, English Heritage, Forestry Commission, Historic Scotland, National Trust and National Trust for Scotland, RSPB, The Wildlife Trust, Scottish Natural Heritage, Natural England, The Countryside Council for Wales. Award winning beaches from 'Blue Flag' and 'Keep Scotland Beautiful' (summer 2018 data): for latest information visit *www.blueflag.org* and *www.keepscotlandbeautiful.org*. Road signs are © Crown Copyright 2019. Reproduced under the terms of the Open Government Licence.

Printer: Elcograf S.p.A, Italy

Scale 1:160,000
or 2.52 miles to 1 inch

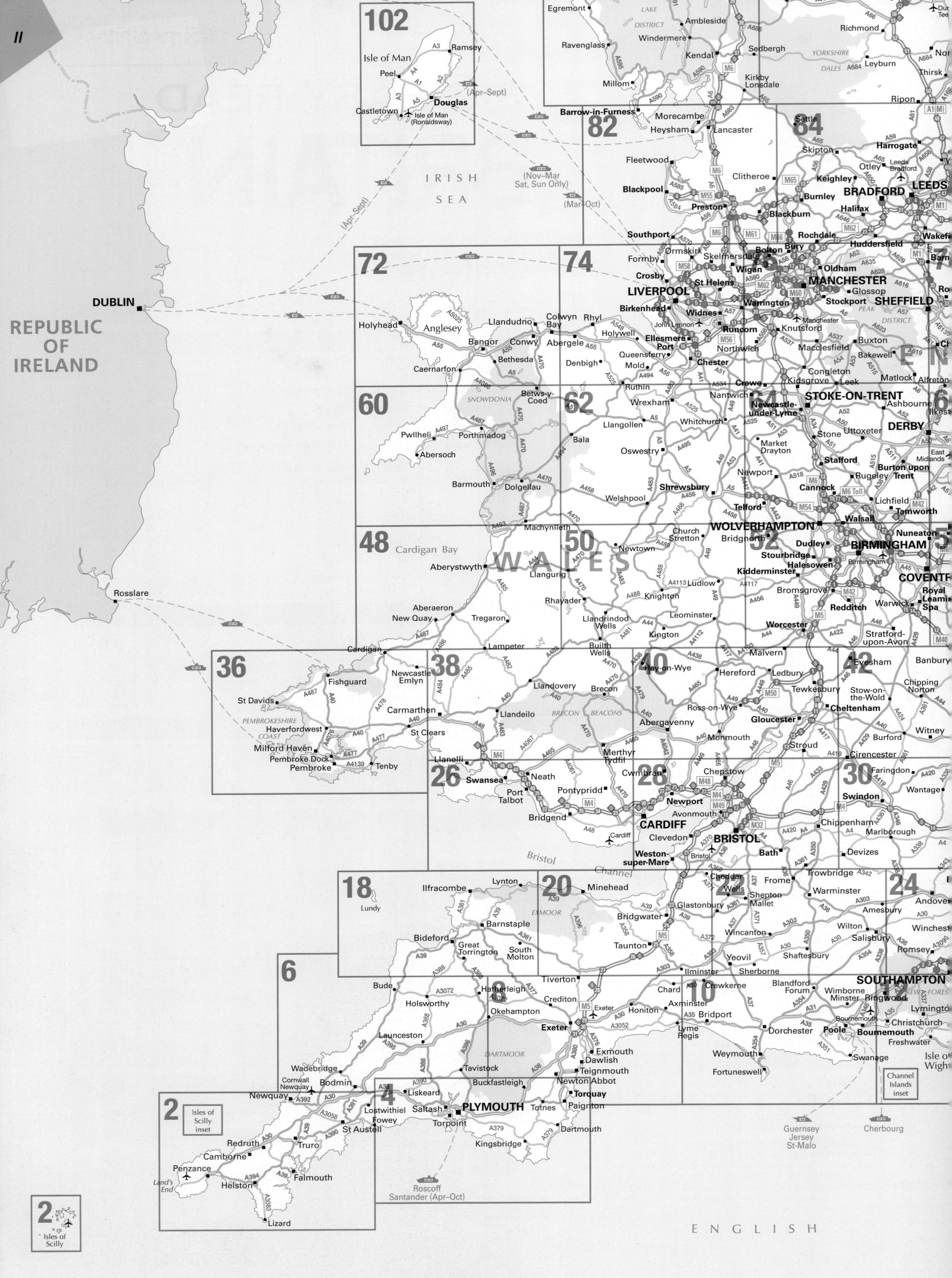

Motorway

Toll motorway

Primary route
dual carriageway

Primary route
single carriageway

Other A road

Vehicle ferry

Fast vehicle ferry
or catamaran

National Park

86 Atlas page
number

| | | | | miles |
|0|10|20|30| |

| | | | | | kilometres |
|0|10|20|30|40| |

BELGIUM

FRANCE

CHANNEL

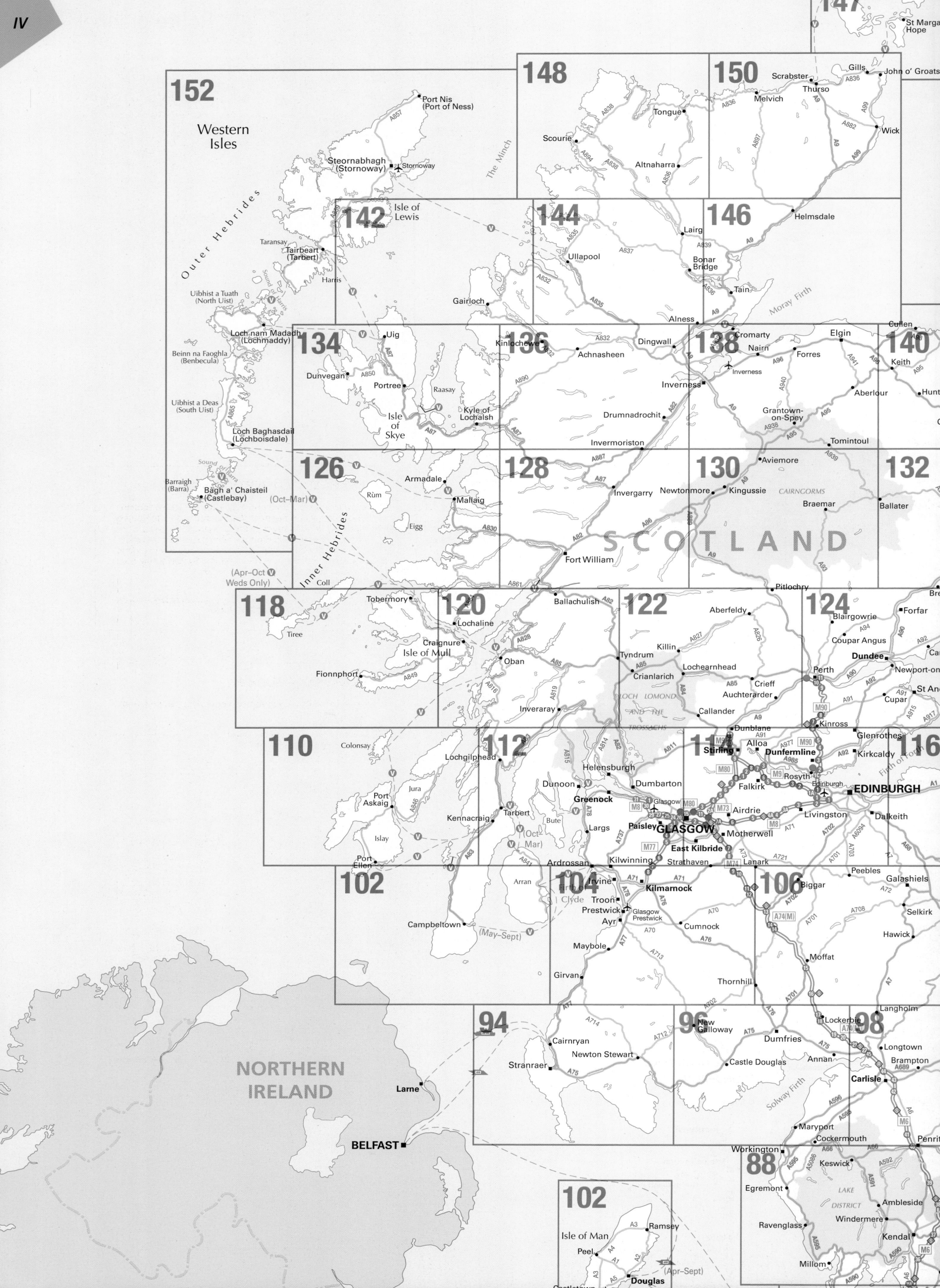

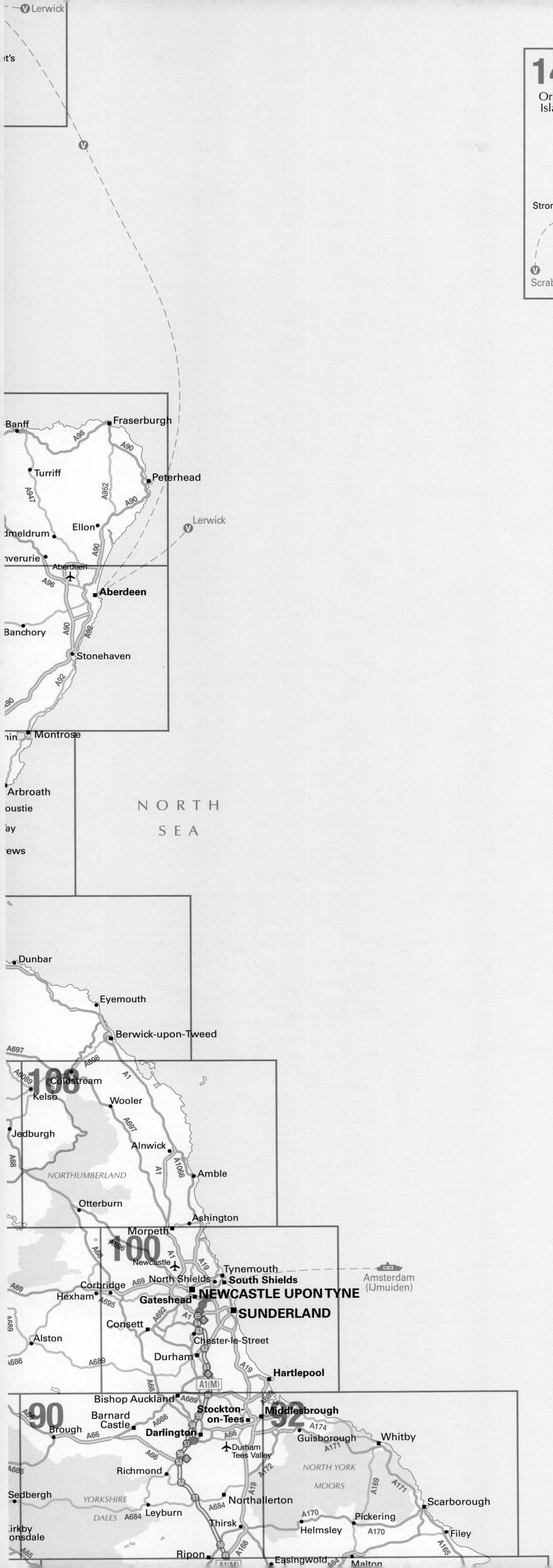

147
Orkney Islands

Papa Westray
North Ronaldsay
Westray
Rousay
Eday
Sanday
Stronsay
Mainland
Shapinsay
Lerwick
Stromness
Kirkwall
Kirkwall
Hoy
St Margaret's Hope
South Ronaldsay
Scrabster
Gills
Aberdeen

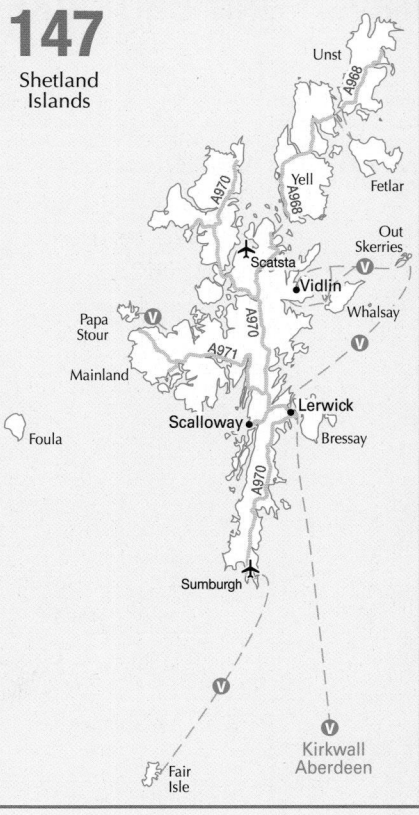

147
Shetland Islands

Unst
Yell
Fetlar
Out Skerries
Scatsta
Vidlin
Whalsay
Papa Stour
Mainland
Scalloway
Lerwick
Bressay
Sumburgh
Fair Isle
Kirkwall
Aberdeen

EMERGENCY DIVERSION ROUTES

In an emergency it may be necessary to close a section of motorway or other main road to traffic, so a temporary sign may advise drivers to follow a diversion route. To help drivers navigate the route, black symbols on yellow patches may be permanently displayed on existing direction signs, including motorway signs. Symbols may also be used on separate signs with yellow backgrounds.

For further information see *theaa.com/breakdown-cover/ advice/emergency-diversion-routes*

FERRY INFORMATION

Information on ferry routes and operators can be found on pages *X–XII*.

Banff
Fraserburgh
Turriff
Peterhead
A947
A90
A952
A90
Ellon
dmeldrum
Lerwick
nverurie
Aberdeen
A96
Aberdeen
Banchory
A92
Stonehaven
A90
Montrose
Arbroath
oustie
ay
ews

NORTH SEA

Dunbar
Eyemouth
Berwick-upon-Tweed
A697
A1
108
Coldstream
Kelso
Wooler
Jedburgh
A697
Alnwick
A68
NORTHUMBERLAND
A1
Amble
Otterburn
Ashington
Morpeth
100
Newcastle
A1
Corbridge
Tynemouth
Amsterdam (IJmuiden)
Hexham
A69
North Shields
South Shields
A695
Gateshead
NEWCASTLE UPON TYNE
Consett
SUNDERLAND
Alston
A689
Chester-le-Street
A686
Durham
A19
Hartlepool
A1(M)
Bishop Auckland
90
Barnard Castle
Stockton-on-Tees
Middlesbrough
92
Brough
A66
Darlington
A174
Guisborough
Whitby
A66
Durham Tees Valley
A171
Richmond
NORTH YORK MOORS
A169
Sedbergh
YORKSHIRE DALES
A684
Leyburn
Northallerton
A19
Scarborough
irkby onsdale
Thirsk
A170
Pickering
A171
Filey
Helmsley
A170
Ripon
Easingwold
Malton

Legend

═══	Motorway
━━━	Toll motorway
═══	Primary route dual carriageway
───	Primary route single carriageway
───	Other A road
🚢 or Ⓥ	Vehicle ferry
⛴	Fast vehicle ferry or catamaran
▢	National Park
96	Atlas page number

0   10   20   30 miles
0 10 20 30 40 kilometres

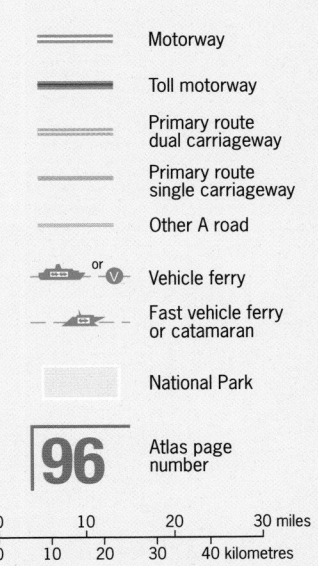

Caravan and camping sites in Britain

These pages list the top 300 AA-inspected Caravan and Camping (C & C) sites in the Pennant rating scheme. **Five Pennant Premier sites are shown in green,** **Four Pennant sites are shown in blue.**

Listings include addresses, telephone numbers and websites together with page and grid references to locate the sites in the atlas. The total number of touring pitches is also included for each site, together with the type of pitch available. The following abbreviations are used: **C = Caravan CV = Campervan T = Tent**

To find out more about the AA's Pennant rating scheme and other rated caravan and camping sites not included on these pages please visit ***theAA.com***

ENGLAND

Alders Caravan Park
Home Farm, Alne, York
YO61 1RY
Tel: 01347 838722 85 P2
alderscaravanpark.co.uk
Total Pitches: 87 (C, CV & T)

Andrewshayes Holiday Park
Dalwood, Axminster
EX13 7DY
Tel: 01404 831225 9 N5
andrewshayes.co.uk
Total Pitches: 150 (C, CV & T)

Apple Tree Park C & C Site
A38, Claypits, Stonehouse
GL10 3AL
Tel: 01452 742362 41 M10
appletreepark.co.uk
Total Pitches: 65 (C, CV & T)

Atlantic Bays Holiday Park
St Merryn, Padstow
PL28 8PY
Tel: 01841 520855 6 C10
atlanticbaysholidaypark.co.uk
Total Pitches: 70 (C, CV & T)

Ayr Holiday Park
St Ives, Cornwall
TR26 1EJ
Tel: 01736 795855 2 E6
ayrholidaypark.co.uk
Total Pitches: 40 (C, CV & T)

Back of Beyond Touring Park
234 Ringwood Road, St Leonards, Dorset
BH24 2SB
Tel: 01202 876968 11 Q4
backofbeyondtouringpark.co.uk
Total Pitches: 80 (C, CV & T)

Bagwell Farm Touring Park
Knights in the Bottom, Chickerell, Weymouth
DT3 4EA
Tel: 01305 782575 10 G8
bagwellfarm.co.uk
Total Pitches: 320 (C, CV & T)

Bardsea Leisure Park
Priory Road, Ulverston
LA12 9QE
Tel: 01229 584712 89 J11
bardsealeisure.co.uk
Total Pitches: 83 (C & CV)

Barn Farm Campsite
Barn Farm, Birchover, Matlock
DE4 2BL
Tel: 01629 650245 77 N11
barnfarmcamping.com
Total Pitches: 62 (C, CV & T)

Bath Chew Valley Caravan Park
Ham Lane, Bishop Sutton
BS39 5TZ
Tel: 01275 332127 29 J10
bathchewvalley.co.uk
Total Pitches: 45 (C, CV & T)

Bay View Holiday Park
Bolton le Sands, Carnforth
LA5 9TN
Tel: 01524 732854 83 L1
holgates.co.uk
Total Pitches: 100 (C, CV & T)

Beacon Cottage Farm Touring Park
Beacon Drive, St Agnes
TR5 0NU
Tel: 01872 552347 2 H4
beaconcottagefarmholidays.co.uk
Total Pitches: 70 (C, CV & T)

Beaconsfield Farm Caravan Park
Battlefield, Shrewsbury
SY4 4AA
Tel: 01939 210370 63 N8
beaconsfieldholidaypark.co.uk
Total Pitches: 60 (C & CV)

Beech Croft Farm
Beech Croft, Blackwell in the Peak, Buxton
SK17 9TQ
Tel: 01298 85330 77 L9
beechcroftfarm.co.uk
Total Pitches: 30 (C, CV & T)

Bellingham C & C Club Site
Brown Rigg, Bellingham
NE48 2JY
Tel: 01434 220175 99 N2
campingandcaravanningclub.co.uk/bellingham
Total Pitches: 64 (C, CV & T)

Beverley Park C & C Park
Goodrington Road, Paignton
TQ4 7JE
Tel: 01803 661961 5 Q5
beverley-holidays.co.uk
Total Pitches: 172 (C, CV & T)

Blue Rose Caravan Country Park
Star Carr Lane, Brandesburton
YO25 8RU
Tel: 01964 543366 87 L6
bluerosepark.com
Total Pitches: 58 (C & CV)

Briarfields Motel & Touring Park
Gloucester Road, Cheltenham
GL51 0SX
Tel: 01242 235324 41 P7
briarfields.net
Total Pitches: 72 (C, CV & T)

Broadhembury C & C Park
Steeds Lane, Kingsnorth, Ashford
TN26 1NQ
Tel: 01233 620859 16 H3
broadhembury.co.uk
Total Pitches: 110 (C, CV & T)

Budemeadows Touring Park
Widemouth Bay, Bude
EX23 0NA
Tel: 01288 361646 7 J4
budemeadows.com
Total Pitches: 145 (C, CV & T)

Burnham-on-Sea Holiday Village
Marine Drive, Burnham-on-Sea
TA8 1LA
Tel: 01278 783391 21 M4
haven.com/burnhamonsea
Total Pitches: 781 (C, CV & T)

Burrowhayes Farm C & C Site & Riding Stables
West Luccombe, Porlock, Minehead
TA24 8HT
Tel: 01643 862463 20 D4
burrowhayes.co.uk
Total Pitches: 120 (C, CV & T)

Burton Constable Holiday Park & Arboretum
Old Lodges, Sproatley, Hull
HU11 4LJ
Tel: 01964 562508 87 M8
burtonconstable.co.uk
Total Pitches: 105 (C, CV & T)

Caister-on-Sea Holiday Park
Ormesby Road, Caister-on-Sea, Great Yarmouth
NR30 5NH
Tel: 01493 728931 71 Q9
haven.com/caister
Total Pitches: 949 (C &CV)

Caistor Lakes Leisure Park
99a Brigg Road, Caistor
LN7 6RX
Tel: 01472 859626 80 B3
caistorlakes.co.uk
Total Pitches: 36 (C &CV)

Cakes & Ale
Abbey Lane, Theberton, Leiston
IP16 4TE
Tel: 01728 831655 59 N8
cakesandale.co.uk
Total Pitches: 55 (C, CV & T)

Calloose C & C Park
Leedstown, Hayle
TR27 5ET
Tel: 01736 850431 2 F7
calloose.co.uk
Total Pitches: 109 (C, CV & T)

Camping Caradon Touring Park
Trelawne, Looe
PL13 2NA
Tel: 01503 272388 4 C6
campingcaradon.co.uk
Total Pitches: 75 (C, CV & T)

Capesthorne Hall
Congleton Road, Siddington, Macclesfield
SK11 9JY
Tel: 01625 861221 76 F9
capesthorne.com
Total Pitches: 50 (C & CV)

Carlyon Bay C & C Park
Bethesda, Cypress Avenue, Carlyon Bay
PL25 3RE
Tel: 01726 812735 3 P4
carlyonbay.net
Total Pitches: 180 (C, CV & T)

Carnon Downs C & C Park
Carnon Downs, Truro
TR3 6JJ
Tel: 01872 862283 3 K6
carnon-downs-caravanpark.co.uk
Total Pitches: 150 (C, CV & T)

Cartref C & C
Cartref, Ford Heath, Shrewsbury
SY5 9GD
Tel: 01743 821688 63 L10
cartrefcaravansite.co.uk
Total Pitches: 44 (C, CV & T)

Carvynick Country Club
Summercourt, Newquay
TR8 5AF
Tel: 01872 510716 3 L3
carvynick.co.uk
Total Pitches: 47 (C & CV)

Castlerigg Hall C & C Park
Castlerigg Hall, Keswick
CA12 4TE
Tel: 017687 74499 89 J2
castlerigg.co.uk
Total Pitches: 68 (C, CV & T)

Charris C & C Park
Candy's Lane, Corfe Mullen, Wimborne
BH21 3EF
Tel: 01202 885970 11 N5
charris.co.uk
Total Pitches: 45 (C, CV & T)

Cheddar Mendip Heights C & C Club Site
Townsend, Priddy, Wells
BA5 3BP
Tel: 01749 870241 22 C3
campingandcaravanningclub.co.uk/cheddar
Total Pitches: 90 (C, CV & T)

Chy Carne Holiday Park
Kuggar, Ruan Minor, Helston
TR12 7LX
Tel: 01326 290200 2 H11
chycarne.co.uk
Total Pitches: 30 (C, CV & T)

Clippesby Hall
Hall Lane, Clippesby, Great Yarmouth
NR29 3BL
Tel: 01493 367800 71 N9
clippesbyhall.com
Total Pitches: 120 (C, CV & T)

Cofton Holidays
Starcross, Dawlish
EX6 8RP
Tel: 01626 890111 8 H8
coftonholidays.co.uk
Total Pitches: 450 (C, CV & T)

Concierge Camping
Ratham Estate, Ratham Lane, West Ashling, Chichester
PO18 8DL
Tel: 01243 573118 13 P3
conciergecamping.co.uk
Total Pitches: 15 (C, CV & T)

Coombe Touring Park
Race Plain, Netherhampton, Salisbury
SP2 8PN
Tel: 01722 328451 23 N7
coombecaravanpark.co.uk
Total Pitches: 50 (C, CV & T)

Corfe Castle C & C Club Site
Bucknowle, Wareham
BH20 5PQ
Tel: 01929 480280 11 M8
campingandcaravanningclub.co.uk/corfecastle
Total Pitches: 80 (C, CV & T)

Cornish Farm Touring Park
Shoreditch, Taunton
TA3 7BS
Tel: 01823 327746 21 K9
cornishfarm.com
Total Pitches: 50 (C, CV & T)

Cosawes Park
Perranarworthal, Truro
TR3 7QS
Tel: 01872 863724 3 J7
cosawes.co.uk
Total Pitches: 59 (C, CV & T)

Cote Ghyll C & C Park
Osmotherley, Northallerton
DL6 3AH
Tel: 01609 883425 91 Q7
coteghyll.com
Total Pitches: 77 (C, CV & T)

Country View Holiday Park
Sand Road, Sand Bay, Weston-super-Mare
BS22 9UJ
Tel: 01934 627595 28 D9
cvhp.co.uk
Total Pitches: 190 (C, CV & T)

Crealy Adventure Park and Resort
Sidmouth Road, Clyst St Mary, Exeter
EX5 1DR
Tel: 01395 234888 9 J6
crealy.co.uk
Total Pitches: 120 (C, CV & T)

Crows Nest Caravan Park
Gristhorpe, Filey
YO14 9PS
Tel: 01723 582206 93 M10
crowsnestcaravanpark.com
Total Pitches: 49 (C, CV & T)

Deepdale Backpackers & Camping
Deepdale Farm, Burnham Deepdale
PE31 8DD
Tel: 01485 210256 69 Q3
deepdalebackpackers.co.uk
Total Pitches: 80 (CV & T)

Dolbeare Park C & C
St Ive Road, Landrake, Saltash
PL12 5AF
Tel: 01752 851332 4 E4
dolbeare.co.uk
Total Pitches: 60 (C, CV & T)

Dornafield
Dornafield Farm, Two Mile Oak, Newton Abbot
TQ12 6DD
Tel: 01803 812732 5 P3
dornafield.com
Total Pitches: 135 (C, CV & T)

East Fleet Farm Touring Park
Chickerell, Weymouth
DT3 4DW
Tel: 01305 785768 10 G9
eastfleet.co.uk
Total Pitches: 400 (C, CV & T)

Eden Valley Holiday Park
Lanlivery, Nr Lostwithiel
PL30 5BU
Tel: 01208 872277 3 Q3
edenvalleyholidaypark.co.uk
Total Pitches: 56 (C, CV & T)

Exe Valley Caravan Site
Mill House, Bridgetown, Dulverton
TA22 9JR
Tel: 01643 851432 20 E7
exevalleycamping.co.uk
Total Pitches: 48 (C, CV & T)

Eye Kettleby Lakes
Eye Kettleby, Melton Mowbray
LE14 2TN
Tel: 01664 565900 67 J9
eyekettlebylakes.com
Total Pitches: 130 (C, CV & T)

Fields End Water Caravan Park & Fishery
Benwick Road, Doddington, March
PE15 0TY
Tel: 01354 740199 56 G2
fieldsendcaravans.co.uk
Total Pitches: 52 (C, CV & T)

Flower of May Holiday Park
Lebberston Cliff, Filey, Scarborough
YO11 3NU
Tel: 01723 584311 93 M10
flowerofmay.com
Total Pitches: 503 (C, CV & T)

Freshwater Beach Holiday Park
Burton Bradstock, Bridport
DT6 4PT
Tel: 01308 897317 10 D7
freshwaterbeach.co.uk
Total Pitches: 750 (C, CV & T)

Glenfield Caravan Park
Blackmoor Lane, Bardsey, Leeds
LS17 9DZ
Tel: 01937 574657 85 M7
glenfieldcaravanpark.co.uk
Total Pitches: 31 (C, CV & T)

Globe Vale Holiday Park
Radnor, Redruth
TR16 4BH
Tel: 01209 891183 2 H5
globevale.co.uk
Total Pitches: 138 (C, CV & T)

Glororum Caravan Park
Glororum Farm, Bamburgh
NE69 7AW
Tel: 01670 860256 109 K3
northumbrianleisure.co.uk
Total Pitches: 213 (C & CV)

Golden Cap Holiday Park
Seatown, Chideock, Bridport
DT6 6JX
Tel: 01308 422139 10 C6
wdlh.co.uk
Total Pitches: 108 (C, CV & T)

Golden Coast Holiday Park
Station Road, Woolacombe
EX34 7HW
Tel: 01271 872302 19 J5
woolacombe.com
Total Pitches: 431 (C, CV & T)

Golden Sands Holiday Park
Quebec Road, Mablethorpe
LN12 1QJ
Tel: 01507 477871 81 J6
haven.com/goldensands
Total Pitches: 1672 (C, CV & T)

Golden Square C & C Park
Oswaldkirk, Helmsley
YO62 5YQ
Tel: 01439 788269 92 C10
goldensquarecaravanpark.com
Total Pitches: 129 (C, CV & T)

Goosewood Holiday Park
Sutton-on-the-Forest, York
YO61 1ET
Tel: 01347 810829 86 B3
flowerofmay.com
Total Pitches: 100 (C & CV)

Green Acres Caravan Park
High Knells, Houghton, Carlisle
CA6 4JW
Tel: 01228 675418 98 E6
caravanpark-cumbria.com
Total Pitches: 35 (C, CV & T)

Greenhill Farm C & C Park
Greenhill Farm, New Road, Landford, Salisbury
SP5 2AZ
Tel: 01794 324117 24 D9
greenhillfarm.co.uk
Total Pitches: 160 (C, CV & T)

Greenhill Leisure Park
Greenhill Farm, Station Road, Bletchingdon, Oxford
OX5 3BQ
Tel: 01869 351600 43 K8
greenhill-leisure-park.co.uk
Total Pitches: 92 (C, CV & T)

Grooby's Pit
Bridgefoot Farm, Steeping Road, Thorpe St Peter
PE24 4QT
Tel: 07427 137463 81 J11
fishskegness.co.uk
Total Pitches: 18 (C & CV)

Grouse Hill Caravan Park
Flask Bungalow Farm, Fylingdales, Robin Hood's Bay
YO22 4QH
Tel: 01947 880543 93 J7
grousehill.co.uk
Total Pitches: 175 (C, CV & T)

Gunvenna Holiday Park
St Minver, Wadebridge
PL27 6QN
Tel: 01208 862405 6 D9
gunvenna.com
Total Pitches: 75 (C, CV & T)

Haggerston Castle Holiday Park
Beal, Berwick-upon-Tweed
TD15 2PA
Tel: 01289 381333 108 G1
haven.com/haggerstoncastle
Total Pitches: 1340 (C & CV)

Harbury Fields
Harbury Fields Farm, Harbury, Nr Leamington Spa
CV33 9JN
Tel: 01926 612457 54 B8
harburyfields.co.uk
Total Pitches: 59 (C & CV)

Harford Bridge Holiday Park
Peter Tavy, Tavistock
PL19 9LS
Tel: 01822 810349 7 P9
harfordbridge.co.uk
Total Pitches: 198 (C, CV & T)

Haw Wood Farm Caravan Park
Hinton, Saxmundham
IP17 3QT
Tel: 01502 359550 59 N6
hawwoodfarm.co.uk
Total Pitches: 60 (C, CV & T)

Heathfield Farm Camping
Heathfield Road, Freshwater, Isle of Wight
PO40 9SH
Tel: 01983 407822 12 E7
heathfieldcamping.co.uk
Total Pitches: 75 (C, CV & T)

Heathland Beach Caravan Park
London Road, Kessingland
NR33 7PJ
Tel: 01502 740337 59 Q3
heathlandbeach.co.uk
Total Pitches: 63 (C, CV & T)

Hele Valley Holiday Park
Hele Bay, Ilfracombe
EX34 9RD
Tel: 01271 862460 19 K4
helevalley.co.uk
Total Pitches: 50 (C, CV & T)

Hendra Holiday Park
Newquay
TR8 4NY
Tel: 01637 875778 3 K2
hendra-holidays.com
Total Pitches: 548 (C, CV & T)

Hidden Valley Park
West Down, Braunton, Ilfracombe
EX34 8NU
Tel: 01271 813837 19 K5
hiddenvalleypark.com
Total Pitches: 100 (C, CV & T)

Highfield Farm Touring Park
Long Road, Comberton, Cambridge
CB23 7DG
Tel: 01223 262308 56 H9
highfieldfarmtouringpark.co.uk
Total Pitches: 120 (C, CV & T)

Highlands End Holiday Park
Eype, Bridport, Dorset
DT6 6AR
Tel: 01308 422139 10 C6
wdlh.co.uk
Total Pitches: 195 (C, CV & T)

Hill Cottage Farm C & C Park
Sandleheath Road, Alderholt, Fordingbridge
SP6 3EG
Tel: 01425 650513 23 P10
hillcottagefarmcampingandcaravanpark.co.uk
Total Pitches: 95 (C, CV & T)

Hill of Oaks & Blakeholme
Windermere
LA12 8NR
Tel: 015395 31578 89 K9
hillofoaks.co.uk
Total Pitches: 43 (C & CV)

Hillside Caravan Park
Canvas Farm, Moor Road, Knayton, Thirsk
YO7 4BR
Tel: 01845 537349 91 Q9
hillsidecaravanpark.co.uk
Total Pitches: 50 (C & CV)

Holiday Resort Unity
Coast Road, Brean Sands, Brean
TA8 2RB
Tel: 01278 751235 21 L3
hru.co.uk
Total Pitches: 1114 (C, CV & T)

Hollins Farm C & C
Far Arnside, Carnforth
LA5 0SL
Tel: 01524 701767 89 M11
holgates.co.uk
Total Pitches: 12 (C, CV & T)

Hylton Caravan Park
Eden Street, Silloth
CA7 4AY
Tel: 016973 31707 97 M7
stanwix.com
Total Pitches: 90 (C, CV & T)

Island Lodge C & C Site
Stumpy Post Cross, Kingsbridge
TQ7 4BL
Tel: 01548 852956 5 M7
islandlodgesite.co.uk
Total Pitches: 30 (C, CV & T)

Isle of Avalon Touring Caravan Park
Godney Road, Glastonbury
BA6 9AF
Tel: 01458 833618 22 C5
avaloncaravanpark.co.uk
Total Pitches: 120 (C, CV & T)

Jasmine Caravan Park
Cross Lane, Snainton, Scarborough
YO13 9BE
Tel: 01723 859240 93 J10
jasminepark.co.uk
Total Pitches: 68 (C, CV & T)

Kenneggy Cove Holiday Park
Higher Kenneggy, Rosudgeon, Penzance
TR20 9AU
Tel: 01736 763453 2 E9
kenneggycove.co.uk
Total Pitches: 40 (C, CV & T)

Kennford International Caravan Park
Kennford, Exeter
EX6 7YN
Tel: 01392 833046 8 G7
kennfordinternational.co.uk
Total Pitches: 87 (C, CV & T)

King's Lynn C & C Park
New Road, North Runcton, King's Lynn
PE33 0RA
Tel: 01553 840004 69 M9
kl-cc.co.uk
Total Pitches: 150 (C, CV & T)

Kloofs Caravan Park
Sandhurst Lane, Bexhill
TN39 4RG
Tel: 01424 842839 16 C9
kloofs.com
Total Pitches: 125 (C, CV & T)

Knepps Farm Holiday Park
River Road, Stanah, Thornton-Cleveleys, Blackpool
FY5 5LR
Tel: 01253 823632 83 J6
kneppsfarm.co.uk
Total Pitches: 40 (C & CV)

Knight Stainforth Hall Caravan & Campsite
Stainforth, Settle
BD24 0DP
Tel: 01729 822200 84 B2
knightstainforth.co.uk
Total Pitches: 100 (C, CV & T)

Ladycross Plantation Caravan Park
Egton, Whitby
YO21 1UA
Tel: 01947 895502 92 G5
ladycrossplantation.co.uk
Total Pitches: 130 (C, CV & T)

Lady's Mile Holiday Park
Dawlish, Devon
EX7 0LX
Tel: 01626 863411 8 H9
ladysmile.co.uk
Total Pitches: 570 (C, CV & T)

Lakeland Leisure Park
Moor Lane, Flookburgh
LA11 7LT
Tel: 01539 558556 89 K12
haven.com/lakeland
Total Pitches: 977 (C, CV & T)

Lamb Cottage Caravan Park
Dalefords Lane, Whitegate, Northwich
CW8 2BN
Tel: 01606 882302 75 Q10
lambcottage.co.uk
Total Pitches: 45 (C & CV)

Langstone Manor C & C Park
Moortown, Tavistock
PL19 9JZ
Tel: 01822 613371 7 P10
langstonemanor.co.uk
Total Pitches: 40 (C, CV & T)

Lanyon Holiday Park
Loscombe Lane, Four Lanes, Redruth
TR16 6LP
Tel: 01209 313474 2 H7
lanyonholidaypark.co.uk
Total Pitches: 25 (C, CV & T)

Lebberston Touring Park
Filey Road, Lebberston, Scarborough
YO11 3PE
Tel: 01723 585723 93 M10
lebberstontouring.co.uk
Total Pitches: 125 (C & CV)

Lickpenny Caravan Site
Lickpenny Lane, Tansley, Matlock
DE4 5GF
Tel: 01629 583040 77 Q11
lickpennycaravanpark.co.uk
Total Pitches: 80 (C & CV)

Lime Tree Park
Dukes Drive, Buxton
SK17 9RP
Tel: 01298 22988 77 K9
limetreeparkbuxton.com
Total Pitches: 106 (C, CV & T)

Lincoln Farm Park Oxfordshire
High Street, Standlake
OX29 7RH
Tel: 01865 300239 43 J11
lincolnfarmpark.co.uk
Total Pitches: 90 (C, CV & T)

Little Lakeland Caravan Park
Wortwell, Harleston
IP20 0EL
Tel: 01986 788646 59 K4
littlelakelandcaravanparkandcamping.co.uk
Total Pitches: 58 (C, CV & T)

Littlesea Holiday Park
Lynch Lane, Weymouth
DT4 9DT
Tel: 01305 774414 10 G9
haven.com/littlesea
Total Pitches: 861 (C, CV & T)

Long Acres Touring Park
Station Road, Old Leake, Boston
PE22 9RF
Tel: 01205 871555 68 G2
long-acres.co.uk
Total Pitches: 40 (C, CV & T)

Longnor Wood Holiday Park
Newtown, Longnor, Nr Buxton
SK17 0NG
Tel: 01298 83648 77 K11
longnorwood.co.uk
Total Pitches: 47 (C, CV & T)

Lower Polladras Touring Park
Carleen, Breage, Helston
TR13 9NX
Tel: 01736 762220 2 F8
lower-polladras.co.uk
Total Pitches: 39 (C, CV & T)

Lowther Holiday Park
Eamont Bridge, Penrith
CA10 2JB
Tel: 01768 863631 89 N1
lowther-holidaypark.co.uk
Total Pitches: 180 (C, CV & T)

Manor Wood Country Caravan Park
Manor Wood, Coddington, Chester
CH3 9EN
Tel: 01829 782990 63 M1
cheshire-caravan-sites.co.uk
Total Pitches: 45 (C, CV & T)

Marton Mere Holiday Village
Mythop Road, Blackpool
FY4 4XN
Tel: 01253 767544 82 H8
haven.com/martonmere
Total Pitches: 782 (C & CV)

Mayfield Park
Cheltenham Road, Cirencester
GL7 7BH
Tel: 01285 831301 42 B10
mayfieldpark.co.uk
Total Pitches: 105 (C, CV & T)

Meadowbank Holidays
Stour Way, Christchurch
BH23 2PQ
Tel: 01202 483597 12 B6
meadowbank-holidays.co.uk
Total Pitches: 41 (C & CV)

Middlewood Farm Holiday Park
Middlewood Lane, Fylingthorpe, Robin Hood's Bay, Whitby
YO22 4UF
Tel: 01947 880414 93 J6
middlewoodfarm.com
Total Pitches: 100 (C, CV & T)

Minnows Touring Park
Holbrook Lane, Sampford Peverell
EX16 7EN
Tel: 01884 821770 20 G10
minnowstouringpark.co.uk
Total Pitches: 59 (C, CV & T)

Monkey Tree Holiday Park
Hendra Croft, Scotland Road, Newquay
TR8 5QR
Tel: 01872 572032 3 K4
monkeytreeholidaypark.co.uk
Total Pitches: 700 (C, CV & T)

Moon & Sixpence
Newbourn Road, Waldringfield, Woodbridge
IP12 4PP
Tel: 01473 736650 47 N3
moonandsixpence.co.uk
Total Pitches: 50 (C & CV)

Moor Lodge Park
Blackmoor Lane, Bardsey, Leeds
LS17 9DZ
Tel: 01937 572424 85 M7
moorlodgecaravanpark.co.uk
Total Pitches: 12 (C & CV)

Moss Wood Caravan Park
Crimbles Lane, Cockerham
LA2 0ES
Tel: 01524 791041 83 L5
mosswood.co.uk
Total Pitches: 25 (C, CV & T)

Naburn Lock Caravan Park
Naburn
YO19 4RU
Tel: 01904 728697 86 B6
naburnlock.co.uk
Total Pitches: 100 (C, CV & T)

New Lodge Farm C & C Site
New Lodge Farm, Bulwick, Corby
NN17 3DU
Tel: 01780 450493 55 N2
newlodgefarm.com
Total Pitches: 72 (C, CV & T)

Newberry Valley Park
Woodlands, Combe Martin
EX34 0AT
Tel: 01271 882334 19 L4
newberryvalleypark.co.uk
Total Pitches: 110 (C, CV & T)

Newlands Holidays
Charmouth, Bridport
DT6 6RB
Tel: 01297 560259 10 B6
newlandsholidays.co.uk
Total Pitches: 240 (C, CV & T)

Newperran Holiday Park
Rejerrah, Newquay
TR8 5QJ
Tel: 01872 572407 3 K4
newperran.co.uk
Total Pitches: 357 (C, CV & T)

Ninham Country Holidays
Ninham, Shanklin, Isle of Wight
PO37 7PL
Tel: 01983 864243 13 J8
ninham-holidays.co.uk
Total Pitches: 135 (C, CV & T)

North Morte Farm C & C Park
North Morte Road, Mortehoe, Woolacombe
EX34 7EG
Tel: 01271 870381 19 J4
northmortefarm.co.uk
Total Pitches: 180 (C, CV & T)

Northam Farm Caravan & Touring Park
Brean, Burnham-on-Sea
TA8 2SE
Tel: 01278 751244 21 M2
northamfarm.co.uk
Total Pitches: 350 (C, CV & T)

Oakdown Country Holiday Park
Gatedown Lane, Weston, Sidmouth
EX10 0PT
Tel: 01297 680387 9 M7
oakdown.co.uk
Total Pitches: 150 (C, CV & T)

Old Hall Caravan Park
Capernwray, Carnforth
LA6 1AD
Tel: 01524 733276 83 M1
oldhallcaravanpark.co.uk
Total Pitches: 38 (C & CV)

Ord House Country Park
East Ord, Berwick-upon-Tweed
TD15 2NS
Tel: 01289 305288 117 L11
ordhouse.co.uk
Total Pitches: 79 (C, CV & T)

Oxon Hall Touring Park
Welshpool Road, Shrewsbury
SY3 5FB
Tel: 01743 340868 63 M9
morris-leisure.co.uk
Total Pitches: 105 (C, CV & T)

Padstow Touring Park
Padstow
PL28 8LE
Tel: 01841 532061 6 C10
padstowtouringpark.co.uk
Total Pitches: 150 (C, CV & T)

Park Cliffe C & C Estate
Birks Road, Tower Wood, Windermere
LA23 3PG
Tel: 015395 31344 89 L8
parkcliffe.co.uk
Total Pitches: 60 (C, CV & T)

Parkers Farm Holiday Park
Higher Mead Farm, Ashburton, Devon
TQ13 7LJ
Tel: 01364 654869 8 E10
parkersfarmholidays.co.uk
Total Pitches: 100 (C, CV & T)

Park Foot C & C Park
Howtown Road, Pooley Bridge
CA10 2NA
Tel: 017684 86309 89 M2
parkfootullswater.co.uk
Total Pitches: 454 (C, CV & T)

Parkland C & C Site
Sorley Green Cross, Kingsbridge
TQ7 4AF
Tel: 01548 852723 5 M7
parklandsite.co.uk
Total Pitches: 50 (C, CV & T)

Pebble Bank Caravan Park
Camp Road, Wyke Regis, Weymouth
DT4 9HF
Tel: 01305 774844 10 G9
pebblebank.co.uk
Total Pitches: 120 (C, CV & T)

Perran Sands Holiday Park
Perranporth, Truro
TR6 0AQ
Tel: 01872 573551 3 J3
haven.com/perransands
Total Pitches: 1012 (C, CV & T)

Petwood Caravan Park
Off Stixwould Road, Woodhall Spa
LN10 6QH
Tel: 01526 354799 80 D11
petwoodcaravanpark.co.uk
Total Pitches: 98 (C, CV & T)

Polmanter Touring Park
Halsetown, St Ives
TR26 3LX
Tel: 01736 795640 2 E7
polmanter.co.uk
Total Pitches: 270 (C, CV & T)

Porthtowan Tourist Park
Mile Hill, Porthtowan, Truro
TR4 8TY
Tel: 01209 890256 2 H5
porthtowantouristpark.co.uk
Total Pitches: 80 (C, CV & T)

Primrose Valley Holiday Park
Filey
YO14 9RF
Tel: 01723 513771 93 M11
haven.com/primrosevalley
Total Pitches: 1549 (C & CV)

Quantock Orchard Caravan Park
Flaxpool, Crowcombe, Taunton
TA4 4AW
Tel: 01984 618618 21 J6
quantock-orchard.co.uk
Total Pitches: 60 (C, CV & T)

Ranch Caravan Park
Station Road, Honeybourne, Evesham
WR11 7PR
Tel: 01386 830744 42 C3
ranch.co.uk
Total Pitches: 120 (C & CV)

Ripley Caravan Park
Knaresborough Road, Ripley, Harrogate
HG3 3AU
Tel: 01423 770050 85 L3
ripleycaravanpark.com
Total Pitches: 60 (C, CV & T)

River Dart Country Park
Holne Park, Ashburton
TQ13 7NP
Tel: 01364 652511 5 M3
riverdart.co.uk
Total Pitches: 170 (C, CV & T)

River Valley Holiday Park
London Apprentice, St Austell
PL26 7AP
Tel: 01726 73533 3 N4
rivervalleyholidaypark.co.uk
Total Pitches: 45 (C, CV & T)

Riverside C & C Park
Marsh Lane, North Molton Road, South Molton
EX36 3HQ
Tel: 01769 579269 19 P8
exmoorriverside.co.uk
Total Pitches: 58 (C, CV & T)

Riverside Caravan Park
High Bentham, Lancaster
LA2 7FJ
Tel: 015242 61272 83 P1
riversidecaravanpark.co.uk
Total Pitches: 61 (C & CV)

Riverside Holiday Park
Southport New Road, Southport
PR9 8DF
Tel: 01704 228886 83 J11
riversideleisurecentre.co.uk
Total Pitches: 615 (C & CV)

Riverside Meadows Country Caravan Park
Ure Bank Top, Ripon
HG4 1JD
Tel: 01765 602964 91 N12
flowerofmay.com
Total Pitches: 80 (C, CV & T)

Robin Hood C & C Park
Green Dyke Lane, Slingsby
YO62 4AP
Tel: 01653 628391 92 E11
robinhoodcaravanpark.co.uk
Total Pitches: 32 (C, CV & T)

Rose Farm Touring & Camping Park
Stepshort, Belton, Nr Great Yarmouth
NR31 9JS
Tel: 01493 738292 71 P11
rosefarmtouringpark.co.uk
Total Pitches: 145 (C, CV & T)

Rosedale Abbey C & C Park
Rosedale Abbey, Pickering
YO18 8SA
Tel: 01751 417272 92 E7
rosedaleabbeycaravanpark.co.uk
Total Pitches: 100 (C, CV & T)

Ross Park
Park Hill Farm, Ipplepen, Newton Abbot
TQ12 5TT
Tel: 01803 812983 5 P3
rossparkcaravanpark.co.uk
Total Pitches: 110 (C, CV & T)

Rudding Holiday Park
Follifoot, Harrogate
HG3 1JH
Tel: 01423 870439 85 L4
ruddingholidaypark.co.uk
Total Pitches: 86 (C, CV & T)

Run Cottage Touring Park
Alderton Road, Hollesley, Woodbridge
IP12 3RQ
Tel: 01394 411309 47 P3
runcottage.co.uk
Total Pitches: 45 (C, CV & T)

Rutland C & C
Park Lane, Greetham, Oakham
LE15 7FN
Tel: 01572 813520 67 M9
rutlandcaravanandcamping.co.uk
Total Pitches: 130 (C, CV & T)

St Helens Caravan Park
Wykeham, Scarborough
YO13 9QD
Tel: 01723 862771 93 K10
sthelenscaravanpark.co.uk
Total Pitches: 250 (C, CV & T)

St Ives Bay Holiday Park
73 Loggans Road, Upton Towans, Hayle
TR27 5BH
Tel: 01736 752274 2 F6
stivesbay.co.uk
Total Pitches: 507 (C, CV & T)

Salcombe Regis C & C Park
Salcombe Regis, Sidmouth
EX10 0JH
Tel: 01395 514303 9 M7
salcombe-regis.co.uk
Total Pitches: 110 (C, CV & T)

Sand le Mere Holiday Village
Southfield Lane, Tunstall
HU12 0JF
Tel: 01964 670403 87 P9
sand-le-mere.co.uk
Total Pitches: 89 (C & CV)

Sandy Balls Holiday Village
Sandy Balls Estate Ltd, Godshill, Fordingbridge
SP6 2JZ
Tel: 01442 508850 24 B10
awayresorts.co.uk
Total Pitches: 225 (C, CV & T)

Searles Leisure Resort
South Beach Road, Hunstanton
PE36 5BB
Tel: 01485 534211 69 M4
searles.co.uk
Total Pitches: 413 (C, CV & T)

Seaview Holiday Park
Preston, Weymouth
DT3 6DZ
Tel: 01305 832271 10 H8
haven.com/seaview
Total Pitches: 347 (C, CV & T)

Seaview International Holiday Park
Boswinger, Mevagissey
PL26 6LL
Tel: 01726 843425 3 N6
seaviewinternational.com
Total Pitches: 201 (C, CV & T)

Severn Gorge Park
Bridgnorth Road, Tweedale, Telford
TF7 4JB
Tel: 01952 684789 64 D11
severngorgepark.co.uk
Total Pitches: 12 (C & CV)

Shamba Holidays
East Moors Lane, St Leonards, Ringwood
BH24 2SB
Tel: 01202 873302 11 Q4
shambaholidays.co.uk
Total Pitches: 150 (C, CV & T)

Shrubbery Touring Park
Rousdon, Lyme Regis
DT7 3XW
Tel: 01297 442227 9 P6
shrubberypark.co.uk
Total Pitches: 120 (C, CV & T)

Silverdale Caravan Park
Middlebarrow Plain, Cove Road, Silverdale, Nr Carnforth
LA5 0SH
Tel: 01524 701508 89 M11
holgates.co.uk
Total Pitches: 80 (C, CV & T)

Skelwith Fold Caravan Park
Ambleside, Cumbria
LA22 0HX
Tel: 015394 32277 89 K6
skelwith.com
Total Pitches: 150 (C & CV)

Skirlington Leisure Park
Driffield, Skipsea
YO25 8SY
Tel: 01262 468213 87 M5
skirlington.com
Total Pitches: 930 (C, CV & T)

Sleningford Watermill Caravan Camping Park
North Stainley, Ripon
HG4 3HQ
Tel: 01765 635201 91 M11
sleningfordwatermill.co.uk
Total Pitches: 135 (C, CV & T)

Somers Wood Caravan Park
Somers Road, Meriden
CV7 7PL
Tel: 01676 522978 53 N4
somerswood.co.uk
Total Pitches: 48 (C & CV)

South Lytchett Manor C & C Park
Dorchester Road, Lytchett Minster, Poole
BH16 6JB
Tel: 01202 622577 11 M6
southlytchettmanor.co.uk
Total Pitches: 150 (C, CV & T)

South Meadows Caravan Park
South Road, Belford
NE70 7DP
Tel: 01668 213326 109 J3
southmeadows.co.uk
Total Pitches: 83 (C, CV & T)

Stanmore Hall Touring Park
Stourbridge Road, Bridgnorth
WV15 6DT
Tel: 01746 761761 52 D2
morris-leisure.co.uk
Total Pitches: 129 (C, CV & T)

Stanwix Park Holiday Centre
Greenrow, Silloth
CA7 4HH
Tel: 016973 32666 97 M7
stanwix.com
Total Pitches: 337 (C, CV & T)

Stowford Farm Meadows
Berry Down, Combe Martin
EX34 0PW
Tel: 01271 882476 19 L5
stowford.co.uk
Total Pitches: 700 (C, CV & T)

Stroud Hill Park
Fen Road, Pidley, St Ives
PE28 3DE
Tel: 01487 741333 56 G5
stroudhillpark.co.uk
Total Pitches: 60 (C, CV & T)

Summer Valley Touring Park
Shortlanesend, Truro
TR4 9DW
Tel: 01872 277878 3 K5
summervalley.co.uk
Total Pitches: 60 (C, CV & T)

Sumners Ponds Fishery & Campsite
Chapel Road, Barns Green, Horsham
RH13 0PR
Tel: 01403 732539 14 G5
sumnersponds.co.uk
Total Pitches: 86 (C, CV & T)

Swiss Farm Touring & Camping
Marlow Road, Henley-on-Thames
RG9 2HY
Tel: 01491 573419 31 Q6
swissfarmhenley.co.uk
Total Pitches: 140 (C, CV & T)

Tanner Farm Touring C & C Park
Tanner Farm, Goudhurst Road, Marden
TN12 9ND
Tel: 01622 832399 16 C3
tannerfarmpark.co.uk
Total Pitches: 120 (C, CV & T)

Tattershall Lakes Country Park
Sleaford Road, Tattershall
LN4 4LR
Tel: 01526 348800 80 D12
tattershall-lakes.com
Total Pitches: 186 (C, CV & T)

Tehidy Holiday Park
Harris Mill, Illogan, Portreath
TR16 4JQ
Tel: 01209 216489 2 H6
tehidy.co.uk
Total Pitches: 18 (C, CV & T)

Tencreek Holiday Park
Polperro Road, Looe
PL13 2JR
Tel: 01503 262447 4 C6
dolphinholidays.co.uk
Total Pitches: 355 (C, CV & T)

Teversal C & C Club Site
Silverhill Lane, Teversal
NG17 3JJ
Tel: 01623 551838 78 D11
campingandcaravanningclub.co.uk/teversal
Total Pitches: 126 (C, CV & T)

The Laurels Holiday Park
Padstow Road, Whitecross, Wadebridge
PL27 7JQ
Tel: 01208 813341 6 D10
thelaurelsholidaypark.co.uk
Total Pitches: 30 (C, CV & T)

The Old Brick Kilns
Little Barney Lane, Barney, Fakenham
NR21 0NL
Tel: 01328 878305 70 E5
old-brick-kilns.co.uk
Total Pitches: 65 (C, CV & T)

The Old Oaks Touring Park
Wick Farm, Wick, Glastonbury
BA6 8JS
Tel: 01458 831437 22 C5
theoldoaks.co.uk
Total Pitches: 98 (C, CV & T)

The Orchards Holiday Caravan Park
Main Road, Newbridge, Yarmouth, Isle of Wight
PO41 0TS
Tel: 01983 531331 12 G7
orchards-holiday-park.co.uk
Total Pitches: 160 (C, CV & T)

The Quiet Site
Ullswater, Watermillock
CA11 0LS
Tel: 07768 727016 89 L2
thequietsite.co.uk
Total Pitches: 100 (C, CV & T)

Thornwick Bay Holiday Village
North Marine Road, Flamborough
YO15 1AU
Tel: 01262 850569 93 P12
haven.com/parks/yorkshire/thornwick-bay
Total Pitches: 72 (C, CV & T)

Thorpe Park Holiday Centre
Cleethorpes
DN35 0PW
Tel: 01472 813395 80 F2
haven.com/thorpepark
Total Pitches: 1491 (C, CV & T)

Treago Farm Caravan Site
Crantock, Newquay
TR8 5QS
Tel: 01637 830277 3 J2
treagofarm.co.uk
Total Pitches: 90 (C, CV & T)

Tregoad Park
St Martin, Looe
PL13 1PB
Tel: 01503 262718 4 D5
tregoadpark.co.uk
Total Pitches: 200 (C, CV & T)

Treloy Touring Park
Newquay
TR8 4JN
Tel: 01637 872063 3 L2
treloy.co.uk
Total Pitches: 223 (C, CV & T)

Trencreek Holiday Park
Hillcrest, Higher Trencreek, Newquay
TR8 4NS
Tel: 01637 874210 3 K2
trencreekholidaypark.co.uk
Total Pitches: 194 (C, CV & T)

Trethem Mill Touring Park
St Just-in-Roseland, Nr St Mawes, Truro
TR2 5JF
Tel: 01872 580504 3 L7
trethem.com
Total Pitches: 84 (C, CV & T)

Trevalgan Touring Park
Trevalgan, St Ives
TR26 3BJ
Tel: 01736 791892 2 D6
trevalgantouringpark.co.uk
Total Pitches: 135 (C, CV & T)

Trevedra Farm C & C Site
Sennen, Penzance
TR19 7BE
Tel: 01736 871818 2 B9
trevedrafarm.co.uk
Total Pitches: 100 (C, CV & T)

Trevella Park
Crantock, Newquay
TR8 5EW
Tel: 01637 830308 3 K3
trevella.co.uk
Total Pitches: 165 (C, CV & T)

Trevornick
Holywell Bay, Newquay
TR8 5PW
Tel: 01637 830531 3 J3
trevornick.co.uk
Total Pitches: 688 (C, CV & T)

Truro C & C Park
Truro
TR4 8QN
Tel: 01872 560274 3 J5
trurocaravanandcampingpark.co.uk
Total Pitches: 51 (C, CV & T)

Tudor C & C
Shepherds Patch, Slimbridge, Gloucester
GL2 7BP
Tel: 01453 890483 41 L11
tudorcaravanpark.com
Total Pitches: 75 (C, CV & T)

Twitchen House Holiday Park
Mortehoe Station Road, Mortehoe, Woolacombe
EX34 7ES
Tel: 01271 872302 19 J4
woolacombe.com
Total Pitches: 569 (C, CV & T)

Two Mills Touring Park
Yarmouth Road, North Walsham
NR28 9NA
Tel: 01692 405829 71 K6
twomills.co.uk
Total Pitches: 81 (C, CV & T)

Ulwell Cottage Caravan Park
Ulwell Cottage, Ulwell, Swanage
BH19 3DG
Tel: 01929 422823 11 N8
ulwellcottagepark.co.uk
Total Pitches: 77 (C, CV & T)

Vale of Pickering Caravan Park
Carr House Farm, Allerston, Pickering
YO18 7PQ
Tel: 01723 859280 92 H10
valeofpickering.co.uk
Total Pitches: 120 (C, CV & T)

Wagtail Country Park
Cliff Lane, Marston, Grantham
NG32 2HU
Tel: 01400 251123 67 M4
wagtailcountrypark.co.uk
Total Pitches: 76 (C & CV)

Waldegraves Holiday Park
Mersea Island, Colchester
CO5 8SE
Tel: 01206 382898 47 J9
waldegraves.co.uk
Total Pitches: 30 (C, CV & T)

Warcombe Farm C & C Park
Station Road, Mortehoe, Woolacombe
EX34 7EJ
Tel: 01271 870690 19 J4
warcombefarm.co.uk
Total Pitches: 250 (C, CV & T)

Wareham Forest Tourist Park
North Trigon, Wareham
BH20 7NZ
Tel: 01929 551393 11 L6
warehamforest.co.uk
Total Pitches: 200 (C, CV & T)

Waren C & C Park
Waren Mill, Bamburgh
NE70 7EE
Tel: 01668 214366 109 J3
meadowhead.co.uk
Total Pitches: 150 (C, CV & T)

Warren Farm Holiday Centre
Brean Sands, Brean, Burnham-on-Sea
TA8 2RP
Tel: 01278 751227 28 D11
warrenfarm.co.uk
Total Pitches: 975 (C, CV & T)

Watergate Bay Touring Park
Watergate Bay, Tregurrian
TR8 4AD
Tel: 01637 860387 6 B11
watergatebaytouringpark.co.uk
Total Pitches: 171 (C, CV & T)

Waterrow Touring Park
Wiveliscombe, Taunton
TA4 2AZ
Tel: 01984 623464 20 G8
waterrowpark.co.uk
Total Pitches: 44 (C, CV & T)

Wayfarers C & C Park
Relubbus Lane, St Hilary, Penzance
TR20 9EF
Tel: 01736 763326 2 E8
wayfarerspark.co.uk
Total Pitches: 32 (C, CV & T)

Wells Touring Park
Haybridge, Wells
BA5 1AJ
Tel: 01749 676869 22 C4
wellstouringpark.co.uk
Total Pitches: 72 (C, CV & T)

Wheathill Touring Park
Wheathill, Bridgnorth
WV16 6QT
Tel: 01584 823456 51 Q4
wheathillpark.co.uk
Total Pitches: 25 (C & CV)

Whitecliff Bay Holiday Park
Hillway Road, Bembridge, Whitecliff Bay
PO35 5PL
Tel: 01983 872671 13 L7
wight-holidays.com
Total Pitches: 653 (C, CV & T)

Whitefield Forest Touring Park
Brading Road, Ryde, Isle of Wight
PO33 1QL
Tel: 01983 617069 13 K7
whitefieldforest.co.uk
Total Pitches: 90 (C, CV & T)

Whitemead Caravan Park
East Burton Road, Wool
BH20 6HG
Tel: 01929 462241 11 K7
whitemeadcaravanpark.co.uk
Total Pitches: 105 (C, CV & T)

Widdicombe Farm Touring Park
Marldon, Paignton
TQ3 1ST
Tel: 01803 558325 5 P4
widdicombefarm.co.uk
Total Pitches: 180 (C, CV & T)

Wild Rose Park
Ormside, Appleby-in-Westmorland
CA16 6EJ
Tel: 017683 51077 90 A3
harrisonholidayhomes.co.uk
Total Pitches: 226 (C & CV)

Wilksworth Farm Caravan Park
Cranborne Road, Wimborne Minster
BH21 4HW
Tel: 01202 885467 11 N4
shorefield.co.uk/camping-touring-holidays/our-parks/wilksworth-caravan-park
Total Pitches: 85 (C, CV & T)

Willowbank Holiday Home & Touring Park
Coastal Road, Ainsdale, Southport
PR8 3ST
Tel: 01704 571566 75 K2
willowbankcp.co.uk
Total Pitches: 87 (C & CV)

Wolds View Touring Park
115 Brigg Road, Caistor
LN7 6RX
Tel: 01472 851099 80 B3
woldsviewtouringpark.co.uk
Total Pitches: 60 (C, CV & T)

Wood Farm C & C Park
Axminster Road, Charmouth
DT6 6BT
Tel: 01297 560697 9 Q6
woodfarm.co.uk
Total Pitches: 175 (C, CV & T)

Wooda Farm Holiday Park
Poughill, Bude
EX23 9HJ
Tel: 01288 352069 7 J3
wooda.co.uk
Total Pitches: 200 (C, CV & T)

Woodclose Caravan Park
High Casterton, Kirkby Lonsdale
LA6 2SE
Tel: 015242 71597 89 Q11
woodclosepark.com
Total Pitches: 22 (C, CV & T)

Woodhall Country Park
Stixwold Road, Woodhall Spa
LN10 6UJ
Tel: 01526 353710 80 D10
woodhallcountrypark.co.uk
Total Pitches: 115 (C, CV & T)

Woodland Springs Adult Touring Park
Venton, Drewsteignton
EX6 6PG
Tel: 01647 231695 8 D6
woodlandsprings.co.uk
Total Pitches: 81 (C, CV & T)

Woodlands Grove C & C Park
Blackawton, Dartmouth
TQ9 7DQ
Tel: 01803 712598 5 N6
woodlandsgrove.co.uk
Total Pitches: 350 (C, CV & T)

Woodovis Park
Gulworthy, Tavistock
PL19 8NY
Tel: 01822 832968 7 N10
woodovis.com
Total Pitches: 50 (C, CV & T)

Yeatheridge Farm Caravan Park
East Worlington, Crediton
EX17 4TN
Tel: 01884 860330 8 E3
yeatheridge.co.uk
Total Pitches: 122 (C, CV & T)

SCOTLAND

Auchenlarie Holiday Park
Gatehouse of Fleet
DG7 2EX
Tel: 01556 506200 95 P8
swalwellholidaygroup.co.uk
Total Pitches: 451 (C, CV & T)

Beecraigs C & C Site
Beecraigs Country Park, The Visitor Centre, Linlithgow
EH49 6PL
Tel: 01506 844516 115 J6
beecraigs.com
Total Pitches: 36 (C, CV & T)

Blair Castle Caravan Park
Blair Atholl, Pitlochry
PH18 5SR
Tel: 01796 481263 130 F11
blaircastlecaravanpark.co.uk
Total Pitches: 226 (C, CV & T)

Brighouse Bay Holiday Park
Brighouse Bay, Borgue, Kirkcudbright
DG6 4TS
Tel: 01557 870267 96 D9
gillespie-leisure.co.uk
Total Pitches: 190 (C, CV & T)

Cairnsmill Holiday Park
Largo Road, St Andrews
KY16 8NN
Tel: 01334 473604 125 K10
cairnsmill.co.uk
Total Pitches: 62 (C, CV & T)

Craig Tara Holiday Park
Ayr
KA7 4LB
Tel: 0800 975 7579 104 E6
haven.com/craigtara
Total Pitches: 1144 (C & CV)

Craigtoun Meadows Holiday Park
Mount Melville, St Andrews
KY16 8PQ
Tel: 01334 475959 125 J10
craigtounmeadows.co.uk
Total Pitches: 56 (C, CV & T)

Faskally Caravan Park
Pitlochry
PH16 5LA
Tel: 01796 472007 130 G12
faskally.co.uk
Total Pitches: 430 (C, CV & T)

Glen Nevis C & C Park
Glen Nevis, Fort William
PH33 6SX
Tel: 01397 702191 128 F10
glen-nevis.co.uk
Total Pitches: 380 (C, CV & T)

Hoddom Castle Caravan Park
Hoddom, Lockerbie
DG11 1AS
Tel: 01576 300251 97 N4
hoddomcastle.co.uk
Total Pitches: 200 (C, CV & T)

Huntly Castle Caravan Park
The Meadow, Huntly
AB54 4UJ
Tel: 01466 794999 140 E8
huntlycastle.co.uk
Total Pitches: 90 (C, CV & T)

Invercoe C & C Park
Ballachulish, Glencoe
PH49 4HP
Tel: 01855 811210 121 L1
invercoe.co.uk
Total Pitches: 66 (C, CV & T)

Linwater Caravan Park
West Clifton, East Calder
EH53 0HT
Tel: 0131 333 3326 115 K7
linwater.co.uk
Total Pitches: 64 (C, CV & T)

Loch Ken Holiday Park
Parton, Castle Douglas
DG7 3NE
Tel: 01644 470282 96 E4
lochkenholidaypark.co.uk
Total Pitches: 40 (C, CV & T)

Lomond Woods Holiday Park
Old Luss Road, Balloch, Loch Lomond
G83 8QP
Tel: 01389 755000 113 M5
woodleisure.co.uk
Total Pitches: 115 (C & CV)

Milton of Fonab Caravan Park
Bridge Road, Pitlochry
PH16 5NA
Tel: 01796 472882 123 N1
fonab.co.uk
Total Pitches: 154 (C, CV & T)

River Tilt Caravan Park
Blair Atholl, Pitlochry
PH18 5TE
Tel: 01796 481467 130 G11
rivertiltpark.co.uk
Total Pitches: 30 (C, CV & T)

Sands of Luce Holiday Park
Sands of Luce, Sandhead, Stranraer
DG9 9JN
Tel: 01776 830456 94 G8
sandsofluceholidaypark.co.uk
Total Pitches: 80 (C, CV & T)

Seaward Caravan Park
Dhoon Bay, Kirkudbright
DG6 4TJ
Tel: 01557 870267 96 D8
gillespie-leisure.co.uk
Total Pitches: 25 (C, CV & T)

Seton Sands Holiday Village
Longniddry
EH32 0QF
Tel: 01875 813333 116 A6
haven.com/setonsands
Total Pitches: 640 (C & CV)

Silver Sands Holiday Park
Covesea, West Beach, Lossiemouth
IV31 6SP
Tel: 01343 813262 147 M11
silver-sands.co.uk
Total Pitches: 140 (C, CV & T)

Skye C & C Club Site
Loch Greshornish, Borve, Arnisort, Edinbane, Isle of Skye
IV51 9PS
Tel: 01470 582230 134 F5
campingandcaravanningclub.co.uk/skye
Total Pitches: 105 (C, CV & T)

Thurston Manor Leisure Park
Innerwick, Dunbar
EH42 1SA
Tel: 01368 840643 116 G6
thurstonmanor.co.uk
Total Pitches: 120 (C & CV)

Trossachs Holiday Park
Aberfoyle
FK8 3SA
Tel: 01877 382614 113 Q2
trossachsholidays.co.uk
Total Pitches: 66 (C, CV & T)

Witches Craig C & C Park
Blairlogie, Stirling
FK9 5PX
Tel: 01786 474947 114 E2
witchescraig.co.uk
Total Pitches: 60 (C, CV & T)

WALES

Bron Derw Touring Caravan Park
Llanrwst
LL26 0YT
Tel: 01492 640494 73 N11
bronderw-wales.co.uk
Total Pitches: 48 (C & CV)

Bron-Y-Wendon Caravan Park
Wern Road, Llanddulas, Colwyn Bay
LL22 8HG
Tel: 01492 512903 74 B8
bronywendon.co.uk
Total Pitches: 130 (C & CV)

Bryn Gloch C & C Park
Betws Garmon, Caernarfon
LL54 7YY
Tel: 01286 650216 73 J12
campwales.co.uk
Total Pitches: 177 (C, CV & T)

Caerfai Bay Caravan & Tent Park
Caerfai Bay, St Davids, Haverfordwest
SA62 6QT
Tel: 01437 720274 36 E5
caerfaibay.co.uk
Total Pitches: 106 (C, CV & T)

Cenarth Falls Holiday Park
Cenarth, Newcastle Emlyn
SA38 9JS
Tel: 01239 710345 37 P2
cenarth-holipark.co.uk
Total Pitches: 30 (C, CV & T)

Daisy Bank Caravan Park
Snead, Montgomery
SY15 6EB
Tel: 01588 620471 51 K2
daisy-bank.co.uk
Total Pitches: 80 (C, CV & T)

Dinlle Caravan Park
Dinas Dinlle, Caernarfon
LL54 5TW
Tel: 01286 830324 72 G12
thornleyleisure.co.uk
Total Pitches: 175 (C, CV & T)

Eisteddfa
Eisteddfa Lodge, Pentrefelin, Criccieth
LL52 0PT
Tel: 01766 522696 61 J4
eisteddfapark.co.uk
Total Pitches: 100 (C, CV & T)

Fforest Fields C & C Park
Hundred House, Builth Wells
LD1 5RT
Tel: 01982 570406 50 F10
fforestfields.co.uk
Total Pitches: 120 (C, CV & T)

Fishguard Bay Resort
Garn Gelli, Fishguard
SA65 9ET
Tel: 01348 811415 37 J3
fishguardbay.com
Total Pitches: 102 (C, CV & T)

Greenacres Holiday Park
Black Rock Sands, Morfa Bychan, Porthmadog
LL49 9YF
Tel: 01766 512781 61 J5
haven.com/greenacres
Total Pitches: 945 (C & CV)

Hafan y Môr Holiday Park
Pwllheli
LL53 6HJ
Tel: 01758 612112 60 G5
haven.com/hafanymor
Total Pitches: 875 (C & CV)

Hendre Mynach Touring C & C Park
Llanaber Road, Barmouth
LL42 1YR
Tel: 01341 280262 61 K8
hendremynach.co.uk
Total Pitches: 240 (C, CV & T)

Home Farm Caravan Park
Marian-Glas, Isle of Anglesey
LL73 8PH
Tel: 01248 410614 72 H7
homefarm-anglesey.co.uk
Total Pitches: 102 (C, CV & T)

Islawrffordd Caravan Park
Tal-y-bont, Barmouth
LL43 2AQ
Tel: 01341 247269 61 K8
islawrffordd.co.uk
Total Pitches: 105 (C, CV & T)

Kiln Park Holiday Centre
Marsh Road, Tenby
SA70 8RB
Tel: 01834 844121 37 M10
haven.com/kilnpark
Total Pitches: 849 (C, CV & T)

Pencelli Castle C & C Park
Pencelli, Brecon
LD3 7LX
Tel: 01874 665451 39 P7
pencelli-castle.com
Total Pitches: 80 (C, CV & T)

Penisar Mynydd Caravan Park
Caerwys Road, Rhuallt, St Asaph
LL17 0TY
Tel: 01745 582227 74 F8
penisarmynydd.co.uk
Total Pitches: 71 (C, CV & T)

Plas Farm Caravan & Lodge Park
Betws-yn-Rhos, Abergele
LL22 8AU
Tel: 01492 680254 74 B9
plasfarmcaravanpark.co.uk
Total Pitches: 54 (C & CV)

Plassey Holiday Park
The Plassey, Eyton, Wrexham
LL13 0SP
Tel: 01978 780277 63 K3
plassey.com
Total Pitches: 90 (C, CV & T)

Pont Kemys C & C Park
Chainbridge, Abergavenny
NP7 9DS
Tel: 01873 880688 40 D10
pontkemys.com
Total Pitches: 65 (C, CV & T)

Presthaven Sands Holiday Park
Gronant, Prestatyn
LL19 9TT
Tel: 01745 856471 74 F7
haven.com/presthavensands
Total Pitches: 1102 (C & CV)

Red Kite Touring Park
Van Road, Llanidloes
SY18 6NG
Tel: 01686 412122 50 C4
redkitetouringpark.co.uk
Total Pitches: 66 (C & CV)

River View Touring Park
The Dingle, Llanedi, Pontarddulais
SA4 0FH
Tel: 01635 844876 38 E10
riverviewtouringpark.com
Total Pitches: 60 (C, CV & T)

Riverside Camping
Seiont Nurseries, Pont Rug, Caernarfon
LL55 2BB
Tel: 01286 678781 72 H11
riversidecamping.co.uk
Total Pitches: 73 (C, CV & T)

The Trotting Mare Caravan Park
Overton, Wrexham
LL13 0LE
Tel: 01978 711963 63 L4
thetrottingmare.co.uk
Total Pitches: 65 (C, CV & T)

Trawsdir Touring C & C Park
Llanaber, Barmouth
LL42 1RR
Tel: 01341 280999 61 K8
barmouthholidays.co.uk
Total Pitches: 70 (C, CV & T)

Trefalun Park
Devonshire Drive, St Florence, Tenby
SA70 8RD
Tel: 01646 651514 37 L10
trefalunpark.co.uk
Total Pitches: 90 (C, CV & T)

Tyddyn Isaf Caravan Park
Lligwy Bay, Dulas, Isle of Anglesey
LL70 9PQ
Tel: 01248 410203 72 H6
tyddynisaf.co.uk
Total Pitches: 80 (C, CV & T)

White Tower Caravan Park
Llandwrog, Caernarfon
LL54 5UH
Tel: 01286 830649 72 G12
whitetowerpark.co.uk
Total Pitches: 52 (C & CV)

CHANNEL ISLANDS

Daisy Cottage Campsite
Route de Vinchelez, St Ouen, Jersey
JE3 2DB
Tel: 01534 481700 13 a1
daisycottagecampsite.com
Total Pitches: 29 (C, CV & T)

Fauxquets Valley Campsite
Castel, Guernsey
GY5 7QL
Tel: 01481 255460 12 c2
fauxquets.co.uk
Total Pitches: 120 (CV & T)

Rozel Camping Park
Summerville Farm, St Martin, Jersey
JE3 6AX
Tel: 01534 855200 13 d1
rozelcamping.com
Total Pitches: 100 (C, CV & T)

Traffic signs

Signs giving orders

Signs with red circles are mostly prohibitive.
Plates below signs qualify their message

 Entry to 20mph zone

 End of 20mph zone

Maximum speed

National speed limit applies

School crossing patrol

Stop and give way

Give way to traffic on major road

Manually operated temporary STOP and GO signs

No entry for vehicular traffic

No vehicles except bicycles being pushed

No cycling

No motor vehicles

No buses (over 8 passenger seats)

No overtaking

No towed caravans

No vehicles carrying explosives

No vehicle or combination of vehicles over length shown

No vehicles over height shown

No vehicles over width shown

Give way to vehicles from opposite direction

No right turn

No left turn

No U-turns

No goods vehicles over maximum gross weight shown (in tonnes) except for loading and unloading

No vehicles over maximum gross weight shown (in tonnes)

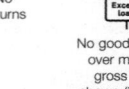 Parking restricted to permit holders

 No stopping at any time except buses

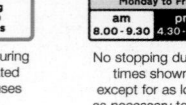 No stopping during period indicated except for buses

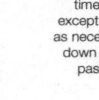 No stopping during times shown except for as long as necessary to set down or pick up passengers

No waiting

No stopping (Clearway)

Signs with blue circles but no red border mostly give positive instruction.

Ahead only

Turn left ahead (right if symbol reversed)

Turn left (right if symbol reversed)

Keep left (right if symbol reversed)

Vehicles may pass either side to reach same destination

Mini-roundabout (roundabout circulation – give way to vehicles from the immediate right)

Route to be used by pedal cycles only

Segregated pedal cycle and pedestrian route

Minimum speed

End of minimum speed

Buses and cycles only

Trams only

Pedestrian crossing point over tramway

One-way traffic (note: compare circular 'Ahead only' sign)

With-flow bus and cycle lane

Contraflow bus lane

With-flow pedal cycle lane

Note: The signs shown in this road atlas are those most commonly in use and are not all drawn to the same scale. In Scotland and Wales bilingual versions of some signs are used, showing both English and Gaelic or Welsh spellings. Some older designs of signs may still be seen on the roads. A comprehensive explanation of the signing system illustrating the vast majority of road signs can be found in the AA's handbook Know Your Road Signs. Where there is a reference to a rule number, this refers to The Highway Code.

Warning signs

Mostly triangular

Distance to 'STOP' line ahead

Dual carriageway ends

Road narrows on right (left if symbol reversed)

Road narrows on both sides

Distance to 'Give Way' line ahead

Crossroads

Junction on bend ahead

T-junction with priority over vehicles from the right

Staggered junction

Traffic merging from left ahead

The priority through route is indicated by the broader line.

Double bend first to left (symbol may be reversed)

Bend to right (or left if symbol reversed)

Roundabout

Uneven road

Plate below some signs

Two-way traffic crosses one-way road

Two-way traffic straight ahead

Opening or swing bridge ahead

Low-flying aircraft or sudden aircraft noise

Falling or fallen rocks

Traffic signals not in use

Traffic signals

Slippery road

Steep hill downwards

Steep hill upwards

Gradients may be shown as a ratio i.e. 20% = 1:5

Tunnel ahead

Trams crossing ahead

Level crossing with barrier or gate ahead

Level crossing without barrier or gate ahead

Level crossing without barrier

School crossing patrol ahead (some signs have amber lights which flash when crossings are in use)

Frail (or blind or disabled if shown) pedestrians likely to cross road ahead

No footway for 400 yds — Pedestrians in road ahead

Zebra crossing

Overhead electric cable; plate indicates maximum height of vehicles which can pass safely

Available width of headroom indicated

Sharp deviation of route to left (or right if chevrons reversed)

Light signals ahead at level crossing, airfield or bridge

Miniature warning lights at level crossings

Cattle

Wild animals

Wild horses or ponies

Accompanied horses or ponies

Cycle route ahead

Risk of ice

Traffic queues likely ahead

Distance over which road humps extend

Other danger; plate indicates nature of danger

Soft verges

Side winds

Hump bridge

Worded warning sign

Quayside or river bank

Risk of grounding

Direction signs

Mostly rectangular
Signs on motorways - blue backgrounds

 At a junction leading directly into a motorway (junction number may be shown on a black background)

 On approaches to junctions (junction number on black background)

 Route confirmatory sign after junction

Downward pointing arrows mean 'Get in lane'
The left-hand lane leads to a different destination from the other lanes.

The panel with the inclined arrow indicates the destinations which can be reached

Signs on primary routes - green backgrounds

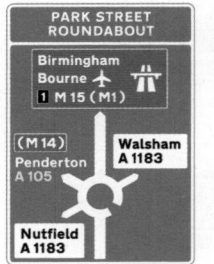 On approaches to junctions

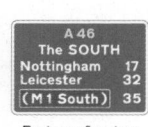 At the junction

 On approaches to junctions

Route confirmatory sign after junction

 On approach to a junction in Wales (bilingual)

Blue panels indicate that the motorway starts at the junction ahead.
Motorways shown in brackets can also be reached along the route indicated.
White panels indicate local or non-primary routes leading from the junction ahead.
Brown panels show the route to tourist attractions.
The name of the junction may be shown at the top of the sign.
The aircraft symbol indicates the route to an airport.
A symbol may be included to warn of a hazard or restriction along that route.

Primary route forming part of a ring road

Signs on non-primary and local routes - black borders

On approaches to junctions

At the junction

Direction to toilets with access for the disabled

Green panels indicate that the primary route starts at the junction ahead.
Route numbers on a blue background show the direction to a motorway.
Route numbers on a green background show the direction to a primary route.

Signs on non-primary and local routes - black borders

Picnic site

Ancient monument in the care of English Heritage

Direction to a car park

Zoo — Tourist attraction

Direction to camping and caravan site

Advisory route for lorries

Route for pedal cycles forming part of a network

Recommended route for pedal cycles to place shown

Route for pedestrians

Emergency diversion routes

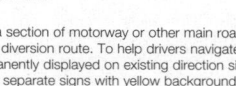 Symbols showing emergency diversion route for motorway and other main road traffic

Diversion route

In an emergency it may be necessary to close a section of motorway or other main road to traffic, so a temporary sign may advise drivers to follow a diversion route. To help drivers navigate the route, black symbols on yellow patches may be permanently displayed on existing direction signs, including motorway signs. Symbols may also be used on separate signs with yellow backgrounds.
For further information visit:
theaa.com/breakdown-cover/advice/emergency-diversion-routes

Information signs

All retangular

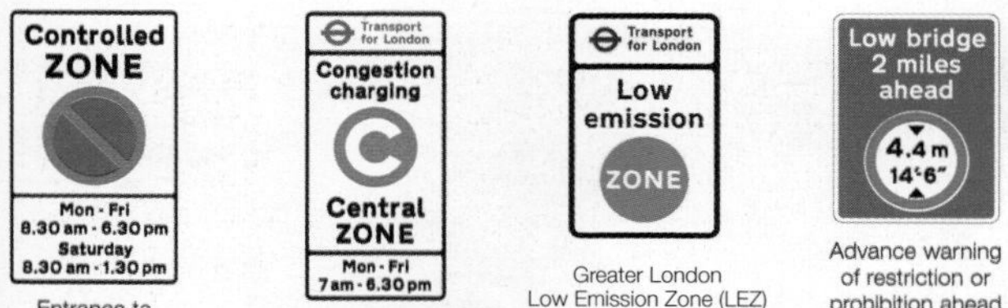
Controlled ZONE
Mon - Fri 8.30 am - 6.30 pm Saturday 8.30 am - 1.30 pm
Transport for London
Congestion charging
Central ZONE
Mon - Fri 7 am - 6.30 pm
Transport for London
Low emission
ZONE
Low bridge 2 miles ahead
4.4 m 14'6"

Entrance to controlled parking zone

Entrance to congestion charging zone

Greater London Low Emission Zone (LEZ)

Advance warning of restriction or prohibition ahead

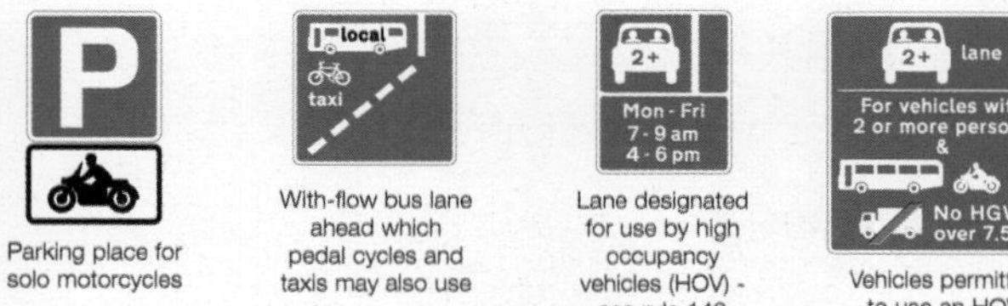
P
local
taxi
2+
Mon - Fri 7 - 9 am 4 - 6 pm
2+ lane
For vehicles with 2 or more persons
No HGVs over 7.5T

Parking place for solo motorcycles

With-flow bus lane ahead which pedal cycles and taxis may also use

Lane designated for use by high occupancy vehicles (HOV) - see rule 142

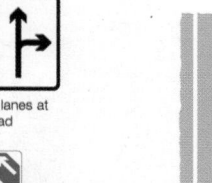

Vehicles permitted to use an HOV lane ahead

M62
Except buses

End of motorway

Start of motorway and point from which motorway regulations apply

Appropriate traffic lanes at junction ahead

Traffic on the main carriageway coming from right has priority over joining traffic

Additional traffic joining from left ahead. Traffic on main carriageway has priority over joining traffic from right hand lane of slip road

Traffic in right hand lane of slip road joining the main carriageway has prority over left hand lane

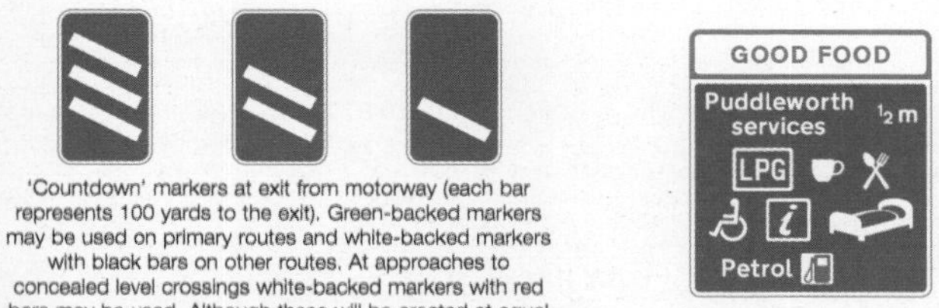
GOOD FOOD
Puddleworth services
½ m
LPG
i
Petrol

'Countdown' markers at exit from motorway (each bar represents 100 yards to the exit). Green-backed markers may be used on primary routes and white-backed markers with black bars on other routes. At approaches to concealed level crossings white-backed markers with red bars may be used. Although these will be erected at equal distances the bars do not represent 100 yard intervals.

Motorway service area sign showing the operator's name

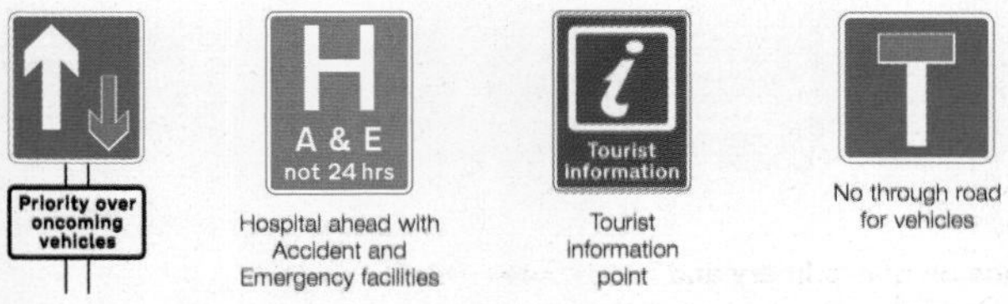
Priority over oncoming vehicles
H
A & E
not 24 hrs
i
Tourist information

Traffic has priority over oncoming vehicles

Hospital ahead with Accident and Emergency facilities

Tourist information point

No through road for vehicles

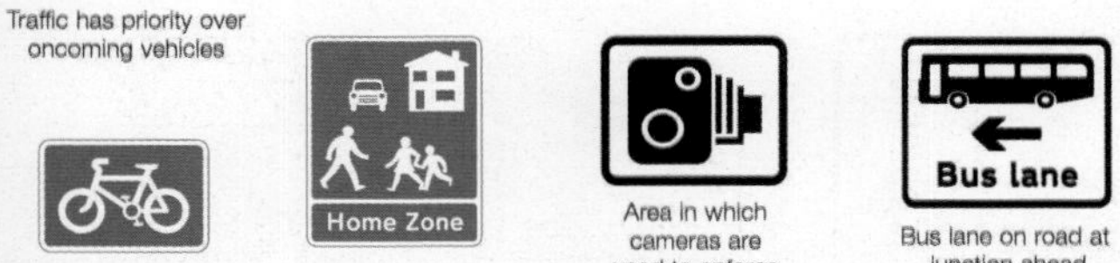
Home Zone
Bus lane

Recommended route for pedal cycles

Home Zone Entry

Area in which cameras are used to enforce traffic regulations

Bus lane on road at junction ahead

*Home Zone Entry – You are entering an area where people could be using the whole street for a range of activities. You should drive slowly and carefully and be prepared to stop to allow people time to move out of the way.

Roadworks signs

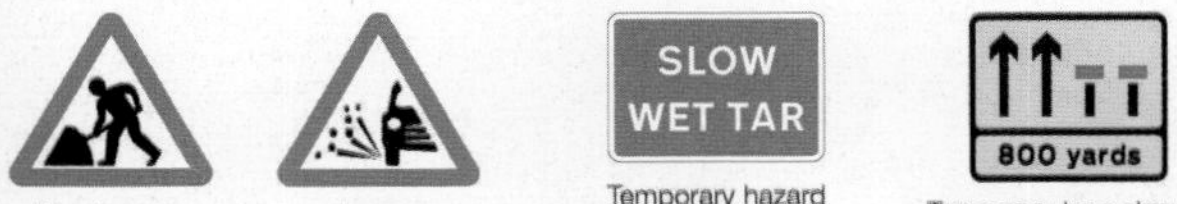
SLOW
WET TAR
800 yards

Road works

Loose chippings

Temporary hazard at roadworks

Temporary lane closure (the number and position of arrows and red bars may be varied according to lanes open and closed)

50
¾ mile ahead
Delays possible until Mar 08
1 mile
Sorry for any delay
End
Authority name

Slow-moving or stationary works vehicle blocking a traffic lane. Pass in the direction shown by the arrow.

Mandatory speed limit ahead

Roadworks 1 mile ahead

End of roadworks and any temporary restrictions including speed limits

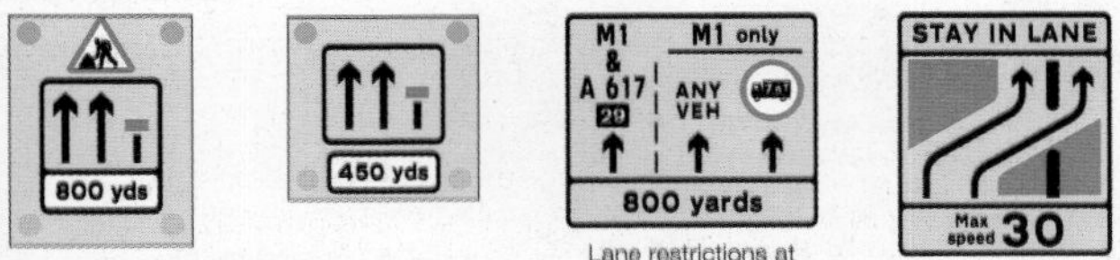
800 yds
450 yds
M1
M1 only
A 617
29
ANY VEH
800 yards
STAY IN LANE
Max speed 30

Signs used on the back of slow-moving or stationary vehicles warning of a lane closed ahead by a works vehicle. There are no cones on the road.

Lane restrictions at roadworks ahead

One lane crossover at contraflow roadworks

Road markings

Across the carriageway

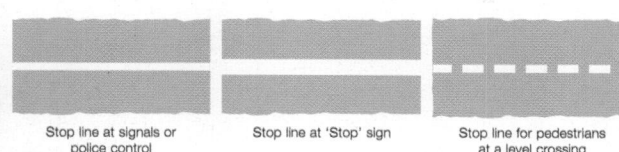

Stop line at signals or police control

Stop line at 'Stop' sign

Stop line for pedestrians at a level crossing

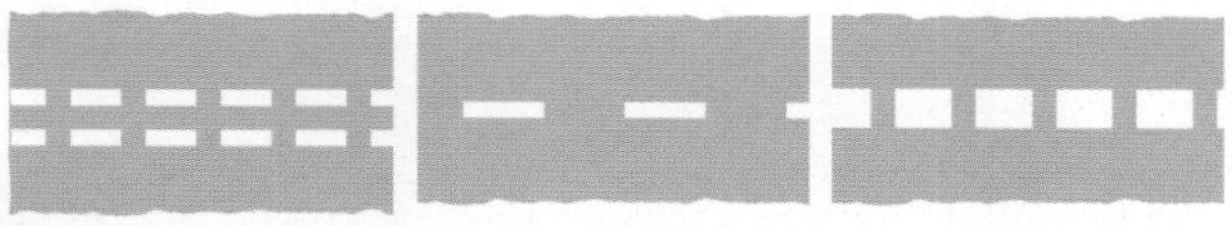

Give way to traffic on major road (can also be used at mini roundabouts)

Give way to traffic from the right at a roundabout

Give way to traffic from the right at a mini-roundabout

Along the carriageway

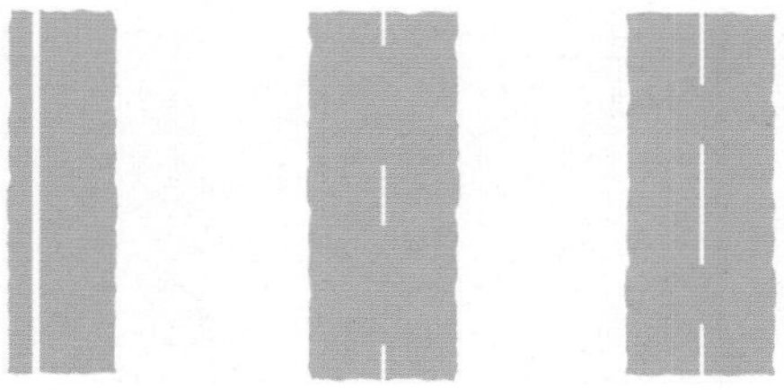

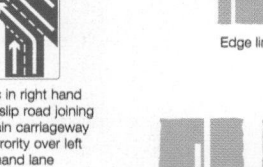

Edge line

Centre line See Rule 127

Hazard warning line See Rule 127

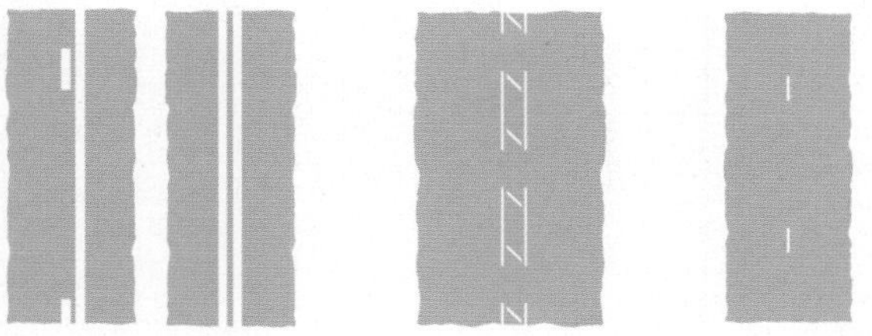

Double white lines See Rules 128 and 129

See Rule 130

Lane line See Rule 131

Along the edge of the carriageway

Waiting restrictions

Waiting restrictions indicated by yellow lines apply to the carriageway, pavement and verge. You may stop to load or unload (unless there are also loading restrictions as described below) or while passengers board or alight. Double yellow lines mean no waiting at any time, unless there are signs that specifically indicate seasonal restrictions. The times at which the restrictions apply for other road markings are shown on nearby plates or on entry signs to controlled parking zones. If no days are shown on the signs, the restrictions are in force every day including Sundays and Bank Holidays. White bay markings and upright signs (see below) indicate where parking is allowed.

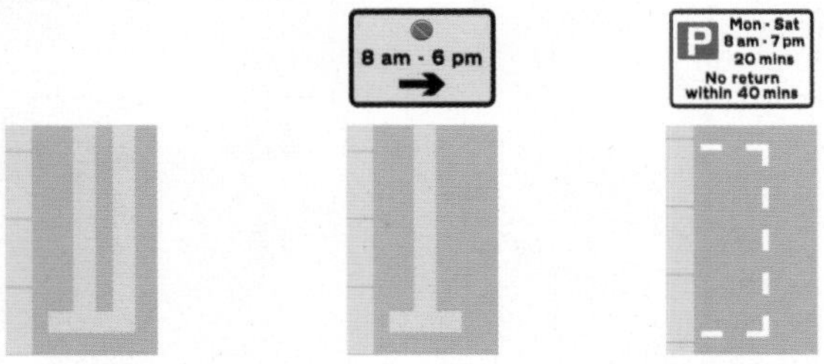
8 am - 6 pm
P
Mon - Sat 8 am - 7 pm 20 mins
No return within 40 mins

No waiting at any time

No waiting during times shown on sign

Waiting is limited to the duration specified during the days and times shown

Red Route stopping controls

Red lines are used on some roads instead of yellow lines. In London the double and single red lines used on Red Routes indicate that stopping to park, load/unload or to board and alight from a vehicle (except for a licensed taxi or if you hold a Blue Badge) is prohibited. The red lines apply to the carriageway, pavement and verge. The times that the red line prohibitions apply are shown on nearby signs, but the double red line ALWAYS means no stopping at any time. On Red Routes you may stop to park, load/unload in specially marked boxes and adjacent signs specify the times and purposes and duration allowed. A box MARKED IN RED indicates that it may only be available for the purpose specified for part of the day (e.g. between busy peak periods). A box MARKED IN WHITE means that it is available throughout the day.

RED AND SINGLE YELLOW LINES CAN ONLY GIVE A GUIDE TO THE RESTRICTIONS AND CONTROLS IN FORCE AND SIGNS, NEARBY OR AT A ZONE ENTRY, MUST BE CONSULTED.

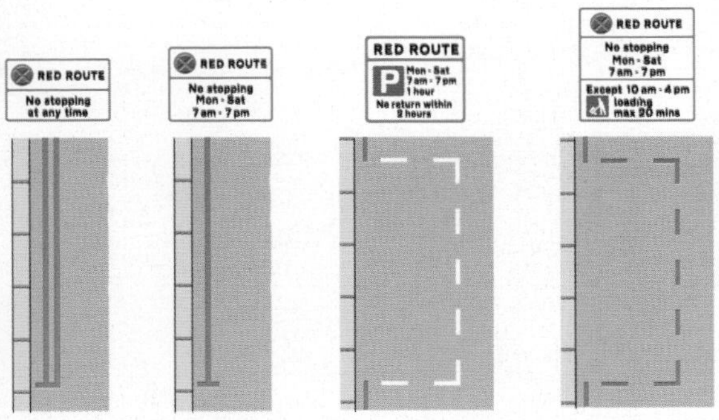
RED ROUTE
No stopping at any time
RED ROUTE
No stopping Mon - Sat 7am - 7pm
RED ROUTE
Mon - Sat 7am - 7pm 1 hour
No return within 2 hours
RED ROUTE
No stopping Mon - Sat 7am - 7pm
Except 10 am - 4 pm loading max 20 mins

No stopping at any time

No stopping during times shown on sign

Parking is limited to the duration specified during the days and times shown

Only loading may take place at the times shown for up to a maximum duration of 20 mins

On the kerb or at the edge of the carriageway

Loading restrictions on roads other than Red Routes

Yellow marks on the kerb or at the edge of the carriageway indicate that loading or unloading is prohibited at the times shown on the nearby black and white plates. You may stop while passengers board or alight. If no days are indicated on the signs the restrictions are in force every day including Sundays and Bank Holidays.

ALWAYS CHECK THE TIMES SHOWN ON THE PLATES.

Lengths of road reserved for vehicles loading and unloading are indicated by a white 'bay' marking with the words 'Loading Only' and a sign with the white on blue 'trolley' symbol. This sign also shows whether loading and unloading is restricted to goods vehicles and the times at which the bay can be used. If no times or days are shown it may be used at any time. Vehicles may not park here if they are not loading or unloading.

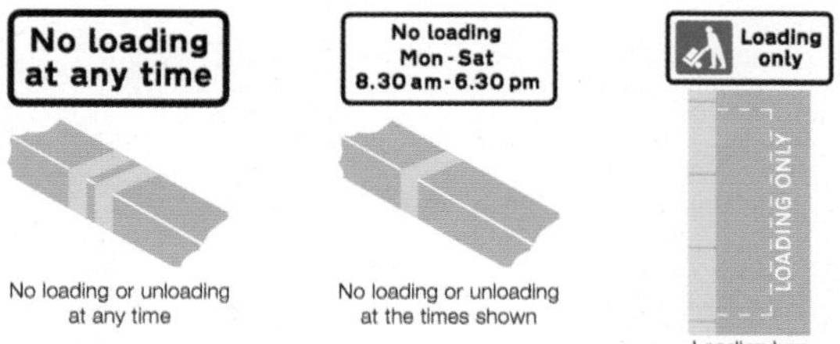
No loading at any time
No loading Mon - Sat 8.30 am - 6.30 pm
Loading only
LOADING ONLY

No loading or unloading at any time

No loading or unloading at the times shown

Loading bay

Other road markings

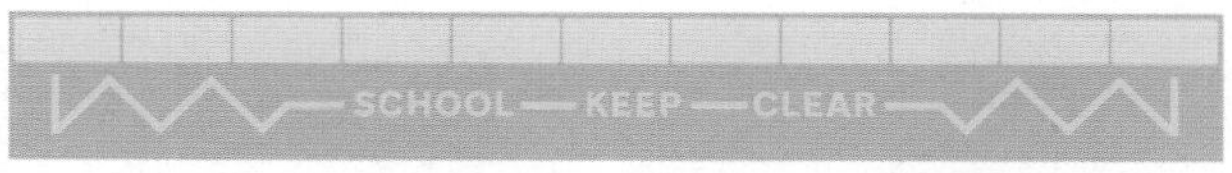
SCHOOL KEEP CLEAR

Keep entrance clear of stationary vehicles, even if picking up or setting down children

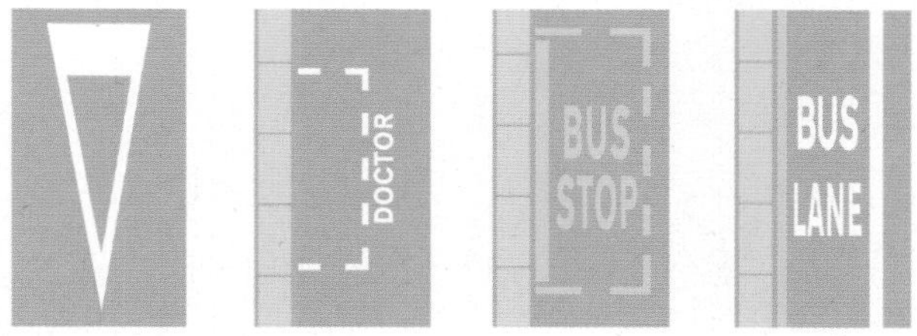
DOCTOR
BUS STOP
BUS LANE

Warning of 'Give Way' just ahead

Parking space reserved for vehicles named

See Rule 243

See Rule 141

KEEP CLEAR
CITY
A3
YORK ST

Box junction - See Rule 174

Do not block that part of the carriageway indicated

Indication of traffic lanes

Light signals controlling traffic

Traffic Light Signals

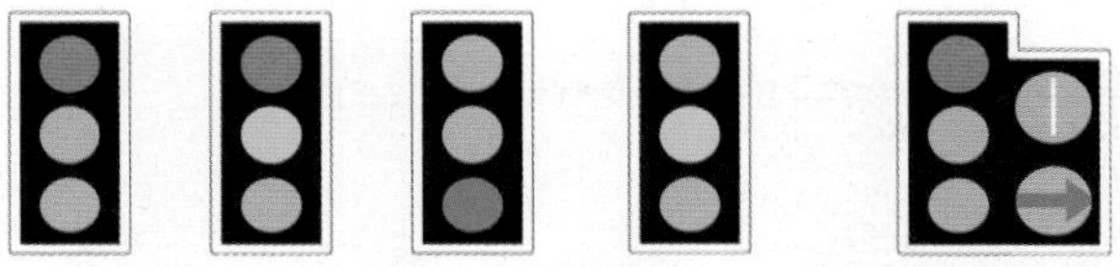

RED means 'Stop'. Wait behind the stop line on the carriageway

RED AND AMBER also means 'Stop'. Do not pass through or start until GREEN shows

GREEN means you may go on if the way is clear. Take special care if you intend to turn left or right and give way to pedestrians who are crossing

AMBER means 'Stop' at the stop line. You may go on only if the AMBER appears after you have crossed the stop line or are so close to it that to pull up might cause an accident

A GREEN ARROW may be provided in addition to the full green signal if movement in a certain direction is allowed before or after the full green phase. If the way is clear you may go but only in the direction shown by the arrow. You may do this whatever other lights may be showing. White light signals may be provided for trams

Flashing red lights

Alternately flashing red lights mean YOU MUST STOP

At level crossings, lifting bridges, airfields, fire stations, etc.

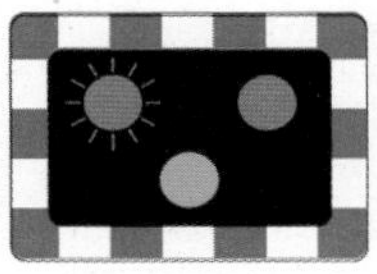

Motorway signals

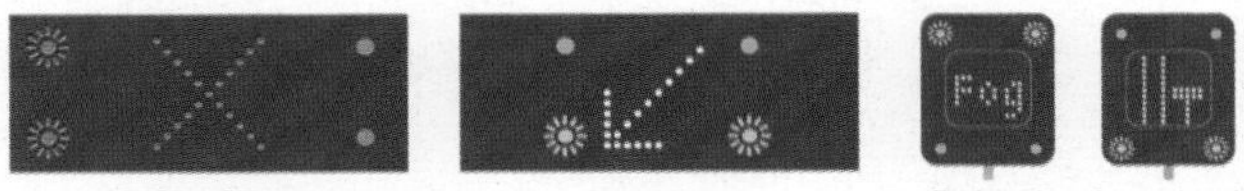
Fog

You MUST NOT proceed further in this lane

Change lane

Reduced visibility ahead

Lane ahead closed

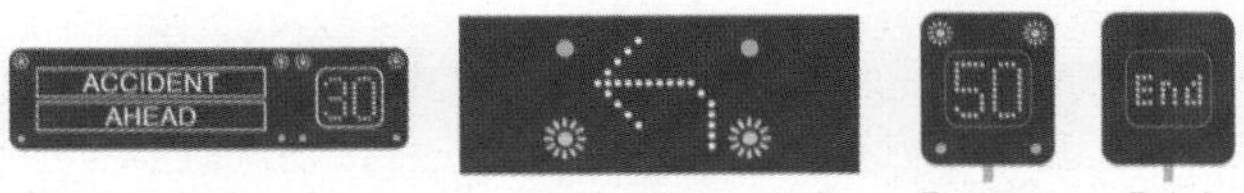
ACCIDENT AHEAD
30
50
End

Temporary maximum speed advised and information message

Leave motorway at next exit

Temporary maximum speed advised

End of restriction

Lane control signals

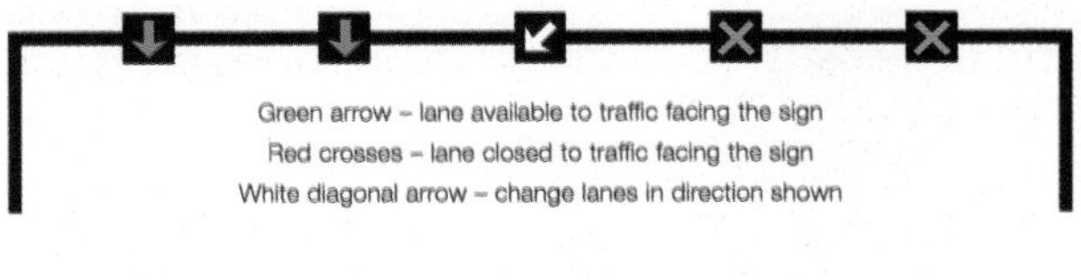

Green arrow – lane available to traffic facing the sign

Red crosses – lane closed to traffic facing the sign

White diagonal arrow – change lanes in direction shown

Channel hopping and the Isle of Wight

For business or pleasure, hopping on a ferry across to France, the Channel Islands or Isle of Wight has never been easier.

The vehicle ferry services listed in the table give you all the options, together with detailed port plans to help you navigate to and from the ferry terminals. Simply choose your preferred route, not forgetting the fast sailings (see ). Bon voyage!

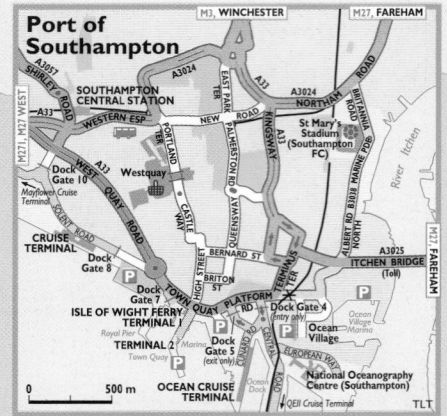

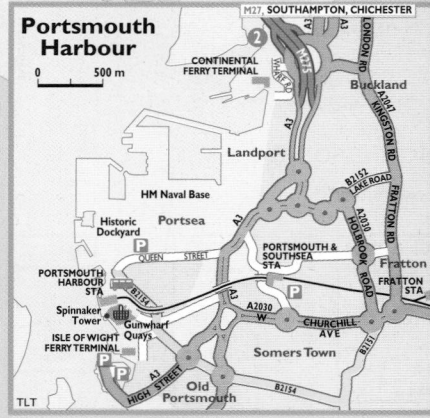

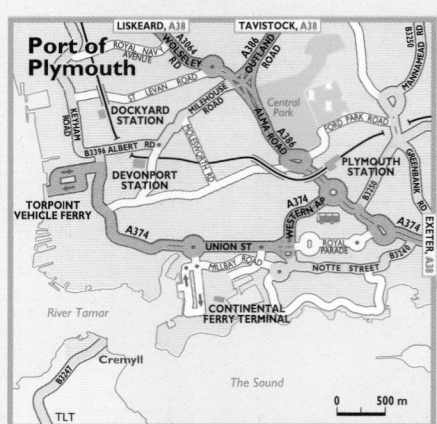

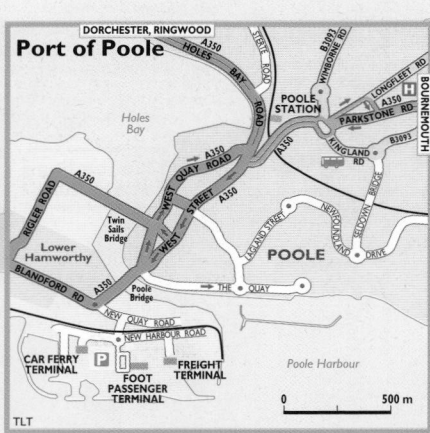

ENGLISH CHANNEL AND ISLE OF WIGHT FERRY CROSSINGS

From	To	Journey time	Operator website
Dover	Calais	1 hr 30 mins	dfdsseaways.co.uk
Dover	Calais	1 hr 30 mins	poferries.com
Dover	Dunkirk	2 hrs	dfdsseaways.co.uk
Folkestone	Calais (Coquelles)	35 mins	eurotunnel.com
Lymington	Yarmouth (IOW)	40 mins	wightlink.co.uk
Newhaven	Dieppe	4 hrs	dfdsseaways.co.uk
Plymouth	Roscoff	6–8 hrs	brittany-ferries.co.uk
Poole	Cherbourg	4 hrs 15 mins	brittany-ferries.co.uk
Poole	Guernsey	3 hrs	condorferries.co.uk
Poole	Jersey	4 hrs 30 mins	condorferries.co.uk
Poole	St-Malo	7–12 hrs (via Channel Is.)	condorferries.co.uk
Portsmouth	Caen (Ouistreham)	6–7 hrs	brittany-ferries.co.uk
Portsmouth	Cherbourg	3 hrs (May–Aug)	brittany-ferries.co.uk
Portsmouth	Fishbourne (IOW)	45 mins	wightlink.co.uk
Portsmouth	Guernsey	7 hrs	condorferries.co.uk
Portsmouth	Jersey	8–11 hrs	condorferries.co.uk
Portsmouth	Le Havre	5 hrs 30 mins	brittany-ferries.co.uk
Portsmouth	St-Malo	9–11 hrs	brittany-ferries.co.uk
Southampton	East Cowes (IOW)	1 hr	redfunnel.co.uk

The information listed is provided as a guide only, as services are liable to change at short notice. Services shown are for vehicle ferries only, operated by conventional ferry unless indicated as a fast ferry service ( ). Please check sailings before planning your journey.

Travelling further afield? For ferry services to Northern Spain see *brittany-ferries.co.uk*.

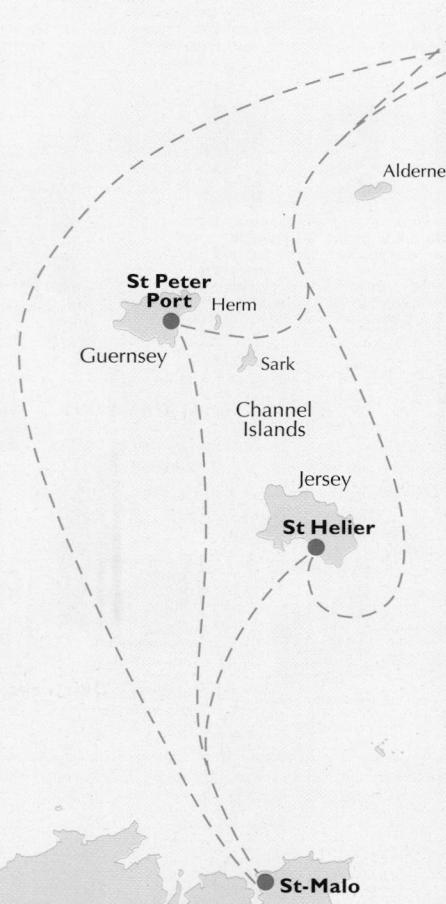

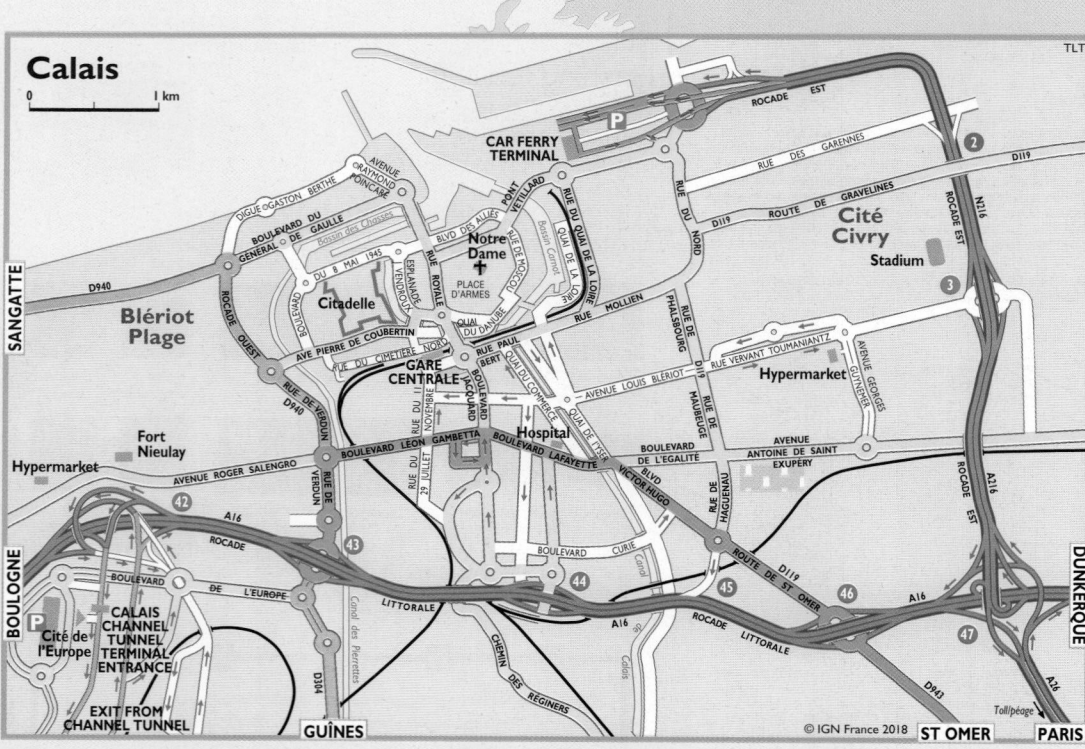

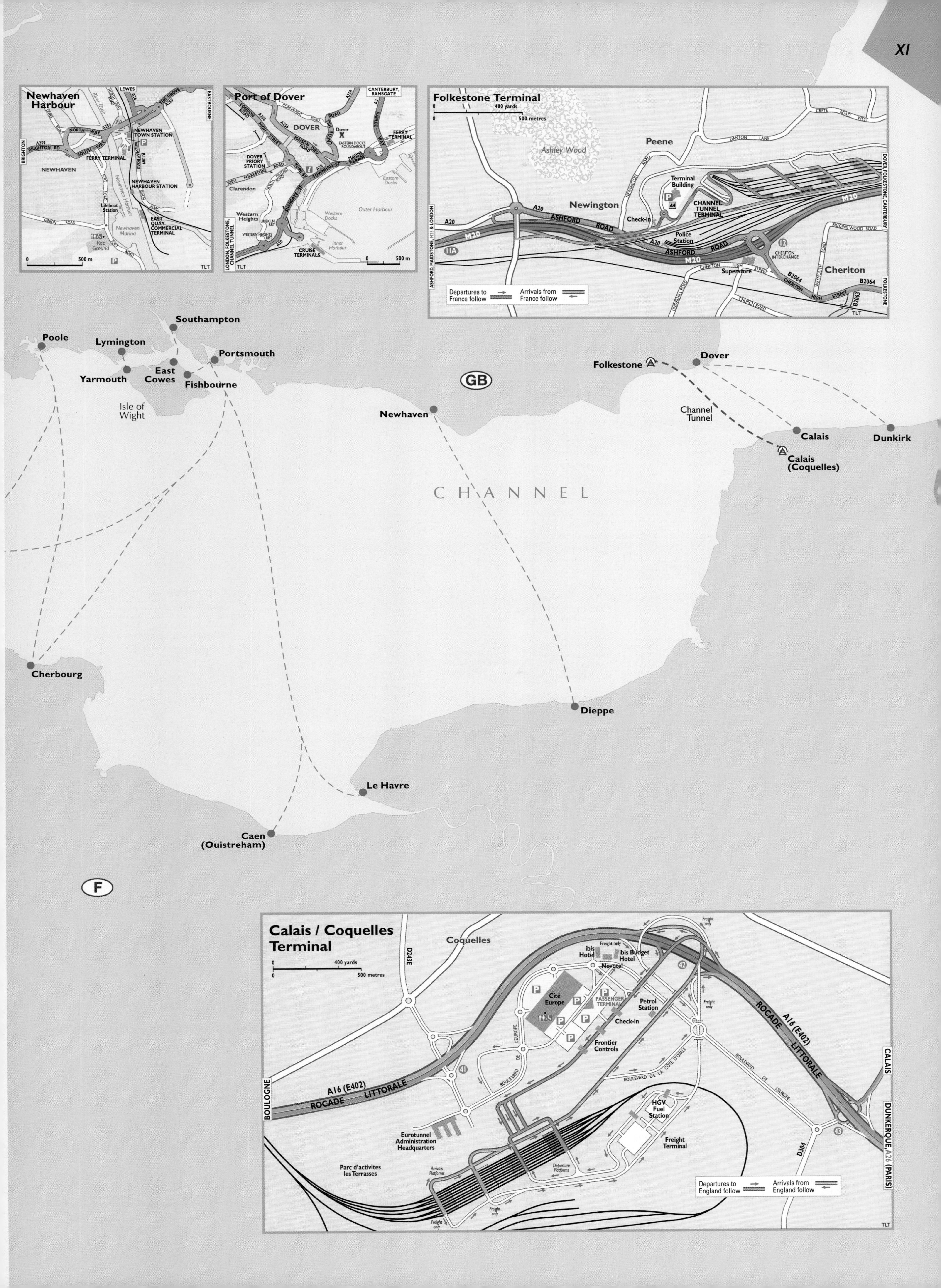

Newhaven Harbour

LEWES
EASTBOURNE
NORTH WAY
SOUTH WAY
BRIGHTON RD
BRIGHTON
NEWHAVEN
NEWHAVEN TOWN STATION
FERRY TERMINAL
NEWHAVEN HARBOUR STATION
Lifeboat Station
Newhaven Marina
Rec Ground
EAST QUAY COMMERCIAL TERMINAL
GIBBON ROAD
THE GROVE
A259
A259
B2109
500 m
TLT

Port of Dover

CANTERBURY, RAMSGATE
CONNAUGHT ROAD
DOVER
Dover ✈
FERRY TERMINAL
EASTERN DOCKS ROUNDABOUT
Eastern Docks
Outer Harbour
DOVER PRIORY STATION
Clarendon
Western Heights
WESTERN HEIGHTS
Western Docks
MARINE PARADE
CRUISE TERMINALS
Inner Harbour
LONDON, FOLKESTONE, CHANNEL TUNNEL
TOWNWALL ST
500 m
TLT

Folkestone Terminal

400 yards
500 metres
Ashley Wood
Peene
Newington
DANTON LANE
CREETE ROAD WEST
Terminal Building
P
Check-in
CHANNEL TUNNEL TERMINAL
Police Station
CHERITON INTERCHANGE
Cheriton
Superstore
ASHFORD ROAD
A20
A20
M20
M20
A20
11A
12
B2064
B2064
CHERITON HIGH STREET
CHURCH ROAD
DOVER FOLKESTONE CANTERBURY
ASHFORD, MAIDSTONE, M25 & LONDON
BIGGINS WOOD ROAD
FOLKESTONE

Departures to France follow →
Arrivals from France follow →

TLT

Poole
Lymington
Southampton
Yarmouth
East Cowes
Fishbourne
Portsmouth
Isle of Wight
Newhaven
Folkestone ✈
Dover
Channel Tunnel
Calais
Calais (Coquelles) ✈
Dunkirk

GB

C H A N N E L

Cherbourg
Dieppe
Le Havre
Caen (Ouistreham)

F

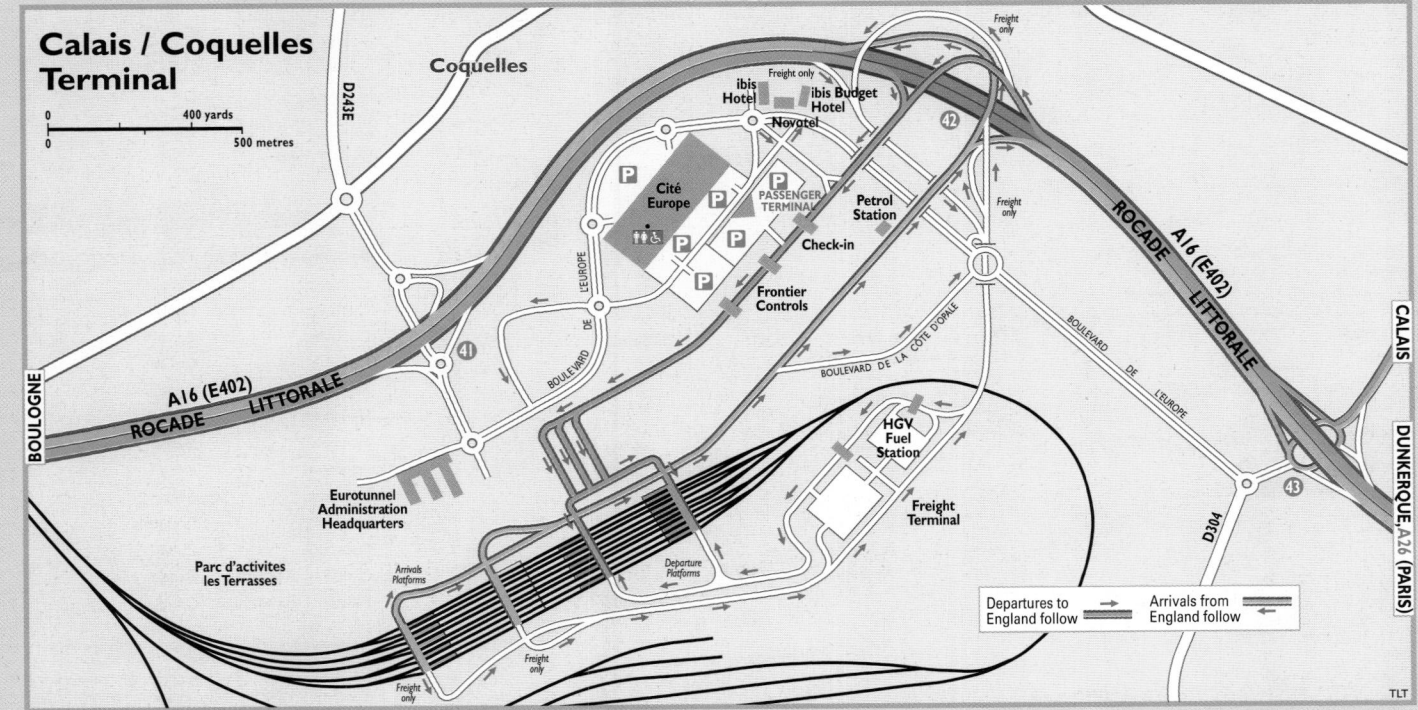

Calais / Coquelles Terminal

Coquelles
400 yards
500 metres
ibis Hotel
ibis Budget Hotel
Novotel
Freight only
Freight only
Cité Europe
P
P
P
P
P
PASSENGER TERMINAL
Check-in
Petrol Station
Frontier Controls
42
Freight only
HGV Fuel Station
Eurotunnel Administration Headquarters
Freight Terminal
Parc d'activités les Terrasses
Arrivals Platforms
Departure Platforms
BOULOGNE
A16 (E402) ROCADE LITTORALE
BOULEVARD DE L'EUROPE
BOULEVARD DE LA CÔTE ROYALE
BOULEVARD DE L'EUROPE
ROCADE LITTORALE A16 (E402)
D243E
D304
41
43
CALAIS
DUNKERQUE A26 (PARIS)
Freight only

Departures to England follow →
Arrivals from England follow →

TLT

SCOTLAND FERRIES

From	To	Journey time	Operator website
Scottish Islands/west coast of Scotland			
Gourock	Dunoon	20 mins	western-ferries.co.uk
Glenelg	Skye	20 mins (Easter–Oct)	skyeferry.co.uk

Numerous and varied sailings from the west coast of Scotland to Scottish islands are provided by Caledonian MacBrayne. Please visit calmac.co.uk for all ferry information, including those of other operators.

From	To	Journey time	Operator website
Orkney Islands			
Aberdeen	Kirkwall	6 hrs	northlinkferries.co.uk
Gills	St Margaret's Hope	1 hr	pentlandferries.co.uk
Scrabster	Stromness	1 hr 30 mins	northlinkferries.co.uk
Lerwick	Kirkwall	5 hrs 30 mins	northlinkferries.co.uk

Inter-island services are operated by Orkney Ferries. Please see orkneyferries.co.uk for details.

From	To	Journey time	Operator website
Shetland Islands			
Aberdeen	Lerwick	12 hrs 30 mins	northlinkferries.co.uk
Kirkwall	Lerwick	7 hrs 45 mins	northlinkferries.co.uk

Inter-island services are operated by Shetland Island Council Ferries. Please see shetland.gov.uk/ferries for details.

Please note that some smaller island services are day dependent and reservations are required for some routes. Book and confirm sailing schedules by contacting the operator.

NORTH SEA FERRY CROSSINGS

From	To	Journey time	Operator website
Harwich	Hook of Holland	7–8 hrs	stenaline.co.uk
Kingston upon Hull	Rotterdam (Europoort)	12 hrs	poferries.com
Kingston upon Hull	Zeebrugge	12 hrs	poferries.com
Newcastle upon Tyne	Amsterdam (IJmuiden)	15 hrs 30 mins	dfdsseaways.co.uk

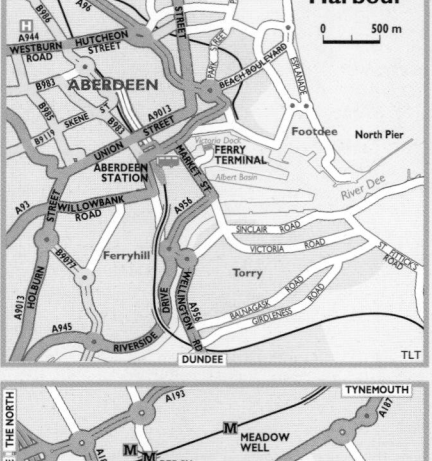

Aberdeen Harbour

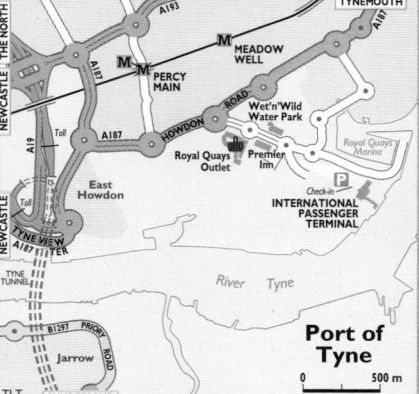

Port of Tyne

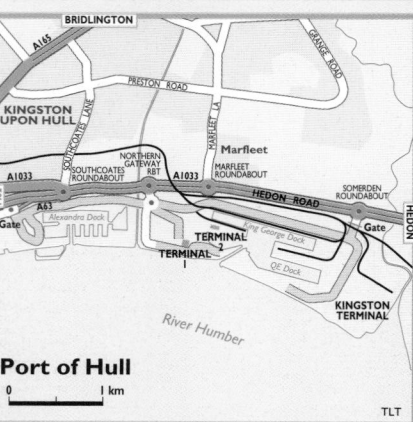

Port of Hull

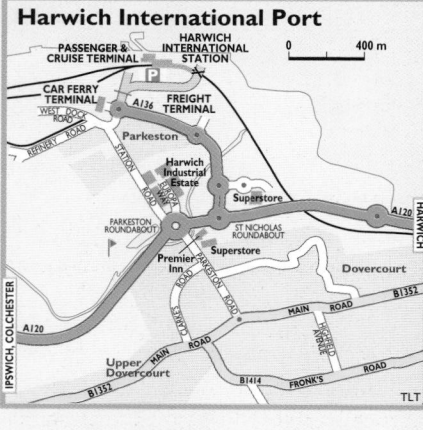

Harwich International Port

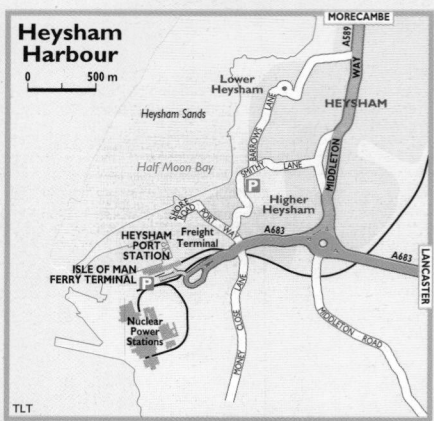

Heysham Harbour

Liverpool Docks

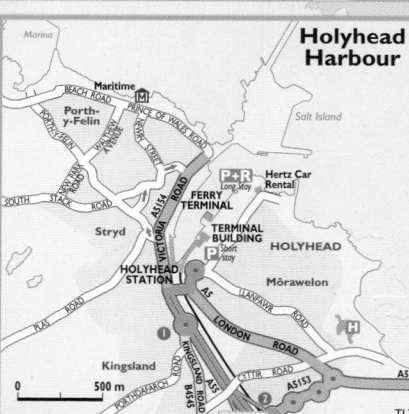

Holyhead Harbour

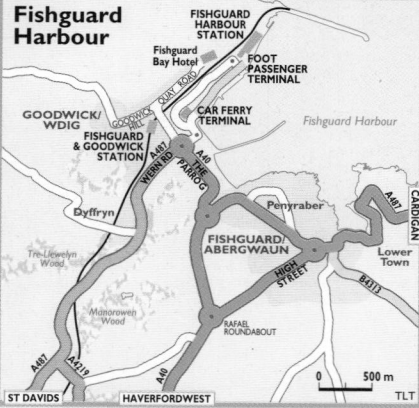

Fishguard Harbour

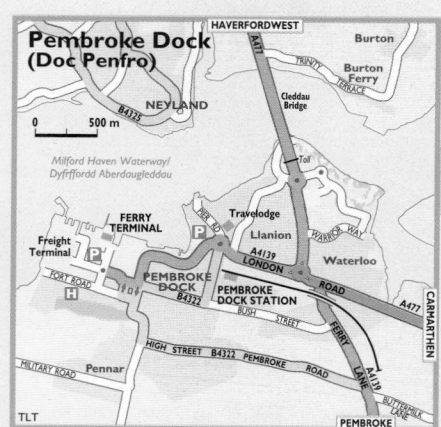

Pembroke Dock (Doc Penfro)

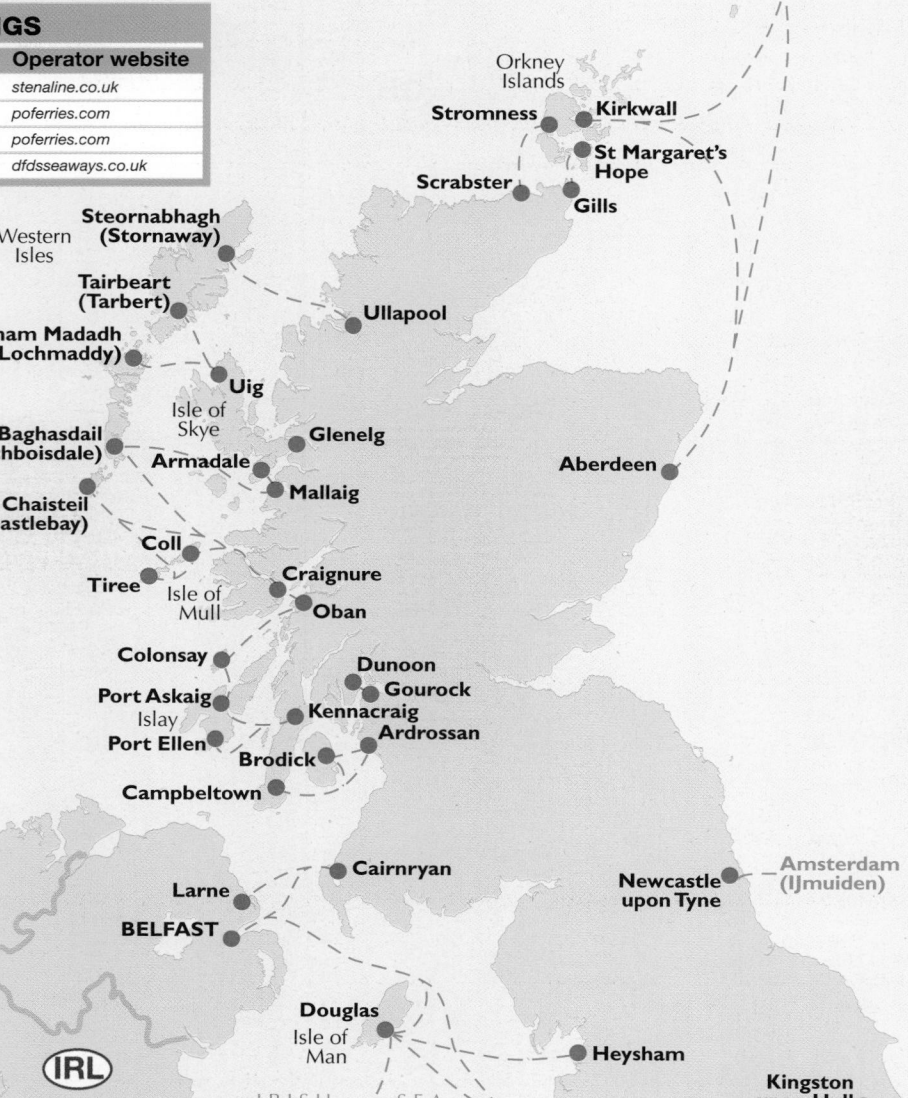

Shetland Islands — Lerwick
Orkney Islands — Stromness, Kirkwall, St Margaret's Hope, Scrabster, Gills
Steornabhagh (Stornaway), Tairbeart (Tarbert), Loch nam Madadh (Lochmaddy), Ullapool
Western Isles
Uig, Isle of Skye, Glenelg, Armadale, Mallaig
Loch Baghasdail (Lochboisdale)
Bàgh a' Chaisteil (Castlebay)
Coll, Craignure, Isle of Mull, Oban
Tiree
Colonsay, Dunoon, Gourock
Port Askaig, Islay, Kennacraig, Ardrossan
Port Ellen, Brodick
Campbeltown
Aberdeen
Cairnryan
Larne, BELFAST
Newcastle upon Tyne — Amsterdam (IJmuiden)
Douglas, Isle of Man, Heysham
Kingston upon Hull — Rotterdam (Europoort), Zeebrugge
IRL
IRISH SEA
DUBLIN
Holyhead, Anglesey, Birkenhead, Liverpool
GB
Rosslare
Fishguard, Pembroke Dock
Harwich — Hook of Holland

IRISH SEA FERRY CROSSINGS

From	To	Journey time	Operator website
Cairnryan	Belfast	2 hrs 15 mins	stenaline.co.uk
Cairnryan	Larne	2 hrs	poferries.com
Douglas	Belfast	2 hrs 45 mins (April–Sept)	steam-packet.com
Douglas	Dublin	2 hrs 55 mins (April–Sept)	steam-packet.com
Fishguard	Rosslare	3 hrs 15 mins	stenaline.co.uk
Heysham	Douglas	3 hrs 45 mins	steam-packet.com
Holyhead	Dublin	2 hrs	irishferries.com
Holyhead	Dublin	3 hrs 15 mins	irishferries.com
Holyhead	Dublin	3 hrs 15 mins	stenaline.co.uk
Liverpool	Douglas	2 hrs 45 mins (Mar–Oct)	steam-packet.com
Liverpool	Dublin	8 hrs–8 hrs 30 mins	poferries.com
Liverpool (Birkenhead)	Belfast	8 hrs	stenaline.co.uk
Liverpool (Birkenhead)	Douglas	4 hrs 15 mins (Nov–Mar Sat, Sun only)	steam-packet.com
Pembroke Dock	Rosslare	4 hrs	irishferries.com

The information listed is provided as a guide only, as services are liable to change at short notice. Services shown are for vehicle ferries only, operated by conventional ferry unless indicated as a fast ferry service (⛴). Please check sailings before planning your journey.

Restricted junctions

Motorway and primary route junctions which have access or exit restrictions are shown on the map pages thus: 3 56

M1 London - Leeds

Junction	Northbound	Southbound
2	Access only from A1 (northbound)	Exit only to A1 (southbound)
4	Access only from A41 (northbound)	Exit only to A41 (southbound)
6A	Access only from M25 (no link from A405)	Exit only to M25 (no link from A405)
7	Access only from A414	Exit only to A414
17	Exit only to M45	Access only from M45
19	Exit only to M6 (northbound)	Exit only to A14 (southbound)
21A	Exit only, no access	Access only, no exit
24A	Access only, no exit	Access only from A50 (eastbound)
35A	Exit only, no access	Access only, no exit
43	Exit only to M621	Access only from M621
48	Exit only to A1(M) (northbound)	Access only from A1(M) (southbound)

M2 Rochester - Faversham

Junction	Westbound	Eastbound
1	No exit to A2 (eastbound)	No access from A2 (westbound)

M3 Sunbury - Southampton

Junction	Northeastbound	Southwestbound
8	Access only from A303, no exit	Exit only to A303, no access
10	Exit only, no access	Access only, no exit
14	Access from M27 only, no exit	No access to M27 (westbound)

M4 London - South Wales

Junction	Westbound	Eastbound
1	Access only from A4 (westbound)	Exit only to A4 (eastbound)
2	Access only from A4 (westbound)	Access only from A4 (eastbound)
21	Exit only to M48	Access only from M48
23	Access only from M48	Exit only to M48
25	Exit only, no access	Access only, no exit
25A	Exit only, no access	Access only, no exit
29	Exit only to A48(M)	Access only from A48(M)
38	Exit only, no access	No restriction
39	Access only, no exit	No access or exit
42	Exit only to A483	Access only from A483

M5 Birmingham - Exeter

Junction	Northeastbound	Southwestbound
10	Access only, no exit	Exit only, no access
11A	Access only from A417 (westbound)	Exit only to A417 (eastbound)
18A	Exit only to M49	Access only from M49
18	Exit only, no access	Access only, no exit

M6 Toll Motorway

Junction	Northwestbound	Southeastbound
T1	Access only, no exit	No access or exit
T2	No access or exit	Exit only, no access
T5	Access only, no exit	Exit only to A5148 (northbound), no access
T7	Exit only, no access	Access only, no exit
T8	Exit only, no access	Access only, no exit

M6 Rugby - Carlisle

Junction	Northbound	Southbound
3A	Exit only to M6 Toll	Access only from M6 Toll
4	Exit only to M42 (southbound) & A446	Exit only to A446
4A	Access only from M42 (southbound)	Exit only to M42
5	Exit only, no access	Access only, no exit
10A	Exit only to M54	Access only from M54
11A	Access only from M6 Toll	Exit only to M6 Toll
with M56 (jct 20A)	No restriction	Access only from M56 (eastbound)
20	Exit only to M56 (westbound)	Access only from M56 (eastbound)
24	Access only, no exit	Exit only, no access
25	Exit only, no access	Access only, no exit
30	Access only from M61	Exit only to M61
31A	Exit only, no access	Access only, no exit
45	Exit only, no access	Access only, no exit

M8 Edinburgh - Bishopton

Junction	Westbound	Eastbound
6	Exit only, no access	Access only, no exit
6A	Access only, no exit	Exit only, no access
7	Access only, no exit	Exit only, no access
7A	Exit only, no access	Access only from A725 (northbound), no exit
8	No access from M73 (southbound) or from A8 (eastbound) & A89	No exit to M73 (northbound) or to A8 (westbound) & A89
9	Access only, no exit	Exit only, no access
13	Access only from M80 (southbound)	Exit only to M80 (northbound)
14	Access only, no exit	Exit only, no access
16	Exit only to A804	Access only from A879
17	Exit only to A82	No restriction
18	Access only from A82 (eastbound)	Exit only to A814
19	No access from A814 (westbound)	Exit only to A814 (westbound)
20	Exit only, no access	Access only, no exit
21	Access only, no exit	Exit only to A8
22	Exit only to M77 (southbound)	Access only from M77 (northbound)
23	Exit only to B768	Access only from B768
25	No access or exit from or to A8	No access or exit from or to A8
25A	Exit only, no access	Access only, no exit
28	Exit only, no access	Access only, no exit
28A	Exit only to A737	Access only from A737
29A	Exit only to A8	Access only, no exit

M9 Edinburgh - Dunblane

Junction	Northwestbound	Southeastbound
2	Access only, no exit	Exit only, no access
3	Exit only, no access	Access only, no exit
6	Access only, no exit	Exit only to A905
8	Exit only to M876 (southwestbound)	Access only from M876 (northeastbound)

M11 London - Cambridge

Junction	Northbound	Southbound
4	Access only from A406 (eastbound)	Exit only to A406
5	Exit only, no access	Access only, no exit
8A	Exit only, no access	No direct access, use jct 8
9	Exit only to A11	Access only from A11
13	Exit only, no access	Access only, no exit
14	Exit only, no access	Access only, no exit

M20 Swanley - Folkestone

Junction	Northwestbound	Southeastbound
2	Staggered junction; follow signs - access only	Staggered junction; follow signs - exit only
3	Exit only to M26 (westbound)	Access only from M26 (eastbound)
5	Access only from A20	For access follow signs - exit only to A20
6	No restriction	For exit follow signs
11A	Access only, no exit	Exit only, no access

M23 Hooley - Crawley

Junction	Northbound	Southbound
7	Exit only to A23 (northbound)	Access only from A23 (southbound)
10A	Access only, no exit	Exit only, no access

M25 London Orbital Motorway

Junction	Clockwise	Anticlockwise
1B	No direct access, use slip road to jct 2 Exit only	Access only, no exit
5	No exit to M26 (eastbound)	No access from M26
19	Exit only, no access	Access only, no exit
21	Access only from M1 (southbound) Exit only to M1 (northbound)	Access only from M1 (southbound) Exit only to M1 (northbound)
31	No exit (use slip road via jct 30), access only	No access (use slip road via jct 30), exit only

M26 Sevenoaks - Wrotham

Junction	Westbound	Eastbound
with M25 (jct 5)	Exit only to clockwise M25 (westbound)	Access only from anticlockwise M25 (eastbound)
with M20 (jct 3)	Access only from M20 (northwestbound)	Exit only to M20 (southeastbound)

M27 Cadnam - Portsmouth

Junction	Westbound	Eastbound
4	Staggered junction; follow signs - access only from M3 (southbound). Exit only to M3 (northbound)	Staggered junction; follow signs - access only from M3 (southbound). Exit only to M3 (northbound)
10	Exit only, no access	Access only, no exit
12	Staggered junction; follow signs - exit only to M275 (southbound)	Staggered junction; follow signs - access only from M275 (northbound)

M40 London - Birmingham

Junction	Northwestbound	Southeastbound
3	Exit only, no access	Access only, no exit
7	Exit only, no access	Access only, no exit
8	Exit only to M40/A40	Access only from M40/A40
13	Exit only, no access	Access only, no exit
14	Access only, no exit	Exit only, no access
16	Access only, no exit	Exit only, no access

M42 Bromsgrove - Measham

Junction	Northeastbound	Southwestbound
1	Access only, no exit	Exit only, no access
7	Exit only to M6 (northwestbound)	Access only from M6 (northwestbound)
7A	Exit only to M6 (southeastbound)	No access or exit
8	Access only from M6 (southeastbound)	Exit only to M6 (northwestbound)

M45 Coventry - M1

Junction	Westbound	Eastbound
Dunchurch (unnumbered)	Access only from A45	Exit only, no access
with M1 (jct 17)	Access only from M1 (northbound)	Exit only to M1 (southbound)

M48 Chepstow

Junction	Westbound	Eastbound
21	Access only from M4 (westbound)	Exit only to M4 (eastbound)
23	No exit to M4 (eastbound)	No access from M4 (westbound)

M53 Mersey Tunnel - Chester

Junction	Northbound	Southbound
11	Access only from M56 (westbound) Exit only to M56 (eastbound)	Access only from M56 (westbound) Exit only to M56 (eastbound)

M54 Telford - Birmingham

Junction	Westbound	Eastbound
with M6 (jct 10A)	Access only from M6 (northbound)	Exit only to M6 (southbound)

M56 Chester - Manchester

Junction	Westbound	Eastbound
1	Access only from M60 (westbound)	Exit only to M60 (eastbound) & A34 (northbound)
2	Exit only, no access	Access only, no exit
3	Access only, no exit	Exit only, no access
4	Exit only, no access	Access only, no exit
7	Exit only, no access	No restriction
8	Access only, no exit	No access or exit
9	No exit to M6 (southbound)	No access from M6 (northbound)
15	Exit only to M53	Access only from M53
16	No access or exit	No restriction

M57 Liverpool Outer Ring Road

Junction	Northwestbound	Southeastbound
3	Access only, no exit	Exit only, no access
5	Access only from A580 (westbound)	Exit only, no access

M58 Liverpool - Wigan

Junction	Westbound	Eastbound
1	Exit only, no access	Access only, no exit

M60 Manchester Orbital

Junction	Clockwise	Anticlockwise
2	Access only, no exit	Exit only, no access
3	No access from M56	Access only from A34 (northbound)
4	Access only from A34 (northbound). Exit only to M56	Access only from M56 (eastbound). Exit only to A34 (southbound)
5	Access and exit only from and to A5103 (northbound)	Access and exit only from and to A5103 (southbound)
7	No direct access, use slip road to jct 8. Exit only to A56	Access only from A56. No exit, use jct 8
14	Access from A580 (eastbound)	Exit only to A580 (westbound)
16	Access only, no exit	Exit only, no access
20	Exit only, no access	Access only, no exit
22	No restriction	Exit only, no access
25	Exit only, no access	No restriction
26	No restriction	Exit only, no access
27	Access only, no exit	Exit only, no access

M61 Manchester - Preston

Junction	Northwestbound	Southeastbound
3	No access or exit	Exit only, no access
with M6 (jct 30)	Exit only to M6 (northbound)	Access only from M6 (southbound)

M62 Liverpool - Kingston upon Hull

Junction	Westbound	Eastbound
23	Access only, no exit	Exit only, no access
32A	No access to A1(M) (southbound)	No restriction

M65 Preston - Colne

Junction	Northeastbound	Southwestbound
9	Exit only, no access	Access only, no exit
11	Access only, no exit	Exit only, no access

M66 Bury

Junction	Northbound	Southbound
with A56	Exit only to A56 (northbound)	Access only from A56 (southbound)
1	Exit only, no access	Access only, no exit

M67 Hyde Bypass

Junction	Westbound	Eastbound
1	Access only, no exit	Exit only, no access
2	Exit only, no access	Access only, no exit
3	Exit only, no access	No restriction

M69 Coventry - Leicester

Junction	Northbound	Southbound
2	Access only, no exit	Exit only, no access

M73 East of Glasgow

Junction	Northbound	Southbound
1	No exit to A74 & A721	No exit to A74 & A721
2	No access from or exit to A89. No access from (eastbound)	No access from or exit to A89. No exit to M8 (westbound)

M74 and A74(M) Glasgow - Gretna

Junction	Northbound	Southbound
3	Exit only, no access	Access only, no exit
3A	Access only, no exit	Exit only, no access
4	No access from A74 & A721	Access only, no exit to A74 & A721
7	Access only, no exit	Exit only, no access
9	No access or exit	Exit only, no access
10	No restriction	Access only, no exit
11	Access only, no exit	Exit only, no access
12	Exit only, no access	Access only, no exit
18	Exit only, no access	Access only, no exit

M77 Glasgow - Kilmarnock

Junction	Northbound	Southbound
with M8 (jct 22)	No exit to M8 (westbound)	No access from M8 (eastbound)
4	Access only, no exit	Exit only, no access
6	Access only, no exit	Exit only, no access
7	Access only, no exit	No restriction
8	Exit only, no access	Exit only, no access

M80 Glasgow - Stirling

Junction	Northbound	Southbound
4A	Exit only, no access	Access only, no exit
6A	Access only, no exit	Exit only, no access
8	Exit only to M876 (northeastbound)	Access only from M876 (southwestbound)

M90 Edinburgh - Perth

Junction	Northbound	Southbound
1	No exit, access only	Exit only to A90 (eastbound)
2A	Exit only to A92 (eastbound)	Access only from A92 (westbound)
7	Access only, no exit	Exit only, no access
8	Exit only, no access	Access only, no exit
10	No access from A912. No exit to A912 (southbound)	No access from A912 (northbound) No exit to A912

M180 Doncaster - Grimsby

Junction	Westbound	Eastbound
1	Access only, no exit	Exit only, no access

M606 Bradford Spur

Junction	Northbound	Southbound
2	Exit only, no access	No restriction

M621 Leeds - M1

Junction	Clockwise	Anticlockwise
2A	Access only, no exit	Exit only, no access
4	No exit or access	No restriction
5	Access only, no exit	Exit only, no access
6	Exit only, no access	Access only, no exit
with M1 (jct 43)	Exit only to M1 (southbound)	Access only from M1 (northbound)

M876 Bonnybridge - Kincardine Bridge

Junction	Northeastbound	Southwestbound
with M80 (jct 5)	Access only from M80 (northeastbound)	Exit only to M80 (southwestbound)
with M9 (jct 8)	Exit only to M9 (eastbound)	Access only from M9 (westbound)

A1(M) South Mimms - Baldock

Junction	Northbound	Southbound
2	Exit only, no access	Access only, no exit
3	No restriction	Exit only, no access
5	Access only, no exit	No access or exit

A1(M) Pontefract - Bedale

Junction	Northbound	Southbound
41	No access to M62 (eastbound)	No restriction
43	Access only from M1 (northbound)	Exit only to M1 (southbound)

A1(M) Scotch Corner - Newcastle upon Tyne

Junction	Northbound	Southbound
57	Exit only to A66(M) (eastbound)	Access only from A66(M) (westbound)
65	No access Exit only to A194(M) & A1 (northbound)	No exit Access only from A194(M) & A1 (southbound)

A3(M) Horndean - Havant

Junction	Northbound	Southbound
1	Access only from A3	Exit only to A3
4	Exit only, no access	Access only, no exit

A38(M) Birmingham, Victoria Road (Park Circus)

Junction	Northbound	Southbound
with B4132	No exit	No access

A48(M) Cardiff Spur

Junction	Westbound	Eastbound
29	Access only from M4 (westbound)	Exit only to M4 (eastbound)
29A	Exit only to A48 (westbound)	Access only from A48 (eastbound)

A57(M) Manchester, Brook Street (A34)

Junction	Westbound	Eastbound
with A34	No exit	No access

A58(M) Leeds, Park Lane and Westgate

Junction	Northbound	Southbound
with A58	No restriction	No access

A64(M) Leeds, Clay Pit Lane (A58)

Junction	Westbound	Eastbound
with A58	No exit (to Clay Pit Lane)	No access (from Clay Pit Lane)

A66(M) Darlington Spur

Junction	Westbound	Eastbound
with A1(M) (jct 57)	Exit only to A1(M) (southbound)	Access only from A1(M) (northbound)

A74(M) Gretna - Abington

Junction	Northbound	Southbound
18	Exit only, no access	No exit

A194(M) Newcastle upon Tyne

Junction	Northbound	Southbound
with A1(M) (jct 65)	Access only from A1(M) (northbound)	Exit only to A1(M) (southbound)

A12 M25 - Ipswich

Junction	Northeastbound	Southwestbound
13	Access only, no exit	No restriction
14	Exit only, no access	Access only, no exit
20A	Exit only, no access	Access only, no exit
20B	Access only, no exit	Exit only, no access
21	No restriction	Access only, no exit
23	Exit only, no access	Access only, no exit
24	Access only, no exit	Exit only, no access
27	Exit only, no access	Access only, no exit
Dedham & Stratford St Mary (unnumbered)	Exit only	Access only

A14 M1 - Felixstowe

Junction	Westbound	Eastbound
with M1/M6 (jct19)	Exit only to M6 and M1 (northbound)	Access only from M6 and M1 (southbound)
4	Exit only, no access	Access only, no exit
31	Exit only to M11 (for London)	Access only, no exit
31A	Exit only to A14 (northbound)	Access only, no exit
34	Access only, no exit	Exit only, no access
36	Exit only to A11, access only from A1303	Access only from A11
38	Access only from A11	Exit only to A11
39	Exit only, no access	Access only, no exit
61	Access only, no exit	Exit only, no access

A55 Holyhead - Chester

Junction	Westbound	Eastbound
8A	Exit only, no access	Access only, no exit
23A	Access only, no exit	Exit only, no access
24A	Exit only, no access	No access or exit
27A	No restriction	No access or exit
33A	Exit only, no access	No access or exit
33B	Exit only, no access	Access only, no exit
36A	Exit only to A5104	Access only from A5104

Refer also to atlas pages 32–33

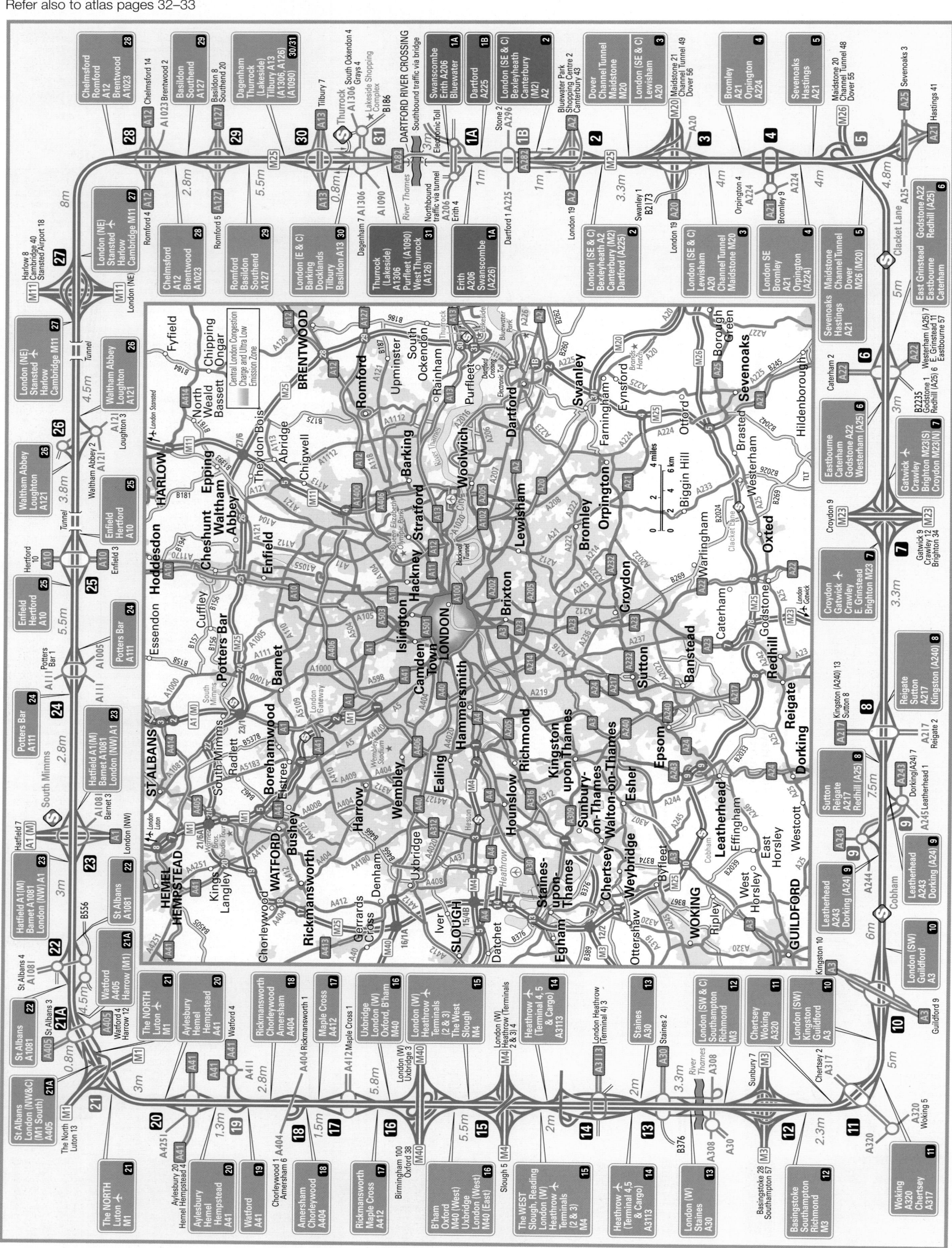

Refer also to atlas pages 53, 64–65

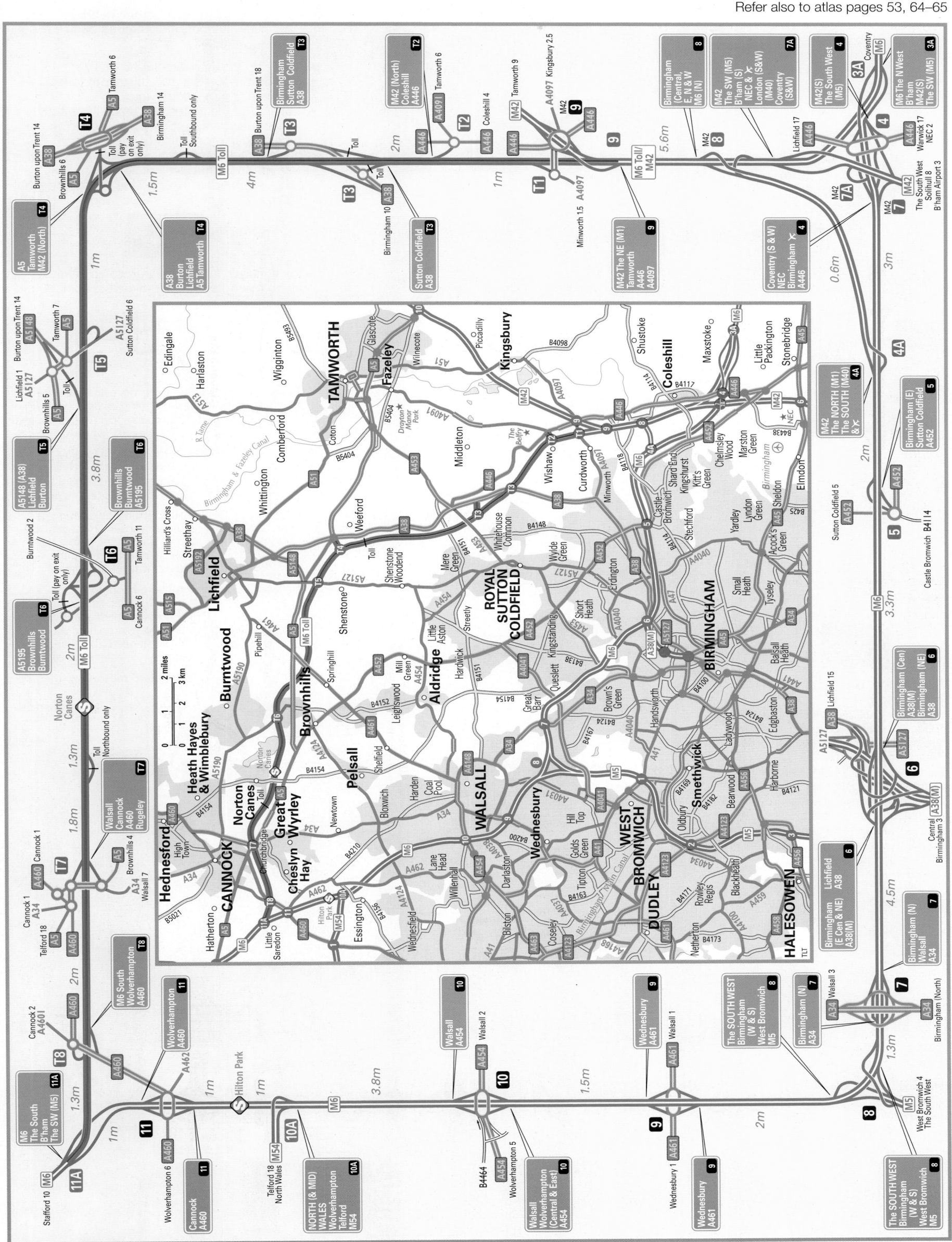

Smart motorways

Since Britain's first motorway (the Preston Bypass) opened in 1958, motorways have changed significantly. A vast increase in car journeys over the last 61 years has meant that motorways quickly filled to capacity. To combat this, the recent development of **smart motorways** uses technology to monitor and actively manage traffic flow and congestion.

How they work

Smart motorways utilise various active traffic management methods, monitored through a regional traffic control centre:

- Traffic flow is monitored using CCTV
- Speed limits are changed to smooth traffic flow and reduce stop-start driving
- Capacity of the motorway can be increased by either temporarily or permanently opening the hard shoulder to traffic
- Warning signs and messages alert drivers to hazards and traffic jams ahead
- Lanes can be closed in the case of an accident or emergency by displaying a red X sign

- Emergency refuge areas are located regularly along the motorway where there is no hard shoulder available

Refuge areas for emergency use only

The map shows the main motorway network with the three different types of smart motorway in operation or planned to open over the next five years:

— **Controlled motorway**
Variable speed limits without hard shoulder (the hard shoulder is used in emergencies only)

— **Hard shoulder running**
Variable speed limits with part-time hard shoulder (the hard shoulder is open to traffic at busy times when signs permit)

— **All lane running**
Variable speed limits with hard shoulder as permanent running lane (there is no hard shoulder); this is standard for all new motorway schemes since 2013

— **Standard motorway**

Quick tips

- Never drive in a lane closed by a red X

- Keep to the speed limit shown on the gantries
- A solid white line indicates the hard shoulder – do not drive in it unless directed or in the case of an emergency
- A broken white line indicates a normal running lane
- Exit the smart motorway where possible if your vehicle is in difficulty. In an emergency, move onto the hard shoulder where there is one, or the nearest emergency refuge area
- Put on your hazard lights if you break down

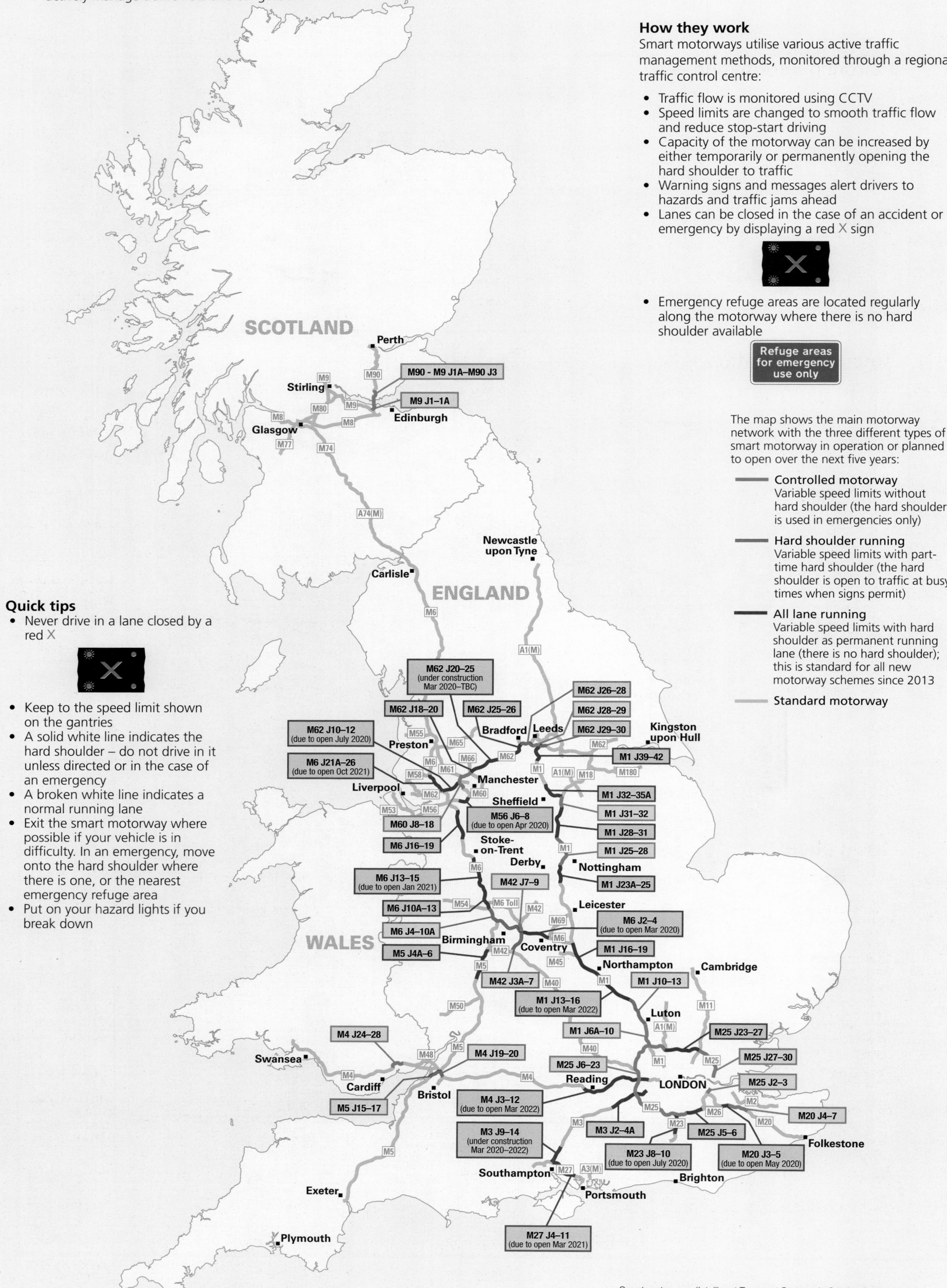

Smart motorways (*Intelligent Transport Systems* in Scotland) are the responsibility of Highways England, Transport Scotland and Transport for Wales

Motoring information

M4	Motorway with number	Primary route junction with and without number	Roundabout	Vehicle ferry	International freight terminal
Toll / T4	Toll motorway with toll station	Restricted primary route junctions	Interchange/junction	Fast vehicle ferry or catamaran	24-hour Accident & Emergency hospital
6	Motorway junction with and without number	Primary route service area	Narrow primary/other A/B road with passing places (Scotland)	Railway line, in tunnel	Crematorium
5	Restricted motorway junctions	BATH — Primary route destination	Road under construction	Railway/tram station, level crossing	Park and Ride (at least 6 days per week)
Fleet / S R	Motorway service area, rest area	A1123 — Other A road single/dual carriageway	Road tunnel	Tourist railway	628 / 637 Lecht Summit — Height in metres, mountain pass
	Motorway and junction under construction	B2070 — B road single/dual carriageway	Road toll, steep gradient (arrows point downhill)	City, town, village or other built-up area	Snow gates (on main routes)
A3	Primary route single/dual carriageway	Minor road more than 4 metres wide, less than 4 metres wide	Distance in miles between symbols	Airport (major/minor), heliport	National boundary, County or administrative boundary

Touring information   To avoid disappointment, check opening times before visiting

Scenic route	Industrial interest	RSPB site	Cave or cavern	National Trust site
Tourist Information Centre	Aqueduct or viaduct	National Nature Reserve (England, Scotland, Wales)	Windmill, monument	National Trust for Scotland site
Tourist Information Centre (seasonal)	Garden	Wildlife Trust reserve	Beach (award winning)	English Heritage site
Visitor or heritage centre	Arboretum	Local nature reserve	Lighthouse	Historic Scotland site
Picnic site	Vineyard	Forest drive	Golf course	Cadw (Welsh heritage) site
Caravan site (AA inspected)	Brewery or distillery	National trail	Football stadium	Other place of interest
Camping site (AA inspected)	Country park	Waterfall	County cricket ground	Boxed symbols indicate attractions within urban areas
Caravan & camping site (AA inspected)	Agricultural showground	Viewpoint	Rugby Union national stadium	World Heritage Site (UNESCO)
Abbey, cathedral or priory	Theme park	Hill-fort	International athletics stadium	National Park and National Scenic Area (Scotland)
Ruined abbey, cathedral or priory	Farm or animal centre	Roman antiquity	Horse racing, show jumping	Forest Park
Castle	Zoological or wildlife collection	Prehistoric monument	Motor-racing circuit	Sandy beach
Historic house or building	Bird collection	Battle site with year / 1066	Air show venue	Heritage coast
Museum or art gallery	Aquarium	Steam railway centre	Ski slope (natural, artificial)	Major shopping centre

Town plans

Motorway and junction	Railway station	Toilet, with facilities for the less able	Tourist Information Centre	Abbey, chapel, church
Primary road single/dual carriageway and numbered junction	Tramway	Building of interest	Visitor or heritage centre	Synagogue
A road single/dual carriageway and numbered junction	London Underground station	Ruined building	Post Office	Mosque
B road single/dual carriageway	London Overground station	City wall	Public library	Golf course
Local road single/dual carriageway	Rail interchange	Cliff lift	Shopping centre	Racecourse
Other road single/dual carriageway, minor road	Docklands Light Railway (DLR) station	Escarpment	Shopmobility	Nature reserve
One-way, gated/closed road	Light rapid transit system station	River/canal, lake	Theatre or performing arts centre	Aquarium
Restricted access	Airport, heliport	Lock, weir	Cinema	World Heritage Site (UNESCO)
Pedestrian area	Railair terminal	Park/sports ground/open space	Museum	English Heritage site
Footpath	Park and Ride (at least 6 days per week)	Cemetery	Castle	Historic Scotland site
Road under construction	Car park, with electric charging point	Woodland	Castle mound	Cadw (Welsh heritage) site
Road tunnel	Bus/coach station	Built-up area	Monument, statue	National Trust site
Level crossing	24-hour Accident & Emergency hospital, other hospital	Beach	Viewpoint	National Trust for Scotland site

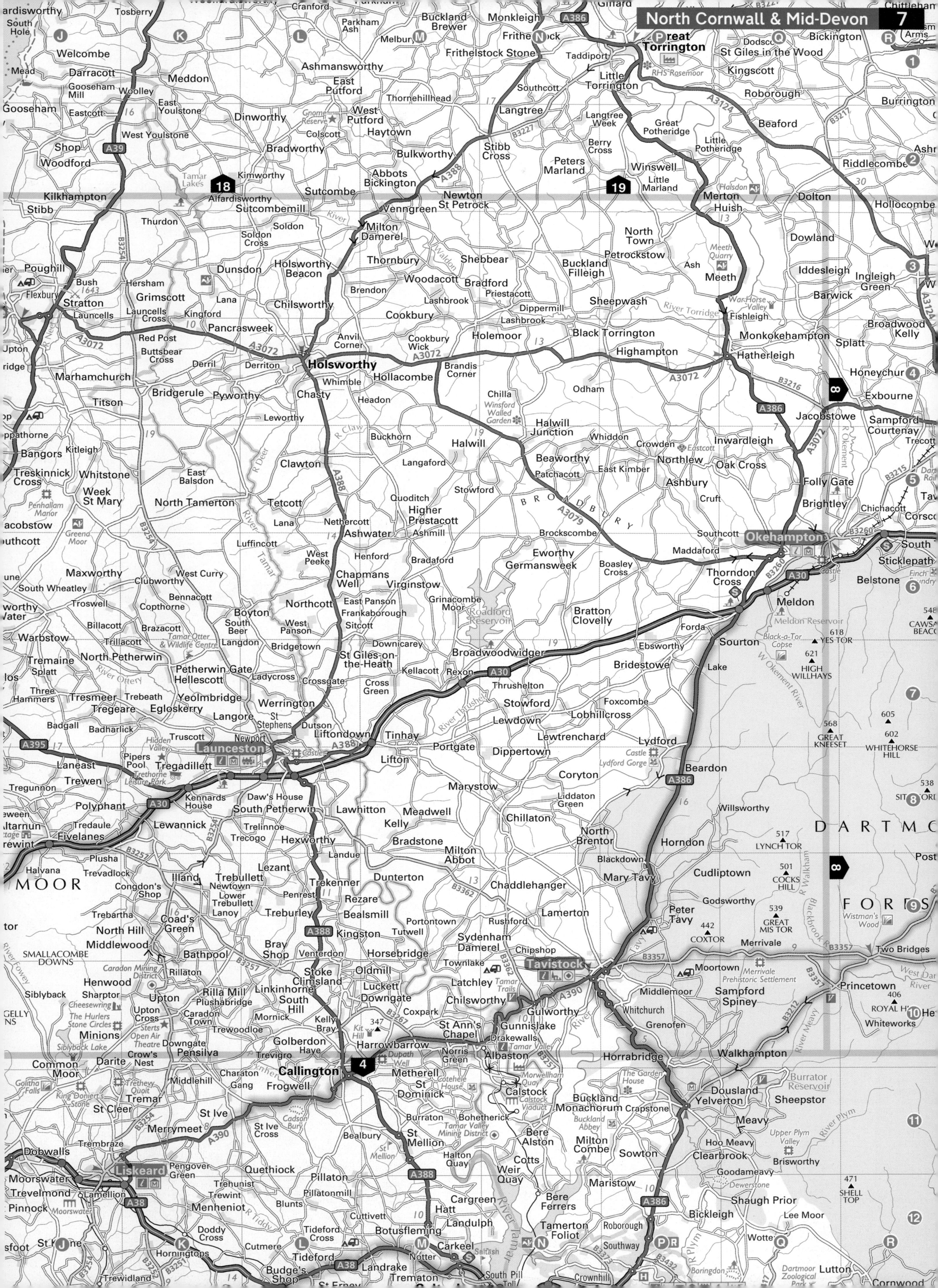

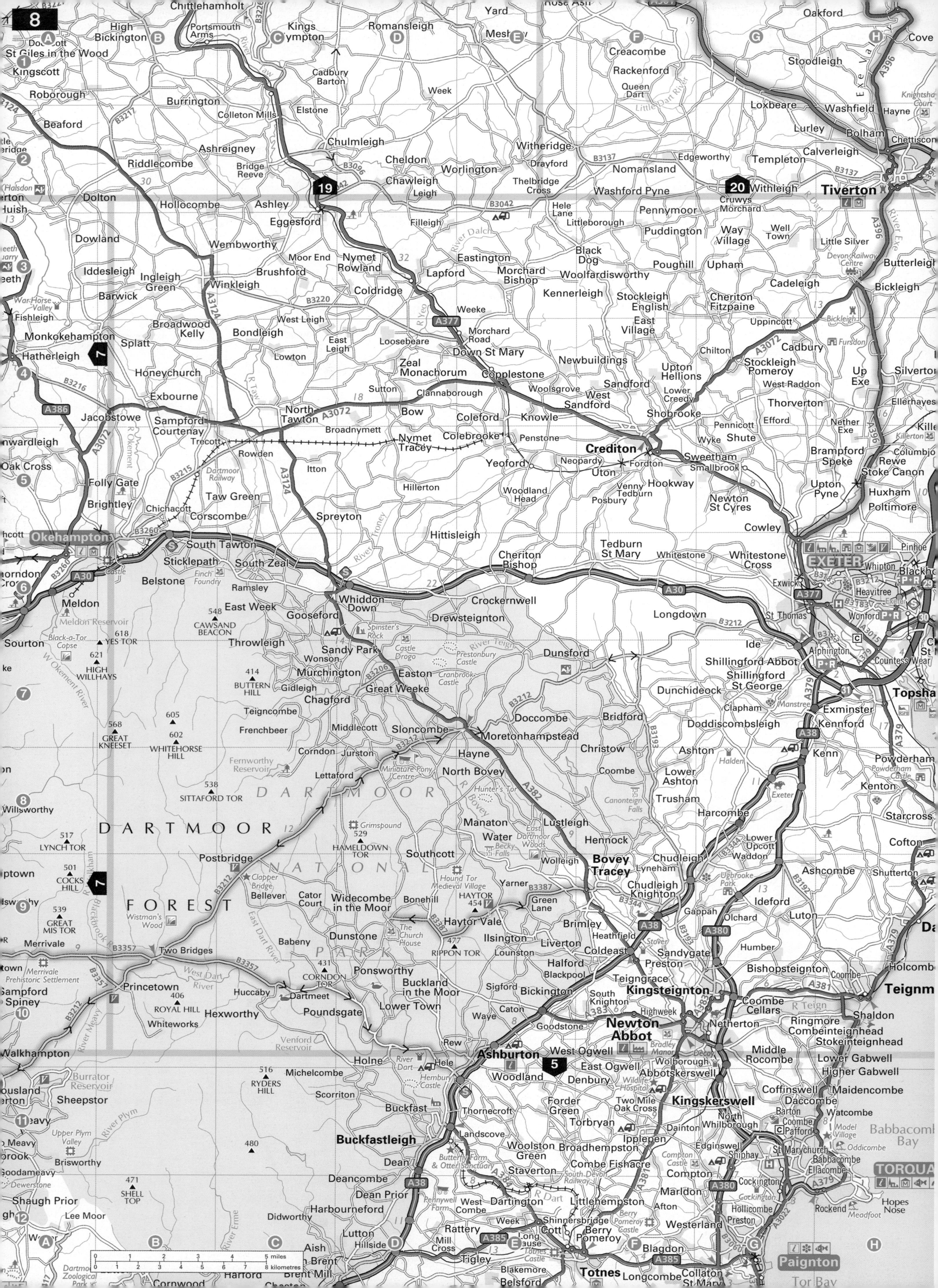

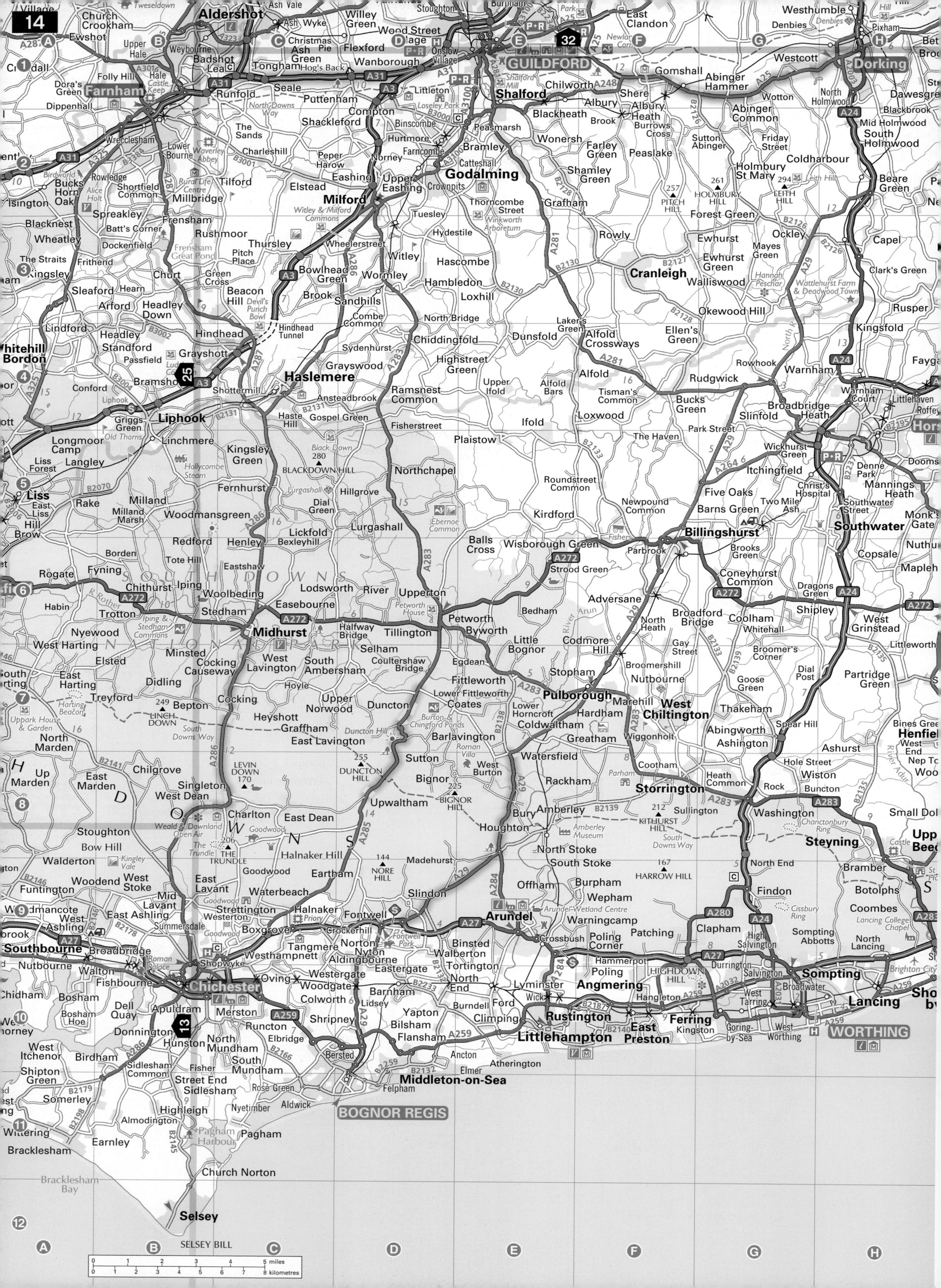

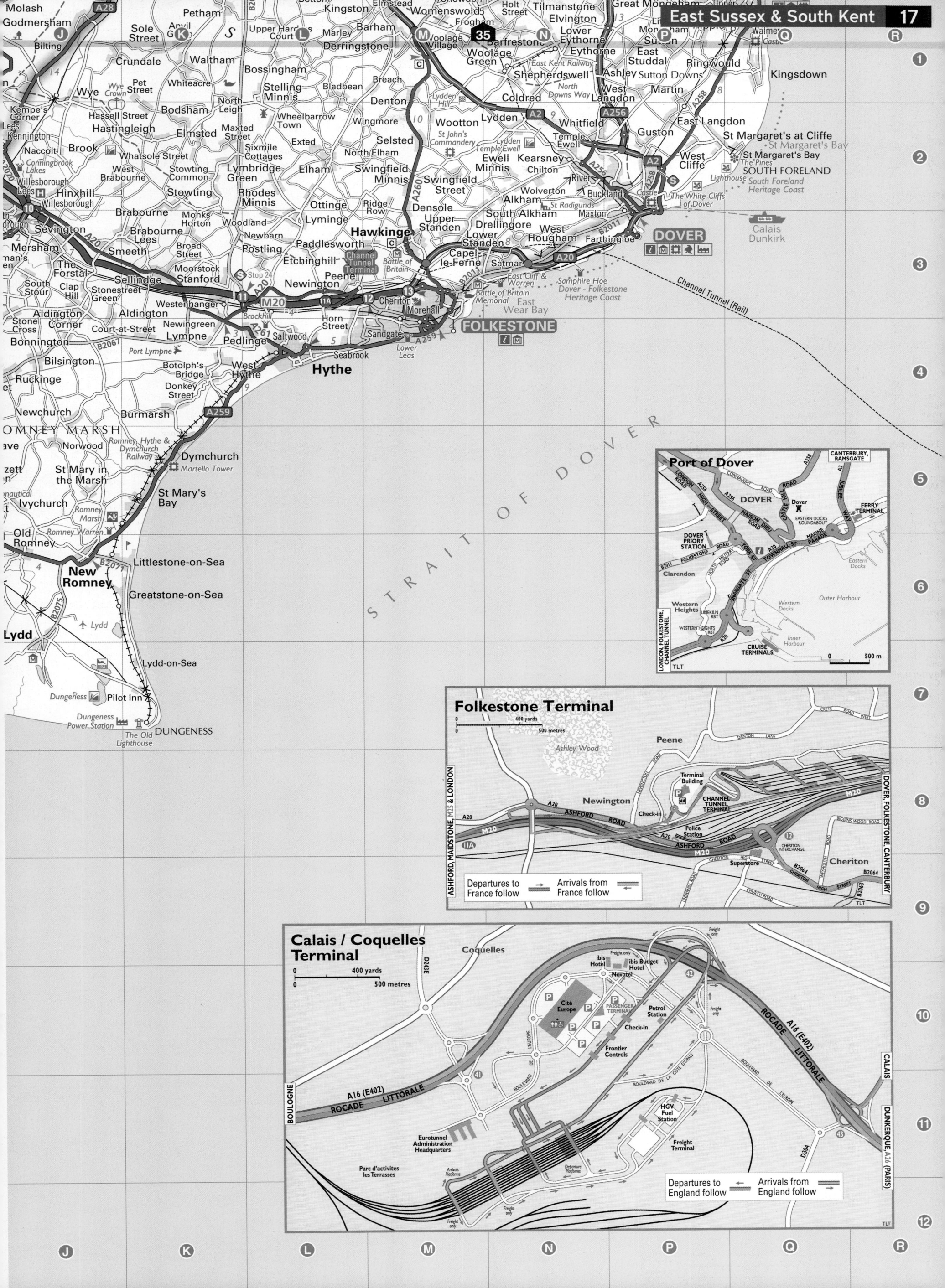

A B C D E F G H

1
2
3
4
5
6
7
8
9
10
11
12

North West Point

Lundy Heritage Coast LUNDY

▲142

Marine Reserve *Marisco*

Shutter Point Surf Point

Morte Point

Woola
Mo
Ba

Baggy Point Putsborc G

Croyde Bay G

Croyde Bay

BARNSTAPLE

OR

BIDEFORD BAY

North Devon Heritage Coast

Northam
Burrows

Westward Ho! Ap

HARTLAND POINT *Shipload Bay*

Titchberry Brownsham

Damehole Point *Hartland Abbey & Gardens*

Stoke Velly Clovelly

Hartland Quay Hartland B3248 4 *B3231* Higher Clovelly Buck's Mills

Speke's Mill Mouth Milford Buck's Cross A39 10

Docton Mill Philham

Elmscott Edistone Woolfardisworthy Cranford

Hardisworthy Tosberry Parkham Ash

South Hole Melbury

Welcombe Darracott Meddon

Mead Gooseham Mill Woolley East Putford Thornehillhead

Gooseham Eastcott 16 East Youlstone Dinworthy Colscott West Putford Haytown

Morwenstow *Gnome Reserve* ★ West Youlstone Bradworthy Bulkworthy

Higher Sharpnose Point Shop A39

South West Coast Path Woodford Kimworthy Abbots Bickington A388

Lower Sharpnose Point *Tamar Lakes* Sutcombe

Steeple Point Kilkhampton Alfardisworthy 7 Sutcombemill Venngreen Newton St Petrock

Stibb Thurdon Soldon Milton Damerel Thornbury Shebbear

Sandy Mouth Soldon Cross *River*

Northcott Mouth Maer Poughill Dunsdon Holsworthy Beacon Woodacott Bradford

Bush 1643 Hersham Lana Brendon Lashbrook

Flexbury Grimscott Chilsworthy Cookbury

Castle Bude Stratton Launcells Kingford Anvil Corner Cookbury Wick

Bude Launcells Cross Red Post Pancrasweek 10

Bude Bay Lynstone Upton Buttsbear Cross Derri Derriton Holsworthy Hollacombe

Helebridge Marhamchurch Whimble Brandis Corner

Widemouth Bay Bridgerule

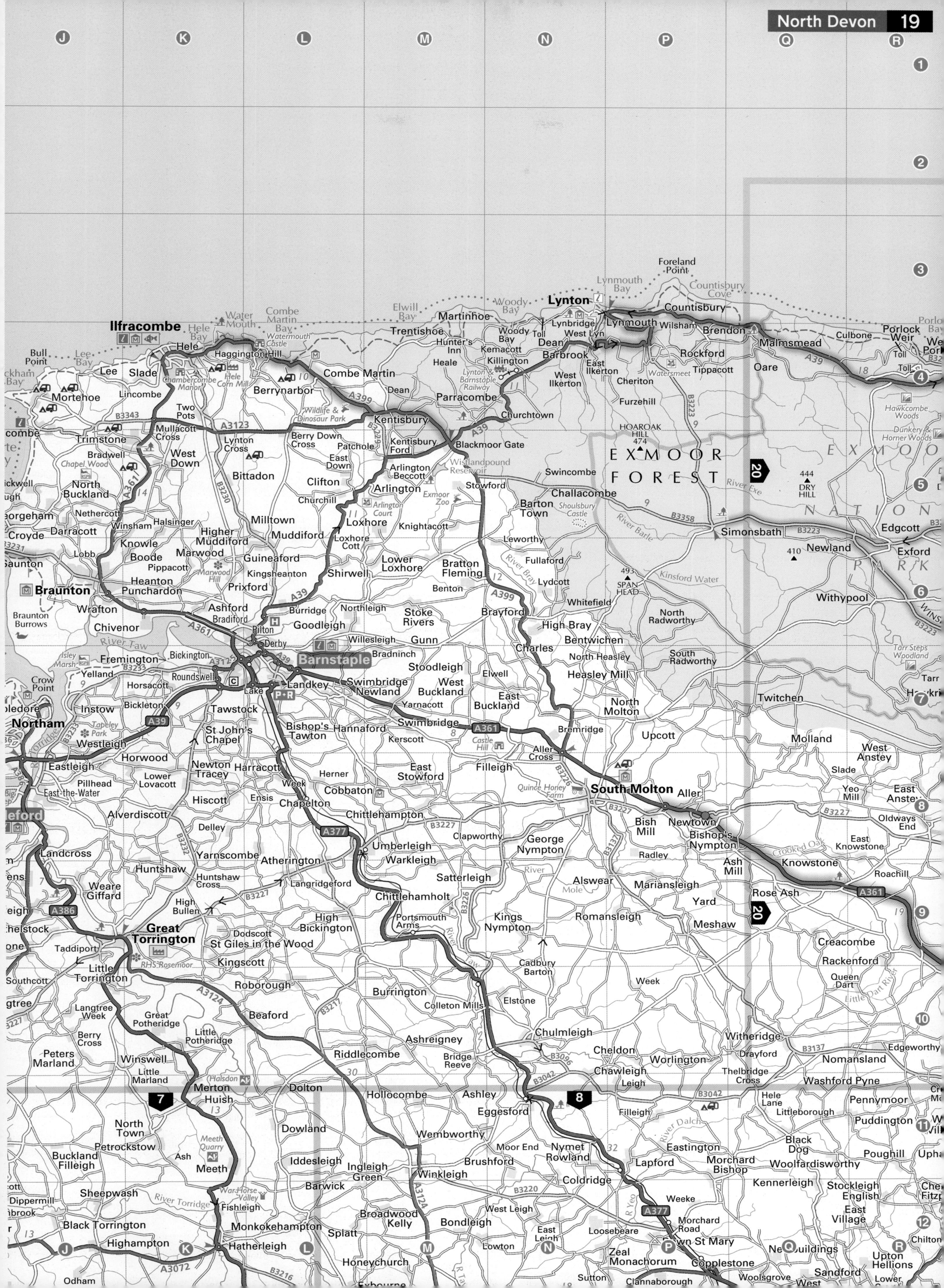

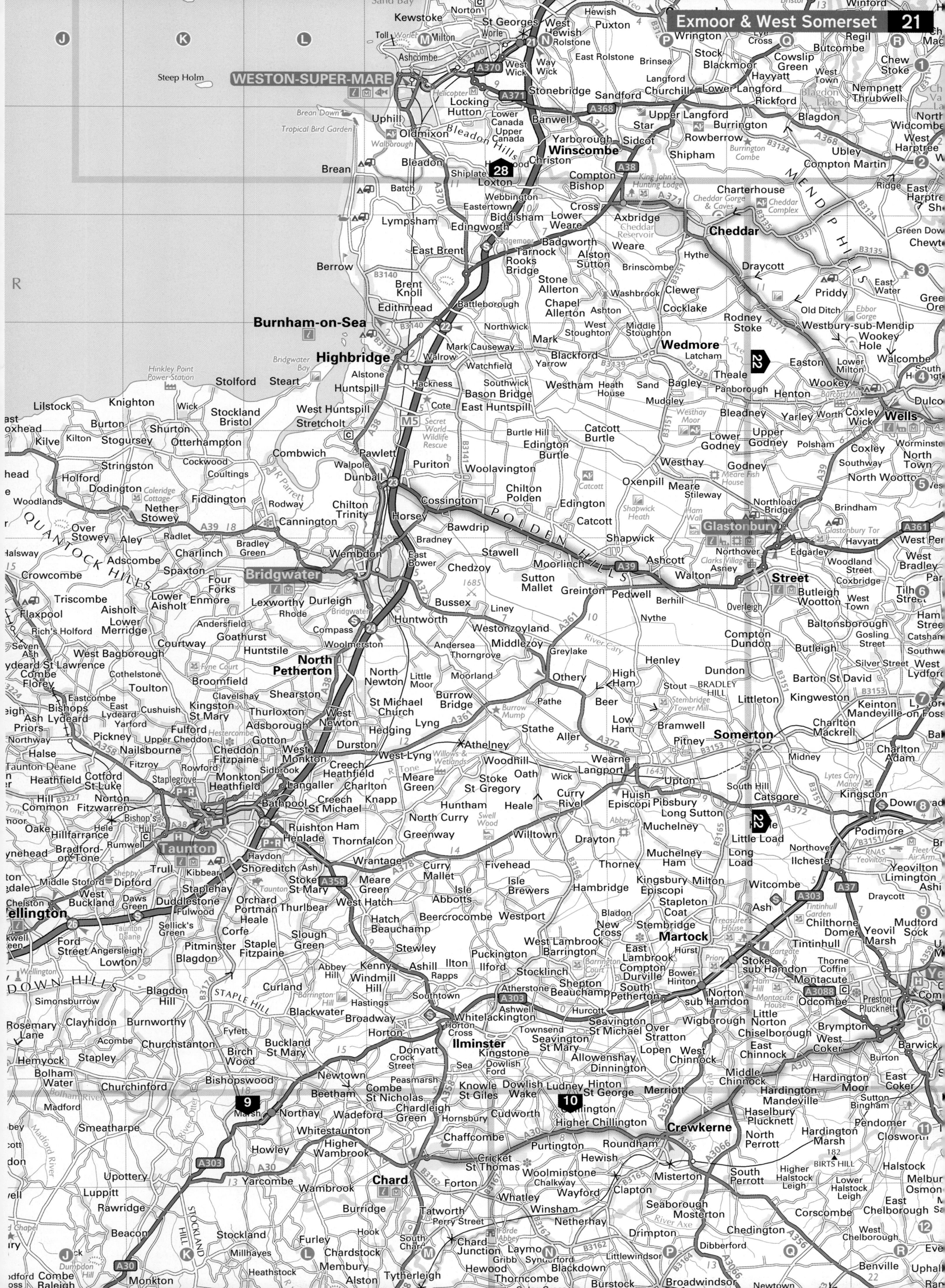

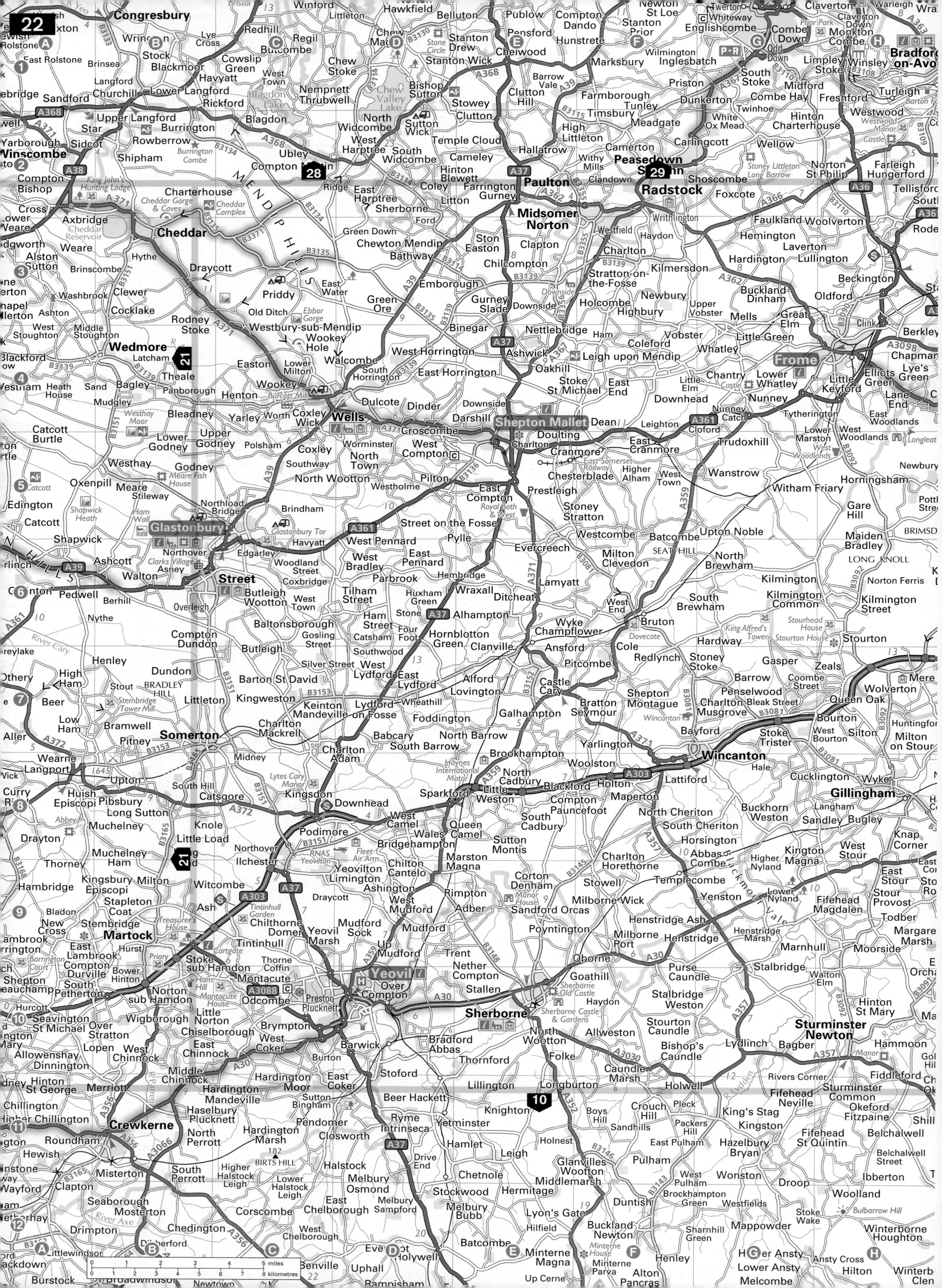

Congresbury
Wrington
Lye Cross
Redhill
Regil
Butcombe
Winford
Littleton
Hawkfield
Belluton
Publow
Compton Dando
Newton St Loe
Stanton Prior
Twerton
Whiteway
Englishcombe
Claverton
Claverton Down
Monkton Combe
Combe Down
Odd Down
Warleigh
Bradford-on-Avon
Rolstone
East Rolstone
Brinsea
Stock
Blackmoor
Cowslip Green
Havyatt
West Town
Chew Magna
Stone Circle
Stanton Drew
Stanton Wick
Pensford
Chelwood
Hunstrete
Marksbury
Wilmington
Inglesbatch
Limpley Stoke
Winsley
South Stoke
Midford
Freshford
Turleigh
Langford
Churchill
Lower Langford
Rickford
Nempnett Thrubwell
Chew Stoke
Chew Valley Lake
Blagdon Lake
Bishop Sutton
Stowey
Clutton Hill
Barrow Vale
Farmborough
Tunley
Priston
Dunkerton
Combe Hay
Twinhoe
Hinton Charterhouse
Westwood
Westwood Manor
Sandford
Upper Langford
Burrington
Blagdon
North Widcombe
Sutton Wick
Clutton
High Littleton
Timsbury
Meadgate
White Ox Mead
Star
Sidcot
Rowberrow
Shipham
Burrington Combe
Ubley
West Harptree
South Widcombe
Temple Cloud
Hallatrow
Cameley
Withy Mills
Camerton
Carlingcott
Wellow
Peasedown St John
Yarborough
Winscombe
Compton Bishop
King John's Hunting Lodge
Compton Martin
Hinton Blewett
Farrington Gurney
Coley
Litton
Paulton
Clandown
Radstock
Shoscombe
Stoney Littleton Long Barrow
Norton St Philip
Farleigh Hungerford
Tellisford
Charterhouse
Cheddar Gorge & Caves
Cheddar Complex
MENDIP HILLS
Ridge
East Harptree
Sherborne
Ford
Midsomer Norton
Foxcote
Writhlington
Faulkland
Woolverton
Rode
Cross
Lower Weare
Axbridge
Cheddar Reservoir
Cheddar
Green Down
Chewton Mendip
Bathway
Ston Easton
Clapton
Westfield
Haydon
Hemington
Laverton
Charlton
Kilmersdon
Hardington
Lullington
Weare
Alston Sutton
Brinscombe
Hythe
Draycott
Priddy
East Water
Emborough
Chilcompton
Stratton-on-the-Fosse
Beckington
Washbrook
Clewer
Cocklake
Ashton
Green Ore
Gurney Slade
Downside
Holcombe
Newbury
Highbury
Buckland Dinham
Upper Vobster
Mells
Great Elm
Oldford
Rodney Stoke
Old Ditch
Ebbor Gorge
Binegar
Nettlebridge
Ham
Vobster
Coleford
Whatley
Little Green
Clink
Berkley
West Stoughton
Middle Stoughton
Westbury-sub-Mendip
Wookey Hole
Walcombe
West Horrington
Ashwick
Leigh upon Mendip
Frome
Chapmanslade
Wedmore
Latcham
Theale
Blackford
Easton
Lower Milton
South Horrington
East Horrington
Oakhill
Stoke St Michael
East End
Little Elm
Chantry
Lower Whatley
Little Keyford
Elliots Green
Lye's Green
Heath House
Sand
Bagley
Panborough
Henton
Wookey
Burcott Mill
Dulcote
Dinder
Downside
Downhead
Nunney
Lane End
Mudgley
Westhay Moor
Bleadney
Yarley
Worth
Coxley Wick
Wells
Croscombe
Darshill
Shepton Mallet
Dean
Leighton
Nunney Catch
Cloford
Tytherington
East Woodlands
Catcott Burtle
Upper Godney
Lower Godney
Polsham
Worminster
West Compton
Charlton
Doulting
Cranmore
East Cranmore
Trudoxhill
Lower Marston
West Woodlands
Longleat
Coxley
North Town
East Somerset Railway
Higher Alham
Westhay
Godney
Meare Fish House
Southway
North Wootton
Pilton
Chesterblade
West Town
Wanstrow
Newbury
Oxenpill
Meare
Stileway
Westholme
East Compton
Prestleigh
Witham Friary
Horningsham
Catcott
Edington
Northload Bridge
Brindham
Royal Bath & West
Stoney Stratton
Gare Hill
Shapwick Heath
Ham Wall
Glastonbury
Glastonbury Tor
A361
Street on the Fosse
Havyatt
West Pennard
Pylle
Evercreech
Westcombe
Batcombe
Upton Noble
Maiden Bradley
BRIMSDOWN HILL
Shapwick
Northover
Edgarley
West Bradley
East Pennard
SEAT HILL
Milton Clevedon
North Brewham
LONG KNOLL
Ashcott
Clarks Village
Asney
Woodland Street
Coxbridge
Parbrook
Hembridge
Wraxall
Lamyatt
Kilmington
Norton Ferris
Walton
Street
Butleigh Wootton
West Town
Tilham Street
Huxham Green
Ditcheat
West End
South Brewham
Kilmington Common
Kilmington Street
Pedwell
Berhill
Overleigh
Ham Street
Stone
Alhampton
Bruton
Stourhead House
Nythe
Baltonsborough
Gosling Street
Catsham
Four Foot
Hornblotton Green
Wyke Champflower
Dovecote
King Alfred's Tower
Stourton House
Stourton
Compton Dundon
Butleigh
Southwood
Clanville
Ansford
Cole
Hardway
River Cary
Henley
Dundon
Silver Street
West Lydford
Alford
Pitcombe
Redlynch
Stoney Stoke
Gasper
Zeals
High Ham
Stout
BRADLEY HILL
Barton St David
East Lydford
Lovington
Castle Cary
Barrow
Coombe Street
Mere
Beer
Stembridge Tower Mill
Littleton
Kingweston
Keinton Mandeville
Lydford-on-Fosse
Wheathill
Bratton Seymour
Shepton Montague
Penselwood
Charlton Musgrove
Bleak Street
Wolverton
Queen Oak
Low Ham
Bramwell
Charlton Mackrell
Foddington
Galhampton
Wincanton Racecourse
Bourton
Pitney
Somerton
Babcary
North Barrow
South Barrow
Bayford
Stoke Trister
West Bourton
Silton
Huntingford
Milton on Stour
Aller
Wearne
Langport
Midney
Charlton Adam
Brookhampton
Yarlington
Woolston
Wincanton
Hale
Cucklington
Wyke
Upton
South Hill
Lytes Cary Manor
Kingsdon
Haynes International Motor Museum
North Cadbury
Little Weston
Blackford
Holton
Lattiford
Maperton
Gillingham
Huish Episcopi
Pibsbury
Long Sutton
Catsgore
Downhead
Sparkford
Compton Pauncefoot
South Cadbury
North Cheriton
South Cheriton
Buckhorn Weston
Langham
Sandley
Bugley
Curry Rivel
Muchelney
Knole
Muchelney Abbey
Little Load
Podimore
West Camel
Queen Camel
Wales
Bridgehampton
Sutton Montis
Horsington
Abbas Combe
Higher Nyland
Kington Magna
West Stour
Knap Corner
Drayton
Muchelney Ham
Thorney
Northover
Ilchester
RNAS Yeovilton
Fleet Air Arm Museum
Yeovilton
Chilton Cantelo
Marston Magna
Corton Denham
Charlton Horethorne
Templecombe
Blackmore Vale
East Stour
Kingsbury Episcopi
Milton
Hambridge
Witcombe
Limington
Ashington
Rimpton
Stowell
Lower Nyland
Yenston
Fifehead Magdalen
Stour Provost
Bladon
Stapleton
Ash
Coat
Tintinhull Garden
Draycott
West Mudford
Adber
Manor House
Sandford Orcas
Milborne Wick
Henstridge Ash
Todber
New Cross
Stembridge
Treasurer's House
Chilthorne Domer
Yeovil Marsh
Mudford Sock
Mudford
Poyntington
Milborne Port
Henstridge
Henstridge Marsh
Marnhull
Moorside
Margaret Marsh
Martock
Tintinhull
Up Mudford
Trent
Oborne
Stalbridge
East Lambrook
Hurst
Priory
Cartgate
Thorne Coffin
Nether Compton
Goathill
Purse Caundle
Walton Elm
Barrington Court
Compton Durville
Bower Hinton
Stoke sub Hamdon
Montacute
Yeovil
Over Compton
Stallen
Sherborne Old Castle
Stalbridge Weston
Shepton Beauchamp
South Petherton
Norton sub Hamdon
Ham Hill
Montacute House
Odcombe
Preston Plucknett
Sherborne
Sherborne Castle & Gardens
Haydon
Hinton St Mary
Hurcott
Seavington St Michael
Over Stratton
Wigborough
Little Norton
Chiselborough
Brympton
West Coker
Bradford Abbas
North Wootton
Allweston
Stourton Caundle
Sturminster Newton
Lopen
West Chinnock
East Chinnock
Barwick
Thornford
Folke
Bishop's Caundle
Lydlinch
Bagber
Hammoon
Allowenshay
Dinnington
Middle Chinnock
Burton
Caundle Marsh
Rivers Corner
Fiddleford
Hinton St George
Merriott
Hardington Moor
East Coker
Stoford
Lillington
Longburton
Holwell
Fifehead Neville
Sturminster Common
Chillington
Higher Chillington
Crewkerne
Hardington Mandeville
Haselbury Plucknett
Sutton Bingham
Beer Hackett
Knighton
Crouch Hill
Pleck
Boys Hill
Sandhills
King's Stag
Okeford Fitzpaine
North Perrott
Pendomer
Ryme Intrinseca
Yetminster
Packers Hill
Kingston
Roundham
Hardington Marsh
Closworth
Hamlet
Holnest
East Pulham
Hazelbury Bryan
Fifehead St Quintin
Belchalwell
Belchalwell Street
Hewish
BIRTS HILL
Leigh
Glanvilles Wootton
Pulham
Misterton
South Perrott
Higher Halstock Leigh
Halstock
Drive End
Middlemarsh
West Pulham
Wonston
Droop
Ibberton
Wayford
Clapton
Lower Halstock Leigh
Melbury Osmond
Chetnole
Hermitage
Brockhampton Green
Westfields
Woolland
Seaborough
Mosterton
Corscombe
East Chelborough
Melbury Sampford
Stockwood
Melbury Bubb
Dunstish
Lyon's Gate
Bulbarrow Hill
Stoke Wake
River Axe
Chedington
West Chelborough
Hilfield
Buckland Newton
Sharnhill Green
Mappowder
Winterborne Houghton
Drimpton
Dibberford
Batcombe
Minterne House
Littlewindsor
Evershot
Holywell
Minterne Magna
Minterne Parva
Henley
Higher Ansty
Lower Ansty
Ansty Cross
Hilton
Burstock
Broadwindsor
Benville
Uphall
Rampisham
Up Cerne
Alton Pancras
Melcombe
Newtown
0 1 2 3 4 5 miles
0 1 2 3 4 5 6 7 8 kilometres

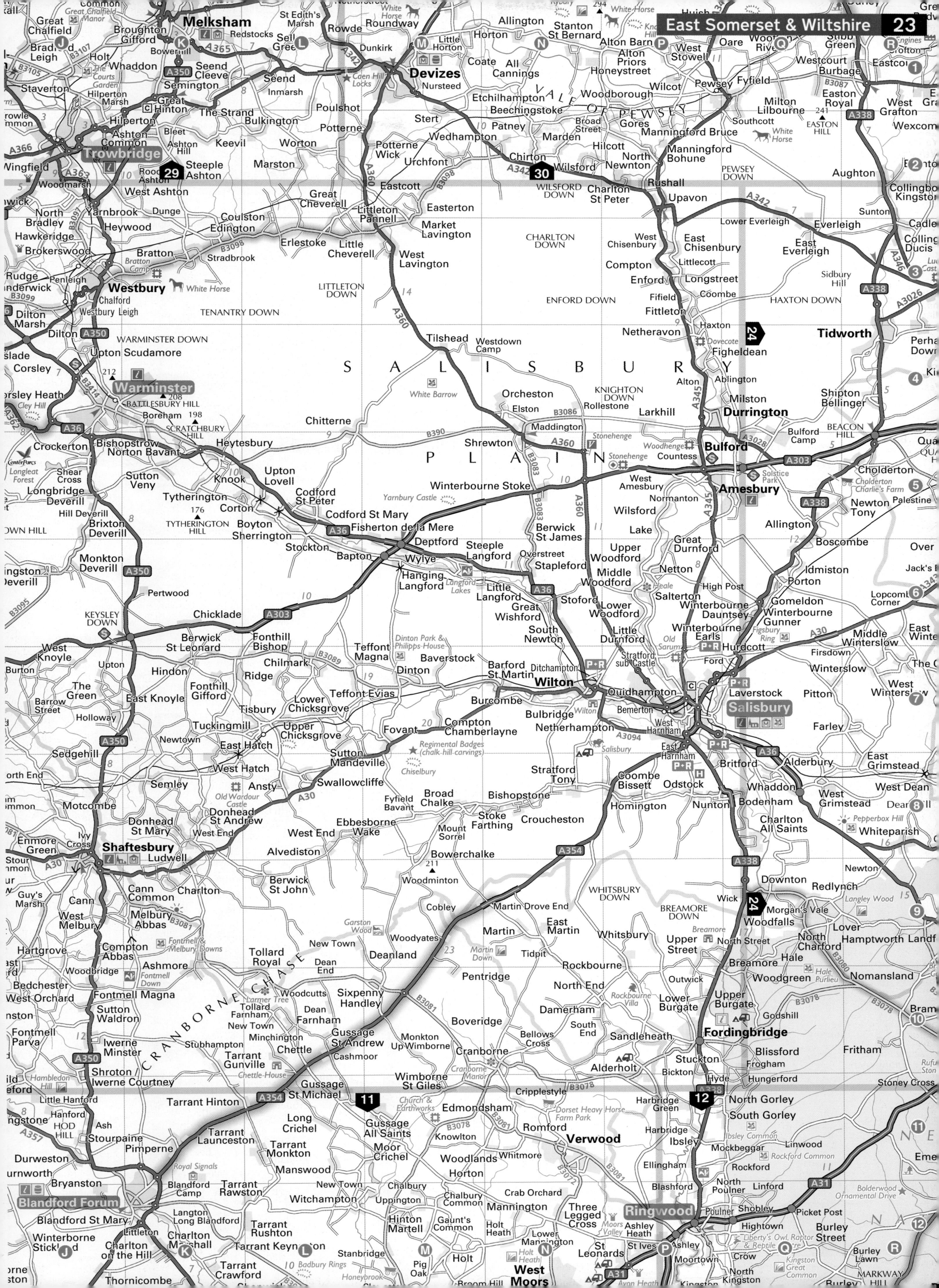

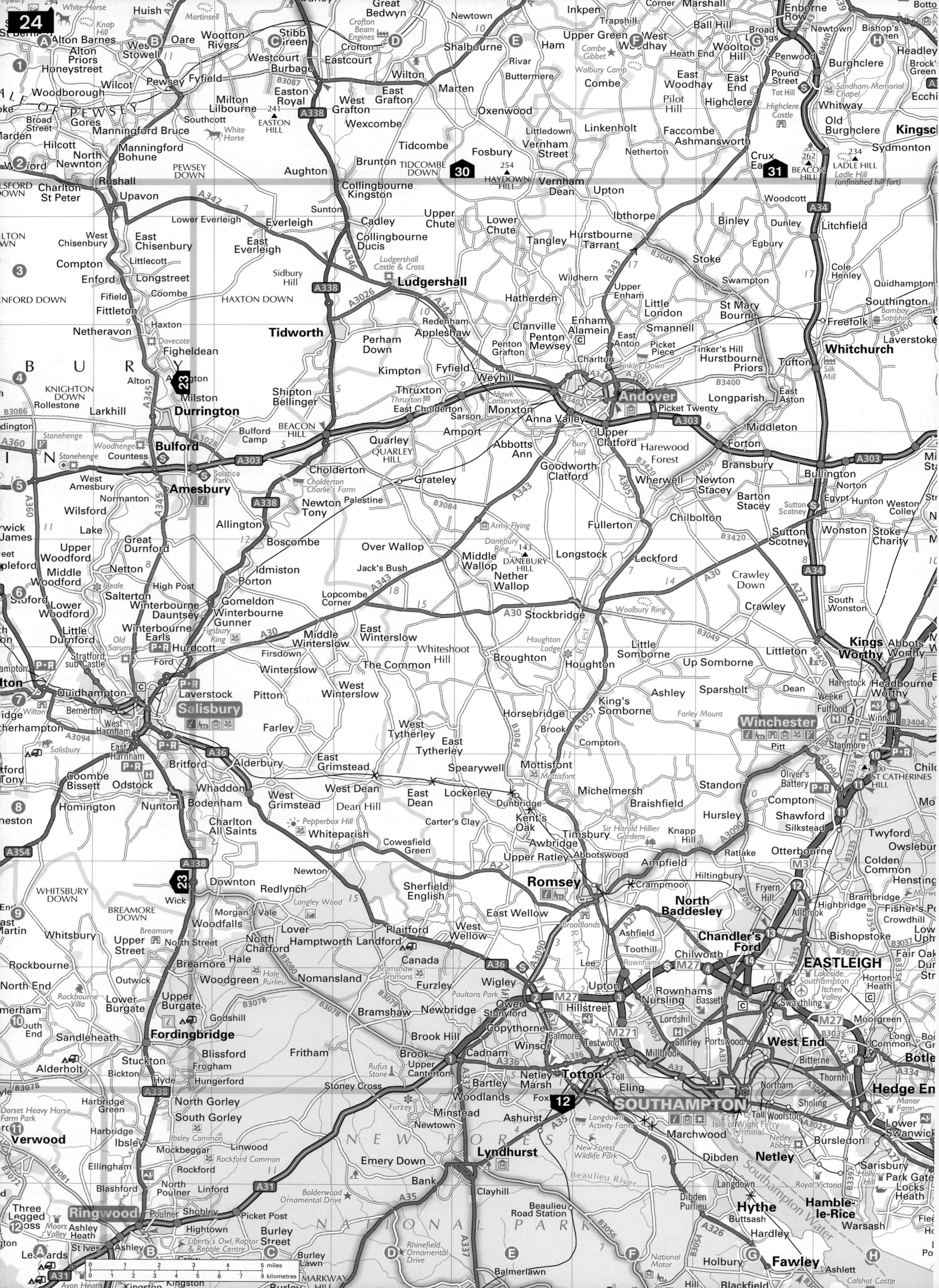

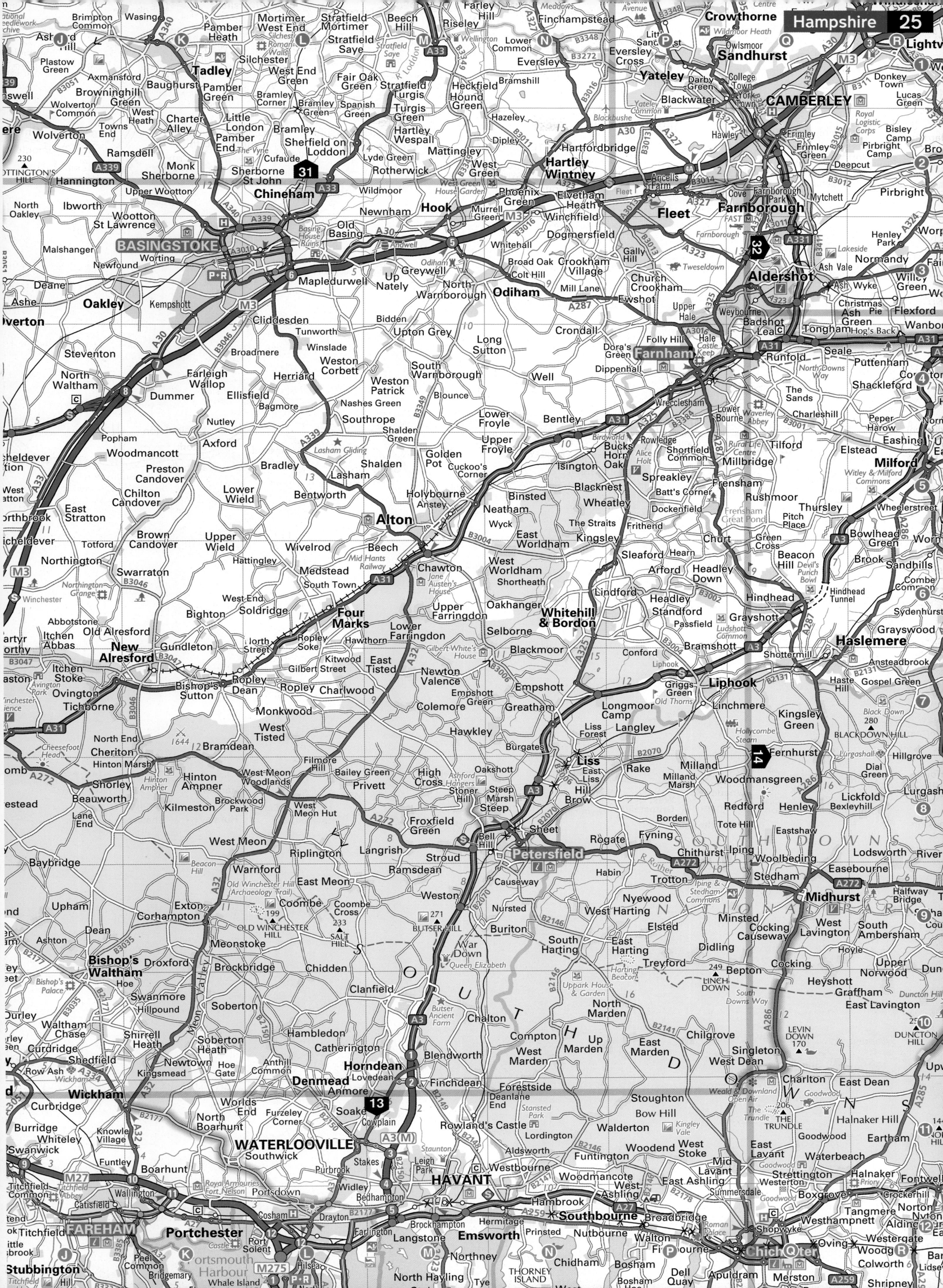

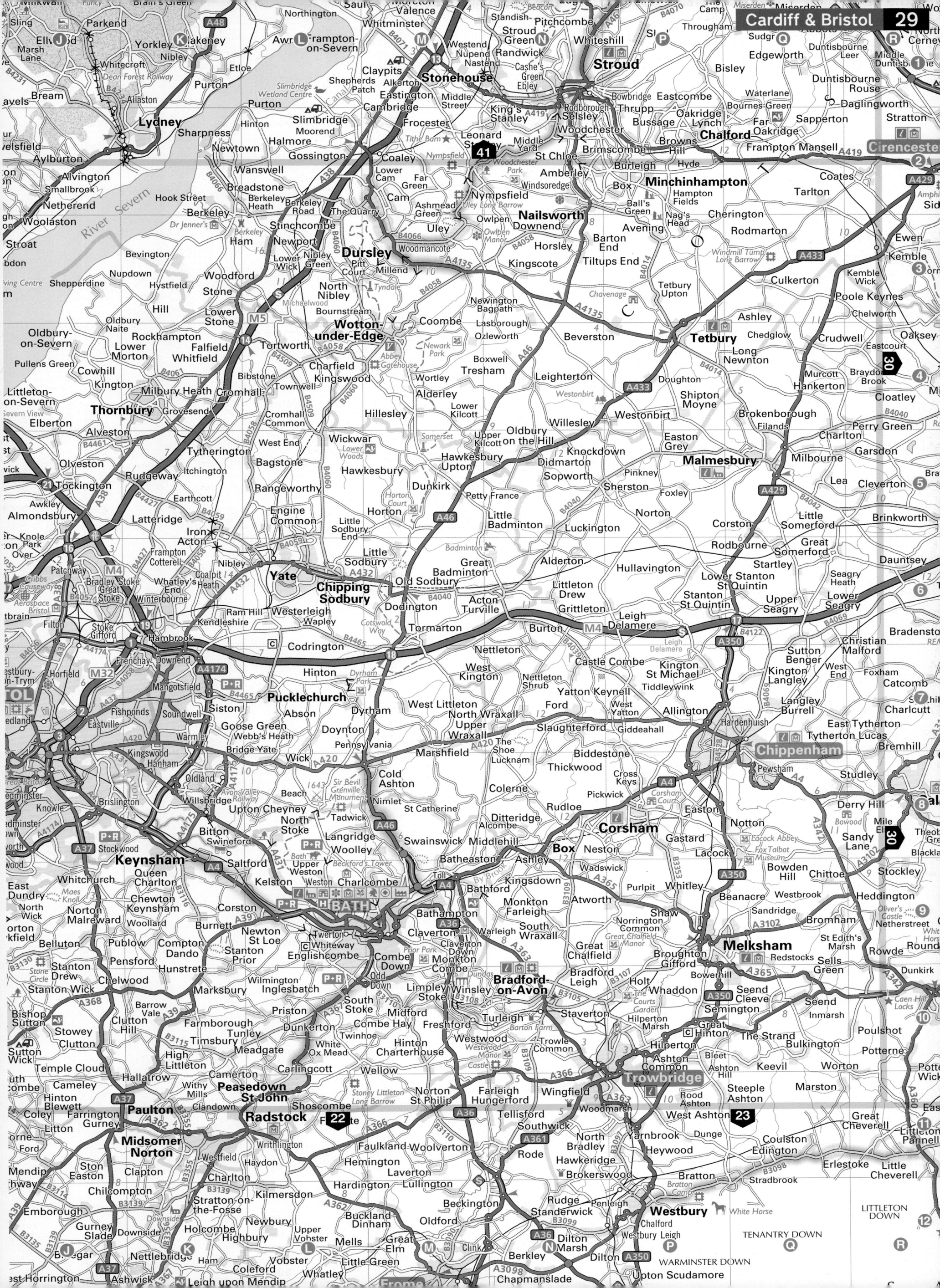

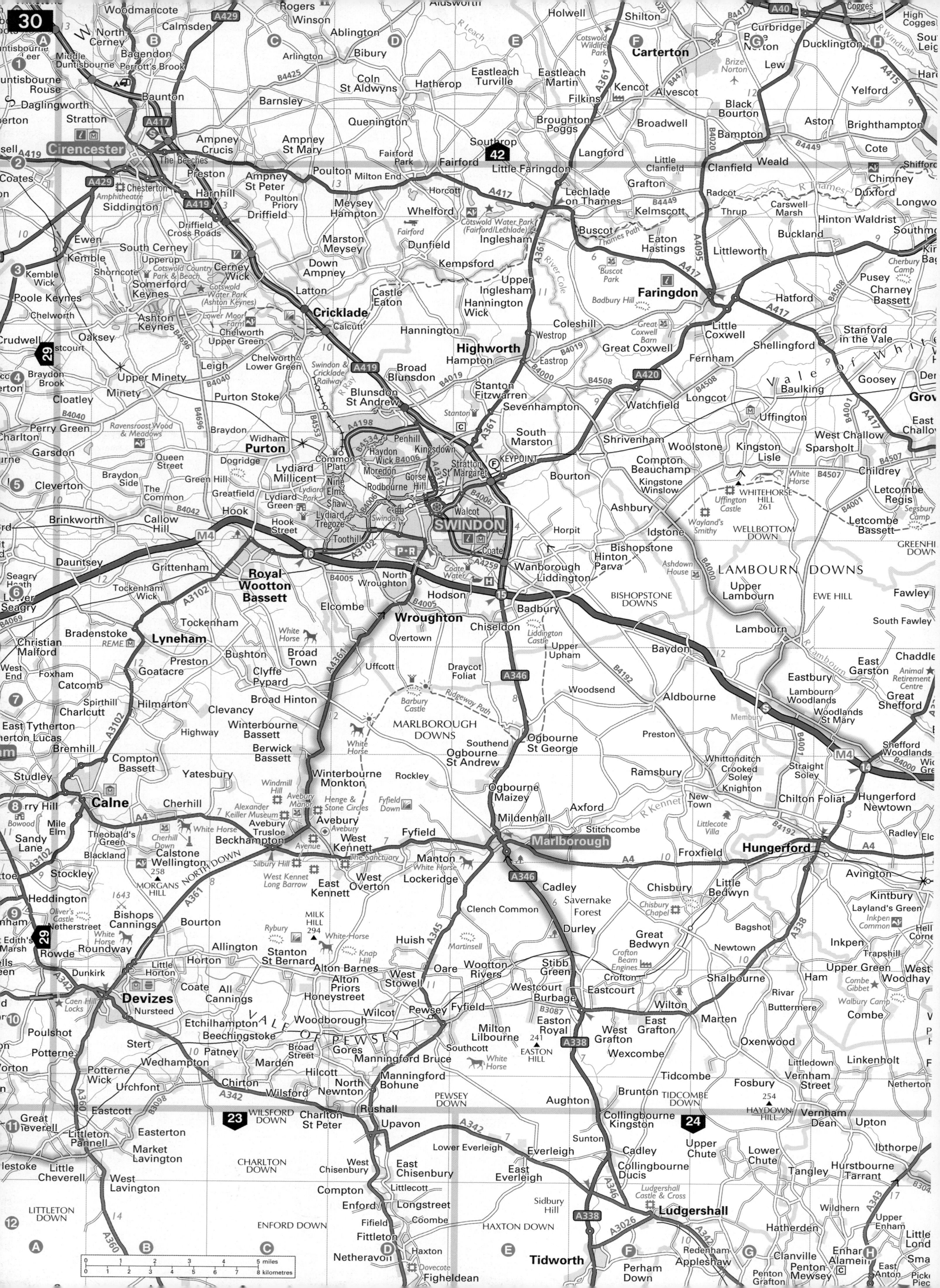

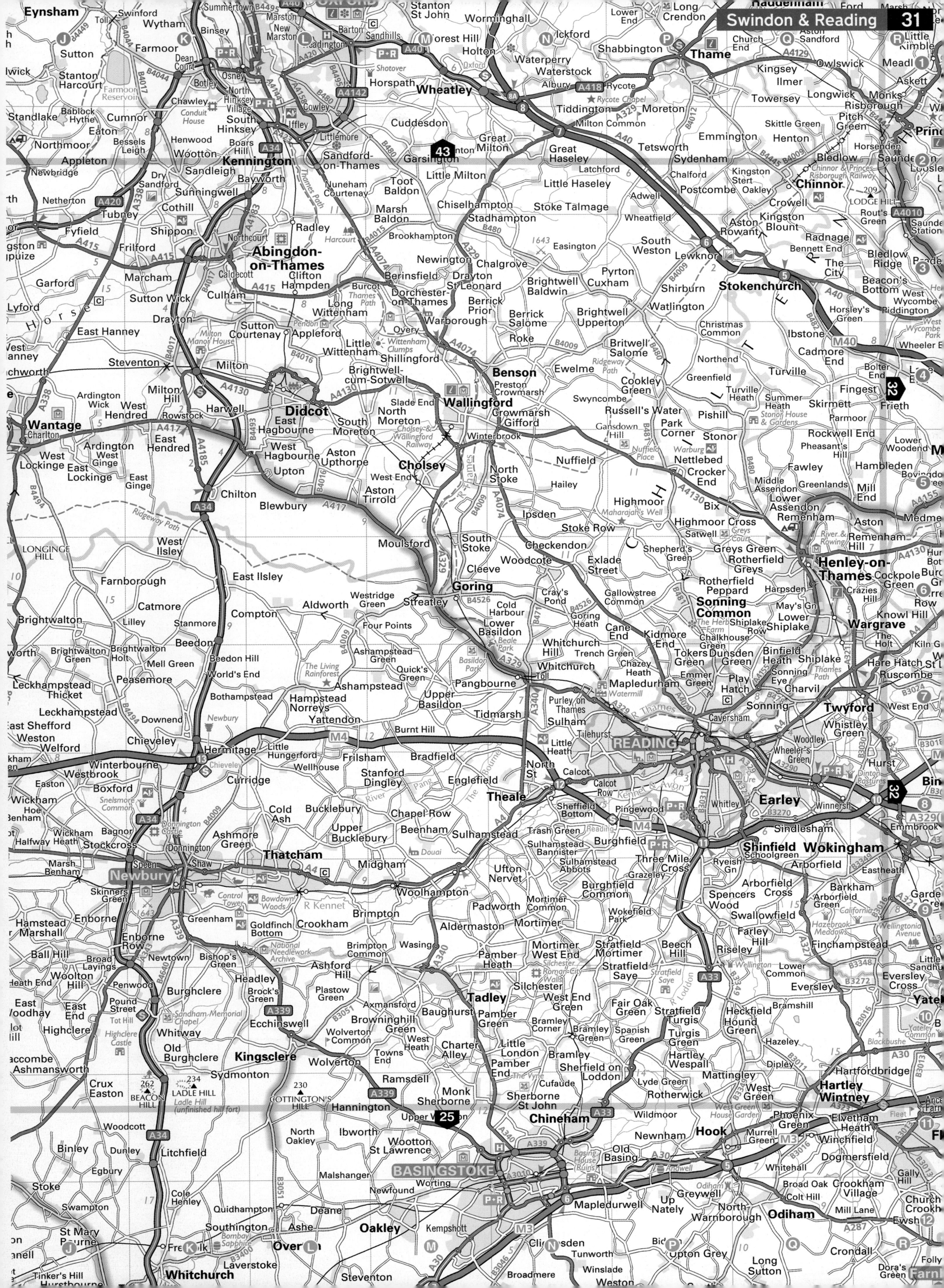

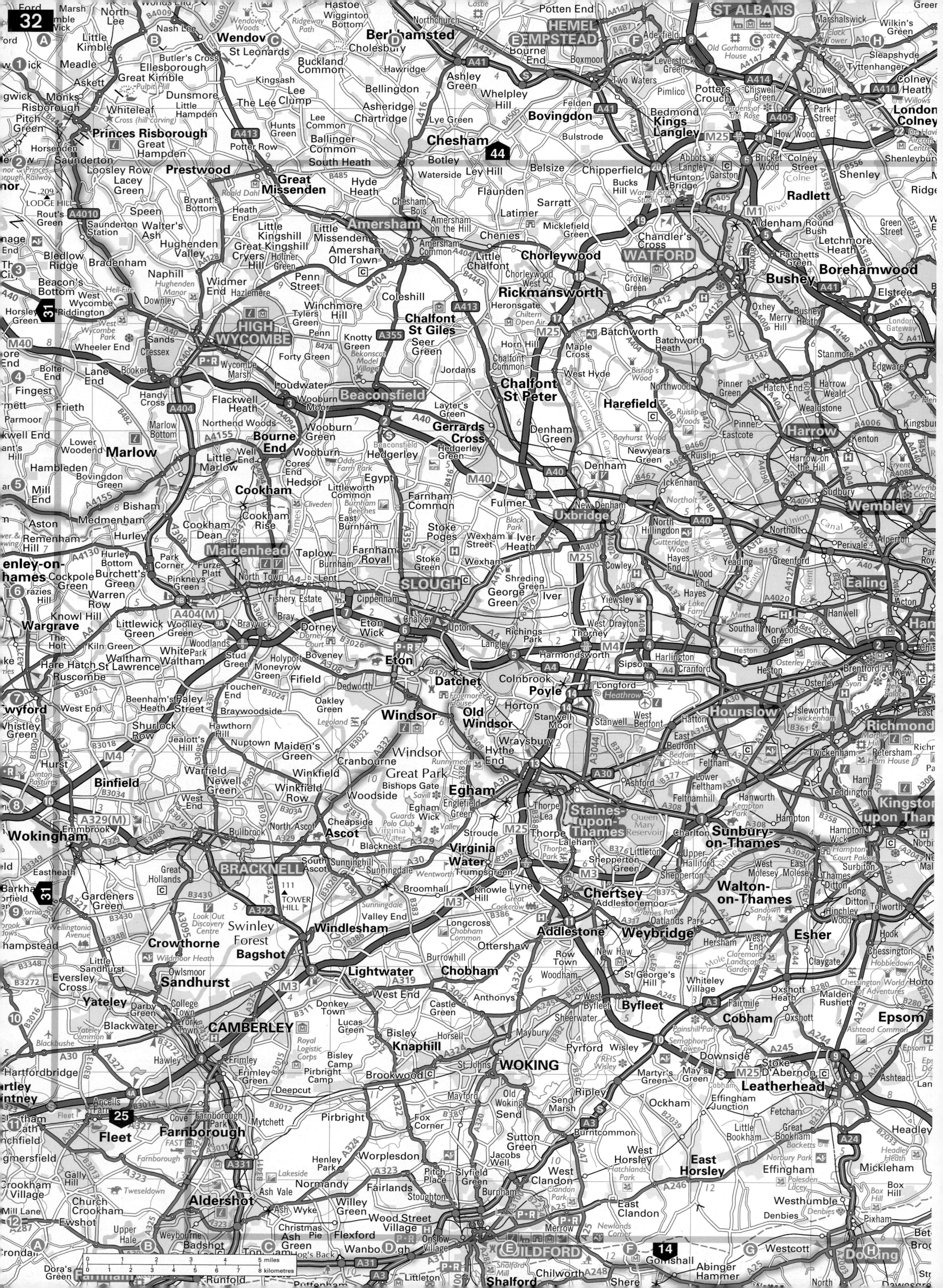

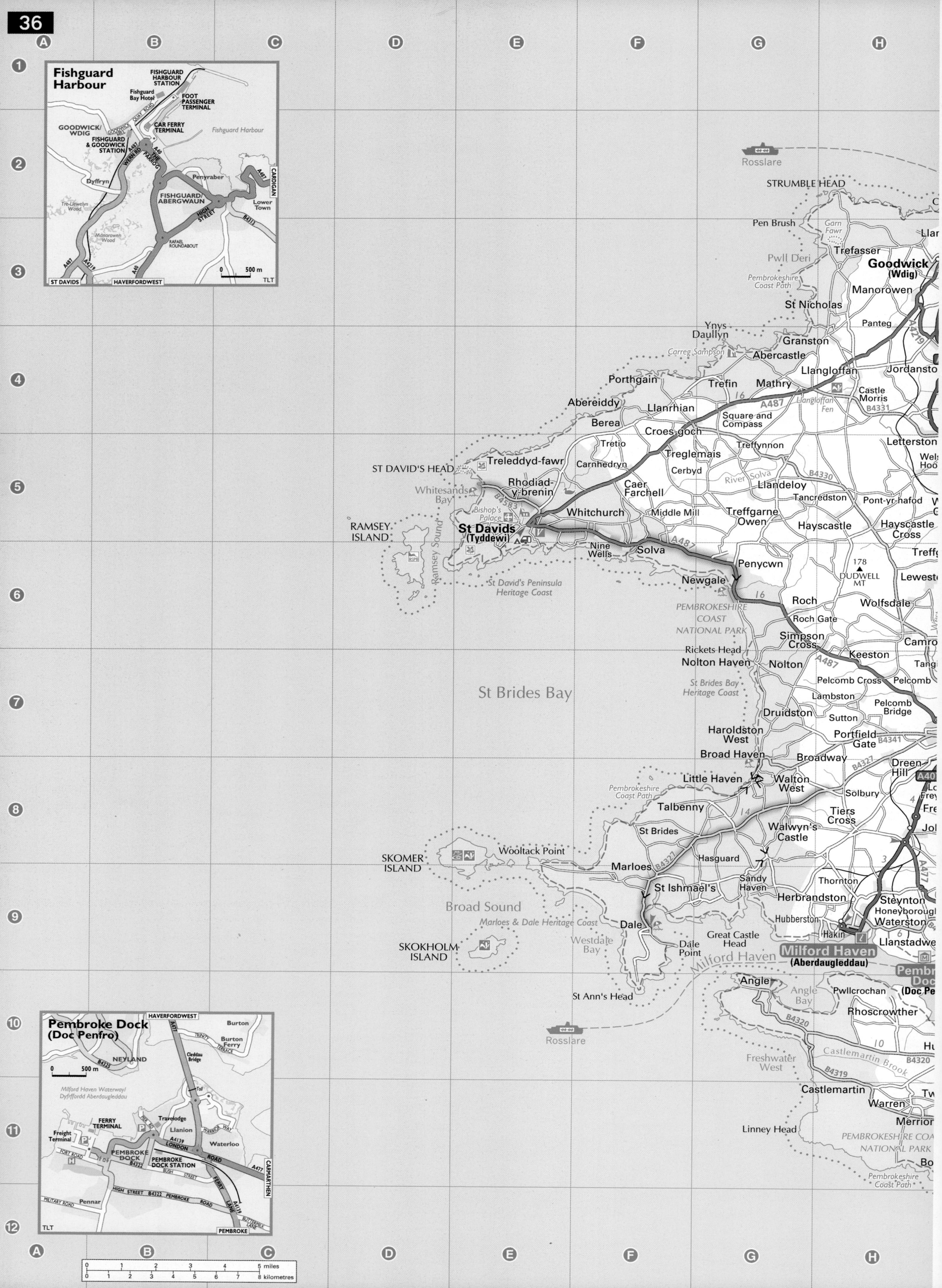

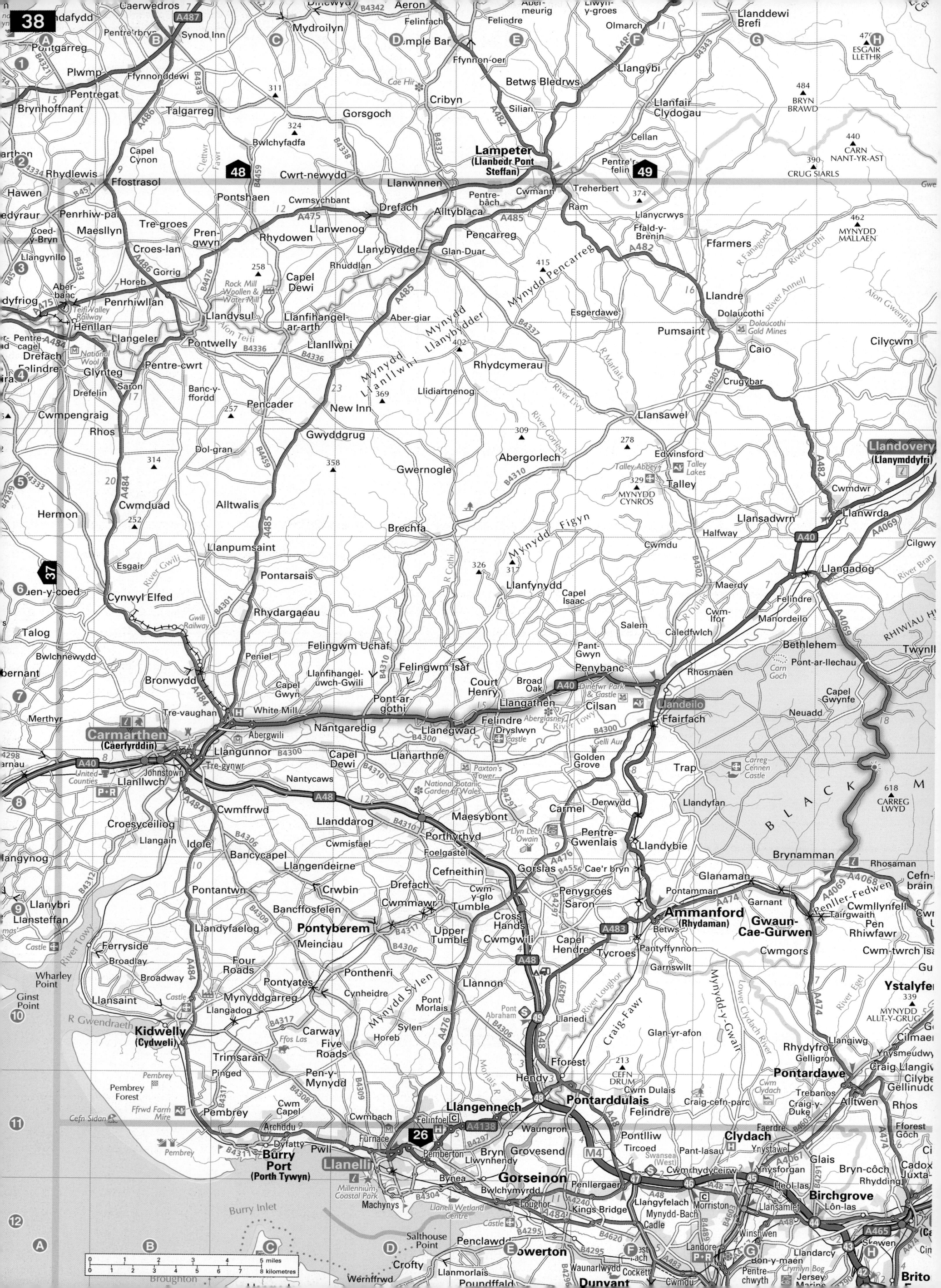

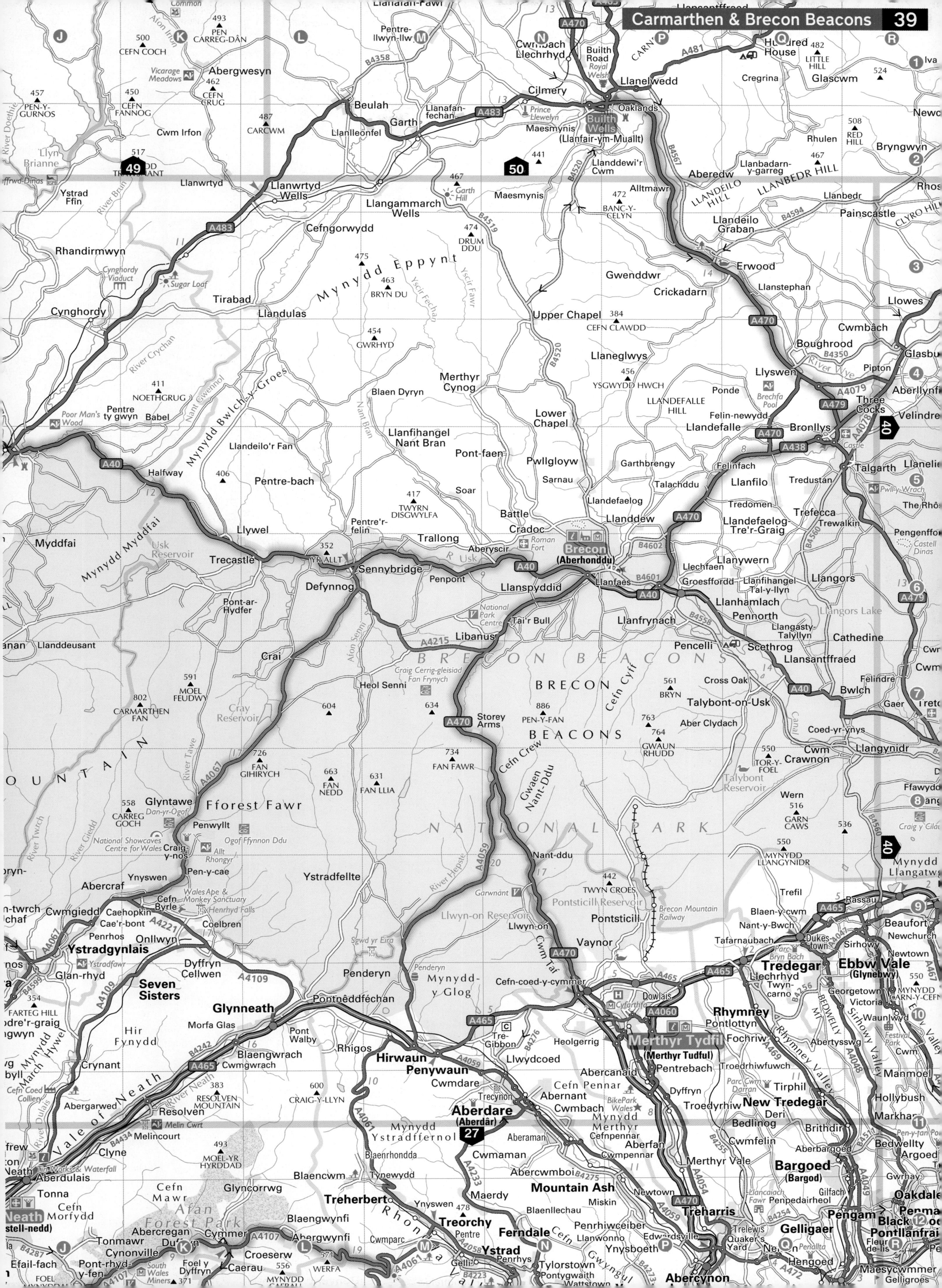

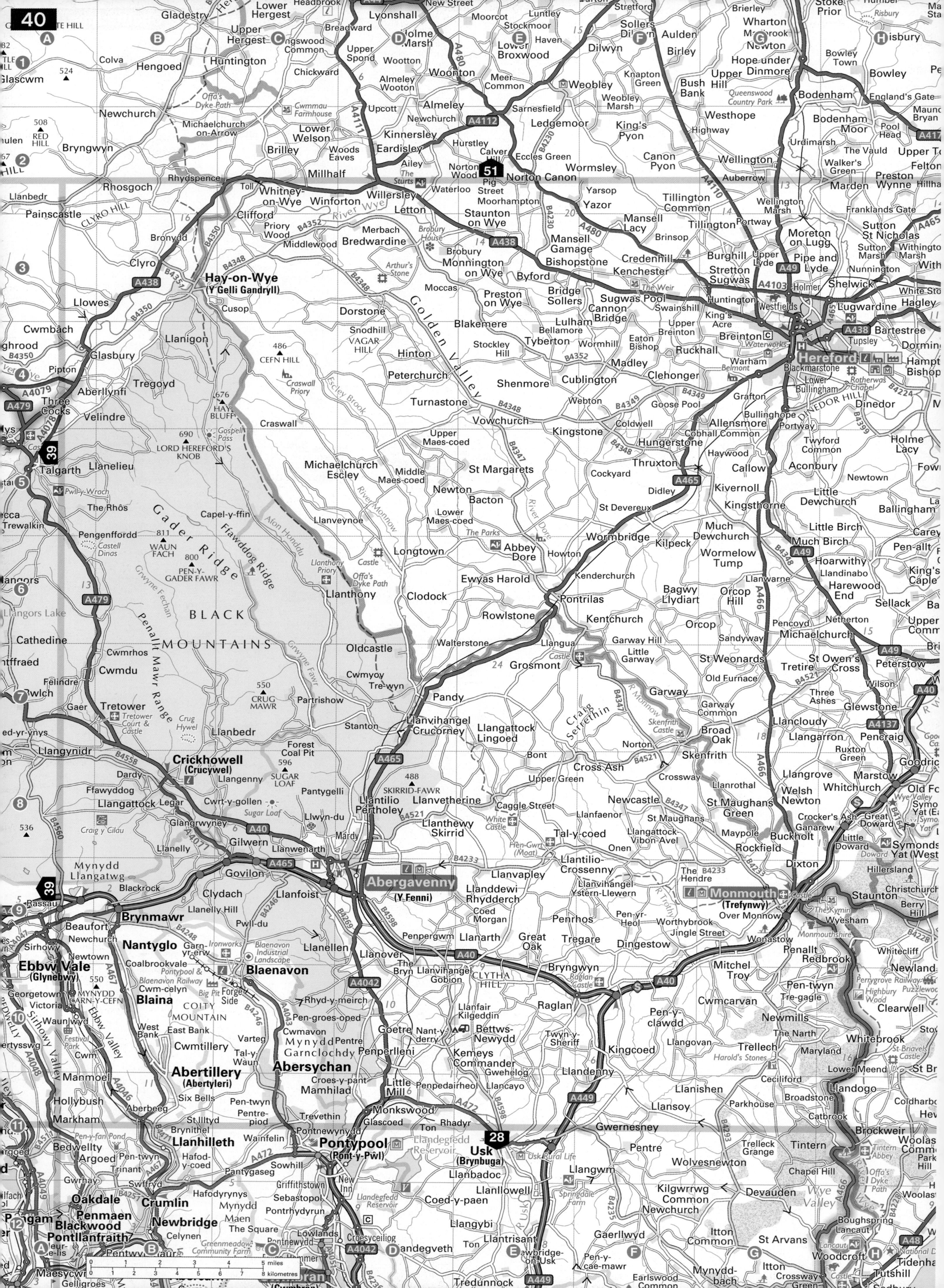

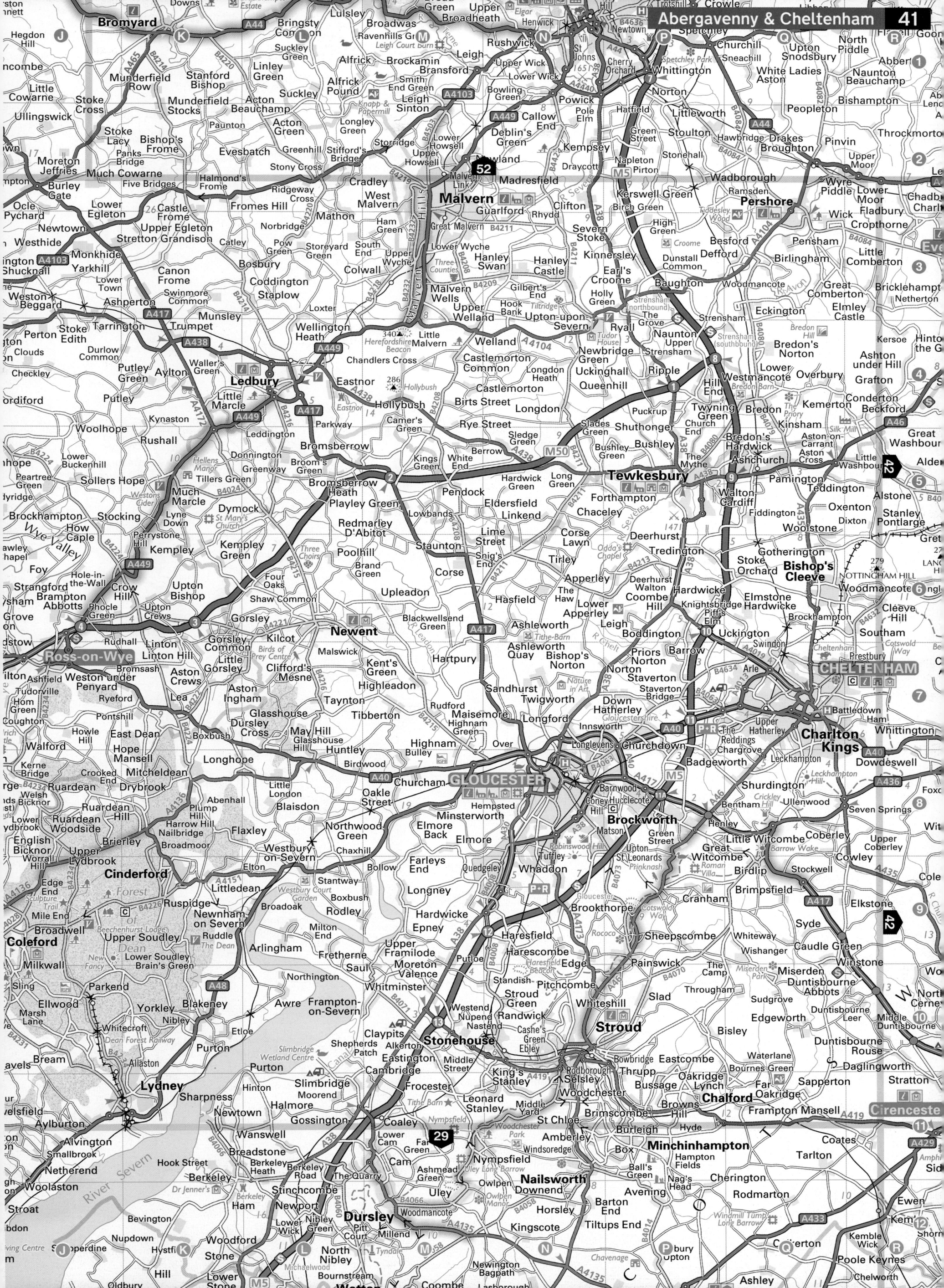

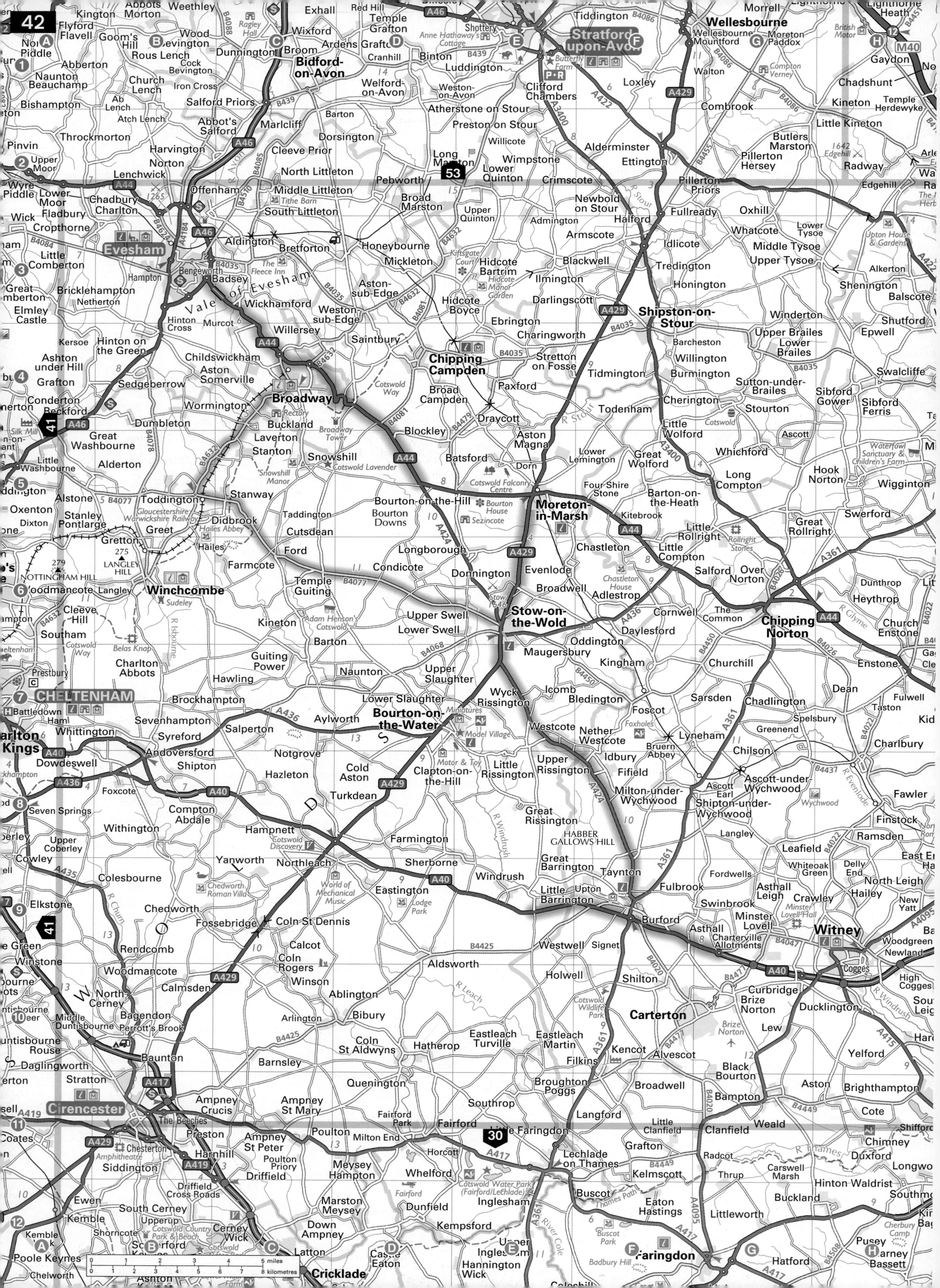

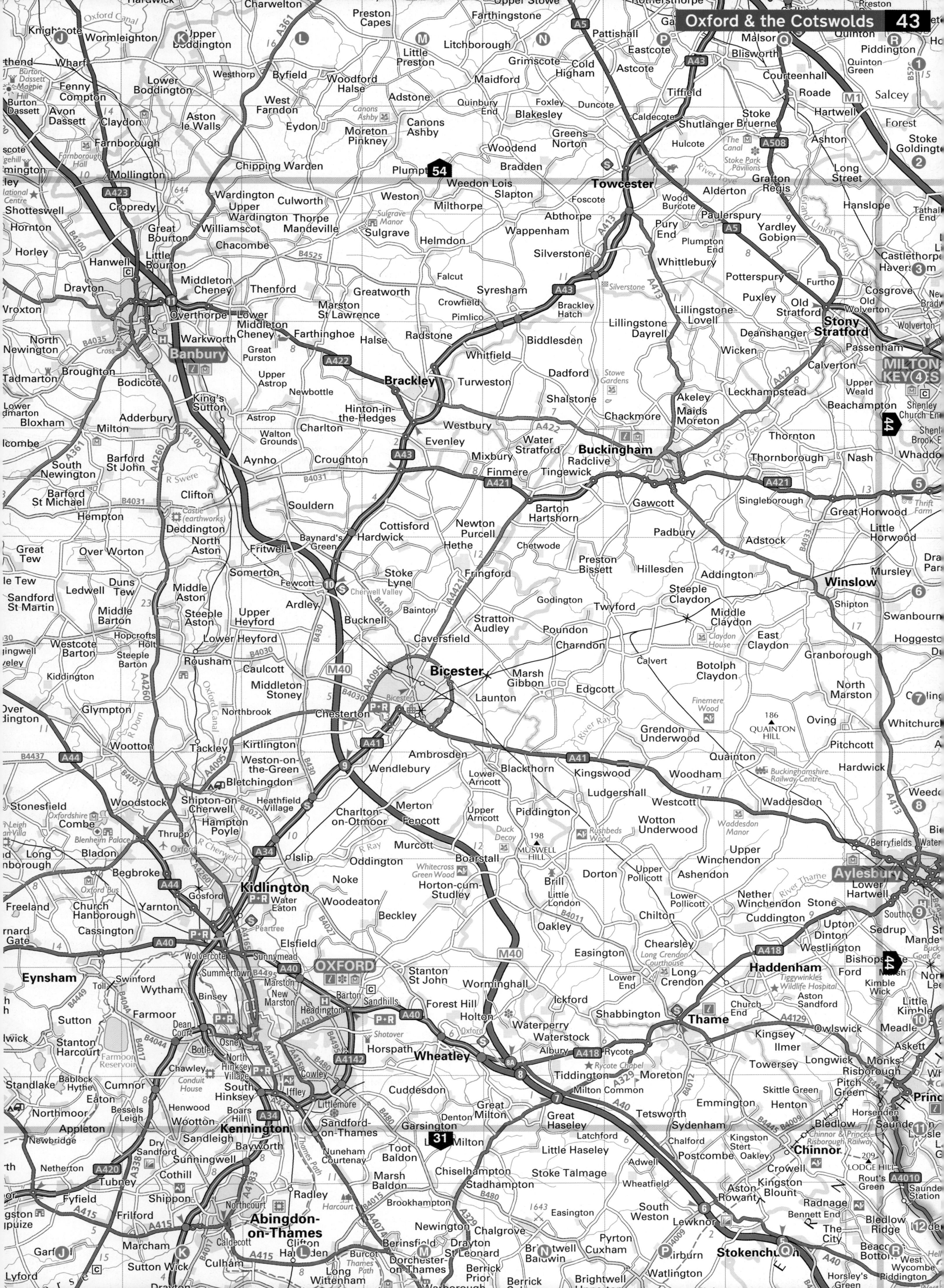

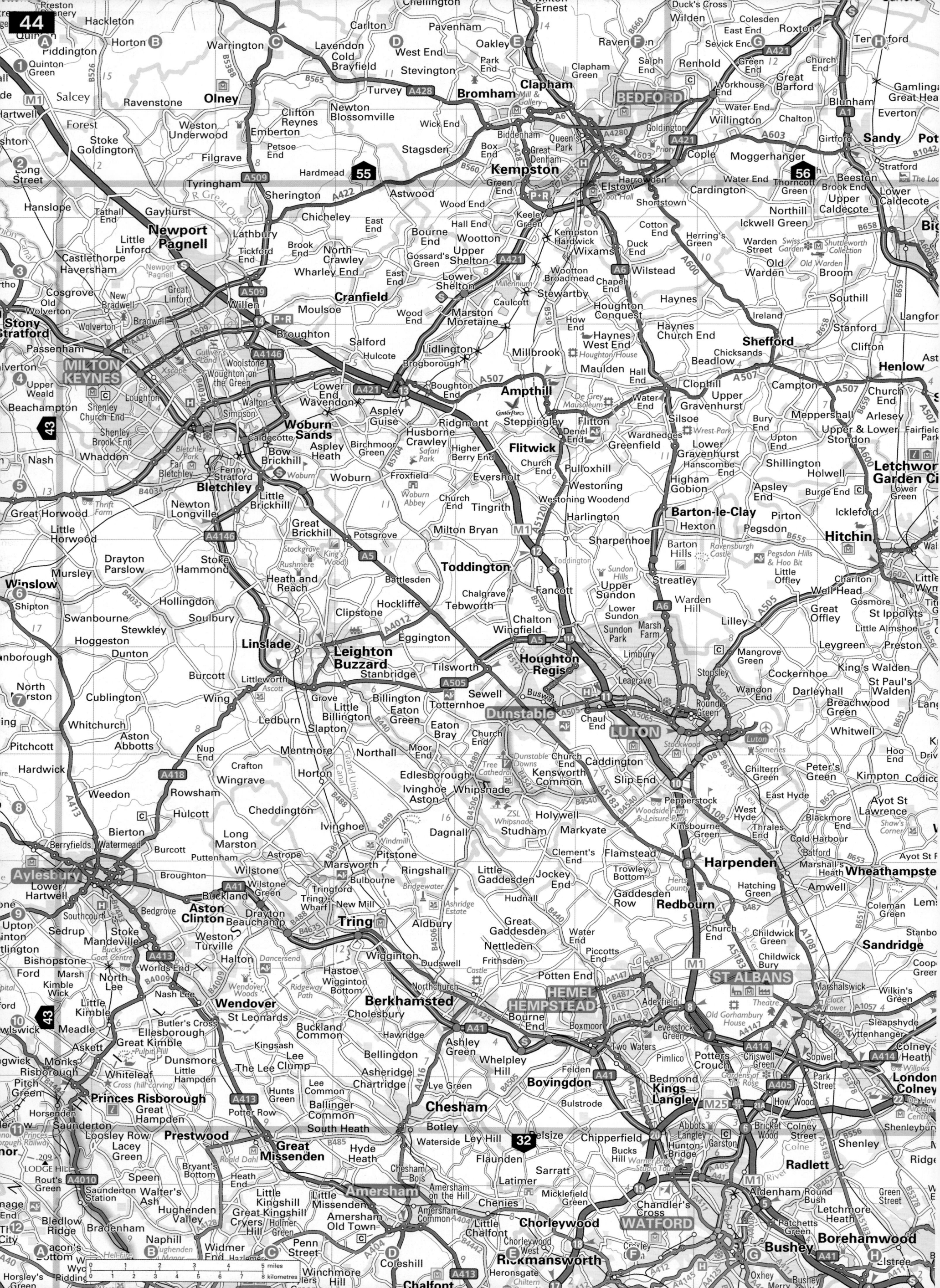

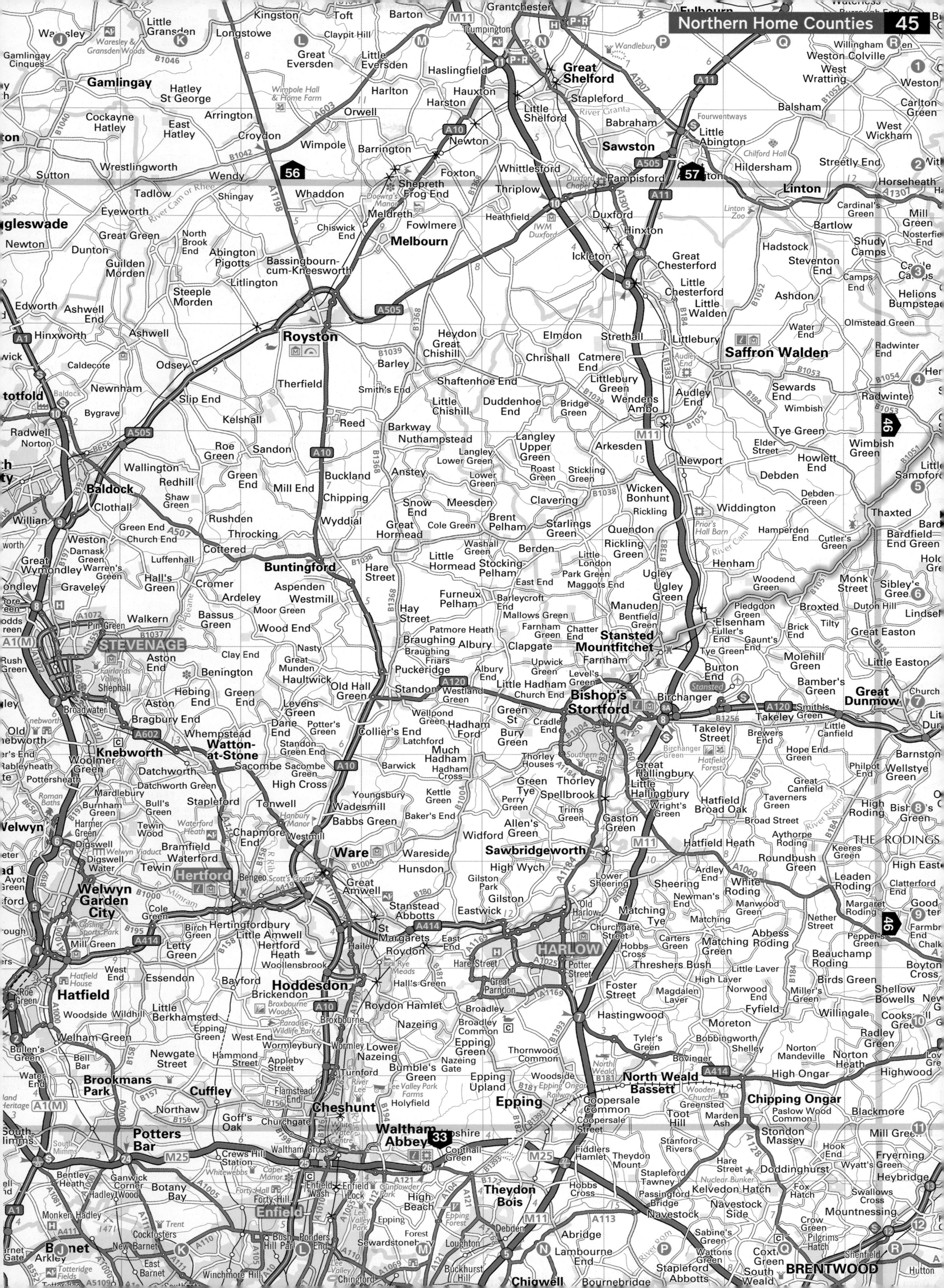

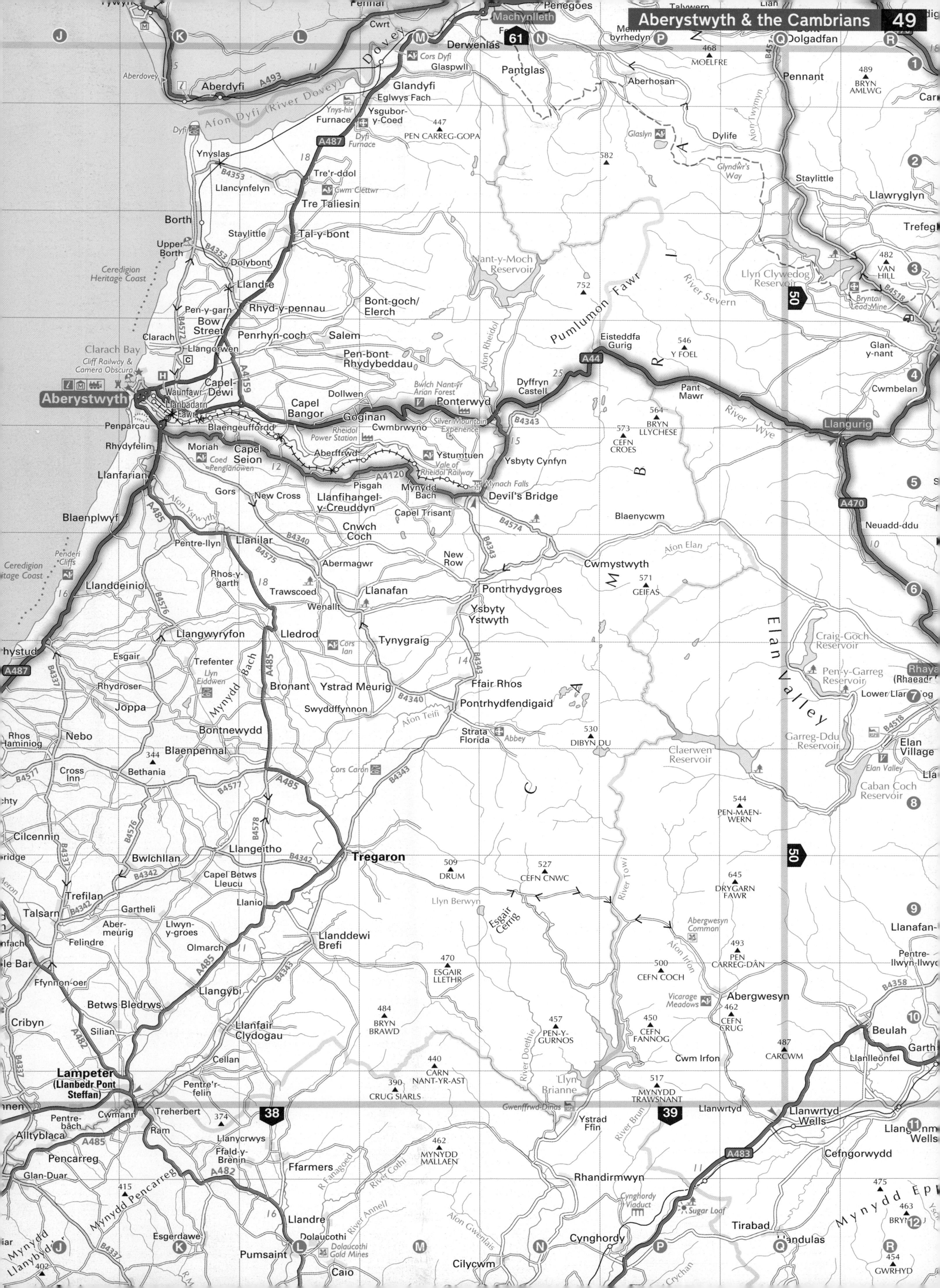

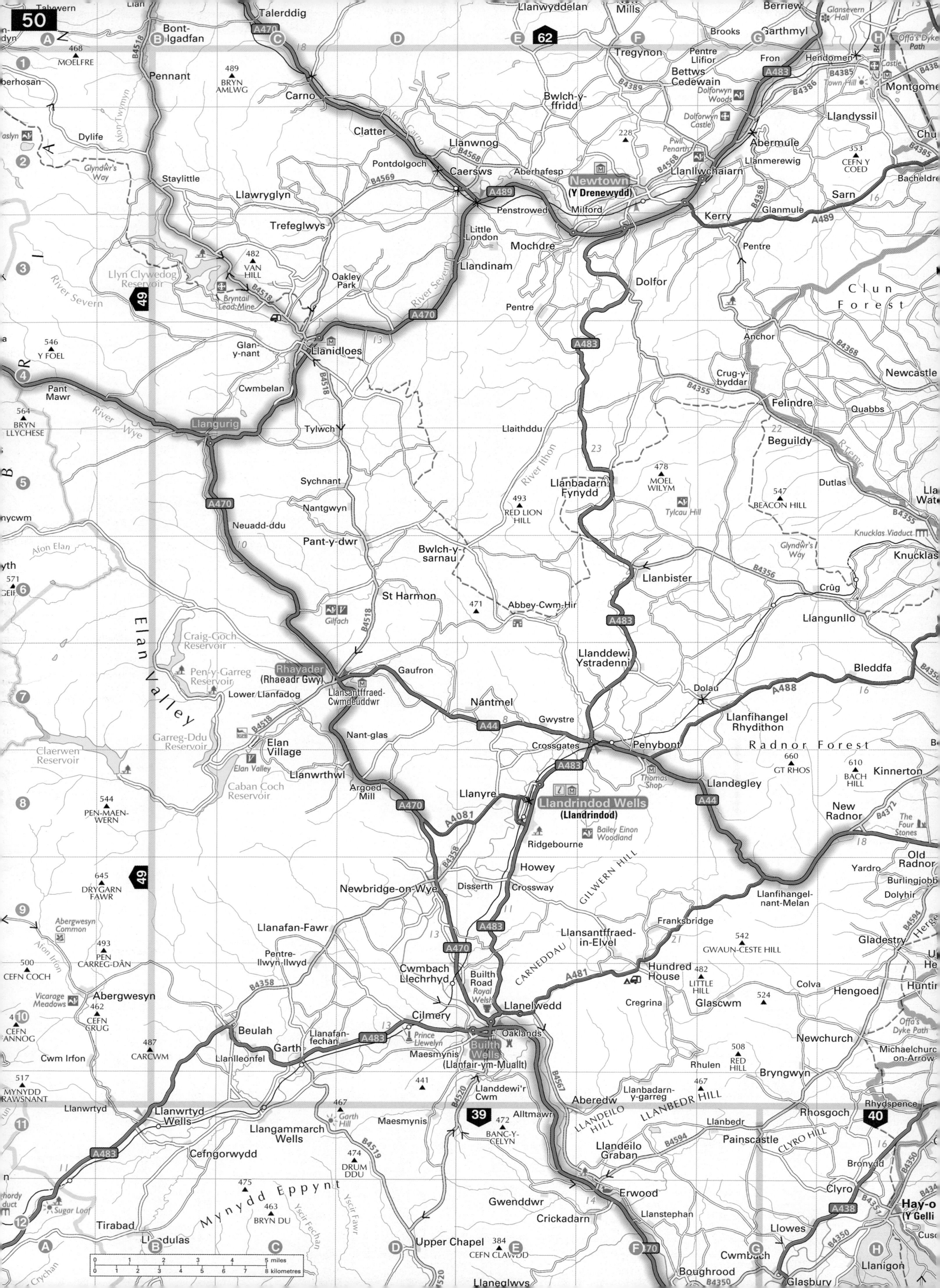

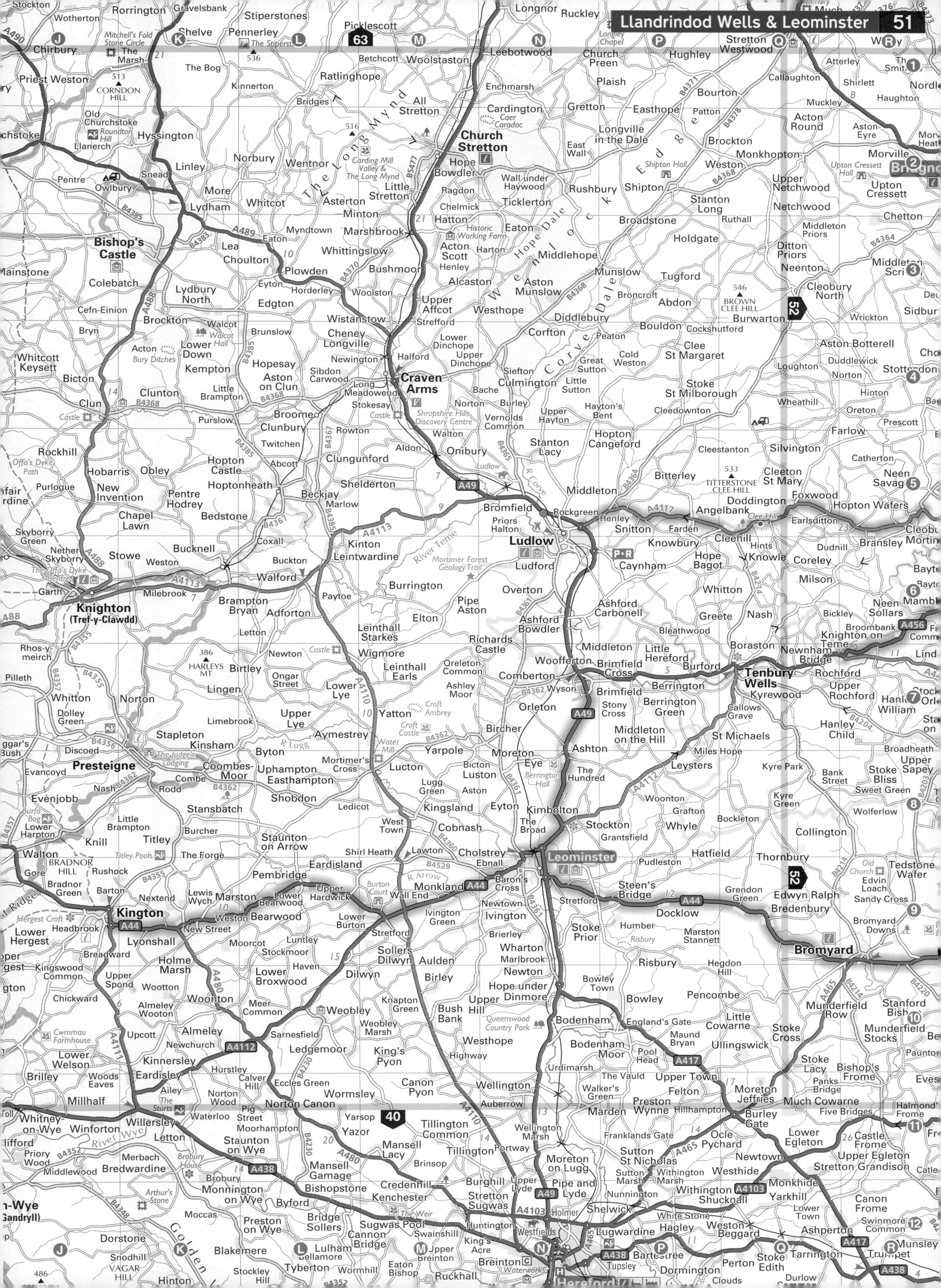

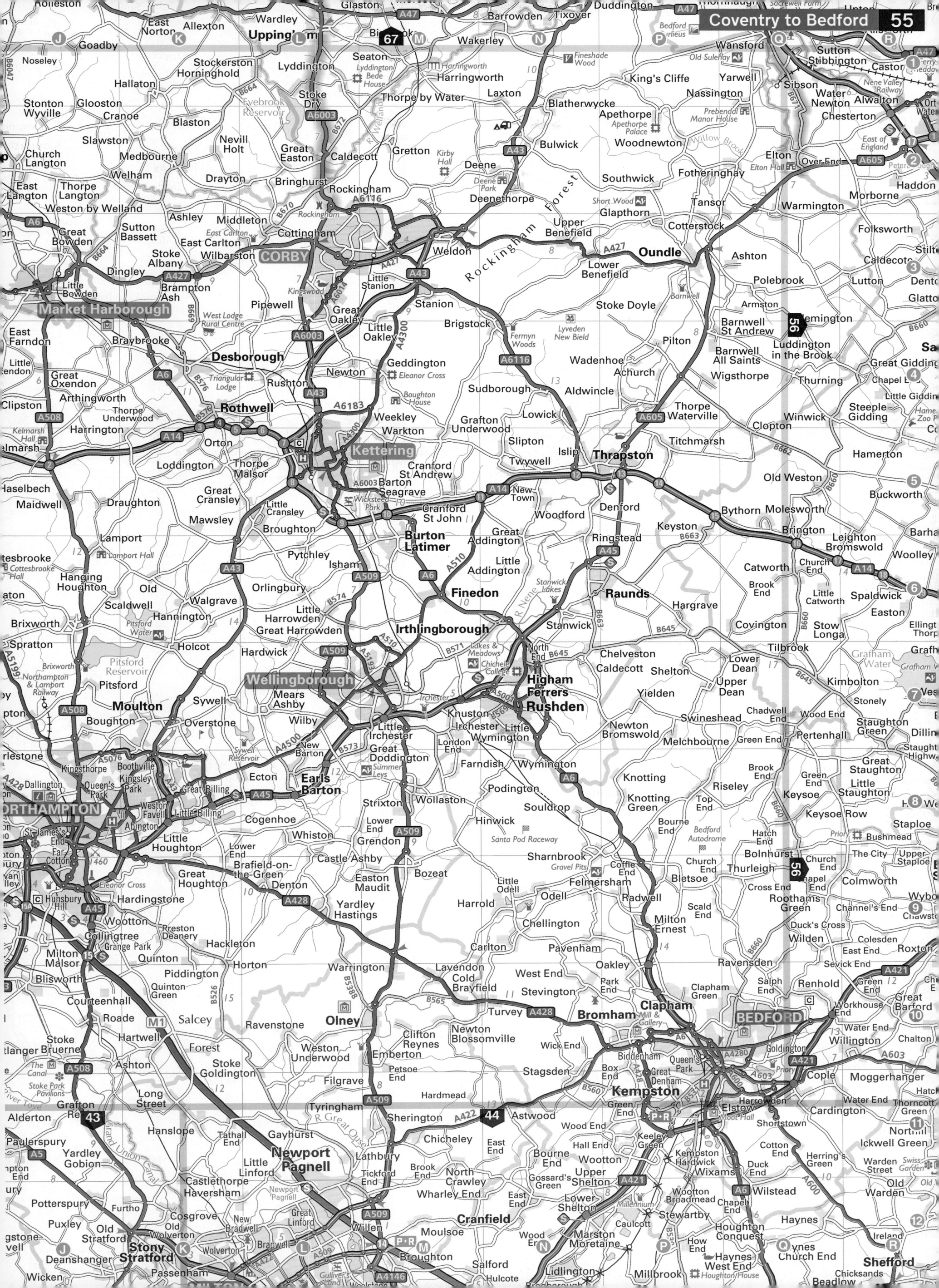

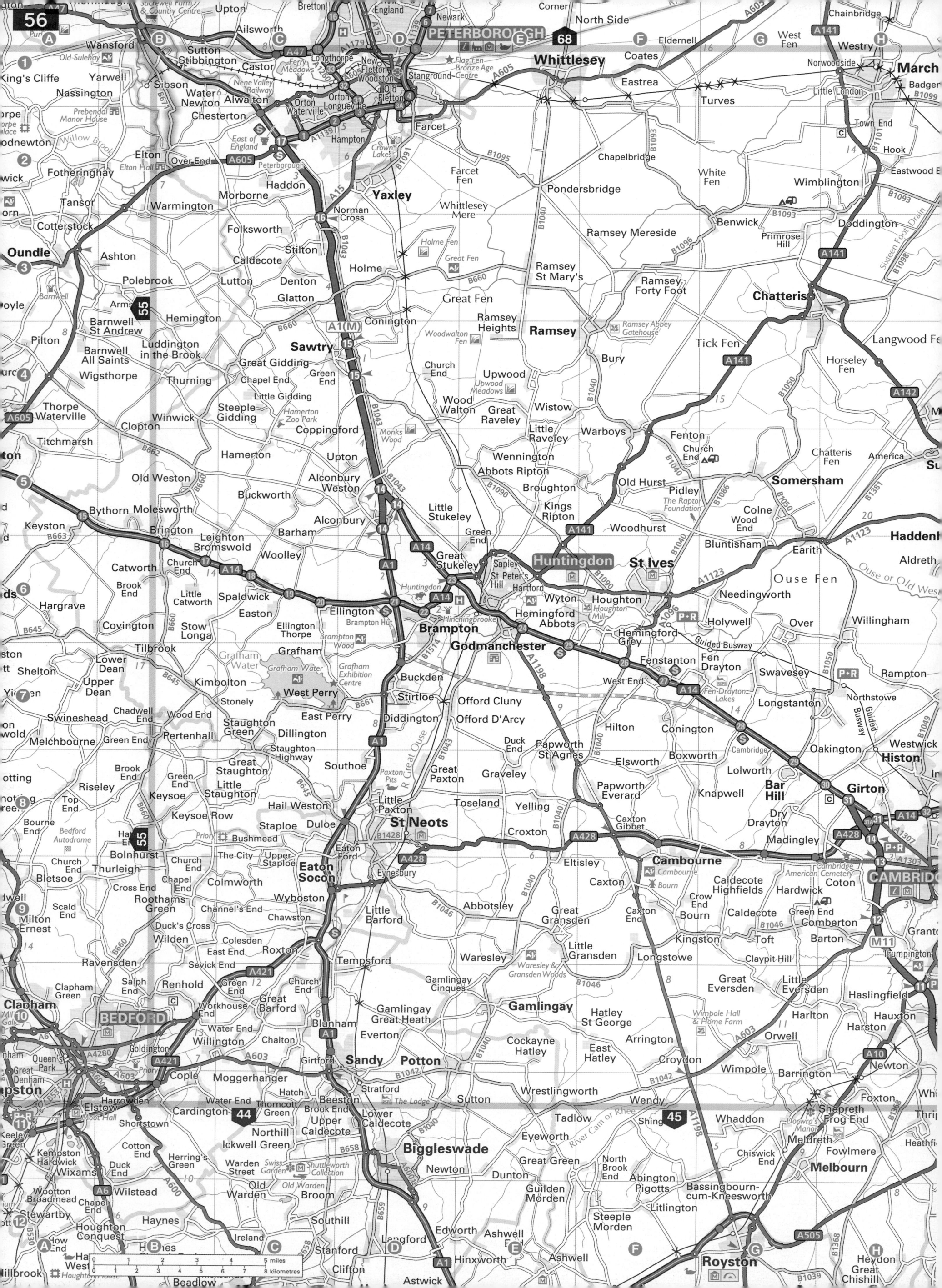

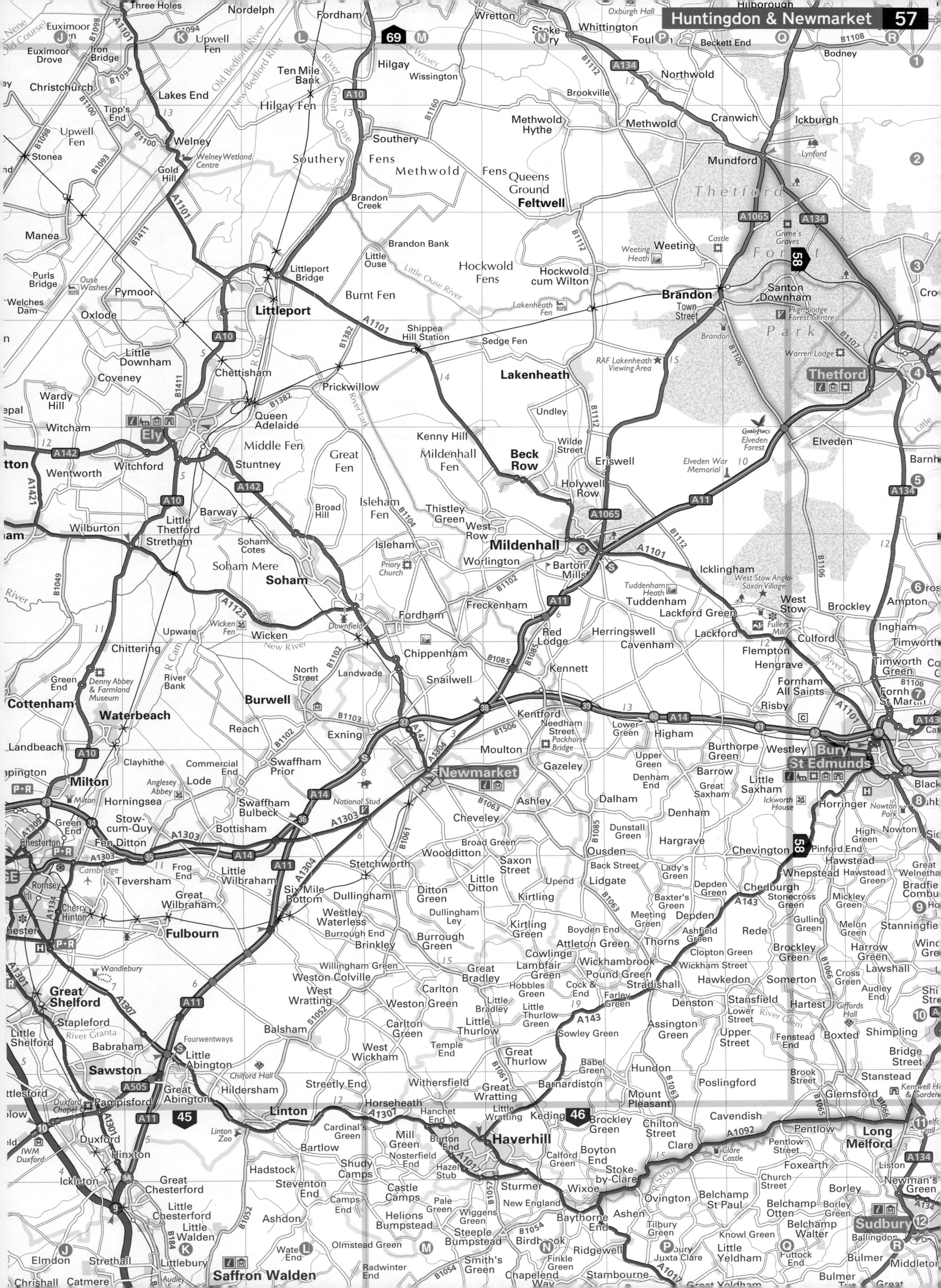

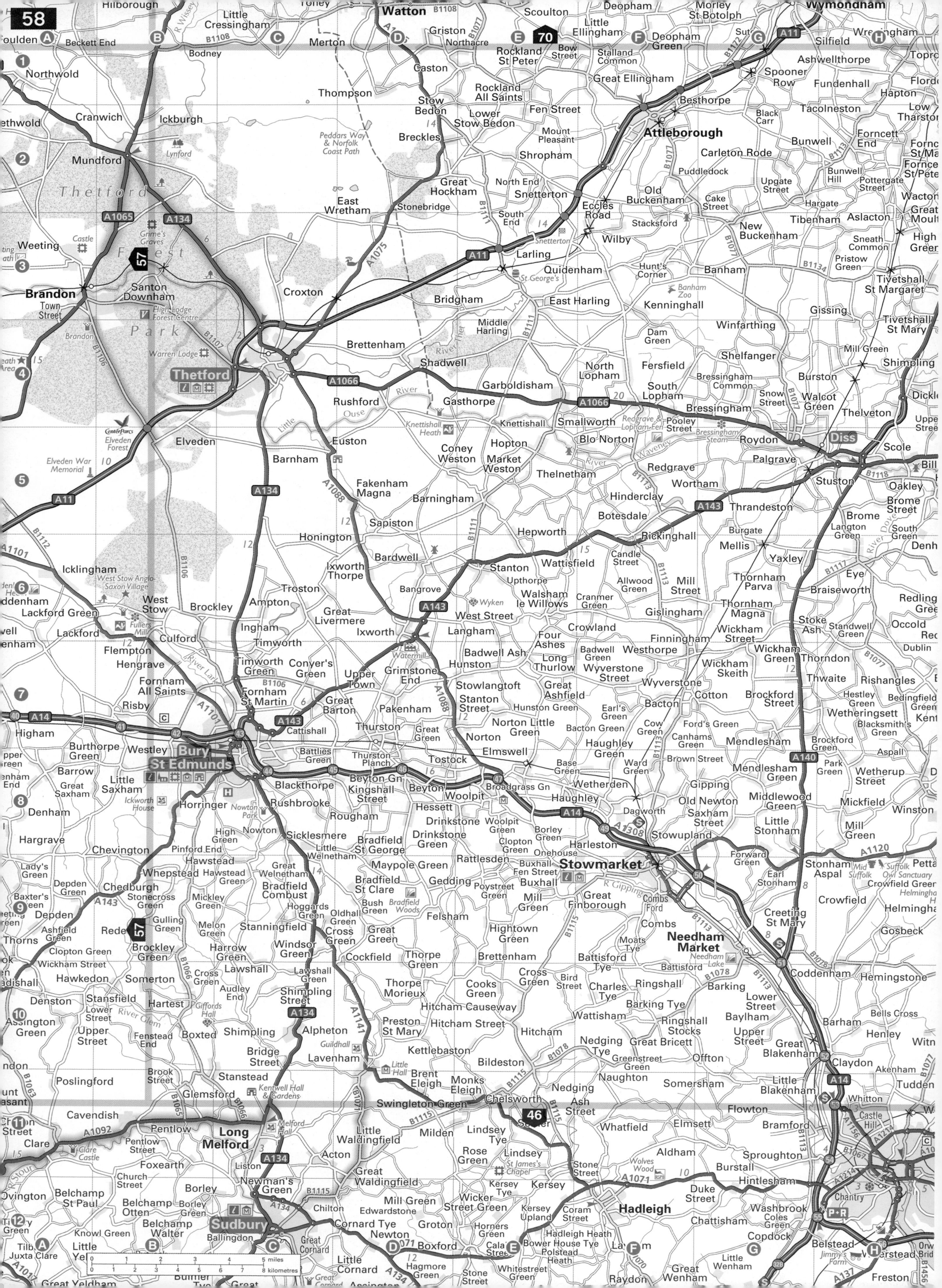

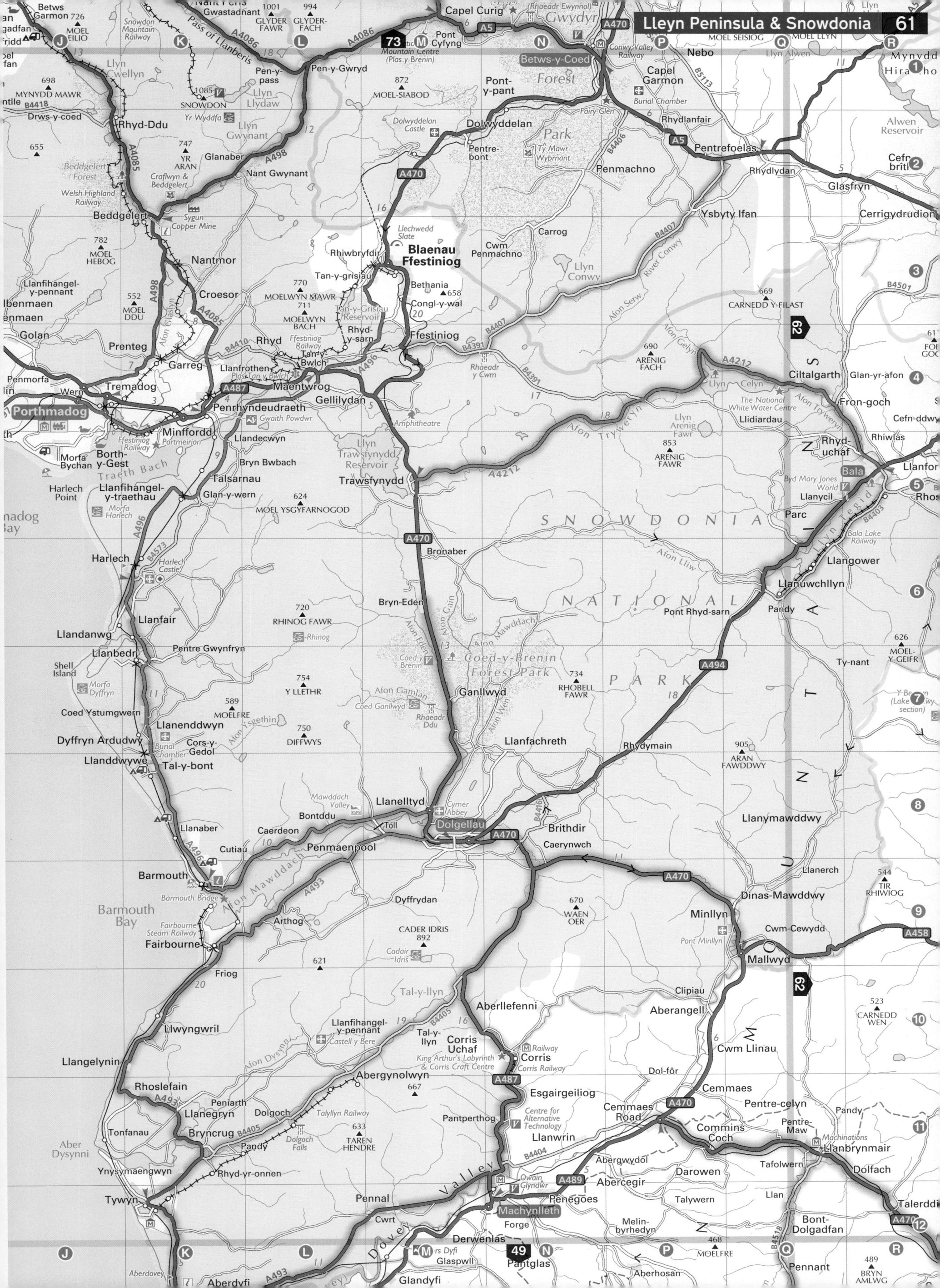

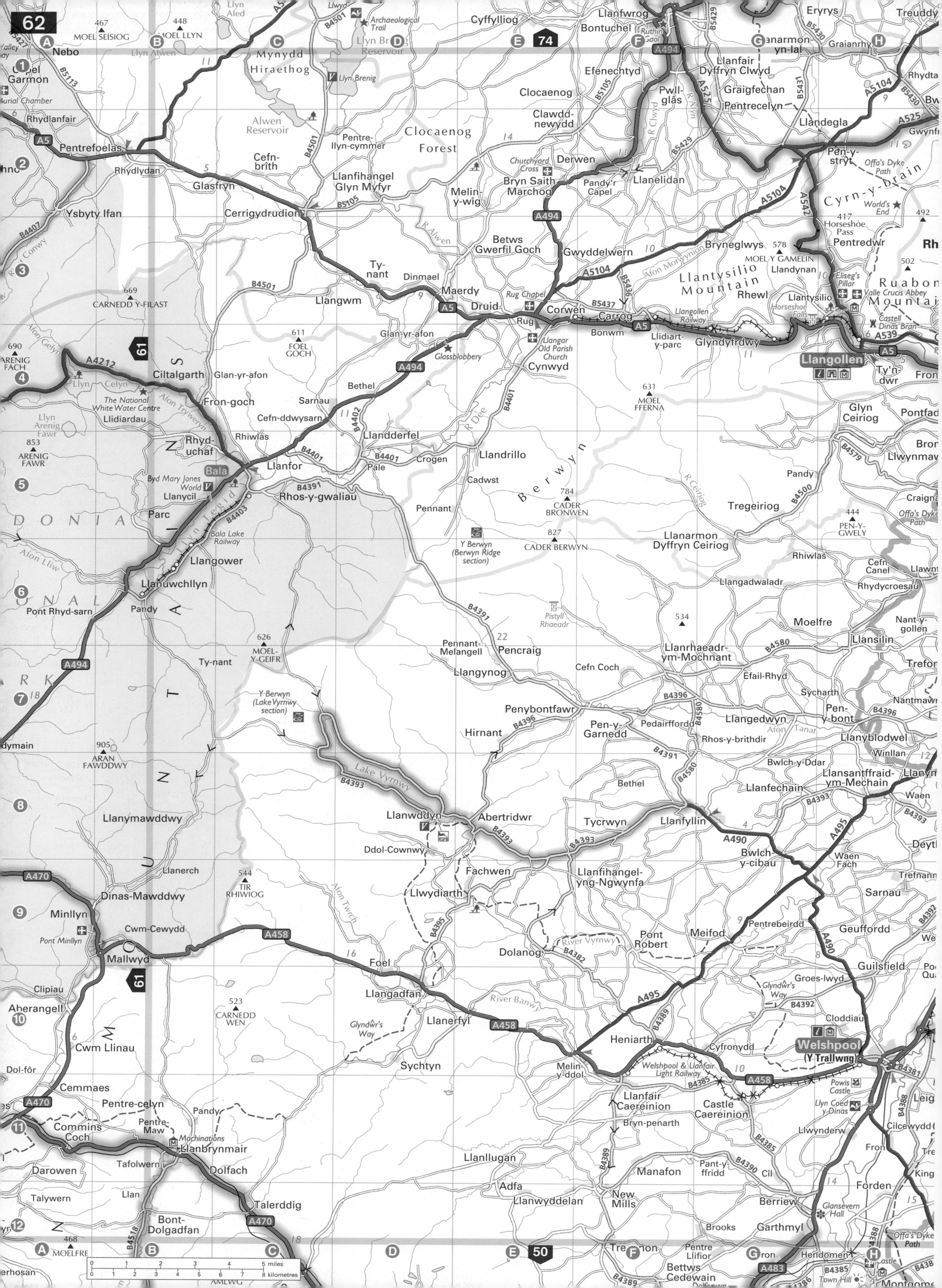

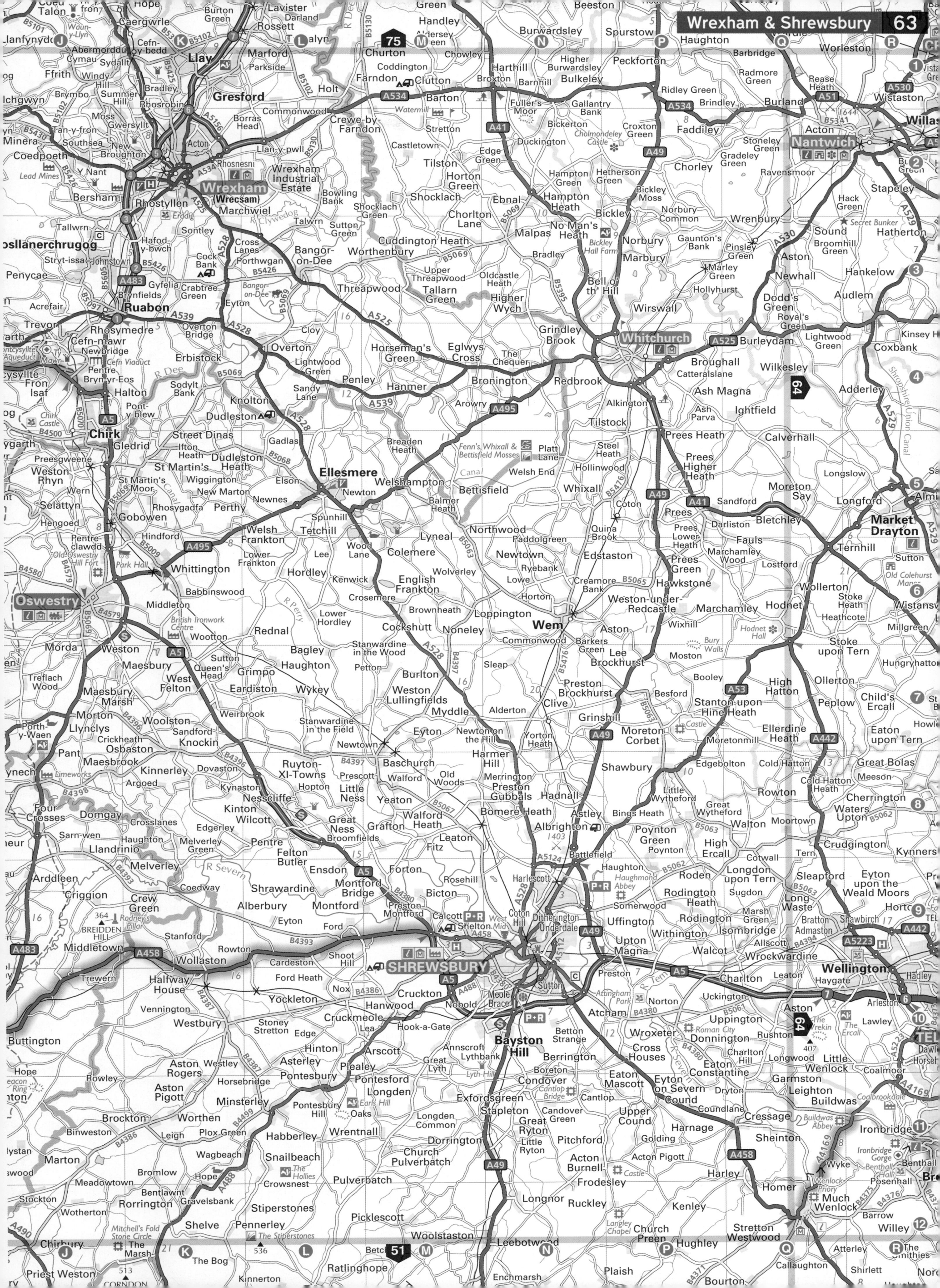

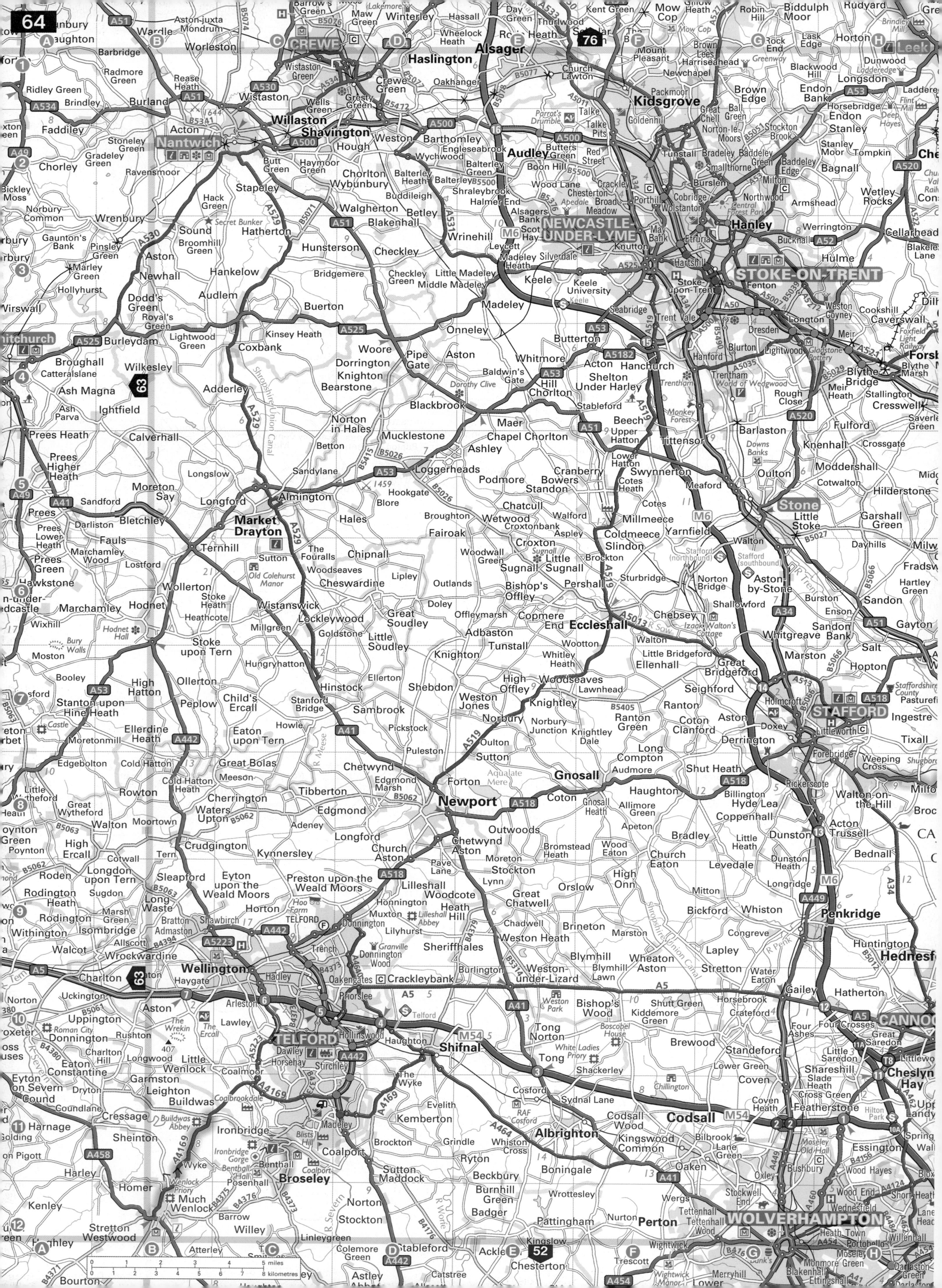

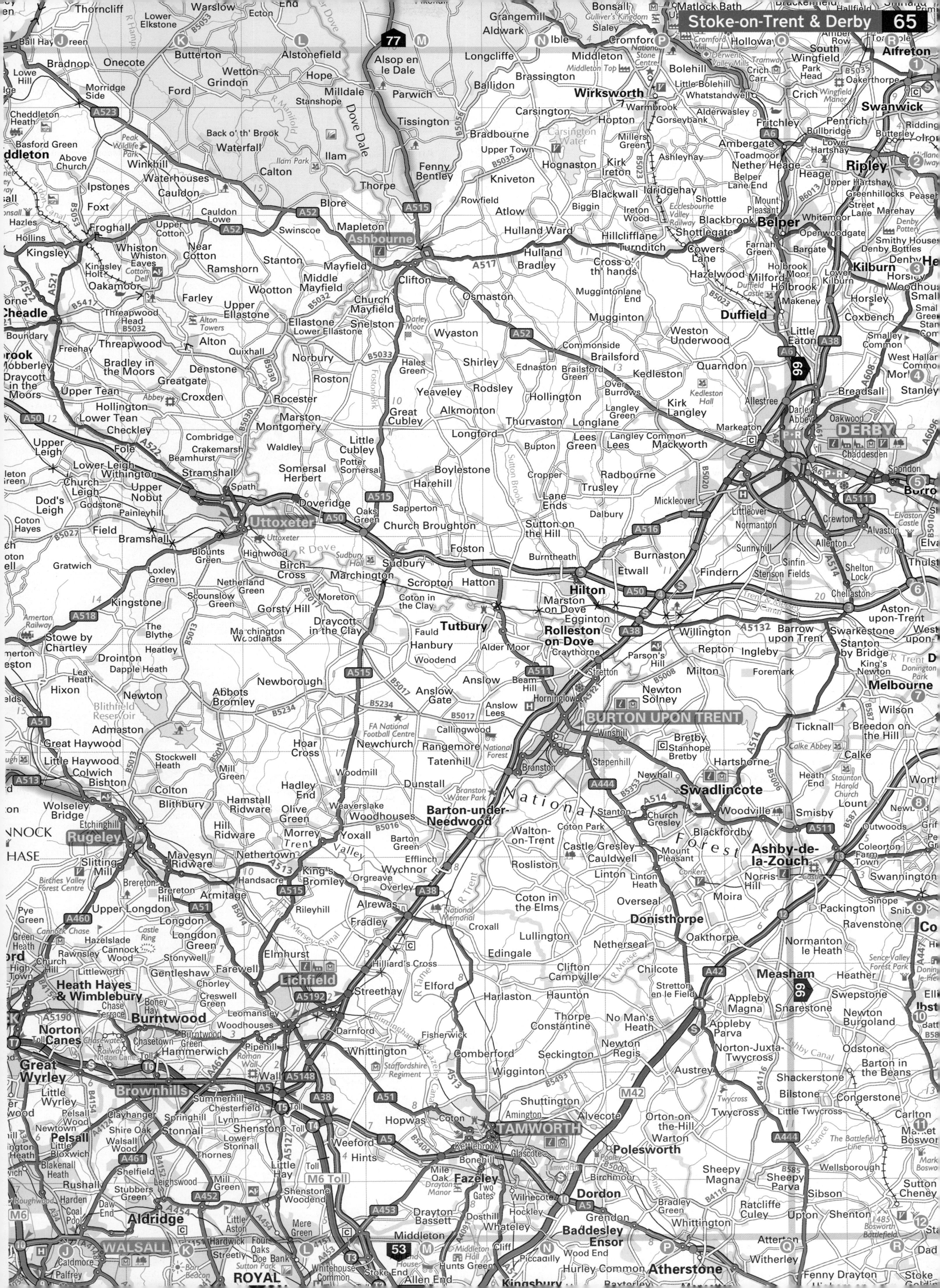

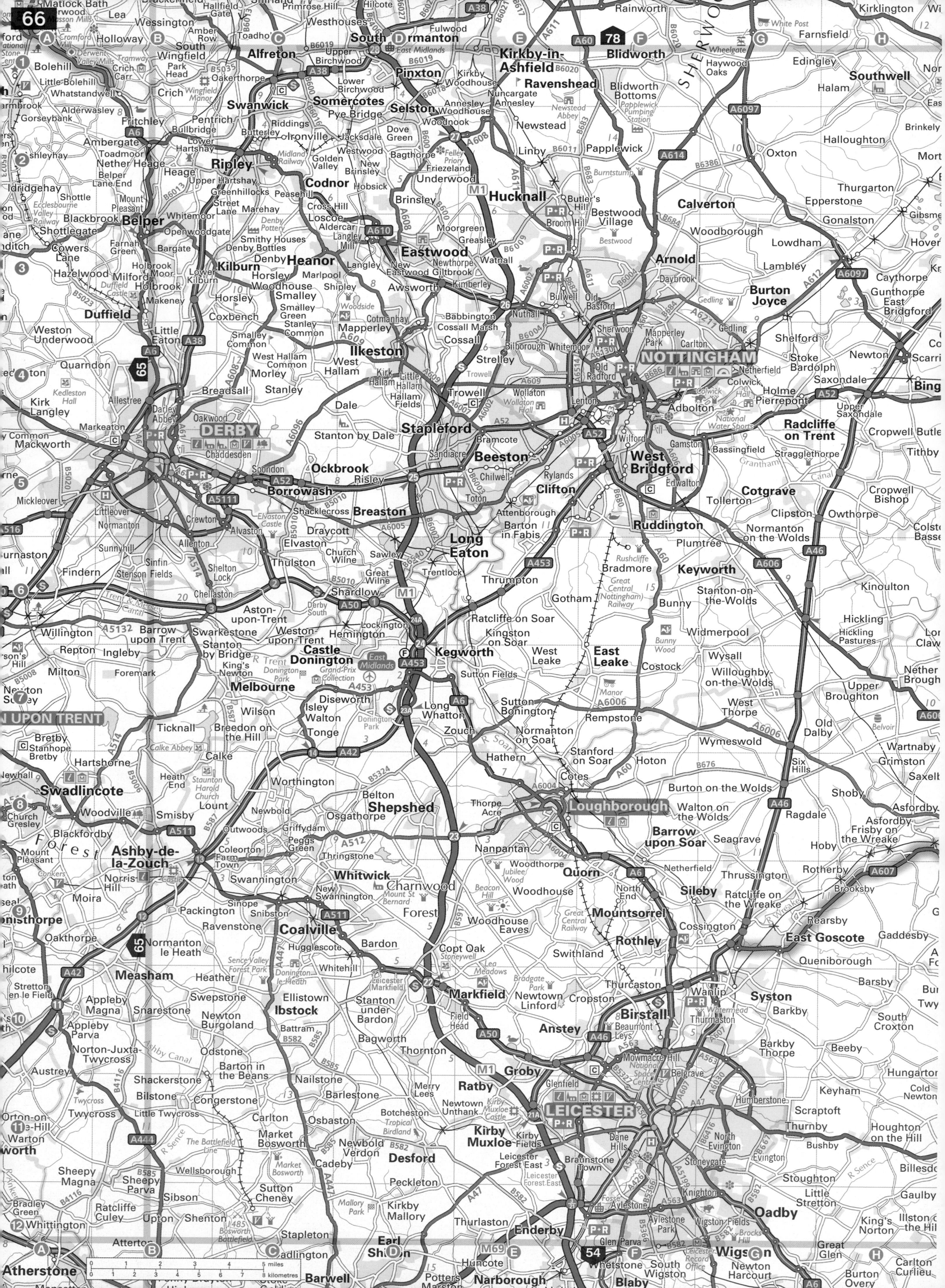

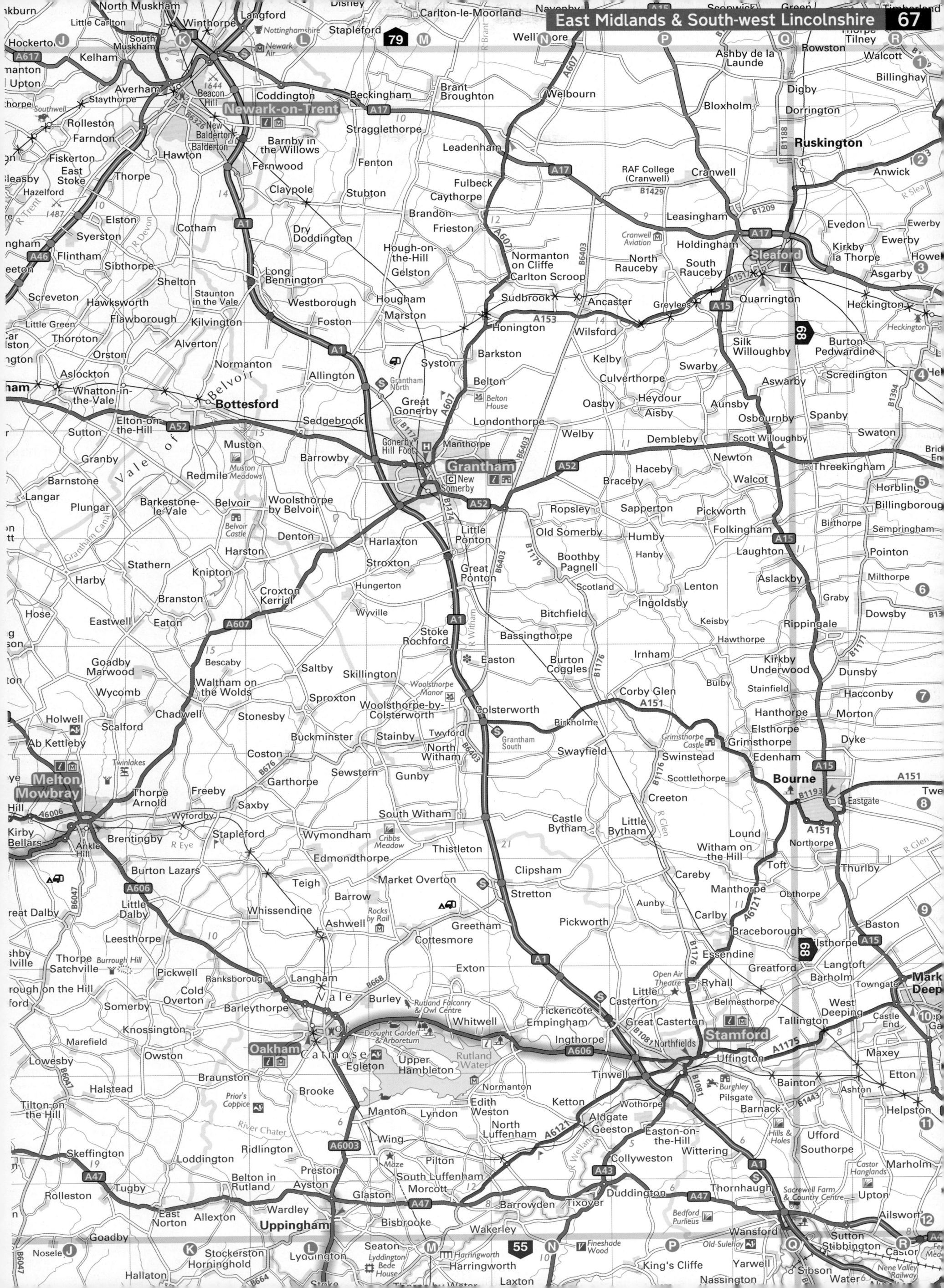

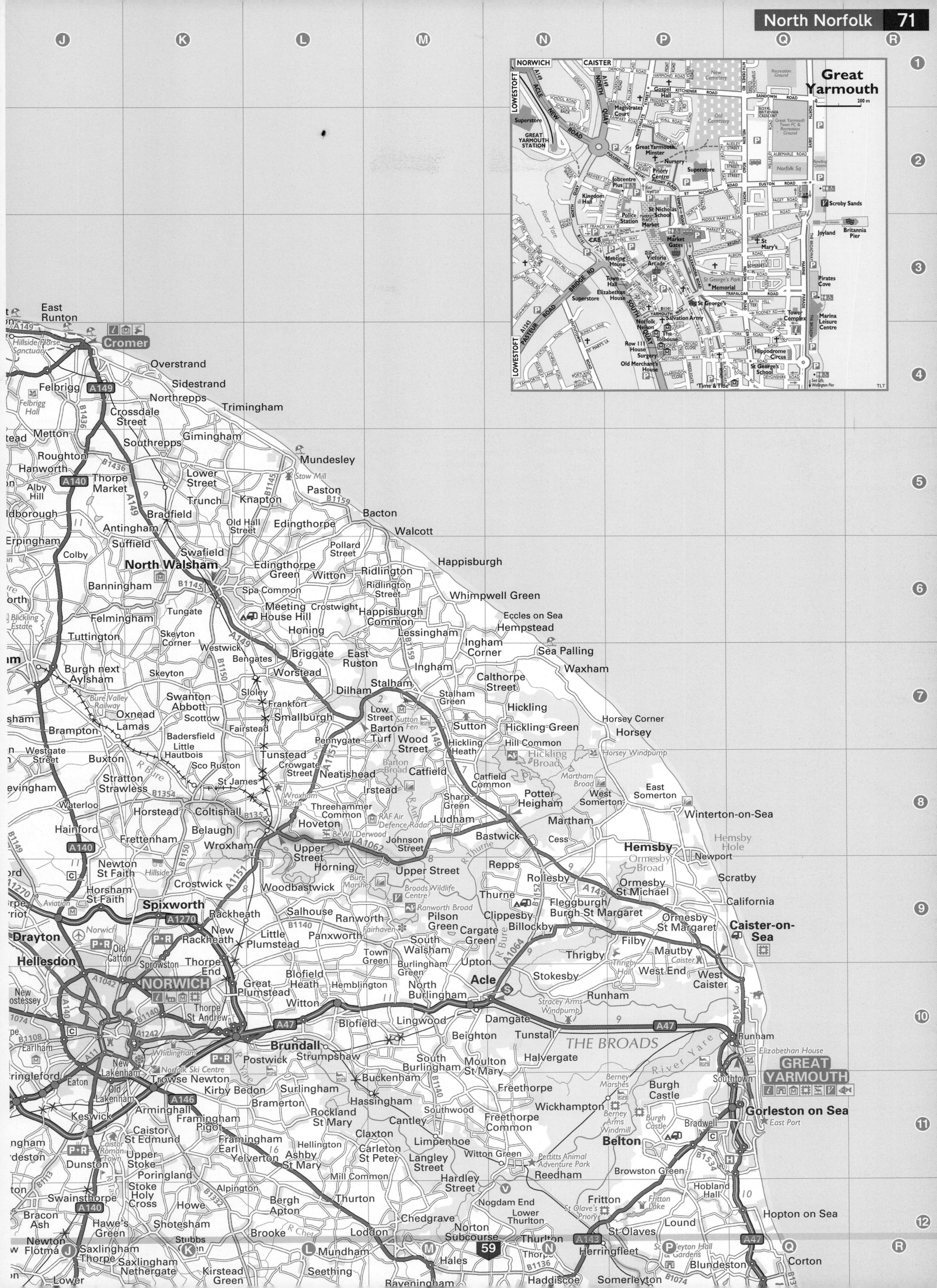

A B C D E F G H

1
2
3
4
5
6
7
8
9
10
11
12

The Skerries

North Anglesey
Heritage Coast

Wylfa
Head   Cemaes
               Bay   Porth
                          Wen
Hen   Cemlyn   Bull Bay
Borth   Bay   Amlwch
                   Cemaes   Llanbadrig   Bull Bay
CARMEL HEAD   Tregele   Llaneilian   Point Lynas
                                                Burwen   Pengorffwysfa
Llanfairynghornwy   Llanfechell   Pentrefelin
                                          Rhosbeirio   Penysarn   Nebo
Holyhead   Llanrhyddlad   Llanfflewyn   Rhosgoch   Bodewryd   Gadfa   Dulas
Bay   Church   Swtan Folk   Carreglefn   Rhosybol   City
            Bay   Llanbabo   Capel   Brynrefail   Dulas
Dublin   Llanfaethlu   Llyn   Parc   Rhôs Lligwy
                                                        Alaw   Din Lligwy
Dublin   Llanddeusant   Gwredog   Elim   Llantrisant   Maenaddwyn
Porth   Llynnon Mill   Stryd-y-   Llanerchymedd   Hebron   Bachau   Capel   Brynteg
Tywynmawr   Facsen   ANGLESEY   Llechcynfarwy   Coch   Tynygongl
North Stack   Breakwater   Llanfwrog   Pen-llyn   Llyn   Capel
Gogarth   Holyhead Mountain   Llywenan   Presaddfed   Llangwyllog   Llanbedrgoch
Bay   Llaingoch   Hut Circles   Llanfigael   B5109   Tregaian   Llanddyfnan
         Holyhead   Rhosmeirch
South Stack   (Caergybi)   Penrhos   Llanfachraeth   Bodedern   Cefni   Oriel
Holyhead Mountain   Ellins   Penrhos Feilw   Penrhos   Trefor   Llynfaes   Reservoir   Ynys Môn   Talwrn
Heritage Coast   Tower   Kingsland   Llanynghenedl   Valley   Bryngwran   Bodffordd   Rhoscefni
Penrhyn Mawr   Trefignath   Valley   Caergeiliog   A55   Gwalchmai   A55   Llangefni
                         A5   Llanfihangel   Heneglwys   Anglesey   Rhostrehwfa
Trearddur Bay   B4545   yn Nhowyn   Llechylched   Dothan   Ceint
HOLY ISLAND   Four Mile   Capel Gwyn   Ty Newydd   Cerrigceinwen   Henblas   Penmynydd
            Bridge   Llanfair-yn-Neubwll   Pencarnisiog   Capel Mawr   Llangristiolus
Rhoscolyn   Plas   Llanfaelog   Ty   Din-Dryfol   Trefdraeth   Pentre Berw   Llanfairpw
Rhoscolyn   Cymyran   Rhosneigr   Bryn Du   Croes   Bethel   Gaerwen   Star
Head   Cymyran   Barclodiad   Bodorgan   Capel   Bryn
         Bay   y Gawres   Porth Trecastell   Hermon   Mawr   Celli Ddu   Llanddaniel Fab
                              Aberffraw   Llangadwaladr   Malltraeth   Bodowyr   Y Felin
                         Anglesey   Caer Lêb   Burial Chamber   Brynsiencyn
                         Circuit   Bodorgan   Castell   Bryn Gwyn   Llanidan
                    Aberffraw   Hermon   Llangaffo   Anglesey
                    Bay   Newborough   Pen-lôn   Bodorgan   Sea Zoo   Bethel
Aberffraw Bay   Malltraeth Bay   Newborough   Foel Farm   A487   Waterloo
Heritage Coast   Warren   Caernarfon   Park   Port
                    Llanddwyn Island   Llanddwyn   Caernarfon   Segontium
                         Bay   Caernarfon Castle   Welsh Highland
                              Abermenai   Railway   Gypsy
                              Point   Airworld   Wood
                         Foryd   Aviation   Bontnewydd
                         Bay   Morfa Dinlle   Llanwnda
C A E R N A R F O N   Dinas Dinlle   Llandwrog   Carmel

Holyhead Harbour

Mariso   Maritime
Porth-   BEACH ROAD   PRINCE OF WALES ROAD
y-Felin   Salt Island
              P+R   Hertz Car
Long Stay   Rental
FERRY
TERMINAL
Stryd   TERMINAL
BUILDING   HOLYHEAD
P   Short Stay
HOLYHEAD   Môrawelon
STATION
Kingsland   LONDON   ROAD
BANGOR   TLT

0 ___ 500 m

0 1 2 3 4 5 miles
0 1 2 3 4 5 6 7 8 kilometres

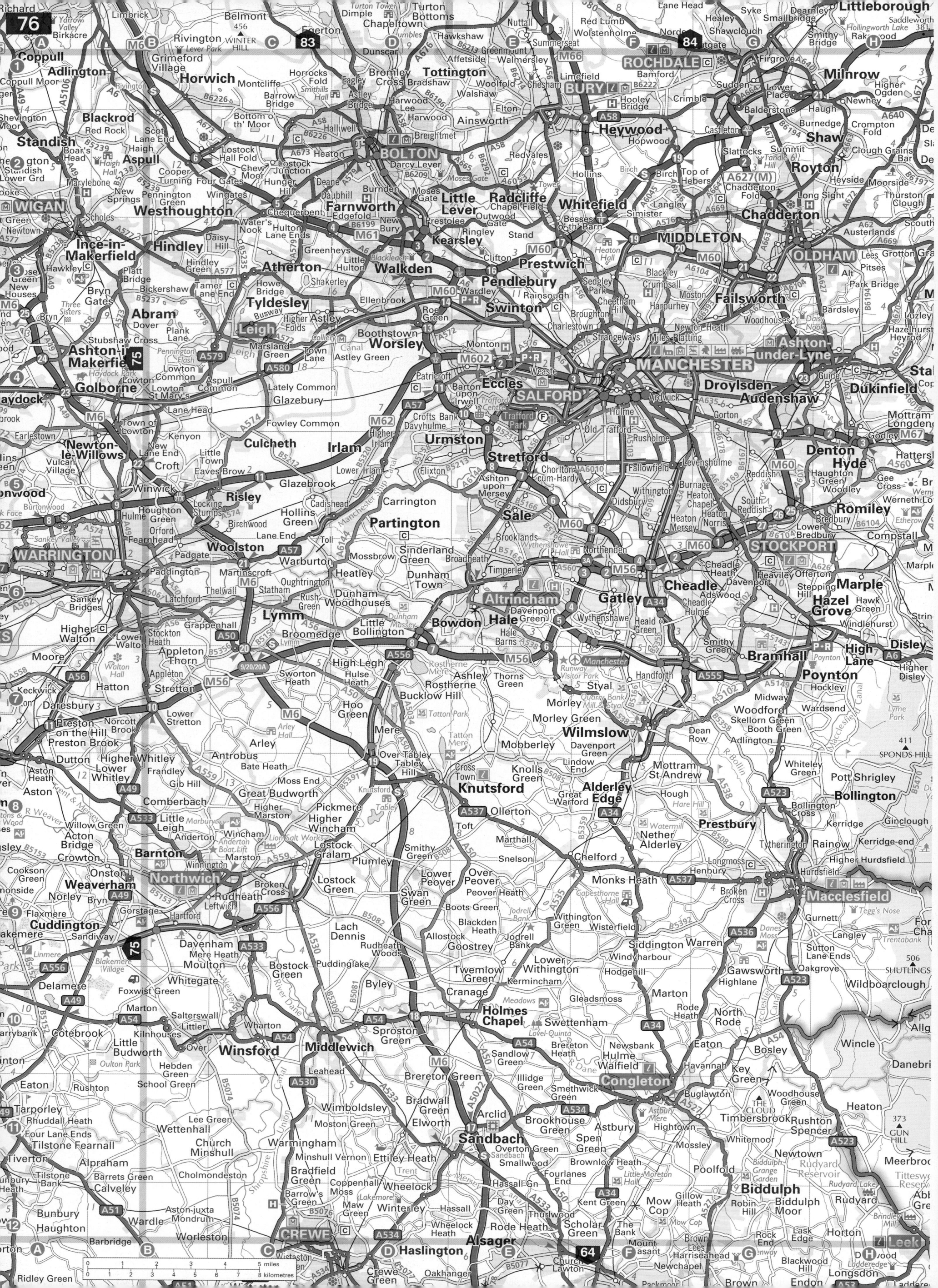

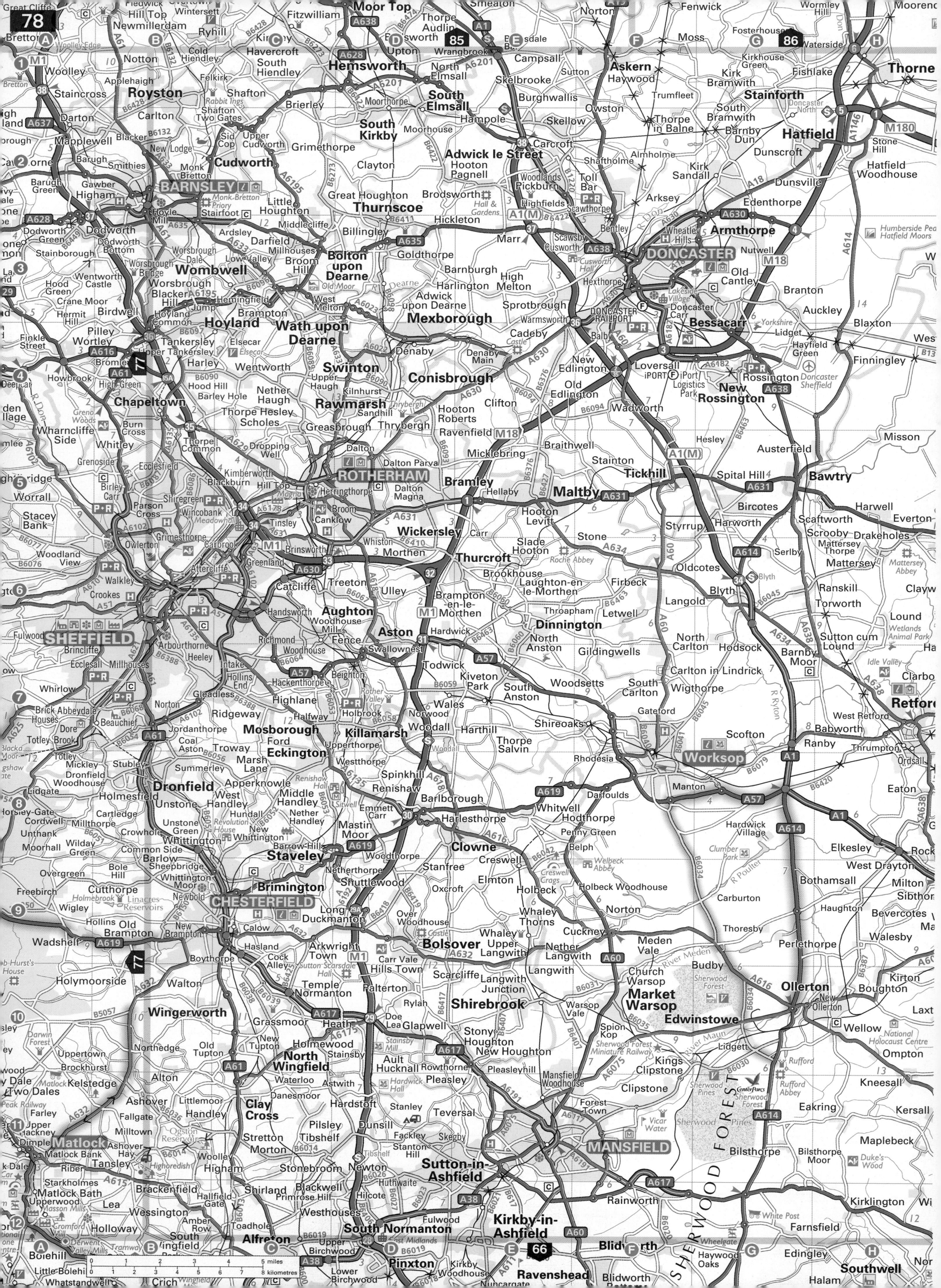

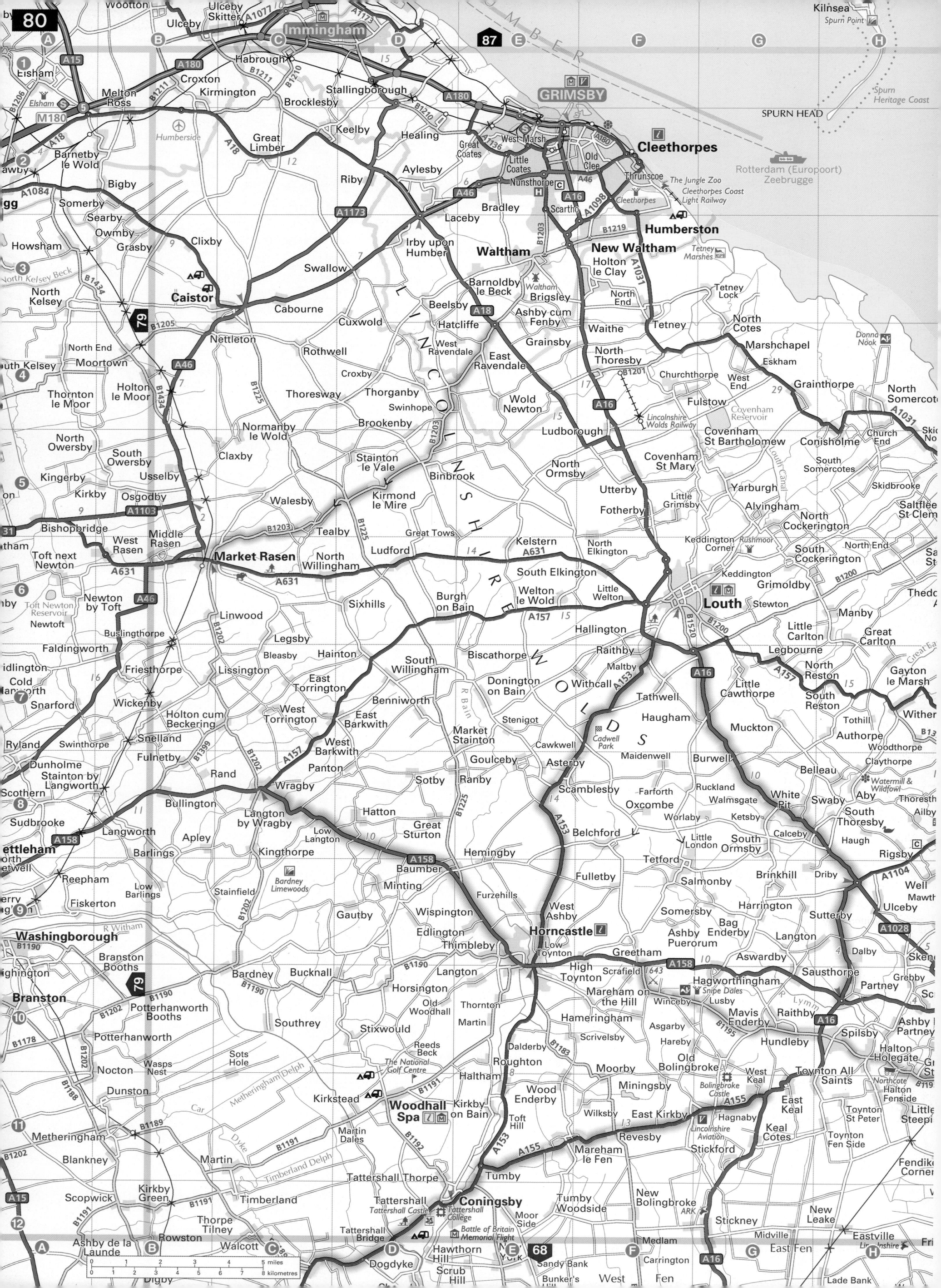

J K L M N P Q R

1
2
3
4

...brooke
...h End
Saltfleet

Saltfleetby -
Theddlethorpe Dunes

...by
...ent

Saltfleetby
All Saints

...tfleetby
...Peter

Theddlethorpe
St Helen

A1031

...lethorpe
...ll Saints

Seal Sanctuary &
Wildlife Centre

5
6

Mablethorpe

Strubby

A1104

Trusthorpe

Thorpe

A52

Sutton on Sea

Maltby
le Marsh

A1111

Sandilands

7

Hagnaby

Beesby
Saleby

Hannah

A52

Markby

Asserby
Turn

Asserby

...orpe

Bilsby
Thurlby

Huttoft

Anderby Creek

8

B1449

X

Alford

Anderby

B1196

Farlesthorpe

Mumby

Authorpe
Row

Chapel Point

Cumberworth

Helsey

I 8

Chapel
St Leonards

9

Bonthorpe

Hogsthorpe

...orpe

Willoughby

Slackholme
End

Claxby

Sloothby

Fantasy Island

...leby

Hasthorpe

Habertoft

Addlethorpe

Ingoldmells

Welton
le Marsh

A52

Ingoldmells
Point

...emby

Candlesby

Lincolnshire Coast
Light Railway

10

...by

Gunby

Orby

Winthorpe

Gunby Hall

Monksthorpe

7

...eeping

Burgh le Marsh

Natureland Seal
Sanctuary

Bratoft

A158

...Irby in the Marsh

11

Firsby

Skegness

Croft

Seacroft

...ng

Thorpe St Peter

Wainfleet
Haven

...Wainfleet
Bank

Wainfleet
All Saints

Gibraltar

Wainfleet
St Mary

A52

Gibraltar Point

12

...kney

J riskney Eaudike K L N P Q R

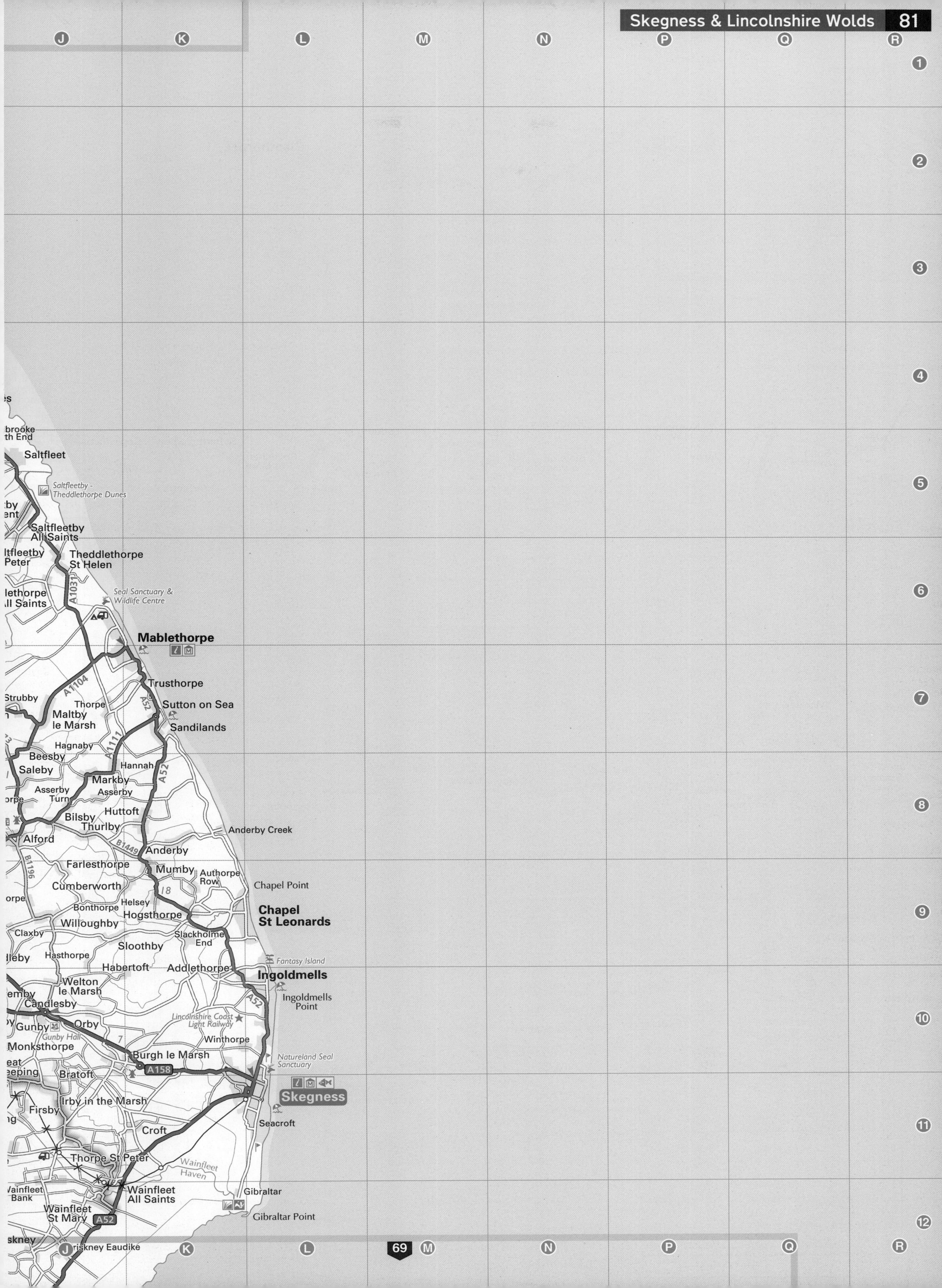

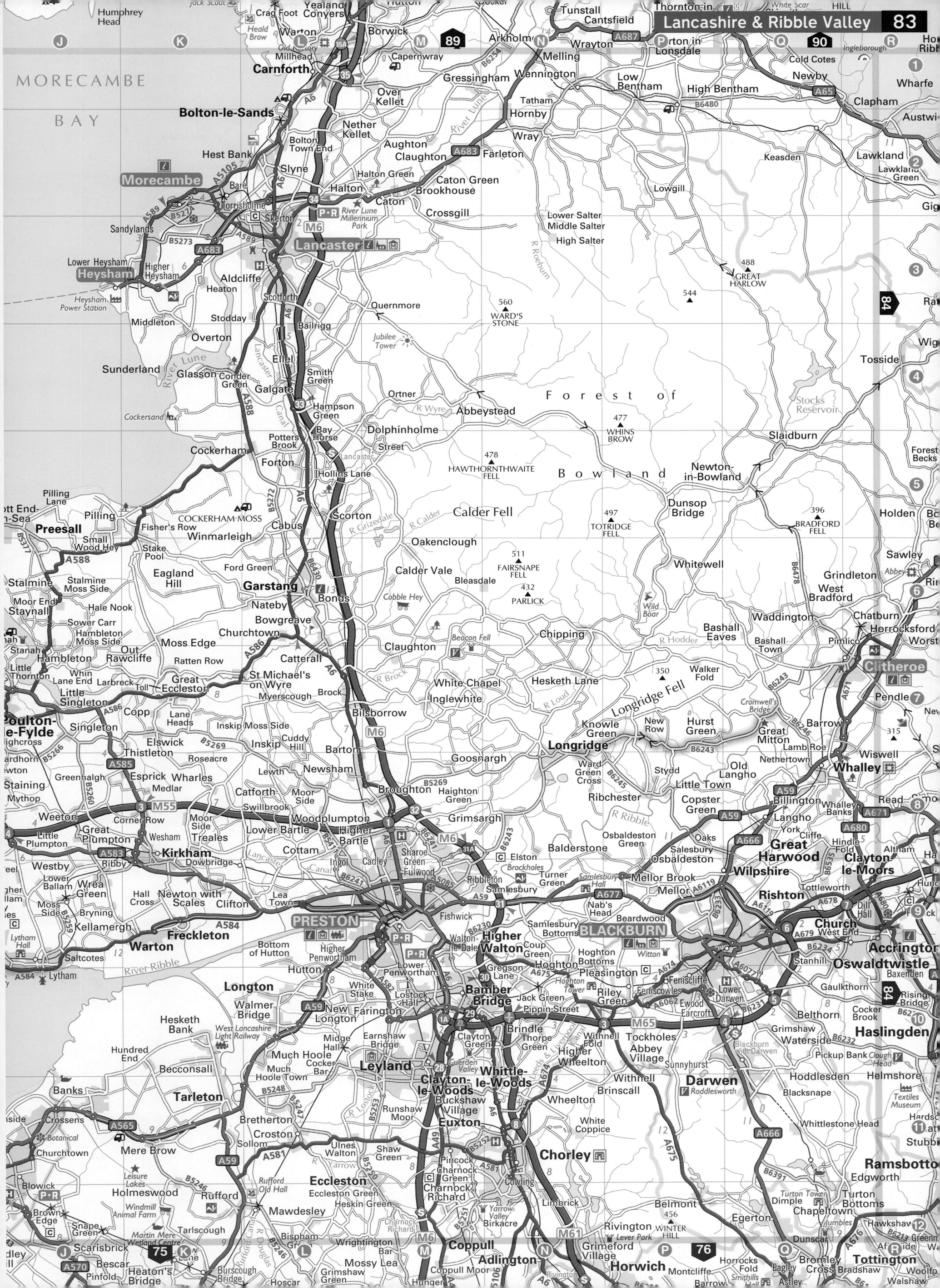

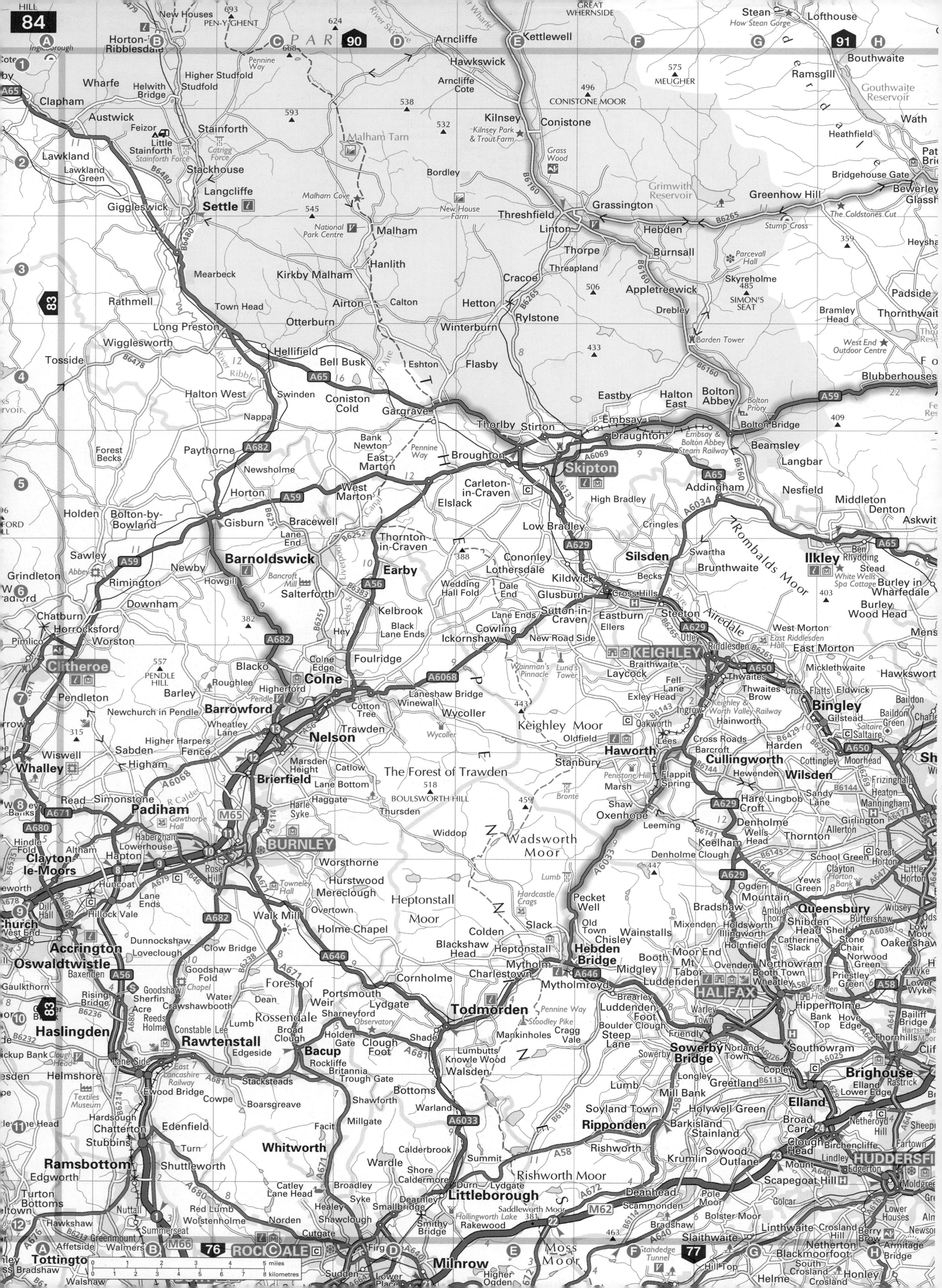

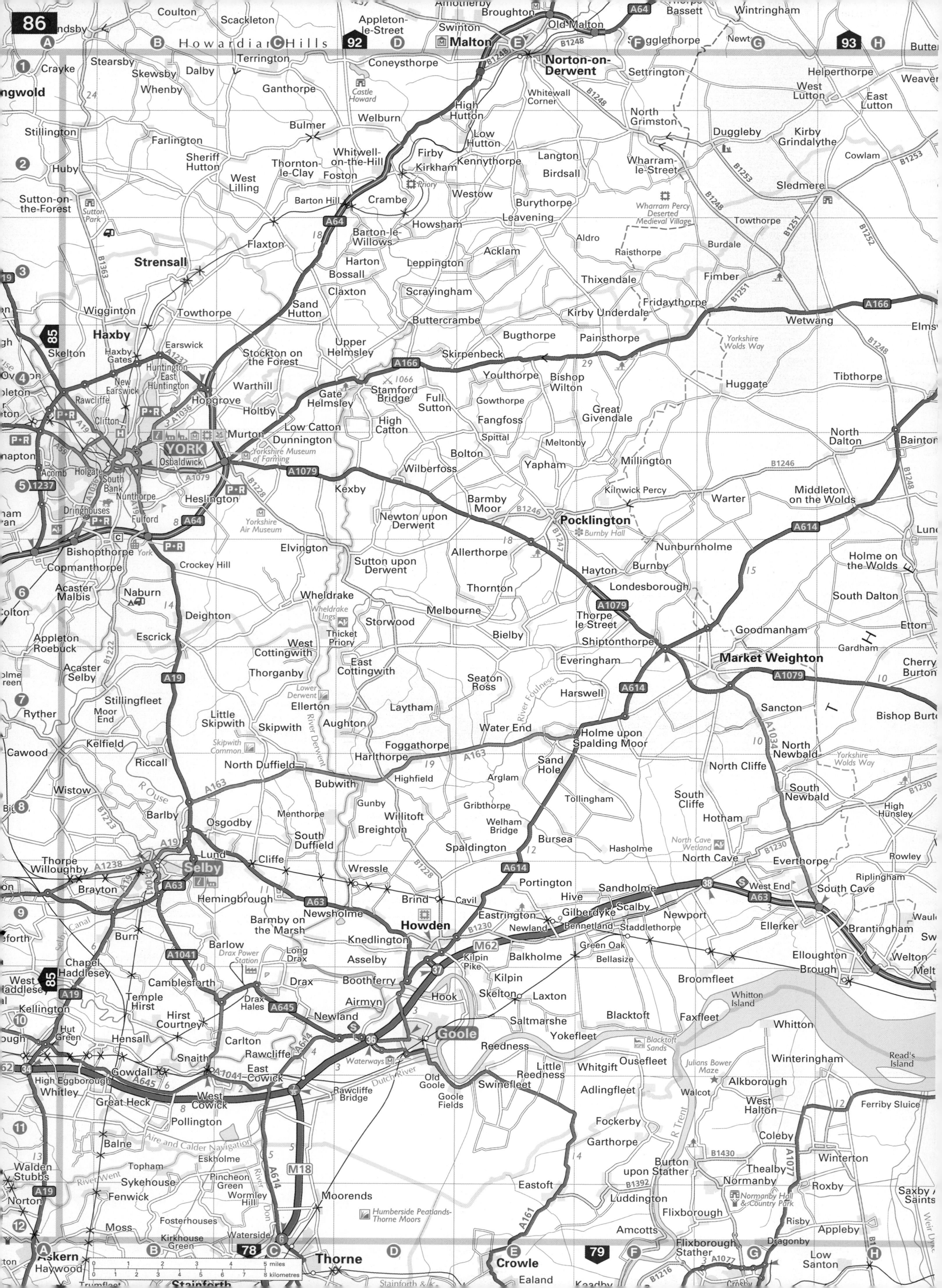

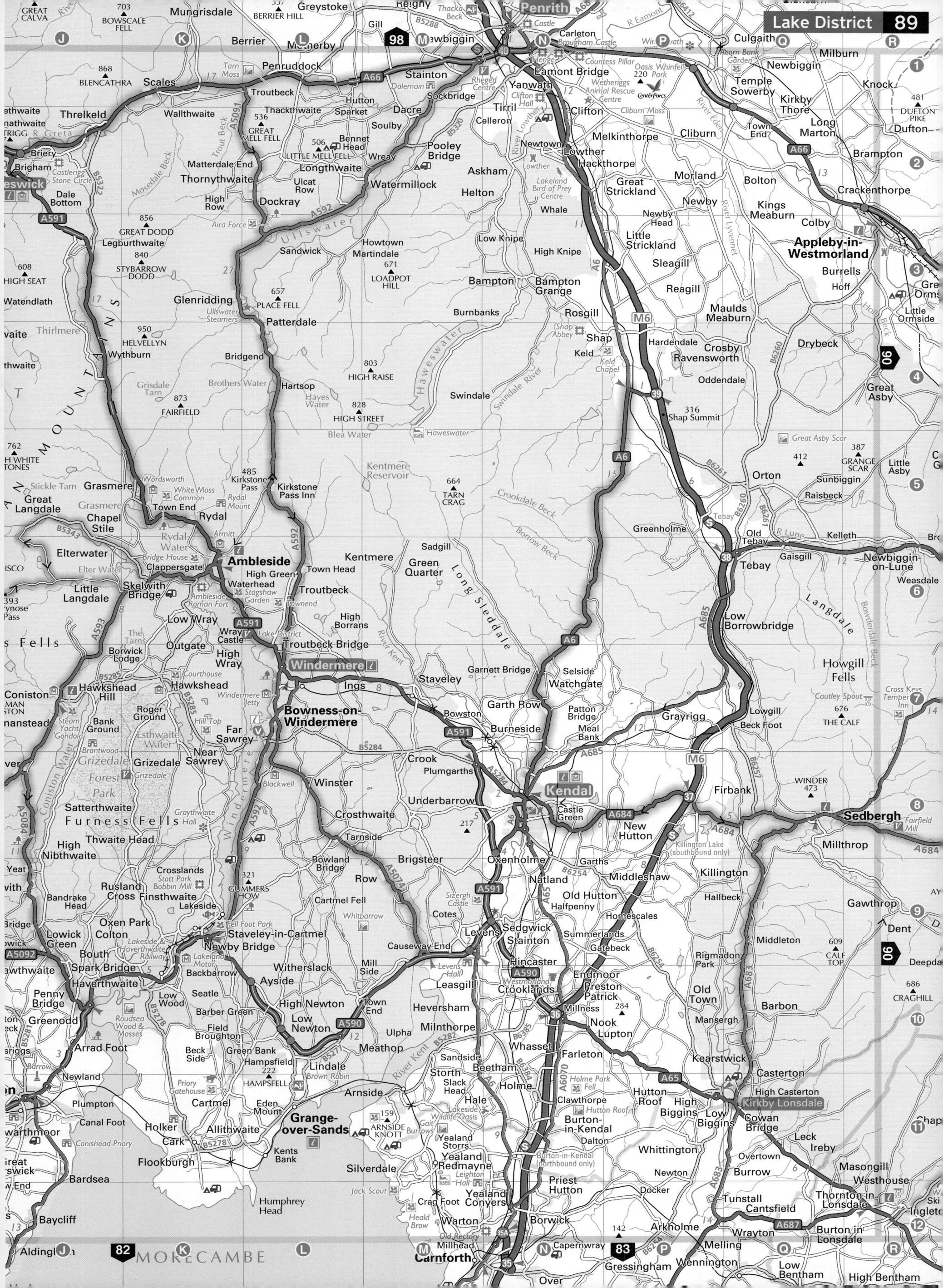

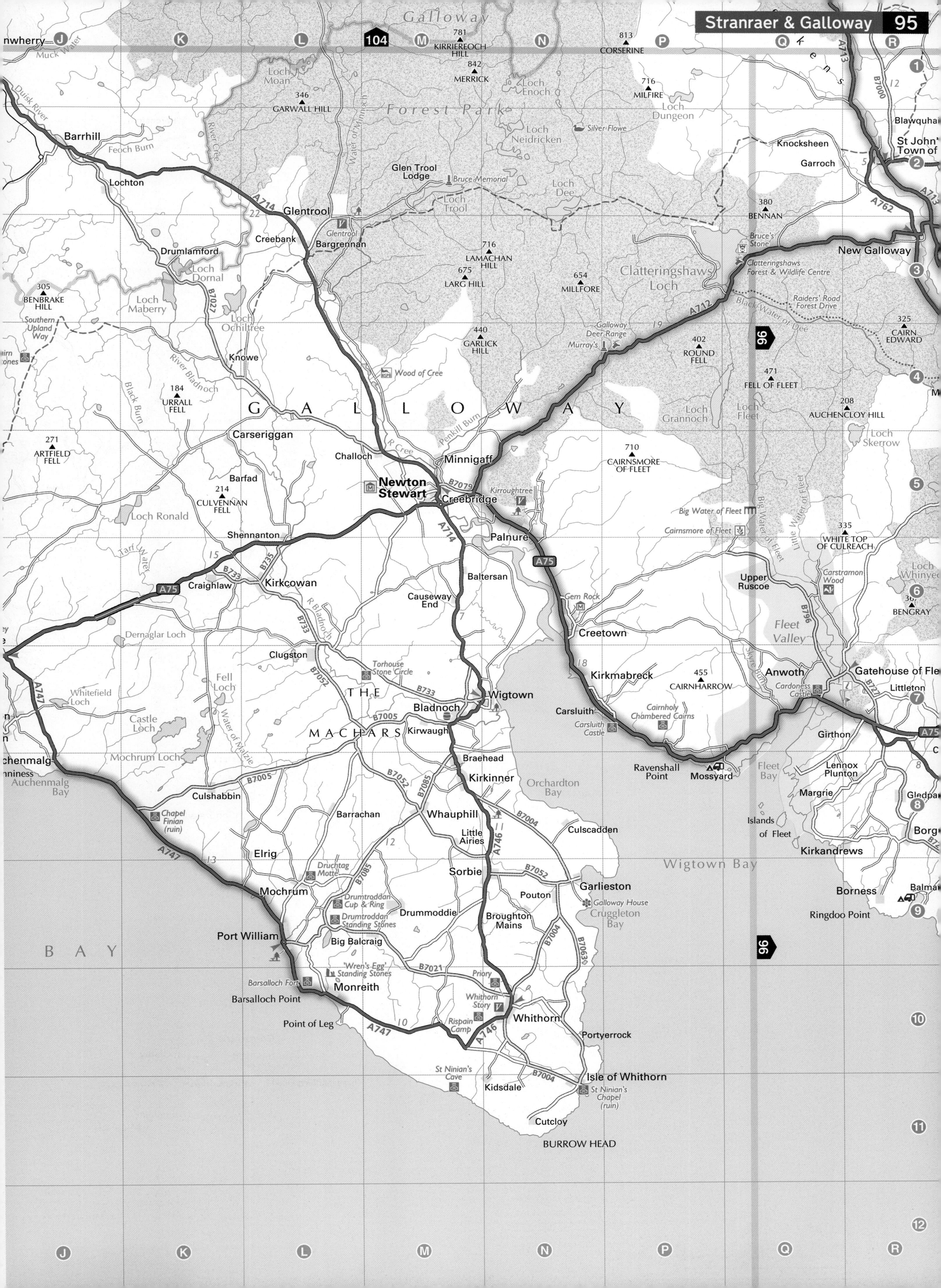

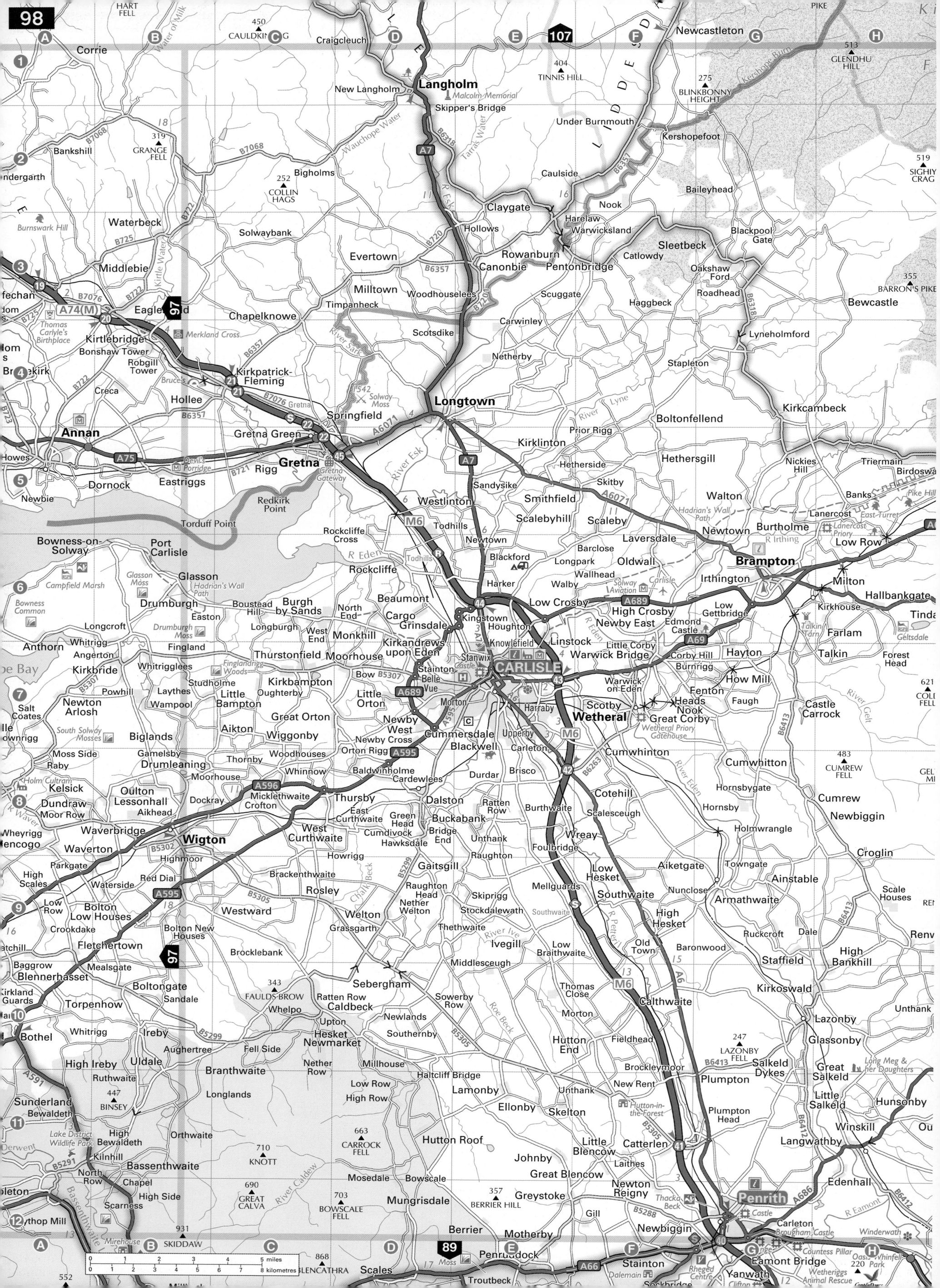

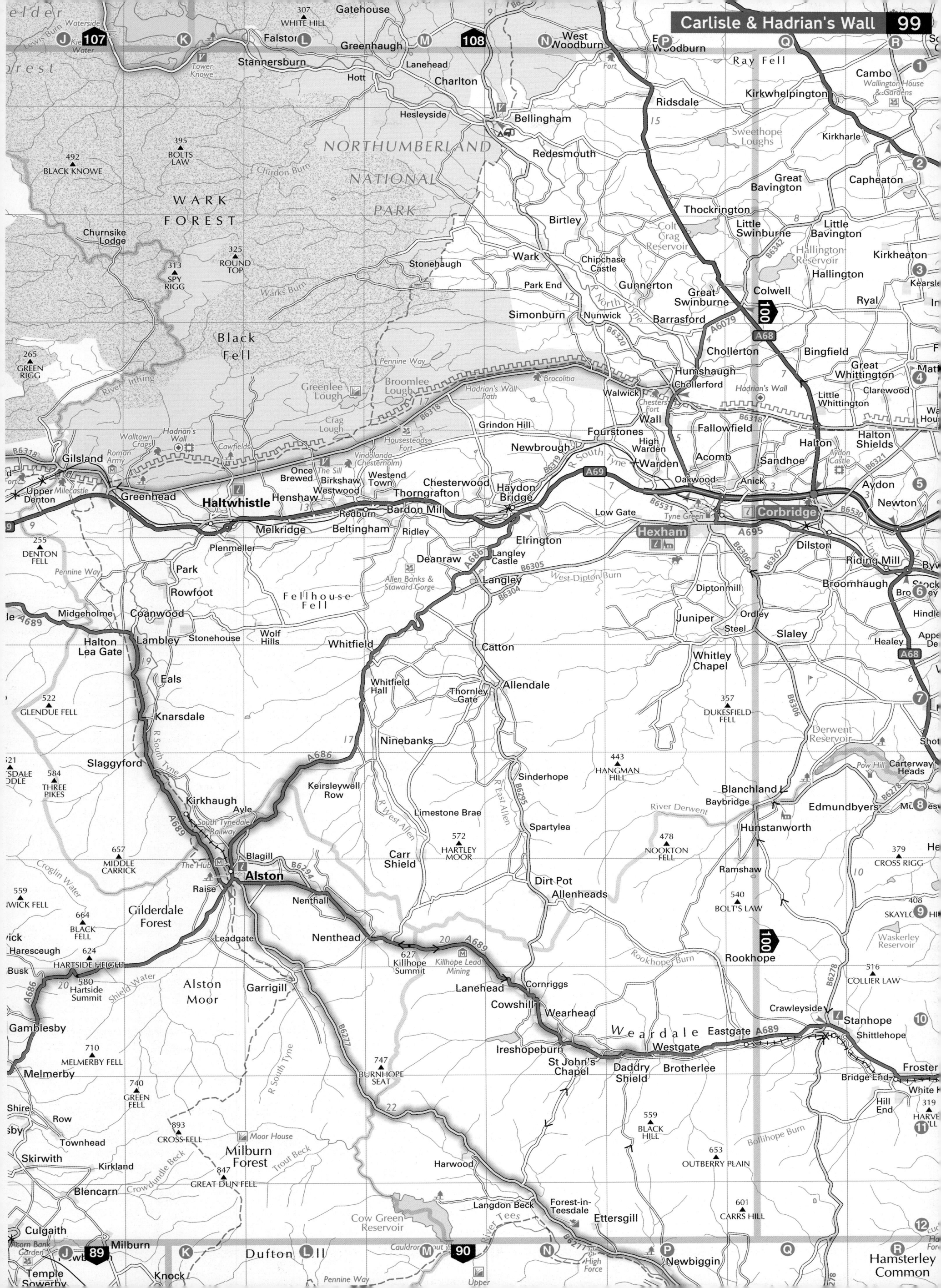

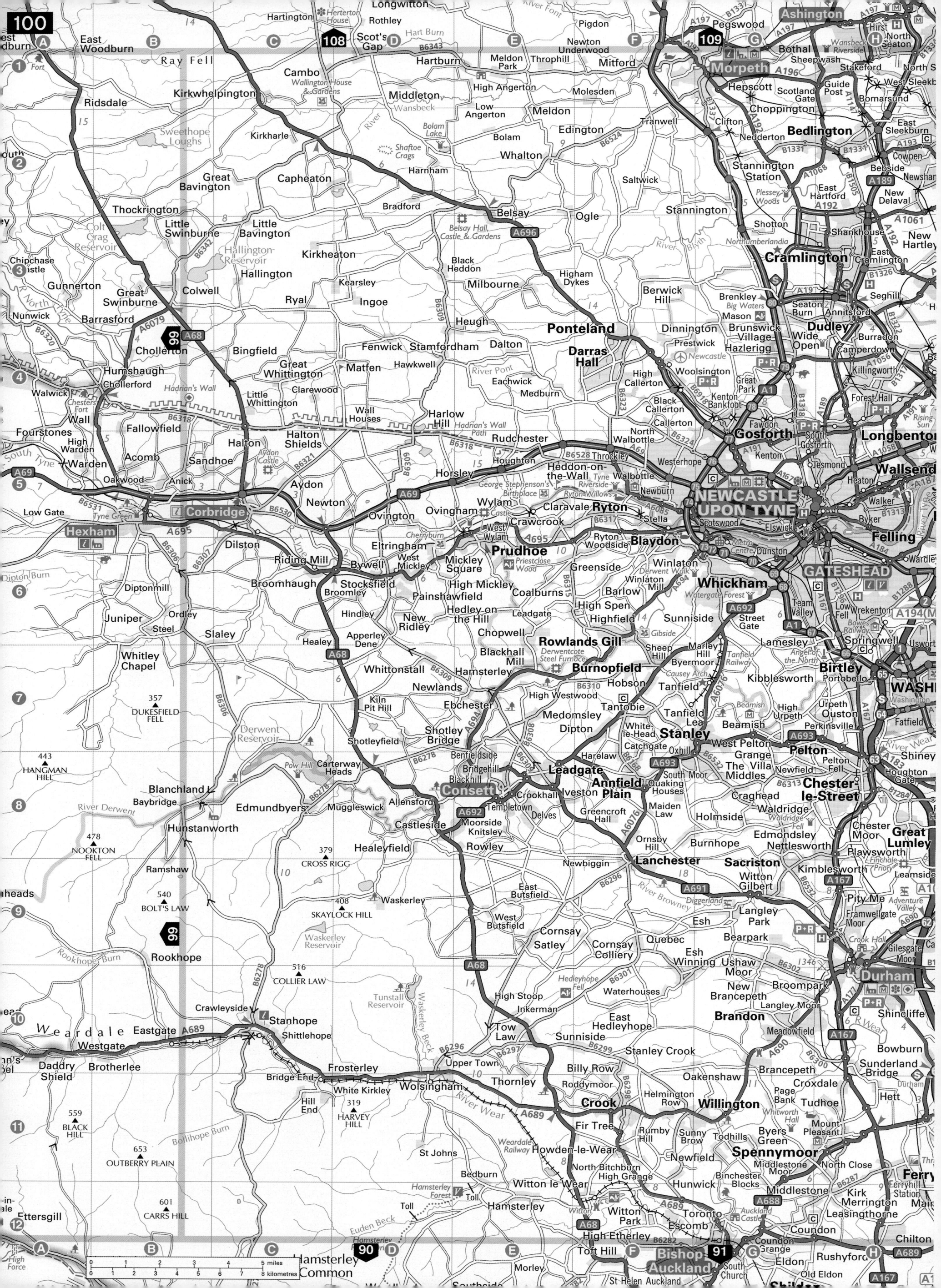

Tayinloan

J 111 K L Grogport M Pirnmill N 112 North Arran P 134 Q R

Penrioch CAISTEAL ABHAIL

1

Barmollack Corrie

Loch Tanna

354 Whitefarland 715 GOATFELL 874

CRUACH BEINN Merkland Point 2

NAN GABHAR BHARRAIN 6

A83 Imachar Brodick Castle, Garden

Muasdale Balliekine 792 & Country Park

Belloch Barr Water BEINN Glen Rosa Brodick

Clan NUIS Bay

MacAlister ARRAN Brodick Strathwhillan

454 Iorsa Water Corriegills 3

Carradale Auchagallon A'CHRUACH

Bridgend B879 Port Right Stone Circle Machrie 512 Clauchlands

Dippen Machrie Point

Waterfoot Bay Tormore 503 Lamlash Margnaheglish

Bellochantuy Torrisdale Carradale Point Machrie Moor BEINN BHREAC Lamlash

Stone Circles Bay Holy Island

408 Moss Farm Road Balmichael Cordon

BORD Saddell Stone Circle Torbeg Shiskine 4

MOR Bay Drumadoon Point Blackwaterfoot Auchencairn Kingscross

Saddell Kilpatrick Knockenkelly

396 Drumadoon Glen Scorrodale Whiting

SGREADAN Bay Kilpatrick Dun Carn Ban Bay

HILL Ugadale Brown Head Whiting Bay

Tangy Loch Glenashdale Largymore 5

Lussa Torr a' Chaisteal Fort Corriecravie Kilmory Water Largybeg

Loch Sliddery Dippin Dippin Head

Glen Lussa Kilmory Bennan

A83 Peninver Lagg Torrylin Kildonan

Ardnacross Cairn

Kilmichael Bay Bennan Head Pladda

Campbeltown

B842 Campbeltown Loch Island Davaar Campbeltown-Ardrossan (May–Sept) 6

B843 B842

Stewarton

Kilkerran

352 Kildalloig 7

BEINN GHUILEAN Achinhoan

Conie Glen Ru Stafnish

Glen Kerran

Cattadale Polliwilline Bay 8

Macharioch

Southend

Dunaverty

Sound of Sanda

Sheep Island

Sanda Island

104 9

Ailsa Craig

340

10

11

12

J K L M N P Q R

0 1 2 3 4 5 miles
0 1 2 3 4 5 6 7 8 kilometres

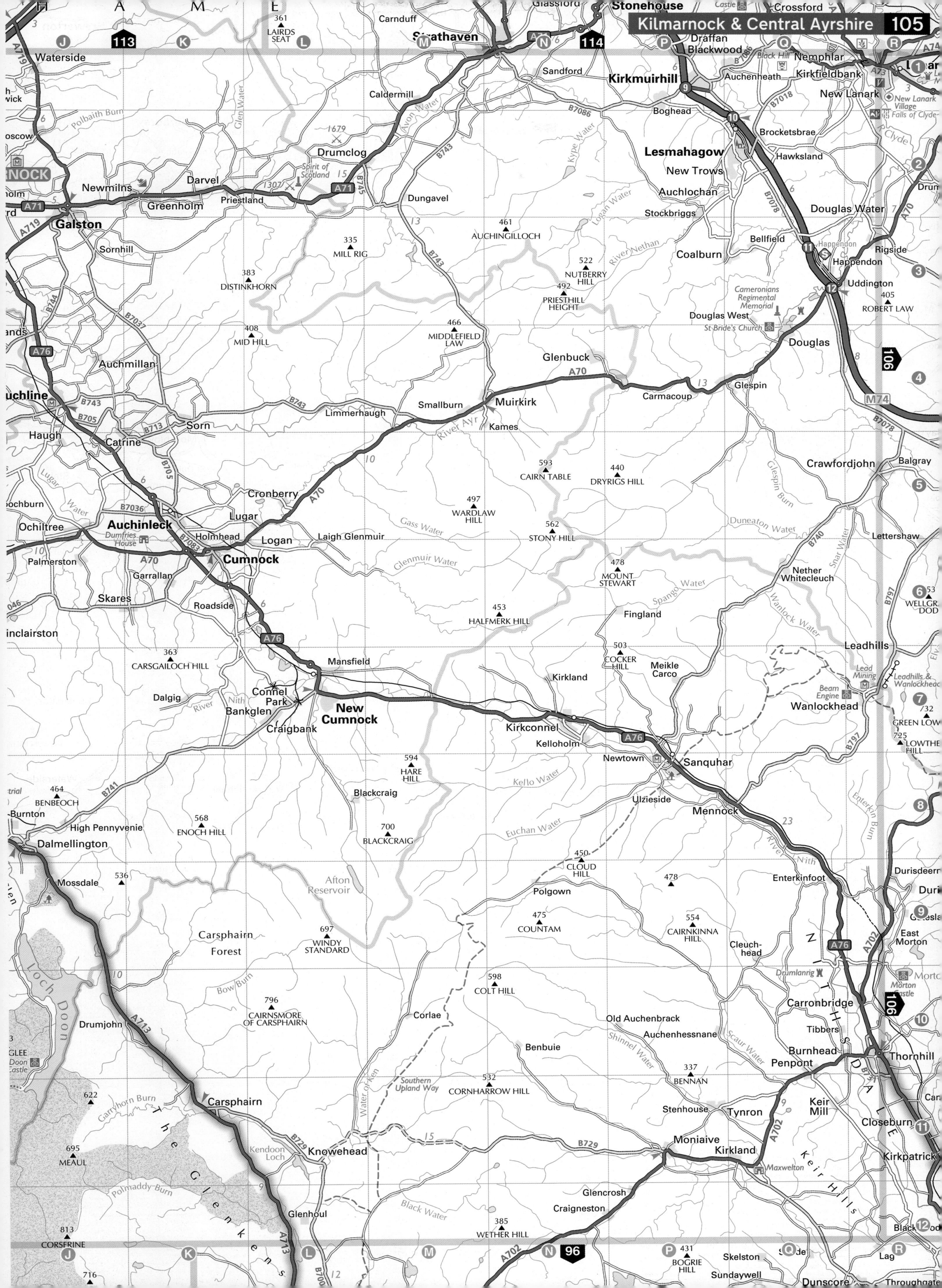

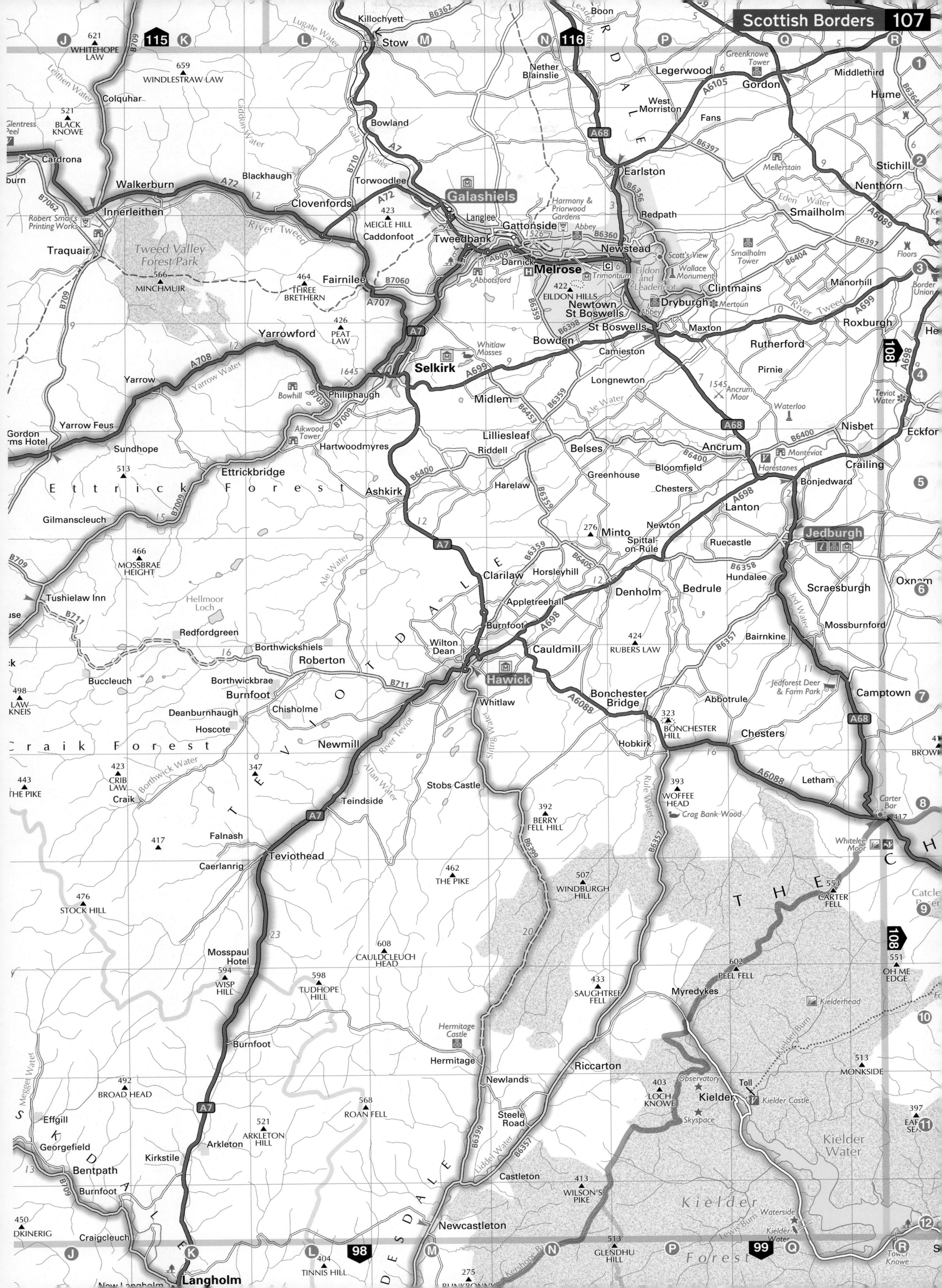

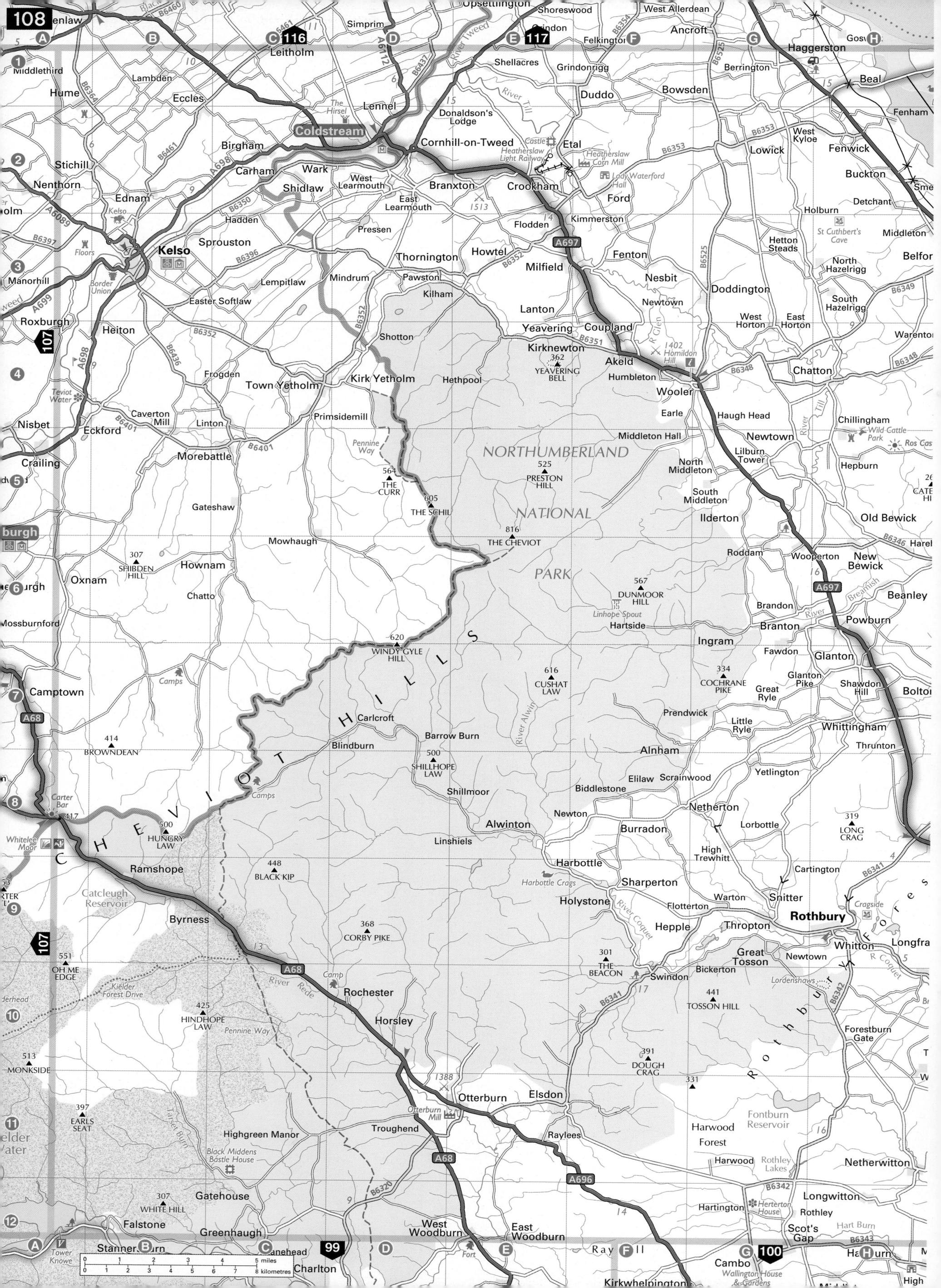

J · K · L · M · N · P · Q · R

117

HOLY ISLAND
Holy Island
Lindisfarne Castle
Lindisfarne Priory
Castle Point
Guile Point

Causeway flooded at high tide

Elwick
Ross
Low Middleton
Easington
Waren Mill
Budle
Bamburgh
Outchester
Spindlestone
Burton
New Shoreston
Bradford
Elford
Seahouses
Bellhill
Lucker
North Sunderland
Adderstone
Newham
Beadnell
Warenford
Swinhoe
Chathill
Tughall
Beadnell Bay
Newstead
Ellingham
Preston
Brunton
Newton-by-the-Sea
Brownieside
Christon Bank
Embleton & Newton Links
North Charlton
Doxford
Embleton
Fallodon
Embleton Bay
West Ditchburn
South Charlton
Dunstan Steads
Dunstanburgh Castle
Eglingham
Rock
Dunstan
East Bolton
Rennington
Stamford
Craster
River Aln
Broxfield
Howick Hall
Howick
Abberwick
Denwick
Littlehoughton
Cullernose Point
Broome Park
Alnwick
Longhoughton
Hawkhill
Boulmer
Castle
Aln Valley Railway
Lesbury
Seaton Point
Edlingham
Bilton
Hipsburn
Alnmouth
Bilton Banks
High Buston
Alnmouth Bay
GLANTLEES HILL
Shilbottle
Low Buston
260
Newton-on-the-Moor
Warkworth Castle & Hermitage
Birling
Swarland
Guyzance
Warkworth
Old Swarland North End
Acklington
Gloster Hill
North Togston
Amble
Felton
Togston
Coquet Island
East Thirston
Radcliffe
High Hauxley
Pauperhaugh
West Thirston
Broomhill
Weldon Bridge
Eshott
South Broomhill
Hadston
Red Row
Druridge Bay
Helm
Druridge Bay
West Chevington
Druridge
Longhorsley
Causey Park
Stobswood
Widdrington
Causey Park Bridge
Earsdon
Widdrington Station
North Northumberland Heritage Coast
Cresswell
Tritlington
Ulgham
Linton
Ellington
Stanton
Fenrother
Lynemouth
Hebron
Longhirst
Woodhorn
Beacon Point
River Font
Pigdon
QE2
Woodhorn Demesne
Newton Underwood
Pegswood
Ashington
Newbiggin-by-the-Sea
Mitford
Bothal
Hirst
North Seaton
Weldon Park
Throphill
Morpeth
Leepwash
Stakeford
North Seaton Colliery
Angerton
Hepscott
Guide Post
West Sleekburn
Molesden
Scotland

A1 · A697 · A1068 · A189 · A197 · A196 · A192 · B1342 · B1340 · B1341 · B6347 · B1339 · B6346 · B6341 · B6345 · B1337 · B1334

FARNE ISLANDS
Longstone
Staple Sound
Inner Sound
North Northumberland Heritage Coast

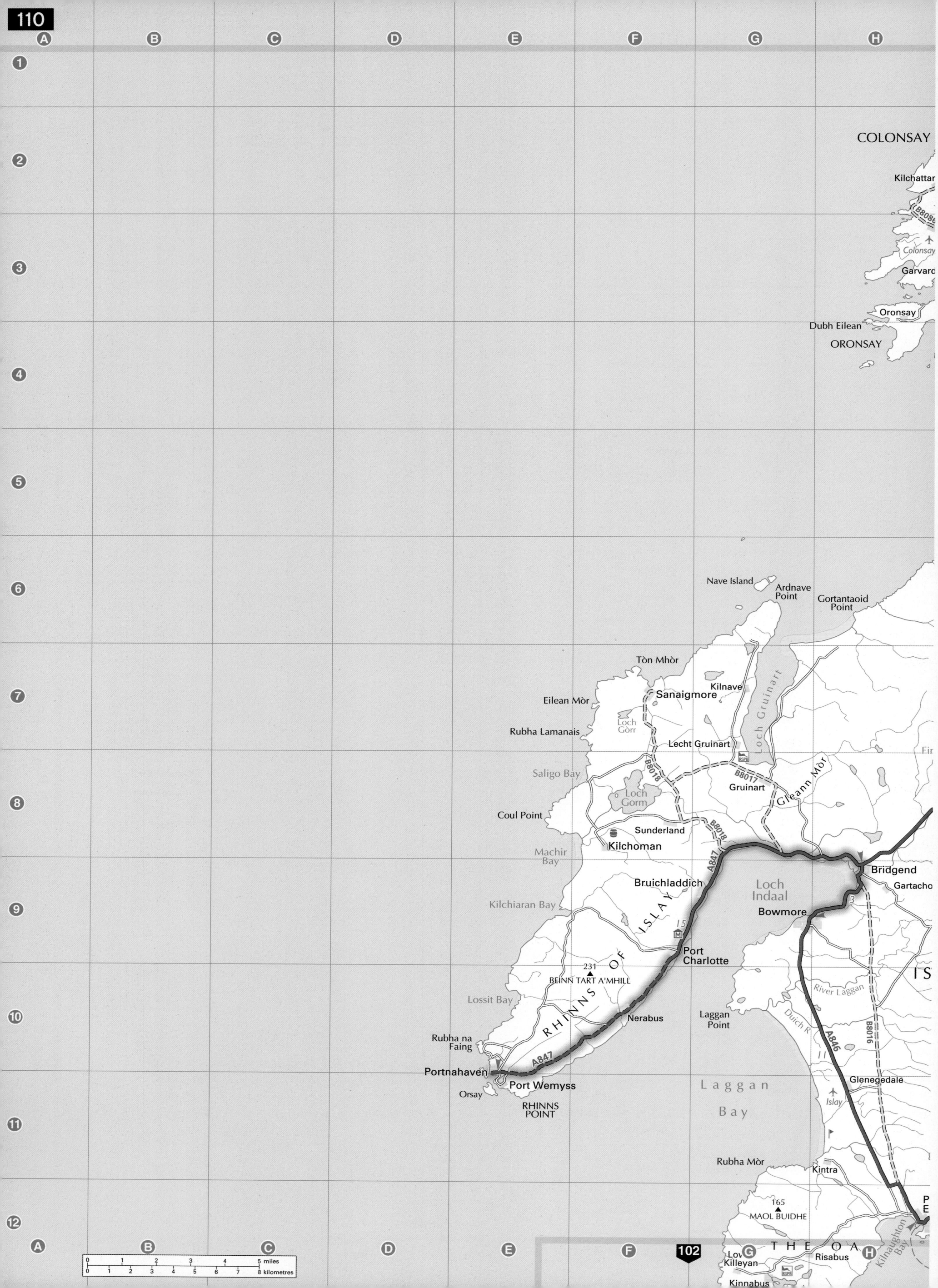

COLONSAY

Kilchattan

Colonsay

Garvard

Oronsay

Dubh Eilean

ORONSAY

Nave Island
Ardnave Point
Gortantaoid Point

Tòn Mhòr

Kilnave

Eilean Mòr
Sanaigmore

Loch Gruinart

Rubha Lamanais
Loch Gòrr
Lecht Gruinart

Saligo Bay
B8018
B8017
Gruinart
Gleann Mòr

Loch Gorm
B8018

Coul Point
Sunderland

Kilchoman
A847

Machir Bay
Bridgend
Gartacho

Bruichladdich
Loch Indaal

Kilchiaran Bay
RHINNS OF ISLAY
Bowmore

Port Charlotte
IS

231
BEINN TART A'MHILL
River Laggan

Lossit Bay
RHINNS OF ISLAY
Nerabus
Laggan Point
Duich R.
A846
B8016

Rubha na Faing
A847
Glenegedale

Portnahaven
Port Wemyss
Laggan
Islay

Orsay
RHINNS POINT
Bay

Rubha Mòr
Kintra
PE

165
MAOL BUIDHE
Kilnaughton Bay

THE OA
Lov Killeyan
Risabus

Kinnabus

0 1 2 3 4 5 miles
0 1 2 3 4 5 6 7 8 kilometres

Eilean
Dubh

CRUACH SCARBA
Ardfern

J

K

119

L

M

N

120

P

Q

R

Gulf of Corryvreckan

Aird

1

Kiloran Bay

Rubh' a' Geodha

Oban

Loch Craignish

▲143
CARNAN
EOIN

Craignish Point

Island
Macaskin
Sle
Temple
Stone C

Kiloran

295
CRUACH NA
SEILCHEIG

2

Scalasaig

Glengarrisdale
Bay

Loch Crinan

Crinan

Machrins

Glendebadel Bay

364
BEN
GARRISDALE

Kilmahumaig

Bellanoch

3

Rubha
Bàn

Corpach Bay

Lussa River

Bárnluas

112

Knapdale

Rubha
Ban

J U R A

466
BEINN
BHREAC

Glen Grundale

Lealt Burn

Eilean
Ghaoideamal

Carsaig Bay

Tayvallich

Achnama

Kilmich
of

4

Shian
Bay

453
RAINBERG MÒR

Ardlussa

Lussa Point
Lussagiven

Táynish

Loch
Right
Mòr

A846

Rubh' an t-Sàilein

Keills Chapel

5

Kilbride
Castle
Sween

466
CRUACH
LUSACH

Rubha a' Mhàil

Loch Tarbert

Danna
Island

Rubha
Bholsa

363
SGARBH
BREAC

St Cormac's
Chapel

Ellary

Lochead

6

Achah

506
SCRINADLE

398
BEINN
TARSUINN

Kilmory

Kilmory Knap
Chapel

Point of Knap

Jura Forest

Kilmory Bay

Bunnahabhain

316
GUIR-
BHEINN

784
BEINN
AN OIR

734

24

Knockrome

Ardfernal

Ormsary

Druimdrishaig

48
DUBH
CHREAG

7

Paps of Jura

Loch a'
Chnuic Bhric

Loch nan
Torran

Jura

Port
Askaig

560
GLAS BHEINN

Feolin Ferry

Keils

Small
Isles

Cretshengan

Coulaghailtro

Finlaggan

Keills

529
DUBH
BHEINN

Craighouse

Rubha na
Caillich

Kilberry
Sculptured
Stones

Kilberry

Loch
laggan

342
BRAT
BHEINN

Ballygrant

A846

Loch Ballygrant

Loch
Lossit

Cabrach

Kilberry Head

Keppoch Point

213
CRUACH AIRDE

8

266
BEINNE
DUBH

Am Fraoch
Eilean

Brosdale
Island

Rubha na Tràille

Tiretigan

Torint

ssan

429
SGÒRR NAM
FAOILEANN

McArthur's
Head

Loch Stornoway

Ardpatrick

112

Kilc

9

Kilennan Burn

471

Port Askaig · Kennacraig

Portachoillan

Clachan

490
BEINN BHEIGEIR

Ronachan Point

Ronachan

10

LAY

Rubha Liath

Loch
Ciàran

Loch
Garasdale

454
BEINN URARAIDH

Ardtalla

Claggain
Bay

Kinerarach

247
CRUACH MHIC
GOUGAIN

11

Loch Uraraidh

Tarbert

346
BEINN SHOLUM

Kintour

Kildalton
Cross

Ardmore
Point

GIGHA

Rhunahaorine
Point

CNOC A
SAMHLA

rt

A846

Ardbeg

Eilean
a' Chùirn

Ardminish

Rhunahaorine

Port Ellen · Kennacraig

Sound of Gigha

Tayinloan

12

Texa

Lagavulin

Laphroaig

Rubha na
Gainmhich

Achamore

Cara

J

K

102

L

M

N

P

103

Q

R

354

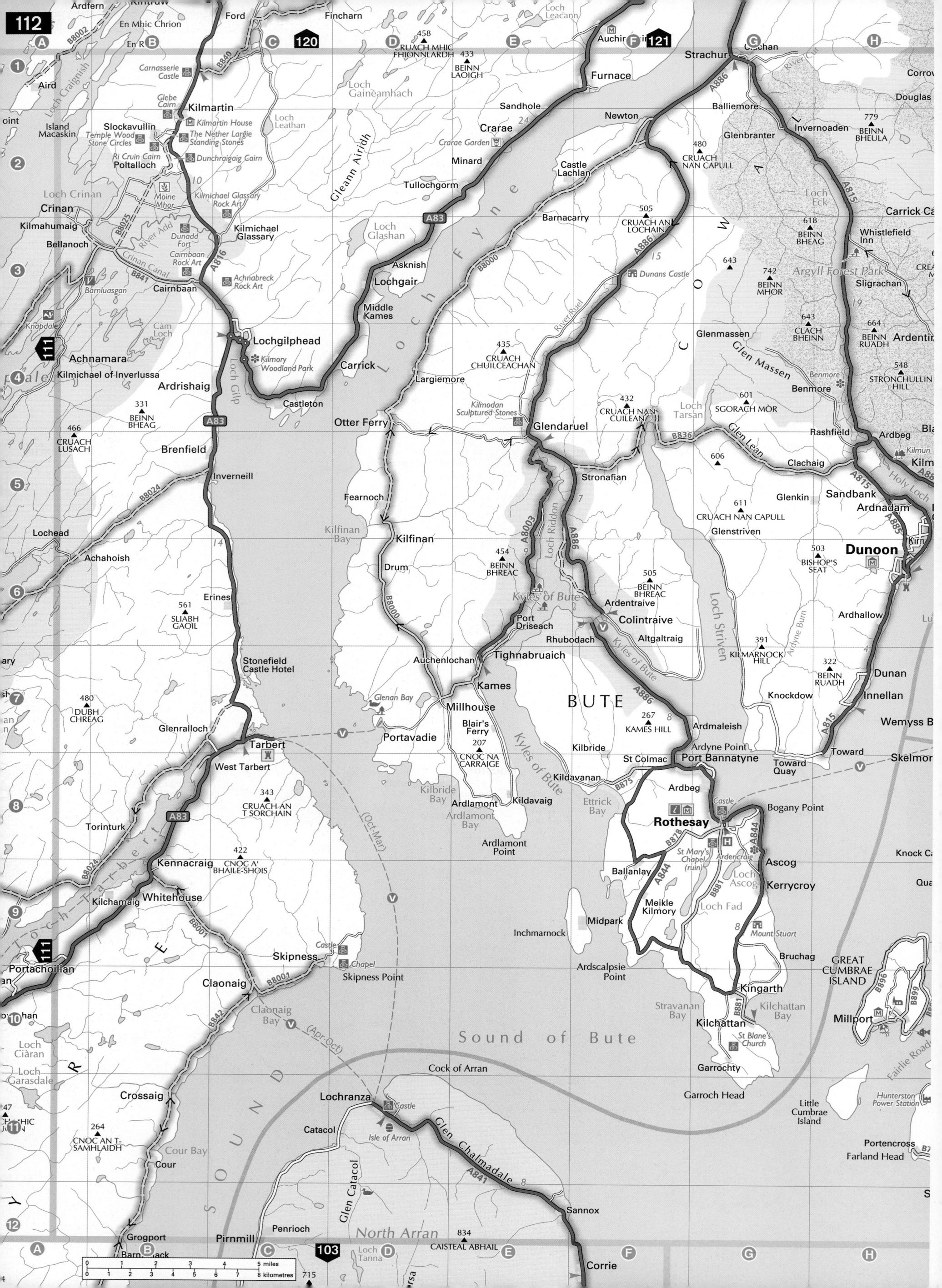

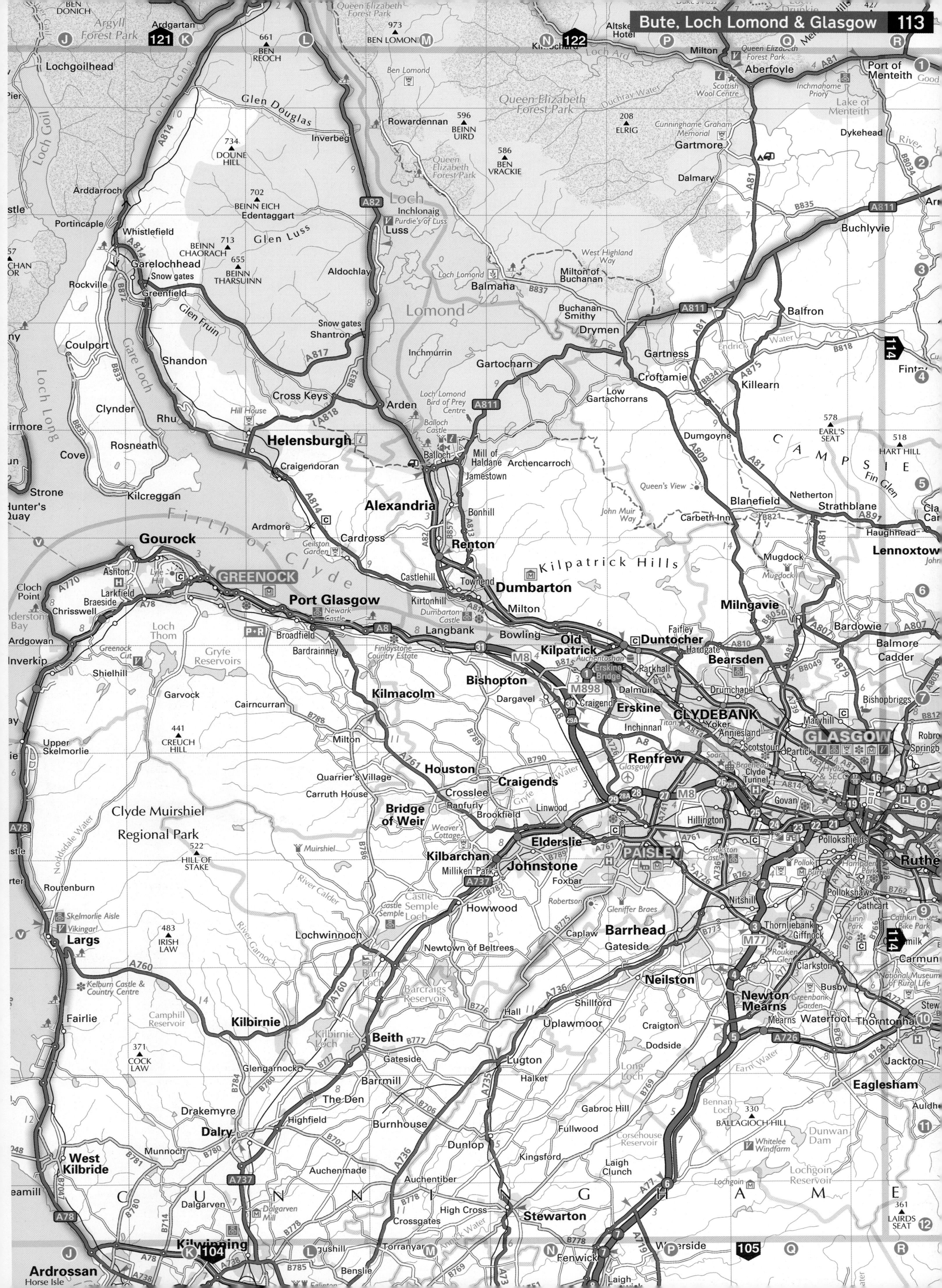

121 K   L   M   N 122   P   Q   R

BEN DONICH

Argyll Forest Park

J

Ardgartan

Lochgoilhead

Loch Goil

Pier

Arddarroch

Portincaple

BEN REOCH 661

973 BEN LOMON

Rowardennan

Ben Lomond

596 BEINN UIRD

Queen Elizabeth Forest Park

Duchray Water

208 ELRIG

Milton

Queen Elizabeth Forest Park

Aberfoyle

Altske Hotel

Scottish Wool Centre

Inchmahome Priory

Cunninghame Graham Memorial

Gartmore

Lake of Menteith

Dykehead

River

Port of Menteith

1

2

3

Castle

Arddarroch

Glen Douglas

734 DOUNE HILL

Inverbeg

Queen Elizabeth Forest Park

586 BEN VRACKIE

Dalmary

A811

B8034

Buchlyvie

Whistlefield

BEINN CHAORACH 713

Edentaggart

702 BEINN EICH

Glen Luss

Loch Lomond

Luss

Purdie's of Luss

Aldochlay

Inchlonaig

Balmaha

West Highland Way

Milton of Buchanan

B837

Buchanan Smithy

Drymen

A811

Gartness

Croftamie

Buchlyvie

Balfron

Killearn

B834

A875

B818

114

4

Garelochhead

Snow gates

Greenfield

BEINN THARSUINN 655

Glen Fruin

Snow gates Shantron

A817

Inchmurrin

Gartocharn

Low Gartachorrans

Dumgoyne

A809

Blanefield

EARL'S SEAT 578

HART HILL

C A M P S I E

HART HILL 518

Fintry

Rockville

Coulport

Shandon

Clynder

Rhu

A818

Cross Keys

B832

Arden

Loch Lomond Bird of Prey Centre

Hill House

Balloch Castle

A811

Netherton

Strathblane

Fin Glen

Cla Car

5

Clyde

Rosneath

Cove

Hunter's Quay

Strone

Kilcreggan

Helensburgh

Craigendoran

Balloch

Mill of Haldane

Archencarroch

Jamestown

Carbeth Inn

John Muir Way

Queen's View

B821

Blanefield

A891

Haughhead

Lennoxtow

John

Firth of Clyde

Ardmore

Cardross

Alexandria

Bonhill

A813

Renton

K i l p a t r i c k   H i l l s

Mugdock

Mugdock

A809

Milngavie

6

Gourock

Ashton

Lyle Hill

C

GREENOCK

Geilston Garden

Castlehill

Townend

Dumbarton

Milton

Kirtonhill

A814

Bardowie

Balmore

Cadder

A807

Cloch Point

A770

Larkfield

Braeside

A78

Chrisswell

Port Glasgow

Newark Castle

Broadfield

A8

Langbank

Bowling

Old Kilpatrick

Dumbarton Castle

Duntocher

Hardgate

Faifley

Parkhall

Bearsden

B8049

B8050

A810

A839

Bishopbriggs

B812

7

Ardgowan

Inverkip

Shielhill

Garvock

Loch Thom

Gryfe Reservoirs

Bardrainney

Finlaystone Country Estate

M8

B815

Erskine Bridge

M898

Auchentoshan

Dalmuir

Drumchapel

Maryhill

C

CLYDEBANK

GLASGOW

Springb

Robro

Bishopton

Dargavel

Erskine

Inchinnan

Yoker

Scotstoun

Partick

A81

A82

Maryhill

16

Braehead

Clyde Tunnel

A814

Hydro & SEC

15

14

8

Upper Skelmorlie

CREUCH HILL 441

Cairncurran

Milton

B788

A761

Houston

B789

Craigends

Crosslee

Gryfe Water

B790

Linwood

Renfrew

Glasgow

26

28A 28

27

M8

25A

Govan

H

25

19

Pollokshields

Pollok

Burrell

Pollokshaws

Ruthe

Clyde

9

Routenburn

Skelmorlie Aisle

Vikingar!

V

Largs

Clyde Muirshiel Regional Park

HILL OF STAKE 522

Muirshiel

B786

Quarrier's Village

Carruth House

Ranfurly

Bridge of Weir

Weaver's Cottage

Brookfield

Elderslie

A761

Hillington

Crookston Castle

24

23

22

21

Crookston

Cardonald

Nitshill

1A

Hampden

Cathcart

B767

Linn Park

B766

Cathkin Bike Park

114

A78

Noddsdale Water

Kelburn Castle & Country Centre

IRISH LAW 483

River Calder

Castle Semple Loch

Kilbarchan

Milliken Park

Johnstone

Foxbar

A737

Howwood

Robertson

Gleniffer Braes

PAISLEY

A726

A736

B762

Thornliebank

Giffnock

M77

Clarkston

National Museum of Rural Life

Carmun

Fairlie

COCK LAW 371

Camphill Reservoir

Kilbirnie

Glengarnock

B780

B784

Lochwinnoch

Newtown of Beltrees

Barr Loch

Barcraigs Reservoir

B776

Caplaw

Barrhead

Gateside

Neilston

Shillford

Craigton

Neilston

4

5

Newton Mearns

Mearns

Waterfoot

Thorntonhal

Busby

Greenbank Garden

A727

Stew

10

West Kilbride

CAMPHILL

River Garnock

Beith

B777

Gateside

B778

B706

Hall

Uplawmoor

B769

Dodside

A726

Bennan Loch

BALLAGIOCH HILL 330

Whitelee Windfarm

Dunwan Dam

Eaglesham

11

Drakemyre

Highfield

Burnhouse

B707

Lugton

Halket

Gabroc Hill

Fullwood

Corsehouse Reservoir

Lochgoin Reservoir

LAIRDS SEAT 361

12

Dalry

Munnoch

Dalgarven

Dalgarven Mill

Glengarnocko

The Den

Barrmill

A736

B778

Dunlop

Kingsford

Laigh Clunch

A77

A719

W rside

West Kilbride

C U N N I N G H A M E

A737

Auchenmede

Auchentiber

High Cross

Crossgates

Stewarton

Fenwick

Laigh

Kilwinning

105 Q R

104 K L M N

Ardrossan

A78

A738

Benslie

B769

B778

A73

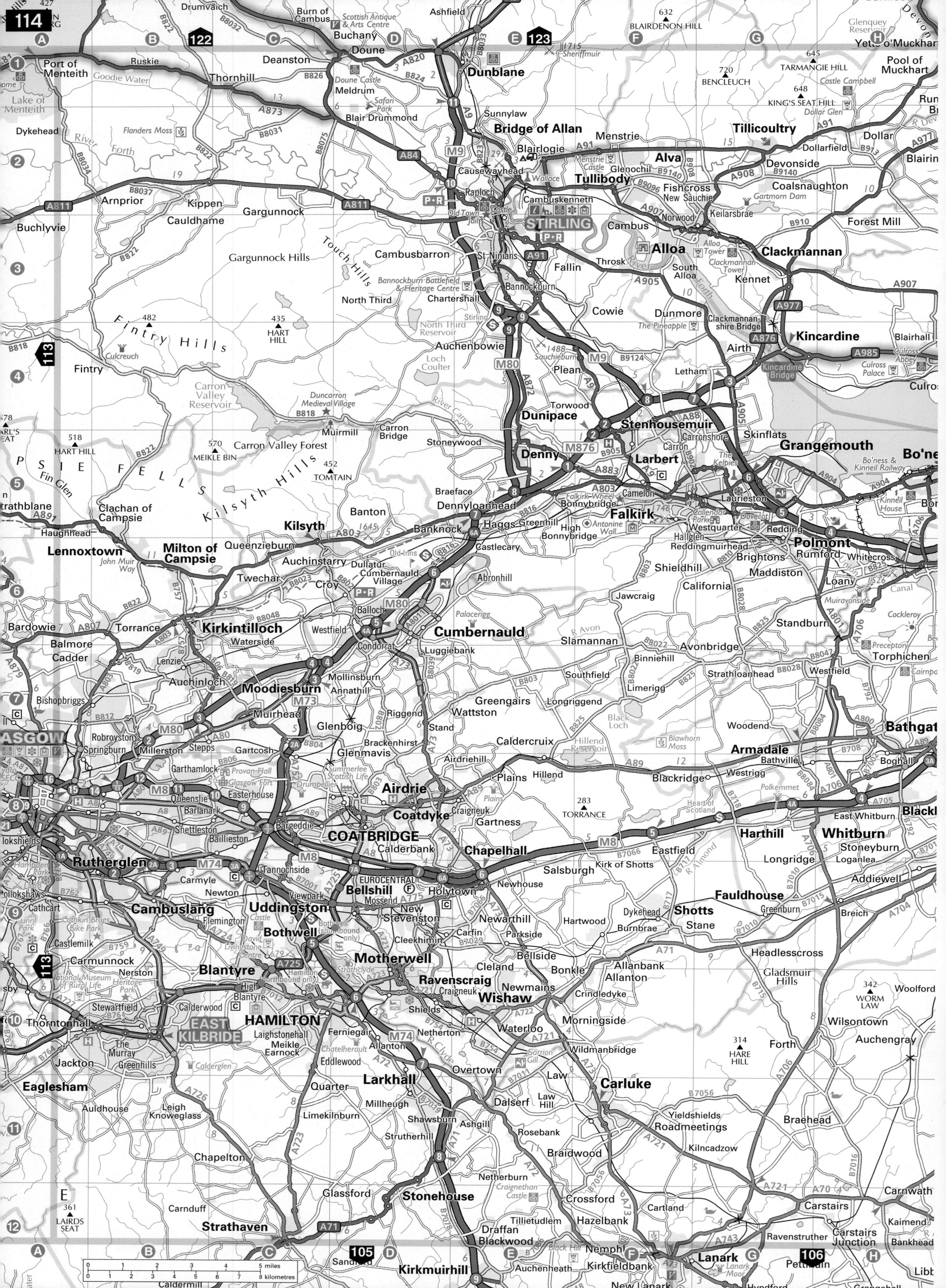

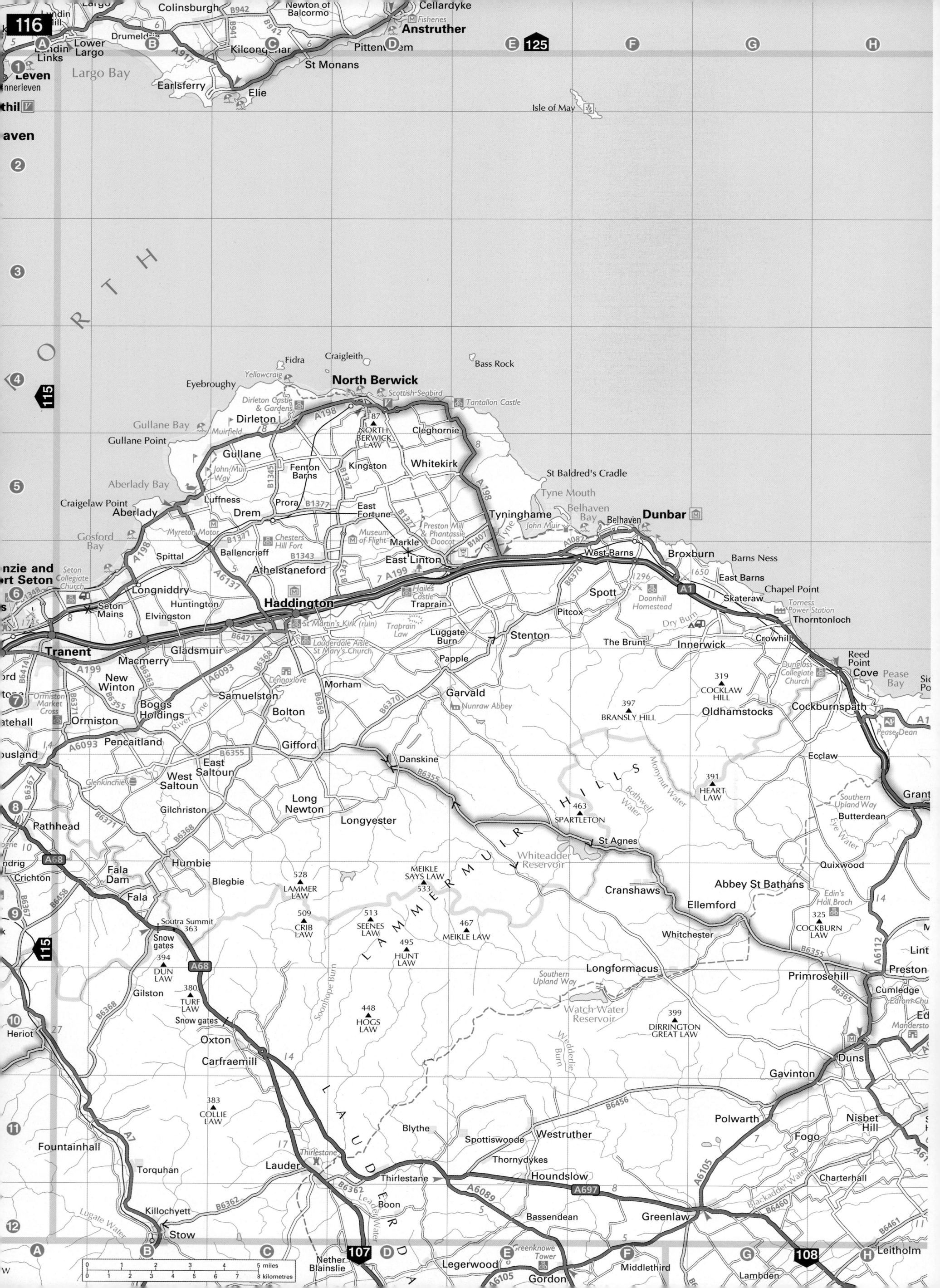

J   K   L   M   N   P   Q   R

1
2
3
4
5
6
7
8
9
10
11
12

car
nt
Fast Castle Head

107

196
BROWN
RIG
Coldingham
Loch

ST ABB'S HEAD

St Abbs

shouse   Coldingham   Coldingham
                                            Bay

Houndwood   B6438   A1107   22
Heugh   Cairncross
Head   Eyemouth

262
HORSELEY HILL   Reston   A1   Ayton   Burnmouth
Auchencrow

arygold
aw   Lamberton

Chirnside   Marshall Meadows Bay
B6355
                   Foulden   North Northumberland
Chirnsidebridge   Heritage Coast
ch   Foulden   1333
rom   Edington   Tithe Barn
Broadhaugh   Whiteadder Water
          Allanton   Hutton   A6105
                                                 Berwick-upon-Tweed
                              Paxton   Castle
Blackadder   B6460   B6461 Town
                                             Ramparts   Barracks &
                                             Tweedmouth Main Guard
Whitsome   Hilton   Loanend
                                        East
inclair's   Ord   Huds
ill   Head
          Horndean   Horncliffe   Spittal
                                             Scremerston
Ladykirk   Castle   Murton   Unthank
Swinton   B6470   Norham A698 Thornton   A1
Upsettlington   Shoreswood   Cheswick
Simprim   Grindon   West Allerdean
                       Felkington   Ancroft   Causeway
                                                     flooded at
                                                     high tide
                                             Goswick
J   K   108   L   M   Berrington N   P   HOLY ISLAND Q   109   R
         Kellacres Grindonrigg   Holy
                                        Beal   Island
                              Bowsden

1

Arnabost

Grishipoll
Clabhach
Loch
Cliad
Hogh Bay   Ballyhaugh   Arinagour

Bàgh a' Chaisteil
(Castlebay)   CO

2   Totronald

(Apr.-Oct. Weds only)   Feall   Arileod   Coll   Acha   B8070
Bay   Uig   Eilean
Ornsay
Calgary Point   Crossapol   Rubha
Bay   Fàsachd
Loch Breachacha
Gunna

3   Rubha Port   Clachan   Caoles   Rubha Dubh
Bhiosd   Mor
Balephetrish   B8069
Loch   Bay   Ruaig   V
Bhasapoll   B8068
Hough   Ballevullin   Cornoigmore   Gott
Bay   Kenovay   Bay
Tiree
Kilkenneth   B8068   Scarinish
Moss   Heylipoll   B8065
4   Middleton   Crossapol   TIREE   TRESHNISH
Barrapoll   B8065   Hynish Bay   ISLES
Loch a'
Phuill   B8067   Balemartine
Rinn   Mannal
Thorbhais   Balephuil   Hynish   Bac M
5   Bay   Bac Beag

6

7

8

Soa Island
9

10

11

12

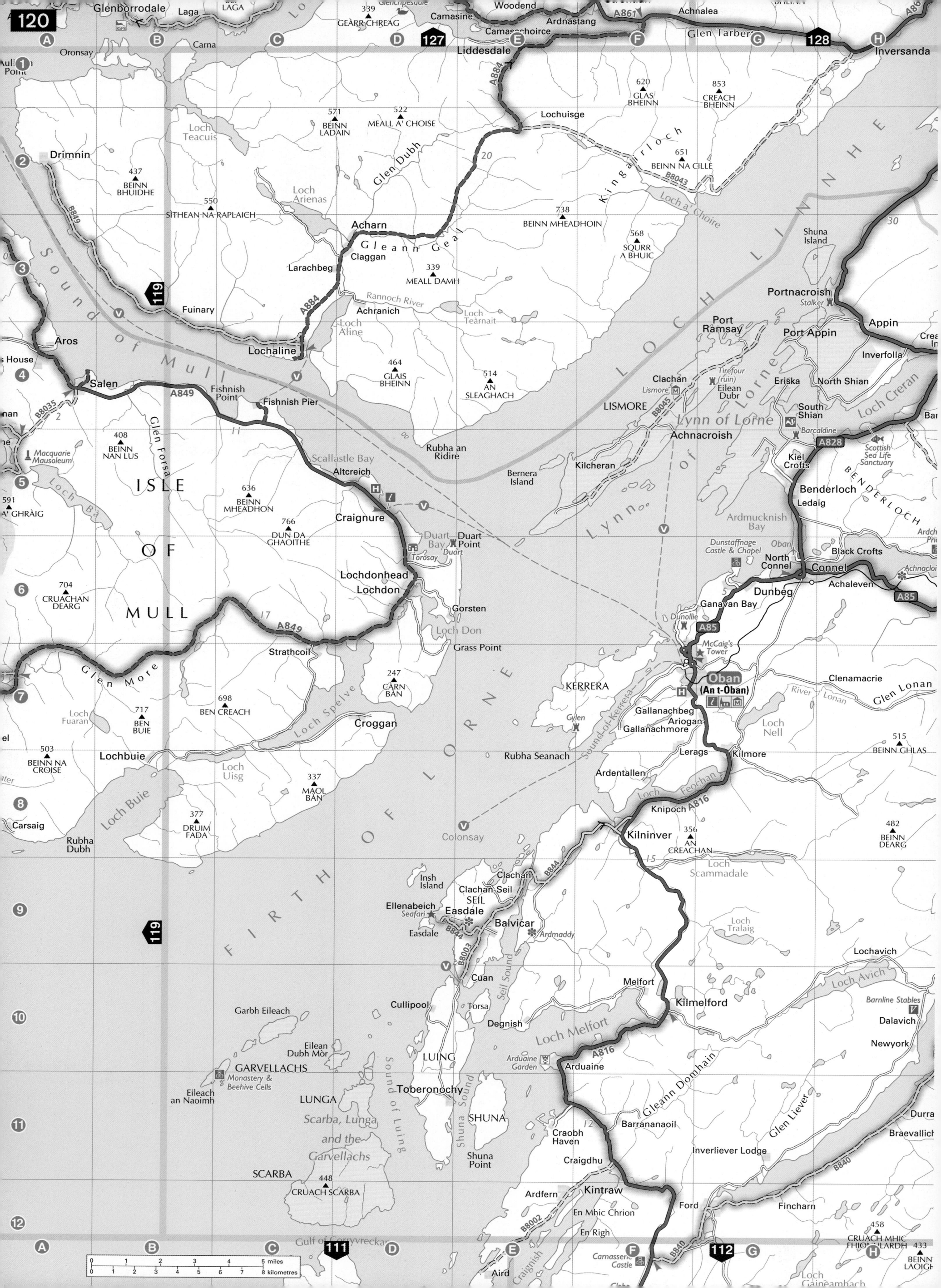

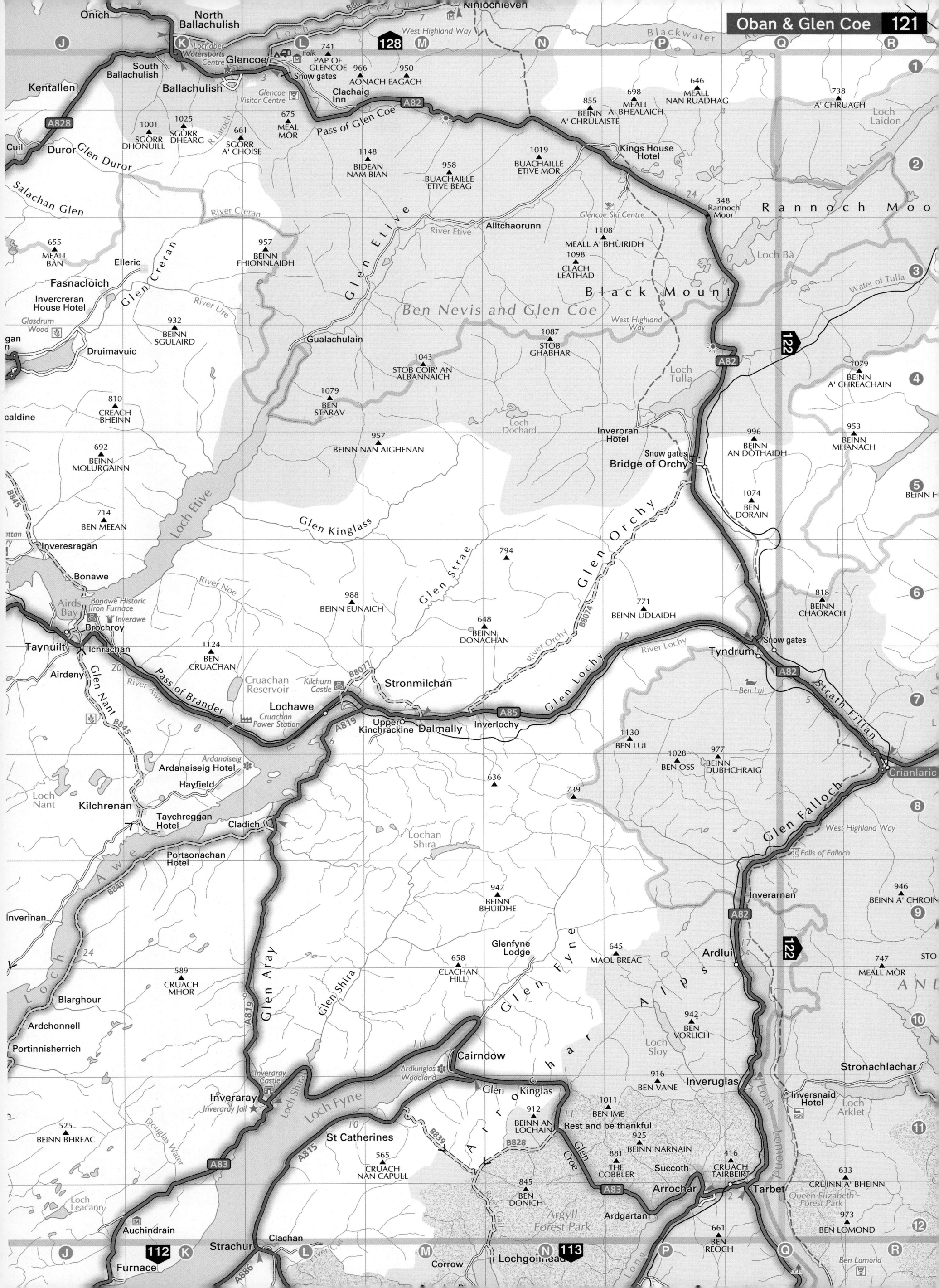

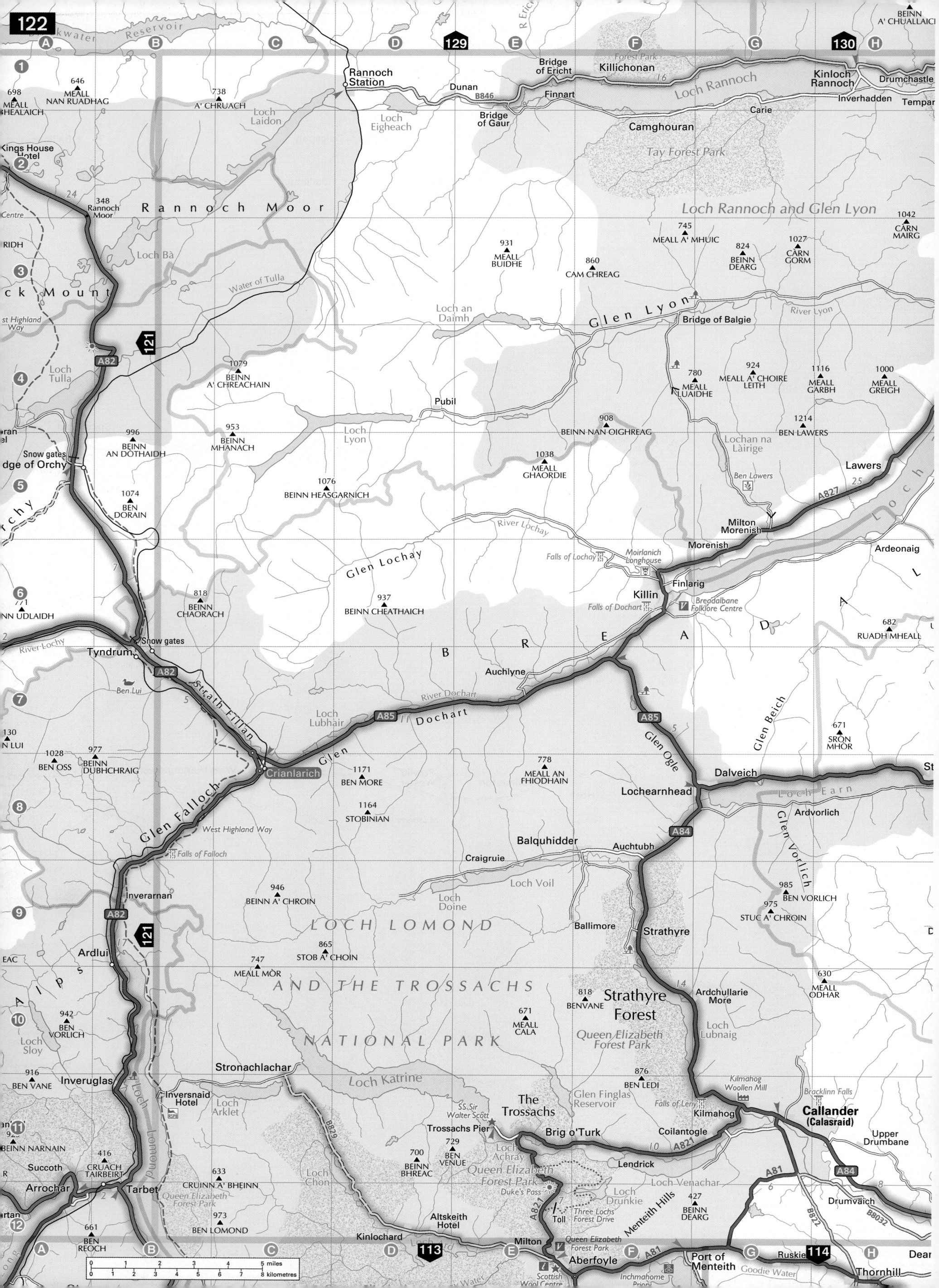

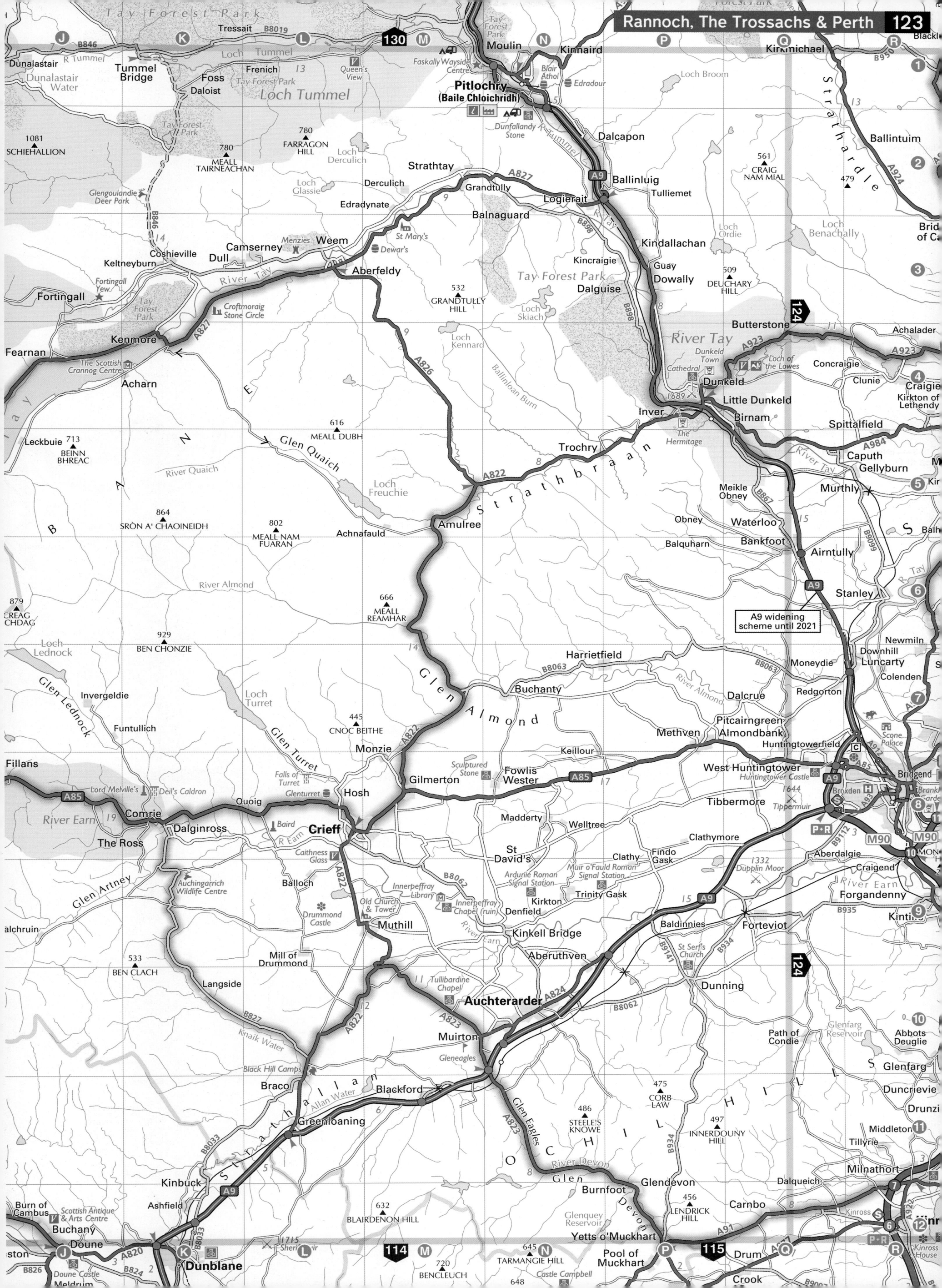

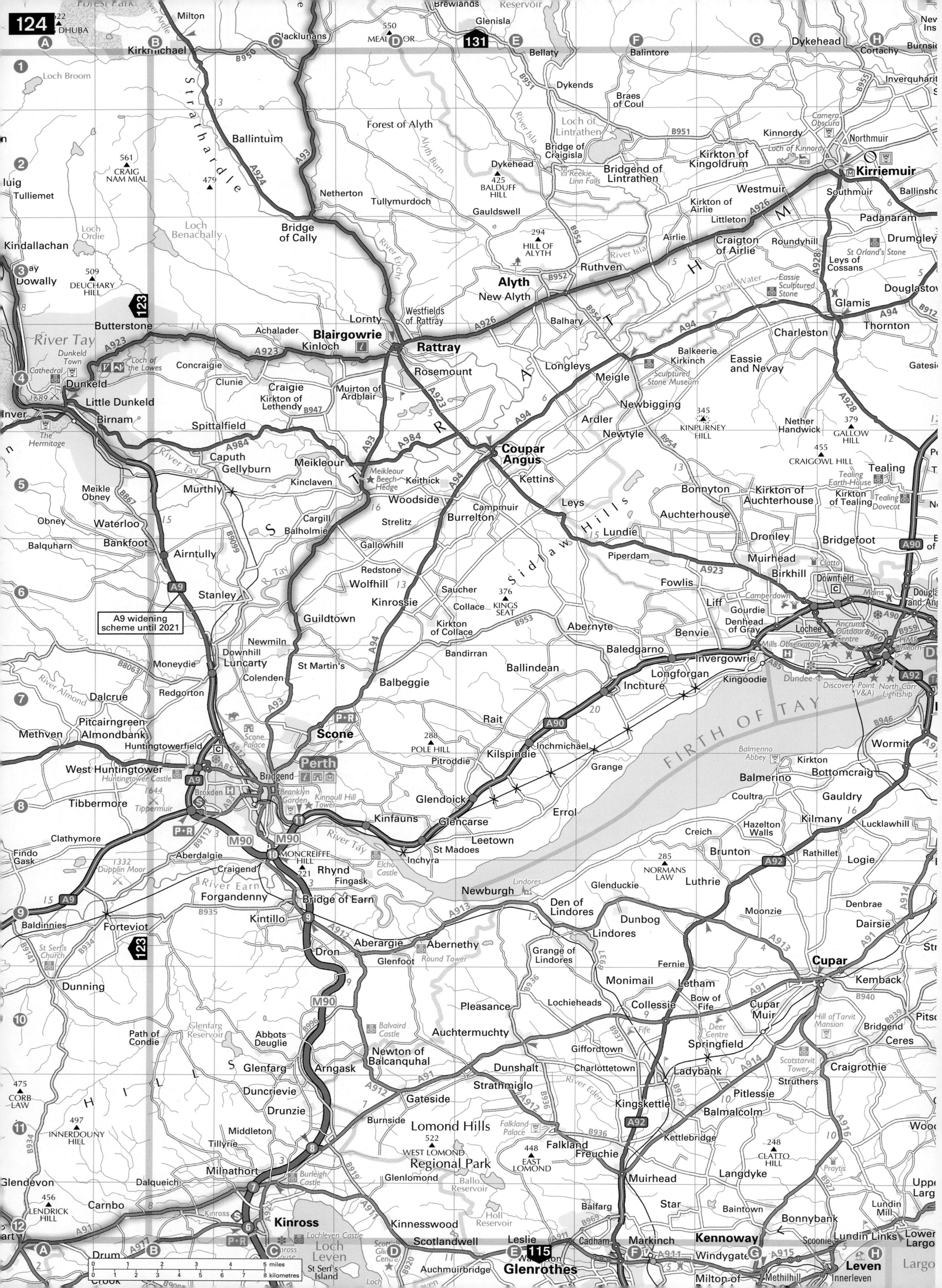

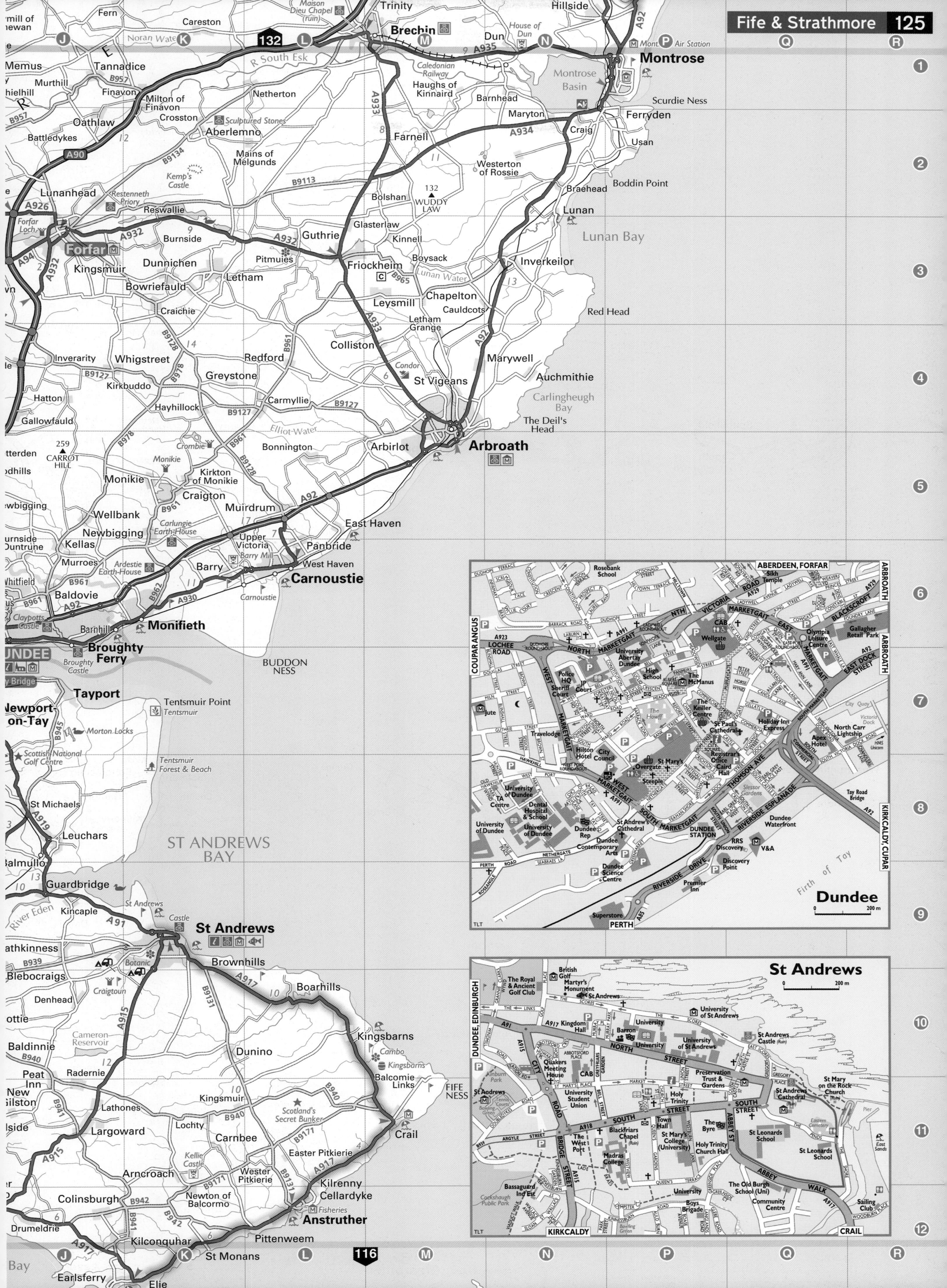

A   B   C   D   E   F 134   G   H

1

Loch Brittr

894
GARS
BHEINN

225
CEANN NA BEINNE

Rubha an Dùnain

Soay Sound

139
BEINN
BHREAC

Mol-chlach

SOAY

2

Loch Baghasdail
(Lochboisdale)

Rubh'
Aonghais

CUILLIN SOUN

3

CANNA

210
CÀRN A' GHAILL

A'Chill

Canna
Harbour

Kilmory
Bay

Rubha
Shamhnan
Insir

Garrisdale Point

Sanday

Canna

Sound of Canna

4

A' Bhrideanach

302
MULLACH
MÒR

Rubha
na Roinne

Loch Scresort

Kinloch

570
ORVAL

5

Oigh-sgeir

Harris
Bay

RÙM

810
ASKIVAL

All vehicles must have
the relevant island
permit prior to travel
to The Small Isles.
Services are seasonal,
day & weather dependent.

6

The Small Isles

763
SGÙRR NAN
GILLEAN

Rubha nam
Meirleach

Sound of Rùm

Bay of
Laig

7

Rubha an
Fhasaidh

Laig

CRU

EIGG

Sound of Eigg

393
AN SGÙRR

8

Eilean
nan Each

MUCK

Port Mòr

9

10

Sanna Point

Sanna
Bay

Sanna

Portuairk

Achnaha

Ardnamurchan
Point

Achosnich

B8007

11

Bàgh a' Chaisteil
(Castlebay)
Loch Baghasdail
(Lochboisdale)
(Oct-Mar)

Eilean Mòr

Rubha
Mòr

Rubha
Sgor-innis

342
BEINN
NA SEILG

Bousd

Sorisdale

Ormsaigmore

Cliad
Bay

B8072

12

Arnabost

Grishipoll

Clab

B8071

A   B   C 118   D   E   F 119   G   H

Ardmore
Point

Sorne
Point

Coll Oban

Arinagour

0   1   2   3   4   5 miles
0 1 2 3 4 5 6 7 8 kilometres

J   K   L   135   M   N   P   Q   R

1

Kirkibost
B8083
Loch Slapin
BEINN NAN CARN
Heast
300
BEN ASLAK
Glenelg Brochs
Glean Beag
Mam
Balvraid

Loch Scavaig
344
BEN MEABOST
Suisnish
Drumfearn
Duisdalemore
Isleornsay
561
BEINN NA SEAMRAIG
Loch na Dal
Sandaig Islands
974
BEINN SGRITHEAL
773
BEINN NAN CAORACH

2
Elgol
Glasnakille
Rubha Suisnish
298
SGORACH BREAC
Loch Eishort
Ord River
Ornsay
Rubha Buidhe
Arnisdale
Glen Arnisdale
Corran
614
709
DRUM FADA

Strathaird Point
Tarskavaig
Tokavaig
Teangue
Knock
Rubha Àrd Slisneach
Invarguseran
784
BEINN NA CAILLICH
Loch Hourn
Barrisdale Bay

3
Tarskavaig
Tarskavaig Bay
Achnacloich
Loch nam Uamph
Ferrindonald
Knock Bay
Airor
518
DRUIM NA CLUAIN-AIRIDHE
Glen Guseran
1019
LADHAR BHEINN

SOUND OF SLEAT
Kilmore
Kilbeg
Sandaig
128

4
Armadale Castle
Ardvasar
Calligarry
Armadale
Sandaig Bay
Inverie
Inverie Bay
KNOYDART
Loch an Dubh-Lochain
940
946
MEALL BUIDHE

Aird of Sleat
Ard Thurinish
Rubha Raonuill
854
BEINN BHUIDHE
1039
SGURR NA CICHE

5
Point of Sleat
Courteachan
Mallaigvaig
547
CÀRN A'GHOBHAIR
Loch an Nostaire
437
SGURR BHUIDHE
723
SGURR BREAC
859
SGURR NAH-AIDE

Mallaig (Malaig)
Glasnacardoch Bay
Beoraidbeg
Morar
Bracora
Bracorina
Tarbet
Swordland
Kylesmorar

6
AN ACHAN
299
B8008
Glenancross
A830
Loch Morar
Lettermorar
Meoble
716
AN STAC
949
SGURR NAN COIREACHAN

Kildonnan
Eilean Ighe
Bunacaimb
503
CÀRN A' MHÀDAIDH-RUAIDH
710
MEITH BHEINN
River Meoble

7
Galmisdale
Back of Keppoch
Arisaig
Luinga Mhòr
600
SIDHEAN MÒR
Prince Charlie's Cairn
Kinlochnanuagh
Loch Beoriad
633
796
SGURR AN UTHA
Glen Finnan

Eilean Chathastail
Rubh' Arisaig
103
Druimindarroch
Arisaig House
9
A830
14

8
CRUACH DOIRE
Loch nan Uamh
Polnish
Lochailort
Inverailort
Loch Eilt
Glenfinnan
Glenfinnan Monument

Sound of Arisaig
Rubha Choalais
Ardnish
A861
877
ROIS-BHEINN
882
BEINN ODHAR BHEAG

9
Smirisary
Glenuig
21
712
664
BEINN GAIRE
Scamodale
758
MEALL MÒR
128

Eilean Shona
Kinlochmoidart
Glen Forsian
754
SGOR AN TARMACHAIN
Loch Shiel

10
Rubha Àird Druimnich
Loch Moidart
Seven Men of Moidart
Tioram
Brunery
239
Ardmolich
Glen Moidart
MOIDART
888
SGURR DHOMHNUILL

Ockle Point
Morar, Moidart and Ardnamurchan
Ardtoe
Shielfoot
Langal
Dalnabreck
Dalelia
Glen Hurich
Loch Doilet
Polloch

11
Kilmory
Ockle
356
BEINN BHREAC
Kentra
B8044
Blain
Mingarrypark
Arevegaig
Acharacle
Claish Moss
846
BEINN RESIPOL
Ariundle Oakwood

Branault
436
MEALL NAN CON
ARDNAMURCHAN
437
SUNART
Anaheilt
884
GARBH BHEINN

12
Kilchoan
Mingary
527
BEN HIANT
Natural History
Glenbeg
512
BEN LAGA
B8007
Salen
Resipole Burn
A861
Woodend
Strontian
A861
Achnalea
Glen Tarbert

Glenborrodale
Ardslignish
Laga
Carna
339
GEÀRR CHREAG
Glencripesdale
Camasine
Camasachoirce
Ardnastang

Rubha nan Gall
Aulist Point
119
Oronsay
Rubha nan Gall
J   K   L   120   M   N   P   Q   R
A884
620
853
Liddesdale

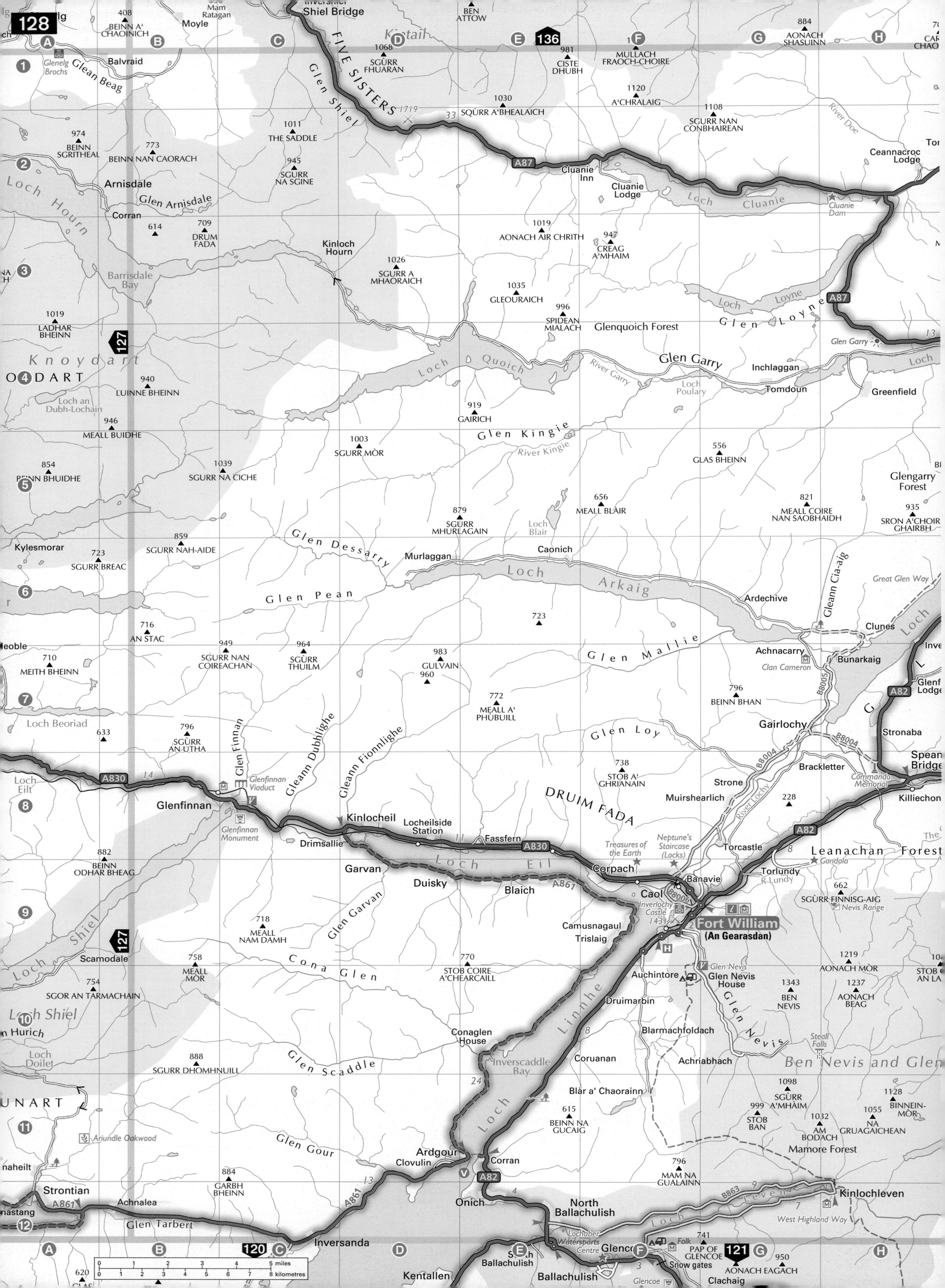

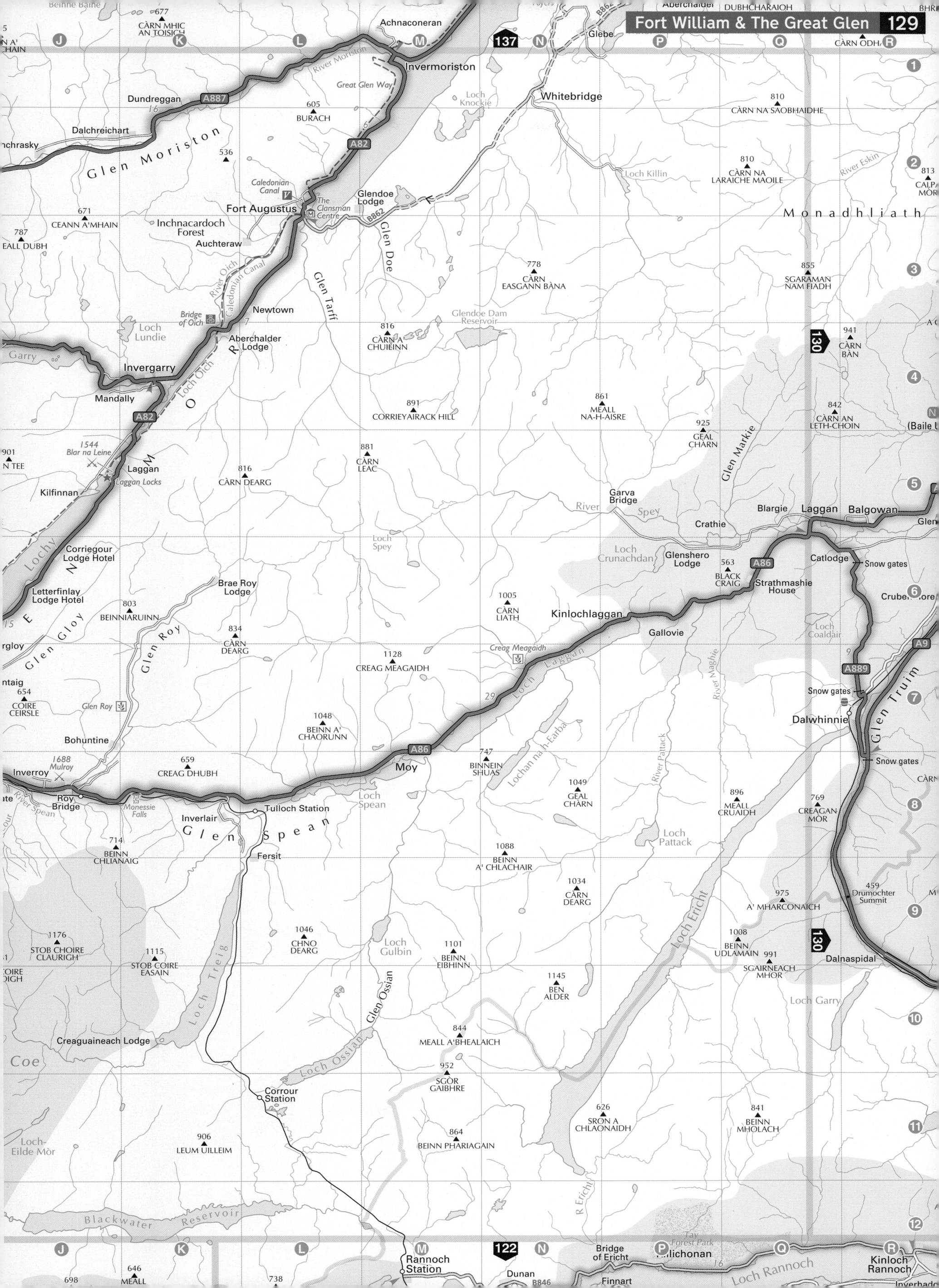

Beinne Baihe
677
CÀRN MHIC
AN TOISICH
J   K   L   M   137   N   P   Q   CÀRN ODH R

Achnaconeran
Aberchalder   DUBHCHARAIOH   BH

Glebe

1

Dundreggan   `A887`   River Moriston   Invermoriston
Great Glen Way

810
CÀRN NA SAOBHAIDHE
Whitebridge

Dalchreichart   605   BURACH
`A82`   Loch Knockie   Glen Moriston

2
813
CALPA
MÒR
nchrasky   Loch Killin   CÀRN NA
LARAICHE MAOILE   River Eskin

536   810

671   CEANN A'MHAIN   Caledonian Canal   Glendoe Lodge   855
SGARAMAN
NAM FIADH   3
787
EALL DUBH   Fort Augustus   The Clansman Centre   B862   Monadhliath
Inchnacardoch Forest   Glen Doe

Auchteraw   River Oich   778   CÀRN
EASGANN BÀNA

Newtown   Glendoe Dam Reservoir   941   CÀRN
BÀN   130

Glen Tarff   816
CÀRN A'
CHUILINN

Bridge of Oich   Loch Lundie   Aberchalder Lodge   4
842
CÀRN AN
LETH-CHOIN
(Baile U

Invergarry   891   CORRIEYAIRACK HILL   861   MEALL
NA-H-AISRE   925
GEAL
CHÀRN

Mandally   `A82`   Glen Markie

1544   Blar na Leine   N   816   CÀRN DEARG   881   CÀRN
LEAC   5
901
N TEE

Laggan   Laggan Locks   River Spey   Garva Bridge   Blargie   Laggan   Balgowan
Gle

Kilfinnan   Crathie   563   BLACK
CRAIG   `A86`   Catlodge   Snow gates
Crubel ore

Corriegour Lodge Hotel   Loch Crunachdan   Glenshero Lodge   Strathmashie House   6

Letterfinlay Lodge Hotel   Glen Gloy   Brae Roy Lodge   1005
CÀRN
LIATH   Kinlochlaggan   Loch Coaldair   `A889`   `A9`

rgloy   803   BEINNIARUINN   Gallovie   7
654   COIRE
CEIRSLE   Glen Roy   834   CÀRN
DEARG   Creag Meagaidh   Snow gates   Glen Truim

ntaig   1128   CREAG MEAGAIDH   Dalwhinnie

Bohuntine   Loch Laggan   8
1048   BEINN A'
CHAORUNN   747   BINNEIN
SHUAS   Lochan na h-Earba   896   769   CREAGAN
MÒR
1688   Mulroy   Inverroy   659   CREAG DHUBH   `A86`   1049   GEAL
CHÀRN   MEALL
CRUAIDH   CÀRN

Roy Bridge   Moy   River Pattack
Monessie Falls   Loch Spean   Loch Pattack   9
714   BEINN
CHLIANAIG   Tulloch Station   1088   BEINN
A' CHLACHAIR   975   Drumochter Summit   459

Inverlair   Glen Spean   1034   CÀRN
DEARG   A' MHARCONAICH   Dalnaspidal
Fersit   1008   BEINN
UDLAMAIN   991

1176   STOB CHOIRE
CLAURIGH   1046   CHNO
DEARG   Loch Gulbin   1101   BEINN
EIBHINN   1145   BEN
ALDER   SGAIRNEACH
MHOR   130   10
1115   STOB COIRE
EASAIN   Loch Treig   Loch Ericht   Loch Garry

COIRE
DIGH   844   MEALL A'BHEALAICH

Coe   Creaguaineach Lodge   Glen Ossian   952   SGÒR
GAIBHRE   11

Loch-Eilde Mòr   906   LEUM UILLEIM   Corrour Station   Loch Ossian   626   SRON A
CHLAONAIDH   841   BEINN
MHOLACH

864   BEINN PHARIAGAIN   Tay
Forest Park   12

Blackwater Reservoir   122
J   K   L   M   N   P   Q   R
646   MEALL   738   Rannoch Station   Dunan   B846   Bridge of Ericht   llichonan   Loch Rannoch   Kinloch
Rannoch
698   Finnart   Inverhadd

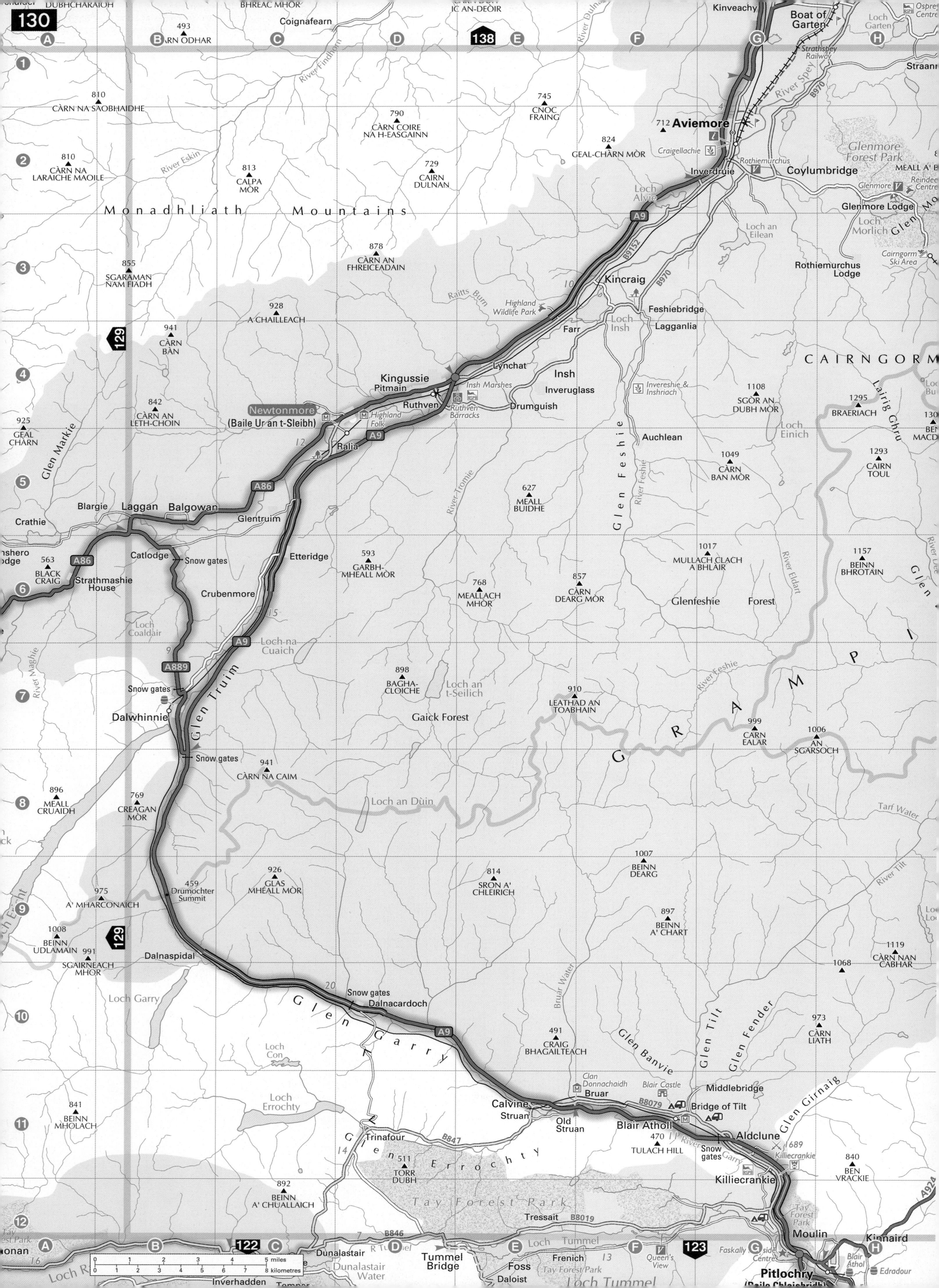

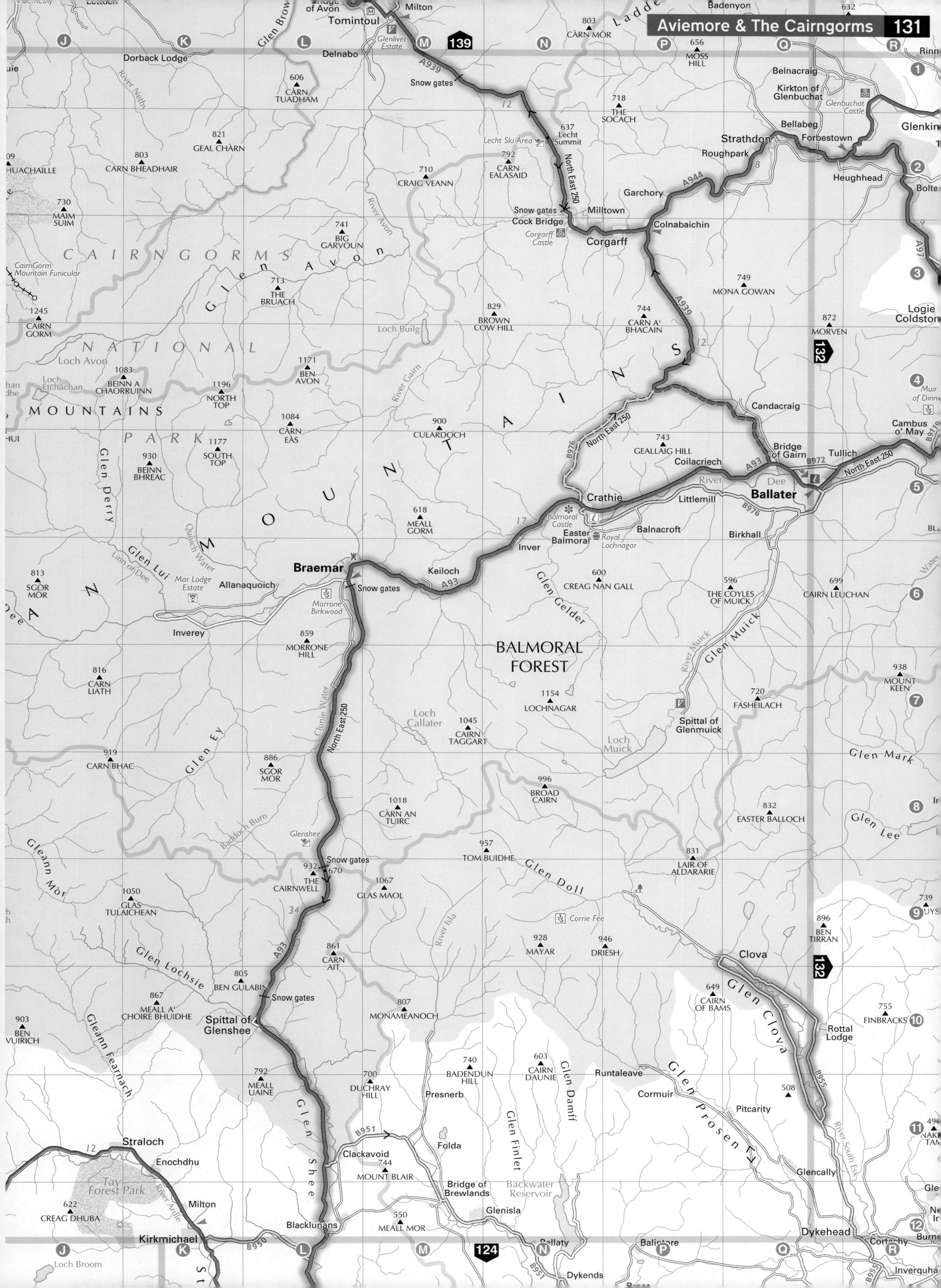

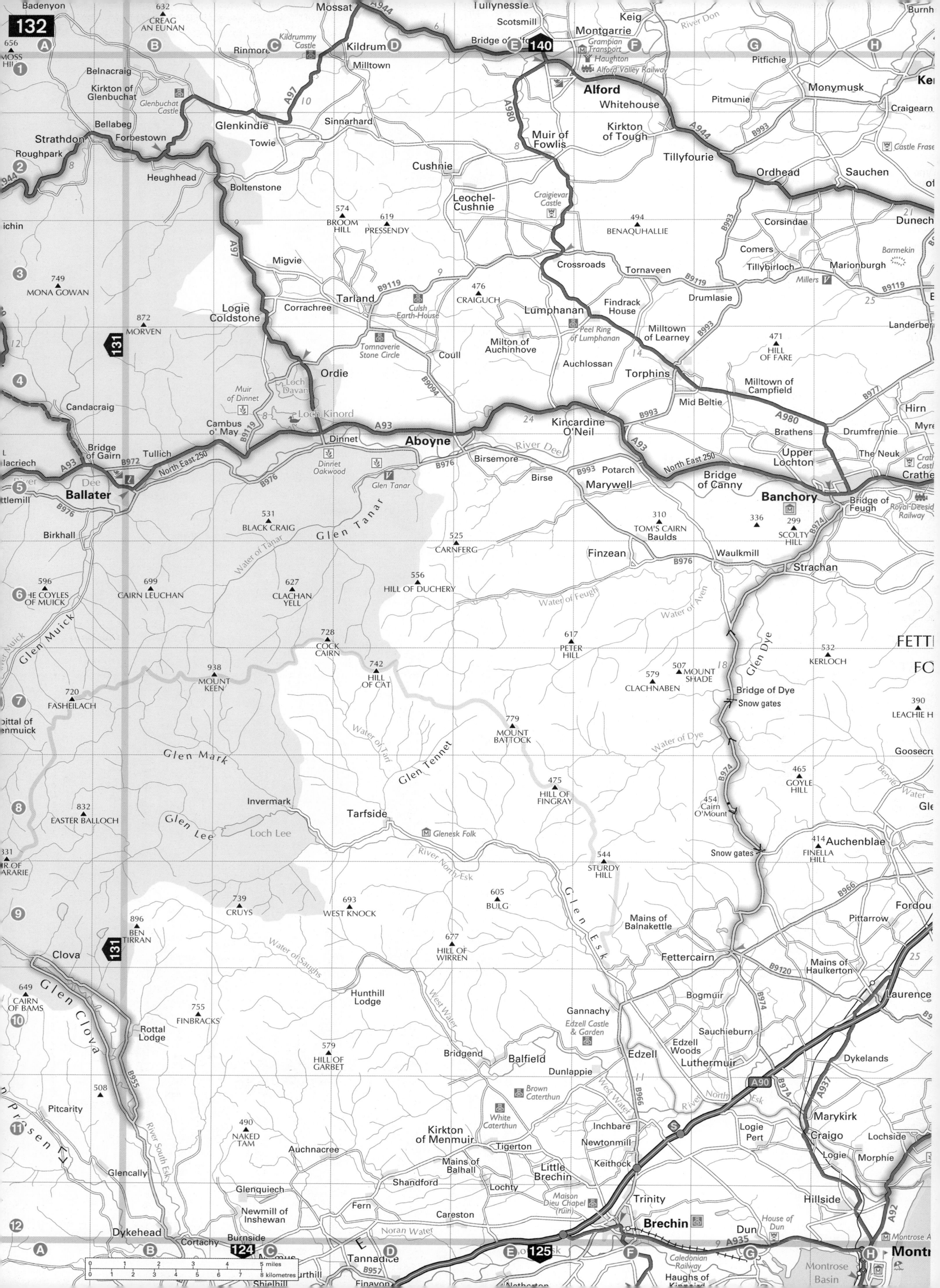

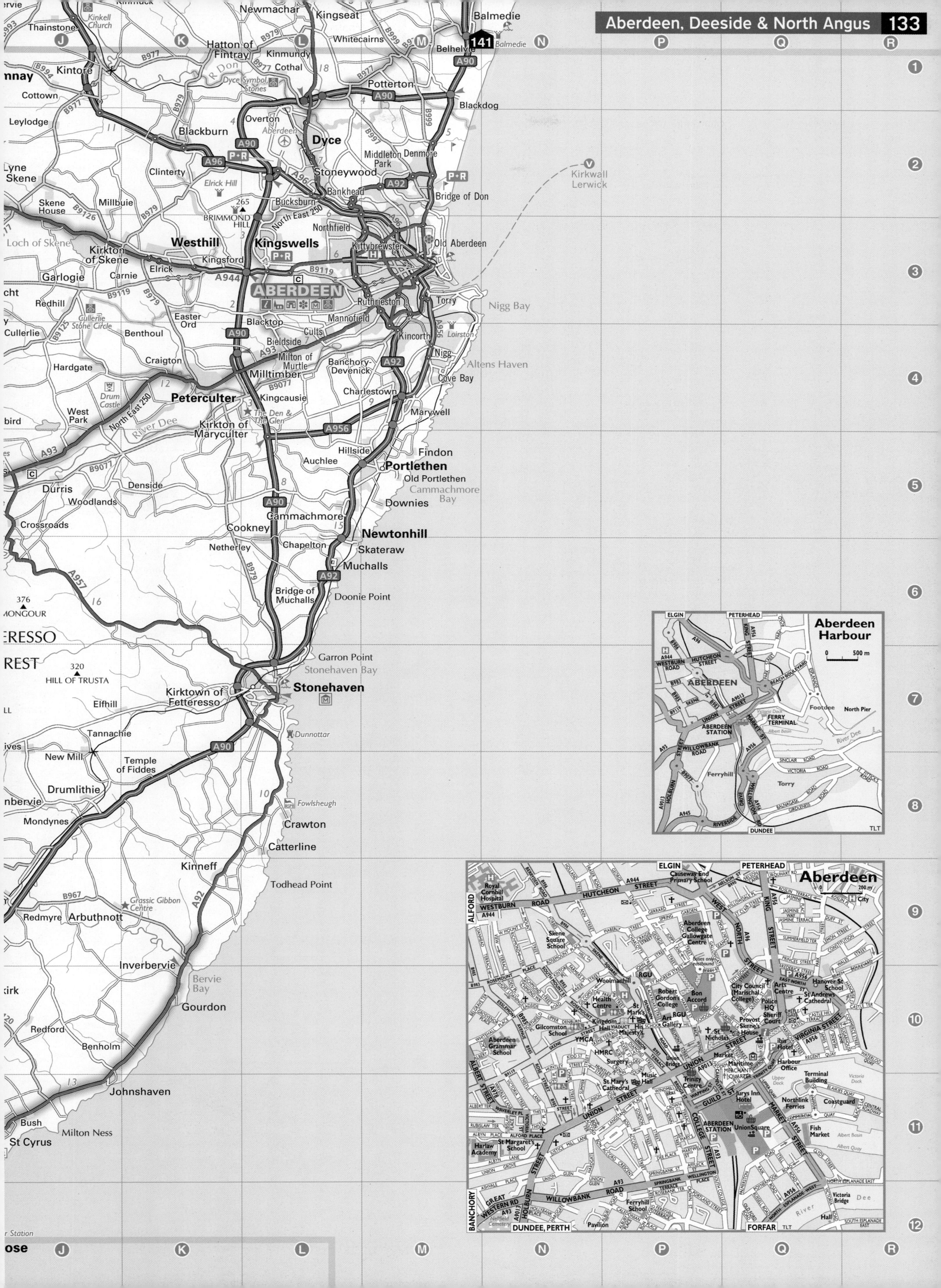

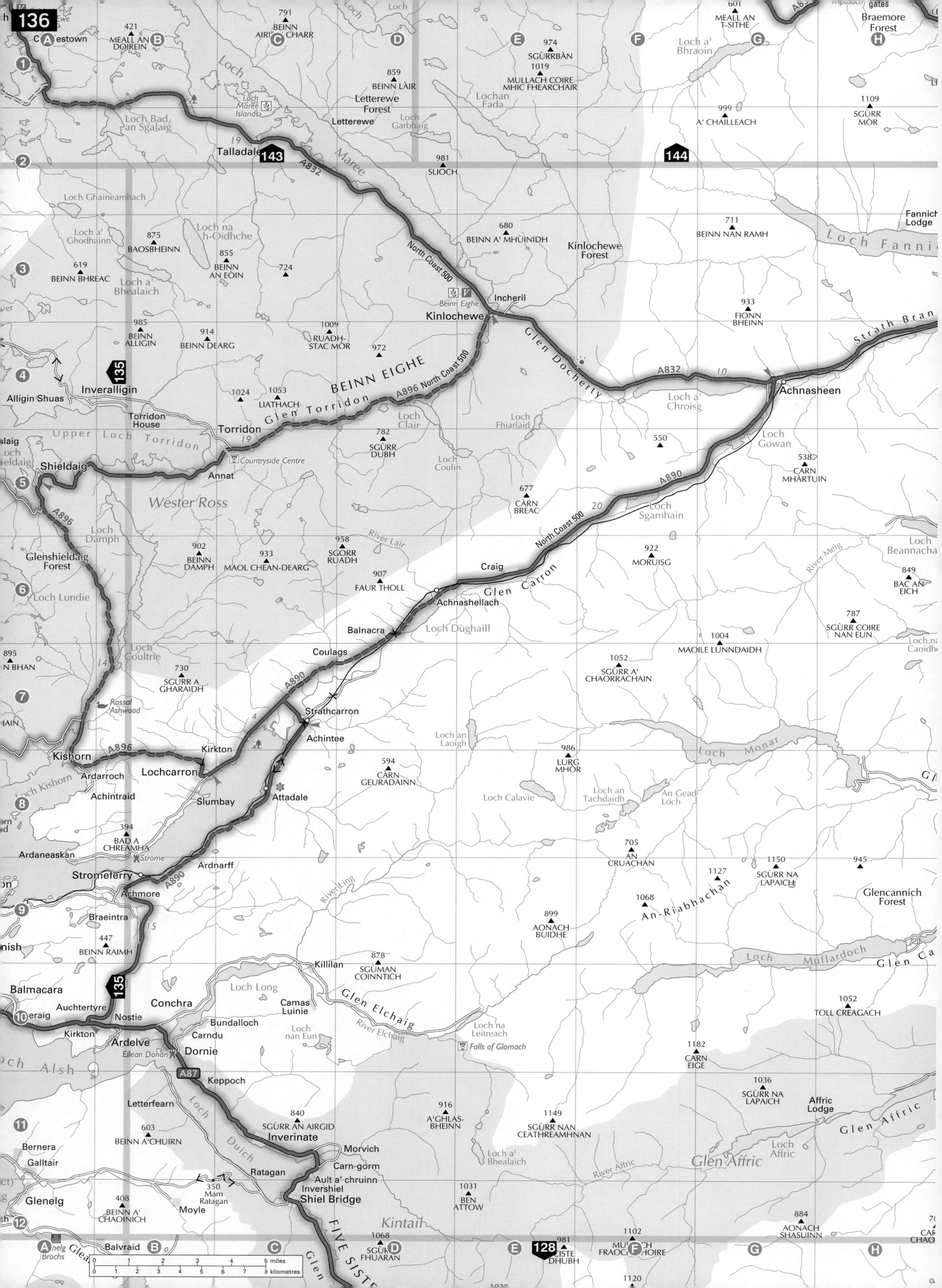

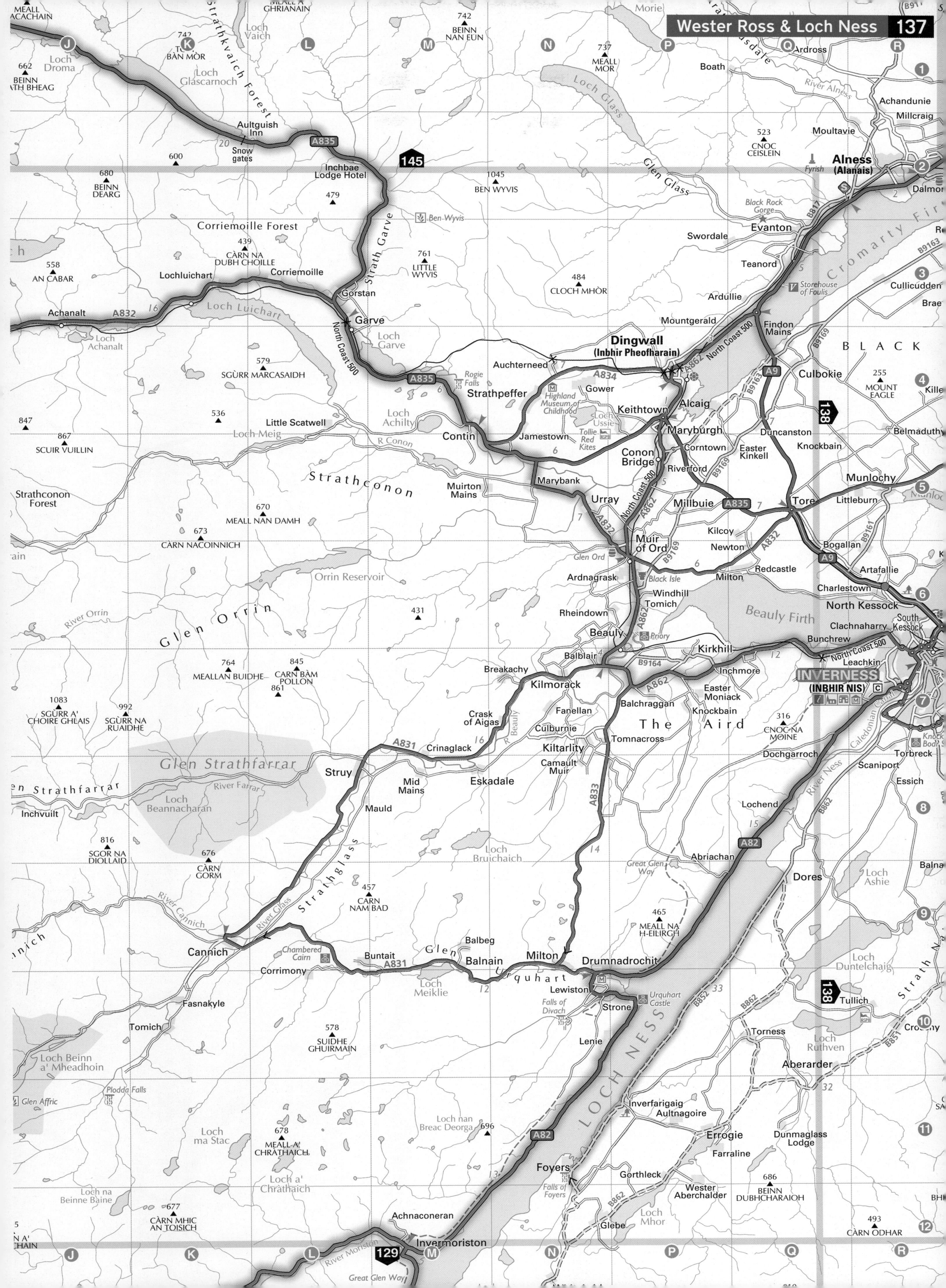

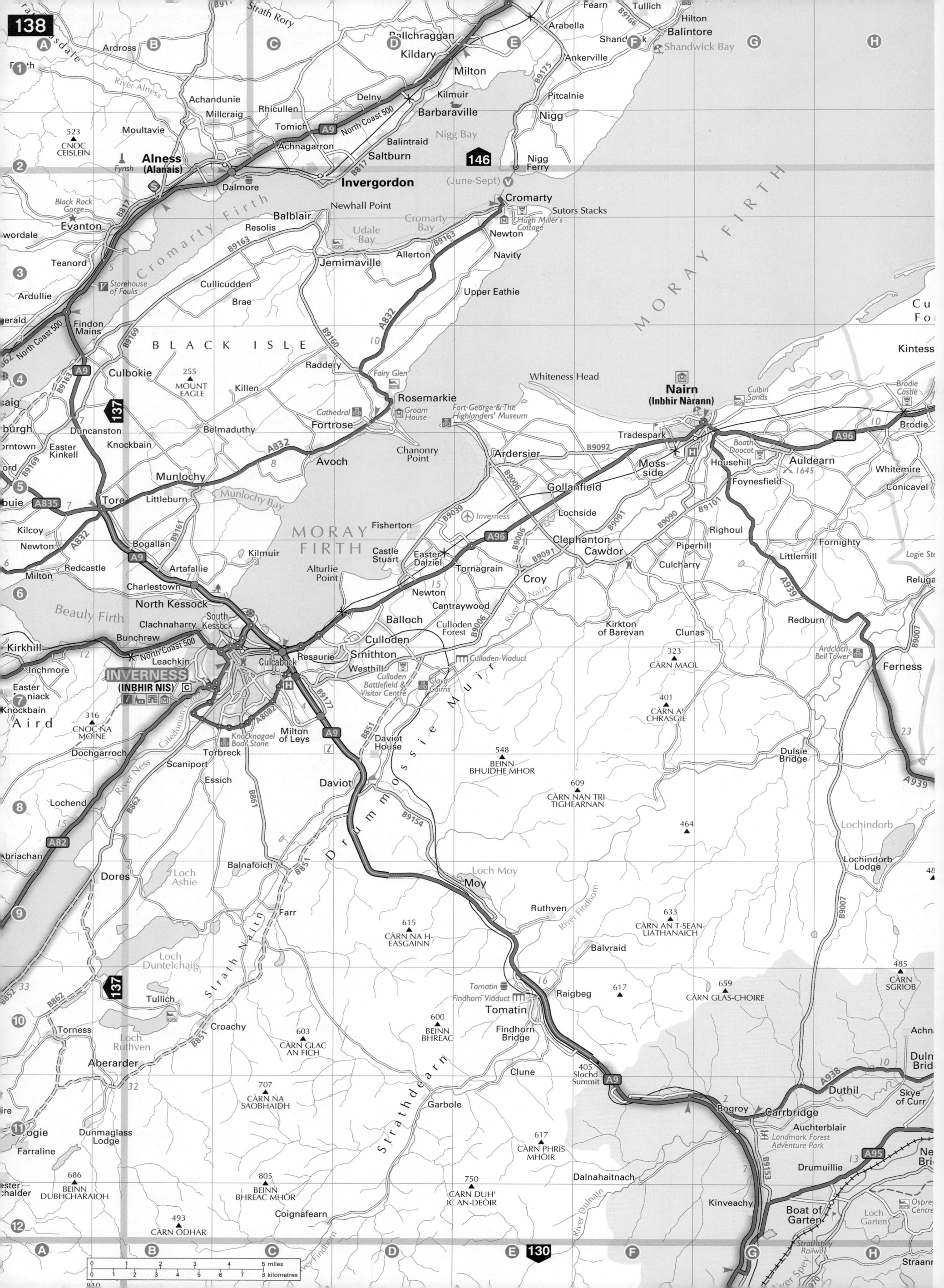

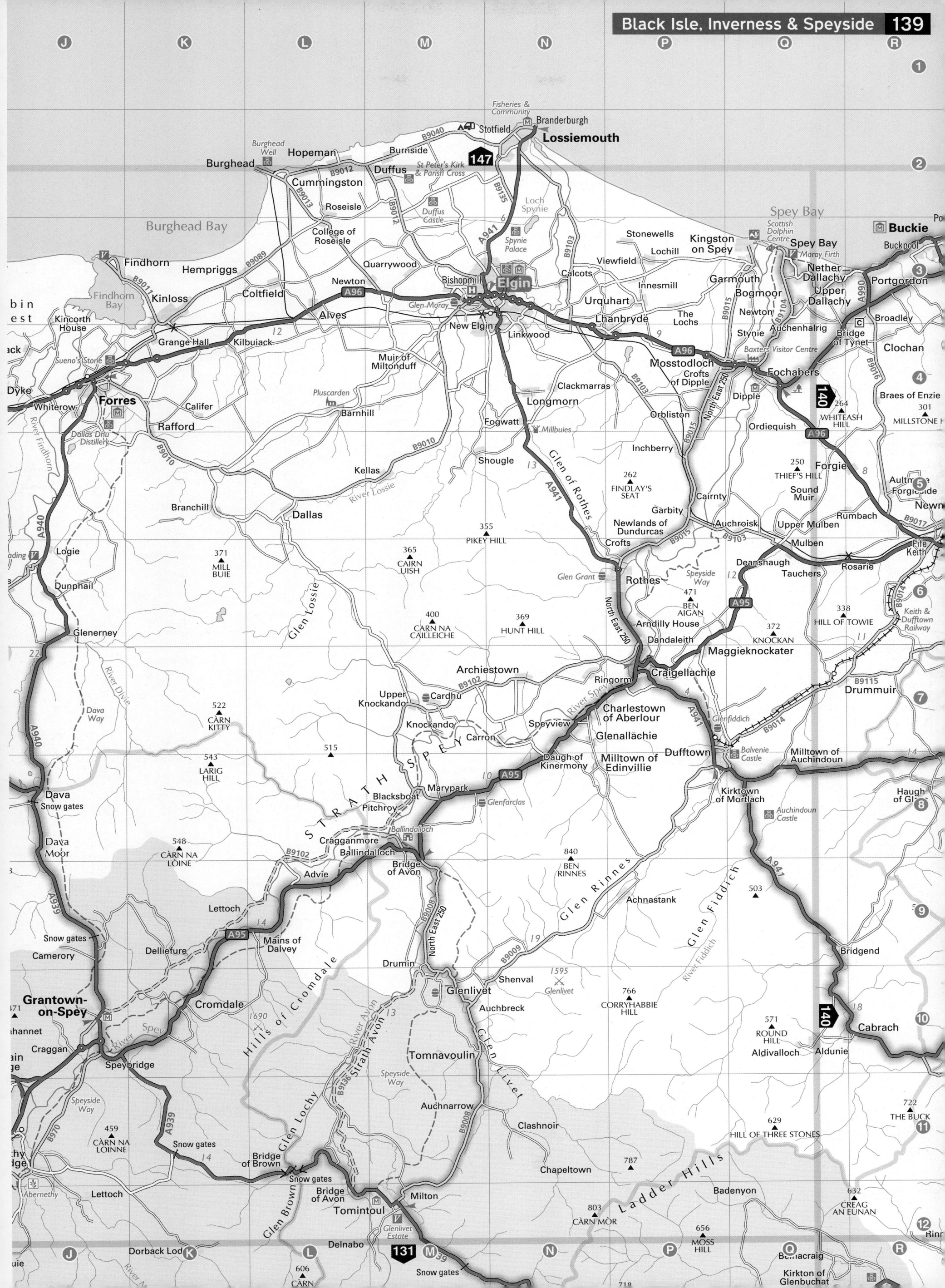

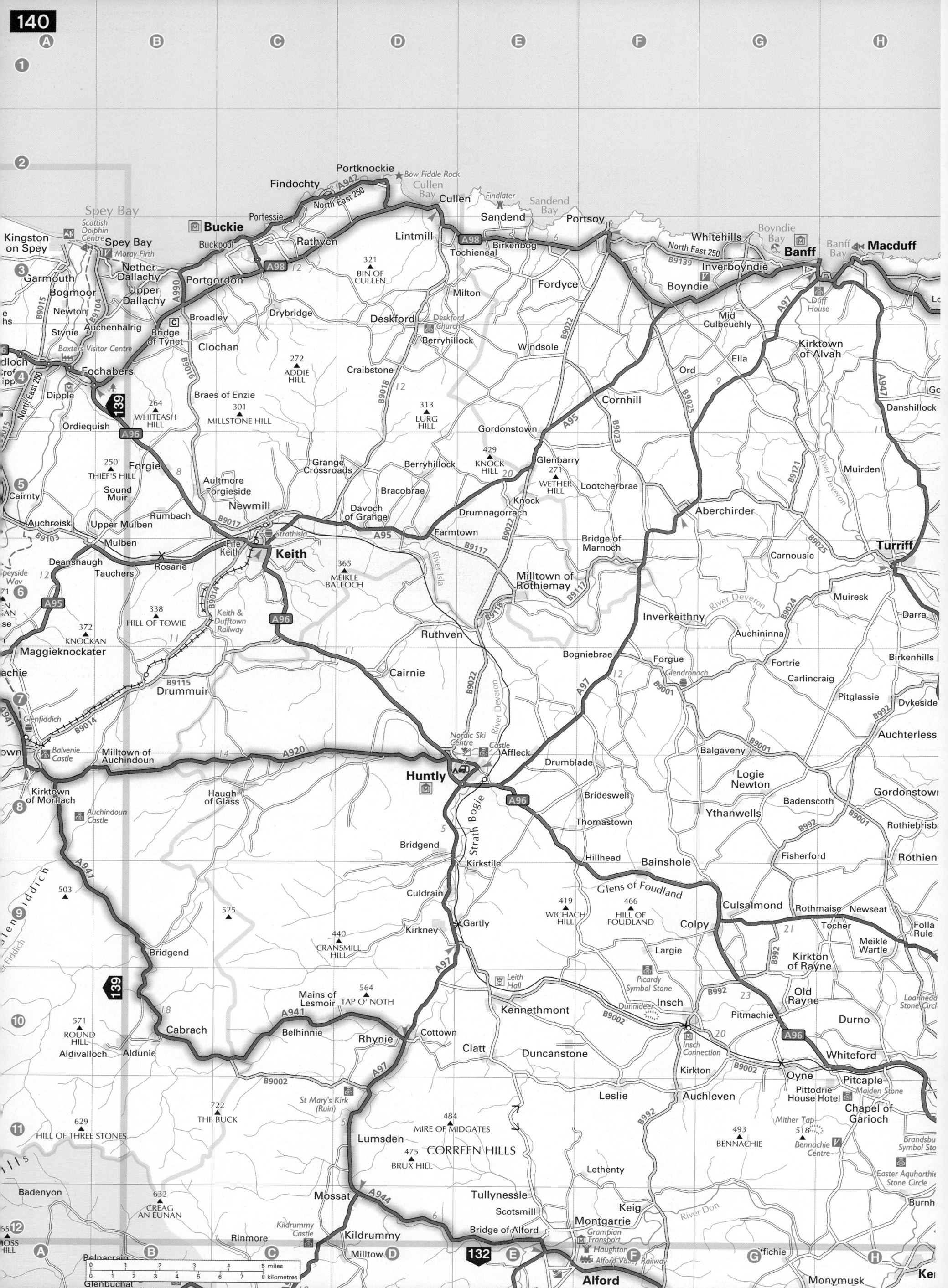

A B C D E F G H

1

Baile Ailein
(Balalla)
Lacasaig
(Laxay)
Cromor
Gearraidh Bhaird
(Garyvard)
dh a Bhruaich
(Aribruach)
Loch Erisort
Cearsiadar
(Kershader)
Marbhig
(Marvig)

2

B8060
Grabhair
(Gravir)
Loch Ouirn
401
MÒR
MHONADH
A' Chabag

152

3

PARK
Eishken
(Eisgein)
Leumrabhagh
(Lemreway)
571
BEINN MHOR
Loch Shell

Loch Claidh

4

Loch
Brollum

Loch Brollum

SOUND OF SHIANT

Reinigeadal
(Rhenigidale)

5

las Scalpaigh
yles Scalpay)

SHIANT
ISLANDS

T H E

6

Sgalpaigh
(Scalpay)

SCALPAY

152

7

The Little Minch

8

9

Fladda-chùain

Eilean Trodday

Rubha Hunish

10

Tairbeart
(Tarbert)
Duntulm
Kilmaluag
A855
Lùb Score
Skye Museum
of Island Life
Flodigarry
Poldorais
Eilean Flodigarry
Borneskitaig
Kilmuir
Heribusta
Kilvaxter
542
MEAL NA
SUIREAMACH
Digg
Staffin Bay
Staffin Island

11

134
Balgown
Brogaig
135
Stenscholl
Staffin
Linicro
464
BIODA
BUIDHE
Trotternish
Maligar
Totscore
Ellishader
Kilt Rock
River Rha

12

Ascrib
Islands
Idrigill
Marishader
Garros
Valtos
atairnis
Uig Bay
D g
(Uige)
Fairy
Glen
River Conon
E
BEINN
EDRA
Garros
Rubha nam Brathai
Culnaknock

A B C D E F G H

283

0   1   2   3   4   5 miles
0 1 2 3 4 5 6 7 8 kilometres

148

Baddidarrach

Inverkirkaig **1**

Rubha Còigeach

Eilean Mòr **2**

Enard Bay

Rubha Mòr
Reiff

Achnahaird

144

Eilean Mullagrach

Altandhu **3**

Loch
Osgaig

Loch Bad
a' Ghaill

Isle Ristol

Polbain

Badentarbet

Glas-leac Mòr

SUMMER ISLES

Achiltibuie

*Badentarbat
Bay*

Polglass

Ben M
Coigac

Tanera Beg

V

Tanera
Mòr

Horse
Island

*Horse
Sound*

Achduart **4**

Steornabhagh
(Stornoway)

Glas-leac Beag

Eilean Dubh

Culnacraig

BEN
CO

Priest
Island

Leac Dhonn

Isle Martin **5**

Greenstone
Point

Cailleach Head

*Annat
Bay*

6

Rubha Beag

Scoraig

Ruigh'riabhach

635
BEINN GHOBHLACH

Mellon
Udrigle

Stattic Point

GRUINARD
ISLAND

Badluarach

Badrallach

A832

Foura

Laide

*Gruinard
Bay*

North Coast 500

Badcaul

32

Rubha Rèidh

Rubha
nan Sasan

Cove

Mellon
Charles

Ormiscaig

Gruinard

Ardessie

Camusnaga **7**

296
AN
CUAIDH

Aultbea

Loch a'
Bhàid-luachraich

Little Gruinard River

764
SAIL
MHÒR

Dundonnel

Melvaig

B8057

ISLE
OF EWE

Gruinard River

347
CREAG-
MHEAL BEAG

Lochan
Gaineamhach

1062
AN TEALLACH **8**

Aultgrishin

Loch Ewe

Loch
Fada

Strathnasheallag Forest

Inverasdale

293
CNOC
BREAC

Naast

250

MEALL NA MEINE

681
BEINN A'
CHAISGEIN BEAG

144

rfield Forest

Loch na
Sealga

906
BEINN DEARG MHOR **9**

Inverewe
Garden

13

North Erradale

B8021

Poolewe

Londubh

Fionn

Wester Ross

Big Sand

A832

Smithstown

Strath

Heritage

Auchtercairn

791
BEINN
AIRIDH CHARR

*Dubh
Loch*

974
SGÙRRBÀN
1019 **10**

Longa
Island

Lonemore

Gairloch
& Loch Ewe

421
MEALL AN
DOIREIN

859
BEINN LÀIR

MULLACH COIRE
MHIC FHEARCHAIR

*Loch
Gairloch*

Gairloch

Charlestown

Letterewe
Forest

Loch

Lochan
Fada

Port
Henderson

B8056

Eilean
Horrisdale

Loch
Maree
Islands

Letterewe

Loch
Garbhaig

Badachro

11

Opinan

981
SLIOCH

South Erradale

*Loch Bad
an Sgalaig*

Talladale

19

A832

*Loch
Maree*

Redpoint

135

136

North Coast 500

680
BEINN A' MHÙINIDH

Kinlochewe
Forest

Red
Point

Loch Ghaineamhach

Loch na
h-Oidhche

875
BAOSBHEINN

855
BEINN
AN EÒIN

724

Beinn Eighe

12

Incheril

619
BEINN BHREAC

Loch a'
Bhealaich

Kinlochewe

Loch
Torridon

Rubha
na Fearn

985

1009

J **K** **L** **M** **N** **P** **Q** **R**

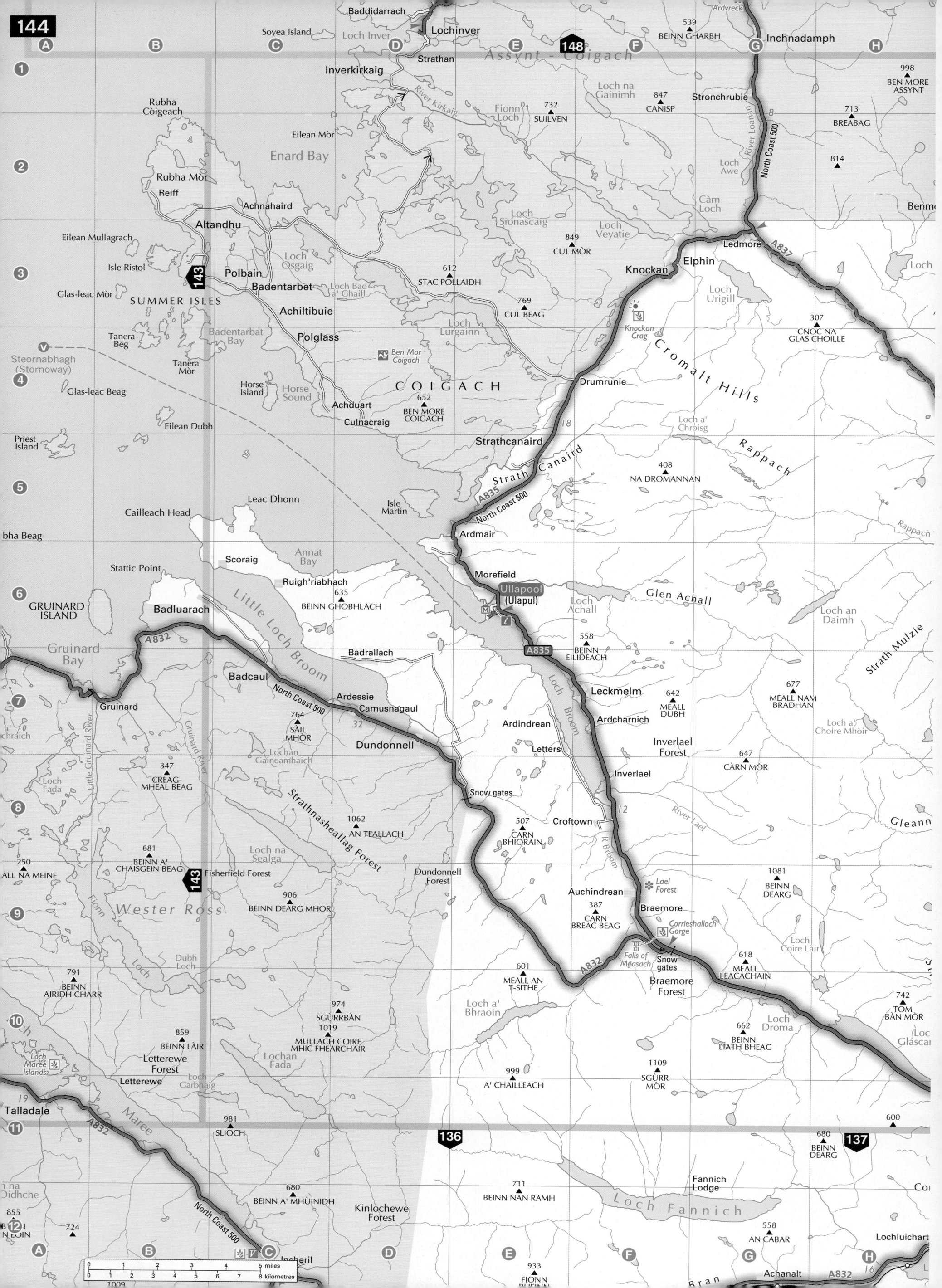

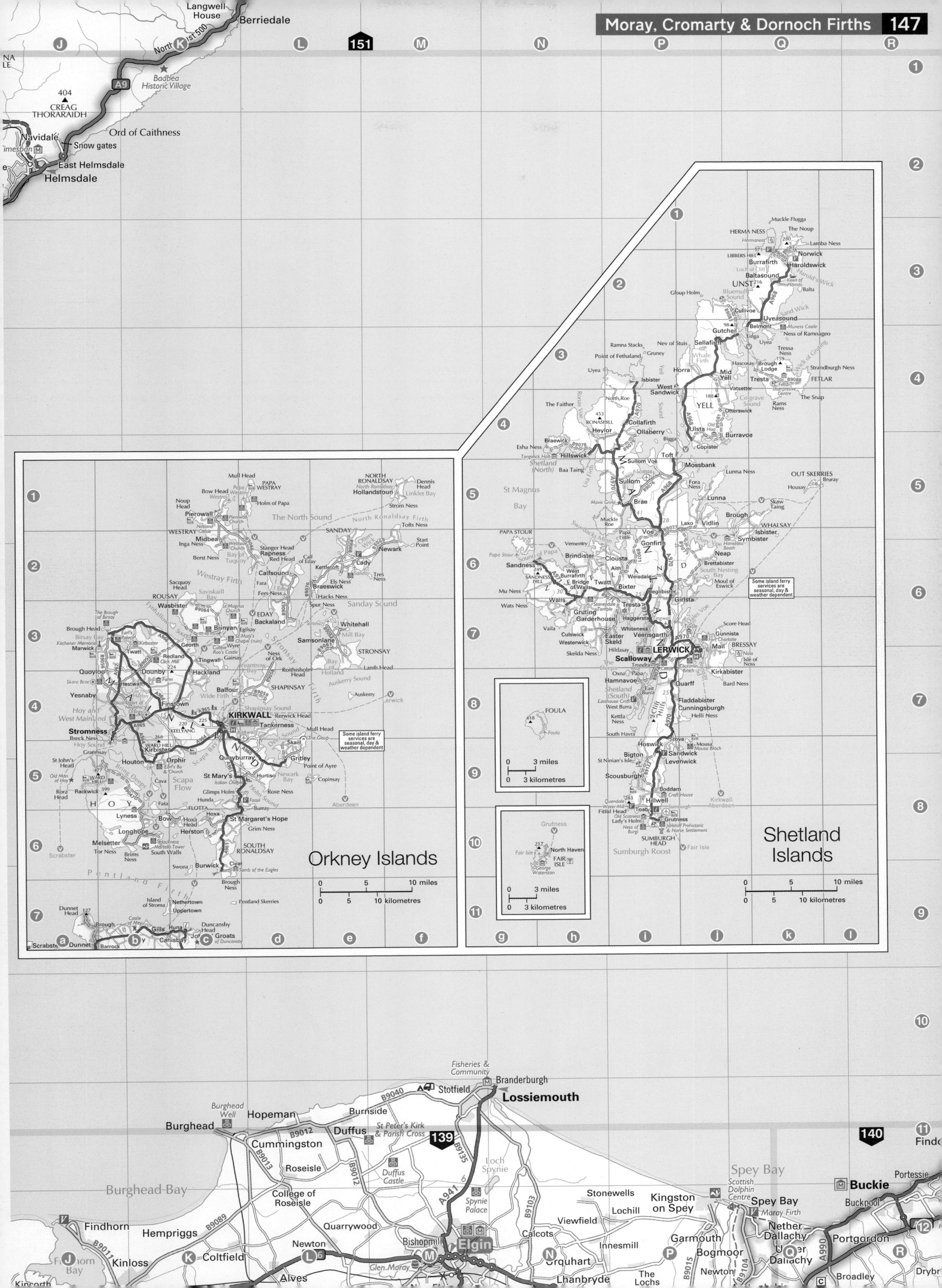

A B C D E F G H

1
2
3
4
5
6
7
8
9
10
11
12

CAPE WRATH

Kearvaig
Bay

Cléit
Dhubh

▲371
SGRIBHIS-
BHEINN

▲297
CNOC A
GHIUBHAIS

▲300
MAOVALLY

Balna
Ba

THE PARPH

Loch Airigh
na Beinne

Bal

Sandwood
Bay

▲457
FASHVEN

Keolo

Sandwood
Loch

▲485
CREAG
RIABACH

Rubh' an Fhir Lèithe

▲468
BEINN
DEARG MHÒR

▲464
MEALL
NA MÒINE

▲331
GHLAS-
BHEINN

Kyle of Du

A838

Sheigra

Strath Shinary

▲521
FARVEALL

19

Balchreick   Blairmore

Oldshoremore

▲355
AN
SOCACH

▲773
BEINN
SPIONNAIDH

Kinlochbervie

Badcall

▲801
CRANSTACKIE

Loch Clash

Loch Inchard

B801

Achriesgill

North Coast 500

Strath Dionard

River Dionard

Rubha Ruadh

Loch na
Claise Càrnaich

Rhiconich

Fanagmore

Skerricha

▲908
FOINAVEN

Tarbet

Loch Laxford

A838

Foindle

North-west Sutherland

Loch na Tuadh

HANDA
ISLAND

7

Laxford
Bridge

▲786
ARKLE

Scourie Bay

Scourie

A894

River Laxford

Loch
Stack

SÀBHAL

Scourie More

▲721
BEN STACK

Upper
Badcall

Lower
Badcall

Strath Stack

Badcall Bay

Loch a'
Mhuilinn

▲386
BEN
AUSKAIRD

Achfary

▲333
BEN
SCREAVIE

▲800

CA
DE

Rubh' a'
Mhucard

North Coast 500

17

A838

Loch More

Point of Stoer

OLDANY
ISLAND

Eddrachillis
Bay

Locha Chàim Bhàin

▲419
BEN
STROME

Loch an
Leathaid Bhuain

Kinloch

Old Man
of Stoer

Culkein
Drumbeg

Kylestrome

Glendhu Forest

Culkein

Clashnessie
Bay

Oldany

Drumbeg

Kylesku

Loch Glendhu

▲525
BEINN AIRD
DA LOCH

▲613
MEALL AN FHEUR

Achnacarnin

Nedd

B869

Glen

Unapool

Loch Glencoul

Clashmore

Clashnessie

Loch
Poll

Loch an
Leothaid

▲776
SAIL
GHORM

Leirg

A894

▲792
BEINN LEOID

Stoer

▲809
QUINAG

Loch-Beag

Clachtoll

Loch
Beannach

▲774
GLAS BHEINN

Eas-a' Chùal Aluinn

B869

Bay of Clachtoll

North Coast 500

11

Rhicarn

Achmelvich
Bay

A837

Loch Assynt

Achmelvich

Baddidarrach

Ardvreck

Soyea Island

Loch Inver

Lochinver

Assynt Coigach

▲539
BEINN GHARBH

Inchnadamph

Strathan

0 1 2 3 4 5 miles
0 1 2 3 4 5 6 7 8 kilometres

Loch na
Gainimh   847   Strech

Dubh

▲998
BEN MORE
ASSYNT

MA

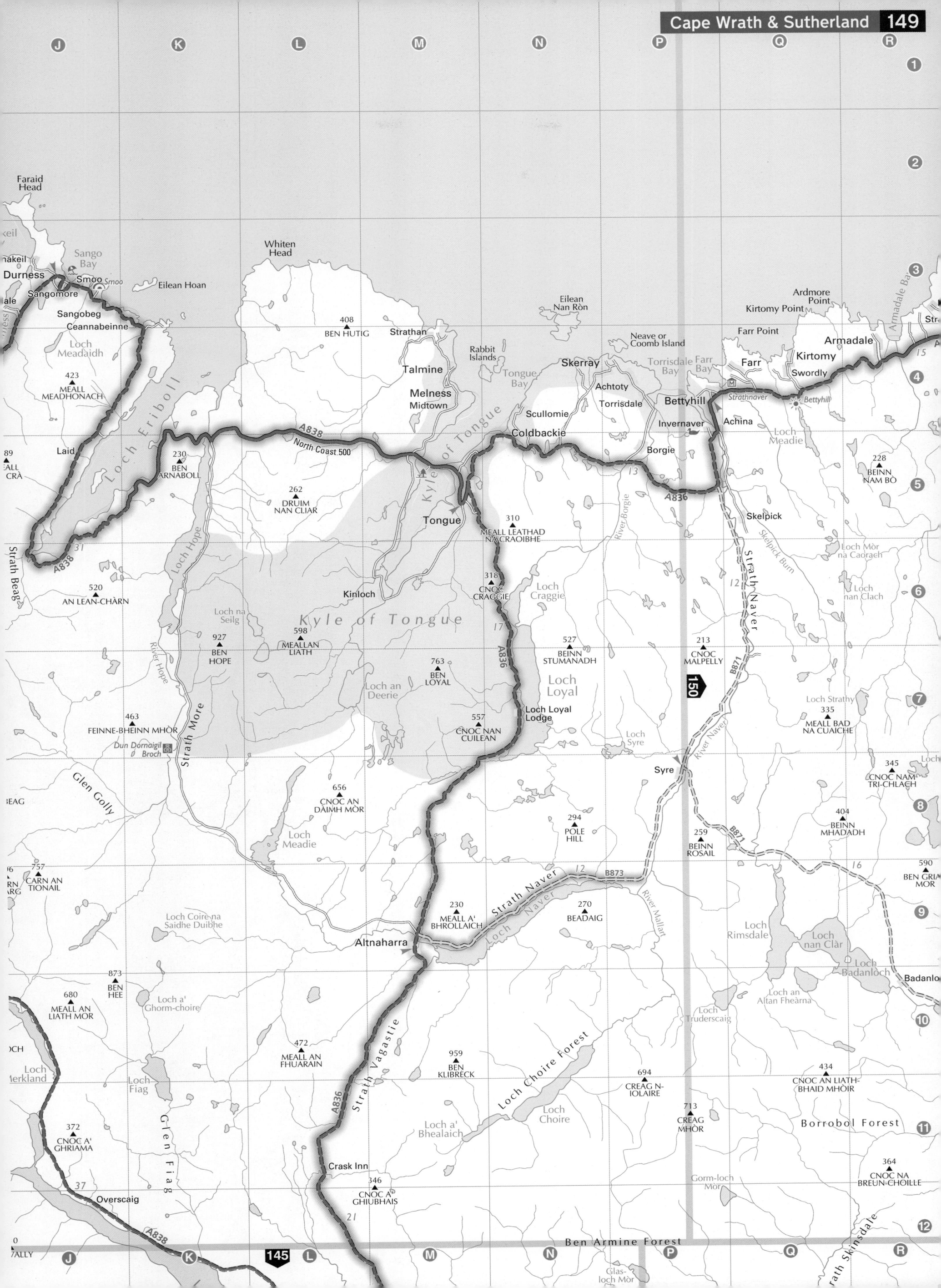

J K L M N P Q R

1

2

Faraid
Head

Sango
Bay   Whiten
                                                       Head

Durness   Smoo Smoo   Eilean Hoan   Armadale Bay   3
Sangomore
                                                                                                                   Ardmore
Sangobeg   Point
Ceannabeinne   Eilean   Kirtomy Point
Loch   Nan Ròn   Farr Point
Meadaidh   408   Torrisdale Farr
                                      ▲   Strathan   Rabbit   Neave or   Bay   Bay   Farr   Armadale
423   BEN HUTIG   Islands   Coomb Island   Kirtomy   4
▲   Talmine   Skerray   Farr   Swordly
MEALL   Achtoty
MEADHONACH   Melness   Torrisdale Bettyhill
                                                 Midtown   Scullomie   Invernaver   Strathnaver Bettyhill
A838   Achina
89   Laid   North Coast 500   Coldbackie   Borgie   Loch   5
LL   Meadie
CRÀ   230   262   River Borgie   A836
                   ▲   ▲   228
                BEN   DRUIM   ▲
                ARNABOLL   NAN CLIAR   310   BEINN
                                                                               ▲   NAM BÒ
31   A838   MEALL LEATHAD   Skelpick
                                                                             NA CRAOIBHE   Loch Mòr
Strath Beag   na Caorach
                                                                      318   Loch   6
520   Kinloch   ▲   Loch   nan Clach
▲   CNOC   Craggie   Strath Naver
AN LEAN-CHÀRN   CRAGGIE   12
                              598   213
                              ▲   Kyle of Tongue   17   527   ▲
927   MEALLAN   ▲   CNOC   7
▲   LIATH   BEINN   MALPELLY   Loch Strathy
BEN   STUMANADH   335
HOPE   Loch   ▲
                                                     763   Loyal   MEALL BAD
463   ▲   Loch   NA CUAICHE
▲   BEN   Syre   150
FEINNE-BHEINN MHÒR   LOYAL   345
                                            Loch an   ▲
Dun Dòrnaigil   Deerie   557   CNOC NAM
Broch   ▲   Loch Loyal   TRI-CHLACH
                                                                   CNOC NAN   Lodge   Syre
Glen Golly   CUILEAN   River Naver   404
                                                                                                               ▲
BEAG   656   BEINN   8
                                              ▲   MHADADH
Strath More   CNOC AN   294   259
757   DÀIMH MÒR   ▲   ▲
▲   POLE   BEINN
CARN AN   Loch   HILL   ROSAIL   B871
TIONAIL   Meadie   16   590
N   ▲
ARG   12   B873   BEN GRIA
                                                                                                                        MÒR
                                                                                                                         9
Loch Coire na   Strath Naver   Loch
Saidhe Duibhe   230   Loch Naver   Rimsdale   Loch
                                             ▲   nan Clàr
873   MEALL A'   270   Loch
▲   BHROLLAICH   ▲   Badanloch
BEN   BEADAIG   Badanlo
HEE   Altnaharra   10
680
▲   Loch an
MEALL AN   Altan Fheàrna
LIATH MOR   Loch a'
               Ghorm-choire
472   Loch   434
▲   Truderscaig   ▲
MEALL AN   959   CNOC AN LIATH-
FHUARAIN   ▲   694   BHAID MHÒR
OCH   BEN   ▲   11
Loch   KLIBRECK   CREAG N-   713
Merkland   Loch   IOLAIRE   ▲
              Fiag   CREAG
372   MHÒR   Borrobol Forest
▲   Glen   Loch a'   Loch
CNOC A'   Fiag   Bhealaich   Choire
GHRIAMA   364
37   ▲
Overscaig   A836   Strath Vagastie   Crask Inn   Loch Choire Forest   Gorm-loch   CNOC NA
                                            346   Mòr   BREUN-CHOILLE
0   ▲
                                         CNOC A'
                                         GHIUBHAIS   21
TALLY   12
                  145   Ben Armine Forest   Strath Skinsdale

J K L M N P Q R

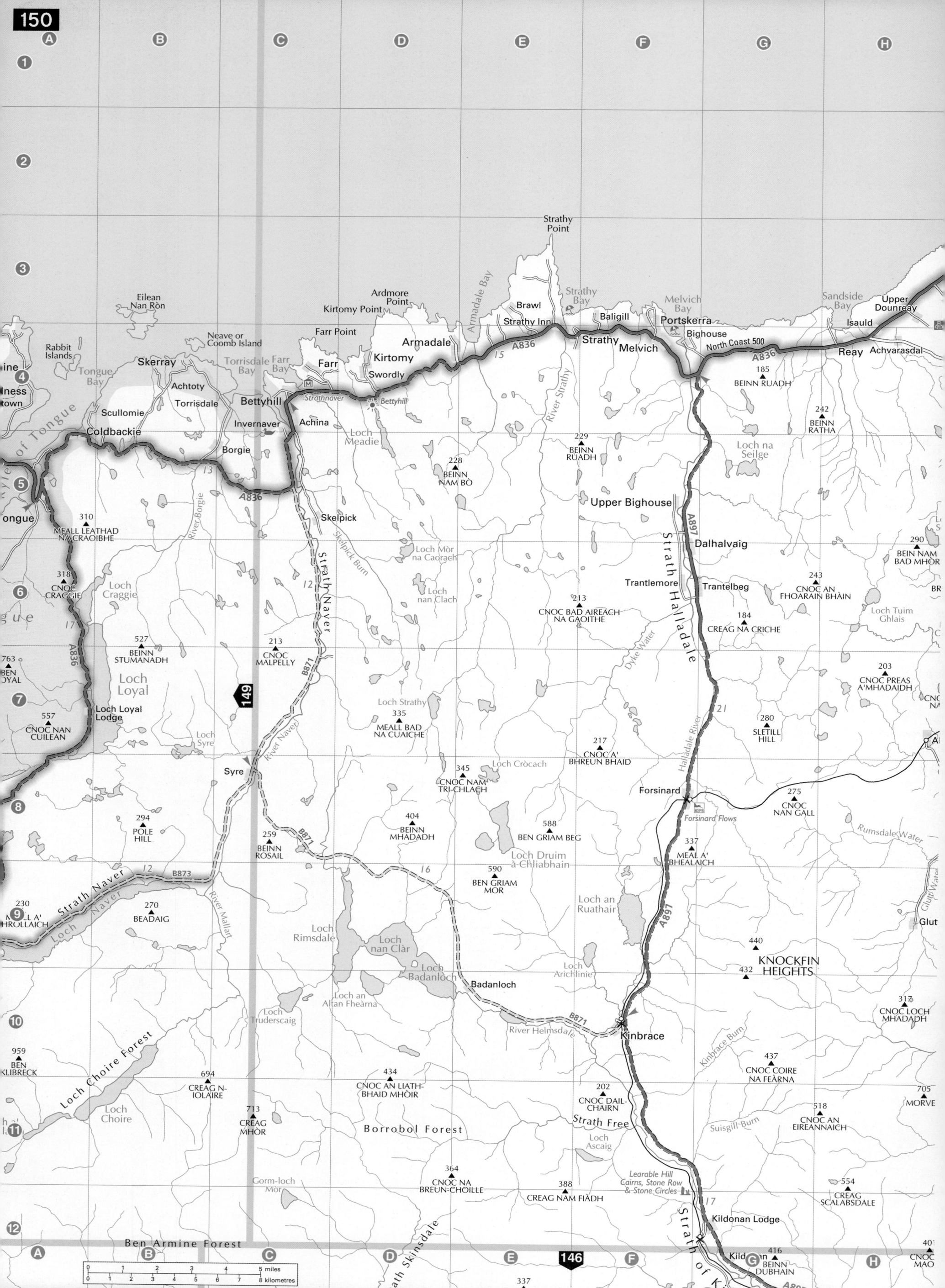

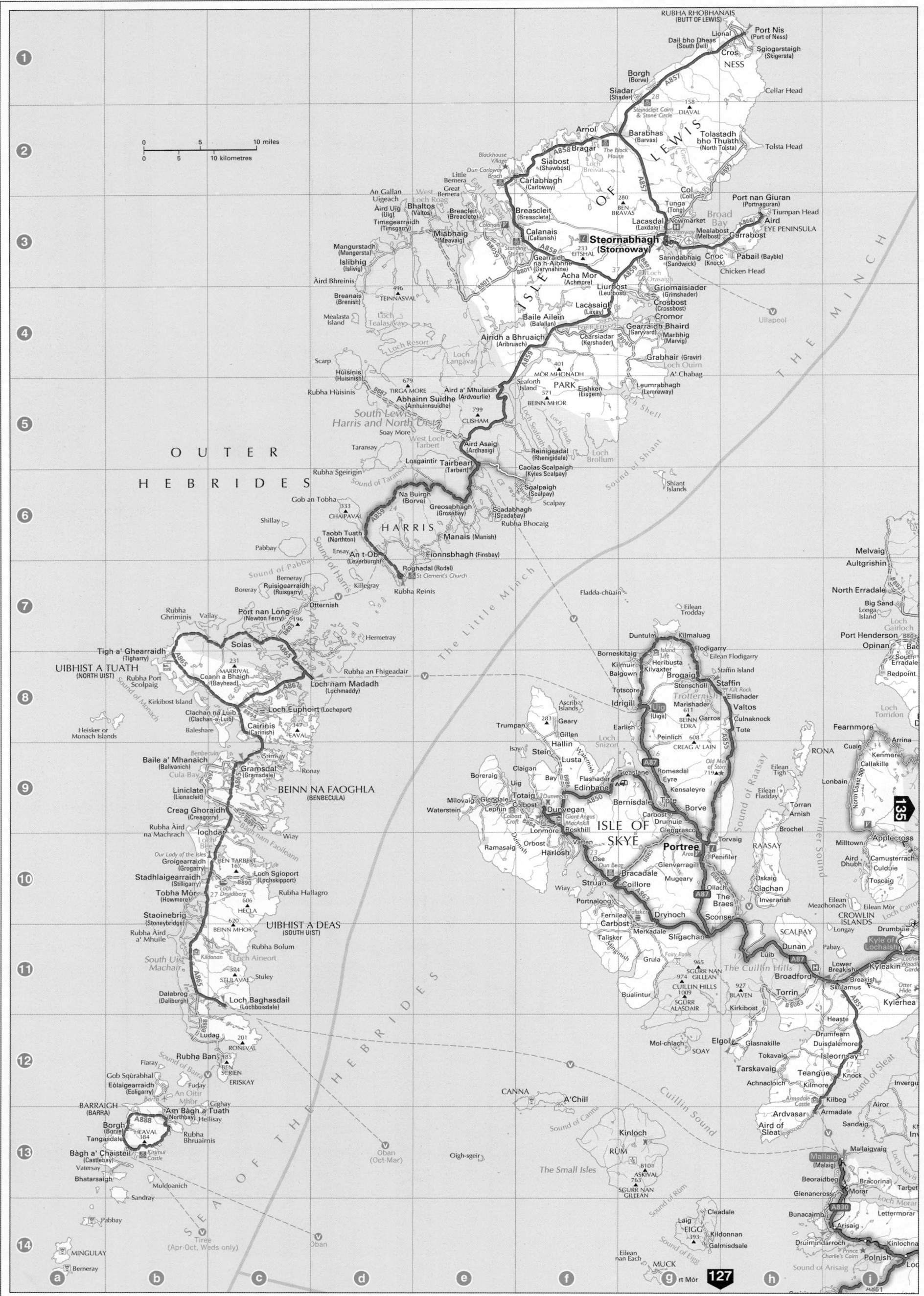

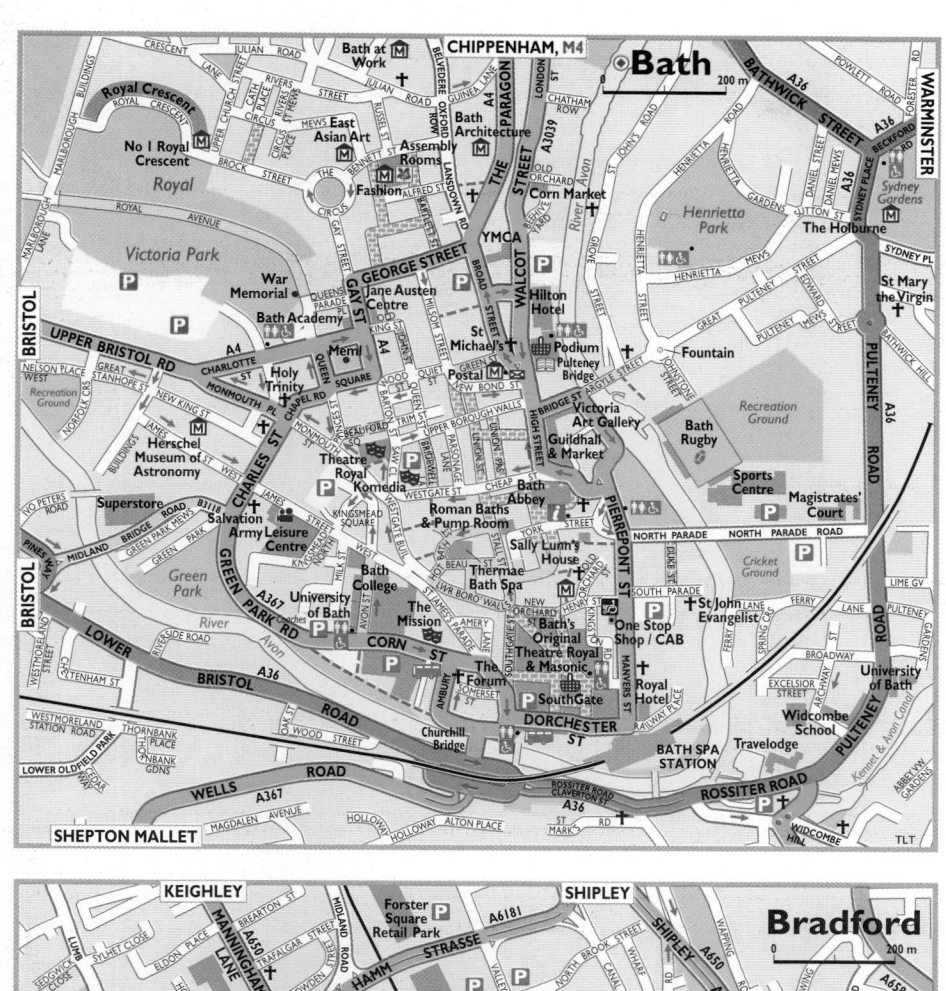

Bath

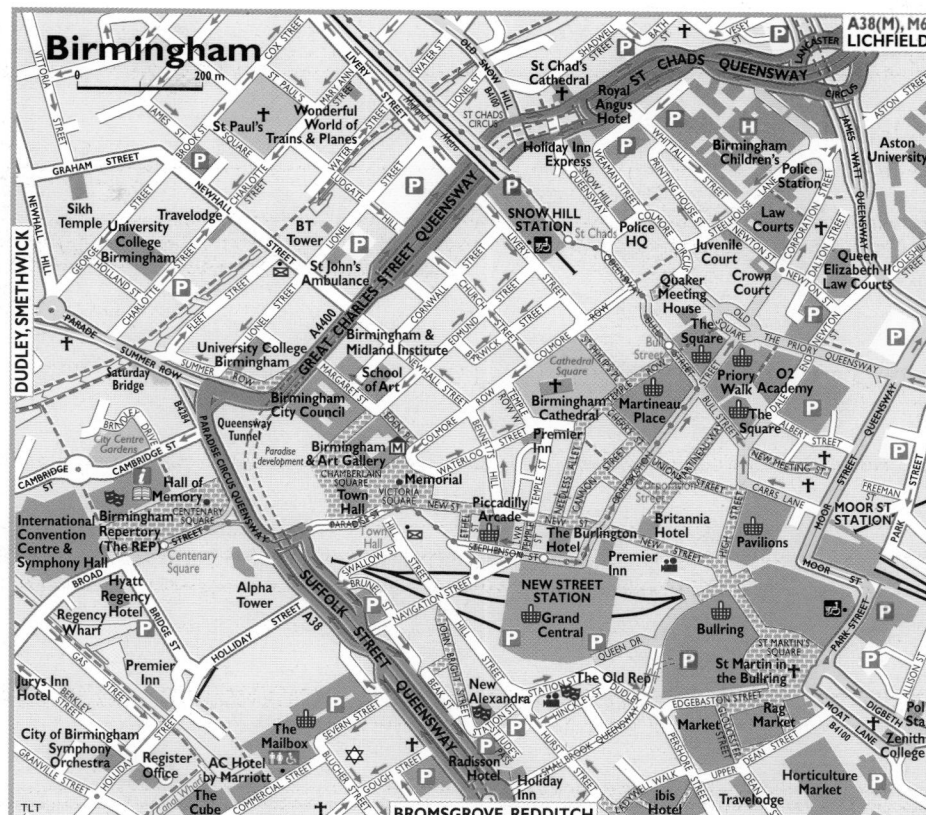

Birmingham

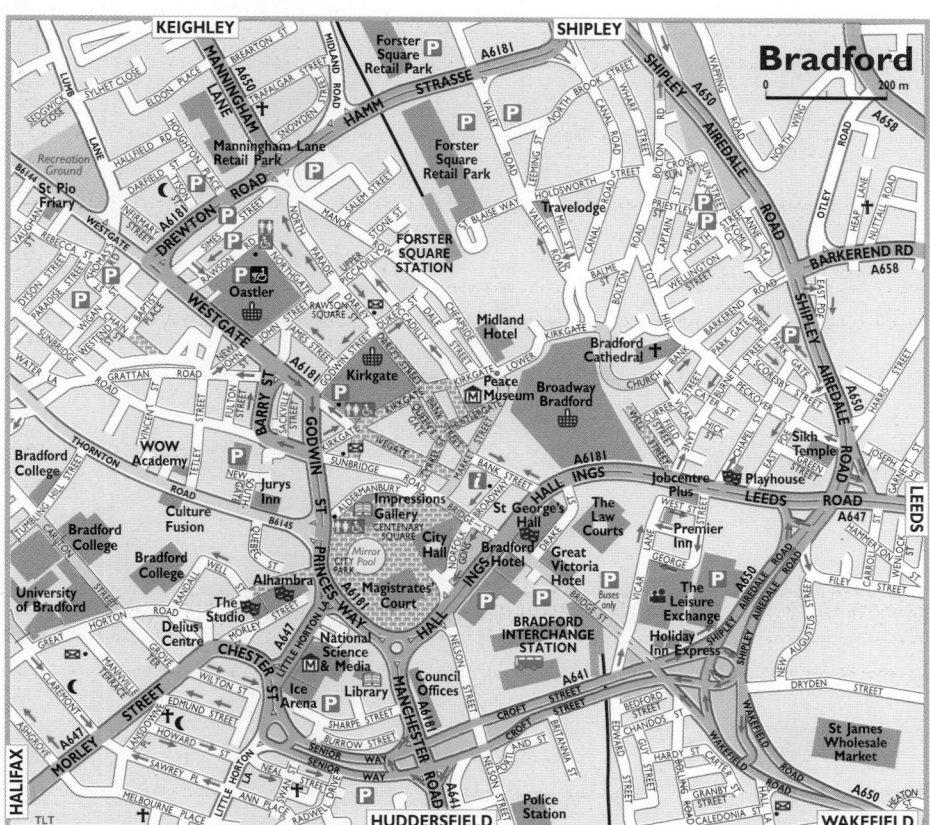

Bradford

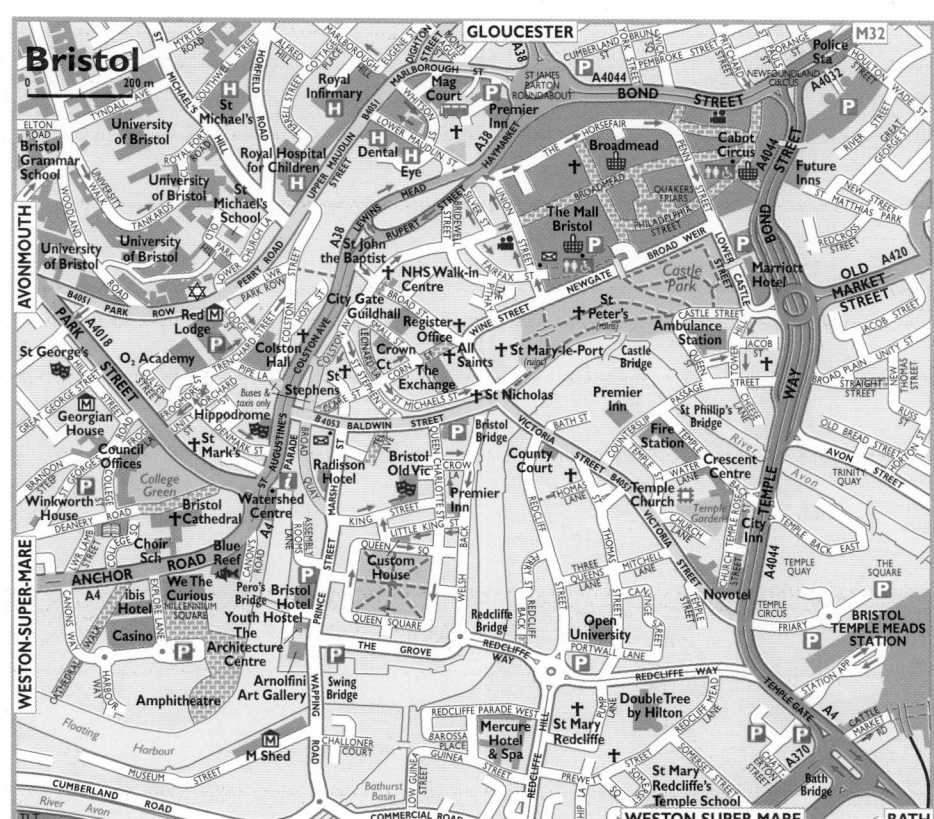

Bristol

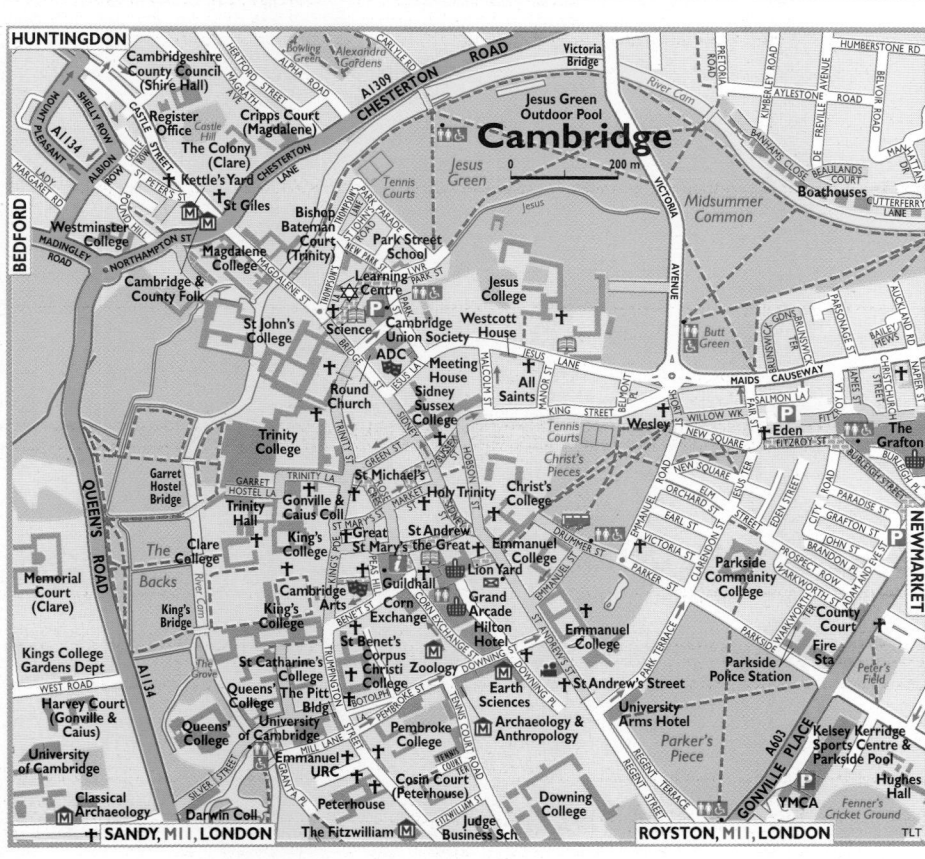

Cambridge

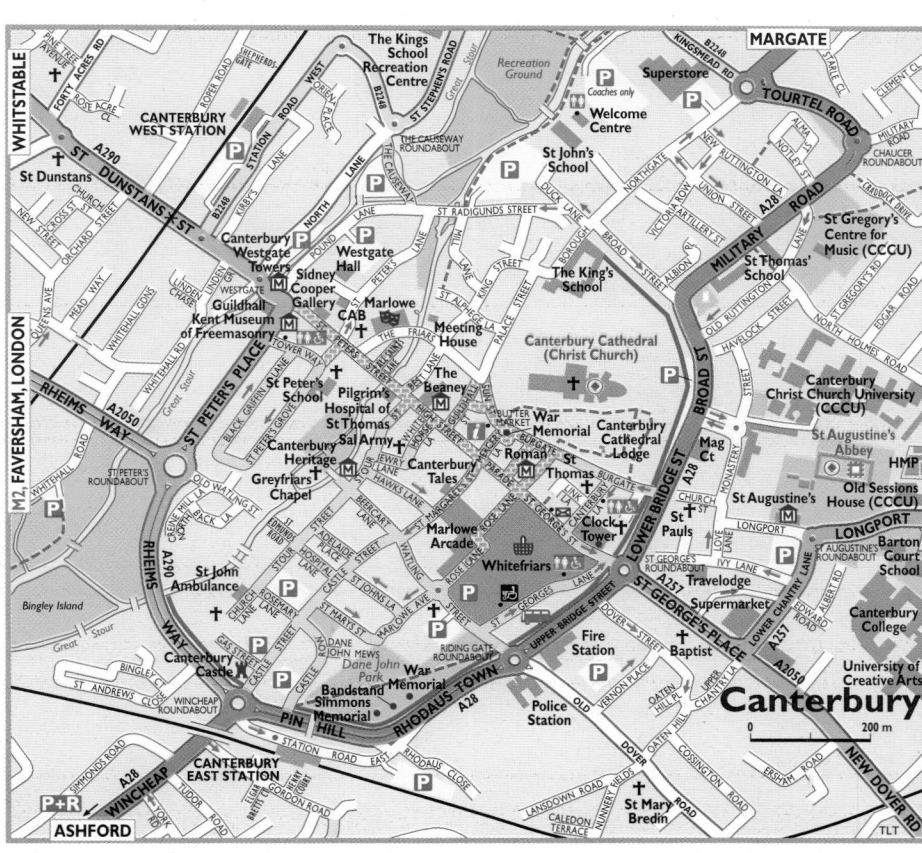

Canterbury

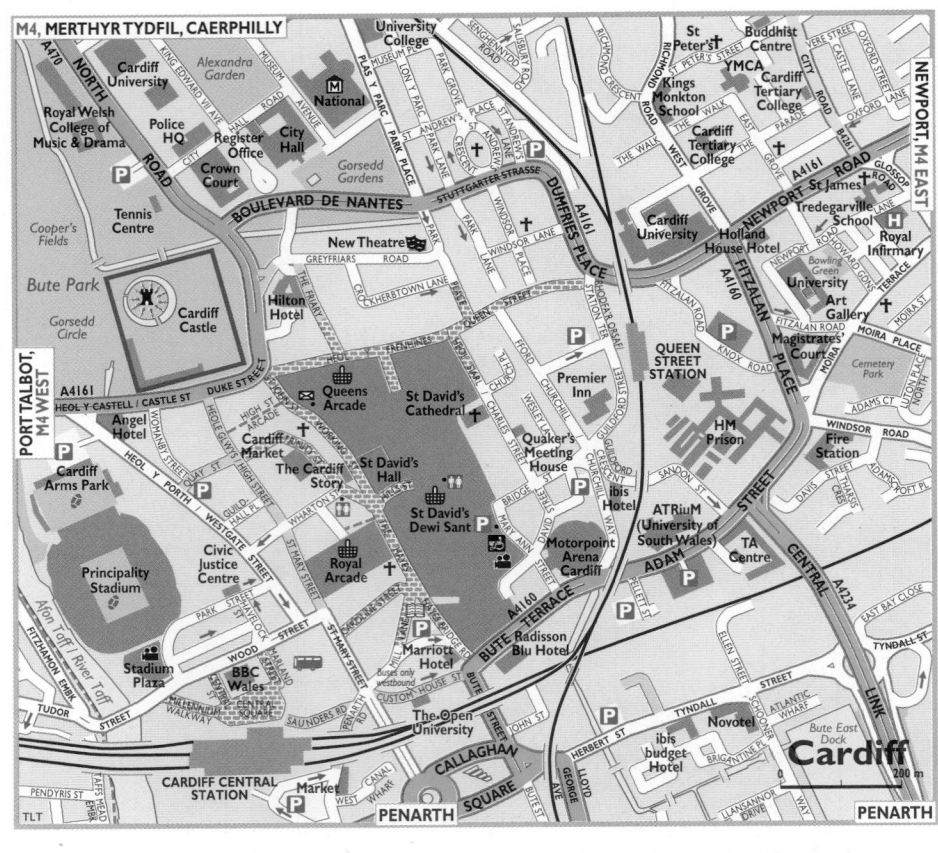

Cardiff

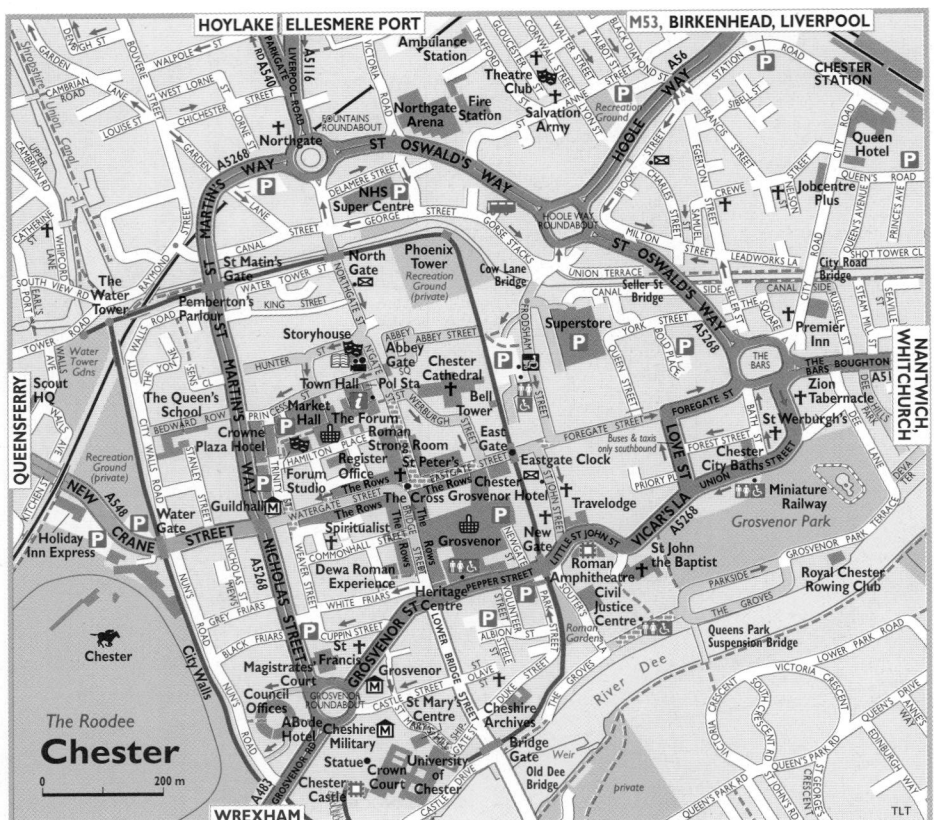

Chester

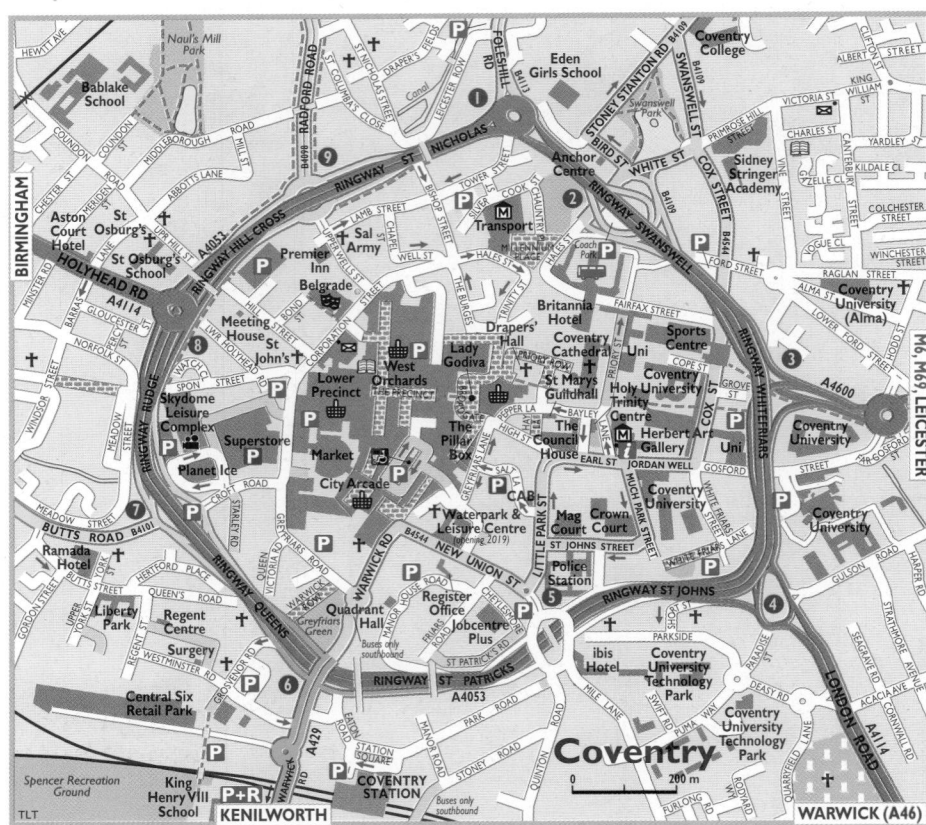

Coventry

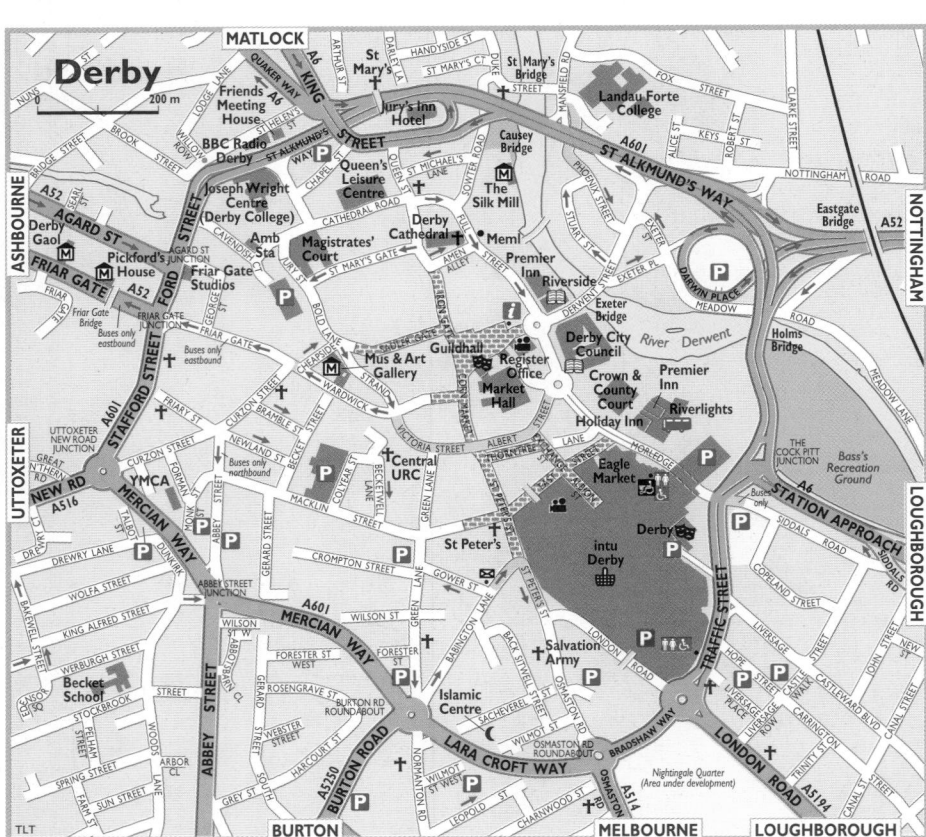

Derby

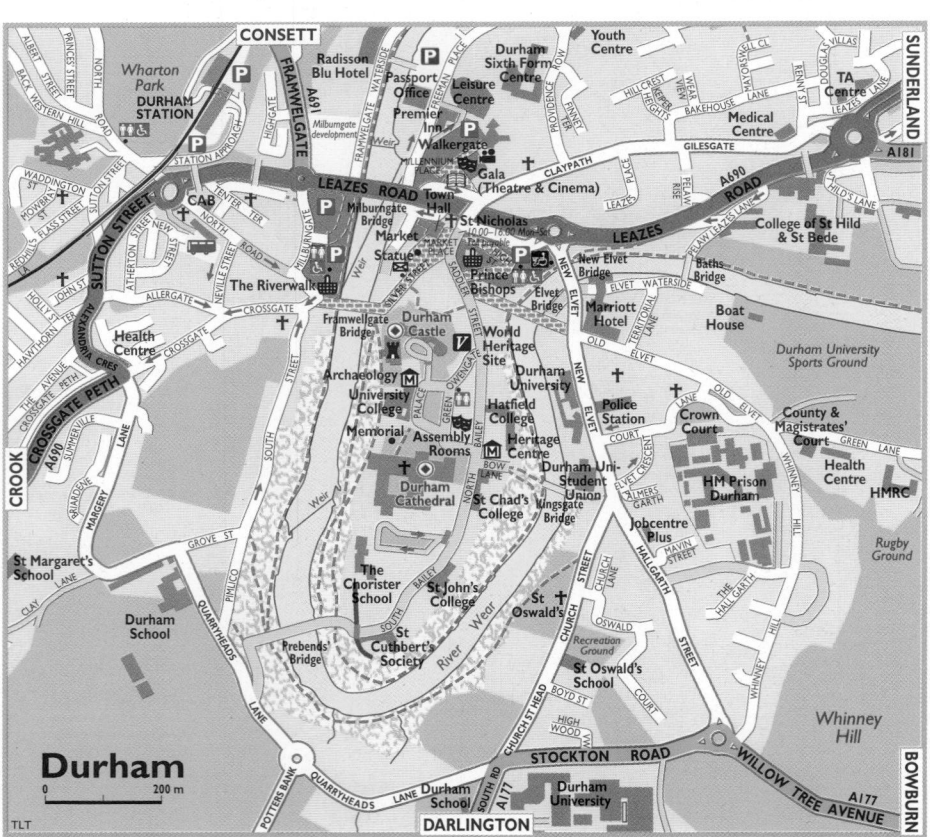

Durham

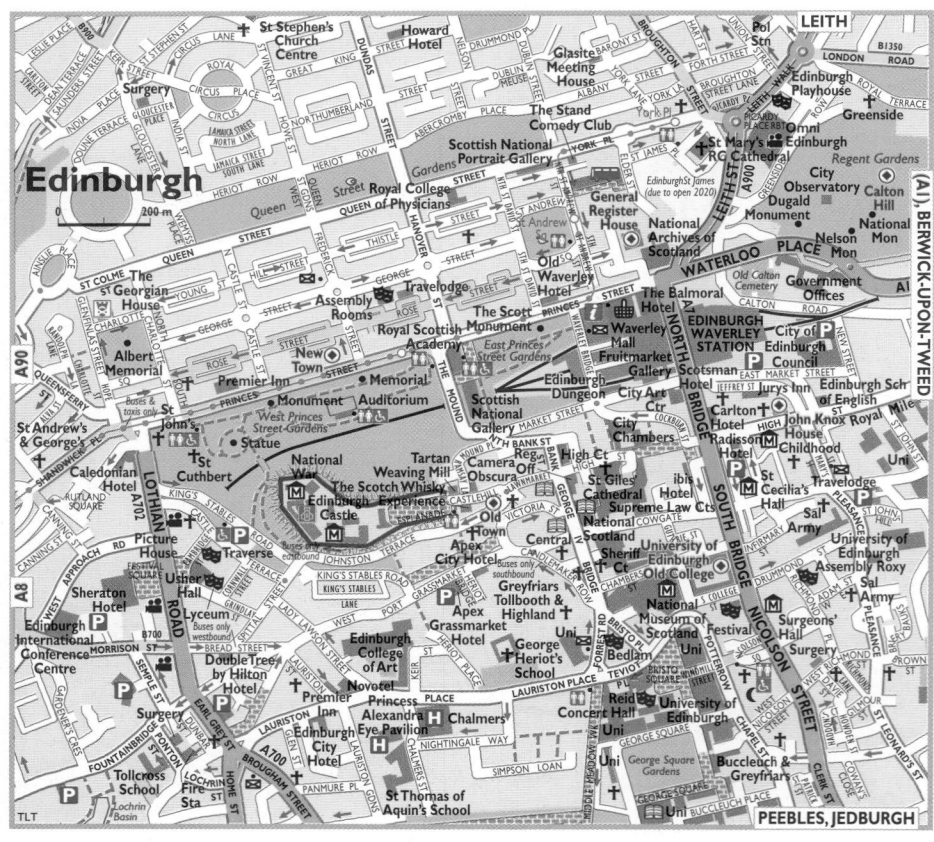

Edinburgh

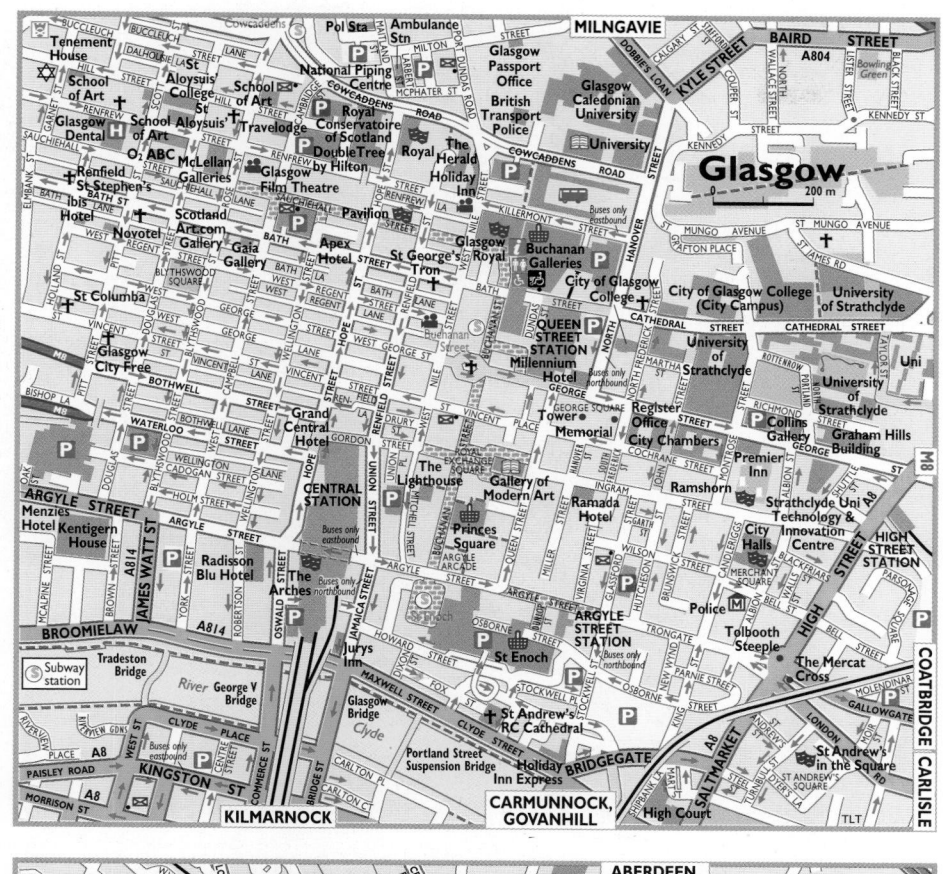

Glasgow

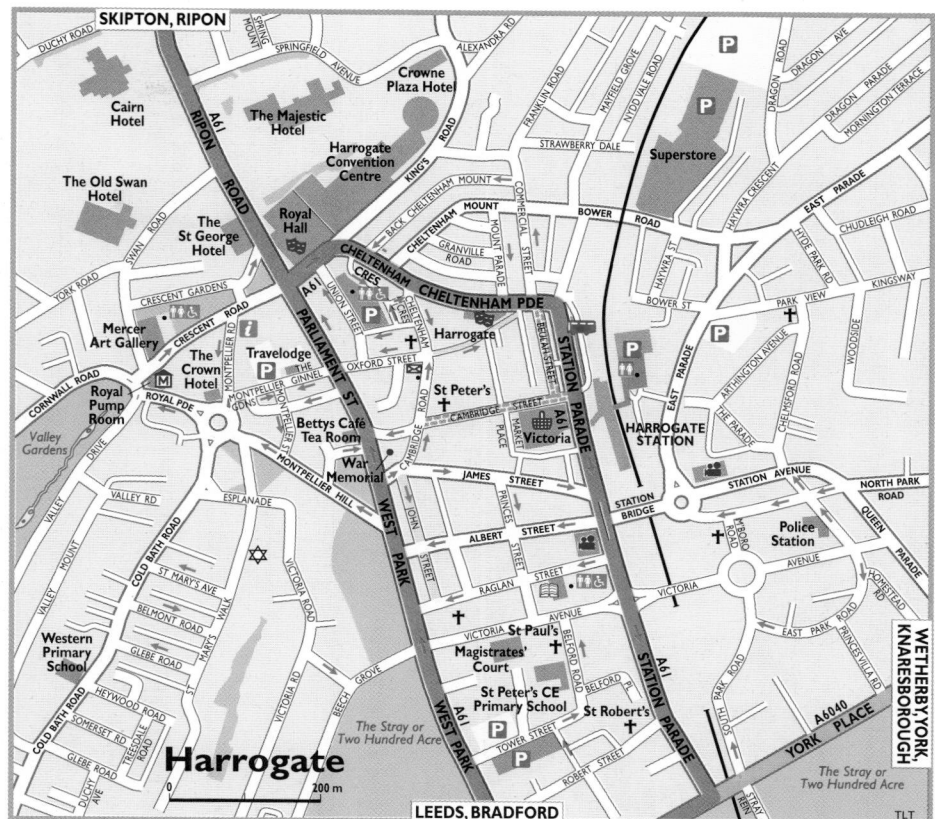

Harrogate

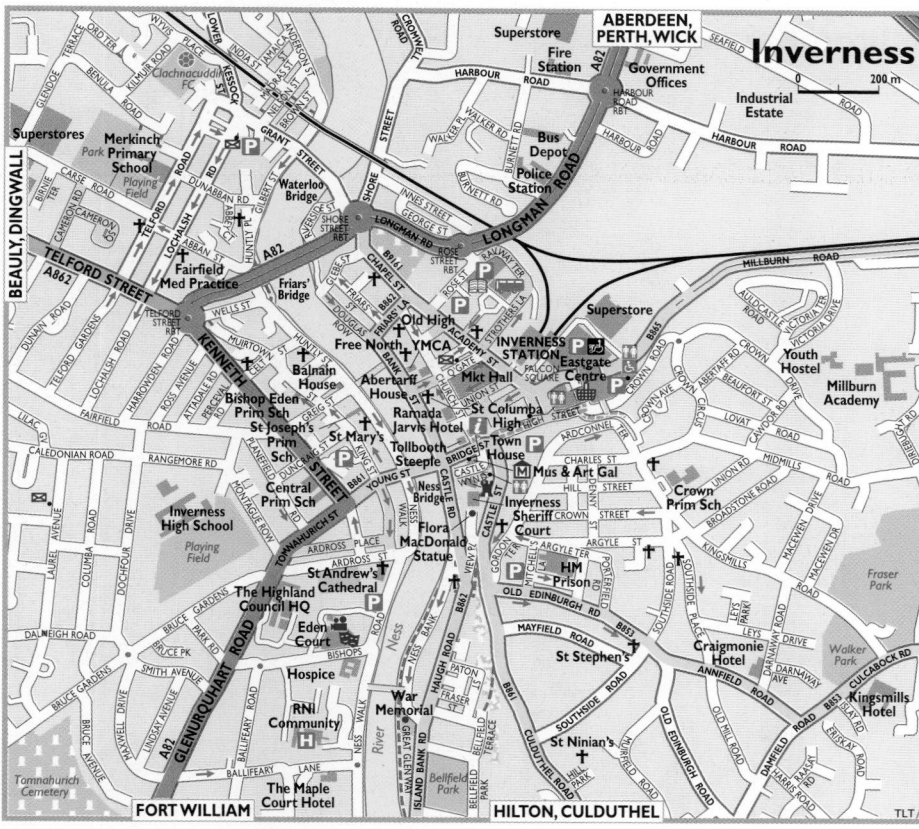

Inverness

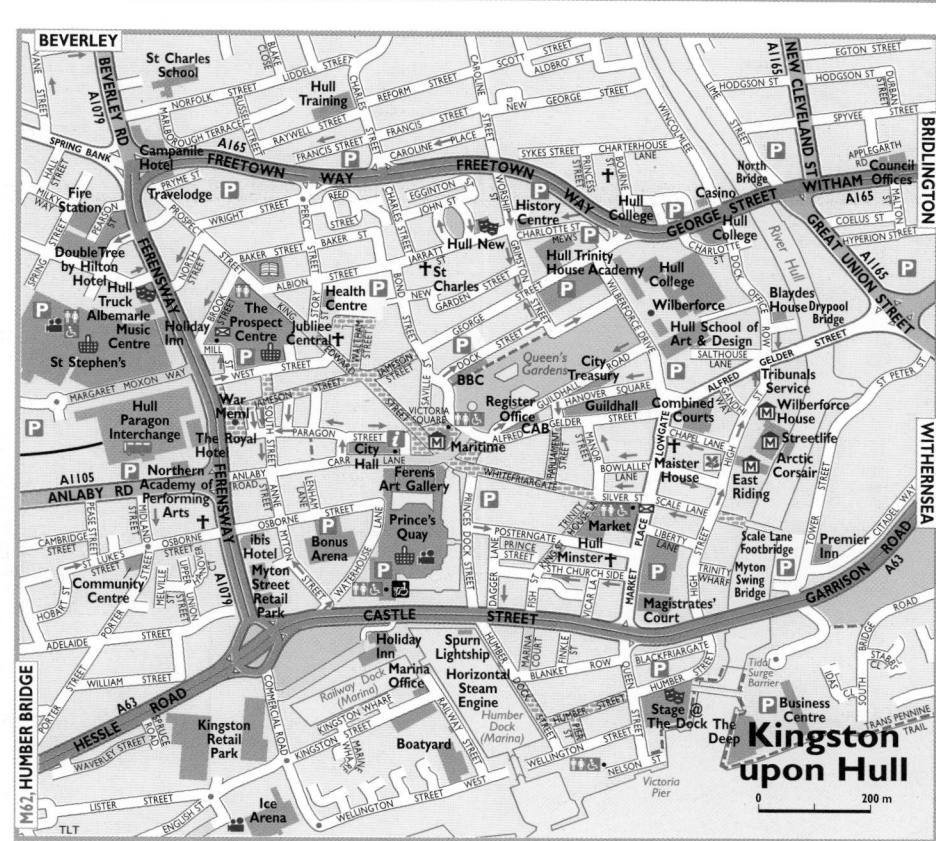

Kingston upon Hull

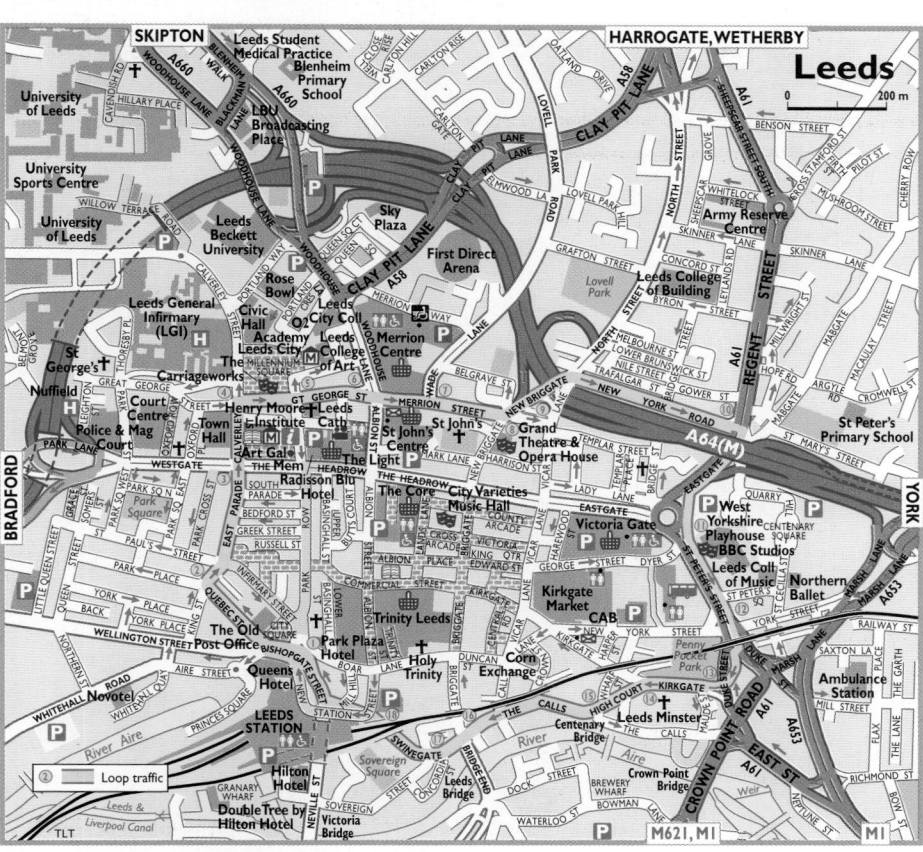

Leeds

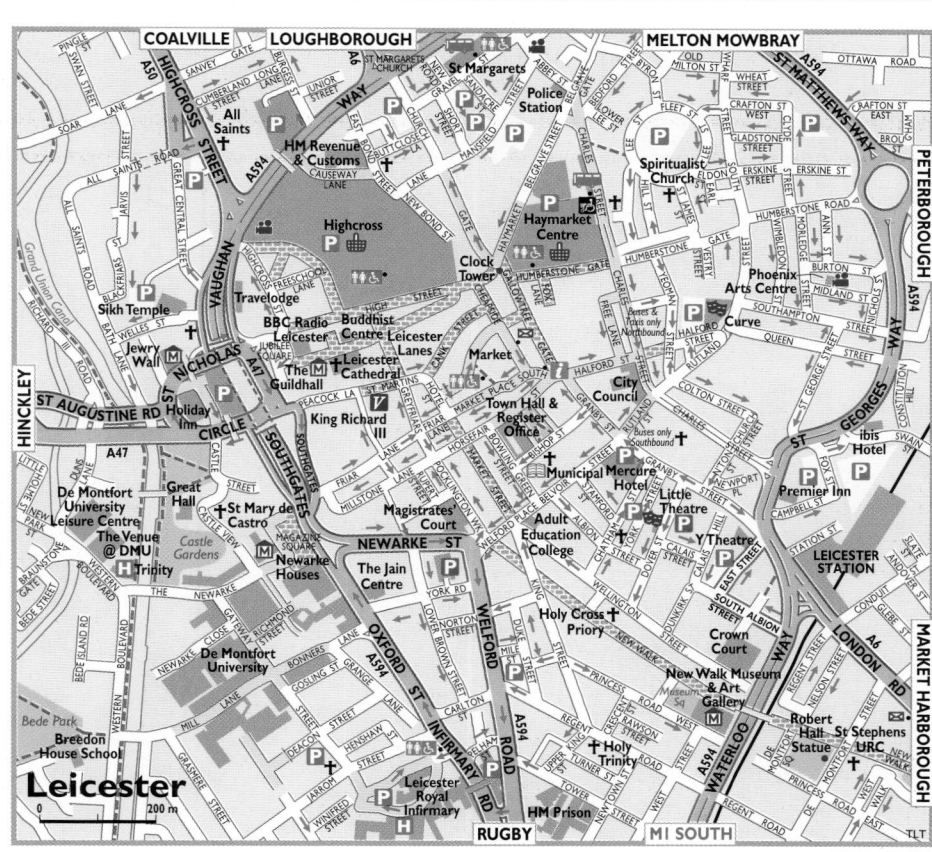

Leicester

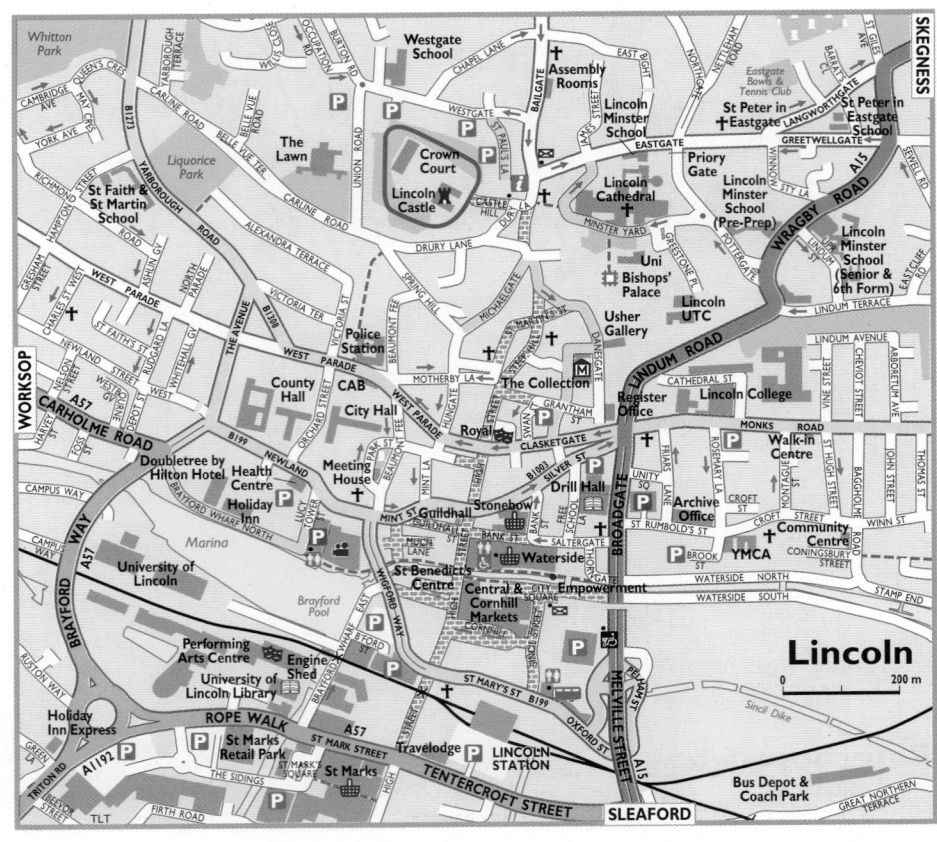

Lincoln

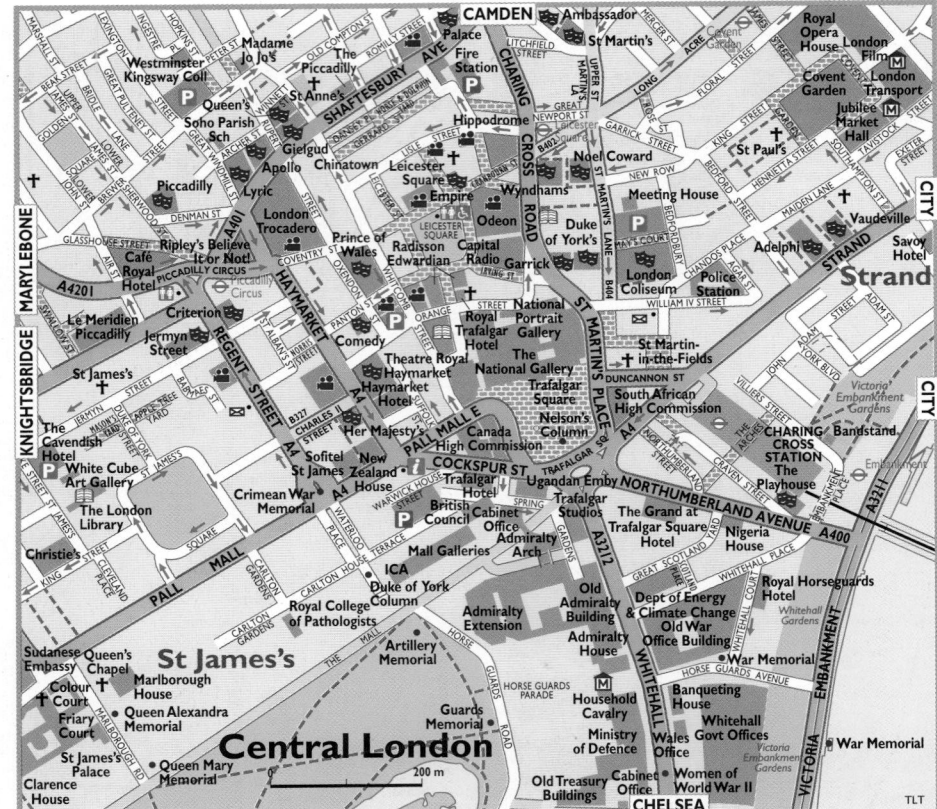

Central London

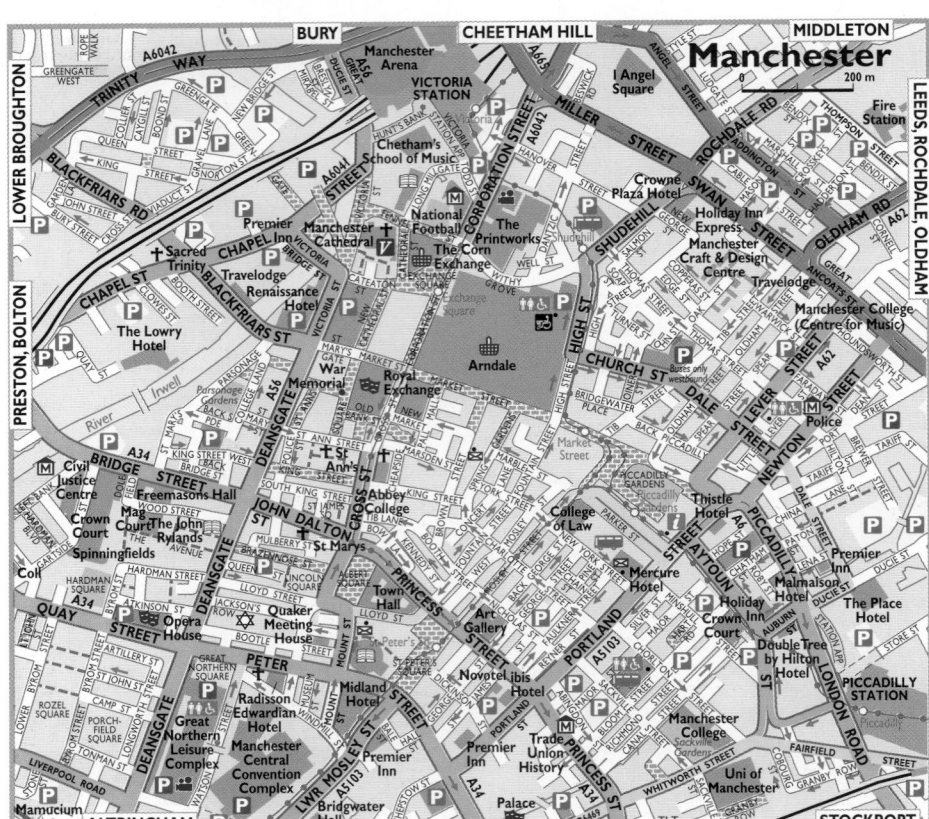

Manchester

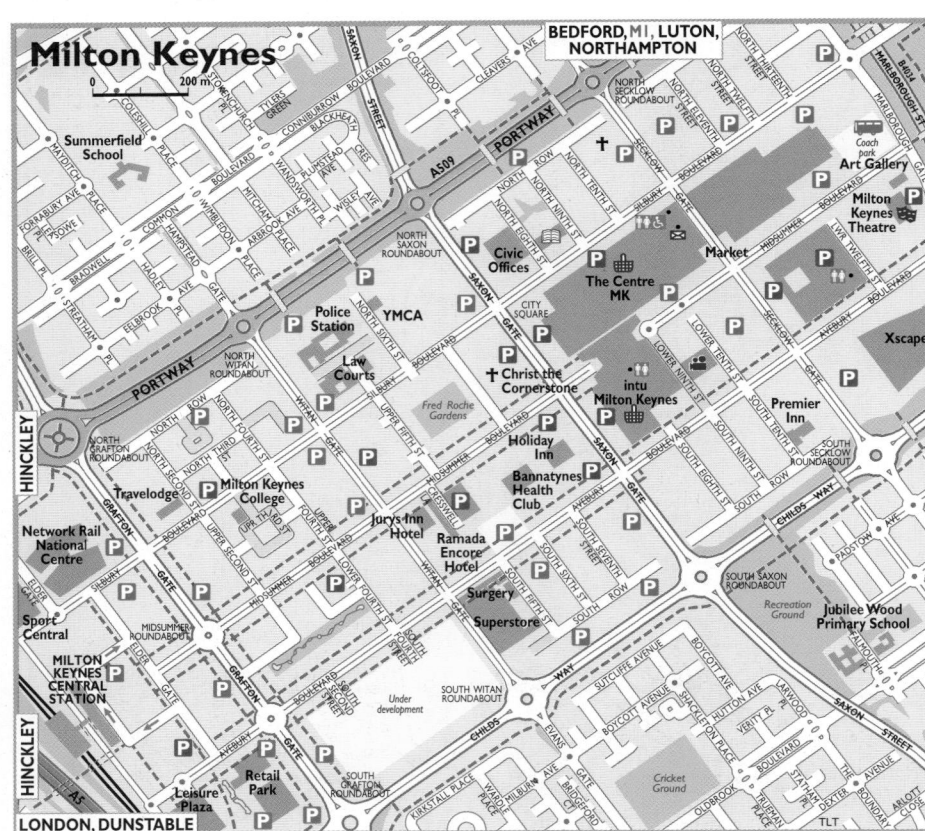

Milton Keynes

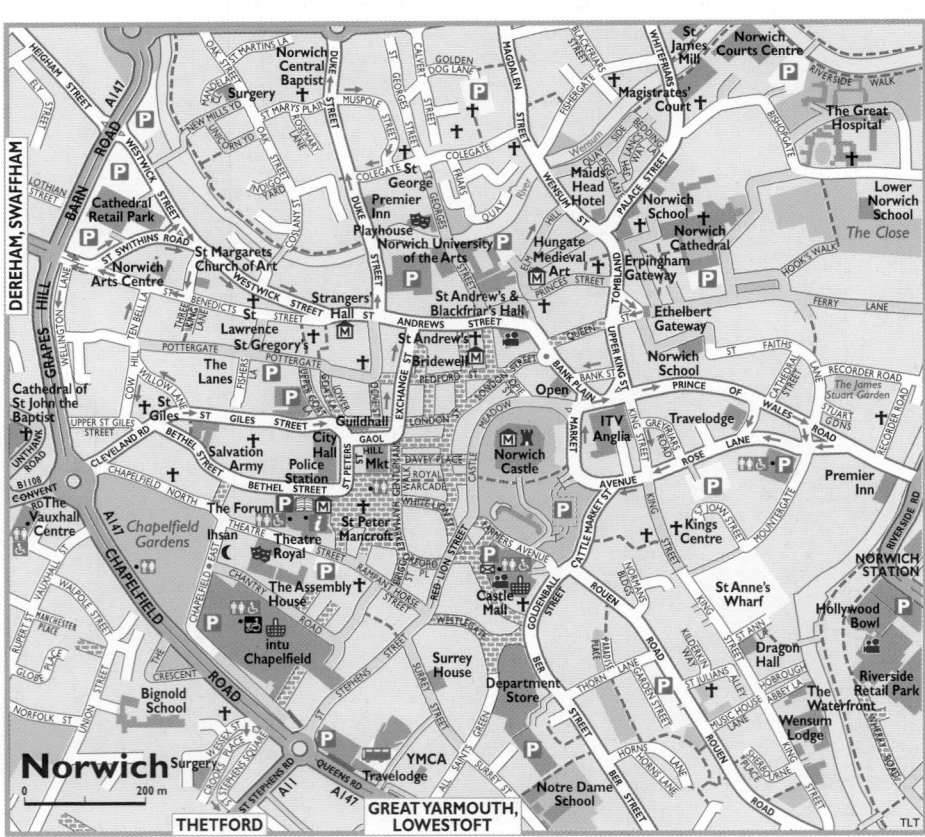

Norwich

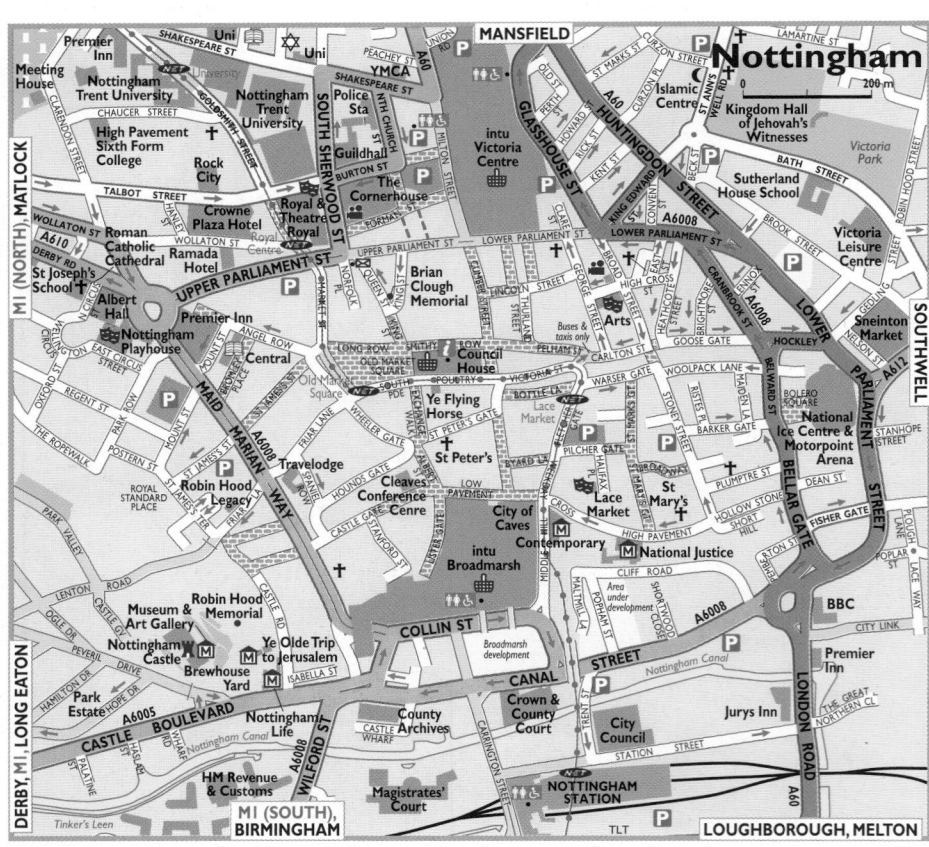

Nottingham

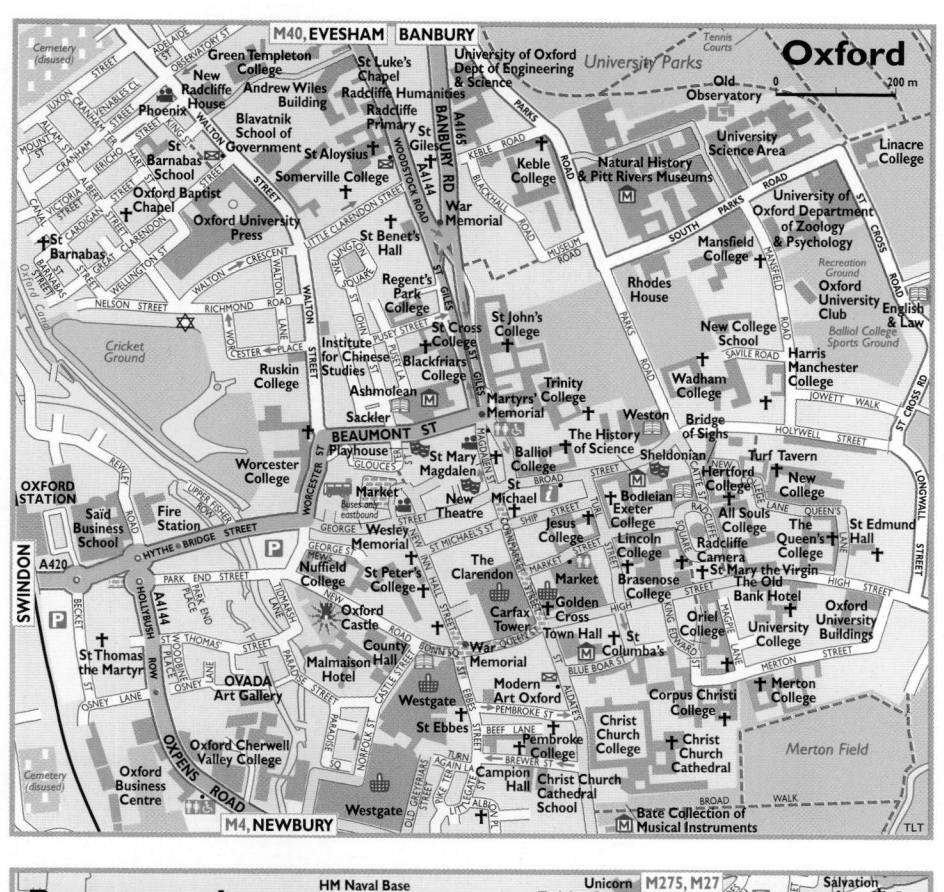

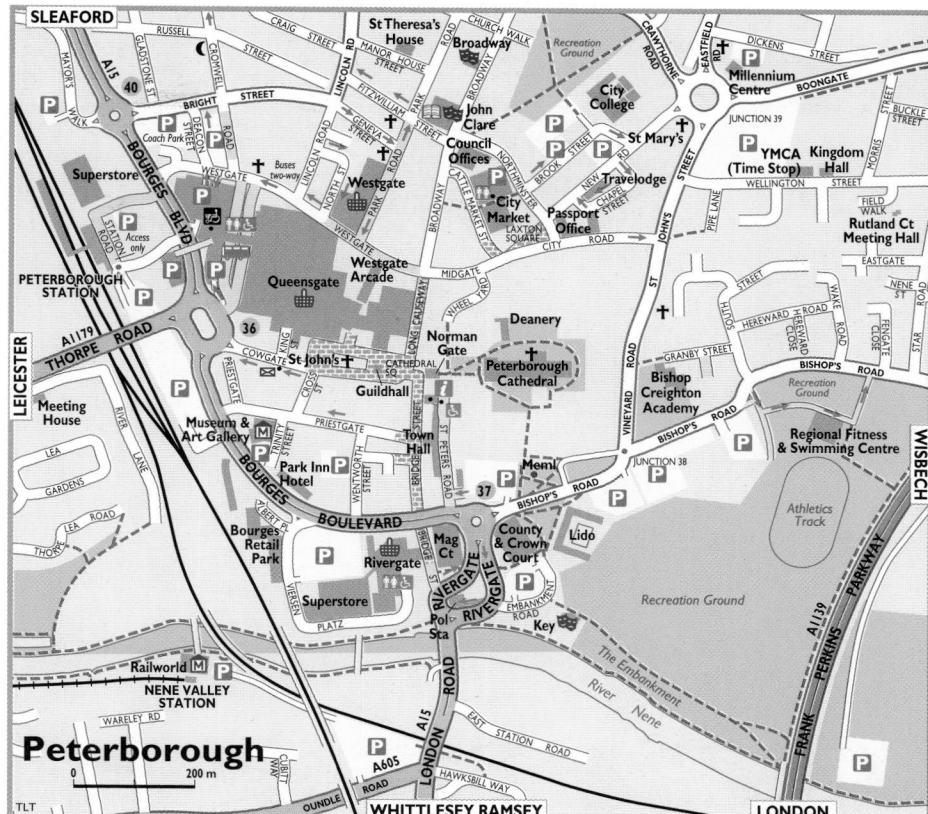

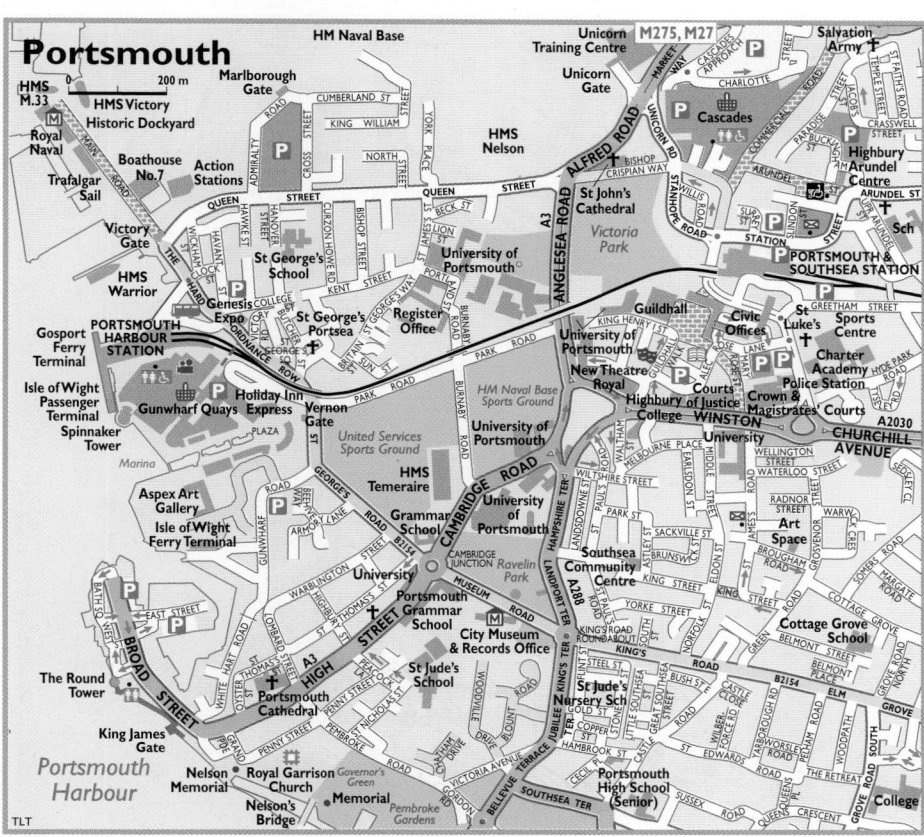

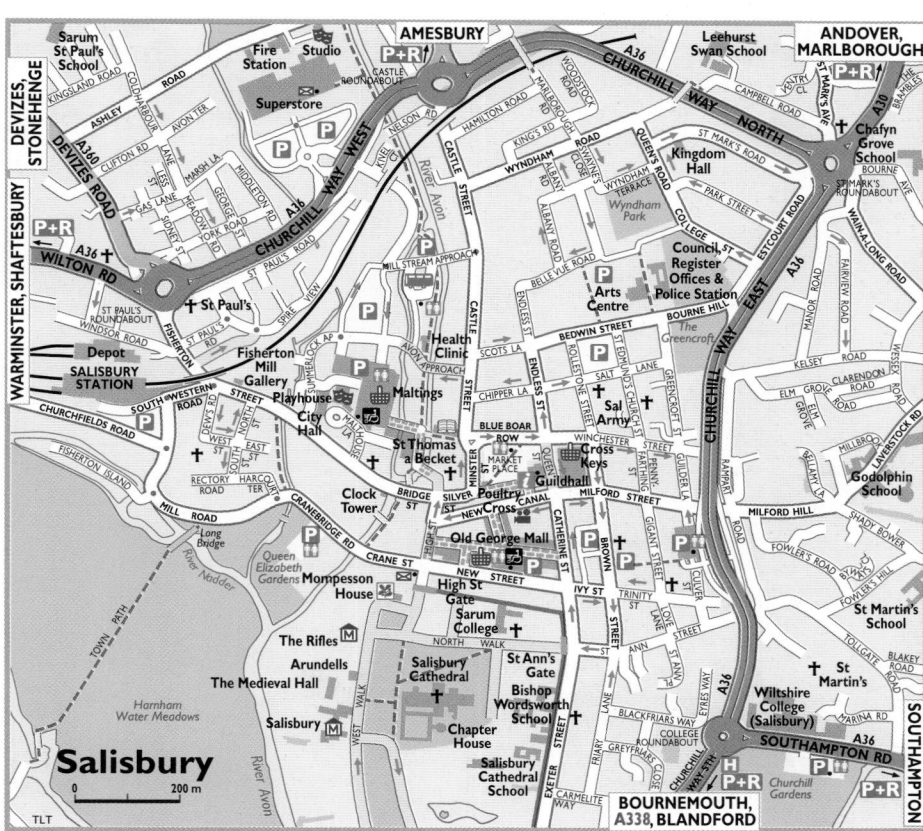

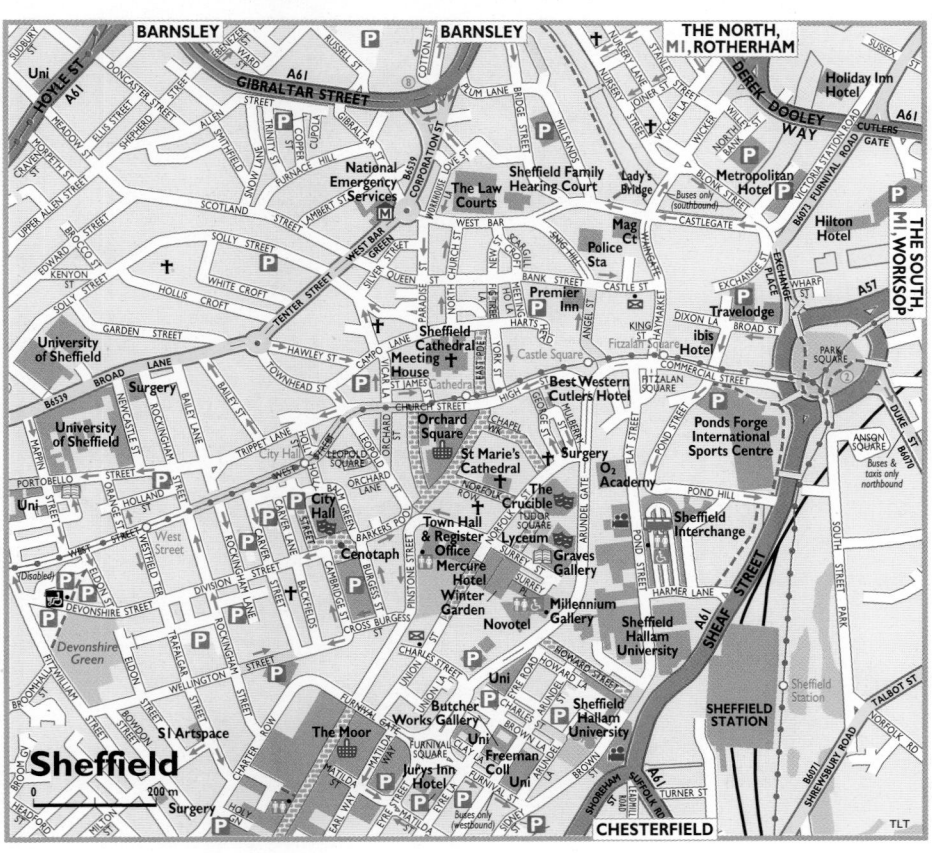

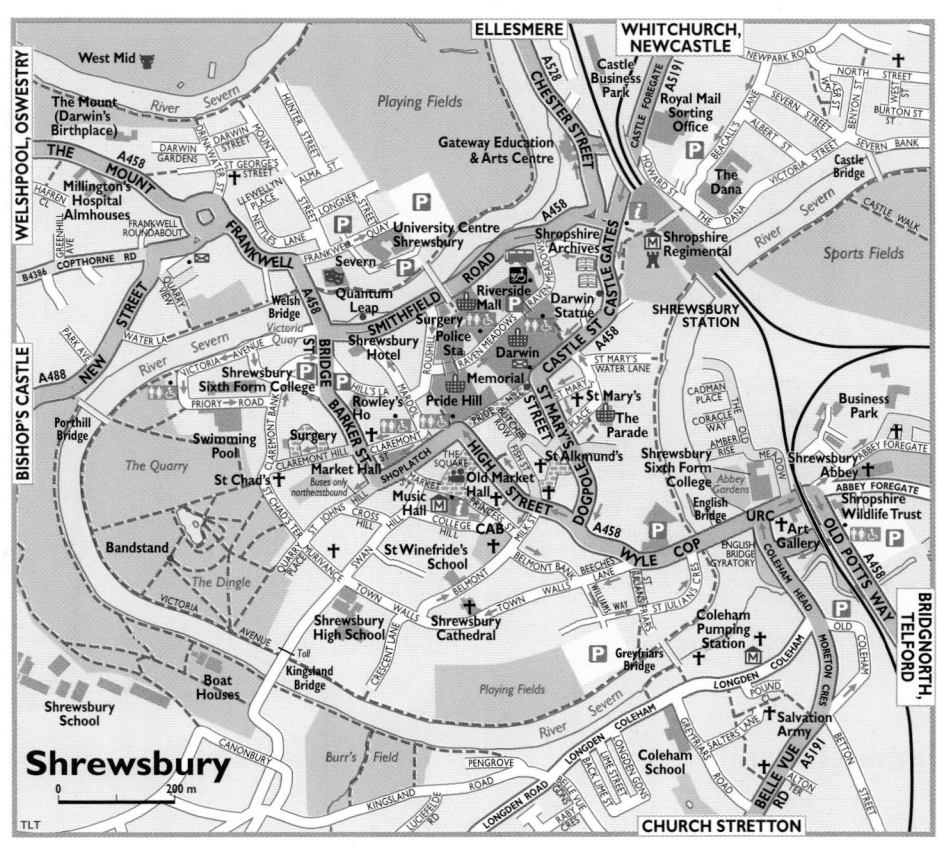

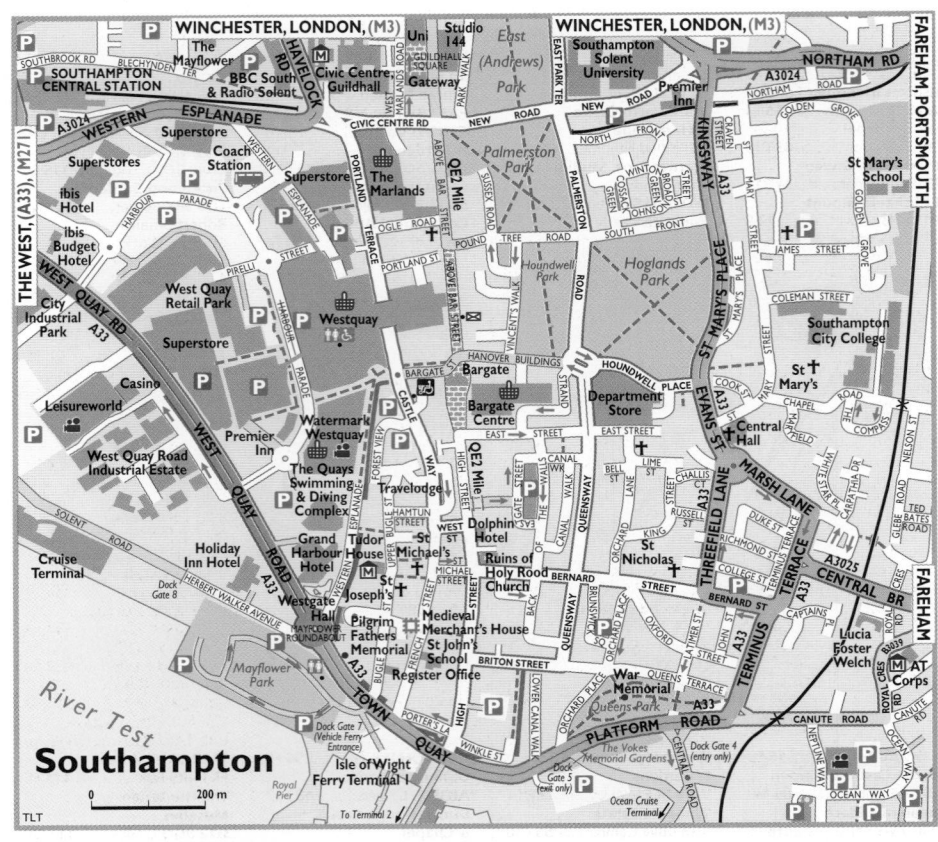

Southampton

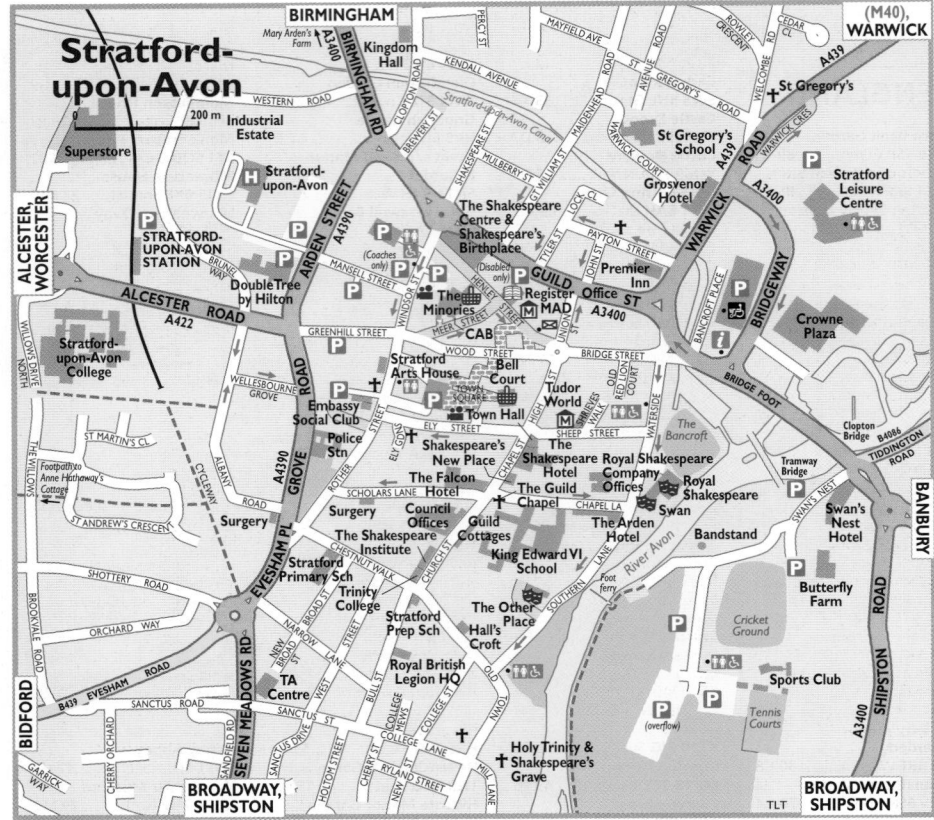

Stratford-upon-Avon

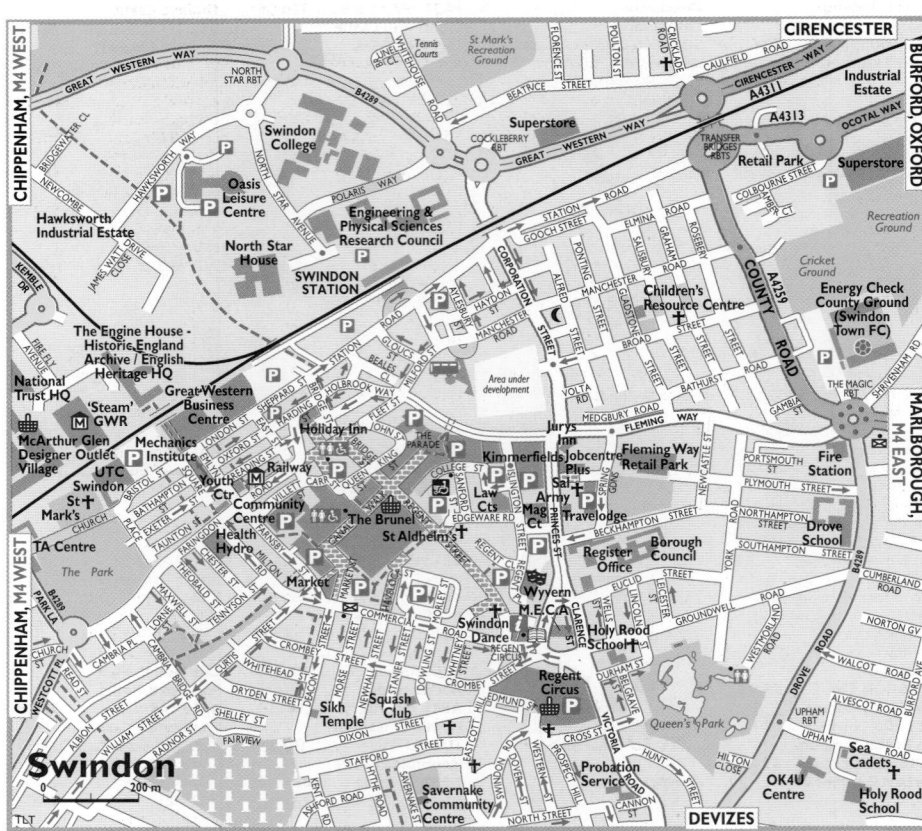

Swindon

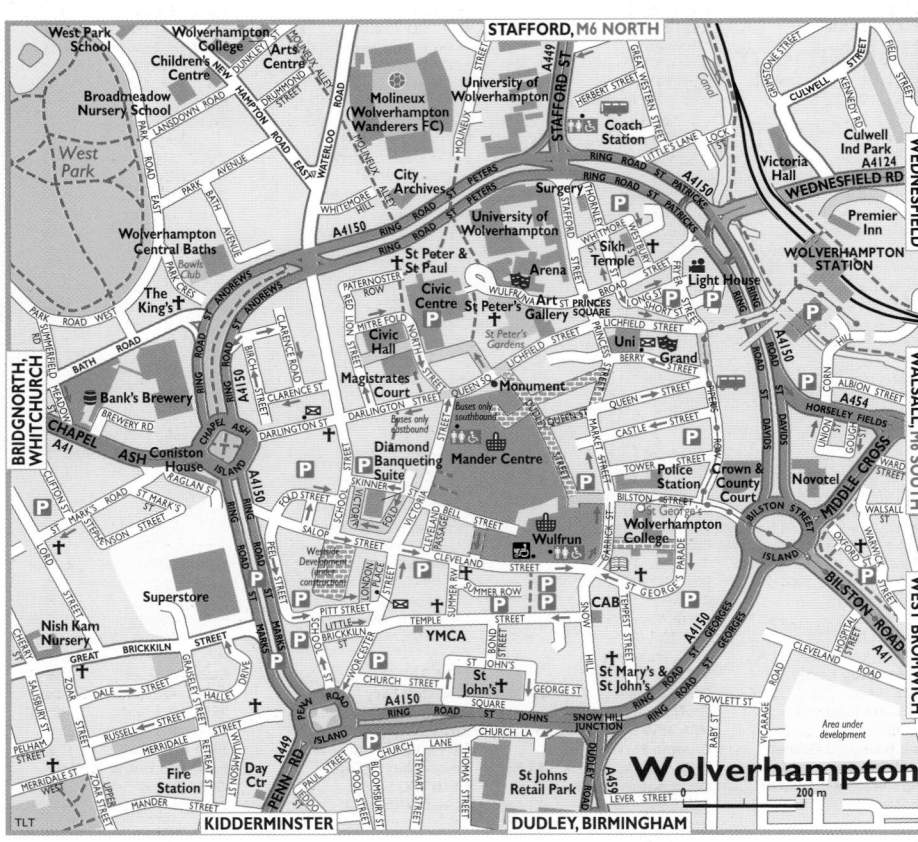

Wolverhampton

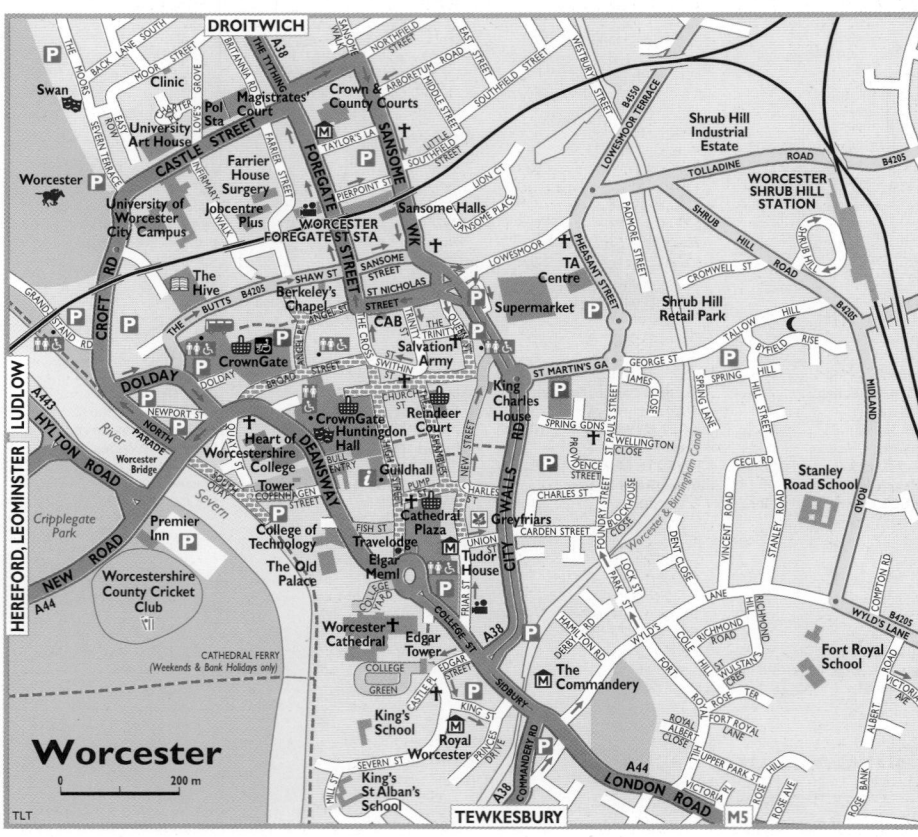

Worcester

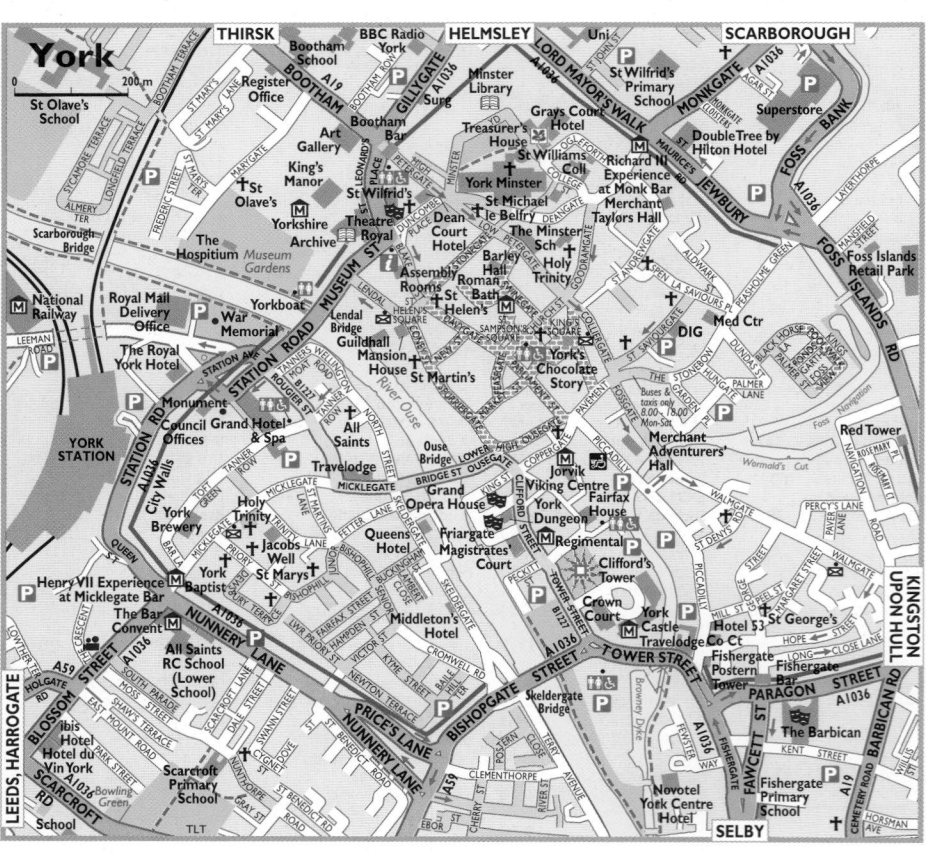

York

ENGLAND

- Acorn Bank Garden CA10 1SP Cumb 89 Q1
- Aldborough Roman Site YO51 9ES N York 85 N2
- Alfriston Clergy House BN26 5TL E Susx 15 P10
- Alton Towers ST10 4DB Staffs 65 K3
- Anglesey Abbey CB25 9EJ Cambs 57 K8
- Anne Hathaway's Cottage CV37 9HH Warwks 53 M9
- Antony House PL11 2QA Cnwll 4 F5
- Appuldurcombe House PO38 3EW IoW 13 J9
- Apsley House W1J 7NT Gt Lon 33 K6
- Arlington Court EX31 4LP Devon 19 M5
- Ascott LU7 0PS Bucks 44 C7
- Ashby-de-la-Zouch Castle LE65 1BR Leics 66 B9
- Athelhampton House & Gardens DT2 7LG Dorset 11 J6
- Attingham Park SY4 4TP Shrops 63 P10
- Audley End House & Gardens CB11 4JF Essex 45 P4
- Avebury Manor & Garden SN8 1RF Wilts 30 C8
- Baconsthorpe Castle NR25 6LN Norfk 70 G4
- Baddesley Clinton Hall B93 0DQ Warwks 53 M6
- Bamburgh Castle NE69 7DF Nthumb 109 K3
- Barnard Castle DL12 8PR Dur 90 H3
- Barrington Court TA19 0NQ Somset 21 N9
- Basildon Park RG8 9NR W Berk 31 M7
- Bateman's TN19 7DS E Susx 16 B6
- Battle of Britain Memorial Flight Visitor Centre LN4 4SY Lincs 80 E12
- Beamish Museum DH9 0RG Dur 100 G7
- Beatrix Potter Gallery LA22 0NS Cumb 89 K7
- Beaulieu SO42 7ZN Hants 12 F4
- Belton House NG32 2LS Lincs 67 M4
- Belvoir Castle NG32 1PE Leics 67 K5
- Bembridge Windmill PO35 5SQ IoW 13 L7
- Beningbrough Hall & Gardens YO30 1DD N York 85 Q3
- Benthall Hall TF12 5RX Shrops 64 C11
- Berkeley Castle GL13 9PJ Gloucs 29 L3
- Berrington Hall HR6 0DW Herefs 51 N8
- Berry Pomeroy Castle TQ9 6LJ Devon 5 P4
- Beth Chatto Gardens CO7 7DB Essex 47 J7
- Biddulph Grange Garden ST8 7SD Staffs 76 G11
- Bishop's Waltham Palace SO32 1DH Hants 25 J10
- Blackpool Zoo FY3 8PP Bpool 82 H8
- Blenheim Palace OX20 1PX Oxon 43 J8
- Blickling Estate NR11 6NF Norfk 70 H6
- Blue John Cavern S33 8WA Derbys 77 L7
- Bodiam Castle TN32 5UA E Susx 16 D6
- Bolsover Castle S44 6PR Derbys 78 D9
- Boscobel House ST19 9AR Staffs 64 F10
- Bovington Tank Museum BH20 6JG Dorset 11 K7
- Bowes Castle DL12 9LD Dur 90 G4
- Bradford Industrial Museum BD2 3HP W York 85 J8
- Bradley Manor TQ12 6BN Devon 8 F10
- Bramber Castle BN44 3WW W Susx 14 H8
- Brinkburn Priory NE65 8AR Nthumb 109 J10
- Bristol Zoo Gardens BS8 3HA Bristl 28 H7
- Brockhampton Estate WR6 5TB Herefs 52 C9
- Brough Castle CA17 4EJ Cumb 90 C4
- Buckfast Abbey TQ11 0EE Devon 5 M3
- Buckingham Palace SW1A 1AA Gt Lon 33 K6
- Buckland Abbey PL20 6EY Devon 4 G3
- Buscot Park SN7 8BU Oxon 30 F3
- Byland Abbey YO61 4BD N York 92 B11
- Cadbury World B30 1JR Birm 53 K4
- Calke Abbey DE73 7LE Derbys 66 B7
- Canons Ashby House NN11 3SD Nhants 54 F10
- Canterbury Cathedral CT1 2EH Kent 35 L10
- Carisbrooke Castle PO30 1XY IoW 12 H7
- Carlyle's House SW3 5HL Gt Lon 33 K7
- Castle Drogo EX6 6PB Devon 8 D7
- Castle Howard YO60 7DA N York 86 D1
- Castle Rising Castle PE31 6AH Norfk 69 M7
- Charlecote Park CV35 9ER Warwks 53 N9
- Chartwell TN16 1PS Kent 33 N12
- Chastleton House GL56 0SU Oxon 42 F6
- Chatsworth DE45 1PP Derbys 77 N9
- Chedworth Roman Villa GL54 3LJ Gloucs 42 B9
- Chessington World of Adventures KT9 2NE Gt Lon 32 H10
- Chester Cathedral CH1 2HU Ches W 75 L10
- Chester Zoo CH2 1EU Ches W 75 L9
- Chesters Roman Fort & Museum NE46 4EU Nthumb 99 P4
- Chiswick House & Gardens W4 2RP Gt Lon 32 H7
- Chysauster Ancient Village TR20 8XA Cnwll 2 D7
- Claremont Landscape Garden KT10 9JG Surrey 32 G9
- Claydon House MK18 2EY Bucks 43 P6
- Cleeve Abbey TA23 0PS Somset 20 G5
- Clevedon Court BS21 6QU N Som 28 F8
- Cliveden SL6 0JA Bucks 32 C5
- Clouds Hill BH20 7NQ Dorset 11 K6
- Clumber Park S80 3AZ Notts 78 G8
- Colchester Zoo CO3 0SL Essex 46 G7
- Coleridge Cottage TA5 1NQ Somset 21 K5
- Coleton Fishacre TQ6 0EQ Devon 5 Q6
- Compton Castle TQ3 1TA Devon 5 P4
- Conisbrough Castle DN12 3BU Donc 78 E4
- Corbridge Roman Town NE45 5NT Nthumb 100 C5
- Corfe Castle BH20 5EZ Dorset 11 M8
- Corsham Court SN13 0BZ Wilts 29 P8
- Cotehele PL12 6TA Cnwll 4 F3
- Coughton Court B49 5JA Warwks 53 K8
- Courts Garden BA14 6RR Wilts 29 P10
- Cragside NE65 7PX Nthumb 108 H9
- Crealy Adventure Park EX5 1DR Devon 9 J6
- Crich Tramway Village DE4 5DP Derbys 65 Q1
- Croft Castle HR6 9PW Herefs 51 M7
- Croome Park WR8 9JS Worcs 41 P3
- Deddington Castle OX15 0TE Oxon 43 K5
- Didcot Railway Centre OX11 7NJ Oxon 31 L4
- Dover Castle CT16 1HU Kent 17 P2
- Drayton Manor Theme Park B78 3SA Staffs 65 M12
- Dudmaston Estate WV15 6QN Shrops 52 D3
- Dunham Massey WA14 4SJ Traffd 76 D6
- Dunstanburgh Castle NE66 3TT Nthumb 109 L5
- Dunster Castle TA24 6SL Somset 20 F5
- Durham Cathedral DH1 3EH Dur 100 H10
- Dyrham Park SN14 8HY S Glos 29 L7
- East Riddlesden Hall BD20 5EL Brad 84 G7
- Eden Project PL24 2SG Cnwll 3 P4
- Eltham Palace & Gardens SE9 5QE Gt Lon 33 M7
- Emmetts Garden TN14 6BA Kent 33 N12
- Exmoor Zoo EX31 4SG Devon 19 M5
- Farleigh Hungerford Castle BA2 7RS Somset 29 N10
- Farnborough Hall OX17 1DU Warwks 54 C10
- Felbrigg Hall NR11 8PR Norfk 71 J4
- Fenton House & Garden NW3 6SP Gt Lon 33 J5
- Finch Foundry EX20 2NW Devon 8 C6
- Finchale Priory DH1 5SH Dur 100 H9
- Fishbourne Roman Palace PO19 3QR W Susx 13 P4
- Flamingo Land YO17 6UX N York 92 F10
- Forde Abbey TA20 4LU Somset 9 Q4
- Fountains Abbey & Studley Royal HG4 3DY N York 85 K1
- Gawthorpe Hall BB12 8UA Lancs 84 B8
- Gisborough Priory TS14 6HG R & Cl 92 C3
- Glendurgan Garden TR11 5JZ Cnwll 3 J9
- Goodrich Castle HR9 6HY Herefs 41 J7
- Great Chalfield Manor & Garden SN12 8NH Wilts 29 P9
- Great Coxwell Barn SN7 7LZ Oxon 30 F3
- Greenway TQ5 0ES Devon 5 P6
- Haddon Hall DE45 1LA Derbys 77 N10
- Hailes Abbey GL54 5PB Gloucs 42 B6
- Ham House & Garden TW10 7RS Gt Lon 32 H8
- Hampton Court Palace KT8 9AU Gt Lon 32 H8
- Hanbury Hall WR9 7EA Worcs 52 H8
- Hardwick Hall S44 5QJ Derbys 78 D11
- Hardy's Cottage DT2 8QJ Dorset 10 H6
- Hare Hill SK10 4PY Ches E 76 G8
- Hatchlands Park GU4 7RT Surrey 32 F12
- Heale Gardens SP4 6NU Wilts 23 P6
- Helmsley Castle YO62 5AB N York 92 C10
- Hereford Cathedral HR1 2NG Herefs 40 G4
- Hergest Croft Gardens HR5 3EG Herefs 51 J9
- Hever Castle & Gardens TN8 7NG Kent 15 N2
- Hidcote Manor Garden GL55 6LR Gloucs 42 E3
- Hill Top LA22 0LF Cumb 89 K7
- Hinton Ampner SO24 0LA Hants 25 K8
- Holkham Hall NR23 1AB Norfk 70 C4
- Housesteads Roman Fort NE47 6NN Nthumb 99 M4
- Howletts Wild Animal Park CT4 5EL Kent 35 M11
- Hughenden Manor HP14 4LA Bucks 32 B3
- Hurst Castle SO41 0TP Hants 12 E7
- Hylands House & Park CM2 8WQ Essex 46 B11
- Ickworth IP29 5QE Suffk 58 B8
- Ightham Mote TN15 0NT Kent 33 Q11
- Ironbridge Gorge Museums TF8 7DQ Wrekin 64 C11
- Kedleston Hall DE22 5JH Derbys 65 P4
- Kenilworth Castle & Elizabethan Garden CV8 1NE Warwks 53 P6
- Kenwood House NW3 7JR Gt Lon 33 K5
- Killerton EX5 3LE Devon 8 H5
- King John's Hunting Lodge BS26 2AP Somset 21 P2
- Kingston Lacy BH21 4EA Dorset 11 N4
- Kirby Hall NN17 3EN Nhants 55 M2
- Knightshayes Court EX16 7RQ Devon 20 E10
- Knole House TN13 1HU Kent 33 P11
- Knowsley Safari Park L34 4AN Knows 75 M5
- Lacock Abbey SN15 2LG Wilts 29 Q8
- Lamb House TN31 7ES E Susx 16 G7
- Lanhydrock House PL30 5AD Cnwll 3 Q2
- Launceston Castle PL15 7DR Cnwll 7 L8
- Leeds Castle ME17 1PB Kent 34 E11
- Legoland SL4 4AY W&M 32 D7
- Lindisfarne Castle TD15 2SH Nthumb 109 J1
- Lindisfarne Priory TD15 2RX Nthumb 109 J1
- Little Moreton Hall CW12 4SD Ches E 76 F11
- Liverpool Cathedral L1 7AZ Lpool 75 K6
- London Zoo ZSL NW1 4RY Gt Lon 33 K6
- Longleat BA12 7NW Wilts 22 H5
- Loseley Park GU3 1HS Surrey 14 D1
- Ludgershall Castle SP11 9QR Wilts 24 D3
- Lydford Castle EX20 4BH Devon 7 P8
- Lyme Park, House & Garden SK12 2NX Ches E 76 H7
- Lytes Cary Manor TA11 7HU Somset 22 C8
- Lyveden New Bield PE8 5AT Nhants 55 N4
- Maiden Castle DT2 9PP Dorset 10 G7
- Mapledurham Estate RG4 7TR Oxon 31 N7
- Marble Hill House TW1 2NL Gt Lon 32 H7
- Marwell Zoo SO21 1JH Hants 24 H9
- Melford Hall CO10 9AA Suffk 46 F2
- Merseyside Maritime Museum L3 4AQ Lpool 75 K6
- Minster Lovell Hall OX29 0RR Oxon 42 G9
- Mompesson House SP1 2EL Wilts 23 P7
- Monk Bretton Priory S71 5QD Barns 78 B2
- Montacute House TA15 6XP Somset 22 C10
- Morwellham Quay PL19 8JL Devon 4 G3
- Moseley Old Hall WV10 7HY Staffs 64 H11
- Mottisfont SO51 0LP Hants 24 E8
- Mottistone Manor Garden PO30 4ED IoW 12 G8
- Mount Grace Priory DL6 3JG N York 91 Q7
- National Maritime Museum SE10 9NF Gt Lon 33 M7
- National Motorcycle Museum B92 0ED Solhll 53 M4
- National Portrait Gallery WC2H 0HE Gt Lon 33 K6
- National Railway Museum YO26 4XJ York 86 B5
- National Space Centre LE4 5NS C Leic 66 F10
- Natural History Museum SW7 5BD Gt Lon 33 K6
- Needles Old Battery PO39 0JH IoW 12 E8
- Nene Valley Railway PE8 6LR Cambs 56 C1
- Netley Abbey SO31 5FB Hants 12 G3
- Newark Air Museum NG24 2NY Notts 79 L12
- Newtown Old Town Hall PO30 4PA IoW 12 G6
- North Leigh Roman Villa OX29 6QB Oxon 43 J8
- Norwich Cathedral NR1 4DH Norfk 71 J10
- Nostell Priory WF4 1QE Wakefd 85 N11
- Nunnington Hall YO62 5UY N York 92 D11
- Nymans House RH17 6EB W Susx 15 K5
- Old Royal Naval College SE10 9NN Gt Lon 33 M7
- Old Sarum SP1 3SD Wilts 23 P7
- Old Wardour Castle SP3 6RR Wilts 23 K8
- Oliver Cromwell's House CB7 4HF Cambs 57 K4
- Orford Castle IP12 2ND Suffk 59 N10
- Ormesby Hall TS3 0SR R & Cl 92 B3
- Osborne House PO32 6JX IoW 13 J6
- Osterley Park & House TW7 4RB Gt Lon 32 G7
- Overbeck's TQ8 8LW Devon 5 M9
- Oxburgh Hall PE33 9PS Norfk 69 P12
- Packwood House B94 6AT Warwks 53 M6
- Paignton Zoo TQ4 7EU Torbay 5 P5
- Paycocke's House & Garden CO6 1NS Essex 46 E7
- Peckover House & Garden PE13 1JR Cambs 69 J10
- Pendennis Castle TR11 4LP Cnwll 3 K8
- Petworth House & Park GU28 0AE W Susx 14 D6
- Pevensey Castle BN24 5LE E Susx 16 B10
- Peveril Castle S33 8WQ Derbys 77 L7
- Polesden Lacey RH5 6BD Surrey 32 G11
- Portland Castle DT5 1AZ Dorset 10 G10
- Portsmouth Historic Dockyard PO1 3LJ C Port 13 L5
- Powderham Castle EX6 8JQ Devon 8 H8
- Prior Park Landscape Garden BA2 5AH BaNES 29 M9
- Prudhoe Castle NE42 6NA Nthumb 100 E5
- Quarry Bank Mill & Styal SK9 4LA Ches E 76 F7
- Quebec House TN16 1TD Kent 33 N11
- Ramsey Abbey Gatehouse PE17 1DH Cambs 56 F4
- Reculver Towers & Roman Fort CT6 6SU Kent 35 M8
- Red House DA6 8JF Gt Lon 33 N7
- Restormel Castle PL22 0EE Cnwll 3 Q2
- Richborough Roman Fort CT13 9JW Kent 35 P10
- Richmond Castle DL10 4QW N York 91 K6
- Roche Abbey S66 8NW Rothm 78 E6
- Rochester Castle ME1 1SW Medway 34 C8
- Rockbourne Roman Villa SP6 3PG Hants 23 P10
- Roman Baths & Pump Room BA1 1LZ BaNES 29 M9
- Royal Botanic Gardens, Kew TW9 3AB Gt Lon 32 H7
- Royal Observatory Greenwich SE10 8XJ Gt Lon 33 M7
- Rufford Old Hall L40 1SG Lancs 83 L12
- Runnymede SL4 2JJ W & M 32 E8
- Rushton Triangular Lodge NN14 1RP Nhants 55 L4
- Rycote Chapel OX9 2PA Oxon 43 P10
- St Leonard's Tower ME19 6PE Kent 34 B11
- St Michael's Mount TR17 0HT Cnwll 2 E8
- St Paul's Cathedral EC4M 8AD Gt Lon 33 L6
- Salisbury Cathedral SP1 2EJ Wilts 23 P7
- Saltram PL7 1UH C Plym 4 H5
- Sandham Memorial Chapel RG20 9JT Hants 31 K10
- Sandringham House & Grounds PE35 6EH Norfk 69 N6
- Saxtead Green Post Mill IP13 9QQ Suffk 59 K8
- Scarborough Castle YO11 1HY N York 93 L9
- Science Museum SW7 2DD Gt Lon 33 K6
- Scotney Castle TN3 8JN Kent 16 B4
- Shaw's Corner AL6 9BX Herts 44 H8
- Sheffield Park & Garden TN22 3QX E Susx 15 M6
- Sherborne Old Castle DT9 3SA Dorset 22 E10
- Sissinghurst Castle Garden TN17 2AB Kent 16 E3
- Sizergh Castle & Garden LA8 8AE Cumb 89 M9
- Smallhythe Place TN30 7NG Kent 16 F5
- Snowshill Manor & Garden WR12 7JU Gloucs 42 C5
- Souter Lighthouse SR6 7NH S Tyne 101 K5
- Speke Hall, Garden & Estate L24 1XD Lpool 75 M7
- Spinnaker Tower, Emirates PO1 3TT C Port 13 L5
- Stokesay Castle SY7 9AH Shrops 51 M4
- Stonehenge SP4 7DE Wilts 23 P5
- Stourhead BA12 6QD Wilts 22 H6
- Stowe Gardens MK18 5EQ Bucks 43 P4
- Sudbury Hall DE6 5HT Derbys 65 M6
- Sulgrave Manor OX17 2SD Nhants 43 M3
- Sunnycroft TF1 2DR Wrekin 64 C10
- Sutton Hoo IP12 3DJ Suffk 59 K10
- Sutton House E9 6JQ Gt Lon 33 L5
- Tate Britain SW1P 4RG Gt Lon 33 K6
- Tate Liverpool L3 4BB Lpoo 75 K6
- Tate Modern SE1 9TG Gt Lon 33 K6
- Tattershall Castle LN4 4LR Lincs 80 D12
- Tatton Park WA16 6QN Ches E 76 D7
- The British Library NW1 2DB Gt Lon 33 K6
- The British Museum WC1B 3DG Gt Lon 33 K6
- The Lost Gardens of Heligan PL26 6EN Cnwll 3 N5
- The Lowry M50 3AZ Salfd 76 E4
- The National Gallery WC2N 5DN Gt Lon 33 K6
- The Vyne RG24 9HL Hants 31 N11
- The Weir Garden HR4 7QF Herefs 40 F3
- Thornton Abbey & Gatehouse DN39 6TU N Linc 87 L11
- Thorpe Park KT16 8PN Surrey 32 E8
- Tilbury Fort RM18 7NR Thurr 34 B7
- Tintagel Castle PL34 0HE Cnwll 6 F7
- Tintinhull Garden BA22 8PZ Somset 22 C9
- Totnes Castle TQ9 5NU Devon 5 N4
- Tower of London EC3N 4AB Gt Lon 33 L6
- Townend LA23 1LB Cumb 89 L6
- Treasurer's House YO1 7JL York 86 B5
- Trelissick Garden TR3 6QL Cnwll 3 K6
- Trengwainton Garden TR20 8RZ Cnwll 2 C8
- Trerice TR8 4PG Cnwll 3 L3
- Twycross Zoo CV9 3PX Leics 65 P11
- Upnor Castle ME2 4XG Medway 34 D8
- Uppark House & Garden GU31 5QR W Susx 25 N10
- Upton House & Garden OX15 6HT Warwks 42 H3
- Victoria & Albert Museum SW7 2RL Gt Lon 33 K6
- Waddesdon Manor HP18 0JH Bucks 43 Q8
- Wakehurst Place RH17 6TN W Susx 15 L4
- Wall Roman Site WS14 0AW Staffs 65 L11
- Wallington NE61 4AR Nthumb 100 C1
- Walmer Castle & Gardens CT14 7LJ Kent 35 Q12
- Warkworth Castle & Hermitage NE65 0UJ Nthumb 109 L8
- Warner Bros. Studio Tour London WD25 7LS Herts 32 F2
- Warwick Castle CV34 4QU Warwks 53 P7
- Washington Old Hall NE38 7LE Sundld 101 J7
- Waterperry Gardens OX33 1LG Oxon 43 N10
- Weeting Castle IP27 0RQ Norfk 57 P3
- Wenlock Priory TF13 6HS Shrops 64 B12
- West Midland Safari & Leisure Park DY12 1LF Worcs 52 E5
- West Wycombe Park HP14 3AJ Bucks 32 B3
- Westbury Court Garden GL14 1PD Gloucs 41 L9
- Westminster Abbey SW1P 3PA Gt Lon 33 K6
- Westonbirt Arboretum GL8 8QS Gloucs 29 N4
- Westwood Manor BA15 2AF Wilts 29 N10
- Whipsnade Zoo ZSL LU6 2LF C Beds 44 E8
- Whitby Abbey YO22 4JT N York 93 J4
- Wicksteed Park NN15 6NJ Nhants 55 L5
- Wightwick Manor & Gardens WV6 8EE Wolves 52 F1
- Wimpole Estate SG8 0BW Cambs 56 F10
- Winchester Cathedral SO23 9LS Hants 24 H7
- Winchester City Mill SO23 0EJ Hants 24 H7
- Windsor Castle SL4 1NJ W & M 32 D7
- Winkworth Arboretum GU8 4AD Surrey 14 E3
- Wisley RHS Garden GU23 6QB Surrey 32 F10
- Woburn Safari Park MK17 9QN C Beds 44 D5
- Wookey Hole Caves BA5 1BA Somset 22 C4
- Woolsthorpe Manor NG33 5PD Lincs 67 M7
- Wordsworth House CA13 9RX Cumb 97 M12
- Wrest Park MK45 4HR C Beds 44 F4
- Wroxeter Roman City SY5 6PR Shrops 63 P10
- WWT Arundel Wetland Centre BN18 9PB W Susx 14 E9
- WWT Slimbridge Wetland Centre GL2 7BT Gloucs 41 L10
- Yarmouth Castle PO41 0PB IoW 12 F7
- York Minster YO1 7HH York 86 B5

SCOTLAND

- Aberdour Castle KY3 0SL Fife 115 M4
- Alloa Tower FK10 1PP Clacks 114 G3
- Arbroath Abbey DD11 1EG Angus 125 M4
- Arduaine Garden PA34 4XQ Ag & B 120 E10
- Bachelors' Club KA5 5RB S Ayrs 104 H4
- Balmoral Castle Grounds AB35 5TB Abers 131 N5
- Balvenie Castle AB55 4DH Moray 139 P7
- Bannockburn Battlefield & Heritage Centre FK7 0LJ Stirlg 114 E3
- Blackness Castle EH49 7NH Falk 115 J5
- Blair Castle PH18 5TL P & K 130 F11
- Bothwell Castle G71 8BL S Lans 114 C9
- Branklyn Garden PH2 7BB P & K 124 C8
- Brodick Castle, Garden & Country Park KA27 8HY N Ayrs 103 Q2
- Brodie Castle IV36 2TE Moray 138 H4
- Broughton House & Garden DG6 4JX D & G 96 D8
- Burleigh Castle KY13 9GG P & K 124 C11
- Caerlaverock Castle DG1 4RU D & G 97 L5
- Cardoness Castle DG7 2EH D & G 96 C7
- Castle Campbell & Garden FK14 7PP Clacks 114 H1
- Castle Fraser, Garden & Estate AB51 7LD Abers 132 H2
- Castle Kennedy & Gardens DG9 8BX D & G 94 G6
- Castle Menzies PH15 2JD P & K 123 L3
- Corgarff Castle AB36 8YP Abers 131 N3
- Craigievar Castle AB33 8JF Abers 132 E2
- Craigmillar Castle EH16 4SY C Edin 115 P7
- Crarae Garden PA32 8YA Ag & B 112 E2
- Crathes Castle & Garden AB31 5QJ Abers 132 H5
- Crichton Castle EH37 5XA Mdloth 115 Q9
- Crossraguel Abbey KA19 8HQ S Ayrs 104 E8
- Culloden Battlefield IV2 5EU Highld 138 D7
- Culross Palace KY12 8JH Fife 114 H4
- Culzean Castle & Country Park KA19 8LE S Ayrs 104 D8
- Dallas Dhu Distillery IV36 2RR Moray 139 J4
- David Livingstone Centre G72 9BY S Lans 114 C9
- Dirleton Castle & Garden EH39 5ER E Loth 116 C4
- Doune Castle FK16 6EA Stirlg 114 D1
- Drum Castle, Garden & Estate AB31 5EY Abers 133 J4
- Dryburgh Abbey TD6 0RQ Border 107 P3
- Duff House AB45 3SX Abers 140 H3
- Dumbarton Castle G82 1JJ W Duns 113 M6
- Dundrennan Abbey DG6 4QH D & G 96 F9
- Dunnottar Castle AB39 2TL Abers 133 L7
- Dunstaffnage Castle & Chapel PA37 1PZ Ag & B 120 G6
- Edinburgh Castle EH1 2NG C Edin 115 N6
- Edinburgh Zoo RZSS EH12 6TS C Edin 115 M6
- Edzell Castle & Garden DD9 7UE Angus 132 F10
- Eilean Donan Castle IV40 8DX Highld 136 B10
- Elgin Cathedral IV30 1HU Moray 139 N3
- Falkland Palace & Garden KY15 7BU Fife 124 E11
- Fort George IV2 7TE Highld 138 D4
- Fyvie Castle AB53 8JS Abers 141 J8
- Georgian House EH2 4DR C Edin 115 N6
- Gladstone's Land EH1 2NT C Edin 115 N6
- Glamis Castle DD8 1RJ Angus 124 H3
- Glasgow Botanic Gardens G12 0UE C Glas 113 Q8
- Glasgow Cathedral G4 0QZ C Glas 114 A8
- Glasgow Science Centre G51 1EA C Glas 113 Q8
- Glen Grant Distillery AB38 7BS Moray 139 N6
- Glenluce Abbey DG8 0AF D & G 94 H6
- Greenbank Garden G76 8RB E Rens 113 Q10
- Haddo House AB41 7EQ Abers 141 L9
- Harmony Garden TD6 9LJ Border 107 N3
- Hermitage Castle TD9 0LU Border 107 M10
- Highland Wildlife Park RZSS PH21 1NL Highld 130 E3
- Hill House G84 9AJ Ag & B 113 L4
- Hill of Tarvit Mansion & Garden KY15 5PB Fife 124 H10
- Holmwood G44 3YG C Glas 113 R9
- House of Dun DD10 9LQ Angus 132 G12
- House of the Binns EH49 7NA W Loth 115 J6
- Huntingtower Castle PH1 3JL P & K 124 B8
- Huntly Castle AB54 4SH Abers 140 E7
- Hutchesons' Hall G1 1EJ C Glas 114 A8
- Inchmahome Priory FK8 3RA Stirlg 113 Q1
- Inveresk Lodge Garden EH21 7TE E Loth 115 Q7
- Inverewe Garden & Estate IV22 2LG Highld 143 M8
- Inverlochy Castle PH33 6SH Highld 128 F9
- Kellie Castle & Garden KY10 2RF Fife 125 K11
- Kildrummy Castle AB33 8RA Abers 132 C1
- Killiecrankie PH16 5LG P & K 130 G11
- Leith Hall Garden & Estate AB54 4NQ Abers 140 E10
- Linlithgow Palace EH49 7AL W Loth 115 J6
- Lochleven Castle KY13 8UF P & K 124 C12
- Logan Botanic Garden DG9 9ND D & G 94 F9
- Malleny Garden EH14 7AF C Edin 115 L8
- Melrose Abbey TD6 9LG Border 107 N3
- National Museum of Scotland EH1 1JF C Edin 115 N6
- Newark Castle PA14 5NH Inver 113 L6
- Palace of Holyroodhouse EH8 8DX C Edin 115 N6
- Pitmedden Garden AB41 7PD Abers 141 L10
- Preston Mill EH40 3DS E Loth 116 E6
- Priorwood Garden TD6 9PX Border 107 N3
- Robert Smail's Printing Works EH44 6HA Border 107 J2
- Rothesay Castle PA20 0DA Ag & B 112 G8
- Royal Botanic Garden Edinburgh EH3 5LR C Edin 115 N6
- Royal Yacht Britannia EH6 6JJ C Edin 115 N6
- St Andrews Aquarium KY16 9AS Fife 125 K9
- Scone Palace PH2 6BD P & K 124 C7
- Smailholm Tower TD5 7PG Border 107 Q3
- Souter Johnnie's Cottage KA19 8HY S Ayrs 104 D8
- Stirling Castle FK8 1EJ Stirlg 114 E2
- Sweetheart Abbey DG2 8BU D & G 97 K5
- Tantallon Castle EH39 5PN E Loth 116 E4
- Tenement House G3 6QN C Glas 113 R8
- The Burrell Collection G43 1AT C Glas 113 Q9
- The Falkirk Wheel FK1 4RS Falk 114 F5
- The Hunterian Museum G12 8QQ C Glas 113 Q8
- Threave Castle DG7 1TJ D & G 96 E6
- Threave Garden DG7 1RX D & G 96 F6
- Tolquhon Castle AB41 7LP Abers 141 L10
- Traquair House EH44 6PW Border 107 J3
- Urquhart Castle IV63 6XJ Highld 137 P10
- Weaver's Cottage PA10 2JG Rens 113 M8
- Whithorn Priory & Museum DG8 8PY D & G 95 N10

WALES

- Aberconwy House LL32 8AY Conwy 73 N8
- Aberdulais Tin Works & Waterfall SA10 8EU Neath 27 J2
- Beaumaris Castle LL58 8AP IoA 73 K8
- Big Pit: National Coal Museum NP4 9XP Torfn 40 B10
- Bodnant Garden LL28 5RE Conwy 73 P9
- Caerleon Roman Fortress & Baths NP18 1AE Newpt 28 D4
- Caernarfon Castle LL55 2AY Gwynd 72 H11
- Caldicot Castle & Country Park NP26 4HU Mons 28 G5
- Cardiff Castle CF10 3RB Cardif 28 A7
- Castell Coch CF15 7JS Cardif 27 Q6
- Chirk Castle LL14 5AF Wrexhm 63 J4
- Colby Woodland Garden SA67 8PP Pembks 37 M9
- Conwy Castle LL32 8AY Conwy 73 N8
- Criccieth Castle LL52 0DP Gwynd 60 H5
- Dinefwr Park & Castle SA19 6RT Carmth 38 F7
- Dolaucothi Gold Mines SA19 8US Carmth 38 G4
- Erddig LL13 0YT Wrexhm 63 K2
- Ffestiniog Railway LL49 9NF Gwynd 61 L4
- Harlech Castle LL46 2YH Gwynd 61 K6
- Llanerchaeron SA48 8DG Cerdgn 48 H8
- National Showcaves Centre for Wales SA9 1GJ Powys 39 K8
- Penrhyn Castle LL57 4HT Gwynd 73 K9
- Plas Newydd LL61 6DQ IoA 73 J9
- Plas yn Rhiw LL53 8AB Gwynd 60 C6
- Portmeirion LL48 6ER Gwynd 61 K5
- Powis Castle & Garden SY21 8RF Powys 62 H11
- Raglan Castle NP15 2BT Mons 40 F10
- Sygun Copper Mine LL55 4NE Gwynd 61 K2
- Tintern Abbey NP16 6SE Mons 28 H2
- Tudor Merchant's House SA70 7BX Pembks 37 M10
- Tŷ Mawr Wybrnant LL25 0HJ Conwy 61 N2
- Valle Crucis Abbey LL20 8DD Denbgs 62 H3

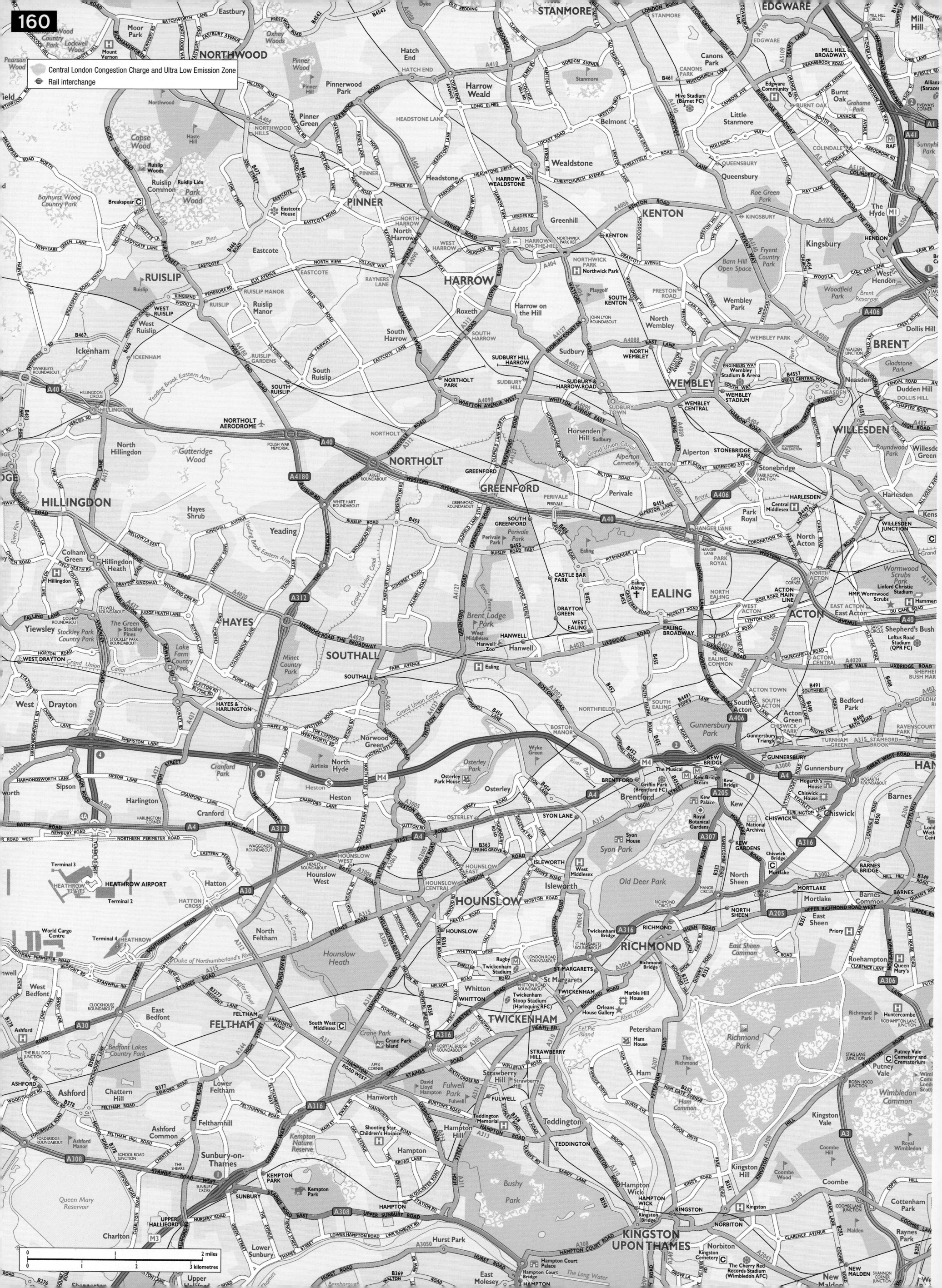

This index lists places appearing in the main map section of the atlas in alphabetical order. The reference following each name gives the atlas page number and grid reference of the square in which the place appears. The map shows counties, unitary authorities and administrative areas, together with a list of the abbreviated name forms used in the index.

The top 100 places of tourist interest are indexed in **red**, World Heritage sites in **green**, motorway service areas in **blue**, airports in blue *italic* and National Parks in green *italic*.

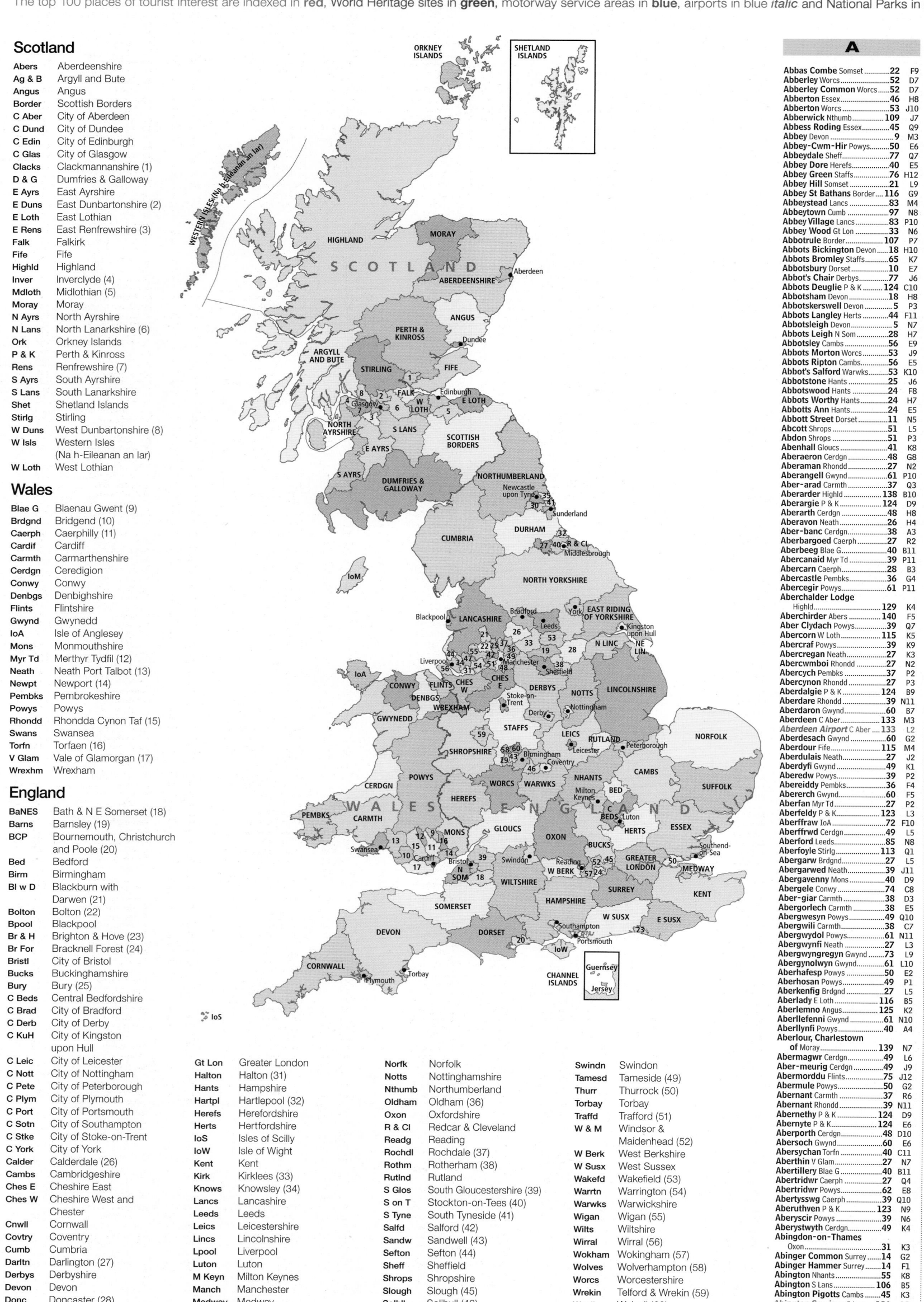

A

Place	County	Page	Grid
Abbas Combe	Somset	22	F9
Abberley	Worcs	52	D7
Abberley Common	Worcs	52	D7
Abberton	Essex	46	H8
Abberton	Worcs	53	J10
Abberwick	Nthumb	109	J7
Abbess Roding	Essex	45	Q9
Abbey	Devon	9	M3
Abbey-Cwm-Hir	Powys	50	E6
Abbeydale	Sheff	77	Q7
Abbey Dore	Herefs	40	E5
Abbey Green	Staffs	76	H12
Abbey Hill	Somset	21	L9
Abbey St Bathans	Border	116	G9
Abbeystead	Lancs	83	M4
Abbeytown	Cumb	97	N8
Abbey Village	Lancs	83	P10
Abbey Wood	Gt Lon	33	N6
Abbotrule	Border	107	P7
Abbots Bickington	Devon	18	H10
Abbots Bromley	Staffs	65	K7
Abbotsbury	Dorset	10	E7
Abbot's Chair	Derbys	77	J6
Abbots Deuglie	P & K	124	C10
Abbotsham	Devon	18	H8
Abbotskerswell	Devon	5	P3
Abbots Langley	Herts	44	F11
Abbotsleigh	Devon	5	N7
Abbots Leigh	N Som	28	N7
Abbotsley	Cambs	56	E9
Abbots Morton	Worcs	53	J9
Abbots Ripton	Cambs	56	E5
Abbot's Salford	Warwks	53	K10
Abbotstone	Hants	25	J6
Abbotswood	Hants	24	F8
Abbots Worthy	Hants	24	H7
Abbotts Ann	Hants	24	E5
Abbott Street	Dorset	11	N5
Abcott	Shrops	51	L5
Abdon	Shrops	51	P3
Abenhall	Gloucs	41	K8
Aberaeron	Cerdgn	48	G8
Aberaman	Rhondd	27	N2
Aberangell	Gwynd	61	P10
Aber-arad	Carmth	37	Q3
Aberarder	Highld	138	B10
Aberargie	P & K	124	D9
Aberarth	Cerdgn	48	H8
Aberavon	Neath	26	H4
Aber-banc	Cerdgn	38	A3
Aberbargoed	Caerph	27	R2
Aberbeeg	Blae G	40	B1
Abercanaid	Myr Td	39	P11
Abercarn	Caerph	28	B3
Abercastle	Pembks	36	G4
Abercegir	Powys	61	P11
Aberchalder Lodge	Highld	129	K4
Aberchirder	Abers	140	F5
Aber Clydach	Powys	39	Q7
Abercorn	W Loth	115	K5
Abercraf	Powys	39	K9
Abercregan	Neath	27	K3
Abercwmboi	Rhondd	27	N2
Abercych	Pembks	37	P2
Abercynon	Rhondd	27	N3
Aberdalgie	P & K	124	B9
Aberdare	Rhondd	39	N11
Aberdaron	Gwynd	60	B7
Aberdeen	C Aber	133	M3
Aberdeen Airport	*C Aber*	*133*	*L2*
Aberdesach	Gwynd	60	G2
Aberdour	Fife	115	M4
Aberdulais	Neath	27	J2
Aberdyfi	Gwynd	49	K3
Aberedw	Powys	39	P2
Abereiddy	Pembks	36	F4
Abererch	Gwynd	60	F5
Aberfan	Myr Td	27	P2
Aberfeldy	P & K	123	L3
Aberffraw	IoA	72	F10
Aberffrwd	Cerdgn	49	L5
Aberford	Leeds	85	N8
Aberfoyle	Stirlg	113	Q1
Abergarw	Brdgnd	27	L5
Abergarwed	Neath	39	J11
Abergavenny	Mons	40	D9
Abergele	Conwy	74	C8
Aber-giar	Carmth	38	D3
Abergorlech	Carmth	38	E5
Abergwesyn	Powys	49	Q10
Abergwili	Carmth	38	C7
Abergwydol	Powys	61	N11
Abergwynfi	Neath	27	L3
Abergwyngregyn	Gwynd	73	L9
Abergynolwyn	Gwynd	61	L10
Aberhafesp	Powys	50	F4
Aberhosan	Powys	49	P1
Aberkenfig	Brdgnd	27	L5
Aberlady	E Loth	116	L9
Aberlemno	Angus	125	K2
Aberllefenni	Gwynd	61	N10
Aberllynfi	Powys	40	A4
Aberlour, Charlestown of	Moray	139	N7
Abermagwr	Cerdgn	49	L6
Aber-meurig	Cerdgn	49	J9
Abermorddu	Flints	75	J12
Abermule	Powys	50	G2
Abernant	Carmth	37	R6
Abernant	Rhondd	39	N11
Abernethy	P & K	124	D9
Abernyte	P & K	124	E6
Aberporth	Cerdgn	48	D10
Abersoch	Gwynd	60	E6
Abersychan	Torfn	40	C11
Aberthin	V Glam	27	N7
Abertillery	Blae G	40	B11
Abertridwr	Caerph	27	Q4
Abertridwr	Powys	62	E8
Abertysswg	Caerph	39	Q10
Aberuthven	P & K	123	N9
Aberyscir	Powys	39	N6
Aberystwyth	Cerdgn	49	K4
Abingdon-on-Thames	Oxon	31	K3
Abinger Common	Surrey	14	G2
Abinger Hammer	Surrey	14	F1
Abington	Nhants	55	K5
Abington	S Lans	106	B5
Abington Pigotts	Cambs	45	K3
Abington Services	*S Lans*	*106*	*B5*
Abingworth	W Susx	14	G7
Ab Kettleby	Leics	67	J10
Ab Lench	Worcs	53	J10
Ablington	Gloucs	42	C10
Ablington	Wilts	23	P4
Abney	Derbys	77	M7
Above Church	Staffs	65	J2
Aboyne	Abers	132	E5
Abhainn Suidhe	W Isls	152	d5
Abram	Wigan	75	Q3
Abriachan	Highld	137	P9
Abridge	Essex	33	N3
Abronhill	N Lans	114	E6
Abson	S Glos	29	L7
Abthorpe	Nhants	43	N2
Aby	Lincs	80	H8
Acaster Malbis	C York	86	A6
Acaster Selby	N York	85	N7
Accrington	Lancs	84	A9
Acha	Ag & B	118	C2
Achahoish	Ag & B	112	A6
Achalader	P & K	124	B3
Achaleven	Ag & B	120	H4
Acha Mor	W Isls	152	f3
Achanalt	Highld	137	J3
Achandunie	Highld	145	P10
Achany	Highld	145	N5
Acharacle	Highld	127	M10
Acharn	Highld	120	D3
Acharn	P & K	123	K4
Achavanich	Highld	151	M8
Achduart	Highld	144	C4
Achfary	Highld	148	G8
A'Chill	Highld	126	C3
Achiltibuie	Highld	144	C3
Achina	Highld	150	C4
Achinhoan	Ag & B	103	K6
Achintee	Highld	136	C7
Achintraid	Highld	135	Q8
Achmelvich	Highld	148	C11
Achmore	Highld	135	Q9
Achmore	W Isls	152	f3
Achnacarnin	Highld	148	C10
Achnacarry	Highld	128	G10
Achnacloich	Highld	127	K3
Achnaconeran	Highld	137	M12
Achnacroish	Ag & B	120	F4
Achnadrish House	Ag & B	119	M2
Achnafauld	P & K	123	M5
Achnagarron	Highld	146	C11
Achnaha	Highld	126	H10
Achnahaird	Highld	144	C2
Achnahannet	Highld	138	H10
Achnairn	Highld	145	M3
Achnalea	Highld	127	Q12
Achnamara	Ag & B	112	A4
Achnasheen	Highld	136	G4
Achnashellach	Highld	136	D6
Achnastank	Moray	139	P9
Achosnich	Highld	126	H10
Achranich	Highld	120	D3
Achreamie	Highld	151	J3
Achriabhach	Highld	128	G10
Achriesgill	Highld	148	F6
Achtoty	Highld	149	P4
Achurch	Nhants	55	P4
Achvaich	Highld	146	C6
Achvarasdal	Highld	150	H4
Ackergill	Highld	151	Q6
Acklam	Middsb	91	R3
Acklam	N York	86	E1
Ackleton	Shrops	52	E1
Acklington	Nthumb	109	L9
Ackton	Wakefd	85	N10
Ackworth Moor Top	Wakefd	85	N12
Acle	Norfk	71	M10
Acock's Green	Birm	53	L4
Acol	Kent	35	P9
Acomb	C York	85	R5
Acomb	Nthumb	99	P5
Acombe	Somset	21	K10
Aconbury	Herefs	40	G5
Acre	Lancs	84	B10
Acrefair	Wrexhm	63	J3
Acton	Ches E	64	B2
Acton	Dorset	11	N9
Acton	Gt Lon	32	H6
Acton	Shrops	51	K4
Acton	Staffs	64	F4
Acton	Suffk	46	F3
Acton	Worcs	52	F7
Acton	Wrexhm	63	K2
Acton Beauchamp	Herefs	52	C10
Acton Bridge	Ches W	75	Q8
Acton Burnell	Shrops	63	P11
Acton Green	Herefs	52	C10
Acton Pigott	Shrops	63	P11
Acton Round	Shrops	52	B2
Acton Scott	Shrops	51	M3
Acton Trussell	Staffs	64	H8
Acton Turville	S Glos	29	N6
Adbaston	Staffs	64	E6
Adber	Dorset	22	D9
Adderbury	Oxon	43	K4
Adderley	Shrops	64	C4
Adderstone	Nthumb	109	J3
Addiewell	W Loth	114	H8
Addingham	C Brad	84	G5
Addington	Bucks	43	Q6
Addington	Gt Lon	33	L9
Addington	Kent	34	B10
Addiscombe	Gt Lon	33	L9
Addlestone	Surrey	32	F9
Addlestonemoor	Surrey	32	F9
Addlethorpe	Lincs	81	K10
Adeney	Wrekin	64	C8
Adeyfield	Herts	44	F10
Adfa	Powys	62	E12
Adforton	Herefs	51	L5
Adisham	Kent	35	M11
Adlestrop	Gloucs	42	F6
Adlingfleet	E R Yk	86	F11
Adlington	Ches E	76	G6
Adlington	Lancs	75	Q1
Admaston	Staffs	65	K7
Admaston	Wrekin	64	B9
Admington	Warwks	42	H3
Adpar	Cerdgn	37	Q2
Adsborough	Somset	21	L7
Adscombe	Somset	21	J6
Adstock	Bucks	43	Q5
Adstone	Nhants	54	F10
Adversane	W Susx	14	F5
Advie	Highld	139	L9
Adwalton	Leeds	85	K9
Adwell	Oxon	31	P2
Adwick le Street	Donc	78	D3
Adwick upon Dearne	Donc	78	B3
Ae	D & G	106	C12
Ae Bridgend	D & G	97	K1
Afan Forest Park	Neath	27	K3
Affetside	Bury	76	D1
Affleck	Abers	140	G8
Affpuddle	Dorset	11	K6
Affric Lodge	Highld	136	H11
Afon-wen	Flints	74	F9
Afon Wen	Gwynd	60	G5
Afton	Devon	5	J4
Afton	IoW	12	F7
Agglethorpe	N York	90	H9
Aigburth	Lpool	75	K6
Aike	E R Yk	87	K6
Aiketgate	Cumb	98	F8

Bickerton – Braeintra 165

Bickerton N York 85 P5
Bickerton Nthumb 108 G9
Bickford Staffs 64 G9
Bickington Devon 8 E10
Bickington Devon 19 K7
Bickleigh Devon 4 H4
Bickleigh Devon 8 H3
Bickleton Devon 19 K7
Bickley Ches W 63 P2
Bickley Gt Lon 33 M8
Bickley N York 93 J8
Bickley Worcs 52 B6
Bickley Moss Ches W 63 P2
Bicknacre Essex 46 D11
Bicknoller Somset 20 H5
Bicknor Kent 34 F10
Bickton Hants 23 P11
Bicton Herefs 51 M8
Bicton Shrops 51 J4
Bicton Shrops 63 M9
Bidborough Kent 15 Q2
Bidden Hants 25 M3
Biddenden Kent 16 E3
Biddenden Green Kent 16 F2
Biddenham Bed 55 P10
Biddestone Wilts 29 P7
Biddisham Somset 21 N3
Biddlesden Bucks 43 N4
Biddlestone Nthumb 108 F8
Biddulph Staffs 76 G12
Biddulph Moor Staffs 76 G12
Bideford Devon 19 J8
Bidford-on-Avon Warwks 53 L10
Bidston Wirral 75 J6
Bielby E R Yk 86 E6
Bieldside C Aber 133 L4
Bierley IoW 12 H9
Bierton Bucks 44 B8
Big Balcraig D & G 95 M9
Bigbury Devon 5 L7
Bigbury-on-Sea Devon 5 K8
Bigby Lincs 79 Q2
Biggar Cumb 82 F2
Biggar S Lans 106 D2
Biggin Derbys 65 N2
Biggin Derbys 77 M11
Biggin N York 85 Q8
Biggin Hill Gt Lon 33 M10
Biggleswade C Beds 44 H3
Bigholms D & G 98 C2
Bighouse Highld 150 F4
Bighton Hants 25 K6
Biglands Cumb 97 Q7
Bignor W Susx 14 D8
Bigrigg Cumb 88 D4
Big Sand Highld 143 K9
Bigton Shet 147 i9
Bilborough C Nott 66 E4
Bilbrook Somset 20 G5
Bilbrook Staffs 64 G11
Bilbrough N York 85 Q6
Bilbster Highld 151 N6
Bildershaw Dur 91 K2
Bildeston Suffk 58 E10
Billacott Cnwll 7 K6
Billericay Essex 34 B3
Billesdon Leics 67 J11
Billesley Warwks 53 L9
Billingborough Lincs 68 C5
Billinge St Hel 75 N4
Billingford Norfk 58 H5
Billingford Norfk 70 F8
Billingham S on T 91 Q2
Billinghay Lincs 68 C1
Billingley Barns 78 D3
Billingshurst W Susx 14 F6
Billingsley Shrops 52 D4
Billington C Beds 44 D7
Billington Lancs 83 Q8
Billington Staffs 64 G8
Billockby Norfk 71 N9
Billy Row Dur 100 F10
Bilsborrow Lancs 83 L7
Bilsby Lincs 81 J8
Bilsham W Susx 14 D10
Bilsington Kent 17 J4
Bilsthorpe Notts 78 G11
Bilsthorpe Moor Notts 78 G11
Bilston Mdloth 115 N8
Bilston Wolves 52 H1
Bilstone Leics 66 B11
Bilting Kent 17 J1
Bilton E R Yk 87 M8
Bilton N York 85 L4
Bilton Nthumb 109 L7
Bilton Warwks 54 D6
Bilton Banks Nthumb 109 K8
Bilton-in-Ainsty N York 85 P5
Binbrook Lincs 80 D5
Binchester Blocks Dur 100 G11
Bincombe Dorset 10 G8
Binegar Somset 22 E3
Bines Green W Susx 14 H7
Binfield Br For 32 B8
Binfield Heath Oxon 31 Q7
Bingfield Nthumb 100 C4
Bingham Notts 66 H4
Bingham's Melcombe Dorset 11 J4
Bingley C Brad 84 G7
Bings Heath Shrops 63 P8
Binham Norfk 70 E4
Binley Covtry 54 C5
Binley Hants 24 G3
Binley Woods Warwks 54 C5
Binnegar Dorset 11 L7
Binniehill Falk 114 F7
Binscombe Surrey 14 D2
Binsey Oxon 43 K10
Binstead IoW 13 K6
Binsted Hants 25 N5
Binsted W Susx 14 D9
Binton Warwks 53 L10
Bintree Norfk 70 F7
Binweston Shrops 63 J11
Birch Essex 46 G7
Birch Rochdl 76 F2
Bircham Newton Norfk 69 P5
Bircham Tofts Norfk 69 P6
Birchanger Essex 45 P7
Birchanger Green Services Essex 45 P7
Birch Cross Staffs 65 L6
Birchencliffe Kirk 84 H11
Bircher Herefs 51 N7
Birchett's Green E Susx 16 B4
Birchfield Birm 53 K2
Birch Green Essex 46 G8
Birch Green Herts 45 K9
Birch Green Worcs 41 P3
Birchgrove Cardif 28 A6
Birchgrove Swans 26 H3
Birchgrove W Susx 15 M5
Birch Heath Ches W 75 P11
Birch Hill Ches W 75 N9
Birchington Kent 35 N8
Birchington-on-Sea Kent 35 N8
Birchley Heath Warwks 53 P2
Birchmoor Warwks 65 N11
Birchmoor Green C Beds 44 D5
Birchover Derbys 77 N11
Birch Services Rochdl 76 F2
Birch Vale Derbys 77 J6
Birchwood Lincs 79 M10
Birch Wood Somset 21 K10
Birchwood Warrtn 76 C5
Bircotes Notts 78 G5
Birdbrook Essex 46 C3
Birdforth N York 91 R11
Birdham W Susx 13 P5
Birdingbury Warwks 54 C7
Birdlip Gloucs 41 Q9
Birdoswald Cumb 99 J5
Birdsall N York 86 F2
Birds Edge Kirk 77 M2
Birds Green Essex 45 Q10
Birdsgreen Shrops 52 E4
Birdsmoorgate Dorset 10 B4
Bird Street Suffk 58 E10
Birdwell Barns 77 Q3
Birdwood Gloucs 41 L8
Birgham Border 108 C2
Birichin Highld 146 D6
Birkacre Lancs 83 M12
Birkby N York 91 N6
Birkdale Sefton 82 H12
Birkenbog Abers 140 E3
Birkenhead Wirral 75 K6
Birkenhead (Queensway) Tunnel Lpool 75 K6
Birkenhills Abers 140 H7
Birkenshaw Kirk 85 J9
Birkhall Abers 131 Q5
Birkhill Angus 124 G6
Birkhill D & G 106 G6
Birkholme Lincs 67 N7
Birkin N York 85 Q10
Birks Leeds 85 K10
Birkshaw Nthumb 99 L5
Birley Herefs 51 M10
Birley Carr Sheff 77 Q5
Birling Kent 34 B10
Birling Nthumb 109 L8
Birling Gap E Susx 15 Q11
Birlingham Worcs 41 Q3
Birmingham Birm 53 K3
Birmingham Airport Solhll 53 M4
Birnam P & K 123 Q4
Birness Abers 141 N9
Birse Abers 132 E5
Birsemore Abers 132 E5
Birstall Kirk 85 K10
Birstall Leics 66 F10
Birstwith N York 85 K3
Birthorpe Lincs 68 B5
Birtley Gatesd 100 H7
Birtley Herefs 51 L7
Birtley Nthumb 99 N3
Birts Street Worcs 41 M4
Bisbrooke Rutlnd 67 M12
Biscathorpe Lincs 80 E7
Biscovey Cnwll 3 P4
Bisham W & M 32 B5
Bishampton Worcs 53 J10
Bish Mill Devon 19 P8
Bishop Auckland Dur 91 L1
Bishopbridge Lincs 79 P5
Bishopbriggs E Duns 114 A7
Bishop Burton E R Yk 87 J7
Bishop Middleham Dur 101 J12
Bishopmill Moray 139 N3
Bishop Monkton N York 85 L2
Bishop Norton Lincs 79 N5
Bishopsbourne Kent 35 L11
Bishops Cannings Wilts 30 B9
Bishop's Castle Shrops 51 K3
Bishop's Caundle Dorset 22 F10
Bishop's Cleeve Gloucs 41 Q6
Bishop's Frome Herefs 52 C11
Bishops Gate Surrey 32 D8
Bishop's Green Essex 46 A8
Bishop's Green Hants 31 K9
Bishop's Hull Somset 21 K8
Bishop's Itchington Warwks 54 C9
Bishops Lydeard Somset 21 J7
Bishop's Norton Gloucs 41 N7
Bishop's Nympton Devon 19 P8
Bishop's Offley Staffs 64 E6
Bishop's Stortford Herts 45 N7
Bishop's Sutton Hants 25 K7
Bishop's Tachbrook Warwks 53 P8
Bishop's Tawton Devon 19 L7
Bishopsteignton Devon 8 G10
Bishopstoke Hants 24 H9
Bishopston Swans 26 E4
Bishopstone Bucks 44 A9
Bishopstone E Susx 15 N10
Bishopstone Herefs 40 F3
Bishopstone Kent 35 M8
Bishopstone Swindn 30 F5
Bishopstone Wilts 23 N8
Bishopstrow Wilts 23 K5
Bishop Sutton BaNES 29 J10
Bishop's Waltham Hants 25 J10
Bishopswood Somset 21 L10
Bishop's Wood Staffs 64 F10
Bishopsworth Bristl 28 H8
Bishop Thornton N York 85 K3
Bishopthorpe C York 86 B6
Bishopton Darltn 91 N2
Bishopton Rens 113 N7
Bishopton Warwks 53 M9
Bishop Wilton E R Yk 86 E4
Bishton Newpt 28 E5
Bishton Staffs 65 J8
Bisley Gloucs 41 P10
Bisley Surrey 32 D10
Bisley Camp Surrey 32 D10
Bispham Bpool 82 H7
Bispham Green Lancs 75 N1
Bissoe Cnwll 3 J6
Bisterne Hants 12 B4
Bitchet Green Kent 33 Q11
Bitchfield Lincs 67 N6
Bittadon Devon 19 K5
Bittaford Devon 5 L5
Bittering Norfk 70 D8
Bitterley Shrops 51 P5
Bitterne C Sotn 24 G10
Bitteswell Leics 54 E3
Bitton S Glos 29 K8
Bix Oxon 31 P5
Bixter Shet 147 i6
Blaby Leics 54 F1
Blackadder Border 117 J10
Blackawton Devon 5 N6
Blackbeck Cumb 88 D5
Blackborough Devon 9 L3
Blackborough End Norfk 69 M9
Black Bourton Oxon 42 G10
Blackboys E Susx 15 P6
Blackbrook Derbys 65 Q3
Blackbrook St Hel 75 P4
Blackbrook Staffs 64 E4
Blackbrook Surrey 14 H1
Blackburn Abers 133 K2
Blackburn Bl w D 83 P9
Blackburn Rothm 78 C5
Blackburn W Loth 114 H8
Blackburn with Darwen Services Bl w D 83 Q10
Black Callerton N u Ty 100 F4
Black Carr Norfk 58 G2
Black Corner W Susx 15 K3
Blackcraig E Ayrs 105 L8
Black Crofts Ag & B 120 H6
Black Cross Cnwll 3 M2
Blackden Heath Ches E 76 E9
Blackdog Abers 133 M1
Black Dog Devon 8 E3
Blackdown Devon 7 P9
Blackdown Dorset 10 B4
Blackdyke Cumb 97 N8
Blacker Barns 77 Q2
Blacker Hill Barns 78 B3
Blackfen Gt Lon 33 N7
Blackfield Hants 12 G4
Blackford Cumb 98 E6
Blackford P & K 123 M11
Blackford Somset 21 N4
Blackford Somset 22 F8
Blackfordby Leics 65 Q8
Blackgang IoW 12 H9
Blackhall C Edin 115 M6
Blackhall Colliery Dur 101 L10
Blackhall Mill Gatesd 100 E7
Blackhall Rocks Dur 101 L10
Blackhaugh Border 107 L2
Blackheath Essex 46 H7
Blackheath Gt Lon 33 M7
Blackheath Sandw 52 H3
Blackheath Suffk 59 N6
Blackheath Surrey 14 E2
Black Heddon Nthumb 100 D3
Blackhill Abers 141 P5
Blackhill Abers 141 Q7
Blackhill Dur 100 E8
Blackhill of Clackriach Abers 141 M6
Blackhorse Devon 9 J6
Blackjack Lincs 68 E4
Blackland Wilts 30 B8
Black Lane Ends Lancs 84 D6
Blacklaw D & G 106 D8
Blackley Manch 76 F3
Blacklunans P & K 131 L12
Blackmarstone Herefs 40 G4
Blackmill Brdgnd 27 M5
Blackmoor Hants 25 N7
Black Moor Leeds 85 L7
Blackmoor N Som 28 G10
Blackmoorfoot Kirk 77 L1
Blackmoor Gate Devon 19 M5
Blackmore Essex 45 R11
Blackmore End Essex 46 C5
Blackmore End Herts 44 H8
Black Mountains 40 C6
Blackness Falk 115 J5
Blacknest Hants 25 P5
Blacknest W & M 32 D8
Black Notley Essex 46 D7
Blacko Lancs 84 C7
Black Pill Swans 26 F4
Blackpool Bpool 82 H8
Blackpool Devon 5 P7
Blackpool Devon 8 F10
Blackpool Gate Cumb 98 G3
Blackpool Zoo Bpool 82 H8
Blackridge W Loth 114 G8
Blackrock Cnwll 2 G7
Blackrock Mons 40 B9
Blackrod Bolton 75 Q2
Blacksboat Moray 139 M8
Blackshaw D & G 97 L5
Blackshaw Head Calder 84 E9
Blacksmith's Green Suffk 58 H7
Blacksnape Bl w D 83 Q11
Blackstone W Susx 15 J7
Black Street Suffk 59 P3
Black Tar Pembks 37 J8
Blackthorn Oxon 43 N8
Blackthorpe Suffk 58 D8
Blacktoft E R Yk 86 F10
Blacktop C Aber 133 L3
Black Torrington Devon 7 N4
Blackwall Derbys 65 N2
Blackwall Tunnel Gt Lon 33 M6
Blackwater Cnwll 3 J5
Blackwater Hants 32 B10
Blackwater IoW 12 H7
Blackwater Somset 21 L10
Blackwaterfoot N Ayrs 103 N4
Blackwell Cumb 98 E7
Blackwell Darltn 91 M4
Blackwell Derbys 77 L9
Blackwell Derbys 78 D12
Blackwell Warwks 42 F3
Blackwell Worcs 53 J6
Blackwellsend Green Gloucs 41 M6
Blackwood Caerph 28 A3
Blackwood D & G 106 B12
Blackwood S Lans 105 P1
Blackwood Hill Staffs 64 G1
Blacon Ches W 75 L10
Bladbean Kent 17 L1
Bladnoch D & G 95 M7
Bladon Oxon 43 K8
Bladon Somset 21 P9
Blaenannerch Cerdgn 48 D11
Blaenau Ffestiniog Gwynd 61 M3
Blaenavon Torfn 40 C10
Blaenavon Industrial Landscape Torfn 40 C10
Blaencwm Rhondd 27 L3
Blaen Dyryn Powys 39 M4
Blaenffos Pembks 37 N3
Blaengarw Brdgnd 27 L4
Blaengeuffordd Cerdgn 49 L4
Blaengwrach Neath 39 K10
Blaengwynfi Neath 27 L3
Blaenllechau Rhondd 27 N3
Blaenpennal Cerdgn 49 K8
Blaenplwyf Cerdgn 49 K5
Blaenporth Cerdgn 48 D11
Blaenrhondda Rhondd 27 M2
Blaenwaun Carmth 37 P5
Blaen-y-coed Carmth 37 R5
Blaen-y-cwm Blae G 39 Q9
Blaenycwm Cerdgn 49 P5
Blagdon N Som 28 G10
Blagdon Somset 21 K9
Blagdon Torbay 5 P4
Blagdon Hill Somset 21 K10
Blagill Cumb 99 L9
Blaguegate Lancs 75 M2
Blaich Highld 128 E9
Blain Highld 127 M10
Blaina Blae G 40 B10
Blair Atholl P & K 130 F11
Blair Drummond Stirlg 114 D2
Blairgowrie P & K 124 D4
Blairhall Fife 114 H4
Blairingone P & K 114 H2
Blairlogie Stirlg 114 E2
Blairmore Ag & B 113 J5
Blairmore Highld 148 E5
Blair's Ferry Ag & B 112 E7
Blaisdon Gloucs 41 L8
Blakebrook Worcs 52 F5
Blakedown Worcs 52 G5
Blake End Essex 46 C7
Blakeley Lane Staffs 64 H3
Blakemere Ches W 75 P9
Blakemere Herefs 40 E3
Blakemore Devon 5 M5
Blakenall Heath Wsall 65 J11
Blakeney Gloucs 41 K10
Blakeney Norfk 70 F3
Blakenhall Ches E 64 D3
Blakenhall Wolves 52 G1
Blakeshall Worcs 52 F4
Blakesley Nhants 54 G10
Blanchland Nthumb 100 B8
Blandford Camp Dorset 11 M3
Blandford Forum Dorset 11 L3
Blandford St Mary Dorset 11 L4
Bland Hill N York 85 J4
Blanefield Stirlg 113 Q5
Blankney Lincs 79 Q11
Blantyre S Lans 114 C9
Blàr a' Chaorainn Highld 128 F11
Blarghour Ag & B 121 J10
Blargie Highld 129 Q5
Blarmachfoldach Highld 128 F10
Blashford Hants 12 B3
Blaston Leics 55 K2
Blatherwycke Nhants 55 N2
Blawith Cumb 89 J9
Blawquhairn D & G 96 C2
Blaxhall Suffk 59 M9
Blaxton Donc 78 H4
Blaydon Gatesd 100 F5
Bleadney Somset 22 B4
Bleadon N Som 28 D11
Bleak Street Somset 22 G7
Blean Kent 35 K10
Bleasby Lincs 80 C7
Bleasby Notts 66 H2
Bleasdale Lancs 83 N6
Bleatarn Cumb 90 B4
Bleathwood Herefs 51 P6
Blebocraigs Fife 124 H10
Bleddfa Powys 50 H7
Bledington Gloucs 42 F7
Bledlow Bucks 43 Q11
Bledlow Ridge Bucks 31 R3
Bleet Wilts 29 P10
Blegbie E Loth 116 C9
Blencarn Cumb 99 J12
Blencogo Cumb 97 P8
Blendworth Hants 25 M10
Blenheim Palace Oxon 43 J8
Blennerhasset Cumb 97 N10
Bletchingdon Oxon 43 L8
Bletchingley Surrey 33 L12
Bletchley M Keyn 44 B5
Bletchley Shrops 64 B5
Bletchley Park Museum M Keyn 44 B5
Bletherston Pembks 37 L6
Bletsoe Bed 55 P9
Blewbury Oxon 31 L5
Blickling Norfk 70 H6
Blidworth Notts 66 F1
Blidworth Bottoms Notts 66 F1
Blindburn Nthumb 108 C7
Blindcrake Cumb 97 N11
Blindley Heath Surrey 15 L2
Blisland Cnwll 6 G10
Blissford Hants 24 B10
Bliss Gate Worcs 52 D6
Blisworth Nhants 55 J10
Blithbury Staffs 65 K8
Blitterlees Cumb 97 M8
Blockley Gloucs 42 D5
Blofield Norfk 71 L10
Blofield Heath Norfk 71 L10
Blo Norton Norfk 58 F5
Bloomfield Border 107 P5
Blore Staffs 64 D5
Blore Staffs 65 L2
Blounce Hants 25 M4
Blounts Green Staffs 65 K6
Blowick Sefton 83 J12
Bloxham Oxon 43 J4
Bloxholm Lincs 67 Q1
Bloxwich Wsall 65 J11
Bloxworth Dorset 11 L6
Blubberhouses N York 85 J4
Blue Anchor Cnwll 3 M3
Blue Anchor Somset 20 G5
Blue Bell Hill Kent 34 D10
Blue John Cavern Derbys 77 L7
Blundellsands Sefton 75 J4
Blundeston Suffk 59 Q1
Blunham C Beds 56 C10
Blunsdon St Andrew Swindn 30 D4
Bluntington Worcs 52 G6
Bluntisham Cambs 56 G6
Blunts Cnwll 4 E4
Blunts Green Warwks 53 L7
Blurton C Stke 64 G4
Blyborough Lincs 79 M5
Blyford Suffk 59 N5
Blymhill Staffs 64 E9
Blymhill Lawn Staffs 64 F10
Blyth Notts 78 G6
Blyth Nthumb 101 J2
Blyth Bridge Border 115 L12
Blythburgh Suffk 59 N5
Blythe Border 116 D11
Blythe Bridge Staffs 64 H4
Blythe End Warwks 53 N2
Blythe Marsh Staffs 64 H4
Blyth Services Notts 78 G6
Blyton Lincs 79 L5
Boarhills Fife 125 L10
Boarhunt Hants 13 K3
Boarley Kent 34 D10
Boarsgreave Lancs 84 C11
Boarshead E Susx 15 P4
Boar's Head Wigan 75 P2
Boars Hill Oxon 43 K11
Boarstall Bucks 43 N9
Boasley Cross Devon 7 P6
Boath Highld 145 N10
Boat of Garten Highld 138 H12
Bobbing Kent 34 F9
Bobbington Staffs 52 E2
Bobbingworth Essex 45 P10
Bocaddon Cnwll 4 B5
Bocking Essex 46 D7
Bocking Churchstreet Essex 46 D6
Bockleton Worcs 51 Q8
Boconnoc Cnwll 4 A4
Boddam Abers 141 Q7
Boddam Shet 147 i9
Boddington Gloucs 41 P6
Bodedern IoA 72 E7
Bodelwyddan Denbgs 74 D8
Bodenham Herefs 51 P10
Bodenham Wilts 23 Q8
Bodenham Moor Herefs 51 P10
Bodewryd IoA 72 F5
Bodfari Denbgs 74 F9
Bodffordd IoA 72 G8
Bodham Norfk 70 H4
Bodiam E Susx 16 D6
Bodicote Oxon 43 K4
Bodieve Cnwll 6 E10
Bodinnick Cnwll 3 R4
Bodle Street Green E Susx 16 B8
Bodmin Cnwll 6 F11
Bodmin Moor Cnwll 6 H9
Bodney Norfk 70 B12
Bodorgan IoA 72 F10
Bodsham Kent 17 K2
Boduan Gwynd 60 E4
Bodwen Cnwll 3 P2
Bodymoor Heath Warwks 53 M1
Bogallan Highld 138 B6
Bogbrae Abers 141 P8
Bogend S Ayrs 104 G3
Boggs Holdings E Loth 116 B7
Boghall Mdloth 115 N8
Boghall W Loth 114 H7
Boghead S Lans 105 P1
Bogmoor Moray 139 Q3
Bogmuir Abers 132 G10
Bogniebrae Abers 140 F7
Bognor Regis W Susx 14 D11
Bogroy Highld 138 G11
Bogue D & G 96 D2
Bohetherick Cnwll 4 F3
Bohortha Cnwll 3 L8
Bohuntine Highld 129 J7
Bojewyan Cnwll 2 C7
Bokiddick Cnwll 3 P2
Bolam Dur 91 K2
Bolam Nthumb 100 E2
Bolberry Devon 5 L9
Bold Heath St Hel 75 P6
Boldmere Birm 53 L2
Boldon Colliery S Tyne 101 J6
Boldre Hants 12 E5
Boldron Dur 90 G4
Bole Notts 79 K6
Bolehill Derbys 65 P1
Bole Hill Derbys 77 Q9
Bolenowe Cnwll 2 G7
Bolham Devon 20 E10
Bolham Water Devon 21 J11
Bolingey Cnwll 3 J4
Bollington Ches E 76 H8
Bollington Cross Ches E 76 G8
Bollow Gloucs 41 M9
Bolney W Susx 15 J6
Bolnhurst Bed 56 B8
Bolnore W Susx 15 L6
Bolshan Angus 125 M2
Bolsover Derbys 78 D9
Bolster Moor Kirk 84 G12
Bolsterstone Sheff 77 P4
Boltby N York 91 R9
Boltenstone Abers 132 C2
Bolter End Bucks 31 R4
Bolton Bolton 76 D2
Bolton Cumb 89 Q2
Bolton E Loth 116 C7
Bolton E R Yk 86 E5
Bolton Nthumb 109 J7
Bolton Abbey N York 84 G4
Bolton Bridge N York 84 G4
Bolton-by-Bowland Lancs 84 B5
Boltonfellend Cumb 98 F4
Boltongate Cumb 97 P10
Bolton-le-Sands Lancs 83 L2
Bolton Low Houses Cumb 97 P9
Bolton New Houses Cumb 97 Q9
Bolton-on-Swale N York 91 L7
Bolton Percy N York 85 Q7
Bolton Town End Lancs 83 L2
Bolton upon Dearne Barns 78 D3
Bolventor Cnwll 6 H9
Bomarsund Nthumb 100 H1
Bomere Heath Shrops 63 M8
Bonar Bridge Highld 145 N7
Bonawe Ag & B 121 J6
Bonby N Linc 87 J12
Boncath Pembks 37 N3
Bonchester Bridge Border 107 P7
Bonchurch IoW 13 K9
Bondleigh Devon 8 C4
Bonds Lancs 83 L6
Bonehill Devon 8 D9
Bonehill Staffs 65 M11
Bo'ness Falk 114 H5
Boney Hay Staffs 65 K10
Bonhill W Duns 113 M5
Boningale Shrops 64 F11
Bonjedward Border 107 Q5
Bonkle N Lans 114 F10
Bonnington Angus 125 L5
Bonnington Kent 17 J4
Bonnybank Fife 124 G12
Bonnybridge Falk 114 E5
Bonnykelly Abers 141 L5
Bonnyrigg Mdloth 115 P8
Bonnyton Angus 124 G5
Bonsall Derbys 77 P12
Bonshaw Tower D & G 97 P4
Bont Mons 40 E8
Bontddu Gwynd 61 L8
Bont-Dolgadfan Powys 62 B12
Bont-goch Cerdgn 49 L3
Bonthorpe Lincs 81 J9
Bontnewydd Cerdgn 49 K7
Bontnewydd Gwynd 72 H11
Bontuchel Denbgs 74 F12
Bonvilston V Glam 27 P7
Bonwm Denbgs 62 F4
Bon-y-maen Swans 26 G3
Boode Devon 19 K6
Booker Bucks 32 B4
Booley Shrops 63 P7
Boon Border 116 D12
Boon Hill Staffs 64 E2
Boorley Green Hants 24 H10
Boosbeck R & Cl 92 D3
Boose's Green Essex 46 E5
Boot Cumb 88 G6
Booth Calder 84 F9
Boothby Graffoe Lincs 79 N11
Boothby Pagnell Lincs 67 N6
Boothferry E R Yk 86 D10
Booth Green Ches E 76 G7
Boothstown Salfd 76 D3
Booth Town Calder 84 G10
Boothville Nhants 55 K8
Bootle Cumb 88 E9
Bootle Sefton 75 K5
Boots Green Ches W 76 D9
Boot Street Suffk 59 J11
Booze N York 90 G6
Boraston Shrops 51 Q6
Bordeaux Guern 12 d1
Borden Kent 34 F9
Borden W Susx 25 P8
Border Cumb 97 N7
Bordley N York 84 E2
Boreham Essex 46 D9
Boreham Wilts 23 K4
Boreham Street E Susx 16 B8
Borehamwood Herts 32 H3
Boreland D & G 106 F11
Boreraig Highld 134 C5
Boreton Shrops 63 N10
Borgh W Isls 152 b13
Borgh W Isls 152 g1
Borgie Highld 149 P5
Borgue D & G 96 D8
Borgue Highld 151 L11
Borley Essex 46 E3
Borley Green Essex 46 E3
Borley Green Suffk 58 E8
Borneskitaig Highld 142 D11
Borness D & G 96 C9
Boroughbridge N York 85 N2
Borough Green Kent 33 R11
Borras Head Wrexhm 63 L2
Borrowash Derbys 66 C5
Borrowby N York 91 P9
Borrowby N York 92 F4
Borrowdale Cumb 88 H3
Borrowstoun Falk 114 H5
Borstal Medway 34 C9
Borth Cerdgn 49 K3
Borthwick Mdloth 115 Q9
Borthwickbrae Border 107 L7
Borthwickshiels Border 107 L6
Borth-y-Gest Gwynd 61 J5
Borve Highld 134 H6
Borve W Isls 152 b13
Borve W Isls 152 d6
Borve W Isls 152 g1
Borwick Lancs 89 N12
Borwick Lodge Cumb 89 K7
Borwick Rails Cumb 88 G10
Bosavern Cnwll 2 B8
Bosbury Herefs 41 L3
Boscarne Cnwll 6 F11
Boscastle Cnwll 6 G6
Boscombe BCP 11 Q6
Boscombe Wilts 24 C5
Boscoppa Cnwll 3 P4
Bosham W Susx 13 P4
Bosham Hoe W Susx 13 P4
Bosherston Pembks 37 J11
Boskednan Cnwll 2 C7
Boskenna Cnwll 2 C9
Bosley Ches E 76 G10
Bosoughan Cnwll 3 L2
Bossall N York 86 D3
Bossiney Cnwll 6 F7
Bossingham Kent 17 L1
Bossington Somset 20 D4
Bostock Green Ches W 76 C10
Boston Lincs 68 F3
Boston Spa Leeds 85 N6
Boswarthan Cnwll 2 C8
Boswinger Cnwll 3 N6
Botallack Cnwll 2 B8
Botany Bay Gt Lon 33 K3
Botcheston Leics 66 D11
Botesdale Suffk 58 F5
Bothal Nthumb 100 G1
Bothampstead W Berk 31 L7
Bothamsall Notts 78 H9
Bothel Cumb 97 N10
Bothenhampton Dorset 10 D6
Bothwell S Lans 114 C9
Bothwell Services S Lans 114 C9
Botley Bucks 44 D11
Botley Hants 24 H10
Botley Oxon 43 K10
Botolph Claydon Bucks 43 Q7
Botolphs W Susx 14 H9
Botolph's Bridge Kent 17 K4
Bottesford Leics 67 K4
Bottesford N Linc 79 M2
Bottisham Cambs 57 K8
Bottomcraig Fife 124 G8
Bottom of Hutton Lancs 83 L9
Bottom o' th' Moor Bolton 76 C1
Bottoms Calder 84 D11
Bottoms Cnwll 2 B9
Botts Green Warwks 53 N2
Botusfleming Cnwll 4 F4
Botwnnog Gwynd 60 D6
Bough Beech Kent 15 P1
Boughrood Powys 39 Q4
Boughspring Gloucs 28 H3
Boughton Nhants 55 J7
Boughton Norfk 69 N11
Boughton Notts 78 H10
Boughton Aluph Kent 17 J1
Boughton End C Beds 44 E4
Boughton Green Kent 34 D12
Boughton Malherbe Kent 34 F12
Boughton Monchelsea Kent 34 D12
Boughton Street Kent 35 J10
Boulby R & Cl 92 F3
Boulder Clough Calder 84 F10
Bouldnor IoW 12 F7
Bouldon Shrops 51 P4
Boulmer Nthumb 109 L7
Boulston Pembks 37 J8
Boultham Lincs 79 N10
Boundary Staffs 64 H4
Bourn Cambs 56 F9
Bournbrook Birm 53 K4
Bourne Lincs 68 B8
Bournebridge Essex 33 P3
Bourne End Bed 55 P8
Bourne End Bucks 32 C5
Bourne End C Beds 44 D3
Bourne End Herts 44 E10
Bournemouth BCP 11 Q6
Bournemouth Airport BCP 11 Q5
Bournes Green Gloucs 41 Q10
Bournes Green Sthend 34 F5
Bournheath Worcs 52 H6
Bournmoor Dur 100 H8
Bournstream Gloucs 29 M3
Bournville Birm 53 K4
Bourton Dorset 22 G7
Bourton N Som 28 E9
Bourton Oxon 30 F5
Bourton Shrops 51 Q1
Bourton Wilts 30 B9
Bourton on Dunsmore Warwks 54 D6
Bourton-on-the-Hill Gloucs 42 E5
Bourton-on-the-Water Gloucs 42 E7
Bousd Ag & B 126 D11
Boustead Hill Cumb 98 C6
Bouth Cumb 89 J9
Bouthwaite N York 84 H1
Bouts Worcs 53 J9
Boveney Bucks 32 D7
Boveridge Dorset 23 N10
Bovey Tracey Devon 8 F9
Bovingdon Herts 44 E11
Bovingdon Green Bucks 32 B5
Bovinger Essex 45 P10
Bovington Dorset 11 K7
Bovington Camp Dorset 11 K7
Bow Cumb 98 D7
Bow Devon 5 N5
Bow Devon 8 D4
Bow Gt Lon 33 L6
Bow Ork 147 c6
Bowbank Dur 90 F2
Bow Brickhill M Keyn 44 C5
Bowbridge Gloucs 41 P10
Bowburn Dur 100 H10
Bowcombe IoW 12 H7
Bowd Devon 9 L7
Bowden Border 107 N4
Bowden Devon 5 P7
Bowden Hill Wilts 29 Q9
Bowdon Traffd 76 E6
Bower Highld 151 N4
Bowerchalke Wilts 23 M8
Bowerhill Wilts 29 Q10
Bower Hinton Somset 21 P10
Bower House Tye Suffk 46 H3
Bowermadden Highld 151 N4
Bowers Staffs 64 F5
Bowers Gifford Essex 34 D5
Bowershall Fife 115 K3
Bower's Row Leeds 85 N9
Bowes Dur 90 G4
Bowgreave Lancs 83 L6
Bowhouse D & G 97 L5
Bowithick Cnwll 6 H8
Bowker's Green Lancs 75 L3
Bowland Border 107 M2
Bowland Bridge Cumb 89 L9
Bowley Herefs 51 P10
Bowley Town Herefs 51 P10
Bowlhead Green Surrey 14 C3
Bowling C Brad 85 J9
Bowling W Duns 113 N6
Bowling Bank Wrexhm 63 L2
Bowling Green Worcs 52 F10
Bowmanstead Cumb 89 J7
Bowmore Ag & B 110 G9
Bowness-on-Solway Cumb 97 P6
Bowness-on-Windermere Cumb 89 L7
Bow of Fife Fife 124 G10
Bowriefauld Angus 125 K3
Bowscale Cumb 98 D12
Bowsden Nthumb 108 G1
Bowston Cumb 89 M7
Bow Street Cerdgn 49 K4
Bow Street Norfk 58 F1
Bowthorpe Norfk 70 H10
Box Gloucs 29 P2
Box Wilts 29 N8
Boxbush Gloucs 41 K7
Boxbush Gloucs 41 M9
Box End Bed 55 P10
Boxford Suffk 46 G4
Boxford W Berk 31 J8
Boxgrove W Susx 14 C9
Box Hill Surrey 32 H12
Boxley Kent 34 D10
Boxmoor Herts 44 F10
Box's Shop Cnwll 7 J4
Boxted Essex 46 H5
Boxted Essex 46 H5
Boxted Suffk 58 B10
Boxted Cross Essex 46 H5
Boxwell Gloucs 29 N4
Boxworth Cambs 56 G8
Boyden End Suffk 57 P9
Boyden Gate Kent 35 M9
Boylestone Derbys 65 M5
Boyndie Abers 140 G3
Boyndlie Abers 141 L3
Boynton E R Yk 87 L2
Boysack Angus 125 M3
Boys Hill Dorset 10 G3
Boythorpe Derbys 78 C9
Boyton Cnwll 7 L6
Boyton Suffk 47 Q2
Boyton Wilts 23 L5
Boyton Cross Essex 46 B10
Boyton End Suffk 46 C3
Bozeat Nhants 55 M9
Braaid IoM 102 d6
Brabling Green Suffk 59 L7
Brabourne Kent 17 K2
Brabourne Lees Kent 17 K3
Brabstermire Highld 151 P3
Bracadale Highld 134 F8
Braceborough Lincs 67 Q9
Bracebridge Heath Lincs 79 N10
Bracebridge Low Fields Lincs 79 N10
Braceby Lincs 67 P5
Bracewell Lancs 84 C5
Brackenfield Derbys 78 B12
Brackenhirst N Lans 114 D7
Brackenthwaite Cumb 98 C9
Brackenthwaite N York 85 L5
Brackla Brdgnd 27 L6
Bracklesham W Susx 13 P5
Brackletter Highld 128 H8
Brackley Nhants 43 M4
Brackley Hatch Nhants 43 N3
Bracknell Br For 32 B8
Braco P & K 123 L11
Bracobrae Moray 140 D5
Bracon Ash Norfk 71 J12
Bracora Highld 127 N6
Bracorina Highld 127 N6
Bradaford Devon 7 M6
Bradbourne Derbys 65 M2
Bradbury Dur 91 N1
Bradden Nhants 54 G11
Braddock Cnwll 4 B4
Bradeley C Stke 64 G2
Bradenham Bucks 32 B3
Bradenstoke Wilts 30 B6
Bradfield Devon 9 K3
Bradfield Essex 47 L5
Bradfield Norfk 71 K5
Bradfield Sheff 77 P5
Bradfield W Berk 31 M8
Bradfield Combust Suffk 58 C9
Bradfield Green Ches E 76 C11
Bradfield Heath Essex 47 L6
Bradfield St Clare Suffk 58 D9
Bradfield St George Suffk 58 D8
Bradford C Brad 84 H8
Bradford Cnwll 6 G9
Bradford Devon 7 M3
Bradford Nthumb 100 D2
Bradford Nthumb 109 J3
Bradford Abbas Dorset 22 D10
Bradford Leigh Wilts 29 N10
Bradford-on-Avon Wilts 29 N10
Bradford-on-Tone Somset 21 J9
Bradford Peverell Dorset 10 G6
Bradiford Devon 19 L6
Brading IoW 13 K7
Bradley Ches W 63 N3
Bradley Derbys 65 N3
Bradley Hants 25 L5
Bradley Kirk 85 J11
Bradley N York 90 G10
Bradley NE Lin 80 E2
Bradley Staffs 64 G8
Bradley Wolves 52 H2
Bradley Worcs 53 J8
Bradley Wrexhm 63 K1
Bradley Green Somset 21 L6
Bradley Green Warwks 65 P12
Bradley Green Worcs 53 J8
Bradley in the Moors Staffs 65 K4
Bradley Stoke S Glos 29 J6
Bradmore Notts 66 F6
Bradney Somset 21 M5
Bradninch Devon 9 J4
Bradninch Devon 19 M7
Bradnop Staffs 65 J1
Bradnor Green Herefs 51 J9
Bradpole Dorset 10 D6
Bradshaw Bolton 76 D1
Bradshaw Calder 84 G9
Bradshaw Kirk 84 G12
Bradstone Devon 7 M8
Bradwall Green Ches E 76 E11
Bradwell Derbys 77 M7
Bradwell Devon 19 K5
Bradwell Essex 46 E7
Bradwell M Keyn 44 B3
Bradwell Norfk 71 P11
Bradwell-on-Sea Essex 46 H10
Bradwell Waterside Essex 46 H10
Bradworthy Devon 18 F10
Brae Highld 138 C3
Brae Shet 147 i5
Braeface Falk 114 E5
Braehead Angus 125 N2
Braehead D & G 95 M8
Braehead S Lans 114 H11
Braeintra Highld 136 B9

166 Braemar – Burnside of Duntrune

Braemar Abers 131 L6
Braemore Highld 144 F9
Braemore Highld 151 K10
Brae Roy Lodge Highld 129 K6
Braeside Inver 113 J6
Braes of Coul Angus 124 F1
Braes of Enzie Moray 140 B4
Braeswick Ork 147 e2
Braevallich Ag & B 120 H11
Braewick Shet 147 h4
Brafferton Darltn 91 M2
Brafferton N York 85 N1
Brafield-on-the-Green Nhants 55 K9
Bragar W Isls 152 f2
Bragbury End Herts 45 K7
Braidwood S Lans 114 F11
Brailsford Derbys 65 N4
Brailsford Green Derbys 65 N4
Brain's Green Gloucs 41 K10
Braintree Essex 46 D7
Braiseworth Suffk 58 H6
Braishfield Hants 24 F8
Braithwaite C Brad 84 F7
Braithwaite Cumb 88 H2
Braithwell Donc 78 E5
Braken Hill Wakefd 85 N12
Bramber W Susx 14 H8
Brambridge Hants 24 H9
Bramcote Notts 66 E5
Bramcote Warwks 54 C3
Bramdean Hants 25 K8
Bramerton Norfk 71 L11
Bramfield Herts 45 K8
Bramfield Suffk 59 M6
Bramford Suffk 47 K2
Bramhall Stockp 76 G7
Bramham Leeds 85 N6
Bramhope Leeds 85 K6
Bramley Hants 31 N10
Bramley Leeds 85 K8
Bramley Rothm 78 D5
Bramley Surrey 14 E2
Bramley Corner Hants 31 N10
Bramley Green Hants 31 N10
Bramley Head N York 84 H4
Bramling Kent 35 M11
Brampford Speke Devon 8 H5
Brampton Cambs 56 D6
Brampton Cumb 89 R2
Brampton Cumb 98 G6
Brampton Lincs 79 L8
Brampton Norfk 71 J7
Brampton Rothm 78 C3
Brampton Suffk 59 N4
Brampton Abbotts Herefs 41 J6
Brampton Ash Nhants 55 K3
Brampton Bryan Herefs 51 L6
Brampton-en-le-Morthen Rothm 78 D6
Bramshall Staffs 65 K5
Bramshaw Hants 24 D10
Bramshill Hants 31 Q10
Bramshott Hants 25 P7
Bramwell Somset 21 P7
Branault Highld 127 J10
Brancaster Norfk 69 P3
Brancaster Staithe Norfk 69 Q3
Brancepeth Dur 100 G10
Branchill Moray 139 K5
Brand End Lincs 68 G3
Branderburgh Moray 147 N11
Brandesburton E R Yk 87 L6
Brandeston Suffk 59 K8
Brand Green Gloucs 41 L6
Brandis Corner Devon 7 M4
Brandiston Norfk 70 H8
Brandon Dur 100 G10
Brandon Lincs 67 M3
Brandon Nthumb 108 G6
Brandon Suffk 57 Q3
Brandon Warwks 54 C5
Brandon Bank Norfk 57 M3
Brandon Creek Norfk 57 L2
Brandon Parva Norfk 70 G10
Brandsby N York 92 C12
Brandy Wharf Lincs 79 P4
Brane Cnwll 2 C9
Bran End Essex 46 B6
Branksome BCP 11 P6
Branksome Park BCP 11 P6
Bransbury Hants 24 G5
Bransby Lincs 79 M8
Branscombe Devon 9 M7
Bransford Worcs 52 E10
Bransgore Hants 12 C5
Bransholme C KuH 87 L8
Bransley Shrops 52 C5
Branson's Cross Worcs 53 K6
Branston Leics 67 K6
Branston Lincs 79 P10
Branston Staffs 65 N8
Branston Booths Lincs 79 Q10
Branstone IoW 13 J8
Brant Broughton Lincs 67 M1
Brantham Suffk 47 K5
Branthwaite Cumb 88 E2
Branthwaite Cumb 98 C10
Brantingham E R Yk 86 H9
Branton Donc 78 G3
Branton Nthumb 108 G6
Branton Green N York 85 N3
Branxton Nthumb 108 E2
Brassey Green Ches W 75 N11
Brassington Derbys 65 N1
Brasted Kent 33 N11
Brasted Chart Kent 33 N11
Brathens Abers 132 G5
Bratoft Lincs 81 J10
Brattleby Lincs 79 N7
Bratton Somset 20 E4
Bratton Wilts 23 K3
Bratton Wrekin 64 B9
Bratton Clovelly Devon 7 N6
Bratton Fleming Devon 19 M6
Bratton Seymour Somset 22 F7
Braughing Herts 45 M6
Braughing Friars Herts 45 M7
Braunston Nhants 54 E7
Braunston Rutlnd 67 L10
Braunstone Town Leics 66 F11
Braunton Devon 19 J6
Brawby N York 92 E11
Brawl Highld 150 E3
Brawlbin Highld 151 K5
Bray W & M 32 C6
Braybrooke Nhants 55 J4
Braydon Wilts 30 B5
Braydon Brook Wilts 30 A4
Braydon Side Wilts 30 B5
Brayford Devon 19 N6
Bray's Hill E Susx 16 B8
Bray Shop Cnwll 7 L10
Braystones Cumb 88 D5
Braythorn N York 85 K5
Brayton N York 86 B9
Braywick W & M 32 C6
Braywoodside W & M 32 C7
Brazacott Cnwll 7 K6
Breach Kent 17 M1
Breach Kent 34 E9
Breachwood Green Herts 44 G7
Breacleit W Isls 152 e3
Breaclete W Isls 152 e3
Breaden Heath Shrops 63 M5
Breadsall Derbys 66 B4
Breadstone Gloucs 29 L2
Breadward Herefs 51 J9
Breage Cnwll 2 F9
Breakachy Highld 137 N7
Breakish Highld 135 M11
Brealangwell Lodge Highld 145 M6
Bream Gloucs 41 J10
Breamore Hants 23 P9
Brean Somset 28 D11
Breanais W Isls 152 d4
Brearley Calder 84 F10
Brearton N York 85 L3
Breascleit W Isls 152 f3
Breasclete W Isls 152 f3
Breaston Derbys 66 D5
Brechfa Carmth 38 D6
Brechin Angus 132 F12
Breckles Norfk 58 D2
Brecon Powys 39 P6
Brecon Beacons National Park 39 N7
Bredbury Stockp 76 G5
Brede E Susx 16 E7
Bredenbury Herefs 51 Q9
Bredfield Suffk 59 K10
Bredgar Kent 34 F10
Bredhurst Kent 34 D10
Bredon Worcs 41 Q4
Bredon's Hardwick Worcs 41 P5
Bredon's Norton Worcs 41 Q4
Bredwardine Herefs 40 D3
Breedon on the Hill Leics 66 C7
Breich W Loth 114 H9
Breightmet Bolton 76 D2
Breighton E R Yk 86 D8
Breinton Herefs 40 G4
Bremhill Wilts 29 R8
Bremridge Devon 19 N7
Brenchley Kent 16 B2
Brendon Devon 7 L3
Brendon Devon 19 P4
Brendon Hill Somset 20 G6
Brenfield Ag & B 112 B5
Brenish W Isls 152 d4
Brenkley N u Ty 100 G3
Brent Cross Gt Lon 33 J5
Brent Eleigh Suffk 58 D11
Brentford Gt Lon 32 H7
Brentingby Leics 67 K8
Brent Knoll Somset 21 M3
Brent Mill Devon 5 L5
Brent Pelham Herts 45 N5
Brentwood Essex 33 Q4
Brenzett Kent 16 H5
Brenzett Green Kent 16 H5
Brereton Staffs 65 K9
Brereton Green Ches E 76 E10
Brereton Heath Ches E 76 E10
Brereton Hill Staffs 65 K9
Bressay Shet 147 j7
Bressingham Norfk 58 G4
Bressingham Common Norfk 58 G4
Bretby Derbys 65 P7
Bretford Warwks 54 C5
Bretforton Worcs 42 C3
Bretherton Lancs 83 L11
Brettabister Shet 147 j6
Brettenham Norfk 58 D4
Brettenham Suffk 58 E10
Bretton C Pete 68 C12
Bretton Derbys 77 M8
Bretton Flints 75 K11
Brewers End Essex 45 Q7
Brewer Street Surrey 33 L12
Brewood Staffs 64 G10
Briantspuddle Dorset 11 K6
Brick End Essex 45 Q6
Brickendon Herts 45 L10
Bricket Wood Herts 44 G11
Brick Houses Sheff 77 P7
Brickkiln Green Essex 46 C5
Bricklehampton Worcs 41 R3
Bride IoM 102 f2
Bridekirk Cumb 97 M11
Bridell Pembks 37 N2
Bridestowe Devon 7 P7
Brideswell Abers 140 F8
Bridford Devon 8 F7
Bridge Kent 35 L11
Bridge End Cumb 88 G10
Bridge End Cumb 98 D8
Bridge End Devon 5 L7
Bridge End Dur 100 C11
Bridge End Essex 46 B5
Bridge End Lincs 68 C5
Bridgefoot Angus 124 H6
Bridgefoot Cumb 97 L12
Bridge Green Essex 45 N4
Bridgehampton Somset 22 D8
Bridge Hewick N York 85 M1
Bridgehill Dur 100 E8
Bridgehouse Gate N York 84 H2
Bridgemary Hants 13 K4
Bridgemere Ches E 64 D3
Bridgend Abers 140 D8
Bridgend Ag & B 103 L2
Bridgend Ag & B 110 H9
Bridgend Angus 132 E10
Bridgend Brdgnd 27 L6
Bridgend Cerdgn 48 B11
Bridgend Cumb 89 L4
Bridgend D & G 106 E8
Bridgend Devon 5 J7
Bridgend Fife 124 H10
Bridgend Moray 140 B9
Bridgend P & K 124 C8
Bridgend W Loth 115 J6
Bridgend of Lintrathen Angus 124 F2
Bridge of Alford Abers 140 E12
Bridge of Allan Stirlg 114 E2
Bridge of Avon Moray 139 L12
Bridge of Avon Moray 139 M8
Bridge of Balgie P & K 122 F3
Bridge of Brewlands Angus 131 M12
Bridge of Brown Highld 139 L11
Bridge of Cally P & K 124 C3
Bridge of Canny Abers 132 G5
Bridge of Craigisla Angus 124 E2
Bridge of Dee D & G 96 E6
Bridge of Don C Aber 133 M2
Bridge of Dye Abers 132 G7
Bridge of Earn P & K 124 C9
Bridge of Ericht P & K 122 E1
Bridge of Feugh Abers 133 H5
Bridge of Gairn Abers 131 Q5
Bridge of Gaur P & K 122 E1
Bridge of Marnoch Abers 140 F6
Bridge of Muchalls Abers 133 L6
Bridge of Orchy Ag & B 121 P5
Bridge of Tilt P & K 130 F11
Bridge of Tynet Moray 140 B4
Bridge of Walls Shet 147 h6
Bridge of Weir Rens 113 M8
Bridge Reeve Devon 19 M10
Bridgerule Devon 7 K4
Bridges Shrops 51 L1
Bridge Sollers Herefs 40 F3
Bridge Street Suffk 58 C10
Bridgetown Cnwll 7 L7
Bridgetown Somset 20 E7
Bridge Trafford Ches W 75 M9
Bridge Yate S Glos 29 K8
Bridgham Norfk 58 E3
Bridgnorth Shrops 52 D2
Bridgwater Somset 21 L6
Bridgwater Services Somset 21 M6
Bridlington E R Yk 87 M2
Bridport Dorset 10 D6
Bridstow Herefs 41 J7
Brierfield Lancs 84 C8
Brierley Barns 78 C2
Brierley Gloucs 41 J8
Brierley Herefs 51 N9
Brierley Hill Dudley 52 G3
Brierlow Bar Derbys 77 K9
Brierton Hartpl 101 L12
Briery Cumb 89 J2
Brigg N Linc 79 P2
Briggate Norfk 71 L7
Briggswath N York 92 H5
Brigham Cumb 89 J2
Brigham Cumb 97 M12
Brigham E R Yk 87 K4
Brighouse Calder 84 H10
Brighstone IoW 12 G8
Brightgate Derbys 77 P11
Brighthampton Oxon 42 H11
Brightholmlee Sheff 77 P5
Brightley Devon 8 B5
Brightling E Susx 16 B6
Brightlingsea Essex 47 K8
Brighton Br & H 15 K10
Brighton Cnwll 3 M4
Brighton City Airport W Susx 14 H9
Brighton le Sands Sefton 75 K4
Brightons Falk 114 G6
Brightwalton W Berk 31 J6
Brightwalton Green W Berk 31 J6
Brightwalton Holt W Berk 31 J7
Brightwell Suffk 47 N3
Brightwell Baldwin Oxon 31 N3
Brightwell-cum-Sotwell Oxon 31 M4
Brightwell Upperton Oxon 31 N3
Brignall Dur 90 H4
Brig o'Turk Stirlg 122 F11
Brigsley NE Lin 80 E3
Brigsteer Cumb 89 M9
Brigstock Nhants 55 N4
Brill Bucks 43 N9
Brill Cnwll 2 H8
Brilley Herefs 51 J11
Brimfield Herefs 51 N7
Brimfield Cross Herefs 51 P7
Brimington Derbys 78 C9
Brimley Devon 8 E9
Brimpsfield Gloucs 41 Q9
Brimpton W Berk 31 L9
Brimpton Common W Berk 31 M9
Brimscombe Gloucs 41 P11
Brimstage Wirral 75 J7
Brincliffe Sheff 77 Q7
Brind E R Yk 86 D9
Brindham Somset 22 C5
Brindister Shet 147 h6
Brindle Lancs 83 N10
Brindley Ches E 63 Q2
Brineton Staffs 64 E9
Bringhurst Leics 55 L2
Bringsty Common Herefs 52 C9
Brington Cambs 56 B5
Briningham Norfk 70 F5
Brinkely Notts 66 H2
Brinkhill Lincs 80 G9
Brinkley Cambs 57 M9
Brinklow Warwks 54 D5
Brinkworth Wilts 30 B5
Brinscall Lancs 83 N11
Brinscombe Somset 21 P3
Brinsea N Som 28 F10
Brinsley Notts 66 D2
Brinsop Herefs 40 F3
Brinsworth Rothm 78 C6
Brinton Norfk 70 F5
Brinyan Ork 147 c3
Brisco Cumb 98 E8
Brisley Norfk 70 D8
Brislington Bristl 29 J8
Brissenden Green Kent 16 G3
Bristol Bristl 29 J8
Bristol Airport N Som 28 G9
Bristol Zoo Gardens Bristl 28 H7
Briston Norfk 70 F6
Brisworthy Devon 5 J4
Britannia Lancs 84 C11
Britford Wilts 23 P8
Brithdir Caerph 39 Q11
Brithdir Gwynd 61 N8
British Legion Village Kent 34 C10
Briton Ferry Neath 26 H3
Britwell Salome Oxon 31 N4
Brixham Torbay 5 Q5
Brixton Devon 5 J6
Brixton Gt Lon 33 K7
Brixton Deverill Wilts 23 J6
Brixworth Nhants 55 J6
Brize Norton Oxon 42 G10
Brize Norton Airport Oxon 42 G10
Broad Alley Worcs 52 G7
Broad Blunsdon Swindn 30 D4
Broadbottom Tamesd 77 J5
Broadbridge W Susx 13 P4
Broadbridge Heath W Susx 14 G4
Broad Campden Gloucs 42 D4
Broad Carr Calder 84 G11
Broad Chalke Wilts 23 M8
Broad Clough Lancs 84 C10
Broadclyst Devon 9 J5
Broadfield Inver 113 L6
Broadfield Pembks 37 M9
Broadford Highld 135 L11
Broad Ford Kent 16 C3
Broadford Bridge W Susx 14 F6
Broadgairhill Border 106 G7
Broadgrass Green Suffk 58 E8
Broad Green Cambs 57 N8
Broad Green Essex 46 F7
Broad Green Worcs 52 E9
Broad Green Worcs 53 J6
Broadhaugh Border 117 J10
Broad Haven Pembks 36 G8
Broadheath Traffd 76 E6
Broadheath Worcs 52 C7
Broadhembury Devon 9 L4
Broadhempston Devon 5 N3
Broad Hill Cambs 57 L5
Broad Hinton Wilts 30 C7
Broadholme Lincs 79 M9
Broadland Row E Susx 16 E7
Broadlay Carmth 38 B10
Broad Layings Hants 31 J10
Broadley Essex 45 M10
Broadley Lancs 84 C12
Broadley Moray 140 B3
Broadley Common Essex 45 M10
Broad Marston Worcs 42 D2
Broadmayne Dorset 10 H7
Broad Meadow Staffs 64 F2
Broadmere Hants 25 K4
Broadmoor Gloucs 41 K8
Broadmoor Pembks 37 L9
Broadnymett Devon 8 D4
Broad Oak Carmth 38 E7
Broad Oak Cumb 88 F8
Broadoak Dorset 10 C5
Broad Oak E Susx 15 R6
Broad Oak E Susx 16 E7
Broadoak Gloucs 41 L9
Broad Oak Hants 25 N3
Broad Oak Herefs 40 G7
Broad Oak Kent 35 L10
Broad Oak St Hel 75 P5
Broadoak Wrexhm 75 L12
Broad Road Suffk 59 K5
Broadsands Torbay 5 Q5
Broad's Green Essex 46 C9
Broadstairs Kent 35 Q9
Broadstone BCP 11 N6
Broadstone Mons 40 G11
Broadstone Shrops 51 P3
Broad Street E Susx 16 F7
Broad Street Essex 45 Q8
Broad Street Kent 17 K3
Broad Street Kent 34 E11
Broad Street Medway 34 D8
Broad Street Wilts 30 C10
Broad Street Green Essex 46 F9
Broad Town Wilts 30 C7
Broadwas Worcs 52 D9
Broadwater Herts 45 J7
Broadwater W Susx 14 G10
Broadwaters Worcs 52 F5
Broadway Carmth 37 Q8
Broadway Carmth 38 B10
Broadway Pembks 36 G8
Broadway Somset 21 M10
Broadway Suffk 59 M5
Broadway Worcs 42 C4
Broadwell Gloucs 41 J9
Broadwell Gloucs 42 E6
Broadwell Oxon 42 F10
Broadwell Warwks 54 D7
Broadwey Dorset 10 G8
Broadwindsor Dorset 10 C4
Broadwood Kelly Devon 8 B3
Broadwoodwidger Devon 7 M7
Brobury Herefs 40 D3
Brochel Highld 135 K6
Brochroy Ag & B 121 J6
Brock Lancs 83 L7
Brockamin Worcs 52 E10
Brockbridge Hants 25 K9
Brockdish Norfk 59 J5
Brockencote Worcs 52 G6
Brockenhurst Hants 12 E4
Brocketsbrae S Lans 105 Q2
Brockford Green Suffk 58 G7
Brockford Street Suffk 58 G7
Brockhall Nhants 54 G8
Brockham Surrey 14 H1
Brockhampton Gloucs 41 Q6
Brockhampton Gloucs 42 B7
Brockhampton Hants 13 M3
Brockhampton Herefs 41 J5
Brockhampton Green Dorset 10 H3
Brockholes Kirk 77 M2
Brockhurst Derbys 77 Q10
Brockhurst Warwks 54 D4
Brocklebank Cumb 98 C9
Brocklesby Lincs 80 C1
Brockley N Som 28 G9
Brockley Suffk 58 B6
Brockley Green Suffk 46 C2
Brockley Green Suffk 58 B9
Brockleymoor Cumb 98 F11
Brockmoor Dudley 52 G3
Brockscombe Devon 7 N6
Brock's Green Hants 31 K10
Brockton Shrops 51 K3
Brockton Shrops 51 P5
Brockton Shrops 63 K11
Brockton Shrops 64 D11
Brockton Staffs 64 F6
Brockweir Gloucs 28 H2
Brockwood Park Hants 25 K8
Brockworth Gloucs 41 P8
Brocton Cnwll 6 E11
Brocton Staffs 64 H8
Brodick N Ayrs 103 Q3
Brodie Moray 138 H4
Brodsworth Donc 78 E2
Brogaig Highld 134 H2
Brogborough C Beds 44 D4
Brokenborough Wilts 29 Q4
Broken Cross Ches E 76 G9
Broken Cross Ches W 76 C9
Brokerswood Wilts 23 J3
Bromborough Wirral 75 K7
Brome Suffk 58 H5
Brome Street Suffk 58 H5
Bromeswell Suffk 59 L10
Bromfield Cumb 97 N9
Bromfield Shrops 51 N5
Bromham Bed 55 P10
Bromham Wilts 29 Q9
Bromley Barns 77 Q4
Bromley Dudley 52 G3
Bromley Gt Lon 33 M8
Bromley Shrops 52 D1
Bromley Common Gt Lon 33 M9
Bromley Cross Bolton 76 D1
Bromley Cross Essex 47 J6
Bromley Green Kent 16 H3
Bromlow Shrops 63 K11
Brompton Medway 34 D8
Brompton N York 91 P7
Brompton-by-Sawdon N York 93 J10
Brompton-on-Swale N York 91 L7
Brompton Ralph Somset 20 H7
Brompton Regis Somset 20 E7
Bromsash Herefs 41 K7
Bromsberrow Gloucs 41 L5
Bromsberrow Heath Gloucs 41 L5
Bromsgrove Worcs 52 H6
Bromstead Heath Staffs 64 E8
Bromyard Herefs 52 C9
Bromyard Downs Herefs 52 C9
Bronaber Gwynd 61 N6
Bronant Cerdgn 49 L7
Broncroft Shrops 51 P3
Brongest Cerdgn 48 E11
Bronington Wrexhm 63 N4
Bronllys Powys 39 Q5
Bronwydd Carmth 38 B7
Bronydd Powys 40 B3
Bronygarth Shrops 63 J5
Brook Carmth 37 P8
Brook Hants 24 D10
Brook Hants 24 E7
Brook IoW 12 F8
Brook Kent 17 J2
Brook Surrey 14 D3
Brook Surrey 14 F2
Brooke Norfk 71 K12
Brooke Rutlnd 67 L11
Brookenby Lincs 80 D5
Brook End Bed 55 Q8
Brook End C Beds 56 C11
Brook End Cambs 55 Q6
Brook End M Keyn 44 C3
Brookfield Rens 113 N8
Brookhampton Oxon 31 M3
Brookhampton Somset 22 E8
Brook Hill Hants 24 D10
Brook House Denbgs 74 E10
Brookhouse Lancs 83 M2
Brookhouse Rothm 78 E6
Brookhouse Green Ches E 76 E11
Brookhouses Derbys 77 J6
Brookland Kent 16 H5
Brooklands Traffd 76 E5
Brookmans Park Herts 45 J11
Brooks Powys 62 G12
Brooksby Leics 66 H9
Brooks End Kent 35 N9
Brooks Green W Susx 14 G6
Brook Street Essex 33 Q4
Brook Street Kent 16 G4
Brook Street Suffk 58 B11
Brook Street W Susx 15 K5
Brookthorpe Gloucs 41 N9
Brookville Norfk 57 P1
Brookwood Surrey 32 D11
Broom C Beds 44 H3
Broom Rothm 78 D5
Broom Warwks 53 K10
Broombank Worcs 52 C6
Broome Norfk 59 M2
Broome Shrops 51 L4
Broome Worcs 52 G5
Broomedge Warrtn 76 D6
Broome Park Nthumb 109 J7
Broomer's Corner W Susx 14 G6
Broomershill W Susx 14 F7
Broomfield Essex 46 C9
Broomfield Kent 34 E11
Broomfield Kent 35 M9
Broomfield Somset 21 K7
Broomfields Shrops 63 M8
Broomfleet E R Yk 86 G9
Broom Green Norfk 70 E7
Broomhall W & M 32 D9
Broomhaugh Nthumb 100 C6
Broom Hill Barns 78 C3
Broom Hill Dorset 11 P4
Broom Hill Notts 66 E3
Broomhill Nthumb 109 L9
Broom Hill Worcs 52 G5
Broomhill Green Ches E 64 B3
Broomley Nthumb 100 D6
Broompark Dur 100 G10
Broom's Green Gloucs 41 L5
Broomsthorpe Norfk 70 C6
Broom Street Kent 35 J10
Brora Highld 146 G4
Broseley Shrops 64 C11
Brotherhouse Bar Lincs 68 E10
Brotherlee Dur 99 P10
Brothertoft Lincs 68 E3
Brotherton N York 85 P10
Brotton R & Cl 92 E3
Broubster Highld 151 J5
Brough Cumb 90 C4
Brough Derbys 77 M7
Brough E R Yk 86 H10
Brough Highld 151 M2
Brough Notts 79 L12
Brough Shet 147 j5
Broughall Shrops 63 P4
Brough Lodge Shet 147 k3
Brough Sowerby Cumb 90 C4
Broughton Border 106 E3
Broughton Bucks 44 B9
Broughton Cambs 56 F5
Broughton Flints 75 K11
Broughton Hants 24 E7
Broughton Lancs 83 M8
Broughton M Keyn 44 C4
Broughton N Linc 79 N2
Broughton N York 84 D5
Broughton N York 92 F12
Broughton Nhants 55 L5
Broughton Oxon 43 J4
Broughton Salfd 76 F3
Broughton Staffs 64 E5
Broughton V Glam 27 L8
Broughton Astley Leics 54 E2
Broughton Beck Cumb 89 J10
Broughton Gifford Wilts 29 P9
Broughton Green Worcs 52 H8
Broughton Hackett Worcs 52 G9
Broughton-in-Furness Cumb 88 G9
Broughton Mains D & G 95 N9
Broughton Mills Cumb 88 H8
Broughton Moor Cumb 97 L11
Broughton Poggs Oxon 42 F11
Broughton Tower Cumb 88 G9
Broughty Ferry C Dund 125 J7
Brough with St Giles N York 91 L7
Brow End Cumb 88 H11
Brownber Cumb 90 B5
Brown Candover Hants 25 K5
Brown Edge Lancs 83 J12
Brown Edge Staffs 64 G1
Brown Heath Ches W 75 M10
Brownheath Shrops 63 M6
Brownhill Abers 141 L8
Brownhills Fife 125 K9
Brownhills Wsall 65 K11
Brownieside Nthumb 109 K5
Browninghill Green Hants 31 M10
Brown Lees Staffs 64 G1
Brownlow Heath Ches E 76 F11
Brownrigg Cumb 88 D3
Brownrigg Cumb 97 N7
Brownsea Island Dorset 11 N7
Brown's Green Birm 53 K2
Brownsham Devon 18 F8
Browns Hill Gloucs 41 P11
Brownsover Warwks 54 E5
Brownston Devon 5 L6
Brown Street Suffk 58 F8
Brow-of-the-Hill Norfk 69 N8
Browston Green Norfk 71 P11
Broxa N York 93 J8
Broxbourne Herts 45 L10
Broxburn E Loth 116 F6
Broxburn W Loth 115 K7
Broxfield Nthumb 109 K6
Broxted Essex 45 Q6
Broxton Ches W 63 N1
Broyle Side E Susx 15 N8
Bruan Highld 151 P8
Bruar P & K 130 F11
Bruchag Ag & B 112 G9
Bruera Ches W 75 M11
Bruern Abbey Oxon 42 F7
Bruichladdich Ag & B 110 G9
Bruisyard Suffk 59 L7
Bruisyard Street Suffk 59 L7
Brumby N Linc 79 M2
Brund Staffs 77 L11
Brundall Norfk 71 L10
Brundish Suffk 59 K7
Brundish Street Suffk 59 K6
Brunery Highld 127 N10
Brunnion Cnwll 2 E7
Brunslow Shrops 51 L4
Brunswick Village N u Ty 100 G4
Bruntcliffe Leeds 85 K10
Brunthwaite C Brad 84 F6
Bruntingthorpe Leics 54 G3
Brunton Fife 124 G8
Brunton Nthumb 109 K5
Brunton Wilts 30 F11
Brushford Devon 8 C3
Brushford Somset 20 E8
Bruton Somset 22 F6
Bryan's Green Worcs 52 G7
Bryanston Dorset 11 L3
Bryant's Bottom Bucks 32 B2
Brydekirk D & G 97 N4
Bryher IoS 2 b1
Brymbo Wrexhm 63 J1
Brympton Somset 22 C10
Bryn Carmth 26 E2
Bryn Ches W 75 Q9
Bryn Neath 27 J4
Bryn Shrops 51 J4
Bryn Wigan 75 P3
Brynamman Carmth 38 H9
Brynberian Pembks 37 L3
Brynbryddan Neath 27 J4
Bryn Bwbach Gwynd 61 K5
Bryncae Rhondd 27 N6
Bryncethin Brdgnd 27 L5
Bryncir Gwynd 60 H3
Bryn-côch Neath 26 H2
Bryncroes Gwynd 60 C6
Bryncrug Gwynd 61 K11
Bryn Du IoA 72 E9
Bryn-Eden Gwynd 61 M6
Bryneglwys Denbgs 62 G3
Brynfields Wrexhm 63 K3
Brynford Flints 74 G9
Bryn Gates Wigan 75 Q3
Bryn Golau Rhondd 27 N5
Bryngwran IoA 72 F8
Bryngwyn Mons 40 E10
Bryngwyn Powys 50 G10
Bryn-Henllan Pembks 37 K3
Brynhoffnant Cerdgn 48 E10
Bryning Lancs 83 J9
Brynithel Blae G 28 B2
Brynmawr Blae G 40 B9
Bryn-mawr Gwynd 60 D5
Brynmenyn Brdgnd 27 L5
Brynmill Swans 26 F4
Brynna Rhondd 27 N6
Bryn-penarth Powys 62 F11
Brynrefail Gwynd 73 J11
Brynrefail IoA 72 H6
Brynsadler Rhondd 27 N6
Bryn Saith Marchog Denbgs 62 E2
Brynsiencyn IoA 72 H10
Brynteg IoA 72 H7
Bryn-y-bal Flints 75 J10
Bryn-y-Maen Conwy 73 P8
Bryn-yr-Eos Wrexhm 63 J4
Bualintur Highld 134 G11
Buarth-draw Flints 74 G8
Bubbenhall Warwks 54 B6
Bubwith E R Yk 86 D8
Buccleuch Border 107 J7
Buchanan Smithy Stirlg 113 N3
Buchanhaven Abers 141 Q6
Buchanty P & K 123 N7
Buchany Stirlg 123 J12
Buchlyvie Stirlg 113 Q2
Buckabank Cumb 98 D8
Buckden Cambs 56 D7
Buckden N York 90 F11
Buckenham Norfk 71 M11
Buckerell Devon 9 L5
Buckfast Devon 5 M3
Buckfastleigh Devon 5 M3
Buckhaven Fife 115 Q2
Buckholt Mons 40 G8
Buckhorn Devon 7 M5
Buckhorn Weston Dorset 22 G8
Buckhurst Hill Essex 33 M3
Buckie Moray 140 C3
Buckingham Bucks 43 P5
Buckland Bucks 44 C9
Buckland Devon 5 L8
Buckland Gloucs 42 C4
Buckland Hants 12 E5
Buckland Herts 45 L5
Buckland Kent 17 P2
Buckland Oxon 30 H3
Buckland Surrey 33 J12
Buckland Brewer Devon 18 H9
Buckland Common Bucks 44 C10
Buckland Dinham Somset 22 G3
Buckland Filleigh Devon 7 N3
Buckland in the Moor Devon 8 D10
Buckland Monachorum Devon 4 H3
Buckland Newton Dorset 10 G4
Buckland Ripers Dorset 10 G8
Buckland St Mary Somset 21 L10
Buckland-Tout-Saints Devon 5 M7
Bucklebury W Berk 31 L8
Bucklers Hard Hants 12 G5
Bucklesham Suffk 47 M3
Buckley Flints 75 J11
Buckley Green Warwks 53 M7
Bucklow Hill Ches E 76 D7
Buckminster Leics 67 L7
Bucknall C Stke 64 G3
Bucknall Lincs 80 D10
Bucknell Oxon 43 M6
Bucknell Shrops 51 K6
Buckpool Moray 140 C3
Bucksburn C Aber 133 L2
Buck's Cross Devon 18 G9
Bucks Green W Susx 14 F4
Buckshaw Village Lancs 83 M11
Bucks Hill Herts 32 F2
Bucks Horn Oak Hants 25 P5
Buck's Mills Devon 18 G8
Buckton E R Yk 93 N12
Buckton Herefs 51 L6
Buckton Nthumb 108 H2
Buckworth Cambs 56 C5
Budby Notts 78 G9
Buddileigh Staffs 64 D2
Bude Cnwll 7 J4
Budge's Shop Cnwll 4 E5
Budlake Devon 9 J5
Budle Nthumb 109 J3
Budleigh Salterton Devon 9 K8
Budlett's Common E Susx 15 N6
Budock Water Cnwll 3 J8
Buerton Ches E 64 C3
Bugbrooke Nhants 54 H9
Bugford Devon 5 P6
Buglawton Ches E 76 G11
Bugle Cnwll 3 P3
Bugley Dorset 22 H8
Bugthorpe E R Yk 86 E4
Buildwas Shrops 64 B11
Builth Road Powys 50 E10
Builth Wells Powys 50 E10
Bulbourne Herts 44 D9
Bulbridge Wilts 23 N7
Bulby Lincs 67 Q7
Bulford Wilts 23 Q5
Bulford Camp Wilts 24 C5
Bulkeley Ches E 63 P1
Bulkington Warwks 54 C3
Bulkington Wilts 29 Q10
Bulkworthy Devon 18 H10
Bullamoor N York 91 P8
Bull Bay IoA 72 G5
Bullbridge Derbys 66 B2
Bullbrook Br For 32 C8
Bullen's Green Herts 45 J10
Bulley Gloucs 41 M8
Bullgill Cumb 97 M10
Bullinghope Herefs 40 G4
Bullington Hants 24 G5
Bullington Lincs 80 B8
Bullockstone Kent 35 L9
Bull's Green Herts 45 K8
Bull's Green Norfk 59 N2
Bulmer Essex 46 E4
Bulmer N York 86 C2
Bulmer Tye Essex 46 E4
Bulphan Thurr 34 B5
Bulstone Devon 9 M7
Bulstrode Herts 44 E11
Bulverhythe E Susx 16 D9
Bulwark Abers 141 M7
Bulwell C Nott 66 E3
Bulwick Nhants 55 N2
Bumble's Green Essex 45 M10
Bunacaimb Highld 127 M6
Bunarkaig Highld 128 H7
Bunbury Ches E 75 P12
Bunbury Heath Ches E 75 P12
Bunchrew Highld 138 B6
Buncton W Susx 14 G8
Bundalloch Highld 136 B10
Bunessan Ag & B 119 L8
Bungay Suffk 59 L3
Bunker's Hill Lincs 68 E1
Bunnahabhain Ag & B 111 J6
Bunny Notts 66 F6
Buntait Highld 137 L9
Buntingford Herts 45 L6
Bunwell Norfk 58 G2
Bunwell Hill Norfk 58 H2
Bupton Derbys 65 N5
Burbage Derbys 77 K9
Burbage Leics 54 D2
Burbage Wilts 30 F10
Burcher Herefs 51 K8
Burchett's Green W & M 32 B6
Burcombe Wilts 23 N7
Burcot Oxon 31 M3
Burcot Worcs 52 H6
Burcote Shrops 52 D2
Burcott Bucks 44 B8
Burcott Bucks 44 C7
Burdale N York 86 G3
Bures Essex 46 F5
Burford Oxon 42 F9
Burford Shrops 51 P7
Burg Ag & B 119 L4
Burgate Suffk 58 G5
Burgates Hants 25 N7
Burge End Herts 44 G5
Burgess Hill W Susx 15 K7
Burgh Suffk 59 J10
Burgh by Sands Cumb 98 C6
Burgh Castle Norfk 71 P11
Burghclere Hants 31 K10
Burghead Moray 139 L2
Burghfield W Berk 31 N8
Burghfield Common W Berk 31 N9
Burgh Heath Surrey 33 J10
Burgh Hill E Susx 16 C5
Burghill Herefs 40 G3
Burgh Island Devon 5 K8
Burgh le Marsh Lincs 81 J10
Burgh next Aylsham Norfk 71 J7
Burgh on Bain Lincs 80 D6
Burgh St Margaret Norfk 71 N9
Burgh St Peter Norfk 59 P2
Burghwallis Donc 78 E1
Burham Kent 34 C10
Buriton Hants 25 M9
Burland Ches E 63 Q2
Burlawn Cnwll 6 E10
Burleigh Gloucs 41 P11
Burlescombe Devon 20 G10
Burleston Dorset 11 J6
Burlestone Devon 5 N7
Burley Hants 12 C4
Burley Rutlnd 67 L10
Burley Shrops 51 N4
Burleydam Ches E 63 Q4
Burley Gate Herefs 41 J2
Burley in Wharfedale C Brad 84 H6
Burley Lawn Hants 12 C4
Burley Street Hants 12 C4
Burley Wood Head C Brad 84 H6
Burlingham Green Norfk 71 M10
Burlingjobb Powys 51 J9
Burlington Shrops 64 E10
Burlton Shrops 63 M7
Burmarsh Kent 17 K4
Burmington Warwks 42 F4
Burn N York 86 B9
Burnage Manch 76 G5
Burnaston Derbys 65 P6
Burnbanks Cumb 89 N3
Burnbrae N Lans 114 F9
Burn Bridge N York 85 L5
Burnby E R Yk 86 F6
Burn Cross Sheff 77 Q4
Burndell W Susx 14 E10
Burnden Bolton 76 D2
Burnedge Rochdl 76 G2
Burneside Cumb 89 N7
Burneston N York 91 M9
Burnett BaNES 29 K9
Burnfoot Border 107 L7
Burnfoot Border 107 N6
Burnfoot D & G 106 C11
Burnfoot D & G 107 J12
Burnfoot D & G 107 K10
Burnfoot P & K 123 P12
Burnham Bucks 32 D6
Burnham N Linc 87 K11
Burnham Deepdale Norfk 69 Q3
Burnham Green Herts 45 J8
Burnham Market Norfk 70 B4
Burnham Norton Norfk 70 B3
Burnham-on-Crouch Essex 34 G3
Burnham-on-Sea Somset 21 M3
Burnham Overy Norfk 70 B4
Burnham Overy Staithe Norfk 70 C3
Burnham Thorpe Norfk 70 C4
Burnhead D & G 105 Q10
Burnhervie Abers 140 H12
Burnhill Green Staffs 64 E12
Burnhope Dur 100 F8
Burnhouse N Ayrs 113 M11
Burniston N York 93 K8
Burnley Lancs 84 C8
Burnmouth Border 117 L9
Burn Naze Lancs 82 H6
Burn of Cambus Stirlg 123 J12
Burnopfield Dur 100 F7
Burnrigg Cumb 98 F7
Burnsall N York 84 F3
Burnside Angus 124 H1
Burnside Angus 125 K3
Burnside Fife 124 D11
Burnside Moray 147 L11
Burnside W Loth 115 K6
Burnside of Duntrune Angus 125 J6

Burntcommon – Chargrove 167

Burntcommon Surrey 32 E11
Burntheath Derbys 65 N6
Burnt Heath Essex 47 J6
Burnt Hill W Berk 31 M7
Burnthouse Cnwll 3 J7
Burnt Houses Dur 91 J2
Burntisland Fife 115 N4
Burnt Oak E Susx 15 P5
Burnton E Ayrs 105 J8
Burntwood Flints 75 J10
Burntwood Staffs 65 K10
Burntwood Green Staffs 65 K10
Burnt Yates N York 85 K3
Burnworthy Somset 21 K10
Burpham Surrey 32 E12
Burpham W Susx 14 E9
Burradon N Tyne 100 H4
Burradon Nthumb 108 F8
Burrafirth Shet 147 k2
Burras Cnwll 2 H7
Burraton Cnwll 4 F3
Burravoe Shet 147 j4
Burrells Cumb 89 R3
Burrelton P & K 124 D5
Burridge Devon 9 Q3
Burridge Devon 19 L6
Burridge Hants 13 J3
Burrill N York 91 L9
Burringham N Linc 79 L2
Burrington Devon 19 M10
Burrington Herefs 51 M6
Burrington N Som 28 G10
Burrough End Cambs 57 M9
Burrough Green Cambs 57 M9
Burrough on the Hill Leics 67 J10
Burrow Lancs 89 Q11
Burrow Somset 20 E5
Burrow Bridge Somset 21 M7
Burrowhill Surrey 32 D9
Burrows Cross Surrey 14 F2
Burry Swans 26 C4
Burry Green Swans 26 C4
Burry Port Carmth 26 C2
Burscough Lancs 75 M1
Burscough Bridge Lancs 75 M1
Bursea E R Yk 86 E8
Burshill E R Yk 87 K5
Bursledon Hants 12 H3
Burslem C Stke 64 F2
Burstall Suffk 47 K3
Burstock Dorset 10 C4
Burston Norfk 58 H4
Burston Staffs 64 H6
Burstow Surrey 15 K3
Burstwick E R Yk 87 N9
Burtersett N York 90 E9
Burtholme Cumb 98 G5
Burthorpe Green Suffk 57 P8
Burthwaite Cumb 98 E8
Burthy Cnwll 3 M3
Burtle Hill Somset 21 N4
Burtoft Lincs 68 E5
Burton BCP 12 B6
Burton Ches W 75 K9
Burton Ches W 75 N11
Burton Dorset 10 G6
Burton Nthumb 109 K3
Burton Pembks 37 J9
Burton Somset 21 K4
Burton Somset 22 C10
Burton Wilts 22 H7
Burton Wilts 29 N6
Burton Agnes E R Yk 87 L3
Burton Bradstock Dorset 10 D7
Burton-by-Lincoln Lincs 79 N9
Burton Coggles Lincs 67 N7
Burton Dassett Warwks 54 C10
Burton End Essex 45 P7
Burton End Suffk 46 B3
Burton Fleming E R Yk 93 M12
Burton Green Warwks 53 P5
Burton Green Wrexhm 75 K12
Burton Hastings Warwks 54 C3
Burton-in-Kendal Cumb 89 N11
Burton-in-Kendal Services Cumb 89 N11
Burton in Lonsdale N York 89 Q12
Burton Joyce Notts 66 G3
Burton Latimer Nhants 55 M6
Burton Lazars Leics 67 J9
Burton Leonard N York 85 L2
Burton on the Wolds Leics 66 F8
Burton Overy Leics 54 H1
Burton Pedwardine Lincs 68 C4
Burton Pidsea E R Yk 87 N9
Burton Salmon N York 85 P9
Burton's Green Essex 46 E6
Burton upon Stather N Linc 86 G11
Burton upon Trent Staffs 65 N7
Burton Waters Lincs 79 M9
Burtonwood Warrtn 75 P5
Burtonwood Services Warrtn 75 P5
Burwardsley Ches W 75 N12
Burwarton Shrops 52 B4
Burwash E Susx 16 B6
Burwash Common E Susx 16 B6
Burwash Weald E Susx 16 B6
Burwell Cambs 57 L7
Burwell Lincs 80 G8
Burwen IoA 72 G5
Burwick Ork 147 c6
Bury Bury 76 E1
Bury Cambs 56 F4
Bury Somset 20 E8
Bury W Susx 14 E8
Bury End C Beds 44 G5
Bury Green Herts 45 N7
Bury St Edmunds Suffk 58 C8
Burythorpe N York 86 E2
Busby E Rens 113 Q10
Busby Stoop N York 91 P10
Buscot Oxon 30 F3
Bush Abers 133 J11
Bush Cnwll 7 J3
Bush Bank Herefs 51 M10
Bushbury Wolves 64 G11
Bushby Leics 66 G11
Bushey Herts 32 G3
Bushey Heath Herts 32 G3
Bush Green Norfk 59 J3
Bush Green Suffk 58 D9
Bush Hill Park Gt Lon 33 L3
Bushley Worcs 41 P5
Bushley Green Worcs 41 P5
Bushmead Bed 56 C8
Bushmoor Shrops 51 M3
Bushton Wilts 30 C7
Busk Cumb 98 H10
Buslingthorpe Lincs 79 Q6
Bussage Gloucs 41 P11
Bussex Somset 21 M6
Butcher's Cross E Susx 15 Q6
Butcombe N Som 28 G10
Bute Ag & B 112 F7
Butleigh Somset 22 C6
Butleigh Wootton Somset 22 C6
Butler's Cross Bucks 44 B10
Butler's Hill Notts 66 E3
Butlers Marston Warwks 53 Q10
Butley Suffk 59 M10
Butley High Corner Suffk 59 M10
Buttercrambe N York 86 D4
Butterdean Border 116 H8
Butterknowle Dur 91 J2
Butterleigh Devon 9 J3
Butterley Derbys 66 C2
Buttermere Cumb 88 G3
Buttermere Wilts 30 H10
Butters Green Staffs 64 E2
Buttershaw C Brad 84 H9
Butterstone P & K 123 Q4
Butterton Staffs 64 F4
Butterton Staffs 77 K12
Butterwick Dur 101 K12
Butterwick Lincs 68 G3
Butterwick N York 87 J1
Butterwick N York 92 E11
Butt Green Ches E 64 C2
Buttington Powys 62 H10
Buttonbridge Shrops 52 D5
Buttonoak Shrops 52 D5
Buttsash Hants 12 G3
Buttsbear Cross Cnwll 7 K4
Butt's Green Essex 46 D11
Buxhall Suffk 58 E9
Buxhall Fen Street Suffk 58 E9
Buxted E Susx 15 P6
Buxton Derbys 77 K9
Buxton Norfk 71 J7
Buxton Heath Norfk 71 J8
Buxworth Derbys 77 J7
Bwlch Powys 39 Q7
Bwlchgwyn Wrexhm 63 J2
Bwlchllan Cerdgn 49 K9
Bwlchnewydd Carmth 38 A7
Bwlchtocyn Gwynd 60 E7
Bwlch-y-cibau Powys 62 G8
Bwlch-y-Ddar Powys 62 G8
Bwlchyfadfa Cerdgn 48 G10
Bwlch-y-ffridd Powys 50 E2
Bwlch-y-groes Pembks 37 P3
Bwlchymyrdd Swans 26 E3
Bwlch-y-sarnau Powys 50 E6
Byermoor Gatesd 100 F7
Byers Green Dur 100 G11
Byfield Nhants 54 E10
Byfleet Surrey 32 F10
Byford Herefs 40 E3
Bygrave Herts 45 K4
Byker N u Ty 100 H5
Byland Abbey N York 92 B11
Bylaugh Norfk 70 F8
Bylchau Conwy 74 D11
Byley Ches W 76 D10
Bynea Carmth 26 E3
Byrness Nthumb 108 C9
Bystock Devon 9 J8
Bythorn Cambs 55 Q5
Byton Herefs 51 L8
Bywell Nthumb 100 D6
Byworth W Susx 14 E6

C

Cabbacott Devon 18 H9
Cabourne Lincs 80 C3
Cabrach Ag & B 111 L8
Cabrach Moray 140 B10
Cabus Lancs 83 L5
Cackle Street E Susx 15 N5
Cackle Street E Susx 16 C7
Cackle Street E Susx 16 E7
Cadbury Devon 8 G4
Cadbury Barton Devon 19 N10
Cadbury World Birm 53 K4
Cadder E Duns 114 B7
Caddington C Beds 44 F8
Caddonfoot Border 107 L3
Cadeby Donc 78 E4
Cadeby Leics 66 C11
Cadeleigh Devon 8 G3
Cade Street E Susx 15 R6
Cadgwith Cnwll 2 H11
Cadham Fife 124 F12
Cadishead Salfd 76 D5
Cadle Swans 26 F3
Cadley Lancs 83 M9
Cadley Wilts 24 D3
Cadley Wilts 30 E9
Cadmore End Bucks 31 R4
Cadnam Hants 24 E10
Cadney N Linc 79 P3
Cadole Flints 74 H11
Cadoxton V Glam 27 Q8
Cadoxton Juxta-Neath Neath 26 H3
Cadwst Denbgs 62 E5
Caeathro Gwynd 72 H11
Caehopkin Powys 39 K9
Caenby Lincs 79 P6
Caerau Brdgnd 27 K3
Caerau Cardif 27 Q7
Cae'r-bont Powys 39 J9
Cae'r bryn Carmth 38 F9
Caerdeon Gwynd 61 L8
Caer Farchell Pembks 36 F5
Caergeiliog IoA 72 E8
Caergwrle Flints 75 J12
Caerhun Conwy 73 N9
Caerlanrig Border 107 K9
Caerleon Newpt 28 D4
Caernarfon Gwynd 72 H11
Caernarfon Castle Gwynd 72 H11
Caerphilly Caerph 27 R5
Caersws Powys 50 E2
Caerwedros Cerdgn 48 F9
Caerwent Mons 28 G4
Caerwys Flints 74 F9
Caerynwch Gwynd 61 N8
Caggle Street Mons 40 E8
Caim IoA 73 K7
Caio Carmth 38 G4
Cairinis W Isls 152 c8
Cairnbaan Ag & B 112 B3
Cairnbulg Abers 141 P3
Cairncross Border 117 K8
Cairncurran Inver 113 L7
Cairndow Ag & B 121 M10
Cairneyhill Fife 115 J4
Cairngarroch D & G 94 F8
Cairngorms National Park 131 K4
Cairnie Abers 140 D7
Cairnorrie Abers 141 L7
Cairnryan D & G 94 F4
Cairnty Moray 139 P5
Caister-on-Sea Norfk 71 Q9
Caistor Lincs 80 C3
Caistor St Edmund Norfk 71 J11
Cakebole Worcs 52 G6
Cake Street Norfk 58 G2
Calais Street Suffk 46 H4
Calanais W Isls 152 f3
Calbourne IoW 12 G7
Calceby Lincs 80 G8
Calcoed Flints 74 G8
Calcot Gloucs 42 C9
Calcot W Berk 31 N8
Calcot Row W Berk 31 P8
Calcots Moray 139 N3
Calcott Kent 35 L9
Calcott Shrops 63 M9
Calcutt N York 85 M4
Calcutt Wilts 30 C4
Caldbeck Cumb 98 C10
Caldbergh N York 91 J9
Caldecote Cambs 56 C3
Caldecote Cambs 56 G9
Caldecote Herts 45 J4
Caldecote Nhants 54 H10
Caldecote Highfields Cambs 56 G9
Caldecott Nhants 55 N7
Caldecott Oxon 31 K3
Caldecott Rutlnd 55 L2
Caldecotte M Keyn 44 C5
Calder Cumb 88 D6
Calderbank N Lans 114 D8
Calder Bridge Cumb 88 D5
Calderbrook Rochdl 84 E11
Caldercruix N Lans 114 E7
Calder Grove Wakefd 85 L11
Caldermill S Lans 105 M1
Caldermore Rochdl 84 D12
Calder Vale Lancs 83 M6
Calderwood S Lans 114 B10
Caldey Island Pembks 37 M11
Caldicot Mons 28 G5
Caldmore Wsall 53 J1
Caldwell N York 91 K4
Caldy Wirral 74 H6
Caledfwlch Carmth 38 G6
Calenick Cnwll 3 K6
Calf of Man IoM 102 a7
Calford Green Suffk 46 C3
Calfsound Ork 147 d2
Calgary Ag & B 119 L2
Califer Moray 139 K4
California Falk 114 G6
California Norfk 71 P9
California Cross Devon 5 L6
Calke Derbys 66 B8
Calke Abbey Derbys 66 B8
Callakille Highld 135 M5
Callander Stirlg 122 G11
Callanish W Isls 152 f3
Callaughton Shrops 52 B1
Callerton N u Ty 100 F4
Callestick Cnwll 3 J4
Calligarry Highld 127 L4
Callington Cnwll 4 E3
Callingwood Staffs 65 M7
Callow Herefs 40 G5
Callow End Worcs 52 F10
Callow Hill Wilts 30 B5
Callow Hill Worcs 52 D6
Callow Hill Worcs 53 J7
Callows Grave Worcs 51 Q7
Calmore Hants 24 E10
Calmsden Gloucs 42 B10
Calne Wilts 30 A8
Calow Derbys 78 C9
Calshot Hants 12 H4
Calstock Cnwll 4 G3
Calstone Wellington Wilts 30 B8
Calthorpe Norfk 71 J6
Calthorpe Street Norfk 71 M7
Calthwaite Cumb 98 F10
Calton N York 84 D3
Calton Staffs 65 L2
Calveley Ches E 75 Q12
Calver Derbys 77 N9
Calverhall Shrops 63 Q5
Calver Hill Herefs 51 L11
Calverleigh Devon 20 E10
Calverley Leeds 85 J8
Calver Sough Derbys 77 N8
Calvert Bucks 43 P7
Calverton M Keyn 43 R4
Calverton Notts 66 G2
Calvine P & K 130 E11
Calvo Cumb 97 N7
Calzeat Border 106 E3
Cam Gloucs 29 M2
Camasachoirce Highld 127 P12
Camasine Highld 127 N12
Camas Luinie Highld 136 C10
Camastianavaig Highld 135 J8
Camault Muir Highld 137 N8
Camber E Susx 16 G7
Camberley Surrey 32 C10
Camberwell Gt Lon 33 L7
Camblesforth N York 86 C10
Cambo Nthumb 100 C1
Cambois Nthumb 100 H2
Camborne Cnwll 2 G6
Camborne & Redruth Mining District Cnwll 2 G6
Cambourne Cambs 56 F8
Cambridge Cambs 57 J9
Cambridge Gloucs 41 M11
Cambridge Airport Cambs 57 J9
Cambrose Cnwll 2 H5
Cambus Clacks 114 F2
Cambusavie Highld 146 D6
Cambusbarron Stirlg 114 E3
Cambuskenneth Stirlg 114 E2
Cambuslang S Lans 114 B9
Cambus o' May Abers 132 C5
Cambuswallace S Lans 106 D2
Camden Town Gt Lon 33 K5
Cameley BaNES 29 J11
Camelford Cnwll 6 G8
Camelon Falk 114 F5
Camerory Highld 139 J9
Camer's Green Worcs 41 M5
Camerton BaNES 29 K11
Camerton Cumb 97 L12
Camghouran P & K 122 F2
Camieston Border 107 P4
Cammachmore Abers 133 L5
Cammeringham Lincs 79 N7
Camore Highld 146 D7
Campbeltown Ag & B 103 K6
Campbeltown Airport Ag & B 103 J5
Camperdown N Tyne 100 H4
Cample D & G 106 B11
Campmuir P & K 124 E5
Camps W Loth 115 K7
Campsall Donc 78 E1
Campsea Ash Suffk 59 L9
Camps End Cambs 45 R3
Campton C Beds 44 G4
Camptown Border 107 R7
Camrose Pembks 36 H6
Camserney P & K 123 L3
Camusnagaul Highld 128 F9
Camusnagaul Highld 144 D7
Camusteel Highld 135 N7
Camusterrach Highld 135 N7
Canada Hants 24 D9
Canal Foot Cumb 89 J11
Canaston Bridge Pembks 37 L7
Candacraig Abers 131 Q4
Candlesby Lincs 81 J10
Candle Street Suffk 58 F6
Candover Green Shrops 63 N11
Candy Mill Border 106 E1
Cane End Oxon 31 P6
Canewdon Essex 34 F3
Canford Bottom Dorset 11 P5
Canford Cliffs BCP 11 P7
Canford Heath BCP 11 P6
Canford Magna BCP 11 P5
Canhams Green Suffk 58 F7
Canisbay Highld 151 Q2
Canklow Rothm 78 C5
Canley Covtry 53 P5
Cann Dorset 23 J9
Canna Highld 126 D3
Cann Common Dorset 23 K9
Cannich Highld 137 K9
Cannington Somset 21 L5
Canning Town Gt Lon 33 M6
Cannock Staffs 64 H10
Cannock Chase Staffs 65 J8
Cannock Wood Staffs 65 K9
Cannon Bridge Herefs 40 F3
Canonbie D & G 98 E3
Canon Frome Herefs 41 K3
Canon Pyon Herefs 51 M11
Canons Ashby Nhants 54 F10
Canonstown Cnwll 2 E7
Canterbury Kent 35 L10
Canterbury Cathedral Kent 35 L10
Cantley Norfk 71 M11
Cantlop Shrops 63 N11
Canton Cardif 27 R7
Cantraywood Highld 138 E6
Cantsfield Lancs 89 Q12
Canvey Island Essex 34 D6
Canwick Lincs 79 N10
Canworthy Water Cnwll 7 J6
Caol Highld 128 F9
Caolas Scalpaigh W Isls 152 f6
Caoles Ag & B 118 E3
Caonich Highld 128 E6
Capel Kent 16 B2
Capel Surrey 14 H3
Capel Bangor Cerdgn 49 L4
Capel Betws Lleucu Cerdgn 49 K9
Capel Coch IoA 72 G7
Capel Curig Conwy 73 M12
Capel Cynon Cerdgn 48 F10
Capel Dewi Carmth 38 C7
Capel Dewi Cerdgn 38 C3
Capel-Dewi Cerdgn 49 K4
Capel Garmon Conwy 61 P1
Capel Green Suffk 59 M10
Capel Gwyn Carmth 38 C7
Capel Gwyn IoA 72 E8
Capel Gwynfe Carmth 38 H7
Capel Hendre Carmth 38 F9
Capel Isaac Carmth 38 E6
Capel Iwan Carmth 37 Q3
Capel-le-Ferne Kent 17 N3
Capelles Guern 12 c2
Capel Llanilltern Cardif 27 P6
Capel Mawr IoA 72 G9
Capel Parc IoA 72 G6
Capel St Andrew Suffk 59 M11
Capel St Mary Suffk 47 K4
Capel Seion Cerdgn 49 L5
Capel Trisant Cerdgn 49 M5
Capeluchaf Gwynd 60 G2
Capelulo Conwy 73 N8
Capel-y-ffin Powys 40 C5
Capel-y-graig Gwynd 73 J10
Capenhurst Ches W 75 L9
Capernwray Lancs 89 N12
Cape Wrath Highld 148 F2
Capheaton Nthumb 100 D2
Caplaw E Rens 113 N9
Capon's Green Suffk 59 K7
Cappercleuch Border 106 H5
Capstone Medway 34 D9
Capton Devon 5 P6
Capton Somset 20 H5
Caputh P & K 124 B5
Caradon Mining District Cnwll 7 K10
Caradon Town Cnwll 7 K10
Carbeth Inn Stirlg 113 Q5
Carbis Cnwll 3 N3
Carbis Bay Cnwll 2 E7
Carbost Highld 134 G6
Carbost Highld 134 G9
Carbrook Sheff 78 C6
Carbrooke Norfk 70 D11
Carburton Notts 78 G9
Carclaze Cnwll 3 P4
Car Colston Notts 67 J4
Carcroft Donc 78 E2
Cardenden Fife 115 M2
Cardeston Shrops 63 L9
Cardewlees Cumb 98 D8
Cardhu Moray 139 M7
Cardiff Cardif 28 A7
Cardiff Airport V Glam 27 P9
Cardiff Gate Services Cardif 28 B6
Cardiff West Services Cardif 27 P6
Cardigan Cerdgn 48 B11
Cardinal's Green Cambs 45 R2
Cardington Bed 56 B11
Cardington Shrops 51 N2
Cardinham Cnwll 6 G11
Cardrain D & G 94 G12
Cardrona Border 107 J2
Cardross Ag & B 113 L6
Cardryne D & G 94 G11
Cardurnock Cumb 97 N6
Careby Lincs 67 P9
Careston Angus 132 E12
Carew Pembks 37 K9
Carew Cheriton Pembks 37 K10
Carew Newton Pembks 37 K9
Carey Herefs 40 H5
Carfin N Lans 114 E9
Carfraemill Border 116 C10
Cargate Green Norfk 71 M9
Cargenbridge D & G 97 J3
Cargill P & K 124 C5
Cargo Cumb 98 D6
Cargreen Cnwll 4 F4
Cargurrel Cnwll 3 L7
Carham Nthumb 108 C2
Carhampton Somset 20 F5
Carharrack Cnwll 3 J6
Carie P & K 122 G1
Carinish W Isls 152 c8
Carisbrooke IoW 12 H7
Cark Cumb 89 K11
Carkeel Cnwll 4 F5
Càrlabhagh W Isls 152 e2
Carland Cross Cnwll 3 L4
Carlbury Darltn 91 L4
Carlby Lincs 67 P9
Carlcroft Nthumb 108 D7
Carlecotes Barns 77 M3
Carleen Cnwll 2 F8
Carlesmoor N York 91 L12
Carleton Cumb 88 D5
Carleton Cumb 98 E7
Carleton Cumb 98 G12
Carleton Lancs 82 H7
Carleton Wakefd 85 P11
Carleton Forehoe Norfk 70 G11
Carleton-in-Craven N York 84 E5
Carleton Rode Norfk 58 G2
Carleton St Peter Norfk 71 L11
Carlidnack Cnwll 3 J8
Carlincraig Abers 140 G7
Carlingcott BaNES 29 L10
Carlin How R & Cl 92 E3
Carlisle Cumb 98 E7
Carlisle Airport Cumb 98 F6
Carloggas Cnwll 6 C11
Carlops Border 115 L10
Carloway W Isls 152 e2
Carlton Barns 78 B2
Carlton Bed 55 N9
Carlton Cambs 57 M10
Carlton Leeds 85 M9
Carlton Leics 66 C11
Carlton N York 86 C10
Carlton N York 90 H10
Carlton N York 92 C9
Carlton Notts 66 G4
Carlton S on T 91 P2
Carlton Suffk 59 M8
Carlton Colville Suffk 59 P3
Carlton Curlieu Leics 54 H1
Carlton Green Cambs 57 M10
Carlton Husthwaite N York 92 A11
Carlton-in-Cleveland N York 92 A6
Carlton in Lindrick Notts 78 F7
Carlton-le-Moorland Lincs 79 M12
Carlton Miniott N York 91 P10
Carlton-on-Trent Notts 79 K11
Carlton Scroop Lincs 67 N3
Carluke S Lans 114 F11
Carlyon Bay Cnwll 3 P4
Carmacoup S Lans 105 P4
Carmarthen Carmth 38 B7
Carmel Carmth 38 E8
Carmel Flints 74 G8
Carmel Gwynd 60 H1
Carmichael S Lans 106 B2
Carmunnock C Glas 114 A9
Carmyle C Glas 114 B9
Carmyllie Angus 125 L4
Carnaby E R Yk 87 L2
Carnbee Fife 125 K11
Carnbo P & K 123 Q12
Carn Brea Cnwll 2 H6
Carnbrogie Abers 141 K10
Carndu Highld 136 B10
Carnduff S Lans 114 B12
Carne Cnwll 3 J9
Carne Cnwll 3 M7
Carne Cnwll 3 N3
Carnell E Ayrs 105 J3
Carnewas Cnwll 6 B11
Carnforth Lancs 83 L1
Carn-gorm Highld 136 C11
Carnhedryn Pembks 36 F5
Carnhell Green Cnwll 2 F7
Carnie Abers 133 K3
Carnkie Cnwll 2 H6
Carnkie Cnwll 2 H7
Carnkiet Cnwll 3 J4
Carno Powys 50 C1
Carnock Fife 115 J3
Carnon Downs Cnwll 3 K6
Carnousie Abers 140 G6
Carnoustie Angus 125 L6
Carnsmerry Cnwll 3 P3
Carnwath S Lans 114 H12
Carnyorth Cnwll 2 B8
Carol Green Solhll 53 N5
Carpalla Cnwll 3 N4
Carperby N York 90 G9
Carr Rothm 78 E6
Carradale Ag & B 103 L2
Carrbridge Highld 138 G11
Carrbrook Tamesd 77 J3
Carrefour Jersey 13 b1
Carreglefn IoA 72 F6
Carr Gate Wakefd 85 L10
Carrhouse N Linc 79 K2
Carrick Ag & B 112 D4
Carrick Castle Ag & B 113 J2
Carriden Falk 115 J5
Carrington Lincs 68 F1
Carrington Mdloth 115 P9
Carrington Traffd 76 D5
Carrog Conwy 61 N3
Carrog Denbgs 62 F3
Carron Falk 114 F5
Carron Moray 139 N7
Carronbridge D & G 105 R10
Carron Bridge Stirlg 114 D4
Carronshore Falk 114 G5
Carrow Hill Mons 28 F4
Carr Shield Nthumb 99 M8
Carrutherstown D & G 97 M4
Carruth House Inver 113 M8
Carr Vale Derbys 78 D9
Carrville Dur 100 H9
Carsaig Ag & B 119 P8
Carseriggan D & G 95 K5
Carsethorn D & G 97 K6
Carshalton Gt Lon 33 K9
Carsington Derbys 65 N2
Carskey Ag & B 103 J8
Carsluith D & G 95 N7
Carsphairn D & G 105 K11
Carstairs S Lans 114 G12
Carstairs Junction S Lans 114 H12
Carswell Marsh Oxon 30 G3
Carter's Clay Hants 24 E8
Carters Green Essex 45 P9
Carterton Oxon 42 G10
Carterway Heads Nthumb 100 D8
Carthew Cnwll 3 N3
Carthorpe N York 91 M10
Cartington Nthumb 108 G9
Cartland S Lans 114 F12
Cartledge Derbys 77 Q8
Cartmel Cumb 89 K11
Cartmel Fell Cumb 89 L9
Carway Carmth 38 C10
Carwinley Cumb 98 E4
Cashe's Green Gloucs 41 N10
Cashmoor Dorset 23 L10
Cassington Oxon 43 K9
Cassop Dur 101 J10
Castallack Cnwll 2 D9
Castel Guern 12 c2
Castell Conwy 73 N10
Castell-y-bwch Torfn 28 C4
Casterton Cumb 89 Q11
Castle Cnwll 3 Q3
Castle Acre Norfk 70 B9
Castle Ashby Nhants 55 L8
Castlebay W Isls 152 b13
Castle Bolton N York 90 G8
Castle Bromwich Solhll 53 L3
Castle Bytham Lincs 67 N8
Castlebythe Pembks 37 K5
Castle Caereinion Powys 62 G11
Castle Camps Cambs 46 A3
Castle Carrock Cumb 98 G7
Castlecary Falk 114 E6
Castle Cary Somset 22 E7
Castle Combe Wilts 29 N7
Castle Donington Leics 66 D7
Castle Douglas D & G 96 F6
Castle Eaton Swindn 30 D3
Castle Eden Dur 101 L10
Castle End C Pete 68 C10
Castleford Wakefd 85 N10
Castle Frome Herefs 41 K3
Castle Gate Cnwll 2 D7
Castle Green Cumb 89 N8
Castle Green Surrey 32 D10
Castle Gresley Derbys 65 P8
Castle Hedingham Essex 46 D4
Castlehill Border 106 G3
Castlehill Highld 151 M3
Castle Hill Kent 16 C2
Castle Hill Suffk 47 L2
Castlehill W Duns 113 M6
Castle Howard N York 86 D1
Castle Kennedy D & G 94 G6
Castle Lachlan Ag & B 112 E2
Castlemartin Pembks 36 H11
Castlemilk C Glas 114 A9
Castle Morris Pembks 36 H4
Castlemorton Worcs 41 M4
Castlemorton Common Worcs 41 M4
Castle O'er D & G 106 H11
Castle Rising Norfk 69 M7
Castleside Dur 100 D8
Castle Stuart Highld 138 D6
Castlethorpe M Keyn 44 A3
Castlethorpe N Linc 79 N2
Castleton Ag & B 112 C4
Castleton Border 107 N11
Castleton Derbys 77 M7
Castleton N York 92 E5
Castleton Newpt 28 C6
Castleton Rochdl 76 G2
Castletown Ches W 63 M2
Castletown Dorset 10 G10
Castletown Highld 151 M3
Castletown IoM 102 c7
Castletown Sundld 101 J6
Castley N York 85 K6
Caston Norfk 58 E1
Castor C Pete 56 C1
Caswell Bay Swans 26 E5
Catacol N Ayrs 112 D11
Cat and Fiddle Derbys 77 J9
Catbrain S Glos 28 H6
Catbrook Mons 40 G11
Catch Flints 74 H9
Catchall Cnwll 2 C9
Catchem's Corner Solhll 53 N5
Catchgate Dur 100 F8
Catcliffe Rothm 78 C6
Catcomb Wilts 30 B7
Catcott Somset 21 N5
Catcott Burtle Somset 21 N5
Caterham Surrey 33 L11
Catfield Norfk 71 M8
Catfield Common Norfk 71 M8
Catford Gt Lon 33 L8
Catforth Lancs 83 L8
Cathcart C Glas 113 R9
Cathedine Powys 39 Q6
Catherine-de-Barnes Solhll 53 M5
Catherine Slack C Brad 84 G9
Catherington Hants 25 M10
Catherston Leweston Dorset 10 B6
Catherton Shrops 52 C5
Catisfield Hants 13 J3
Catley Herefs 41 K3
Catley Lane Head Rochdl 84 C12
Catlodge Highld 130 B6
Catlow Lancs 84 C8
Catlowdy Cumb 98 F3
Catmere End Essex 45 P4
Catmore W Berk 31 K6
Caton Devon 8 E10
Caton Lancs 83 M2
Caton Green Lancs 83 M2
Cator Court Devon 8 C9
Catrine E Ayrs 105 K5
Cat's Ash Newpt 28 E4
Catsfield E Susx 16 C8
Catsfield Stream E Susx 16 C8
Catsgore Somset 22 C8
Catsham Somset 22 D6
Catshill Worcs 52 H6
Catstree Shrops 52 D1
Cattadale Ag & B 103 J7
Cattal N York 85 P4
Cattawade Suffk 47 K5
Catterall Lancs 83 L6
Catteralslane Shrops 63 P4
Catterick N York 91 L7
Catterick Bridge N York 91 L7
Catterick Garrison N York 91 K7
Catterlen Cumb 98 F11
Catterline Abers 133 L8
Catterton N York 85 Q6
Catteshall Surrey 14 D2
Catthorpe Leics 54 F5
Cattishall Suffk 58 C7
Cattistock Dorset 10 F5
Catton N York 91 N11
Catton Nthumb 99 M7
Catwick E R Yk 87 L6
Catworth Cambs 56 B6
Caudle Green Gloucs 41 Q9
Caulcott C Beds 44 E3
Caulcott Oxon 43 L7
Cauldcots Angus 125 N3
Cauldhame Stirlg 114 B2
Cauldmill Border 107 N6
Cauldon Staffs 65 K2
Cauldon Lowe Staffs 65 K3
Cauldwell Derbys 65 N9
Caulkerbush D & G 97 J7
Caulside D & G 98 F2
Caundle Marsh Dorset 22 F10
Caunsall Worcs 52 F4
Caunton Notts 79 J11
Causeway Hants 25 N9
Causeway End Cumb 89 M9
Causeway End D & G 95 M6
Causeway End Essex 46 B8
Causewayend S Lans 106 D2
Causewayhead Cumb 97 M7
Causewayhead Stirlg 114 E2
Causeyend Abers 141 M12
Causey Park Nthumb 109 K10
Causey Park Bridge Nthumb 109 K10
Cavendish Suffk 46 E2
Cavenham Suffk 57 P6
Caversfield Oxon 43 M6
Caversham Readg 31 P7
Caverswall Staffs 64 H4
Caverton Mill Border 108 B5
Cavil E R Yk 86 E9
Cawdor Highld 138 F6
Cawkwell Lincs 80 F7
Cawood N York 86 A8
Cawsand Cnwll 4 F6
Cawston Norfk 70 H7
Cawston Warwks 54 D6
Cawthorn N York 92 F9
Cawthorne Barns 77 P2
Cawton N York 92 D11
Caxton Cambs 56 F9
Caxton End Cambs 56 F9
Caxton Gibbet Cambs 56 F8
Caynham Shrops 51 P6
Caythorpe Lincs 67 M2
Caythorpe Notts 66 H3
Cayton N York 93 L10
Ceannabeinne Highld 149 K3
Ceann a Bhaigh W Isls 152 b8
Ceannacroc Lodge Highld 128 H2
Cearsiadar W Isls 152 f4
Ceciliford Mons 40 G11
Cefn Newpt 28 C5
Cefn Berain Conwy 74 D10
Cefn-brîth Conwy 62 C2
Cefn-bryn-brain Carmth 38 H9
Cefn Byrle Powys 39 K9
Cefn Canel Powys 62 H6
Cefn Coch Powys 62 F7
Cefn-coed-y-cymmer Myr Td 39 N10
Cefn Cribwr Brdgnd 27 K6
Cefn Cross Brdgnd 27 K6
Cefn-ddwysarn Gwynd 62 C4
Cefn-Einion Shrops 51 J3
Cefneithin Carmth 38 E9
Cefngorwydd Powys 39 L3
Cefn-mawr Wrexhm 63 J4
Cefnpennar Rhondd 27 N2
Cefn-y-bedd Flints 63 K1
Cefn-y-pant Carmth 37 N5
Ceint IoA 72 H8
Cellan Cerdgn 49 K10
Cellardyke Fife 125 L12
Cellarhead Staffs 64 H3
Celleron Cumb 89 M2
Celynen Caerph 28 B3
Cemaes IoA 72 F5
Cemmaes Powys 61 P11
Cemmaes Road Powys 61 P11
Cenarth Cerdgn 37 P2
Cerbyd Pembks 36 F5
Ceres Fife 124 H10
Cerne Abbas Dorset 10 G4
Cerney Wick Gloucs 30 C3
Cerrigceinwen IoA 72 G9
Cerrigydrudion Conwy 62 C2
Cess Norfk 71 N8
Ceunant Gwynd 73 J11
Chaceley Gloucs 41 P5
Chacewater Cnwll 3 J5
Chackmore Bucks 43 P4
Chacombe Nhants 43 K3
Chadbury Worcs 42 B2
Chadderton Oldham 76 G3
Chadderton Fold Oldham 76 G2
Chaddesden C Derb 66 C5
Chaddesley Corbett Worcs 52 G6
Chaddlehanger Devon 7 N9
Chaddleworth W Berk 31 J7
Chadlington Oxon 42 G7
Chadshunt Warwks 53 Q10
Chadwell Leics 67 K7
Chadwell Shrops 64 E9
Chadwell End Bed 55 Q7
Chadwell Heath Gt Lon 33 N5
Chadwell St Mary Thurr 34 B6
Chadwick Worcs 52 F7
Chadwick End Solhll 53 N6
Chadwick Green St Hel 75 N4
Chaffcombe Somset 9 Q3
Chafford Hundred Thurr 33 R6
Chagford Devon 8 D7
Chailey E Susx 15 M7
Chainbridge Cambs 68 H12
Chainhurst Kent 16 C1
Chalbury Dorset 11 N3
Chalbury Common Dorset 11 P3
Chaldon Surrey 33 K11
Chaldon Herring Dorset 11 J8
Chale IoW 12 H9
Chale Green IoW 12 H9
Chalfont Common Bucks 32 E4
Chalfont St Giles Bucks 32 E4
Chalfont St Peter Bucks 32 E4
Chalford Gloucs 41 P11
Chalford Oxon 31 P2
Chalford Wilts 23 J3
Chalgrave C Beds 44 E6
Chalgrove Oxon 31 N3
Chalk Kent 34 B8
Chalk End Essex 46 A9
Chalkhouse Green Oxon 31 P6
Chalkway Somset 10 B3
Chalkwell Kent 34 F9
Challaborough Devon 5 K8
Challacombe Devon 19 N5
Challoch D & G 95 M5
Challock Kent 34 H12
Chalmington Dorset 10 F4
Chalton C Beds 44 E6
Chalton C Beds 56 C10
Chalton Hants 25 M10
Chalvey Slough 32 D6
Chalvington E Susx 15 P9
Chambers Green Kent 16 G2
Chandler's Cross Herts 32 F3
Chandlers Cross Worcs 41 M4
Chandler's Ford Hants 24 G9
Channel's End Bed 56 B9
Channel Tunnel Terminal Kent 17 L3
Chantry Somset 22 G4
Chantry Suffk 47 L3
Chapel Cumb 97 P12
Chapel Fife 115 N3
Chapel Allerton Leeds 85 L8
Chapel Allerton Somset 21 N3
Chapel Amble Cnwll 6 E9
Chapel Brampton Nhants 55 J7
Chapelbridge Cambs 56 F2
Chapel Chorlton Staffs 64 E5
Chapel Cross E Susx 15 R7
Chapel End Bed 56 B9
Chapel End C Beds 44 F3
Chapel End Cambs 56 C4
Chapel End Warwks 53 Q2
Chapelend Way Essex 46 C4
Chapel-en-le-Frith Derbys 77 K7
Chapel Field Bury 76 E2
Chapelgate Lincs 68 H7
Chapel Green Warwks 53 P4
Chapel Green Warwks 54 D8
Chapel Haddlesey N York 86 A10
Chapelhall N Lans 114 E8
Chapel Hill Abers 141 P9
Chapel Hill Lincs 68 D1
Chapel Hill Mons 28 H2
Chapel Hill N York 85 M6
Chapelhope Border 106 G6
Chapelknowe D & G 98 C4
Chapel Lawn Shrops 51 K5
Chapel-le-Dale N York 90 B11
Chapel Leigh Somset 20 H7
Chapel Milton Derbys 77 K7
Chapel of Garioch Abers 140 H11
Chapel Rossan D & G 94 G9
Chapel Row E Susx 16 B8
Chapel Row Essex 34 D2
Chapel Row W Berk 31 M8
Chapels Cumb 88 H10
Chapel St Leonards Lincs 81 L9
Chapel Stile Cumb 89 J6
Chapelton Abers 133 L6
Chapelton Angus 125 M3
Chapelton Devon 19 L8
Chapelton S Lans 114 C11
Chapeltown Bl w D 83 Q12
Chapel Town Cnwll 3 L3
Chapeltown Moray 139 N11
Chapeltown Sheff 78 B4
Chapmanslade Wilts 23 J4
Chapmans Well Devon 7 L6
Chapmore End Herts 45 L8
Chappel Essex 46 F6
Charaton Cnwll 4 D3
Chard Somset 9 Q3
Chard Junction Somset 9 Q4
Chardleigh Green Somset 9 Q3
Chardstock Devon 9 Q4
Charfield S Glos 29 L4
Chargrove Gloucs 41 Q8

168 Charing – Colmonell

Charing Kent 16 G1
Charing Heath Kent 16 G1
Charing Hill Kent 34 G12
Charingworth Gloucs 42 E4
Charlbury Oxon 42 H7
Charlcombe BaNES 29 M9
Charlcutt Wilts 30 A7
Charlecote Warwks 53 P9
Charlemont Sandw 53 J2
Charles Devon 19 N7
Charleshill Surrey 14 C2
Charleston Angus 124 H4
Charlestown C Aber 133 M4
Charlestown C Brad 84 H7
Charlestown Calder 84 E10
Charlestown Cnwll 3 P4
Charlestown Cnwll 3 P4
Charlestown Derbys 77 J5
Charlestown Dorset 10 G9
Charlestown Fife 115 K4
Charlestown Highld 138 B6
Charlestown Highld 143 L10
Charlestown Salfd 76 E4
Charlestown of Aberlour Moray 139 N7
Charles Tye Suffk 58 F10
Charlesworth Derbys 77 J5
Charlinch Somset 21 K6
Charlottetown Fife 124 F10
Charlton Gt Lon 33 M7
Charlton Hants 24 F4
Charlton Herts 44 H6
Charlton Nhants 43 L4
Charlton Nthumb 99 M1
Charlton Oxon 31 J5
Charlton Somset 21 L8
Charlton Somset 22 E5
Charlton Somset 22 F3
Charlton Surrey 32 F8
Charlton W Susx 14 C8
Charlton Wilts 23 K9
Charlton Wilts 29 Q4
Charlton Worcs 42 B3
Charlton Worcs 52 F6
Charlton Wrekin 63 Q10
Charlton Abbots Gloucs 42 B7
Charlton Adam Somset 22 C7
Charlton All Saints Wilts 24 B8
Charlton Down Dorset 10 G6
Charlton Hill Shrops 63 P10
Charlton Horethorne Somset 22 F8
Charlton Kings Gloucs 41 Q7
Charlton Mackrell Somset 22 C7
Charlton Marshall Dorset 11 L4
Charlton Musgrove Somset 22 G7
Charlton-on-Otmoor Oxon 43 M8
Charlton on the Hill Dorset 11 L4
Charlton St Peter Wilts 30 D11
Charlwood Hants 25 L7
Charlwood Surrey 15 J3
Charminster Dorset 10 G6
Charmouth Dorset 10 B6
Charndon Bucks 43 P7
Charney Bassett Oxon 30 H3
Charnock Green Lancs 83 M11
Charnock Richard Lancs 83 M12
Charnock Richard Services Lancs 83 M12
Charsfield Suffk 59 K9
Chart Corner Kent 34 D12
Charter Alley Hants 31 M10
Charterhall Border 116 H11
Charterhouse Somset 22 C2
Chartershall Stirlg 114 E3
Charterville Allotments Oxon 42 G9
Chartham Kent 35 K11
Chartham Hatch Kent 35 K11
Chart Hill Kent 16 D1
Chartridge Bucks 44 D11
Chart Sutton Kent 16 E1
Chartway Street Kent 34 E12
Charvil Wokham 31 Q7
Charwelton Nhants 54 E9
Chase Terrace Staffs 65 J10
Chasetown Staffs 65 K10
Chastleton Oxon 42 F6
Chasty Devon 7 L4
Chatburn Lancs 84 A6
Chatcull Staffs 64 E5
Chatham Caerph 28 B4
Chatham Medway 34 D9
Chatham Green Essex 46 C8
Chathill Nthumb 109 K4
Chatley Worcs 52 F8
Chatsworth House Derbys 77 N9
Chattenden Medway 34 D8
Chatter End Essex 45 N6
Chatteris Cambs 56 H3
Chatterton Lancs 84 B11
Chattisham Suffk 47 K3
Chatto Border 108 C6
Chatton Nthumb 108 H4
Chaul End C Beds 44 F7
Chawleigh Devon 19 N11
Chawley Oxon 43 K10
Chawston Bed 56 C9
Chawton Hants 25 M6
Chaxhill Gloucs 41 L9
Chazey Heath Oxon 31 P7
Cheadle Staffs 65 J3
Cheadle Stockp 76 F6
Cheadle Heath Stockp 76 G6
Cheadle Hulme Stockp 76 G6
Cheam Gt Lon 33 J9
Cheapside W & M 32 D8
Chearsley Bucks 43 P9
Chebsey Staffs 64 F6
Checkendon Oxon 31 N6
Checkley Ches E 64 D3
Checkley Herefs 41 J4
Checkley Staffs 65 J5
Checkley Green Ches E 64 D3
Chedburgh Suffk 57 Q9
Cheddar Somset 21 P3
Cheddington Bucks 44 C8
Cheddleton Staffs 64 H2
Cheddleton Heath Staffs 65 J2
Cheddon Fitzpaine Somset 21 K8
Chedglow Wilts 29 Q4
Chedgrave Norfk 71 M12
Chedington Dorset 10 D4
Chediston Suffk 59 M5
Chediston Green Suffk 59 M5
Chedworth Gloucs 42 B9
Chedzoy Somset 21 M6
Cheeseman's Green Kent 17 J3
Cheetham Hill Manch 76 F3
Cheldon Devon 19 P10
Chelford Ches E 76 F9
Chellaston C Derb 66 B6
Chellington Bed 55 N9
Chelmarsh Shrops 52 D3
Chelmick Shrops 51 M2
Chelmondiston Suffk 47 M4
Chelmorton Derbys 77 L9
Chelmsford Essex 46 C10
Chelmsley Wood Solhll 53 M3
Chelsea Gt Lon 33 K7
Chelsfield Gt Lon 33 N9
Chelsham Surrey 33 L10
Chelston Somset 21 J9
Chelsworth Suffk 58 E11
Cheltenham Gloucs 41 Q7
Chelveston Nhants 55 N7
Chelvey N Som 28 G8
Chelwood BaNES 29 K10
Chelwood Common E Susx 15 M5
Chelwood Gate E Susx 15 M5
Chelworth Wilts 29 R3
Chelworth Lower Green Wilts 30 C4
Chelworth Upper Green Wilts 30 C4
Cheney Longville Shrops 51 M4
Chenies Bucks 32 E3
Chepstow Mons 28 H4
Chequerbent Bolton 76 C2
Chequers Corner Norfk 69 J10
Cherhill Wilts 30 B8
Cherington Gloucs 29 P3
Cherington Warwks 42 G4
Cheriton Devon 19 P4
Cheriton Hants 25 K7
Cheriton Kent 17 M3
Cheriton Pembks 37 J11
Cheriton Swans 26 C4
Cheriton Bishop Devon 8 E6
Cheriton Fitzpaine Devon 8 G3
Cherrington Wrekin 64 C8
Cherry Burton E R Yk 87 J7
Cherry Hinton Cambs 57 J9
Cherry Orchard Worcs 52 F10
Cherry Willingham Lincs 79 P9
Chertsey Surrey 32 F9
Cherwell Valley Services Oxon 43 L6
Cheselbourne Dorset 11 J5
Chesham Bucks 44 D11
Chesham Bury 76 E1
Chesham Bois Bucks 32 D2
Cheshunt Herts 45 L11
Chesil Beach Dorset 10 F9
Chesley Kent 34 E9
Cheslyn Hay Staffs 64 H10
Chessetts Wood Warwks 53 M6
Chessington Gt Lon 32 H9
Chessington World of Adventures Gt Lon 32 H10
Chester Ches W 75 L10
Chesterblade Somset 22 F5
Chesterfield Derbys 78 C9
Chesterfield Staffs 65 L11
Chesterhill Mdloth 115 Q8
Chester-le-Street Dur 100 H8
Chester Moor Dur 100 H8
Chesters Border 107 P5
Chesters Border 107 Q7
Chester Services Ches W 75 M8
Chesterton Cambs 56 C2
Chesterton Cambs 57 J8
Chesterton Gloucs 30 B2
Chesterton Oxon 43 M7
Chesterton Shrops 52 E1
Chesterton Staffs 64 F2
Chesterton Green Warwks 54 B9
Chesterwood Nthumb 99 M5
Chester Zoo Ches W 75 L9
Chestfield Kent 35 K9
Chestnut Street Kent 34 F9
Cheston Devon 5 L5
Cheswardine Shrops 64 D6
Cheswick Nthumb 117 M12
Cheswick Green Solhll 53 L5
Chetnole Dorset 10 F3
Chettiscombe Devon 20 F10
Chettisham Cambs 57 K4
Chettle Dorset 23 L10
Chetton Shrops 52 C3
Chetwode Bucks 43 N6
Chetwynd Wrekin 64 D8
Chetwynd Aston Wrekin 64 D8
Cheveley Cambs 57 N8
Chevening Kent 33 N10
Cheverton IoW 12 G8
Chevington Suffk 57 Q8
Cheviot Hills 108 B8
Chevithorne Devon 20 F10
Chew Magna BaNES 29 J9
Chew Moor Bolton 76 C2
Chew Stoke BaNES 28 H10
Chewton Keynsham BaNES 29 K9
Chewton Mendip Somset 22 D3
Chichacott Devon 8 B5
Chicheley M Keyn 44 C2
Chichester W Susx 14 B10
Chickerell Dorset 10 G8
Chickering Suffk 59 J5
Chicklade Wilts 23 K6
Chicksands C Beds 44 G4
Chickward Herefs 51 J10
Chidden Hants 25 L10
Chiddingfold Surrey 14 D4
Chiddingly E Susx 15 Q8
Chiddingstone Kent 15 P2
Chiddingstone Causeway Kent 15 P1
Chiddingstone Hoath Kent 15 P2
Chideock Dorset 10 C6
Chidham W Susx 13 N4
Chidswell Kirk 85 K10
Chieveley W Berk 31 K7
Chieveley Services W Berk 31 K8
Chignall St James Essex 46 B9
Chignall Smealy Essex 46 B9
Chigwell Essex 33 N3
Chigwell Row Essex 33 N4
Chilbolton Hants 24 F5
Chilcomb Hants 24 H7
Chilcombe Dorset 10 E6
Chilcompton Somset 22 E3
Chilcote Leics 65 P10
Childer Thornton Ches W 75 L8
Child Okeford Dorset 23 J10
Childrey Oxon 30 H5
Child's Ercall Shrops 64 C7
Childswickham Worcs 42 C4
Childwall Lpool 75 L6
Childwick Bury Herts 44 G9
Childwick Green Herts 44 G9
Chilfrome Dorset 10 F5
Chilgrove W Susx 25 P10
Chilham Kent 35 J11
Chilla Devon 7 N4
Chillaton Devon 7 N8
Chillenden Kent 35 N11
Chillerton IoW 12 H8
Chillesford Suffk 59 M10
Chillingham Nthumb 108 H5
Chillington Devon 5 N8
Chillington Somset 10 B3
Chilmark Wilts 23 L7
Chilmington Green Kent 16 H3
Chilson Oxon 42 G8
Chilsworthy Cnwll 7 M10
Chilsworthy Devon 7 L3
Chiltern Green C Beds 44 G8
Chiltern Hills 31 Q3
Chilthorne Domer Somset 22 C9
Chilton Bucks 43 P9
Chilton Devon 8 G4
Chilton Dur 100 H12
Chilton Kent 17 N2
Chilton Oxon 31 K5
Chilton Suffk 46 F3
Chilton Candover Hants 25 K5
Chilton Cantelo Somset 22 D9
Chilton Foliat Wilts 30 G8
Chilton Polden Somset 21 N5
Chilton Street Suffk 46 D2
Chilton Trinity Somset 21 L5
Chilwell Notts 66 E5
Chilworth Hants 24 G9
Chilworth Surrey 14 E1
Chimney Oxon 30 H2
Chineham Hants 25 L2
Chingford Gt Lon 33 M3
Chinley Derbys 77 K7
Chinnor Oxon 31 Q2
Chipchase Castle Nthumb 99 N3
Chipnall Shrops 64 D6
Chippenham Cambs 57 M6
Chippenham Wilts 29 Q7
Chipperfield Herts 44 F11
Chipping Herts 45 L5
Chipping Lancs 83 N6
Chipping Campden Gloucs 42 D4
Chipping Hill Essex 46 E8
Chipping Norton Oxon 42 G6
Chipping Ongar Essex 45 Q11
Chipping Sodbury S Glos 29 L6
Chipping Warden Nhants 54 E11
Chipshop Devon 7 N9
Chipstable Somset 20 G8
Chipstead Kent 33 P11
Chipstead Surrey 33 K11
Chirbury Shrops 51 J1
Chirk Wrexhm 63 J5
Chirnside Border 117 J10
Chirnsidebridge Border 117 J10
Chirton Wilts 30 C11
Chisbury Wilts 30 F9
Chiselborough Somset 21 P10
Chiseldon Swindn 30 E6
Chiselhampton Oxon 31 M2
Chisholme Border 107 L7
Chislehurst Gt Lon 33 N8
Chislet Kent 35 M9
Chisley Calder 84 F9
Chiswell Green Herts 44 G10
Chiswick Gt Lon 33 J7
Chiswick End Cambs 45 L3
Chisworth Derbys 77 J5
Chitcombe E Susx 16 E7
Chithurst W Susx 25 P8
Chittering Cambs 57 J7
Chitterne Wilts 23 L5
Chittlehamholt Devon 19 M9
Chittlehampton Devon 19 M8
Chittoe Wilts 29 Q9
Chivelstone Devon 5 N9
Chivenor Devon 19 K6
Chiverton Cross Cnwll 3 J5
Chlenry D & G 94 G6
Chobham Surrey 32 D10
Cholderton Wilts 24 C5
Cholesbury Bucks 44 D10
Chollerford Nthumb 99 P4
Chollerton Nthumb 99 P4
Cholmondeston Ches E 76 B11
Cholsey Oxon 31 M5
Cholstrey Herefs 51 M9
Chop Gate N York 92 B7
Choppington Nthumb 100 H2
Chopwell Gatesd 100 E6
Chorley Ches E 63 P2
Chorley Lancs 83 N11
Chorley Shrops 52 C4
Chorley Staffs 65 K10
Chorleywood Herts 32 E3
Chorleywood West Herts 32 E3
Chorlton Ches E 64 D2
Chorlton-cum-Hardy Manch 76 E5
Chorlton Lane Ches W 63 M3
Choulton Shrops 51 L3
Chowley Ches W 75 N12
Chrishall Essex 45 N4
Chrisswell Inver 113 J6
Christchurch BCP 12 B6
Christchurch Cambs 57 J1
Christchurch Gloucs 40 H9
Christchurch Newpt 28 D4
Christian Malford Wilts 29 Q6
Christleton Ches W 75 M10
Christmas Common Oxon 31 P4
Christmas Pie Surrey 32 C12
Christon N Som 28 E11
Christon Bank Nthumb 109 K5
Christow Devon 8 F8
Christ's Hospital W Susx 14 G5
Chuck Hatch E Susx 15 N4
Chudleigh Devon 8 G9
Chudleigh Knighton Devon 8 F9
Chulmleigh Devon 19 N10
Chunal Derbys 77 J5
Church Lancs 83 R9
Churcham Gloucs 41 M8
Church Aston Wrekin 64 D8
Church Brampton Nhants 55 J7
Church Brough Cumb 90 C4
Church Broughton Derbys 65 M5
Church Cove Cnwll 2 H12
Church Crookham Hants 25 P3
Churchdown Gloucs 41 P7
Church Eaton Staffs 64 F8
Church End Bed 55 P9
Church End Bed 56 B9
Church End Bucks 43 Q10
Church End C Beds 44 D5
Church End C Beds 44 E5
Church End C Beds 44 E7
Church End C Beds 44 E8
Church End C Beds 44 H4
Church End C Beds 56 C10
Church End Cambs 56 B6
Church End Cambs 56 D4
Church End Cambs 56 F5
Churchend Essex 34 H4
Church End Essex 46 A7
Church End Essex 46 C6
Church End Essex 46 C8
Church End Gloucs 41 P4
Church End Gt Lon 33 J4
Church End Herts 44 G9
Church End Herts 45 K6
Church End Herts 45 N7
Church End Lincs 68 E5
Church End Lincs 80 H4
Church End Warwks 53 N2
Church End Warwks 53 P2
Church Enstone Oxon 42 H6
Church Fenton N York 85 Q8
Churchfield Sandw 53 J2
Churchgate Herts 45 L11
Churchgate Street Essex 45 N9
Church Green Devon 9 M5
Church Gresley Derbys 65 P8
Church Hanborough Oxon 43 J9
Church Hill Staffs 65 J10
Church Houses N York 92 D7
Churchill Devon 9 P4
Churchill Devon 19 L5
Churchill N Som 28 F10
Churchill Oxon 42 G7
Churchill Worcs 52 G10
Churchill Worcs 52 G5
Churchinford Somset 21 K11
Church Knowle Dorset 11 M8
Church Laneham Notts 79 K8
Church Langton Leics 55 J2
Church Lawford Warwks 54 D5
Church Lawton Ches E 64 F1
Church Leigh Staffs 65 J5
Church Lench Worcs 53 J10
Church Mayfield Staffs 65 M3
Church Minshull Ches E 76 C11
Church Norton W Susx 14 B11
Churchover Warwks 54 E4
Church Preen Shrops 51 P1
Church Pulverbatch Shrops 63 M11
Churchstanton Somset 21 K10
Churchstoke Powys 51 J2
Churchstow Devon 5 M7
Church Stowe Nhants 54 G9
Church Street Essex 46 D3
Church Street Kent 34 C7
Church Street Suffk 59 P4
Church Stretton Shrops 51 M2
Churchthorpe Lincs 80 F4
Churchtown Bpool 82 H7
Churchtown Cnwll 6 G9
Churchtown Derbys 77 P11
Churchtown Devon 19 N4
Churchtown IoM 102 f3
Churchtown Lancs 83 L6
Church Town N Linc 79 K2
Churchtown Sefton 83 J11
Church Village Rhondd 27 P5
Church Warsop Notts 78 F10
Church Wilne Derbys 66 D6
Churnsike Lodge Nthumb 99 K3
Churston Ferrers Torbay 5 Q5
Churt Surrey 25 Q6
Churton Ches W 75 M12
Churwell Leeds 85 K9
Chwilog Gwynd 60 G4
Chyandour Cnwll 2 D8
Chyanvounder Cnwll 2 G10
Chyeowling Cnwll 3 K6
Chyvarloe Cnwll 2 G10
Cîl Powys 62 G11
Cilcain Flints 74 G10
Cilcennin Cerdgn 49 J8
Cilcewydd Powys 62 H11
Cilfrew Neath 27 J2
Cilfynydd Rhondd 27 P4
Cilgerran Pembks 37 N2
Cilgwyn Carmth 38 H6
Cilgwyn Gwynd 60 H1
Ciliau-Aeron Cerdgn 48 H9
Cilmaengwyn Neath 38 H10
Cilmery Powys 50 D10
Cilrhedyn Pembks 37 Q3
Cilsan Carmth 38 F7
Ciltalgarth Gwynd 62 B4
Cilycwm Carmth 38 H4
Cimla Neath 27 J3
Cinderford Gloucs 41 K9
Cinder Hill Wolves 52 H2
Cippenham Slough 32 D6
Cirencester Gloucs 30 B2
Citadilla N York 91 L7
City Gt Lon 33 L6
City V Glam 27 N7
City Airport Gt Lon 33 M6
City Dulas IoA 72 H6
Clabhach Ag & B 118 G1
Clachaig Ag & B 112 G5
Clachaig Inn Highld 121 L1
Clachan Ag & B 111 Q10
Clachan Ag & B 112 G1
Clachan Ag & B 120 E9
Clachan Ag & B 120 F4
Clachan Highld 135 K8
Clachan-a-Luib W Isls 152 c8
Clachan Mor Ag & B 118 D3
Clachan na Luib W Isls 152 c8
Clachan of Campsie E Duns 114 A5
Clachan-Seil Ag & B 120 E9
Clachnaharry Highld 138 B6
Clachtoll Highld 148 C11
Clackavoid P & K 131 L11
Clacket Lane Services Surrey 33 M11
Clackmannan Clacks 114 G3
Clackmannanshire Bridge Fife 114 G4
Clackmarras Moray 139 N4
Clacton-on-Sea Essex 47 L8
Cladich Ag & B 121 L8
Cladswell Worcs 53 K9
Claggan Highld 120 D3
Claigan Highld 134 D5
Clandown BaNES 22 F2
Clanfield Hants 25 M10
Clanfield Oxon 42 G11
Clannaborough Devon 8 D4
Clanville Hants 24 E4
Clanville Somset 22 E7
Claonaig Ag & B 112 C10
Clapgate Dorset 11 N4
Clapgate Herts 45 N7
Clapham Bed 55 P10
Clapham Devon 8 G7
Clapham Gt Lon 33 K7
Clapham N York 83 R1
Clapham W Susx 14 G9
Clapham Green Bed 55 P10
Clap Hill Kent 17 J3
Clappersgate Cumb 89 K6
Clapton Somset 10 C3
Clapton Somset 22 E3
Clapton-in-Gordano N Som 28 G7
Clapton-on-the-Hill Gloucs 42 D8
Clapworthy Devon 19 N8
Clarach Cerdgn 49 K4
Claravale Gatesd 100 E5
Clarbeston Pembks 37 K6
Clarbeston Road Pembks 37 K6
Clarborough Notts 79 J7
Clare Suffk 46 D3
Clarebrand D & G 96 F5
Clarencefield D & G 97 M4
Clarewood Nthumb 100 C4
Clarilaw Border 107 N6
Clark's Green Surrey 14 H3
Clarkston E Rens 113 Q9
Clashmore Highld 146 D7
Clashmore Highld 148 B10
Clashnessie Highld 148 C10
Clashnoir Moray 139 N11
Clathy P & K 123 P9
Clathymore P & K 123 P8
Clatt Abers 140 E10
Clatter Powys 50 D2
Clatterford End Essex 46 A9
Clatworthy Somset 20 G7
Claughton Lancs 83 M2
Claughton Lancs 83 M7
Claughton Wirral 75 J6
Clavelshay Somset 21 L7
Claverdon Warwks 53 M7
Claverham N Som 28 F9
Clavering Essex 45 N5
Claverley Shrops 52 E2
Claverton BaNES 29 M9
Claverton Down BaNES 29 M9
Clawdd-coch V Glam 27 P7
Clawdd-newydd Denbgs 62 E2
Clawthorpe Cumb 89 N11
Clawton Devon 7 L5
Claxby Lincs 80 C5
Claxby Lincs 81 J9
Claxton N York 86 C3
Claxton Norfk 71 L11
Claybrooke Magna Leics 54 E3
Clay Common Suffk 59 P4
Clay Coton Nhants 54 F5
Clay Cross Derbys 78 C11
Claydon Oxon 54 D10
Claydon Suffk 58 H10
Clay End Herts 45 K7
Claygate D & G 98 E2
Claygate Kent 16 C2
Claygate Surrey 32 H9
Claygate Cross Kent 33 R11
Clayhall Gt Lon 33 M4
Clayhanger Devon 20 G9
Clayhanger Wsall 65 K11
Clayhidon Devon 21 J10
Clayhill E Susx 16 E6
Clayhill Hants 12 E3
Clayhithe Cambs 57 J8
Clayock Highld 151 L5
Claypit Hill Cambs 56 G9
Claypits Gloucs 41 M10
Claypole Lincs 67 L2
Claythorpe Lincs 80 H8
Clayton C Brad 84 H9
Clayton Donc 78 D2
Clayton W Susx 15 K8
Clayton Green Lancs 83 N10
Clayton-le-Moors Lancs 83 R9
Clayton-le-Woods Lancs 83 M10
Clayton West Kirk 77 N2
Clayworth Notts 79 J6
Cleadale Highld 126 H6
Cleadon S Tyne 101 K6
Clearbrook Devon 4 H4
Clearwell Gloucs 40 H10
Cleasby N York 91 L4
Cleat Ork 147 c6
Cleatlam Dur 91 J3
Cleator Cumb 88 D4
Cleator Moor Cumb 88 D4
Cleckheaton Kirk 85 J10
Cleedownton Shrops 51 P4
Cleehill Shrops 51 Q5
Cleekhimin N Lans 114 D9
Clee St Margaret Shrops 51 P4
Cleestanton Shrops 51 P5
Cleethorpes NE Lin 80 F2
Cleeton St Mary Shrops 51 Q5
Cleeve N Som 28 F9
Cleeve Oxon 31 M6
Cleeve Hill Gloucs 41 R6
Cleeve Prior Worcs 53 K10
Cleghornie E Loth 116 D5
Clehonger Herefs 40 F4
Cleish P & K 115 K2
Cleland N Lans 114 E9
Clement's End C Beds 44 E8
Clement Street Kent 33 P8
Clenamacrie Ag & B 120 H7
Clench Common Wilts 30 E9
Clenchwarton Norfk 69 L8
Clenerty Abers 141 J4
Clent Worcs 52 H5
Cleobury Mortimer Shrops 52 C5
Cleobury North Shrops 52 B3
Cleongart Ag & B 103 J3
Clephanton Highld 138 E6
Clerkhill D & G 106 H10
Cleuch-head D & G 105 Q9
Clevancy Wilts 30 B7
Clevedon N Som 28 F8
Cleveley Oxon 42 H7
Cleveleys Lancs 82 H6
Cleverton Wilts 29 R5
Clewer Somset 21 P3
Cley next the Sea Norfk 70 F3
Cliburn Cumb 89 P2
Cliddesden Hants 25 L3
Cliff Warwks 53 N1
Cliffe Lancs 83 Q8
Cliffe Medway 34 C7
Cliffe N York 86 C9
Cliffe N York 91 L4
Cliff End E Susx 16 F8
Cliffe Woods Medway 34 C7
Clifford Herefs 40 C3
Clifford Leeds 85 N6
Clifford Chambers Warwks 53 M10
Clifford's Mesne Gloucs 41 L7
Cliffsend Kent 35 P9
Clifton Bristl 28 H7
Clifton C Beds 44 H4
Clifton C Nott 66 E5
Clifton C York 86 B5
Clifton Calder 84 H10
Clifton Cumb 89 N1
Clifton Derbys 65 M3
Clifton Devon 19 L5
Clifton Donc 78 E4
Clifton Lancs 83 L9
Clifton N York 85 J5
Clifton Nthumb 100 G2
Clifton Oxon 43 K5
Clifton Salfd 76 E3
Clifton Worcs 41 N2
Clifton Campville Staffs 65 N10
Clifton Hampden Oxon 31 L3
Clifton Reynes M Keyn 55 M10
Clifton upon Dunsmore Warwks 54 E5
Clifton upon Teme Worcs 52 D8
Cliftonville Kent 35 Q8
Climping W Susx 14 E10
Clink Somset 22 H4
Clint N York 85 K3
Clinterty C Aber 133 K2
Clint Green Norfk 70 F10
Clintmains Border 107 P3
Clipiau Gwynd 61 P10
Clippesby Norfk 71 N9
Clipsham Rutlnd 67 N9
Clipston Nhants 54 H4
Clipston Notts 66 G5
Clipstone C Beds 44 D6
Clipstone Notts 78 F11
Clitheroe Lancs 83 R7
Clive Shrops 63 N7
Cliveden Bucks 32 C5
Clixby Lincs 80 B3
Cloatley Wilts 29 R4
Clocaenog Denbgs 62 E1
Clochan Moray 140 B4
Clock Face St Hel 75 N5
Cloddiau Powys 62 H10
Clodock Herefs 40 D6
Cloford Somset 22 G4
Clola Abers 141 N7
Clophill C Beds 44 F4
Clopton Nhants 55 Q5
Clopton Suffk 59 J10
Clopton Corner Suffk 59 J9
Clopton Green Suffk 57 P9
Clopton Green Suffk 58 E8
Clos du Valle Guern 12 d1
Closeburn D & G 106 B11
Closeburnmill D & G 106 B10
Closeclark IoM 102 c6
Closworth Somset 10 E3
Clothall Herts 45 K5
Clotton Ches W 75 N11
Cloudesley Bush Warwks 54 D3
Clouds Herefs 41 J4
Clough Oldham 76 H2
Clough Foot Calder 84 D10
Clough Head Calder 84 G11
Cloughton N York 93 K8
Cloughton Newlands N York 93 K7
Clousta Shet 147 h6
Clova Angus 131 Q9
Clovelly Devon 18 F8
Clovenfords Border 107 L2
Clovulin Highld 128 D11
Clow Bridge Lancs 84 B9
Clowne Derbys 78 D8
Clows Top Worcs 52 D6
Cloy Wrexhm 63 L4
Cluanie Inn Highld 128 F2
Cluanie Lodge Highld 128 F2
Clubworthy Cnwll 7 K6
Clugston D & G 95 L7
Clun Shrops 51 J4
Clunas Highld 138 G6
Clunbury Shrops 51 L4
Clunderwen Carmth 37 M6
Clune Highld 138 E10
Clunes Highld 128 H6
Clungunford Shrops 51 L5
Clunie P & K 124 C4
Clunton Shrops 51 K4
Cluny Fife 115 N2
Clutton BaNES 29 J10
Clutton Ches W 63 M1
Clutton Hill BaNES 29 K10
Clwt-y-bont Gwynd 73 K11
Clydach Mons 40 B9
Clydach Swans 26 G2
Clydach Vale Rhondd 27 M4
Clydebank W Duns 113 P7
Clydey Pembks 37 P3
Clyffe Pypard Wilts 30 C7
Clynder Ag & B 113 K4
Clyne Neath 27 J2
Clynnog Fawr Gwynd 60 G2
Clyro Powys 40 B3
Clyst Honiton Devon 9 J6
Clyst Hydon Devon 9 K4
Clyst St George Devon 9 J7
Clyst St Lawrence Devon 9 K5
Clyst St Mary Devon 9 J6
Cnoc W Isls 152 g3
Cnwch Coch Cerdgn 49 L6
Coad's Green Cnwll 7 K9
Coal Aston Derbys 78 B8
Coalbrookvale Blae G 40 B10
Coalburn S Lans 105 Q3
Coalburns Gatesd 100 E6
Coaley Gloucs 41 M11
Coalhill Essex 34 D3
Coalmoor Wrekin 64 C10
Coalpit Heath S Glos 29 K6
Coal Pool Wsall 65 J12
Coalport Wrekin 64 C11
Coalsnaughton Clacks 114 G2
Coal Street Suffk 59 J6
Coaltown of Balgonie Fife 115 P1
Coaltown of Wemyss Fife 115 P2
Coalville Leics 66 C9
Coanwood Nthumb 99 K6
Coat Somset 21 P9
Coatbridge N Lans 114 D8
Coatdyke N Lans 114 D8
Coate Swindn 30 E6
Coate Wilts 30 B10
Coates Cambs 56 F1
Coates Gloucs 29 R2
Coates Lincs 79 M7
Coates Notts 79 K7
Coates W Susx 14 E7
Coatham R & Cl 92 C2
Coatham Mundeville Darltn 91 M3
Cobbaton Devon 19 M8
Coberley Gloucs 41 Q8
Cobhall Common Herefs 40 F5
Cobham Kent 34 B8
Cobham Surrey 32 G10
Cobham Services Surrey 32 G10
Coblers Green Essex 46 C8
Cobley Dorset 23 M9
Cobnash Herefs 51 M8
Cobo Guern 12 c2
Cobridge C Stke 64 G2
Coburby Abers 141 M3
Cock Alley Derbys 78 C9
Cockayne N York 92 C7
Cockayne Hatley C Beds 56 E10
Cock Bank Wrexhm 63 K3
Cock Bevington Warwks 53 K10
Cock Bridge Abers 131 N3
Cockburnspath Border 116 H7
Cock Clarks Essex 46 E11
Cock & End Suffk 57 N10
Cockenzie and Port Seton E Loth 115 R6
Cocker Bar Lancs 83 L10
Cocker Brook Lancs 83 R10
Cockerham Lancs 83 L5
Cockermouth Cumb 97 M12
Cockernhoe Herts 44 G7
Cockersdale Leeds 85 K9
Cockett Swans 26 F3
Cockfield Dur 91 J2
Cockfield Suffk 58 D9
Cockfosters Gt Lon 33 K3
Cock Green Essex 46 C7
Cocking W Susx 14 C7
Cocking Causeway W Susx 14 C7
Cockington Torbay 5 Q4
Cocklake Somset 21 P3
Cockley Beck Cumb 88 H6
Cockley Cley Norfk 69 Q11
Cock Marling E Susx 16 F7
Cockpole Green Wokham 31 R6
Cocks Cnwll 3 J4
Cockshutford Shrops 51 P3
Cockshutt Shrops 63 M6
Cock Street Kent 34 D12
Cockthorpe Norfk 70 E4
Cockwells Cnwll 2 E7
Cockwood Devon 9 J8
Cockwood Somset 21 K5
Cockyard Derbys 77 K7
Cockyard Herefs 40 F5
Coddenham Suffk 58 H9
Coddington Ches W 63 M1
Coddington Herefs 41 L3
Coddington Notts 67 L1
Codford St Mary Wilts 23 L5
Codford St Peter Wilts 23 L5
Codicote Herts 45 J8
Codmore Hill W Susx 14 F7
Codnor Derbys 66 C2
Codrington S Glos 29 L6
Codsall Staffs 64 F11
Codsall Wood Staffs 64 F11
Coedely Rhondd 27 N5
Coed Hirwaun Neath 27 K5
Coedkernew Newpt 28 C6
Coed Morgan Mons 40 E9
Coedpoeth Wrexhm 63 J2
Coed Talon Flints 75 J11
Coedway Powys 63 K9
Coed-y-Bryn Cerdgn 48 F11
Coed-y-caerau Newpt 28 E4
Coed-y-Cwm Rhondd 27 P4
Coed-y-paen Mons 28 D3
Coed-yr-ynys Powys 39 R7
Coed Ystumgwern Gwynd 61 K7
Coelbren Powys 39 K9
Coffinswell Devon 5 Q3
Coffle End Bed 55 P9
Cofton Devon 8 H8
Cofton Hackett Worcs 53 J5
Cogan V Glam 28 A8
Cogenhoe Nhants 55 L8
Cogges Oxon 42 H9
Coggeshall Essex 46 E7
Coggin's Mill E Susx 15 Q5
Coignafearn Highld 138 C12
Coilacriech Abers 131 P5
Coilantogle Stirlg 122 G11
Coillore Highld 134 F8
Coity Brdgnd 27 L6
Col W Isls 152 g3
Colaboll Highld 145 N3
Colan Cnwll 3 L2
Colaton Raleigh Devon 9 K7
Colbost Highld 134 D6
Colburn N York 91 K7
Colby Cumb 89 Q3
Colby IoM 102 c7
Colby Norfk 71 J6
Colchester Essex 46 H6
Colchester Zoo Essex 46 G7
Cold Ash W Berk 31 L8
Cold Ashby Nhants 54 G5
Cold Ashton S Glos 29 M8
Cold Aston Gloucs 42 D8
Coldbackie Highld 149 N5
Coldbeck Cumb 90 B6
Cold Blow Pembks 37 M8
Cold Brayfield M Keyn 55 M10
Cold Cotes N York 83 Q1
Coldean Br & H 15 L9
Coldeast Devon 8 F9
Colden Calder 84 E9
Colden Common Hants 24 H9
Coldfair Green Suffk 59 N8
Coldham Cambs 68 H11
Cold Hanworth Lincs 79 P7
Coldharbour Cnwll 3 J5
Coldharbour Devon 20 G11
Coldharbour Gloucs 40 H11
Cold Harbour Herts 44 G8
Cold Harbour Oxon 31 N6
Coldharbour Surrey 14 G2
Cold Hatton Wrekin 64 B8
Cold Hatton Heath Wrekin 64 B8
Cold Hesledon Dur 101 K9
Cold Hiendley Wakefd 78 B1
Cold Higham Nhants 54 H10
Coldingham Border 117 K8
Cold Kirby N York 92 B10
Coldmeece Staffs 64 F6
Cold Newton Leics 66 H11
Cold Northcott Cnwll 7 J7
Cold Norton Essex 34 E2
Cold Overton Leics 67 K10
Coldred Kent 17 N1
Coldridge Devon 8 D3
Coldstream Border 108 D2
Coldwaltham W Susx 14 E7
Coldwell Herefs 40 F4
Coldwells Abers 141 M8
Cold Weston Shrops 51 P4
Cole Somset 22 F6
Colebatch Shrops 51 K3
Colebrook C Plym 4 H5
Colebrook Devon 9 J3
Colebrooke Devon 8 E5
Coleby Lincs 79 N11
Coleby N Linc 86 G11
Cole End Warwks 53 M3
Coleford Devon 8 E4
Coleford Gloucs 41 J9
Coleford Somset 22 F4
Coleford Water Somset 20 H6
Colegate End Norfk 59 J3
Cole Green Herts 45 K9
Cole Green Herts 45 M5
Cole Henley Hants 24 H3
Colehill Dorset 11 P4
Coleman Green Herts 44 H9
Coleman's Hatch E Susx 15 N4
Colemere Shrops 63 M6
Colemore Hants 25 M7
Colemore Green Shrops 52 D1
Colenden P & K 124 C7
Coleorton Leics 66 C9
Colerne Wilts 29 N8
Colesbourne Gloucs 42 B9
Cole's Cross Devon 5 N7
Coles Cross Dorset 10 B4
Colesden Bed 56 C9
Coles Green Suffk 47 K3
Coleshill Bucks 32 D3
Coleshill Oxon 30 F4
Coleshill Warwks 53 M3
Colestocks Devon 9 L5
Coley BaNES 22 D2
Colgate W Susx 15 J4
Colinsburgh Fife 125 J12
Colinton C Edin 115 M7
Colintraive Ag & B 112 F6
Colkirk Norfk 70 D7
Coll Ag & B 118 H1
Coll W Isls 152 g3
Collace P & K 124 D6
Collafirth Shet 147 i4
Coll Airport Ag & B 118 G2
Collaton Devon 5 M9
Collaton St Mary Torbay 5 P5
College of Roseisle Moray 139 L3
College Town Br For 32 B10
Collessie Fife 124 F10
Colleton Mills Devon 19 N10
Collier Row Gt Lon 33 P4
Collier's End Herts 45 L7
Collier's Green E Susx 16 D6
Colliers Green Kent 16 D3
Collier Street Kent 16 C2
Colliery Row Sundld 101 J8
Collieston Abers 141 P10
Collin D & G 97 L3
Collingbourne Ducis Wilts 24 D3
Collingbourne Kingston Wilts 24 D2
Collingham Leeds 85 N6
Collingham Notts 79 L11
Collington Herefs 52 C8
Collingtree Nhants 55 J9
Collins Green Warrtn 75 P5
Collins Green Worcs 52 D9
Colliston Angus 125 M4
Colliton Devon 9 L4
Collyweston Nhants 67 N11
Colmonell S Ayrs 94 G1

Colmworth – Culpho 169

Colmworth Bed 56 B9
Colnabaichin Abers 131 P3
Colnbrook Slough 32 E7
Colne Cambs 56 G5
Colne Lancs 84 D7
Colne Bridge Kirk 85 J11
Colne Edge Lancs 84 D7
Colne Engaine Essex 46 E5
Colney Norfk 70 H10
Colney Heath Herts 44 H10
Colney Street Herts 44 H11
Coln Rogers Gloucs 42 C9
Coln St Aldwyns Gloucs 42 D10
Coln St Dennis Gloucs 42 C9
Colonsay Ag & B 111 J2
Colonsay Airport Ag & B 110 H3
Colpy Abers 140 G9
Colquhar Border 107 J1
Colquite Cnwll 6 F10
Colscott Devon 18 G10
Colsterdale N York 91 J10
Colsterworth Lincs 67 M7
Colston Bassett Notts 66 H5
Coltfield Moray 139 L3
Colt Hill Hants 25 N3
Coltishall Norfk 71 K8
Colton Cumb 89 J9
Colton Leeds 85 M8
Colton N York 85 Q6
Colton Norfk 70 G10
Colton Staffs 65 K8
Colt's Hill Kent 16 B2
Columbjohn Devon 8 H5
Colva Powys 50 H10
Colvend D & G 96 H7
Colwall Herefs 41 M3
Colwell Nthumb 99 Q3
Colwich Staffs 65 J8
Colwick Notts 66 G4
Colwinston V Glam 27 M7
Colworth W Susx 14 C10
Colwyn Bay Conwy 73 P8
Colyford Devon 9 N6
Colyton Devon 9 N6
Combe Devon 5 M9
Combe Herefs 51 K8
Combe Oxon 43 J8
Combe W Berk 30 H10
Combe Almer Dorset 11 M5
Combe Common Surrey 14 D4
Combe Down BaNES 29 M10
Combe Fishacre Devon 5 P4
Combe Florey Somset 21 J7
Combe Hay BaNES 29 L10
Combeinteignhead Devon 8 G10
Combe Martin Devon 19 L4
Combe Raleigh Devon 9 M4
Comberbach Ches W 76 B8
Comberford Staffs 65 M10
Comberton Cambs 56 G9
Comberton Herefs 51 N7
Combe St Nicholas Somset 9 P2
Combpyne Devon 9 P6
Combridge Staffs 65 K5
Combrook Warwks 53 P10
Combs Derbys 77 K8
Combs Suffk 58 F9
Combs Ford Suffk 58 F9
Combwich Somset 21 L5
Comers Abers 132 G3
Comhampton Worcs 52 F7
Commercial End Cambs 57 K8
Commins Coch Powys 61 P11
Commondale N York 92 D5
Common Edge Bpool 82 H8
Common End Cumb 88 D2
Common Moor Cnwll 4 C3
Common Platt Wilts 30 C5
Commonside Ches W 75 P9
Commonside Derbys 65 N4
Common Side Derbys 77 Q8
Commonwood Shrops 63 N6
Commonwood Wrexhm 63 L1
Compass Somset 21 L6
Compstall Stockp 76 H5
Compstonend D & G 96 D8
Compton Devon 5 P4
Compton Hants 24 F7
Compton Hants 24 H8
Compton Staffs 52 F4
Compton Surrey 14 D1
Compton W Berk 31 L6
Compton W Susx 25 N10
Compton Wilts 23 P3
Compton Abbas Dorset 23 J9
Compton Abdale Gloucs 42 C8
Compton Bassett Wilts 30 B8
Compton Beauchamp Oxon 30 F5
Compton Bishop Somset 21 N2
Compton Chamberlayne Wilts 23 M7
Compton Dando BaNES 29 K9
Compton Dundon Somset 22 C7
Compton Durville Somset 21 P10
Compton Greenfield S Glos 28 H6
Compton Martin BaNES 28 H11
Compton Pauncefoot Somset 22 E8
Compton Valence Dorset 10 F6
Comrie Fife 115 J3
Comrie P & K 123 K8
Conaglen House Highld 128 E10
Conchra Highld 136 B10
Concraigie P & K 124 C4
Conder Green Lancs 83 K4
Conderton Worcs 41 Q4
Condicote Gloucs 42 D6
Condorrat N Lans 114 D6
Condover Shrops 63 N11
Coney Hill Gloucs 41 N8
Coneyhurst Common W Susx 14 G6
Coneysthorpe N York 86 D1
Coneythorpe N York 85 N3
Coney Weston Suffk 58 E5
Conford Hants 25 P7
Congdon's Shop Cnwll 7 K9
Congerstone Leics 66 B11
Congham Norfk 69 N7
Congleton Ches E 76 F11
Congl-y-wal Gwynd 61 M3
Congresbury N Som 28 F9
Congreve Staffs 64 G9
Conheath D & G 97 K4
Conicavel Moray 138 H5
Coningsby Lincs 80 D12
Conington Cambs 56 D3
Conington Cambs 56 F7
Conisbrough Donc 78 E4
Conisholme Lincs 80 H4
Coniston Cumb 89 J7
Coniston E R Yk 87 M8
Coniston Cold N York 84 D4
Conistone N York 84 E2
Connah's Quay Flints 75 J10
Connel Ag & B 120 G6
Connel Park E Ayrs 105 L7
Connor Downs Cnwll 2 F6
Conon Bridge Highld 137 P5
Cononley N York 84 E6
Consall Staffs 64 H2
Consett Dur 100 E8
Constable Burton N York 91 K8
Constable Lee Lancs 84 B10
Constantine Cnwll 3 J8
Constantine Bay Cnwll 6 C10
Contin Highld 137 M4
Conwy Conwy 73 N8
Conwy Castle Conwy 73 N8
Conyer Kent 34 G9
Conyer's Green Suffk 58 C7
Cooden E Susx 16 C9
Cookbury Devon 7 M3
Cookbury Wick Devon 7 M4
Cookham W & M 32 C5
Cookham Dean W & M 32 B5
Cookham Rise W & M 32 C5
Cookhill Worcs 53 K9
Cookley Suffk 59 L5
Cookley Worcs 52 F5
Cookley Green Oxon 31 P4
Cookney Abers 133 L6
Cooksbridge E Susx 15 M8
Cooksey Green Worcs 52 G7
Cook's Green Essex 47 L8
Cooks Green Suffk 58 E10
Cookshill Staffs 64 H3
Cooksland Cnwll 6 F11
Cooksmill Green Essex 46 B10
Cookson Green Ches W 75 P9
Coolham W Susx 14 G6
Cooling Medway 34 D7
Cooling Street Medway 34 D7
Coombe Cnwll 2 G6
Coombe Cnwll 3 K6
Coombe Cnwll 3 M4
Coombe Devon 8 F8
Coombe Devon 8 H10
Coombe Devon 9 L6
Coombe Gloucs 29 M3
Coombe Hants 25 L9
Coombe Wilts 23 P3
Coombe Bissett Wilts 23 P8
Coombe Cellars Devon 8 G10
Coombe Cross Hants 25 L9
Coombe Hill Gloucs 41 P6
Coombe Keynes Dorset 11 K8
Coombe Pafford Torbay 5 Q3
Coombes W Susx 14 H9
Coombes-Moor Herefs 51 L8
Coombe Street Somset 22 G7
Coombeswood Dudley 52 H3
Coopersale Common Essex 45 N11
Coopersale Street Essex 45 N11
Cooper's Corner Kent 33 P12
Coopers Green E Susx 15 N6
Coopers Green Herts 44 H9
Cooper Street Kent 35 P10
Cooper Turning Bolton 76 B2
Cootham W Susx 14 F8
Copdock Suffk 47 K3
Copford Green Essex 46 G7
Copgrove N York 85 M3
Copister Shet 147 j4
Cople Bed 56 B11
Copley Calder 84 G10
Copley Dur 90 H2
Copley Tamesd 76 H4
Coplow Dale Derbys 77 M8
Copmanthorpe C York 85 R6
Copmere End Staffs 64 E6
Copp Lancs 83 K7
Coppathorne Cnwll 7 J5
Coppenhall Staffs 64 G8
Coppenhall Moss Ches E 76 L12
Copperhouse Cnwll 2 F7
Coppicegate Shrops 52 D5
Coppingford Cambs 56 C5
Coppins Corner Kent 16 G1
Copplestone Devon 8 E4
Coppull Lancs 83 M12
Coppull Moor Lancs 75 P1
Copsale W Susx 14 H6
Copster Green Lancs 83 P8
Copston Magna Warwks 54 D3
Cop Street Kent 35 N10
Copthall Green Essex 33 M2
Copt Heath Solhll 53 M5
Copt Hewick N York 85 M1
Copthorne Cnwll 7 K6
Copthorne W Susx 15 K3
Copt Oak Leics 66 D9
Copy's Green Norfk 70 D4
Copythorne Hants 24 E10
Coram Street Suffk 46 H3
Corbets Tey Gt Lon 33 Q5
Corbière Jersey 13 a3
Corbridge Nthumb 100 C5
Corby Nhants 55 M3
Corby Glen Lincs 67 P7
Corby Hill Cumb 98 F7
Cordon N Ayrs 103 Q4
Cordwell Derbys 77 P8
Coreley Shrops 52 B6
Cores End Bucks 32 C5
Corfe Somset 21 K9
Corfe Castle Dorset 11 M8
Corfe Mullen Dorset 11 N5
Corfton Shrops 51 N4
Corgarff Abers 131 P3
Corhampton Hants 25 K9
Corks Pond Kent 16 B3
Corlae D & G 105 M10
Corley Warwks 53 P4
Corley Ash Warwks 53 P3
Corley Moor Warwks 53 P4
Corley Services Warwks 53 P3
Cormuir Angus 131 P11
Cornard Tye Suffk 46 F3
Corndon Devon 8 C7
Corner Row Lancs 83 K8
Corney Cumb 88 F8
Cornforth Dur 101 J11
Cornhill Abers 140 F4
Cornhill-on-Tweed Nthumb 108 D2
Cornholme Calder 84 D10
Cornish Hall End Essex 46 B4
Cornoigmore Ag & B 118 D3
Cornriggs Dur 99 N10
Cornsay Dur 100 F9
Cornsay Colliery Dur 100 F9
Corntown Highld 137 P5
Corntown V Glam 27 L7
Cornwall Airport Newquay Cnwll 3 L2
Cornwell Oxon 42 F6
Cornwood Devon 5 K5
Cornworthy Devon 5 P5
Corpach Highld 128 F9
Corpusty Norfk 70 G6
Corrachree Abers 132 D3
Corran Highld 127 Q2
Corran Highld 128 E11
Corrany IoM 102 f4
Corrie D & G 97 P1
Corrie N Ayrs 103 Q1
Corriecravie N Ayrs 103 N5
Corriegills N Ayrs 103 Q3
Corriegour Lodge Hotel Highld 129 J6
Corriemoille Highld 137 L3
Corrimony Highld 137 L10
Corringham Lincs 79 L5
Corringham Thurr 34 C5
Corris Gwynd 61 N10
Corris Uchaf Gwynd 61 M10
Corrow Ag & B 113 J1
Corry Highld 135 L11
Corscombe Devon 8 B5
Corscombe Dorset 10 D4
Corse Gloucs 41 M6
Corse Lawn Gloucs 41 N5
Corsham Wilts 29 P8
Corsindae Abers 132 G3
Corsley Wilts 23 J4
Corsley Heath Wilts 22 H4
Corsock D & G 96 F3
Corston BaNES 29 L9
Corston Wilts 29 Q5
Corstorphine C Edin 115 M7
Cors-y-Gedol Gwynd 61 K7
Cortachy Angus 132 B12
Corton Suffk 59 Q1
Corton Wilts 23 K5
Corton Denham Somset 22 E9
Coruanan Highld 128 E10
Corwen Denbgs 62 E3
Coryates Dorset 10 F7
Coryton Devon 7 N8
Coryton Thurr 34 C6
Cosby Leics 54 F2
Coseley Dudley 52 H2
Cosford Shrops 64 E11
Cosgrove Nhants 43 R3
Cosham C Port 13 L4
Cosheston Pembks 37 K10
Coshieville P & K 123 K3
Cossall Notts 66 D4
Cossall Marsh Notts 66 D4
Cossington Leics 66 G9
Cossington Somset 21 M5
Costessey Norfk 70 H9
Costock Notts 66 F7
Coston Leics 67 L8
Coston Norfk 70 F11
Cote Oxon 42 H11
Cote Somset 21 M4
Cotebrook Ches W 75 P10
Cotehill Cumb 98 F8
Cotes Cumb 89 M9
Cotes Leics 66 F8
Cotes Staffs 64 F5
Cotesbach Leics 54 E4
Cotes Heath Staffs 64 F5
Cotford St Luke Somset 21 J8
Cotgrave Notts 66 G5
Cothal Abers 133 L1
Cotham Notts 67 K3
Cothelstone Somset 21 J7
Cotherstone Dur 90 G3
Cothill Oxon 31 K2
Cotleigh Devon 9 N4
Cotmanhay Derbys 66 D3
Coton Cambs 56 H9
Coton Nhants 54 H6
Coton Shrops 63 P5
Coton Staffs 64 E8
Coton Staffs 64 H6
Coton Staffs 65 M11
Coton Clanford Staffs 64 F7
Coton Hayes Staffs 65 J5
Coton Hill Shrops 63 N9
Coton in the Clay Staffs 65 M6
Coton in the Elms Derbys 65 N9
Coton Park Derbys 65 P8
Cotswolds 42 A10
Cotswold Wildlife Park & Gardens Oxon 42 F10
Cott Devon 5 N4
Cottam E R Yk 87 J2
Cottam Lancs 83 L8
Cottam Notts 79 K8
Cottenham Cambs 57 J7
Cotterdale N York 90 D8
Cottered Herts 45 K6
Cotteridge Birm 53 K5
Cotterstock Nhants 55 P3
Cottesbrooke Nhants 54 H6
Cottesmore Rutlnd 67 M9
Cottingham E R Yk 87 K8
Cottingham Nhants 55 L3
Cottingley C Brad 84 H8
Cottisford Oxon 43 M5
Cotton Suffk 58 G7
Cotton End Bed 44 F3
Cotton Tree Lancs 84 D7
Cottown Abers 133 J1
Cottown Abers 140 D10
Cottown of Gight Abers 141 K8
Cotts Devon 4 G4
Cotwall Wrekin 63 Q8
Cotwalton Staffs 64 H5
Couch's Mill Cnwll 4 A5
Coughton Herefs 41 J7
Coughton Warwks 53 K8
Coulaghailtro Ag & B 111 Q8
Coulags Highld 136 D7
Coulderton Cumb 88 C5
Coull Abers 132 D4
Coulport Ag & B 113 J4
Coulsdon Gt Lon 33 K10
Coulston Wilts 23 L3
Coulter S Lans 106 D3
Coultershaw Bridge W Susx 14 D7
Coultings Somset 21 K5
Coulton N York 92 D12
Coultra Fife 124 G8
Cound Shrops 63 P11
Coundlane Shrops 63 P11
Coundon Dur 100 G12
Coundon Grange Dur 91 L1
Countersett N York 90 E9
Countess Wilts 23 P5
Countess Cross Essex 46 F5
Countess Wear Devon 8 H7
Countesthorpe Leics 54 F2
Countisbury Devon 19 P3
Coupar Angus P & K 124 E5
Coup Green Lancs 83 N9
Coupland Cumb 90 B3
Coupland Nthumb 108 F4
Cour Ag & B 112 B11
Court-at-Street Kent 17 K4
Courteachan Highld 127 M5
Courteenhall Nhants 55 J10
Court Henry Carmth 38 E7
Courtsend Essex 35 J4
Courtway Somset 21 K6
Cousland Mdloth 115 Q7
Cousley Wood E Susx 16 B4
Cove Ag & B 113 J5
Cove Border 116 H7
Cove Devon 20 E9
Cove Hants 25 Q2
Cove Highld 143 L7
Cove Bay C Aber 133 M4
Cove Bottom Suffk 59 P5
Covehithe Suffk 59 Q4
Coven Staffs 64 G11
Coveney Cambs 57 J4
Covenham St Bartholomew Lincs 80 G5
Covenham St Mary Lincs 80 G5
Coven Heath Staffs 64 G11
Coventry Covtry 53 Q5
Coverack Cnwll 3 J11
Coverack Bridges Cnwll 2 G8
Coverham N York 91 J9
Covington Cambs 55 Q6
Covington S Lans 106 C2
Cowan Bridge Lancs 89 Q11
Cowbeech E Susx 16 A8
Cowbit Lincs 68 E8
Cowbridge V Glam 27 N7
Cowdale Derbys 77 K9
Cowden Kent 15 N3
Cowdenbeath Fife 115 L3
Cowden Pound Kent 15 N2
Cowden Station Kent 15 N2
Cowers Lane Derbys 65 P3
Cowes IoW 12 H5
Cowesby N York 91 Q9
Cowesfield Green Wilts 24 D8
Cowfold W Susx 15 J6
Cowgill Cumb 90 C9
Cow Green Suffk 58 F7
Cowhill S Glos 29 J4
Cowie Stirlg 114 F3
Cowlam E R Yk 86 H2
Cowley Devon 8 G5
Cowley Gloucs 41 Q8
Cowley Gt Lon 32 F6
Cowley Oxon 43 L11
Cowling Lancs 83 N11
Cowling N York 84 E6
Cowling N York 91 L9
Cowlinge Suffk 57 N10
Cowmes Kirk 85 J12
Cowpe Lancs 84 C11
Cowpen Nthumb 100 H2
Cowpen Bewley S on T 91 Q2
Cowplain Hants 13 M3
Cowshill Dur 99 N10
Cowslip Green N Som 28 G10
Cowthorpe N York 85 N5
Coxall Herefs 51 L6
Coxbank Ches E 64 C4
Coxbench Derbys 66 B3
Coxbridge Somset 22 C6
Cox Common Suffk 59 M4
Coxford Cnwll 6 H5
Coxford Norfk 70 C6
Coxgreen Staffs 52 E3
Coxheath Kent 34 C12
Coxhoe Dur 101 J11
Coxley Somset 22 C5
Coxley Wakefd 85 K11
Coxley Wick Somset 22 C4
Coxpark Cnwll 7 M10
Coxtie Green Essex 33 Q3
Coxwold N York 92 B11
Coychurch Brdgnd 27 M6
Coylton S Ayrs 104 H6
Coylumbridge Highld 130 G2
Coytrahen Brdgnd 27 L5
Crabbs Cross Worcs 53 K7
Crab Orchard Dorset 11 Q3
Crabtree W Susx 15 J6
Crabtree Green Wrexhm 63 K3
Crackenthorpe Cumb 89 Q2
Crackington Haven Cnwll 6 G5
Crackley Staffs 64 F2
Crackley Warwks 53 P6
Crackleybank Shrops 64 E10
Crackpot N York 90 F7
Cracoe N York 84 E3
Craddock Devon 20 H11
Cradle End Herts 45 N7
Cradley Dudley 52 H4
Cradley Herefs 41 L2
Cradley Heath Sandw 52 H3
Cradoc Powys 39 N5
Crafthole Cnwll 4 E6
Crafton Bucks 44 C8
Crag Foot Lancs 89 M12
Craggan Highld 139 J10
Cragganmore Moray 139 M8
Cragg Hill Leeds 85 K7
Cragg Vale Calder 84 F10
Craghead Dur 100 G8
Cragside House & Garden Nthumb 108 H9
Crai Powys 39 L7
Craibstone Moray 140 D4
Craichie Angus 125 K3
Craig Angus 125 N2
Craig Highld 136 E6
Craigbank E Ayrs 105 L7
Craigburn Border 115 N10
Craig-cefn-parc Swans 38 G11
Craigcleuch D & G 107 K12
Craigdam Abers 141 K10
Craigdhu Ag & B 120 F11
Craigearn Abers 132 H2
Craigellachie Moray 139 P7
Craigend P & K 124 C9
Craigend Rens 113 N7
Craigendoran Ag & B 113 L5
Craigends Rens 113 N8
Craighlaw D & G 95 K6
Craighouse Ag & B 111 L8
Craigie P & K 124 C4
Craigie S Ayrs 104 H3
Craigiefold Abers 141 M3
Craigley D & G 96 F6
Craig Llangiwg Neath 38 H10
Craiglockhart C Edin 115 M7
Craigmillar C Edin 115 P7
Craignant Shrops 63 J5
Craigneston D & G 105 N12
Craigneuk N Lans 114 D10
Craigneuk N Lans 114 D8
Craignure Ag & B 120 D5
Craigo Angus 132 H11
Craig Penllyn V Glam 27 M7
Craigrothie Fife 124 H10
Craigruie Stirlg 122 E9
Craig's End Essex 46 C4
Craigton Angus 125 K5
Craigton C Aber 133 K4
Craigton E Rens 113 P10
Craigton of Airlie Angus 124 G3
Craig-y-Duke Neath 38 H11
Craig-y-nos Powys 39 K8
Craik Border 107 K8
Crail Fife 125 M11
Crailing Border 107 R5
Craiselound N Linc 79 J4
Crakehall N York 91 L9
Crakehill N York 91 Q12
Crakemarsh Staffs 65 K5
Crambe N York 86 D2
Cramlington Nthumb 100 H3
Cramond C Edin 115 M6
Cramond Bridge C Edin 115 M6
Crampmoor Hants 24 F9
Cranage Ches E 76 D10
Cranberry Staffs 64 F5
Cranborne Dorset 23 N10
Cranbourne Br For 32 C8
Cranbrook Devon 9 J6
Cranbrook Kent 16 D4
Cranbrook Common Kent 16 D3
Crane Moor Barns 77 P3
Crane's Corner Norfk 70 D9
Cranfield C Beds 44 D3
Cranford Devon 18 G9
Cranford Gt Lon 32 G7
Cranford St Andrew Nhants 55 M5
Cranford St John Nhants 55 M5
Cranham Gloucs 41 P9
Cranham Gt Lon 33 Q5
Cranhill Warwks 53 L10
Crank St Hel 75 N4
Cranleigh Surrey 14 F3
Cranmer Green Suffk 58 F6
Cranmore IoW 12 F7
Cranmore Somset 22 F5
Cranoe Leics 55 J2
Cransford Suffk 59 L7
Cranshaws Border 116 F9
Cranstal IoM 102 f2
Cranswick E R Yk 87 J5
Crantock Cnwll 3 K2
Cranwell Lincs 67 P2
Cranwich Norfk 57 P2
Cranworth Norfk 70 E11
Craobh Haven Ag & B 120 E11
Crapstone Devon 4 H3
Crarae Ag & B 112 E2
Crask Inn Highld 149 L11
Crask of Aigas Highld 137 N7
Craster Nthumb 109 L6
Craswall Herefs 40 C4
Crateford Staffs 64 G10
Cratfield Suffk 59 L5
Crathes Abers 133 J5
Crathie Abers 131 N5
Crathie Highld 129 Q5
Crathorne N York 91 Q5
Craven Arms Shrops 51 M4
Crawcrook Gatesd 100 E5
Crawford Lancs 75 N3
Crawford S Lans 106 C5
Crawfordjohn S Lans 106 A5
Crawley Hants 24 G6
Crawley Oxon 42 H9
Crawley W Susx 15 K3
Crawley Down W Susx 15 L3
Crawleyside Dur 100 C10
Crawshawbooth Lancs 84 B10
Crawton Abers 133 L8
Craxe's Green Essex 46 G8
Cray N York 90 F11
Crayford Gt Lon 33 P7
Crayke N York 85 R1
Craymere Beck Norfk 70 F6
Crays Hill Essex 34 C4
Cray's Pond Oxon 31 N6
Craythorne Staffs 65 N7
Craze Lowman Devon 20 F10
Crazies Hill Wokham 31 R6
Creacombe Devon 20 C9
Creagan Inn Ag & B 121 J4
Creag Ghoraidh W Isls 152 c9
Creagorry W Isls 152 c9
Creaguaineach Lodge Highld 129 K10
Creamore Bank Shrops 63 N6
Creaton Nhants 54 H6
Creca D & G 97 P4
Credenhill Herefs 40 F3
Crediton Devon 8 F5
Creebank D & G 95 L3
Creebridge D & G 95 M5
Creech Dorset 11 M8
Creech Heathfield Somset 21 L8
Creech St Michael Somset 21 L8
Creed Cnwll 3 M5
Creekmoor BCP 11 N6
Creekmouth Gt Lon 33 N6
Creeksea Essex 34 G3
Creeting St Mary Suffk 58 G9
Creeton Lincs 67 P8
Creetown D & G 95 N6
Cregneash IoM 102 b7
Creg ny Baa IoM 102 e5
Cregrina Powys 50 F10
Creich Fife 124 G8
Creigiau Cardif 27 P6
Cremyll Cnwll 4 G6
Cressage Shrops 63 Q11
Cressbrook Derbys 77 M9
Cresselly Pembks 37 L9
Cressex Bucks 32 B4
Cressing Essex 46 D7
Cresswell Nthumb 109 M11
Cresswell Pembks 37 K9
Cresswell Staffs 64 H4
Creswell Derbys 78 E9
Creswell Green Staffs 65 K10
Cretingham Suffk 59 J8
Cretshengan Ag & B 111 Q8
Crewe Ches E 64 D1
Crewe-by-Farndon Ches W 63 M2
Crewe Green Ches E 64 D1
Crew Green Powys 63 K9
Crewkerne Somset 10 C3
Crews Hill Station Gt Lon 33 K2
Crewton C Derb 66 B5
Crianlarich Stirlg 122 C8
Cribyn Cerdgn 49 J10
Criccieth Gwynd 60 H4
Crich Derbys 65 Q1
Crich Carr Derbys 65 Q1
Crichton Mdloth 115 Q9
Crick Mons 28 G4
Crick Nhants 54 F6
Crickadarn Powys 39 P3
Cricket St Thomas Somset 10 B3
Crickheath Shrops 63 J7
Crickhowell Powys 40 B8
Cricklade Wilts 30 C4
Cricklewood Gt Lon 33 J5
Cridling Stubbs N York 85 Q11
Crieff P & K 123 L8
Criggan Cnwll 3 P2
Criggion Powys 63 J9
Crigglestone Wakefd 85 L12
Crimble Rochdl 76 F1
Crimond Abers 141 P4
Crimplesham Norfk 69 M11
Crimscote Warwks 42 F2
Crinaglack Highld 137 M8
Crinan Ag & B 112 A2
Crindledyke N Lans 114 E10
Cringleford Norfk 71 J11
Cringles C Brad 84 F5
Crinow Pembks 37 M7
Cripplesease Cnwll 2 D7
Cripplestyle Dorset 23 N11
Cripp's Corner E Susx 16 D6
Croachy Highld 138 B10
Croanford Cnwll 6 F10
Crockenhill Kent 33 P9
Crocker End Oxon 31 P5
Crockerhill W Susx 14 C9
Crockernwell Devon 8 E6
Crocker's Ash Herefs 40 H8
Crockerton Wilts 23 J5
Crocketford D & G 96 G4
Crockey Hill C York 86 B6
Crockham Hill Kent 33 N12
Crockhurst Street Kent 16 A2
Crockleford Heath Essex 47 J6
Crock Street Somset 21 M10
Croeserw Neath 27 K3
Croes-goch Pembks 36 F4
Croes-lan Cerdgn 38 B3
Croesor Gwynd 61 L3
Croesyceiliog Carmth 38 B8
Croesyceiliog Torfn 28 D3
Croes-y-mwyalch Torfn 28 D4
Croes-y-pant Mons 40 D11
Croft Leics 54 E1
Croft Lincs 81 K11
Croft Warrtn 76 B5
Croftamie Stirlg 113 P4
Croft Mitchell Cnwll 2 G7
Crofton Cumb 98 C8
Crofton Wakefd 85 M11
Crofton Wilts 30 F10
Croft-on-Tees N York 91 M5
Croftown Highld 144 F8
Crofts Moray 139 P6
Crofts Bank Traffd 76 E4
Crofts of Dipple Moray 139 P4
Crofts of Savoch Abers 141 P4
Crofty Swans 26 D3
Crogen Gwynd 62 D5
Croggan Ag & B 120 D7
Croglin Cumb 98 H9
Croick Highld 145 L7
Cromarty Highld 138 E2
Crombie Fife 115 J4
Cromdale Highld 139 K10
Cromer Herts 45 K6
Cromer Norfk 71 J4
Cromford Derbys 77 P12
Cromhall S Glos 29 L4
Cromhall Common S Glos 29 L4
Cromor W Isls 152 g4
Crompton Fold Oldham 76 H2
Cromwell Notts 79 K11
Cronberry E Ayrs 105 L5
Crondall Hants 25 N4
Cronkbourne IoM 102 e6
Cronk-y-Voddy IoM 102 d4
Cronton Knows 75 N6
Crook Cumb 89 M7
Crook Dur 100 F11
Crookdake Cumb 97 P9
Crooke Wigan 75 P2
Crooked End Gloucs 41 J8
Crookedholm E Ayrs 104 H2
Crooked Soley Wilts 30 G8
Crookes Sheff 77 Q6
Crookhall Dur 100 E8
Crookham Nthumb 108 E2
Crookham W Berk 31 L9
Crookham Village Hants 25 N3
Crook Inn Border 106 E4
Crooklands Cumb 89 N10
Crook of Devon P & K 115 J1
Cropper Derbys 65 N5
Cropredy Oxon 43 K2
Cropston Leics 66 F10
Cropthorne Worcs 42 A3
Cropton N York 92 F9
Cropwell Bishop Notts 66 H5
Cropwell Butler Notts 66 H5
Cros W Isls 152 h1
Crosbost W Isls 152 g4
Crosby Cumb 97 M10
Crosby IoM 102 d5
Crosby N Linc 79 M1
Crosby Sefton 75 K4
Crosby Garret Cumb 90 B5
Crosby Ravensworth Cumb 89 Q4
Crosby Villa Cumb 97 M10
Croscombe Somset 22 D4
Crosemere Shrops 63 M6
Crosland Edge Kirk 77 L1
Crosland Hill Kirk 84 H12
Cross Somset 21 N2
Crossaig Ag & B 112 B11
Crossapol Ag & B 118 D4
Cross Ash Mons 40 F8
Cross-at-Hand Kent 16 D2
Crossbost W Isls 152 g4
Crossbush W Susx 14 E9
Crosscanonby Cumb 97 L10
Cross Coombe Cnwll 2 H4
Crossdale Street Norfk 71 J4
Cross End Bed 55 Q9
Cross End Essex 46 F5
Crossens Sefton 83 J11
Cross Flatts C Brad 84 G7
Crossford Fife 115 K4
Crossford S Lans 114 E12
Crossgate Cnwll 7 L7
Crossgate Lincs 68 E7
Crossgate Staffs 64 H5
Crossgatehall E Loth 115 Q7
Crossgates E Ayrs 113 M12
Crossgates Fife 115 L3
Cross Gates Leeds 85 M8
Crossgates N York 93 L10
Crossgates Powys 50 F7
Crossgill Lancs 83 M3
Cross Green Devon 7 M7
Cross Green Leeds 85 L9
Cross Green Staffs 64 G11
Cross Green Suffk 58 B10
Cross Green Suffk 58 C9
Cross Green Suffk 58 E10
Crosshands Carmth 37 N6
Cross Hands Carmth 38 E9
Crosshands E Ayrs 105 J4
Cross Hands Pembks 37 L8
Cross Hill Derbys 66 C2
Crosshill Fife 115 M2
Crosshill S Ayrs 104 F8
Cross Hills N York 84 F6
Crosshouse E Ayrs 104 G2
Cross Houses Shrops 52 C2
Cross Houses Shrops 63 P10
Cross in Hand E Susx 15 Q6
Cross Inn Cerdgn 48 F9
Cross Inn Cerdgn 49 J8
Cross Inn Pembks 37 L9
Cross Inn Rhondd 27 P6
Cross Keys Ag & B 113 L4
Crosskeys Caerph 28 B4
Cross Keys Wilts 29 P8
Crosskirk Highld 151 J3
Crosslands Cumb 89 K9
Cross Lane IoW 12 H7
Cross Lane Head Shrops 52 D2
Cross Lanes Cnwll 2 H10
Cross Lanes Cnwll 3 J6
Cross Lanes N York 85 Q2
Crosslanes Shrops 63 K8
Cross Lanes Wrexhm 63 L3
Crosslee Rens 113 N8
Crossley Kirk 85 J11
Crossmichael D & G 96 E5
Cross Oak Powys 39 Q7
Cross of Jackston Abers 141 J9
Cross o' th' hands Derbys 65 P3
Crosspost W Susx 15 J6
Crossroads Abers 132 E3
Crossroads Abers 133 J5
Cross Roads C Brad 84 F7
Cross Street Suffk 59 J5
Crosston Angus 125 K2
Cross Town Ches E 76 D8
Crossway Mons 40 F8
Crossway Powys 50 E9
Crossway Green Mons 28 H3
Crossway Green Worcs 52 F7
Crossways Dorset 11 J7
Crosswell Pembks 37 M3
Crosthwaite Cumb 89 L8
Croston Lancs 83 L11
Crostwick Norfk 71 K9
Crostwight Norfk 71 L6
Crouch Kent 34 A11
Crouch Kent 35 J10
Crouch End Gt Lon 33 K5
Croucheston Wilts 23 N8
Crouch Hill Dorset 10 H3
Crough House Green Kent 15 N2
Croughton Nhants 43 L5
Crovie Abers 141 K3
Crow Hants 12 B4
Crowan Cnwll 2 G7
Crowborough E Susx 15 P4
Crowborough Warren E Susx 15 P5
Crowcombe Somset 21 J6
Crowdecote Derbys 77 L10
Crowden Derbys 77 K4
Crowden Devon 7 P5
Crowdhill Hants 24 H9
Crowdleham Kent 33 Q10
Crow Edge Barns 77 M3
Crowell Oxon 31 Q2
Crow End Cambs 56 F9
Crowfield Nhants 43 N3
Crowfield Suffk 58 H9
Crowfield Green Suffk 58 H9
Crowgate Street Norfk 71 L8
Crow Green Essex 33 Q3
Crowhill E Loth 116 G6
Crow Hill Herefs 41 K6
Crowhole Derbys 77 Q8
Crowhurst E Susx 16 D8
Crowhurst Surrey 15 M1
Crowhurst Lane End Surrey 15 M1
Crowland Lincs 68 E10
Crowland Suffk 58 F6
Crowlas Cnwll 2 E8
Crowle N Linc 79 K1
Crowle Worcs 52 G9
Crowle Green Worcs 52 G9
Crowmarsh Gifford Oxon 31 N4
Crown Corner Suffk 59 K6
Crownhill C Plym 4 G5
Crownpits Surrey 14 D2
Crownthorpe Norfk 70 G11
Crowntown Cnwll 2 G8
Crows-an-Wra Cnwll 2 C9
Crow's Green Essex 46 C6
Crowshill Norfk 70 D11
Crow's Nest Cnwll 4 C3
Crowsnest Shrops 63 L11
Crowthorne Wokham 32 B9
Crowton Ches W 75 P9
Croxall Staffs 65 M9
Croxby Lincs 80 D4
Croxdale Dur 100 H11
Croxden Staffs 65 K4
Croxley Green Herts 32 F3
Croxteth Lpool 75 L4
Croxton Cambs 56 E8
Croxton N Linc 80 B1
Croxton Norfk 58 C3
Croxton Norfk 70 E6
Croxton Staffs 64 E6
Croxtonbank Staffs 64 E6
Croxton Green Ches E 63 P2
Croxton Kerrial Leics 67 L6
Croy Highld 138 E6
Croy N Lans 114 D6
Croyde Devon 19 J5
Croyde Bay Devon 18 H5
Croydon Cambs 56 F10
Croydon Gt Lon 33 L9
Crubenmore Highld 130 C6
Cruckmeole Shrops 63 M10
Cruckton Shrops 63 M10
Cruden Bay Abers 141 Q8
Crudgington Wrekin 64 B8
Crudie Abers 141 J4
Crudwell Wilts 29 Q4
Cruft Devon 7 P5
Crûg Powys 50 G6
Crugmeer Cnwll 6 C9
Crugybar Carmth 38 G4
Crug-y-byddar Powys 50 G4
Crumlin Caerph 28 B3
Crumplehorn Cnwll 4 B6
Crumpsall Manch 76 F3
Crundale Kent 17 J1
Crundale Pembks 37 J7
Crunwere Pembks 37 N8
Cruwys Morchard Devon 20 D11
Crux Easton Hants 31 J11
Cruxton Dorset 10 F5
Crwbin Carmth 38 C9
Cryers Hill Bucks 32 C3
Crymych Pembks 37 N4
Crynant Neath 39 J10
Crystal Palace Gt Lon 33 L8
Cuaig Highld 135 N4
Cuan Ag & B 120 E10
Cubbington Warwks 53 Q7
Cubert Cnwll 3 J3
Cubley Barns 77 N3
Cublington Bucks 44 B7
Cublington Herefs 40 E4
Cuckfield W Susx 15 K6
Cucklington Somset 22 G8
Cuckney Notts 78 F9
Cuckoo Bridge Lincs 68 D8
Cuckoo's Corner Hants 25 N5
Cuckoo's Nest Ches W 75 L11
Cuddesdon Oxon 43 M11
Cuddington Bucks 43 Q9
Cuddington Ches W 75 Q9
Cuddington Heath Ches W 63 M3
Cuddy Hill Lancs 83 L8
Cudham Gt Lon 33 N10
Cudliptown Devon 7 P9
Cudnell BCP 11 P5
Cudworth Barns 78 C2
Cudworth Somset 10 B3
Cuerdley Cross Warrtn 75 P6
Cufaude Hants 31 N11
Cuffley Herts 45 K11
Cuil Highld 121 J2
Culbokie Highld 137 Q4
Culbone Somset 20 C4
Culburnie Highld 137 N7
Culcabock Highld 138 C7
Culcharry Highld 138 F6
Culcheth Warrtn 76 C5
Culdrain Abers 140 D9
Culduie Highld 135 N8
Culford Suffk 58 B6
Culgaith Cumb 99 J12
Culham Oxon 31 L3
Culkein Highld 148 B10
Culkein Drumbeg Highld 148 D10
Culkerton Gloucs 29 Q3
Cullen Moray 140 D2
Cullercoats N Tyne 101 J4
Cullerlie Abers 133 J4
Cullicudden Highld 138 B3
Cullingworth C Brad 84 G8
Cuillin Hills Highld 134 H11
Cullipool Ag & B 120 D10
Cullivoe Shet 147 j2
Culloden Highld 138 D6
Cullompton Devon 9 J3
Cullompton Services Devon 9 J3
Culm Davy Devon 20 H10
Culmington Shrops 51 N4
Culmstock Devon 20 H10
Culnacraig Highld 144 D4
Culnaightrie D & G 96 F8
Culnaknock Highld 135 J3
Culpho Suffk 59 J10

170 Culrain – Dunkeswell

Culrain Highld 145 N6
Culross Fife 114 H4
Culroy S Ayrs 104 F7
Culsalmond Abers 140 G9
Culscadden D & G 95 N8
Culshabbin D & G 95 K8
Culswick Shet 147 h7
Cultercullen Abers 141 M11
Cults C Aber 133 L4
Culverstone Green Kent 34 B9
Culverthorpe Lincs 67 P4
Culworth Nhants 43 L2
Culzean Castle & Country Park S Ayrs 104 D8
Cumbernauld N Lans 114 D6
Cumbernauld Village N Lans 114 D6
Cumberworth Lincs 81 K9
Cumdivock Cumb 98 D8
Cuminestown Abers 141 K6
Cumledge Border 116 H10
Cummersdale Cumb 98 E7
Cummertrees D & G 97 N5
Cummingston Moray 139 L2
Cumnock E Ayrs 105 K6
Cumnor Oxon 43 K11
Cumrew Cumb 98 G8
Cumrue D & G 97 L1
Cumwhinton Cumb 98 F7
Cumwhitton Cumb 98 G8
Cundall N York 91 P12
Cunninghamhead N Ayrs 104 G1
Cunningsburgh Shet 147 i8
Cupar Fife 124 G10
Cupar Muir Fife 124 G10
Curbar Derbys 77 N9
Curbridge Hants 13 J2
Curbridge Oxon 42 G10
Curdridge Hants 25 J10
Curdworth Warwks 53 M2
Curland Somset 21 L10
Curridge W Berk 31 K8
Currie C Edin 115 M8
Curry Mallet Somset 21 M9
Curry Rivel Somset 21 N8
Curteis Corner Kent 16 E3
Curtisden Green Kent 16 C3
Curtisknowle Devon 5 M6
Cury Cnwll 2 H10
Cushnie Abers 132 D2
Cushuish Somset 21 K7
Cusop Herefs 40 C3
Cusworth Donc 78 F3
Cutcloy D & G 95 N11
Cutcombe Somset 20 E5
Cutgate Rochdl 84 C12
Cuthill Highld 146 D7
Cutiau Gwynd 61 L8
Cutler's Green Essex 45 Q5
Cutmadoc Cnwll 3 Q2
Cutmere Cnwll 4 E4
Cutnall Green Worcs 52 G7
Cutsdean Gloucs 42 C6
Cutsyke Wakefd 85 N10
Cutthorpe Derbys 77 Q9
Cuttivett Cnwll 4 E4
Cuxham Oxon 31 N3
Cuxton Medway 34 C9
Cuxwold Lincs 80 D3
Cwm Blae G 40 B10
Cwm Denbgs 74 E8
Cwmafan Neath 27 J4
Cwmaman Rhondd 27 N2
Cwmann Carmth 38 E2
Cwmavon Torfn 40 C10
Cwmbach Carmth 37 P5
Cwmbach Carmth 38 D11
Cwmbâch Powys 40 A4
Cwmbach Rhondd 39 N11
Cwmbach Llechrhyd Powys 50 D10
Cwmbelan Powys 50 C4
Cwmbran Torfn 28 C3
Cwmbrwyno Cerdgn 49 M4
Cwm Capel Carmth 38 C11
Cwmcarn Caerph 28 B4
Cwmcarvan Mons 40 G10
Cwm-celyn Blae G 40 B10
Cwm-Cewydd Gwynd 61 Q9
Cwm-cou Cerdgn 37 Q2
Cwm Crawnon Powys 39 Q7
Cwmdare Rhondd 39 N11
Cwmdu Carmth 38 F6
Cwmdu Powys 40 A7
Cwmdu Swans 26 F3
Cwmduad Carmth 38 B5
Cwm Dulais Swans 38 F11
Cwmdwr Carmth 38 H5
Cwmfelin Brdgnd 27 K4
Cwmfelin Myr Td 27 P2
Cwmfelin Boeth Carmth 37 N7
Cwmfelinfach Caerph 28 B4
Cwmfelin Mynach Carmth 37 P5
Cwmffrwd Carmth 38 B8
Cwmgiedd Powys 39 J9
Cwmgorse Carmth 38 G9
Cwm Gwaun Pembks 37 K4
Cwmgwili Carmth 38 E9
Cwmgwrach Neath 39 K10
Cwmhiraeth Carmth 37 R3
Cwm-Ifor Carmth 38 G6
Cwm Irfon Powys 49 Q10
Cwmisfael Carmth 38 D8
Cwm Llinau Powys 61 P10
Cwmllynfell Neath 38 H9
Cwmmawr Carmth 38 D9
Cwm Morgan Carmth 37 Q3
Cwmparc Rhondd 27 M3
Cwmpengraig Carmth 37 R3
Cwm Penmachno Conwy 61 N3
Cwmpennar Rhondd 27 N2
Cwmrhos Powys 40 B7
Cwmrhydyceirw Swans 26 G2
Cwmsychbant Cerdgn 38 C2
Cwmtillery Blae G 40 B10
Cwm-twrch Isaf Powys 39 J9
Cwm-twrch Uchaf Powys 38 H9
Cwm-y-glo Carmth 38 E9
Cwm-y-glo Gwynd 73 J11
Cwmyoy Mons 40 D7
Cwmystwyth Cerdgn 49 N6
Cwrt Gwynd 61 M12
Cwrt-newydd Cerdgn 48 H11
Cwrt-y-gollen Powys 40 B8
Cyfarthfa Castle Museum Myr Td 39 P10
Cyffylliog Denbgs 74 E12
Cyfronydd Powys 62 G10
Cylibebyll Neath 38 H11
Cymau Flints 63 J1
Cymmer Neath 27 K3
Cymmer Rhondd 27 N4
Cynghordy Carmth 39 J4
Cynheidre Carmth 38 D10
Cynonville Neath 27 K3
Cynwyd Denbgs 62 E4
Cynwyl Elfed Carmth 38 B6

D

Daccombe Devon 5 Q3
Dacre Cumb 89 M1
Dacre N York 85 J3
Dacre Banks N York 85 J3
Daddry Shield Dur 99 P10
Dadford Bucks 43 N4
Dadlington Leics 54 C1
Dafen Carmth 26 D2
Daffy Green Norfk 70 E10
Dagenham Gt Lon 33 P5
Daglingworth Gloucs 42 A10
Dagnall Bucks 44 E8
Dagworth Suffk 58 F8
Dail bho Dheas W Isls 152 g1
Dailly S Ayrs 104 E9
Dainton Devon 5 P3
Dairsie Fife 124 H9
Daisy Hill Bolton 76 C3
Daisy Hill Leeds 85 K9
Dalabrog W Isls 152 b11
Dalavich Ag & B 120 H10
Dalbeattie D & G 96 G6
Dalbury Derbys 65 N5
Dalby IoM 102 b5
Dalby Lincs 80 H9
Dalby N York 86 B1
Dalcapon P & K 123 N2
Dalchalm Highld 146 G4
Dalchreichart Highld 129 J2
Dalchruin P & K 123 J9
Dalcrue P & K 123 Q7
Dalderby Lincs 80 E10
Dalditch Devon 9 K8
Dale Cumb 98 G9
Dale Derbys 66 C4
Dale Pembks 36 F9
Dale Bottom Cumb 89 J2
Dale End Derbys 77 N11
Dale End N York 84 E6
Dale Hill E Susx 16 C5
Dalehouse N York 92 F3
Dalelia Highld 127 N10
Dalgarven N Ayrs 113 K12
Dalgety Bay Fife 115 L4
Dalgig E Ayrs 105 K7
Dalginross P & K 123 K8
Dalguise P & K 123 P3
Dalhalvaig Highld 150 F6
Dalham Suffk 57 N8
Daliburgh W Isls 152 b11
Dalkeith Mdloth 115 Q8
Dallas Moray 139 L5
Dallinghoo Suffk 59 K9
Dallington E Susx 16 B7
Dallington Nhants 55 J8
Dallow N York 91 K12
Dalmally Ag & B 121 M7
Dalmary Stirlg 113 P2
Dalmellington E Ayrs 105 J8
Dalmeny C Edin 115 L6
Dalmore Highld 138 C2
Dalmuir W Duns 113 P7
Dalnabreck Highld 127 M10
Dalnacardoch P & K 130 D10
Dalnahaitnach Highld 138 F11
Dalnaspidal P & K 130 B9
Dalnawillan Lodge Highld 151 J8
Daloist P & K 123 K1
Dalqueich P & K 124 B12
Dalquhairn S Ayrs 104 F10
Dalreavoch Highld 146 D3
Dalry N Ayrs 113 K11
Dalrymple E Ayrs 104 F7
Dalserf S Lans 114 E11
Dalsmeran Ag & B 102 H7
Dalston Cumb 98 D8
Dalston Gt Lon 33 L5
Dalswinton D & G 97 J1
Dalton Cumb 89 N11
Dalton D & G 97 M3
Dalton Lancs 75 N2
Dalton N York 91 J5
Dalton N York 91 Q11
Dalton Nthumb 100 E4
Dalton Rothm 78 D5
Dalton-in-Furness Cumb 88 H12
Dalton-le-Dale Dur 101 K8
Dalton Magna Rothm 78 D5
Dalton-on-Tees N York 91 M5
Dalton Parva Rothm 78 D5
Dalton Piercy Hartpl 101 L12
Dalveich Stirlg 122 G8
Dalwhinnie Highld 130 B7
Dalwood Devon 9 N5
Damask Green Herts 45 J6
Damerham Hants 23 N10
Damgate Norfk 71 M10
Dam Green Norfk 58 F4
Damnaglaur D & G 94 G11
Danaway Kent 34 F9
Danbury Essex 46 D10
Danby N York 92 E5
Danby Bottom N York 92 E6
Danby Wiske N York 91 N7
Dandaleith Moray 139 P6
Danderhall Mdloth 115 P7
Danebridge Ches E 76 H10
Dane End Herts 45 L7
Danegate E Susx 15 Q4
Danehill E Susx 15 M5
Dane Hills C Leic 66 F11
Danemoor Green Norfk 70 F11
Danesford Shrops 52 D2
Danesmoor Derbys 78 C11
Dane Street Kent 35 J11
Daniel's Water Kent 16 G3
Danshillock Abers 140 H4
Danskine E Loth 116 D8
Danthorpe E R Yk 87 N8
Danzey Green Warwks 53 L7
Dapple Heath Staffs 65 K7
Darby Green Hants 32 B10
Darcy Lever Bolton 76 D2
Dardy Powys 40 B8
Darenth Kent 33 Q8
Daresbury Halton 75 P7
Darfield Barns 78 C3
Darfoulds Notts 78 F8
Dargate Kent 35 K10
Dargavel Rens 113 N7
Darite Cnwll 4 C3
Darland Medway 34 D9
Darland Wrexhm 75 L12
Darlaston Wsall 52 H1
Darlaston Green Wsall 52 H1
Darley N York 85 J3
Darley Abbey C Derb 66 B4
Darley Bridge Derbys 77 P11
Darley Dale Derbys 77 P11
Darley Green Solhll 53 M6
Darleyhall Herts 44 G7
Darley Head N York 85 J3
Darlingscott Warwks 42 F3
Darlington Darltn 91 M4
Darliston Shrops 63 P6
Darlton Notts 79 K9
Darnford Staffs 65 L10
Darnick Border 107 N3
Darowen Powys 61 P11
Darra Abers 140 H6
Darracott Devon 18 H9
Darracott Devon 19 J5
Darras Hall Nthumb 100 F4
Darrington Wakefd 85 P11
Darsham Suffk 59 N6
Darshill Somset 22 E4
Dartford Kent 33 P7
Dartford Crossing Kent 33 Q7
Dartington Devon 5 N4
Dartmeet Devon 8 C10
Dartmoor National Park Devon 8 D9
Dartmouth Devon 5 P6
Darton Barns 77 P2
Darvel E Ayrs 105 K2
Darwell Hole E Susx 16 C7
Darwen Bl w D 83 Q10
Datchet W & M 32 E7
Datchworth Herts 45 K8
Datchworth Green Herts 45 K8
Daubhill Bolton 76 C2
Daugh of Kinermony Moray 139 N7
Dauntsey Wilts 30 A6
Dava Highld 139 J8
Davenham Ches W 76 C9
Davenport Stockp 76 G6
Davenport Green Ches E 76 F8
Davenport Green Traffd 76 E6
Daventry Nhants 54 F8
Davidson's Mains C Edin 115 M6
Davidstow Cnwll 6 H7
David Street Kent 34 B9
Davington D & G 106 H9
Davington Hill Kent 34 H10
Daviot Abers 141 J10
Daviot Highld 138 D8
Daviot House Highld 138 D7
Davis's Town E Susx 15 P7
Davoch of Grange Moray 140 D5
Davyhulme Traffd 76 D4
Daw End Wsall 65 J12
Dawesgreen Surrey 15 J1
Dawley Wrekin 64 C10
Dawlish Devon 8 H9
Dawlish Warren Devon 9 J9
Dawn Conwy 73 Q9
Daws Green Somset 21 K9
Daws Heath Essex 34 E5
Daw's House Cnwll 7 L8
Dawsmere Lincs 68 H6
Daybrook Notts 66 F3
Day Green Ches E 76 E12
Dayhills Staffs 64 H5
Dayhouse Bank Worcs 52 H5
Daylesford Gloucs 42 F6
Ddol Flints 74 G9
Ddol-Cownwy Powys 62 D8
Deal Kent 35 Q12
Dean Cumb 88 E2
Dean Devon 5 M4
Dean Devon 19 M4
Dean Devon 19 N4
Dean Dorset 23 L10
Dean Hants 24 G5
Dean Hants 25 J9
Dean Lancs 84 C10
Dean Oxon 42 H7
Dean Somset 22 F5
Dean Bottom Kent 33 Q8
Deanburnhaugh Border 107 K7
Deancombe Devon 5 M4
Dean Court Oxon 43 K10
Deane Bolton 76 C2
Deane Hants 25 J3
Dean End Dorset 23 L10
Dean Head Barns 77 P4
Deanhead Kirk 84 F12
Deanland Dorset 23 M9
Deanlane End W Susx 25 N11
Dean Prior Devon 5 M4
Deanraw Nthumb 99 M6
Dean Row Ches E 76 G7
Deans W Loth 115 J7
Deanscales Cumb 88 E1
Deanshanger Nhants 43 Q4
Deanshaugh Moray 139 Q6
Deanston Stirlg 114 C1
Dean Street Kent 34 D11
Dearham Cumb 97 L11
Dearnley Rochdl 84 D12
Debach Suffk 59 K10
Debden Essex 33 N3
Debden Essex 45 Q5
Debden Green Essex 45 Q5
Debenham Suffk 58 H8
Deblin's Green Worcs 52 E11
Dechmont W Loth 115 J7
Dechmont Road W Loth 115 J7
Deddington Oxon 43 K5
Dedham Essex 47 J5
Dedham Heath Essex 47 J5
Dedworth W & M 32 D7
Deene Nhants 55 N2
Deenethorpe Nhants 55 N2
Deepcar Sheff 77 P4
Deepcut Surrey 32 C11
Deepdale Cumb 90 B9
Deepdale N York 90 E10
Deeping Gate C Pete 68 C10
Deeping St James Lincs 68 C10
Deeping St Nicholas Lincs 68 D9
Deerhurst Gloucs 41 P6
Deerhurst Walton Gloucs 41 P6
Deerton Street Kent 34 H9
Defford Worcs 41 Q3
Defynnog Powys 39 L6
Deganwy Conwy 73 N8
Degnish Ag & B 120 E10
Deighton C York 86 B6
Deighton N York 91 N6
Deiniolen Gwynd 73 K11
Delabole Cnwll 6 F8
Delamere Ches W 75 P10
Delfrigs Abers 141 M11
Delley Devon 19 K8
Delliefure Highld 139 K9
Dell Quay W Susx 13 P4
Delly End Oxon 42 H9
Delnabo Moray 139 L12
Delny Highld 146 D10
Delph Oldham 77 J2
Delves Dur 100 E8
Delvin End Essex 46 D5
Dembleby Lincs 67 P5
Demelza Cnwll 3 N2
Denaby Donc 78 D4
Denaby Main Donc 78 D4
Denbies Surrey 32 G12
Denbigh Denbgs 74 E10
Denbrae Fife 124 H9
Denbury Devon 5 N3
Denby Derbys 66 C3
Denby Bottles Derbys 66 C3
Denby Dale Kirk 77 N2
Denchworth Oxon 30 H4
Dendron Cumb 82 G1
Denel End C Beds 44 E4
Denfield P & K 123 N9
Denford Nhants 55 N5
Dengie Essex 46 H11
Denham Bucks 32 F5
Denham Suffk 57 P8
Denham Suffk 59 J6
Denham End Suffk 57 P8
Denham Green Bucks 32 F5
Denham Green Suffk 59 J6
Denhead Abers 141 N5
Denhead Fife 125 J10
Denhead of Gray C Dund 124 G6
Denholm Border 107 P6
Denholme C Brad 84 G8
Denholme Clough C Brad 84 G8
Denio Gwynd 60 F5
Denmead Hants 25 L11
Denmore C Aber 133 M2
Denne Park W Susx 14 H5
Dennington Suffk 59 K7
Denny Falk 114 E5
Dennyloanhead Falk 114 E5
Den of Lindores Fife 124 E9
Denshaw Oldham 76 H2
Denside Abers 133 K5
Densole Kent 17 M2
Denston Suffk 57 P10
Denstone Staffs 65 L4
Denstroude Kent 35 K10
Dent Cumb 90 B9
Denton Cambs 56 C3
Denton Darltn 91 L3
Denton E Susx 15 N10
Denton Kent 17 M1
Denton Kent 34 B7
Denton Lincs 67 L6
Denton N York 84 H5
Denton Nhants 55 L9
Denton Norfk 59 K3
Denton Oxon 43 M11
Denton Tamesd 76 G5
Denver Norfk 69 L11
Denwick Nthumb 109 K7
Deopham Norfk 70 F12
Deopham Green Norfk 70 F12
Depden Suffk 57 P9
Depden Green Suffk 57 P9
Deptford Gt Lon 33 L7
Deptford Wilts 23 M6
Derby C Derb 66 B5
Derby Devon 19 L6
Derbyhaven IoM 102 c7
Derculich P & K 123 M2
Dereham Norfk 70 E9
Deri Caerph 27 Q2
Derril Devon 7 K4
Derringstone Kent 35 M12
Derrington Staffs 64 G7
Derriton Devon 7 L4
Derry Hill Wilts 29 Q8
Derrythorpe N Linc 79 K2
Dersingham Norfk 69 N6
Dervaig Ag & B 119 M2
Derwen Denbgs 62 E2
Derwenlas Powys 61 M12
Derwent Valley Mills Derbys 65 P1
Derwent Water Cumb 88 H3
Derwydd Carmth 38 F8
Desborough Nhants 55 K4
Desford Leics 66 D11
Deskford Moray 140 D3
Detchant Nthumb 108 H2
Detling Kent 34 D10
Deuxhill Shrops 52 C3
Devauden Mons 28 G3
Devil's Bridge Cerdgn 49 M5
Devitts Green Warwks 53 P3
Devizes Wilts 30 B10
Devonport C Plym 4 G6
Devonside Clacks 114 G2
Devoran Cnwll 3 K7
Devoran & Perran Cnwll 3 K7
Dewarton Mdloth 115 Q8
Dewlish Dorset 11 J5
Dewsbury Kirk 85 K11
Dewsbury Moor Kirk 85 K10
Deytheur Powys 62 H8
Dial N Som 28 H9
Dial Green W Susx 14 C5
Dial Post W Susx 14 H7
Dibberford Dorset 10 D4
Dibden Hants 12 G3
Dibden Purlieu Hants 12 G3
Dickens Heath Solhll 53 L5
Dickleburgh Norfk 58 H4
Didbrook Gloucs 42 B5
Didcot Oxon 31 L4
Diddington Cambs 56 D7
Diddlebury Shrops 51 N3
Didley Herefs 40 F5
Didling W Susx 25 P9
Didmarton Gloucs 29 N5
Didsbury Manch 76 F5
Didworthy Devon 5 L4
Digby Lincs 67 Q1
Digg Highld 134 H2
Diggle Oldham 77 J2
Digmoor Lancs 75 N3
Digswell Herts 45 J8
Digswell Water Herts 45 J8
Dihewyd Cerdgn 48 H9
Dilham Norfk 71 L7
Dilhorne Staffs 64 H3
Dill Hall Lancs 83 R9
Dillington Cambs 56 C7
Dilston Nthumb 100 C5
Dilton Wilts 23 J4
Dilton Marsh Wilts 23 J3
Dilwyn Herefs 51 L9
Dimple Bolton 83 Q12
Dimple Derbys 77 P11
Dinas Carmth 37 P4
Dinas Cnwll 6 C10
Dinas Gwynd 60 D5
Dinas Gwynd 72 H12
Dinas Rhondd 27 N4
Dinas Cross Pembks 37 K3
Dinas Dinlle Gwynd 72 G12
Dinas-Mawddwy Gwynd 61 Q9
Dinas Powys V Glam 27 R8
Dinder Somset 22 D4
Dinedor Herefs 40 H4
Dingestow Mons 40 F9
Dingle Lpool 75 L6
Dingleden Kent 16 E5
Dingley Nhants 55 K3
Dingwall Highld 137 P4
Dinmael Conwy 62 D3
Dinnet Abers 132 C5
Dinnington N u Ty 100 G4
Dinnington Rothm 78 E6
Dinnington Somset 21 N10
Dinorwic Gwynd 73 K11
Dinton Bucks 43 Q9
Dinton Wilts 23 M7
Dinwoodie D & G 106 E11
Dinworthy Devon 18 F10
Dipford Somset 21 K9
Dipley Hants 31 Q11
Dippen Ag & B 103 L2
Dippenhall Surrey 25 P4
Dippermill Devon 7 M3
Dippertown Devon 7 N8
Dippin N Ayrs 103 Q5
Dipple Moray 139 Q4
Dipple S Ayrs 104 D9
Diptford Devon 5 M5
Dipton Dur 100 F7
Diptonmill Nthumb 99 P6
Dirleton E Loth 116 C4
Dirt Pot Nthumb 99 N9
Discoed Powys 51 J8
Diseworth Leics 66 D7
Dishforth N York 85 N1
Disley Ches E 76 H7
Diss Norfk 58 G4
Disserth Powys 50 E9
Distington Cumb 88 D2
Ditchampton Wilts 23 N7
Ditcheat Somset 22 E6
Ditchingham Norfk 59 L2
Ditchling E Susx 15 L8
Ditherington Shrops 63 N9
Ditteridge Wilts 29 N8
Dittisham Devon 5 P6
Ditton Kent 34 C10
Ditton Green Cambs 57 M9
Ditton Priors Shrops 51 Q3
Dixton Gloucs 41 R5
Dixton Mons 40 G9
Dizzard Cnwll 6 H5
Dobcross Oldham 77 J2
Dobwalls Cnwll 4 C4
Doccombe Devon 8 E7
Dochgarroch Highld 138 B7
Dockenfield Surrey 25 P5
Docker Lancs 89 P11
Docking Norfk 69 P5
Docklow Herefs 51 P9
Dockray Cumb 89 L2
Dockray Cumb 98 B8
Dodbrooke Devon 5 M8
Doddinghurst Essex 33 Q3
Doddington Cambs 56 H3
Doddington Kent 34 G11
Doddington Lincs 79 M9
Doddington Nthumb 108 G3
Doddington Shrops 52 B5
Doddiscombsleigh Devon 8 F7
Dodd's Green Ches E 63 Q3
Doddshill Norfk 69 N6
Doddy Cross Cnwll 4 D4
Dodford Nhants 54 G8
Dodford Worcs 52 H6
Dodington S Glos 29 M6
Dodington Somset 21 J5
Dodleston Ches W 75 K11
Dodscott Devon 19 K9
Dodside E Rens 113 P10
Dod's Leigh Staffs 65 J5
Dodworth Barns 77 P3
Dodworth Bottom Barns 77 Q3
Dodworth Green Barns 77 P3
Doe Bank Birm 53 L1
Doe Lea Derbys 78 D10
Dogdyke Lincs 80 D12
Dogley Lane Kirk 85 J12
Dogmersfield Hants 25 N3
Dogridge Wilts 30 C5
Dogsthorpe C Pete 68 D12
Dog Village Devon 9 J5
Dolanog Powys 62 E9
Dolau Powys 50 G7
Dolaucothi Carmth 38 F3
Dolbenmaen Gwynd 60 H4
Doley Staffs 64 D6
Dolfach Powys 62 B11
Dolfor Powys 50 F3
Dol-för Powys 61 P11
Dolgarrog Conwy 73 N10
Dolgellau Gwynd 61 M8
Dolgoch Gwynd 61 L11
Dol-gran Carmth 38 C5
Doll Highld 146 F4
Dollar Clacks 114 H2
Dollarfield Clacks 114 H2
Dolley Green Powys 51 J7
Dollwen Cerdgn 49 M4
Dolphin Flints 74 H9
Dolphinholme Lancs 83 M4
Dolphinton S Lans 115 K12
Dolton Devon 19 L11
Dolwen Conwy 73 Q9
Dolwyddelan Conwy 61 M2
Dolybont Cerdgn 49 K3
Dolyhir Powys 50 H9
Domgay Powys 63 J8
Donaldson's Lodge Nthumb 108 D1
Doncaster Donc 78 F3
Doncaster Carr Donc 78 F3
Doncaster North Services Donc 78 H2
Doncaster Sheffield Airport Donc 78 G4
Donhead St Andrew Wilts 23 K8
Donhead St Mary Wilts 23 K8
Donibristle Fife 115 L3
Doniford Somset 20 H5
Donington Lincs 68 D5
Donington on Bain Lincs 80 E7
Donington Park Services Leics 66 D7
Donington Southing Lincs 68 D5
Donisthorpe Leics 65 P9
Donkey Street Kent 17 K4
Donkey Town Surrey 32 D10
Donnington Gloucs 42 E6
Donnington Herefs 41 L5
Donnington Shrops 63 P10
Donnington W Berk 31 K8
Donnington W Susx 13 Q4
Donnington Wrekin 64 D9
Donnington Wood Wrekin 64 D9
Donyatt Somset 21 M10
Doomsday Green W Susx 14 H5
Doonfoot S Ayrs 104 F6
Dora's Green Hants 25 P4
Dorback Lodge Highld 131 K1
Dorchester Dorset 10 H6
Dorchester-on-Thames Oxon 31 M3
Dordon Warwks 65 N12
Dore Sheff 77 P7
Dores Highld 137 Q9
Dorking Surrey 14 H1
Dorking Tye Suffk 46 G4
Dormansland Surrey 15 M2
Dormans Park Surrey 15 M2
Dormington Herefs 41 J4
Dormston Worcs 53 J9
Dorn Gloucs 42 E5
Dorney Bucks 32 D6
Dornie Highld 136 B10
Dornoch Highld 146 E7
Dornock D & G 97 P5
Dorrery Highld 151 K6
Dorridge Solhll 53 M6
Dorrington Lincs 67 Q2
Dorrington Shrops 63 N11
Dorrington Shrops 64 D4
Dorsington Warwks 53 L10
Dorstone Herefs 40 D3
Dorton Bucks 43 P9
Dosthill Staffs 65 N12
Dothan IoA 72 F9
Dottery Dorset 10 C6
Doublebois Cnwll 4 B4
Doughton Gloucs 29 P4
Douglas IoM 102 e6
Douglas S Lans 105 Q4
Douglas and Angus C Dund 124 H6
Douglas Pier Ag & B 113 J1
Douglastown Angus 124 H3
Douglas Water S Lans 105 Q3
Douglas West S Lans 105 Q4
Doulting Somset 22 E5
Dounby Ork 147 b4
Doune Highld 145 L5
Doune Stirlg 114 D1
Dounepark S Ayrs 104 C10
Dounie Highld 145 N7
Dousland Devon 4 H3
Dovaston Shrops 63 K8
Dove Dale Derbys 65 L2
Dove Green Notts 66 D2
Dove Holes Derbys 77 K8
Dovenby Cumb 97 M11
Dover Kent 17 P2
Dover Wigan 75 Q4
Dover Castle Kent 17 P2
Dovercourt Essex 47 N5
Doverdale Worcs 52 F7
Doveridge Derbys 65 L5
Doversgreen Surrey 15 J1
Dowally P & K 123 P3
Dowbridge Lancs 83 K9
Dowdeswell Gloucs 42 B7
Dowlais Myr Td 39 P10
Dowland Devon 7 Q3
Dowlish Ford Somset 21 M10
Dowlish Wake Somset 21 N10
Down Ampney Gloucs 30 C3
Downderry Cnwll 4 D6
Downe Gt Lon 33 M10
Downend Gloucs 29 N3
Downend IoW 13 J7
Downend S Glos 29 K7
Downend W Berk 31 K7
Downfield C Dund 124 H6
Downgate Cnwll 7 K10
Downgate Cnwll 7 L10
Downham Essex 34 C3
Downham Gt Lon 33 M8
Downham Lancs 84 B6
Downham Market Norfk 69 L11
Down Hatherley Gloucs 41 P7
Downhead Somset 22 D8
Downhead Somset 22 F4
Downhill Cnwll 6 B11
Downhill P & K 124 C7
Downholland Cross Lancs 75 L2
Downholme N York 91 J7
Downicarey Devon 7 M7
Downies Abers 133 M5
Downing Flints 74 G8
Downley Bucks 32 B3
Down St Mary Devon 8 D4
Downside Somset 22 E3
Downside Somset 22 E4
Downside Surrey 32 G10
Down Thomas Devon 4 H7
Downton Hants 12 D6
Downton Wilts 24 C9
Dowsby Lincs 68 C6
Dowsdale Lincs 68 F10
Doxey Staffs 64 G7
Doxford Nthumb 109 K5
Doynton S Glos 29 L7
Draethen Caerph 28 B5
Draffan S Lans 114 E12
Dragonby N Linc 79 M1
Dragons Green W Susx 14 G6
Drakeholes Notts 78 H5
Drakelow Worcs 52 F4
Drakemyre N Ayrs 113 K11
Drakes Broughton Worcs 52 H11
Drakewalls Cnwll 7 N10
Draughton N York 84 F5
Draughton Nhants 55 J5
Drax N York 86 C10
Drax Hales N York 86 C10
Draycote Warwks 54 D6
Draycot Foliat Swindn 30 E7
Draycott Derbys 66 D5
Draycott Gloucs 42 E4
Draycott Shrops 52 E2
Draycott Somset 21 Q3
Draycott Somset 22 D9
Draycott Worcs 52 F11
Draycott in the Clay Staffs 65 M6
Draycott in the Moors Staffs 64 H4
Drayford Devon 19 Q10
Drayton C Port 13 L4
Drayton Leics 55 L2
Drayton Lincs 68 E4
Drayton Norfk 71 J9
Drayton Oxon 31 K3
Drayton Oxon 43 J3
Drayton Somset 21 N8
Drayton Worcs 52 G5
Drayton Bassett Staffs 65 M12
Drayton Beauchamp Bucks 44 C9
Drayton Manor Park Staffs 65 M12
Drayton Parslow Bucks 44 B6
Drayton St Leonard Oxon 31 M3
Drebley N York 84 F3
Dreemskerry IoM 102 f4
Dreen Hill Pembks 36 H7
Drefach Carmth 38 A4
Drefach Carmth 38 D9
Drefach Cerdgn 38 D3
Drefelin Carmth 38 A4
Dreghorn N Ayrs 104 F2
Drellingore Kent 17 M3
Drem E Loth 116 C5
Dresden C Stke 64 G4
Drewsteignton Devon 8 D6
Driby Lincs 80 G9
Driffield E R Yk 87 J4
Driffield Gloucs 30 C2
Driffield Cross Roads Gloucs 30 C3
Drift Cnwll 2 C9
Drigg Cumb 88 E7
Drighlington Leeds 85 K9
Drimnin Highld 119 P2
Drimpton Dorset 10 C4
Drimsallie Highld 128 D8
Dringhouses C York 86 A5
Drinkstone Suffk 58 E8
Drinkstone Green Suffk 58 E8
Drive End Dorset 10 F3
Driver's End Herts 45 J7
Drointon Staffs 65 J7
Droitwich Spa Worcs 52 G8
Dron P & K 124 C9
Dronfield Derbys 78 B8
Dronfield Woodhouse Derbys 77 Q8
Drongan E Ayrs 104 H6
Dronley Angus 124 G6
Droop Dorset 11 J3
Dropping Well Rothm 78 C5
Droxford Hants 25 K9
Droylsden Tamesd 76 G4
Druid Denbgs 62 E3
Druidston Pembks 36 G7
Druimarbin Highld 128 F10
Druimavuic Ag & B 121 J4
Druimdrishaig Ag & B 111 Q7
Druimindarroch Highld 127 M7
Drum Ag & B 112 D6
Drum P & K 115 J1
Drumalbin S Lans 106 B2
Drumbeg Highld 148 D10
Drumblade Abers 140 F8
Drumbreddon D & G 94 F9
Drumbuie Highld 135 P9
Drumburgh Cumb 98 B6
Drumburn D & G 96 H7
Drumburn D & G 97 K6
Drumchapel C Glas 113 Q7
Drumchastle P & K 122 H1
Drumclog S Lans 105 M2
Drumeldrie Fife 125 J12
Drumelzier Border 106 F3
Drumfearn Highld 127 M1
Drumfrennie Abers 132 H5
Drumgley Angus 124 H3
Drumguish Highld 130 E4
Drumin Moray 139 M10
Drumjohn D & G 105 J10
Drumlamford S Ayrs 95 K3
Drumlasie Abers 132 G3
Drumleaning Cumb 98 B8
Drumlemble Ag & B 103 J6
Drumlithie Abers 133 J8
Drummoddie D & G 95 M9
Drummore D & G 94 G11
Drummuir Moray 140 B7
Drumnadrochit Highld 137 N10
Drumnagorrach Moray 140 E5
Drumpark D & G 96 H2
Drumrunie Highld 144 F4
Drumshang S Ayrs 104 E7
Drumuie Highld 134 H6
Drumuillie Highld 138 H11
Drumvaich Stirlg 122 H12
Drunzie P & K 124 C11
Druridge Nthumb 109 M10
Drury Flints 75 J10
Drws-y-coed Gwynd 61 J1
Drybeck Cumb 89 Q4
Drybridge Moray 140 C3
Drybridge N Ayrs 104 G2
Drybrook Gloucs 41 K8
Dryburgh Border 107 P3
Dry Doddington Lincs 67 L3
Dry Drayton Cambs 56 G8
Drymen Stirlg 113 P3
Drymuir Abers 141 L6
Drynoch Highld 134 G9
Dry Sandford Oxon 31 K2
Dryslwyn Carmth 38 E7
Dry Street Essex 34 B5
Dryton Shrops 63 P11
Dubford Abers 141 J3
Dublin Suffk 58 H7
Duchally Highld 145 J2
Duck End Bed 44 F3
Duck End Cambs 56 E8
Duck End Essex 46 B5
Duck End Essex 46 B6
Duckend Green Essex 46 C7
Duckington Ches W 63 N2
Ducklington Oxon 42 H10
Duck's Cross Bed 56 B9
Duddenhoe End Essex 45 N4
Duddingston C Edin 115 P7
Duddington Nhants 67 N12
Duddlestone Somset 21 K9
Duddleswell E Susx 15 N5
Duddlewick Shrops 52 C4
Duddo Nthumb 108 F1
Duddon Ches W 75 N10
Duddon Bridge Cumb 88 G9
Duddon Common Ches W 75 N10
Dudleston Shrops 63 K4
Dudleston Heath Shrops 63 L5
Dudley Dudley 52 H3
Dudley N Tyne 100 H3
Dudley Hill C Brad 85 J9
Dudley Port Sandw 52 H2
Dudnill Shrops 52 C6
Dudsbury Dorset 11 P5
Dudswell Herts 44 D9
Duffield Derbys 65 Q3
Duffryn Neath 27 K3
Dufftown Moray 139 P8
Duffus Moray 139 M2
Dufton Cumb 90 A2
Duggleby N York 86 G2
Duirinish Highld 135 P9
Duisdalemore Highld 127 M2
Duisky Highld 128 D9
Dukestown Blae G 39 Q9
Duke Street Suffk 47 J3
Dukinfield Tamesd 76 H4
Dulas IoA 72 H6
Dulcote Somset 22 D4
Dulford Devon 9 K3
Dull P & K 123 K3
Dullatur N Lans 114 D6
Dullingham Cambs 57 M9
Dullingham Ley Cambs 57 M9
Dulnain Bridge Highld 139 J11
Duloe Bed 56 C8
Duloe Cnwll 4 C5
Dulsie Bridge Highld 138 G7
Dulverton Somset 20 E8
Dulwich Gt Lon 33 L7
Dumbarton W Duns 113 M6
Dumbleton Gloucs 42 B4
Dumfries D & G 97 K3
Dumgoyne Stirlg 113 Q5
Dummer Hants 25 K4
Dumpton Kent 35 Q9
Dun Angus 132 G12
Dunalastair P & K 123 J1
Dunan Ag & B 112 H7
Dunan Highld 135 K10
Dunan P & K 122 D1
Dunaverty Ag & B 103 J8
Dunball Somset 21 M5
Dunbar E Loth 116 F5
Dunbeath Highld 151 L10
Dunbeg Ag & B 120 G6
Dunblane Stirlg 114 E1
Dunbog Fife 124 F9
Dunbridge Hants 24 E8
Duncanston Highld 137 Q4
Duncanstone Abers 140 E10
Dunchideock Devon 8 G7
Dunchurch Warwks 54 D6
Duncote Nhants 54 H10
Duncow D & G 97 K2
Duncrievie P & K 124 C11
Duncton W Susx 14 D7
Dundee C Dund 124 H7
Dundee Airport C Dund 124 H7
Dundon Somset 22 B7
Dundonald S Ayrs 104 G3
Dundonnell Highld 144 D7
Dundraw Cumb 97 P8
Dundreggan Highld 129 K1
Dundrennan D & G 96 F8
Dundry N Som 28 H9
Dunecht Abers 133 J2
Dunfermline Fife 115 K4
Dunfield Gloucs 30 D3
Dunford Bridge Barns 77 M3
Dungate Kent 34 G10
Dungavel S Lans 105 M2
Dunge Wilts 23 K2
Dungeness Kent 17 K7
Dungworth Sheff 77 P6
Dunham Massey Traffd 76 D6
Dunham-on-the-Hill Ches W 75 M9
Dunham-on-Trent Notts 79 K9
Dunhampstead Worcs 52 G8
Dunhampton Worcs 52 F7
Dunham Town Traffd 76 D6
Dunham Woodhouses Traffd 76 D6
Dunholme Lincs 79 P8
Dunino Fife 125 K10
Dunipace Falk 114 E4
Dunkeld P & K 123 P4
Dunkerton BaNES 29 L10
Dunkeswell Devon 9 M3

I

J

K

178 Laverstock – Llangadwaladr

Laverstock Wilts 23 P7
Laverstoke Hants 24 H4
Laverton Gloucs 42 C4
Laverton N York 91 L12
Laverton Somset 22 H3
La Villette Guern 12 c3
Lavister Wrexhm 75 L12
Law S Lans 114 E10
Lawers P & K 122 H5
Lawford Essex 47 K5
Lawford Somset 21 J6
Law Hill S Lans 114 E11
Lawhitton Cnwll 7 L8
Lawkland N York 84 A2
Lawkland Green N York 84 B2
Lawley Wrekin 64 C10
Lawnhead Staffs 64 F7
Lawrence Weston Bristl 28 H6
Lawrenny Pembks 37 K9
Lawshall Suffk 58 C10
Lawshall Green Suffk 58 C10
Lawton Herefs 51 M9
Laxay W Isls 152 f4
Laxdale W Isls 152 g3
Laxey IoM 102 f5
Laxfield Suffk 59 L6
Laxford Bridge Highld 148 F7
Laxo Shet 147 j5
Laxton E R Yk 86 E10
Laxton Nhants 55 N1
Laxton Notts 79 J10
Laycock C Brad 84 F7
Layer Breton Essex 46 G8
Layer-de-la-Haye Essex 46 G7
Layer Marney Essex 46 G8
Layham Suffk 47 J4
Layland's Green W Berk 30 H9
Laymore Dorset 10 B4
Layter's Green Bucks 32 E4
Laytham E R Yk 86 D7
Laythes Cumb 97 P7
Lazenby R & Cl 92 C3
Lazonby Cumb 98 G10
Lea Derbys 77 Q12
Lea Herefs 41 K7
Lea Lincs 79 L6
Lea Shrops 51 K3
Lea Shrops 63 L10
Lea Wilts 29 Q5
Leachkin Highld 138 B7
Leadburn Border 115 N10
Leadenham Lincs 67 N2
Leaden Roding Essex 45 Q9
Leadgate Cumb 99 K9
Leadgate Dur 100 E8
Leadgate Nthumb 100 E6
Leadhills S Lans 106 A7
Leadingcross Green Kent 34 F12
Leadmill Derbys 77 N7
Leafield Oxon 42 G8
Leagrave Luton 44 F7
Leahead Ches W 76 C10
Lea Heath Staffs 65 J7
Leake N York 91 Q8
Leake Common Side Lincs 68 H2
Lealholm N York 92 F5
Lealholm Side N York 92 F5
Lealt Highld 135 J4
Leam Derbys 77 N8
Lea Marston Warwks 53 M2
Leamington Hastings Warwks 54 D7
Leamington Spa Warwks 53 Q7
Leamside Dur 101 J9
Leap Cross E Susx 15 Q9
Leasgill Cumb 89 M10
Leasingham Lincs 67 Q2
Leasingthorne Dur 100 H12
Leatherhead Surrey 32 H11
Leathley N York 85 K6
Leaton Shrops 63 M8
Leaton Wrekin 63 Q10
Lea Town Lancs 83 L9
Leaveland Kent 34 H11
Leavenheath Suffk 46 G4
Leavening N York 86 E3
Leaves Green Gt Lon 33 M10
Lea Yeat Cumb 90 C9
Lebberston N York 93 M10
Le Bigard Guern 12 b3
Le Bourg Guern 12 c3
Le Bourg Jersey 13 d3
Lechlade on Thames Gloucs 30 E2
Lecht Gruinart Ag & B 110 G7
Leck Lancs 89 Q11
Leckbuie P & K 123 J5
Leckford Hants 24 F6
Leckhampstead Bucks 43 P4
Leckhampstead W Berk 31 J7
Leckhampstead Thicket W Berk 31 J7
Leckhampton Gloucs 41 Q8
Leckmelm Highld 144 F7
Leckwith V Glam 27 R7
Leconfield E R Yk 87 J6
Ledaig Ag & B 120 G5
Ledburn Bucks 44 C7
Ledbury Herefs 41 L4
Leddington Gloucs 41 L5
Ledgemoor Herefs 51 L10
Ledicot Herefs 51 L8
Ledmore Highld 144 G3
Ledsham Ches W 75 K9
Ledsham Leeds 85 P9
Ledston Leeds 85 N9
Ledstone Devon 5 M7
Ledston Luck Leeds 85 N9
Ledwell Oxon 43 J6
Lee Devon 19 J4
Lee Gt Lon 33 M7
Lee Hants 24 F9
Lee Shrops 63 L6
Leebotwood Shrops 51 N1
Lee Brockhurst Shrops 63 P7
Leece Cumb 82 G1
Lee Chapel Essex 34 C5
Lee Clump Bucks 44 C10
Lee Common Bucks 44 C11
Leeds Kent 34 E11
Leeds Leeds 85 L8
Leeds Bradford Airport Leeds 85 K7
Leeds Castle Kent 34 E11
Leedstown Cnwll 2 F7
Lee Green Ches E 76 C11
Leek Staffs 77 J12
Leek Wootton Warwks 53 P7
Lee Mill Devon 5 J5
Leeming C Brad 84 F8
Leeming N York 91 M9
Leeming Bar N York 91 M8
Lee Moor Devon 5 J4
Lee-on-the-Solent Hants 13 J5
Lees C Brad 84 F7
Lees Derbys 65 N5
Lees Oldham 76 H3
Lees Green Derbys 65 N5
Leesthorpe Leics 67 K9
Leeswood Flints 75 J11
Leetown P & K 124 E8
Leftwich Ches W 76 C9
Legar Powys 40 B8
Legbourne Lincs 80 G7
Legburthwaite Cumb 89 J3
Legerwood Border 107 P1
Legoland W & M 32 D7
Le Gron Guern 12 b3
Legsby Lincs 80 C6
Le Haguais Jersey 13 c3
Le Hocq Jersey 13 d3
Leicester C Leic 66 F11
Leicester Forest East Leics 66 E11
Leicester Forest East Services Leics 66 E11
Leigh Devon 19 P11
Leigh Dorset 10 F3
Leigh Gloucs 41 P6
Leigh Kent 15 Q2
Leigh Shrops 63 K11
Leigh Surrey 15 J1
Leigh Wigan 76 C4
Leigh Wilts 30 C4
Leigh Worcs 52 E10
Leigh Beck Essex 34 E6
Leigh Delamere Wilts 29 P6
Leigh Delamere Services Wilts 29 P6
Leigh Green Kent 16 F4
Leigh Knoweglass S Lans 114 B11
Leighland Chapel Somset 20 G6
Leigh-on-Sea Sthend 34 E5
Leigh Park Dorset 11 P5
Leigh Park Hants 13 M3
Leigh Sinton Worcs 52 E10
Leighswood Wsall 65 K12
Leighterton Gloucs 29 N4
Leighton N York 91 K11
Leighton Powys 62 H11
Leighton Shrops 63 Q11
Leighton Somset 22 F4
Leighton Bromswold Cambs 56 C5
Leighton Buzzard C Beds 44 C6
Leigh upon Mendip Somset 22 F4
Leigh Woods N Som 28 H8
Leinthall Earls Herefs 51 M7
Leinthall Starkes Herefs 51 M7
Leintwardine Herefs 51 L6
Leire Leics 54 E3
Leiston Suffk 59 N8
Leith C Edin 115 N6
Leitholm Border 108 C1
Lelant Cnwll 2 E7
Lelley E R Yk 87 N8
Lem Hill Worcs 52 D5
Lempitlaw Border 108 C3
Lemreway W Isls 152 g5
Lemsford Herts 45 J9
Lenchwick Worcs 42 B2
Lendalfoot S Ayrs 104 C11
Lendrick Stirlg 122 F11
Lendrum Terrace Abers 141 Q7
Lenham Kent 34 F12
Lenham Heath Kent 34 G12
Lenie Highld 137 N10
Lennel Border 108 D2
Lennox Plunton D & G 96 C8
Lennoxtown E Duns 114 B6
Lent Bucks 32 D6
Lenton C Nott 66 F4
Lenton Lincs 67 P6
Lenwade Norfk 70 G8
Lenzie E Duns 114 B7
Leochel-Cushnie Abers 132 E2
Leomansley Staffs 65 L10
Leominster Herefs 51 N9
Leonard Stanley Gloucs 41 N11
Leoville Jersey 13 a1
Lepe Hants 12 G5
Lephin Highld 134 C6
Leppington N York 86 E3
Lepton Kirk 85 J12
Lerags Ag & B 120 F7
L'Erée Guern 12 b2
Lerryn Cnwll 4 A5
Lerwick Shet 147 j7
Les Arquêts Guern 12 b3
Lesbury Nthumb 109 L7
Les Hubits Guern 12 c3
Leslie Abers 140 F11
Leslie Fife 115 N1
Les Lohiers Guern 12 b2
Lesmahagow S Lans 105 Q2
Les Murchez Guern 12 b3
Lesnewth Cnwll 6 G6
Les Nicolles Guern 12 c3
Les Quartiers Guern 12 c2
Les Quennevais Jersey 13 a2
Les Sages Guern 12 b3
Lessingham Norfk 71 M6
Lessonhall Cumb 97 P8
Lestowder Cnwll 3 K9
Les Villets Guern 12 b3
Leswalt D & G 94 E5
L'Etacq Jersey 13 a1
Letchmore Heath Herts 32 G3
Letchworth Garden City Herts 45 J5
Letcombe Bassett Oxon 30 H5
Letcombe Regis Oxon 30 H5
Letham Angus 125 K3
Letham Border 107 Q8
Letham Falk 114 G4
Letham Fife 124 F10
Letham Grange Angus 125 M4
Lethenty Abers 140 F11
Lethenty Abers 141 K8
Letheringham Suffk 59 K9
Letheringsett Norfk 70 F4
Lettaford Devon 8 D8
Letterewe Highld 143 P11
Letterfearn Highld 136 B11
Letterfinlay Lodge Hotel Highld 129 J6
Lettermorar Highld 127 N6
Letters Highld 144 E7
Lettershaw S Lans 106 B6
Letterston Pembks 36 H4
Lettoch Highld 139 J12
Lettoch Highld 139 K9
Letton Herefs 40 D2
Letton Herefs 51 L6
Lett's Green Kent 33 N10
Letty Green Herts 45 K9
Letwell Rothm 78 F6
Leuchars Fife 125 J8
Leumrabhagh W Isls 152 g5
Leurbost W Isls 152 g4
Levalsa Meor Cnwll 3 N5
Levedale Staffs 64 G9
Level's Green Essex 45 N7
Leven E R Yk 87 L6
Leven Fife 115 Q1
Levens Cumb 89 M9
Levens Green Herts 45 L7
Levenshulme Manch 76 G5
Levenwick Shet 147 i9
Leverburgh W Isls 152 d6
Leverington Cambs 68 H10
Leverstock Green Herts 44 F10
Leverton Lincs 68 H3
Le Villocq Guern 12 c2
Levington Suffk 47 M4
Levisham N York 92 G8
Lew Oxon 42 G10
Lewannick Cnwll 7 K8
Lewdown Devon 7 N7
Lewes E Susx 15 M9
Leweston Pembks 36 H6
Lewisham Gt Lon 33 M7
Lewiston Highld 137 N10
Lewistown Brdgnd 27 M5
Lewis Wych Herefs 51 K9
Lewknor Oxon 31 P3
Leworthy Devon 7 L4
Leworthy Devon 19 N6
Lewson Street Kent 34 G10
Lewth Lancs 83 L8
Lewtrenchard Devon 7 N7
Lexden Essex 46 G6
Lexworthy Somset 21 L6
Ley Cnwll 4 B3
Leybourne Kent 34 B10
Leyburn N York 91 J8
Leycett Staffs 64 E3
Leygreen Herts 44 H7
Ley Hill Bucks 44 E11
Leyland Lancs 83 M10
Leyland Green St Hel 75 P4
Leylodge Abers 133 J2
Leys Abers 141 N5
Leys P & K 124 E5
Leysdown-on-Sea Kent 35 J8
Leysmill Angus 125 M3
Leys of Cossans Angus 124 H3
Leysters Herefs 51 P8
Leyton Gt Lon 33 M5
Leytonstone Gt Lon 33 M5
Lezant Cnwll 7 L9
Lezerea Cnwll 2 H8
Lhanbryde Moray 139 P4
Libanus Powys 39 N6
Libberton S Lans 106 C1
Libbery Worcs 52 H9
Liberton C Edin 115 N7
Lichfield Staffs 65 L10
Lickey Worcs 53 J5
Lickey End Worcs 52 H6
Lickey Rock Worcs 52 H6
Lickfold W Susx 14 C5
Liddaton Green Devon 7 N8
Liddesdale Highld 127 P12
Liddington Swindn 30 E6
Lidgate Derbys 77 P8
Lidgate Suffk 57 N9
Lidget Donc 78 G4
Lidgett Notts 78 G10
Lidham Hill E Susx 16 E7
Lidlington C Beds 44 E4
Lidsey W Susx 14 D10
Lidsing Kent 34 D10
Liff Angus 124 G6
Lifford Birm 53 K5
Lifton Devon 7 M8
Liftondown Devon 7 L7
Lighthorne Warwks 53 Q9
Lighthorne Heath Warwks 54 B9
Lightwater Surrey 32 D10
Lightwater Valley Theme Park N York 91 M11
Lightwood C Stke 64 G4
Lightwood Green Ches E 64 B4
Lightwood Green Wrexhm 63 L4
Lilbourne Nhants 54 F5
Lilburn Tower Nthumb 108 G5
Lilleshall Wrekin 64 D9
Lilley Herts 44 G6
Lilley W Berk 31 J6
Lilliesleaf Border 107 N5
Lillingstone Dayrell Bucks 43 P4
Lillingstone Lovell Bucks 43 P4
Lillington Dorset 22 E11
Lilliput BCP 11 P7
Lilstock Somset 21 J4
Lilyhurst Shrops 64 D9
Limbrick Lancs 83 N12
Limbury Luton 44 F7
Limebrook Herefs 51 L7
Limefield Bury 76 E1
Limekilnburn S Lans 114 C11
Limekilns Fife 115 K5
Limerigg Falk 114 F7
Limerstone IoW 12 G8
Limestone Brae Nthumb 99 M8
Lime Street Worcs 41 N5
Limington Somset 22 C9
Limmerhaugh E Ayrs 105 L4
Limpenhoe Norfk 71 M11
Limpley Stoke Wilts 29 M10
Limpsfield Surrey 33 M11
Limpsfield Chart Surrey 33 M12
Linby Notts 66 E2
Linchmere W Susx 14 B5
Lincluden D & G 97 K3
Lincoln Lincs 79 N9
Lincomb Worcs 52 F7
Lincombe Devon 5 M8
Lincombe Devon 19 K4
Lindale Cumb 89 L10
Lindal in Furness Cumb 88 H11
Lindfield W Susx 15 L6
Lindford Hants 25 P6
Lindley Kirk 84 H11
Lindley N York 85 K5
Lindores Fife 124 F9
Lindow End Ches E 76 F8
Lindridge Worcs 52 C7
Lindsell Essex 46 B6
Lindsey Suffk 46 H3
Lindsey Tye Suffk 46 H3
Liney Somset 21 N6
Linford Hants 12 C3
Linford Thurr 34 B6
Lingbob C Brad 84 G8
Lingdale R & Cl 92 D3
Lingen Herefs 51 L7
Lingfield Surrey 15 M2
Lingwood Norfk 71 M10
Liniclate W Isls 152 c9
Linicro Highld 134 G2
Linkend Worcs 41 N5
Linkenholt Hants 30 H10
Linkhill Kent 16 E5
Linkinhorne Cnwll 7 L10
Linktown Fife 115 N3
Linkwood Moray 139 N4
Linley Shrops 51 K2
Linley Green Herefs 52 C10
Linleygreen Shrops 52 C1
Linlithgow W Loth 114 H6
Linshiels Nthumb 108 E8
Linsidemore Highld 145 M5
Linslade C Beds 44 C7
Linstead Parva Suffk 59 L5
Linstock Cumb 98 E6
Linthurst Worcs 53 J6
Linthwaite Kirk 84 G12
Lintlaw Border 117 J9
Lintmill Moray 140 D3
Linton Border 108 C4
Linton Cambs 45 Q2
Linton Derbys 65 P9
Linton Herefs 41 K6
Linton Kent 34 D12
Linton Leeds 85 N6
Linton N York 84 E3
Linton Nthumb 109 L11
Linton Heath Derbys 65 P9
Linton Hill Herefs 41 K7
Linton-on-Ouse N York 85 P3
Linwood Hants 12 C3
Linwood Lincs 80 B6
Linwood Rens 113 N8
Lionacleit W Isls 152 c9
Lìonal W Isls 152 h1
Lions Green E Susx 15 Q7
Liphook Hants 25 P7
Lipley Shrops 64 D6
Liscard Wirral 75 J5
Liscombe Somset 20 D7
Liskeard Cnwll 4 C4
Lismore Ag & B 120 F4
Liss Hants 25 N8
Lissett E R Yk 87 L4
Liss Forest Hants 25 N7
Lissington Lincs 80 B7
Liston Essex 46 E3
Lisvane Cardif 28 B6
Liswerry Newpt 28 D5
Litcham Norfk 70 C8
Litchborough Nhants 54 G10
Litchfield Hants 24 G3
Litherland Sefton 75 K4
Litlington Cambs 45 K3
Litlington E Susx 15 P10
Little Abington Cambs 57 K10
Little Addington Nhants 55 N6
Little Airies D & G 95 M8
Little Almshoe Herts 44 H6
Little Alne Warwks 53 L8
Little Altcar Sefton 75 J2
Little Amwell Herts 45 L9
Little Asby Cumb 90 A5
Little Aston Staffs 65 K12
Little Atherfield IoW 12 H9
Little Ayton N York 92 B5
Little Baddow Essex 46 D10
Little Badminton S Glos 29 N5
Little Bampton Cumb 98 B7
Little Bardfield Essex 46 B5
Little Barford Bed 56 D9
Little Barningham Norfk 70 H5
Little Barrington Gloucs 42 E9
Little Barrow Ches W 75 M9
Little Barugh N York 92 F10
Little Bavington Nthumb 100 C3
Little Bealings Suffk 59 J11
Littlebeck N York 92 H6
Little Bedwyn Wilts 30 G9
Little Bentley Essex 47 K6
Little Berkhamsted Herts 45 K10
Little Billing Nhants 55 K8
Little Billington C Beds 44 D7
Little Birch Herefs 40 G5
Little Bispham Bpool 82 H7
Little Blakenham Suffk 58 G11
Little Blencow Cumb 98 F11
Little Bloxwich Wsall 65 J11
Little Bognor W Susx 14 E7
Little Bolehill Derbys 65 P1
Little Bollington Ches E 76 D6
Little Bookham Surrey 32 G11
Littleborough Devon 8 F3
Littleborough Notts 79 K7
Littleborough Rochdl 84 D12
Littlebourne Kent 35 M10
Little Bourton Oxon 43 K3
Little Bowden Leics 55 J3
Little Bradley Suffk 57 N10
Little Brampton Herefs 51 J8
Little Brampton Shrops 51 L4
Little Braxted Essex 46 E8
Little Brechin Angus 132 F11
Littlebredy Dorset 10 F7
Little Brickhill M Keyn 44 C5
Little Bridgeford Staffs 64 G7
Little Brington Nhants 54 H8
Little Bromley Essex 47 K6
Little Broughton Cumb 97 M11
Little Budworth Ches W 75 Q10
Littleburn Highld 138 B5
Little Burstead Essex 34 B4
Littlebury Essex 45 P4
Littlebury Green Essex 45 P4
Little Bytham Lincs 67 P8
Little Canfield Essex 45 Q7
Little Carlton Lincs 80 H6
Little Carlton Notts 79 K12
Little Casterton Rutlnd 67 P10
Little Catwick E R Yk 87 L6
Little Catworth Cambs 56 B6
Little Cawthorpe Lincs 80 G7
Little Chalfont Bucks 32 E3
Little Chart Kent 16 G2
Little Chesterford Essex 45 P3
Little Cheveney Kent 16 C2
Little Cheverell Wilts 23 L3
Little Chishill Cambs 45 M4
Little Clacton Essex 47 L8
Little Clanfield Oxon 30 F2
Little Clifton Cumb 88 E1
Little Coates NE Lin 80 E2
Little Comberton Worcs 41 Q3
Little Common E Susx 16 C9
Little Comp Kent 34 B11
Little Compton Warwks 42 F6
Little Corby Cumb 98 F7
Little Cornard Suffk 46 F4
Littlecott Wilts 23 P3
Little Cowarne Herefs 51 Q10
Little Coxwell Oxon 30 G4
Little Crakehall N York 91 L8
Little Cransley Nhants 55 L5
Little Cressingham Norfk 70 C12
Little Crosby Sefton 75 K3
Little Crosthwaite Cumb 88 H1
Little Cubley Derbys 65 M5
Little Dalby Leics 67 K9
Littledean Gloucs 41 K9
Little Dewchurch Herefs 40 H5
Little Ditton Cambs 57 M9
Little Doward Herefs 40 H8
Littledown Hants 30 H10
Little Downham Cambs 57 K4
Little Driffield E R Yk 87 J4
Little Dunham Norfk 70 C9
Little Dunkeld P & K 123 P4
Little Dunmow Essex 46 B7
Little Durnford Wilts 23 P6
Little Easton Essex 45 R7
Little Eaton Derbys 66 B4
Little Ellingham Norfk 70 E12
Little Elm Somset 22 F4
Little Everdon Nhants 54 F9
Little Eversden Cambs 56 G10
Little Faringdon Oxon 30 F2
Little Fencote N York 91 M8
Little Fenton N York 85 Q8
Littleferry Highld 146 E6
Little Fransham Norfk 70 D9
Little Gaddesden Herts 44 E9
Little Garway Herefs 40 F7
Little Gidding Cambs 56 C4
Little Glemham Suffk 59 L9
Little Gorsley Herefs 41 L7
Little Gransden Cambs 56 E9
Little Green Notts 67 J3
Little Green Somset 22 G4
Little Grimsby Lincs 80 F5
Little Gringley Notts 79 J7
Little Habton N York 92 F11
Little Hadham Herts 45 N7
Little Hale Lincs 68 C4
Little Hallam Derbys 66 D4
Little Hallingbury Essex 45 P8
Littleham Devon 9 K8
Littleham Devon 18 H8
Little Hampden Bucks 44 B11
Littlehampton W Susx 14 E10
Little Hanford Dorset 11 K2
Little Harrowden Nhants 55 L6
Little Haseley Oxon 31 N2
Little Hatfield E R Yk 87 M6
Little Hautbois Norfk 71 K8
Little Haven Pembks 36 G8
Littlehaven W Susx 14 H4
Little Hay Staffs 65 L11
Little Hayfield Derbys 77 J6
Little Haywood Staffs 65 J8
Little Heath Staffs 64 G8
Little Heath W Berk 31 N7
Littlehempston Devon 5 N4
Little Hereford Herefs 51 P7
Little Horkesley Essex 46 G5
Little Hormead Herts 45 M6
Little Horsted E Susx 15 N7
Little Horton C Brad 84 H9
Little Horton Wilts 30 B10
Little Horwood Bucks 43 R5
Little Houghton Barns 78 C2
Little Houghton Nhants 55 K8
Littlehoughton Nthumb 109 L6
Little Hucklow Derbys 77 M8
Little Hulton Salfd 76 D3
Little Hungerford W Berk 31 L7
Little Hutton N York 91 Q11
Little Irchester Nhants 55 M7
Little Kelk E R Yk 87 L3
Little Keyford Somset 22 H4
Little Kimble Bucks 44 B10
Little Kineton Warwks 53 Q10
Little Kingshill Bucks 32 C3
Little Knox D & G 96 G6
Little Langdale Cumb 89 J6
Little Langford Wilts 23 N6
Little Laver Essex 45 Q9
Little Leigh Ches W 76 B8
Little Leighs Essex 46 C8
Little Lever Bolton 76 D2
Little Linford M Keyn 44 B3
Little Load Somset 21 P8
Little London Bucks 43 N9
Little London Cambs 56 H1
Little London E Susx 15 Q7
Little London Essex 45 N6
Little London Essex 46 B5
Little London Gloucs 41 L8
Little London Hants 24 F3
Little London Hants 31 N10
Little London Leeds 85 J7
Little London Lincs 68 E8
Little London Lincs 68 H7
Little London Lincs 80 F8
Little London Norfk 69 L8
Little London Powys 50 E3
Little Longstone Derbys 77 M9
Little Madeley Staffs 64 E3
Little Malvern Worcs 41 M4
Little Mancot Flints 75 K10
Little Maplestead Essex 46 E5
Little Marcle Herefs 41 K4
Little Marland Devon 19 K11
Little Marlow Bucks 32 C5
Little Massingham Norfk 69 Q7
Little Melton Norfk 70 H10
Littlemill Abers 131 P5
Littlemill Highld 138 G6
Little Mill Mons 40 D11
Little Milton Oxon 31 N2
Little Missenden Bucks 32 C3
Little Mongeham Kent 35 P12
Littlemoor Derbys 78 B11
Little Moor Somset 21 M7
Littlemore Oxon 43 L11
Little Musgrave Cumb 90 C4
Little Ness Shrops 63 L8
Little Neston Ches W 75 J8
Little Newcastle Pembks 37 J5
Little Newsham Dur 91 J3
Little Norton Somset 21 Q10
Little Oakley Essex 47 M6
Little Oakley Nhants 55 M3
Little Odell Bed 55 N9
Little Offley Herts 44 G6
Little Ormside Cumb 90 B3
Little Orton Cumb 98 D7
Little Ouse Cambs 57 M3
Little Ouseburn N York 85 P3
Littleover C Derb 65 Q5
Little Oxendon Nhants 55 J4
Little Packington Warwks 53 N4
Little Pattenden Kent 16 C2
Little Paxton Cambs 56 D8
Little Petherick Cnwll 6 C10
Little Plumpton Lancs 83 J8
Little Plumstead Norfk 71 L9
Little Ponton Lincs 67 M6
Littleport Cambs 57 L3
Littleport Bridge Cambs 57 L3
Little Posbrook Hants 13 J4
Little Potheridge Devon 19 K10
Little Preston Leeds 85 M9
Little Preston Nhants 54 F10
Littler Ches W 76 B10
Little Raveley Cambs 56 E5
Little Reedness E R Yk 86 E10
Little Ribston N York 85 M4
Little Rissington Gloucs 42 E7
Little Rollright Oxon 42 G6
Little Rowsley Derbys 77 N10
Little Ryburgh Norfk 70 E6
Little Ryle Nthumb 108 G7
Little Ryton Shrops 63 N11
Little Salkeld Cumb 98 H11
Little Sampford Essex 46 B5
Little Sandhurst Br For 32 B10
Little Saredon Staffs 64 H10
Little Saughall Ches W 75 L10
Little Saxham Suffk 57 Q8
Little Scatwell Highld 137 L4
Little Shelford Cambs 57 J10
Little Shrewley Warwks 53 N7
Little Silver Devon 8 G3
Little Singleton Lancs 83 J7
Little Skipwith N York 86 C7
Little Smeaton N York 85 Q11
Little Snoring Norfk 70 D6
Little Sodbury S Glos 29 M6
Little Sodbury End S Glos 29 M5
Little Somborne Hants 24 F7
Little Somerford Wilts 29 Q5
Little Soudley Shrops 64 D6
Little Stainforth N York 84 B2
Little Stainton Darltn 91 N3
Little Stanion Nhants 55 M3
Little Stanney Ches W 75 L9
Little Staughton Bed 56 B8
Little Steeping Lincs 80 H11
Little Stoke Staffs 64 G5
Littlestone-on-Sea Kent 17 K6
Little Stonham Suffk 58 G8
Little Stretton Leics 66 H12
Little Stretton Shrops 51 M2
Little Strickland Cumb 89 P3
Little Stukeley Cambs 56 D5
Little Sugnall Staffs 64 E6
Little Sutton Ches W 75 L8
Little Sutton Shrops 51 N4
Little Swinburne Nthumb 99 Q3
Little Sypland D & G 96 E7
Little Tew Oxon 42 H6
Little Tey Essex 46 F7
Little Thetford Cambs 57 K5
Little Thirkleby N York 91 Q11
Little Thornage Norfk 70 F4
Little Thornton Lancs 83 J7
Little Thorpe Dur 101 L9
Littlethorpe Leics 54 E1
Littlethorpe N York 85 L1
Little Thurlow Suffk 57 N10
Little Thurlow Green Suffk 57 N10
Little Thurrock Thurr 34 A7
Littleton Angus 124 G3
Littleton BaNES 28 H9
Littleton Ches W 75 M10
Littleton D & G 96 D7
Littleton Dorset 11 L4
Littleton Hants 24 G7
Littleton Somset 22 C7
Littleton Surrey 14 D1
Littleton Surrey 32 F8
Littleton Drew Wilts 29 N6
Littleton-on-Severn S Glos 29 J4
Littleton Pannell Wilts 23 M3
Little Torrington Devon 19 J10
Little Totham Essex 46 F9
Little Town Cumb 88 H3
Littletown Dur 101 J9
Little Town Lancs 83 P8
Little Town Warrtn 76 B5
Little Twycross Leics 65 Q11
Little Urswick Cumb 88 H12
Little Wakering Essex 34 G5
Little Walden Essex 45 Q3
Little Waldingfield Suffk 46 G3
Little Walsingham Norfk 70 D5
Little Waltham Essex 46 C9
Little Warley Essex 33 R4
Little Washbourne Gloucs 42 A5
Little Weighton E R Yk 87 J8
Little Welnetham Suffk 58 C8
Little Welton Lincs 80 F6
Little Wenham Suffk 47 K4
Little Wenlock Wrekin 64 C10
Little Weston Somset 22 E8
Little Whitefield IoW 13 K7
Little Whittingham Green Suffk 59 K5
Little Whittington Nthumb 100 C4
Littlewick Green W & M 32 B6
Little Wilbraham Cambs 57 K9
Littlewindsor Dorset 10 C4
Little Witcombe Gloucs 41 P8
Little Witley Worcs 52 E8
Little Wittenham Oxon 31 M4
Little Wolford Warwks 42 F5
Littlewood Staffs 64 H10
Little Woodcote Gt Lon 33 K10
Littleworth Bucks 44 C7
Littleworth Oxon 30 G3
Littleworth Staffs 64 H7
Littleworth Staffs 65 J10
Littleworth W Susx 14 H7
Littleworth Worcs 52 G10
Littleworth Worcs 53 J8
Littleworth Common Bucks 32 D5
Little Wratting Suffk 46 C2
Little Wymington Bed 55 N7
Little Wymondley Herts 45 J6
Little Wyrley Staffs 65 J11
Little Wytheford Shrops 63 P8
Little Yeldham Essex 46 D4
Littley Green Essex 46 C8
Litton Derbys 77 M8
Litton N York 90 E12
Litton Somset 22 D2
Litton Cheney Dorset 10 E6
Liurbost W Isls 152 g4
Liverpool Lpool 75 K5
Liverpool Maritime Mercantile City Lpool 75 K6
Liversedge Kirk 85 J10
Liverton Devon 8 E9
Liverton R & Cl 92 E4
Liverton Mines R & Cl 92 E3
Liverton Street Kent 34 F12
Livingston W Loth 115 K7
Livingston Village W Loth 115 J8
Lixwm Flints 74 G9
Lizard Cnwll 2 H12
Llaingoch IoA 72 C7
Llaithddu Powys 50 E5
Llan Powys 61 Q12
Llanaber Gwynd 61 K8
Llanaelhaearn Gwynd 60 F3
Llanafan Cerdgn 49 M6
Llanafan-Fawr Powys 50 C9
Llanafan-fechan Powys 50 D10
Llanallgo IoA 72 H6
Llanarmon Gwynd 60 G4
Llanarmon Dyffryn Ceiriog Wrexhm 62 G6
Llanarmon-yn-Ial Denbgs 74 G12
Llanarth Cerdgn 48 G9
Llanarth Mons 40 E9
Llanarthne Carmth 38 D7
Llanasa Flints 74 F7
Llanbabo IoA 72 F6
Llanbadarn Fawr Cerdgn 49 K4
Llanbadarn Fynydd Powys 50 F5
Llanbadarn-y-garreg Powys 50 F11
Llanbadoc Mons 28 E2
Llanbadrig IoA 72 F5
Llanbeder Newpt 28 E4
Llanbedr Gwynd 61 K7
Llanbedr Powys 39 Q2
Llanbedr Powys 40 B7
Llanbedr-Dyffryn-Clwyd Denbgs 74 G11
Llanbedrgoch IoA 72 H7
Llanbedrog Gwynd 60 E6
Llanbedr-y-Cennin Conwy 73 N10
Llanberis Gwynd 73 K11
Llanbethêry V Glam 27 N8
Llanbister Powys 50 F6
Llanblethian V Glam 27 N7
Llanboidy Carmth 37 N6
Llanbradach Caerph 27 Q4
Llanbrynmair Powys 62 B11
Llancadle V Glam 27 N8
Llancarfan V Glam 27 P8
Llancayo Mons 40 E11
Llancloudy Herefs 40 G7
Llancynfelyn Cerdgn 49 L2
Llandaff Cardif 27 R7
Llandanwg Gwynd 61 J6
Llandarcy Neath 26 H3
Llandawke Carmth 37 Q8
Llanddaniel Fab IoA 72 H9
Llanddarog Carmth 38 D8
Llanddeiniol Cerdgn 49 J6
Llanddeiniolen Gwynd 73 J10
Llandderfel Gwynd 62 D5
Llanddeusant Carmth 39 J7
Llanddeusant IoA 72 E6
Llanddew Powys 39 P5
Llanddewi Swans 26 C4
Llanddewi Brefi Cerdgn 49 L9
Llanddewi'r Cwm Powys 50 E11
Llanddewi Rhydderch Mons 40 D9
Llanddewi Velfrey Pembks 37 M7
Llanddewi Ystradenni Powys 50 F7
Llanddoged Conwy 73 P11
Llanddona IoA 73 J8
Llanddowror Carmth 37 P7
Llanddulas Conwy 74 B8
Llanddwywe Gwynd 61 K8
Llanddyfnan IoA 72 H8
Llandecwyn Gwynd 61 K5
Llandefaelog Powys 39 N5
Llandefaelog-Tre'r-Graig Powys 39 Q6
Llandefalle Powys 39 Q4
Llandegfan IoA 73 J9
Llandegla Denbgs 62 H2
Llandegley Powys 50 G8
Llandegveth Mons 28 D3
Llandegwning Gwynd 60 D6
Llandeilo Carmth 38 F7
Llandeilo Graban Powys 39 P3
Llandeilo'r Fan Powys 39 L5
Llandeloy Pembks 36 G5
Llandenny Mons 40 F11
Llandevaud Newpt 28 E4
Llandevenny Mons 28 F5
Llandinabo Herefs 40 G6
Llandinam Powys 50 E3
Llandissilio Pembks 37 M6
Llandogo Mons 40 H11
Llandough V Glam 27 N8
Llandough V Glam 27 R8
Llandovery Carmth 39 J5
Llandow V Glam 27 M7
Llandre Carmth 38 G3
Llandre Cerdgn 49 K3
Llandre Isaf Pembks 37 M5
Llandrillo Denbgs 62 E5
Llandrillo-yn-Rhos Conwy 73 P7
Llandrindod Wells Powys 50 E8
Llandrinio Powys 63 J8
Llandudno Conwy 73 N7
Llandudno Junction Conwy 73 N8
Llandulas Powys 39 L3
Llandwrog Gwynd 60 G1
Llandybie Carmth 38 F8
Llandyfaelog Carmth 38 B9
Llandyfan Carmth 38 F8
Llandyfriog Cerdgn 37 Q2
Llandyfrydog IoA 72 G6
Llandygai Gwynd 73 K9
Llandygwydd Cerdgn 37 P2
Llandynan Denbgs 62 G3
Llandyrnog Denbgs 74 F10
Llandyssil Powys 50 H2
Llandysul Cerdgn 38 B3
Llanedeyrn Cardif 28 B6
Llanedi Carmth 38 E10
Llaneglwys Powys 39 P4
Llanegryn Gwynd 61 K11
Llanegwad Carmth 38 D7
Llaneilian IoA 72 H5
Llanelian-yn-Rhôs Conwy 73 Q8
Llanelidan Denbgs 62 F2
Llanelieu Powys 40 A5
Llanellen Mons 40 D9
Llanelli Carmth 26 D2
Llanelltyd Gwynd 61 M8
Llanelly Mons 40 B8
Llanelly Hill Mons 40 B9
Llanelwedd Powys 50 E10
Llanenddwyn Gwynd 61 K7
Llanengan Gwynd 60 E7
Llanerch Gwynd 62 B9
Llanerch Powys 51 J2
Llanerchymedd IoA 72 G7
Llanerfyl Powys 62 E10
Llanfachraeth IoA 72 E7
Llanfachreth Gwynd 61 N7
Llanfaelog IoA 72 E9
Llanfaelrhys Gwynd 60 C7
Llanfaenor Mons 40 F8
Llanfaes IoA 73 K8
Llanfaes Powys 39 N6
Llanfaethlu IoA 72 E6
Llanfair Gwynd 61 K6
Llanfair Caereinion Powys 62 F11
Llanfair Clydogau Cerdgn 49 K10
Llanfair Dyffryn Clwyd Denbgs 62 F1
Llanfairfechan Conwy 73 L9
Llanfair Kilgeddin Mons 40 D10
Llanfair-Nant-Gwyn Pembks 37 M3
Llanfairpwllgwyngyll IoA 73 J9
Llanfair Talhaiarn Conwy 74 C9
Llanfair Waterdine Shrops 50 H5
Llanfairynghornwy IoA 72 E5
Llanfair-yn-Neubwll IoA 72 E8
Llanfallteg Carmth 37 M6
Llanfallteg West Carmth 37 M6
Llanfarian Cerdgn 49 K5
Llanfechain Powys 62 G8
Llanfechell IoA 72 F5
Llanferres Denbgs 74 G11
Llanfflewyn IoA 72 F6
Llanfigael IoA 72 E7
Llanfihangel-ar-arth Carmth 38 C4
Llanfihangel Glyn Myfyr Conwy 62 D2
Llanfihangel Nant Bran Powys 39 M5
Llanfihangel-nant-Melan Powys 50 G9
Llanfihangel Rhydithon Powys 50 G7
Llanfihangel Rogiet Mons 28 F5
Llanfihangel Tal-y-llyn Powys 39 Q6
Llanfihangel-uwch-Gwili Carmth 38 D7
Llanfihangel-y-Creuddyn Cerdgn 49 L5
Llanfihangel-yng-Ngwynfa Powys 62 E9
Llanfihangel yn Nhowyn IoA 72 E8
Llanfihangel-y-pennant Gwynd 61 J3
Llanfihangel-y-pennant Gwynd 61 L10
Llanfihangel-y-traethau Gwynd 61 K5
Llanfilo Powys 39 Q5
Llanfoist Mons 40 C9
Llanfor Gwynd 62 C5
Llanfrechfa Torfn 28 D4
Llanfrothen Gwynd 61 K4
Llanfrynach Powys 39 P6
Llanfwrog Denbgs 74 F12
Llanfwrog IoA 72 E7
Llanfyllin Powys 62 G8
Llanfynydd Carmth 38 E6
Llanfynydd Flints 75 J12
Llanfyrnach Pembks 37 P4
Llangadfan Powys 62 D10
Llangadog Carmth 38 B10
Llangadog Carmth 38 H6
Llangadwaladr IoA 72 F10
Llangadwaladr Powys 62 G6

Llangaffo – Maeshafn 179

Llangaffo IoA 72 G10
Llangain Carmth 38 B8
Llangammarch Wells Powys 39 M2
Llangan V Glam 27 M7
Llangarron Herefs 40 H7
Llangasty-Talyllyn Powys 39 Q6
Llangathen Carmth 38 E7
Llangattock Powys 40 B8
Llangattock Lingoed Mons 40 E7
Llangattock-Vibon-Avel Mons 40 F8
Llangedwyn Powys 62 G7
Llangefni IoA 72 G8
Llangeinor Brdgnd 27 L5
Llangeitho Cerdgn 49 K8
Llangeler Carmth 38 B4
Llangelynin Gwynd 61 K10
Llangendeirne Carmth 38 C9
Llangennech Carmth 26 E2
Llangennith Swans 26 C4
Llangenny Powys 40 C8
Llangernyw Conwy 73 Q10
Llangian Gwynd 60 E6
Llangiwg Neath 38 H10
Llangloffan Pembks 36 H4
Llanglydwen Carmth 37 N5
Llangoed IoA 73 K8
Llangoedmor Cerdgn 48 C11
Llangollen Denbgs 62 H4
Llangolman Pembks 37 M5
Llangors Powys 39 Q6
Llangorwen Cerdgn 49 K4
Llangovan Mons 40 F10
Llangower Gwynd 62 B6
Llangrannog Cerdgn 48 E10
Llangristiolus IoA 72 G9
Llangrove Herefs 40 H8
Llangua Mons 40 E6
Llangunllo Powys 50 H6
Llangunnor Carmth 38 C7
Llangurig Powys 50 B5
Llangwm Conwy 62 C3
Llangwm Mons 28 F2
Llangwm Pembks 37 J8
Llangwnnadl Gwynd 60 C5
Llangwyfan Denbgs 74 F10
Llangwyllog IoA 72 G8
Llangwyryfon Cerdgn 49 K6
Llangybi Cerdgn 49 K10
Llangybi Gwynd 60 G4
Llangybi Mons 28 E3
Llangyfelach Swans 26 F3
Llangynhafal Denbgs 74 F11
Llangynidr Powys 39 R8
Llangynin Carmth 37 P6
Llangynllo Cerdgn 37 R2
Llangynog Carmth 37 R7
Llangynog Powys 62 E7
Llangynwyd Brdgnd 27 K5
Llanhamlach Powys 39 P6
Llanharan Rhondd 27 N6
Llanharry Rhondd 27 N6
Llanhennock Mons 28 E4
Llanhilleth Blae G 28 B2
Llanidan IoA 72 H10
Llanidloes Powys 50 C4
Llaniestyn Gwynd 60 D5
Llanigon Powys 40 B4
Llanilar Cerdgn 49 K6
Llanilid Rhondd 27 M6
Llanina Cerdgn 48 F8
Llanio Cerdgn 49 L9
Llanishen Cardif 28 A6
Llanishen Mons 40 G11
Llanllechid Gwynd 73 K10
Llanlleonfel Powys 50 C10
Llanllowell Mons 28 E3
Llanllugan Powys 62 E11
Llanllwch Carmth 38 B8
Llanllwchaiarn Powys 50 F2
Llanllwni Carmth 38 D4
Llanllyfni Gwynd 60 H2
Llanmadoc Swans 26 C4
Llanmaes V Glam 27 M8
Llanmartin Newpt 28 E4
Llanmerewig Powys 50 G2
Llanmihangel V Glam 27 M8
Llanmiloe Carmth 37 P9
Llanmorlais Swans 26 D3
Llannefydd Conwy 74 D9
Llannon Carmth 38 E10
Llannor Gwynd 60 F5
Llanon Cerdgn 48 H7
Llanover Mons 40 D10
Llanpumsaint Carmth 38 B6
Llanrhaeadr-ym-Mochnant Powys 62 F7
Llanrhian Pembks 36 F4
Llanrhidian Swans 26 D4
Llanrhos Conwy 73 N7
Llanrhychwyn Conwy 73 N11
Llanrhyddlad IoA 72 E6
Llanrhystud Cerdgn 49 J7
Llanrothal Herefs 40 G8
Llanrug Gwynd 73 J11
Llanrumney Cardif 28 B6
Llanrwst Conwy 73 P11
Llansadurnen Carmth 37 Q8
Llansadwrn Carmth 38 G5
Llansadwrn IoA 73 J8
Llansaint Carmth 38 B10
Llansamlet Swans 26 G3
Llansanffraid Glan Conwy Conwy 73 P8
Llansannan Conwy 74 C10
Llansannor V Glam 27 N7
Llansantffraed Powys 39 Q7
Llansantffraed-Cwmdeuddwr Powys 50 C7
Llansantffraed-in-Elvel Powys 50 F9
Llansantffraid Cerdgn 49 J7
Llansantffraid-ym-Mechain Powys 62 H8
Llansawel Carmth 38 F4
Llansilin Powys 62 H6
Llansoy Mons 40 F11
Llanspyddid Powys 39 N6
Llanstadwell Pembks 37 J9
Llansteffan Carmth 37 R8
Llanstephan Powys 39 Q3
Llantarnam Torfn 28 D4
Llanteg Pembks 37 N8
Llanthewy Skirrid Mons 40 D8
Llanthony Mons 40 C6
Llantilio-Crossenny Mons 40 E8
Llantilio Pertholey Mons 40 D8
Llantood Pembks 37 M2
Llantrisant IoA 72 F7
Llantrisant Mons 28 E3
Llantrisant Rhondd 27 P6
Llantrithyd V Glam 27 P8
Llantwit Fardre Rhondd 27 P5
Llantwit Major V Glam 27 M8
Llantysilio Denbgs 62 H3
Llanuwchllyn Gwynd 61 Q6
Llanvaches Newpt 28 F4
Llanvair Discoed Mons 28 F4
Llanvapley Mons 40 E9
Llanvetherine Mons 40 E8
Llanveynoe Herefs 40 D5
Llanvihangel Crucorney Mons 40 D7
Llanvihangel Gobion Mons 40 D9
Llanvihangel-Ystern-Llewern Mons 40 F9
Llanwarne Herefs 40 G6
Llanwddyn Powys 62 D8
Llanwenarth Mons 40 C8
Llanwenog Cerdgn 38 D3
Llanwern Newpt 28 E5
Llanwinio Carmth 37 P5
Llanwnda Gwynd 72 H12
Llanwnda Pembks 36 H3
Llanwnnen Cerdgn 38 D2
Llanwnog Powys 50 D2
Llanwonno Rhondd 27 N3
Llanwrda Carmth 38 H5
Llanwrin Powys 61 N11
Llanwrthwl Powys 50 D8
Llanwrtyd Powys 49 Q11
Llanwrtyd Wells Powys 39 L2
Llanwyddelan Powys 62 E12
Llanyblodwel Shrops 62 H7
Llanybri Carmth 37 R8
Llanybydder Carmth 38 D3
Llanycefn Pembks 37 L6
Llanychaer Pembks 37 J3
Llanycil Gwynd 62 B5
Llanycrwys Carmth 38 F3
Llanymawddwy Gwynd 62 B8
Llanymynech Powys 63 J8
Llanynghenedl IoA 72 E7
Llanynys Denbgs 74 F11
Llan-y-pwll Wrexhm 63 L2
Llanyre Powys 50 E8
Llanystumdwy Gwynd 60 H4
Llanywern Powys 39 Q6
Llawhaden Pembks 37 L7
Llawnt Shrops 62 H6
Llawryglyn Powys 50 C2
Llay Wrexhm 63 K1
Llechcynfarwy IoA 72 F7
Llechfaen Powys 39 P6
Llechrhyd Caerph 39 Q10
Llechryd Cerdgn 37 N2
Llechylched IoA 72 E8
Lledrod Cerdgn 49 L6
Lleyn Peninsula Gwynd 60 E5
Llidiardau Gwynd 61 Q4
Llidiartnenog Carmth 38 E4
Llidiart-y-parc Denbgs 62 F3
Llithfaen Gwynd 60 F4
Lloc Flints 74 G8
Llowes Powys 40 B3
Llwydcoed Rhondd 39 N10
Llwydiarth Powys 62 E9
Llwyn Denbgs 74 E10
Llwyncelyn Cerdgn 48 G8
Llwyndafydd Cerdgn 48 F9
Llwynderw Powys 62 H11
Llwyn-drain Pembks 37 P4
Llwyn-du Mons 40 C8
Llwyndyrys Gwynd 60 F4
Llwyngwril Gwynd 61 K10
Llwynhendy Carmth 26 E2
Llwynmawr Wrexhm 62 H5
Llwyn-on Myr Td 39 N9
Llwyn-y-brain Carmth 37 N7
Llwyn-y-groes Cerdgn 49 K9
Llwynypia Rhondd 27 N4
Llynclys Shrops 63 J7
Llynfaes IoA 72 G8
Llyn-y-pandy Flints 74 H10
Llysfaen Conwy 74 B8
Llyswen Cerdgn 48 G8
Llyswen Powys 39 Q4
Llysworney V Glam 27 M7
Llys-y-frân Pembks 37 K6
Llywel Powys 39 K6
Load Brook Sheff 77 P6
Loan Falk 114 H6
Loanend Nthumb 117 L11
Loanhead Mdloth 115 P8
Loaningfoot D & G 97 J7
Loans S Ayrs 104 F3
Lobb Devon 19 J6
Lobhillcross Devon 7 N7
Lochailort Highld 127 P8
Lochaline Highld 120 C4
Lochans D & G 94 F7
Locharbriggs D & G 97 K2
Lochavich Ag & B 120 H9
Lochawe Ag & B 121 L7
Loch Baghasdail W Isls 152 c11
Lochboisdale W Isls 152 c11
Lochbuie Ag & B 119 Q8
Lochcarron Highld 136 B8
Lochdon Ag & B 120 D6
Lochdonhead Ag & B 120 D6
Lochead Ag & B 111 R6
Lochearnhead Stirlg 122 G8
Lochee C Dund 124 H6
Locheilside Station Highld 128 D8
Lochend Highld 137 Q8
Locheport W Isls 152 c8
Loch Euphoirt W Isls 152 c8
Lochfoot D & G 96 H3
Lochgair Ag & B 112 D3
Lochgelly Fife 115 M3
Lochgilphead Ag & B 112 C4
Lochgoilhead Ag & B 113 J1
Lochieheads Fife 124 E10
Lochill Moray 139 P3
Lochindorb Lodge Highld 138 H9
Lochinver Highld 148 C12
Loch Lomond and The Trossachs National Park 122 D10
Loch Loyal Lodge Highld 149 N7
Lochluichart Highld 137 K3
Lochmaben D & G 97 M2
Lochmaddy W Isls 152 d8
Loch nam Madadh W Isls 152 d8
Loch Ness Highld 137 P10
Lochore Fife 115 M2
Lochranza N Ayrs 112 D11
Loch Sgioport W Isls 152 c10
Lochside Abers 132 H11
Lochside D & G 97 J3
Lochside Highld 138 E5
Lochskipport W Isls 152 c10
Lochslin Highld 146 F9
Lochton S Ayrs 95 J2
Lochty Angus 132 E11
Lochty Fife 125 K11
Lochuisge Highld 120 E2
Lochwinnoch Rens 113 L9
Lochwood D & G 106 E10
Lockengate Cnwll 3 P2
Lockerbie D & G 97 N2
Lockeridge Wilts 30 D9
Lockerley Hants 24 E8
Locking N Som 28 E10
Locking Stumps Warrtn 76 B5
Lockington E R Yk 87 J6
Lockington Leics 66 D6
Lockleywood Shrops 64 C6
Locksbottom Gt Lon 33 M9
Locksgreen IoW 12 G6
Locks Heath Hants 12 H3
Lockton N York 92 G9
Loddington Leics 67 K11
Loddington Nhants 55 K5
Loddiswell Devon 5 M7
Loddon Norfk 71 M12
Lode Cambs 57 K8
Lode Heath Solhll 53 M4
Loders Dorset 10 D6
Lodsworth W Susx 14 D6
Lofthouse Leeds 85 L10
Lofthouse N York 91 J12
Lofthouse Gate Wakefd 85 L10
Loftus R & Cl 92 E3
Logan E Ayrs 105 L6
Loganbeck Cumb 88 G8
Loganlea W Loth 114 H9
Loggerheads Staffs 64 D5
Logie Angus 132 H11
Logie Fife 124 H8
Logie Moray 139 J6
Logie Coldstone Abers 132 C3
Logie Newton Abers 140 G8
Logie Pert Angus 132 G11
Logierait P & K 123 N2
Logierieve Abers 141 M10
Login Carmth 37 M6
Lolworth Cambs 56 G8
Lonbain Highld 135 M5
Londesborough E R Yk 86 F6
London Gt Lon 33 L6
London Apprentice Cnwll 3 N4
London Beach Kent 16 F3
London Colney Herts 44 H11
Londonderry N York 91 M9
London End Nhants 55 M7
London Gateway Services Gt Lon 32 H3
London Gatwick Airport W Susx 15 K3
London Heathrow Airport Gt Lon 32 F7
London Luton Airport Luton 44 G7
London Oxford Airport Oxon 43 K8
London Southend Airport Essex 34 F4
London Stansted Airport Essex 45 Q7
Londonthorpe Lincs 67 N4
London Zoo ZSL Gt Lon 33 K6
Londubh Highld 143 M9
Lonemore Highld 143 L9
Long Ashton N Som 28 H8
Long Bank Worcs 52 E6
Long Bennington Lincs 67 L3
Longbenton N Tyne 100 H4
Longborough Gloucs 42 E6
Long Bredy Dorset 10 E7
Longbridge Birm 53 J5
Longbridge Warwks 53 P8
Longbridge Deverill Wilts 23 J5
Long Buckby Nhants 54 G7
Longburgh Cumb 98 C6
Longburton Dorset 22 E10
Long Cause Devon 5 N4
Long Clawson Leics 67 J7
Longcliffe Derbys 65 N1
Longcombe Devon 5 P5
Long Common Hants 24 H10
Long Compton Staffs 64 F7
Long Compton Warwks 42 G5
Longcot Oxon 30 F4
Long Crendon Bucks 43 P10
Long Crichel Dorset 11 N3
Longcroft Cumb 97 P6
Longcross Surrey 32 E9
Longden Shrops 63 M11
Longden Common Shrops 63 M11
Long Ditton Surrey 32 H9
Longdon Staffs 65 K9
Longdon Worcs 41 N4
Longdon Green Staffs 65 K9
Longdon Heath Worcs 41 N4
Longdon upon Tern Wrekin 63 Q9
Longdown Devon 8 G6
Longdowns Cnwll 3 J7
Long Drax N York 86 C9
Long Duckmanton Derbys 78 D9
Long Eaton Derbys 66 D5
Longfield Kent 33 R8
Longford Covtry 54 B4
Longford Derbys 65 N5
Longford Gloucs 41 N7
Longford Gt Lon 32 F7
Longford Kent 33 P11
Longford Shrops 64 B5
Longford Wrekin 64 D8
Longforgan P & K 124 F7
Longformacus Border 116 F10
Longframlington Nthumb 109 J9
Long Green Ches W 75 N9
Long Green Worcs 41 N5
Longham Dorset 11 P5
Longham Norfk 70 D9
Long Hanborough Oxon 43 J9
Longhaven Abers 141 Q8
Long Hedges Lincs 68 G3
Longhirst Nthumb 109 L12
Longhope Gloucs 41 L8
Longhope Ork 147 b6
Longhorsley Nthumb 109 J11
Longhoughton Nthumb 109 L7
Long Itchington Warwks 54 C7
Longlands Cumb 98 B11
Longlane Derbys 65 N4
Long Lawford Warwks 54 D5
Longleat Safari & Adventure Park Wilts 22 H4
Longlevens Gloucs 41 N8
Longley Calder 84 G10
Longley Kirk 77 L2
Longley Green Worcs 52 D10
Longleys P & K 124 F4
Long Load Somset 21 P8
Longmanhill Abers 140 H3
Long Marston Herts 44 C8
Long Marston N York 85 Q5
Long Marston Warwks 53 M11
Long Marton Cumb 89 Q2
Long Meadowend Shrops 51 L4
Long Melford Suffk 46 F3
Longmoor Camp Hants 25 N7
Longmorn Moray 139 N4
Longmoss Ches E 76 G9
Long Newnton Gloucs 29 P4
Longnewton Border 107 P4
Long Newton E Loth 116 C8
Longnewton S on T 91 P3
Longney Gloucs 41 M9
Longniddry E Loth 116 B6
Longnor Shrops 63 N12
Longnor Staffs 77 K10
Longparish Hants 24 G4
Longpark Cumb 98 E6
Long Preston N York 84 C4
Longridge Lancs 83 N8
Longridge Staffs 64 G9
Longridge W Loth 114 H9
Longriggend N Lans 114 E7
Long Riston E R Yk 87 L7
Longrock Cnwll 2 D8
Longsdon Staffs 64 H1
Longshaw Wigan 75 P3
Longside Abers 141 P6
Long Sight Oldham 76 G2
Longslow Shrops 64 C5
Longstanton Cambs 56 H7
Longstock Hants 24 F6
Longstone Pembks 37 M8
Longstowe Cambs 56 F9
Long Stratton Norfk 59 J2
Long Street M Keyn 55 K11
Longstreet Wilts 23 P3
Long Sutton Hants 25 M4
Long Sutton Lincs 68 H7
Long Sutton Somset 21 P8
Longthorpe C Pete 56 C1
Long Thurlow Suffk 58 E7
Longthwaite Cumb 89 L2
Longton C Stke 64 G3
Longton Lancs 83 L10
Longtown Cumb 98 D4
Longtown Herefs 40 D6
Longueville Jersey 13 c3
Longville in the Dale Shrops 51 P2
Long Waste Wrekin 64 B9
Long Whatton Leics 66 D7
Longwick Bucks 43 R10
Long Wittenham Oxon 31 L4
Longwitton Nthumb 108 H12
Longwood D & G 96 E6
Longwood Shrops 63 Q10
Longworth Oxon 30 H2
Longyester E Loth 116 D8
Lôn-las Swans 26 H3
Lonmay Abers 141 N4
Lonmore Highld 134 E6
Looe Cnwll 4 C6
Loose Kent 34 D12
Loosebeare Devon 8 D4
Loosegate Lincs 68 F7
Loosley Row Bucks 32 B2
Lootcherbrae Abers 140 F5
Lopcombe Corner Wilts 24 D6
Lopen Somset 21 P10
Loppington Shrops 63 M6
Lorbottle Nthumb 108 G8
Lordington W Susx 13 N3
Lordsbridge Norfk 69 L9
Lordshill C Sotn 24 F10
Lords Wood Medway 34 D10
Lornty P & K 124 D4
Loscoe Derbys 66 C3
Loscombe Dorset 10 D5
Losgaintir W Isls 152 e6
Lossiemouth Moray 147 N11
Lostford Shrops 64 B6
Lostock Gralam Ches W 76 C8
Lostock Green Ches W 76 C9
Lostock Hall Lancs 83 M10
Lostock Hall Fold Bolton 76 C2
Lostock Junction Bolton 76 C2
Lostwithiel Cnwll 3 Q3
Lothbeg Highld 146 G3
Lothersdale N York 84 E6
Lothmore Highld 146 H3
Loudwater Bucks 32 C4
Loughborough Leics 66 E8
Loughor Swans 26 E3
Loughton Essex 33 M3
Loughton M Keyn 44 B4
Loughton Shrops 52 B4
Lound Lincs 67 Q8
Lound Notts 78 H6
Lound Suffk 71 P12
Lounston Devon 8 E9
Lount Leics 66 C8
Louth Lincs 80 F6
Loveclough Lancs 84 B9
Lovedean Hants 25 L10
Lover Wilts 24 C9
Loversall Donc 78 F4
Loves Green Essex 46 B10
Lovesome Hill N York 91 N7
Loveston Pembks 37 L9
Lovington Somset 22 D7
Low Ackworth Wakefd 85 P11
Low Angerton Nthumb 100 E1
Lowbands Gloucs 41 M5
Low Barbeth D & G 94 E5
Low Barlings Lincs 80 B9
Low Bell End N York 92 E7
Low Bentham N York 83 P1
Low Biggins Cumb 89 P11
Low Borrowbridge Cumb 89 P6
Low Bradfield Sheff 77 N5
Low Bradley N York 84 F5
Low Braithwaite Cumb 98 E10
Low Burnham N Linc 79 K3
Low Buston Nthumb 109 L8
Lowca Cumb 88 C2
Low Catton E R Yk 86 D4
Low Coniscliffe Darltn 91 L4
Low Crosby Cumb 98 F6
Lowdham Notts 66 H3
Low Dinsdale Darltn 91 N4
Lowe Shrops 63 N6
Lowe Hill Staffs 65 J1
Low Ellington N York 91 L10
Lower Aisholt Somset 21 K6
Lower Ansty Dorset 11 J4
Lower Apperley Gloucs 41 P6
Lower Arboll Highld 146 F9
Lower Arncott Oxon 43 M8
Lower Ashton Devon 8 F8
Lower Assendon Oxon 31 Q5
Lower Badcall Highld 148 E8
Lower Ballam Lancs 83 J9
Lower Bartle Lancs 83 L8
Lower Basildon W Berk 31 M6
Lower Bearwood Herefs 51 L9
Lower Beeding W Susx 15 J5
Lower Benefield Nhants 55 N3
Lower Bentley Worcs 53 J7
Lower Beobridge Shrops 52 E2
Lower Birchwood Derbys 66 C1
Lower Boddington Nhants 54 D10
Lower Boscaswell Cnwll 2 B7
Lower Bourne Surrey 25 P4
Lower Brailes Warwks 42 G4
Lower Breakish Highld 135 M11
Lower Bredbury Stockp 76 G5
Lower Broadheath Worcs 52 E9
Lower Broxwood Herefs 51 L9
Lower Buckenhill Herefs 41 J5
Lower Bullingham Herefs 40 G4
Lower Burgate Hants 23 P10
Lower Burrowton Devon 9 J5
Lower Burton Herefs 51 M9
Lower Caldecote C Beds 44 H2
Lower Cam Gloucs 29 M2
Lower Canada N Som 28 E10
Lower Catesby Nhants 54 E9
Lower Chapel Powys 39 N4
Lower Chicksgrove Wilts 23 L7
Lower Chute Wilts 24 E3
Lower Clapton Gt Lon 33 L5
Lower Clent Worcs 52 G5
Lower Common Hants 31 Q10
Lower Creedy Devon 8 F4
Lower Crossings Derbys 77 K7
Lower Cumberworth Kirk 77 N2
Lower Darwen Bl w D 83 Q10
Lower Dean Bed 55 Q7
Lower Denby Kirk 77 N2
Lower Diabaig Highld 135 P4
Lower Dicker E Susx 15 Q8
Lower Dinchope Shrops 51 M4
Lower Down Shrops 51 K4
Lower Dunsforth N York 85 N2
Lower Egleton Herefs 41 J3
Lower Elkstone Staffs 77 K12
Lower Ellastone Staffs 65 L4
Lower End Bucks 43 P10
Lower End M Keyn 44 D4
Lower End Nhants 55 K9
Lower End Nhants 55 L8
Lower Everleigh Wilts 24 C2
Lower Exbury Hants 12 G5
Lower Eythorne Kent 35 N12
Lower Failand N Som 28 G7
Lower Farringdon Hants 25 M6
Lower Feltham Gt Lon 32 F8
Lower Fittleworth W Susx 14 E7
Lower Foxdale IoM 102 c5
Lower Frankton Shrops 63 L6
Lower Freystrop Pembks 37 J8
Lower Froyle Hants 25 N4
Lower Gabwell Devon 5 Q3
Lower Gledfield Highld 145 N7
Lower Godney Somset 21 Q5
Lower Gornal Dudley 52 G2
Lower Gravenhurst C Beds 44 G5
Lower Green Herts 44 H5
Lower Green Herts 45 M5
Lower Green Kent 15 Q3
Lower Green Kent 16 A2
Lower Green Norfk 70 E5
Lower Green Staffs 64 G10
Lower Green Suffk 57 P7
Lower Hacheston Suffk 59 L9
Lower Halstock Leigh Dorset 10 E3
Lower Halstow Kent 34 F9
Lower Hamworthy BCP 11 N6
Lower Hardres Kent 35 L11
Lower Harpton Herefs 51 J8
Lower Hartlip Kent 34 E9
Lower Hartshay Derbys 66 C2
Lower Hartwell Bucks 43 R9
Lower Hatton Staffs 64 F5
Lower Hawthwaite Cumb 88 G9
Lower Hergest Herefs 51 J9
Lower Heyford Oxon 43 K7
Lower Heysham Lancs 83 K3
Lower Higham Kent 34 C8
Lower Holbrook Suffk 47 L5
Lower Hordley Shrops 63 L6
Lower Horncroft W Susx 14 E7
Lowerhouse Lancs 84 B8
Lower Houses Kirk 84 H12
Lower Howsell Worcs 52 E11
Lower Irlam Salfd 76 D5
Lower Kilburn Derbys 66 B3
Lower Kilcott Gloucs 29 M4
Lower Killeyan Ag & B 102 B1
Lower Kingcombe Dorset 10 E5
Lower Kingswood Surrey 33 J11
Lower Kinnerton Ches W 75 K11
Lower Langford N Som 28 F10
Lower Largo Fife 124 H12
Lower Leigh Staffs 65 J5
Lower Lemington Gloucs 42 E5
Lower Llanfadog Powys 50 C7
Lower Lovacott Devon 19 K8
Lower Loxhore Devon 19 M6
Lower Lydbrook Gloucs 41 J8
Lower Lye Herefs 51 L7
Lower Machen Newpt 28 B5
Lower Maes-coed Herefs 40 D5
Lower Mannington Dorset 11 P4
Lower Marston Somset 22 G4
Lower Meend Gloucs 40 H10
Lower Merridge Somset 21 K6
Lower Middleton Cheney Nhants 43 L3
Lower Milton Somset 22 C4
Lower Moor Worcs 41 R2
Lower Morton S Glos 29 K4
Lower Nazeing Essex 45 M10
Lower Norton Warwks 53 N8
Lower Nyland Dorset 22 G9
Lower Penarth V Glam 28 A8
Lower Penn Staffs 52 G1
Lower Pennington Hants 12 E6
Lower Penwortham Lancs 83 M10
Lower Peover Ches E 76 D9
Lower Place Rochdl 76 G1
Lower Pollicott Bucks 43 P9
Lower Quinton Warwks 42 E2
Lower Rainham Medway 34 E9
Lower Raydon Suffk 47 J4
Lower Roadwater Somset 20 G5
Lower Salter Lancs 83 N3
Lower Seagry Wilts 29 Q6
Lower Sheering Essex 45 P9
Lower Shelton C Beds 44 E3
Lower Shiplake Oxon 31 Q6
Lower Shuckburgh Warwks 54 D8
Lower Slaughter Gloucs 42 D7
Lower Soothill Kirk 85 K10
Lower Soudley Gloucs 41 K9
Lower Standen Kent 17 M3
Lower Stanton St Quintin Wilts 29 Q6
Lower Stoke Medway 34 E7
Lower Stondon C Beds 44 H5
Lower Stone Gloucs 29 K3
Lower Stonnall Staffs 65 K11
Lower Stow Bedon Norfk 58 E2
Lower Street Dorset 11 K5
Lower Street E Susx 16 C8
Lower Street Norfk 71 K5
Lower Street Suffk 57 Q10
Lower Street Suffk 58 G10
Lower Stretton Warrtn 76 B7
Lower Stroud Dorset 10 C5
Lower Sundon C Beds 44 F6
Lower Swanwick Hants 12 H3
Lower Swell Gloucs 42 E6
Lower Tadmarton Oxon 43 J4
Lower Tale Devon 9 K4
Lower Tasburgh Norfk 59 J1
Lower Tean Staffs 65 J4
Lower Thurlton Norfk 71 N12
Lower Town Cnwll 2 G8
Lower Town Devon 8 D10
Lower Town Herefs 41 K3
Lower Town Pembks 37 J3
Lower Trebullett Cnwll 7 L9
Lower Treluswell Cnwll 3 J7
Lower Tysoe Warwks 42 H3
Lower Ufford Suffk 59 L10
Lower Upcott Devon 8 G8
Lower Upham Hants 25 J9
Lower Upnor Medway 34 D8
Lower Vexford Somset 20 H6
Lower Walton Warrtn 75 Q6
Lower Waterston Dorset 10 H6
Lower Weare Somset 21 N3
Lower Weedon Nhants 54 G9
Lower Welson Herefs 51 J10
Lower Westmancote Worcs 41 Q4
Lower Whatcombe Dorset 11 K4
Lower Whatley Somset 22 G4
Lower Whitley Ches W 75 Q8
Lower Wick Gloucs 29 L3
Lower Wick Worcs 52 F10
Lower Wield Hants 25 L5
Lower Willingdon E Susx 15 Q10
Lower Withington Ches E 76 E9
Lower Woodend Bucks 32 B5
Lower Woodford Wilts 23 P6
Lower Wraxhall Dorset 10 E4
Lower Wyche Worcs 41 M3
Lower Wyke C Brad 84 H10
Lowesby Leics 67 J10
Lowestoft Suffk 59 Q2
Loweswater Cumb 88 F3
Low Fell Gatesd 100 H6
Lowfield Heath W Susx 15 K3
Low Gartachorrans Stirlg 113 P4
Low Gate Nthumb 99 P5
Low Gettbridge Cumb 98 G6
Lowgill Cumb 89 Q7
Lowgill Lancs 83 P2
Low Grantley N York 85 K1
Low Green N York 85 J3
Low Habberley Worcs 52 E5
Low Ham Somset 21 P7
Low Harrogate N York 85 L4
Low Hawsker N York 93 J5
Low Hesket Cumb 98 F9
Low Hutton N York 86 E2
Lowick Cumb 89 J9
Lowick Nhants 55 N4
Lowick Nthumb 108 G2
Lowick Bridge Cumb 89 J9
Lowick Green Cumb 89 J9
Low Knipe Cumb 89 N3
Low Laithe N York 85 J2
Lowlands Dur 91 J2
Lowlands Torfn 28 C3
Low Langton Lincs 80 C8
Low Leighton Derbys 77 J6
Low Lorton Cumb 88 F2
Low Marishes N York 92 G11
Low Marnham Notts 79 K10
Low Middleton Nthumb 109 J3
Low Mill N York 92 D7
Low Moor C Brad 84 H9
Low Moorsley Sundld 101 J9
Low Moresby Cumb 88 D3
Low Newton Cumb 89 L10
Low Row Cumb 97 P9
Low Row Cumb 98 D11
Low Row Cumb 98 H6
Low Row N York 90 G7
Low Salchrie D & G 94 E5
Low Santon N Linc 79 N1
Lowsonford Warwks 53 M7
Low Street Norfk 71 L7
Low Street Thurr 34 B7
Low Tharston Norfk 59 J2
Lowther Cumb 89 N2
Lowthorpe E R Yk 87 K3
Lowton Devon 8 C4
Lowton Somset 21 K9
Lowton Wigan 75 Q4
Lowton Common Wigan 76 B4
Lowton St Mary's Wigan 76 B4
Low Torry Fife 115 J4
Low Toynton Lincs 80 E9
Low Valley Barns 78 C3
Low Wood Cumb 89 K10
Low Worsall N York 91 P5
Low Wray Cumb 89 K6
Loxbeare Devon 20 E10
Loxhill Surrey 14 E3
Loxhore Devon 19 M5
Loxhore Cott Devon 19 M6
Loxley Warwks 53 N10
Loxley Green Staffs 65 K6
Loxter Herefs 41 L3
Loxton N Som 21 N2
Loxwood W Susx 14 E4
Lubenham Leics 54 H3
Lucasgate Lincs 68 H3
Lucas Green Surrey 32 D10
Luccombe Somset 20 E5
Luccombe Village IoW 13 K9
Lucker Nthumb 109 J4
Luckett Cnwll 7 M10
Lucking Street Essex 46 E5
Luckington Wilts 29 N5
Lucklawhill Fife 124 H8
Lucknam Wilts 29 N8
Luckwell Bridge Somset 20 D5
Lucton Herefs 51 M8
Lucy Cross N York 91 L4
Ludag W Isls 152 c12
Ludborough Lincs 80 F4
Ludbrook Devon 5 L6
Ludchurch Pembks 37 M8
Luddenden Calder 84 F10
Luddenden Foot Calder 84 F10
Luddenham Court Kent 34 H9
Luddesdown Kent 34 B9
Luddington N Linc 86 F12
Luddington Warwks 53 M10
Luddington in the Brook Nhants 56 B4
Ludford Lincs 80 D6
Ludford Shrops 51 N6
Ludgershall Bucks 43 N8
Ludgershall Wilts 24 D3
Ludgvan Cnwll 2 D8
Ludham Norfk 71 M8
Ludlow Shrops 51 N5
Ludney Somset 21 N11
Ludwell Wilts 23 K9
Ludworth Dur 101 J10
Luffenhall Herts 45 K6
Luffincott Devon 7 L6
Luffness E Loth 116 B5
Lugar E Ayrs 105 L5
Luggate Burn E Loth 116 E6
Lugg Green Herefs 51 M8
Luggiebank N Lans 114 D7
Lugton E Ayrs 113 N10
Lugwardine Herefs 40 H3
Luib Highld 135 K10
Luing Ag & B 120 D10
Lulham Herefs 40 F3
Lullington Derbys 65 N9
Lullington E Susx 15 P10
Lullington Somset 22 H3
Lulsgate Bottom N Som 28 G9
Lulsley Worcs 52 D9
Lulworth Camp Dorset 11 K8
Lumb Calder 84 F11
Lumb Lancs 84 C10
Lumbutts Calder 84 E10
Lumby N York 85 P9
Lumphanan Abers 132 F3
Lumphinnans Fife 115 M3
Lumsden Abers 140 D11
Lunan Angus 125 N2
Lunanhead Angus 125 J2
Luncarty P & K 124 C7
Lund E R Yk 86 H5
Lund N York 86 C8
Lundie Angus 124 F5
Lundin Links Fife 124 H12
Lundin Mill Fife 124 H12
Lundy Devon 18 C4
Lundy Green Norfk 59 K2
Lunga Ag & B 120 D11
Lunna Shet 147 j5
Lunsford Kent 34 C10
Lunsford's Cross E Susx 16 C8
Lunt Sefton 75 K3
Luntley Herefs 51 L9
Luppitt Devon 9 M3
Lupridge Devon 5 M6
Lupset Wakefd 85 L11
Lupton Cumb 89 N10
Lurgashall W Susx 14 D5
Lurley Devon 20 E10
Lusby Lincs 80 G10
Luscombe Devon 5 N5
Luson Devon 5 J7
Luss Ag & B 113 M3
Lussagiven Ag & B 111 N4
Lusta Highld 134 E4
Lustleigh Devon 8 E8
Luston Herefs 51 N8
Luthermuir Abers 132 G10
Luthrie Fife 124 G9
Lutley Dudley 52 H4
Luton Devon 8 G9
Luton Devon 9 K4
Luton Luton 44 F7
Luton Medway 34 D9
Luton Airport Luton 44 G7
Lutterworth Leics 54 E4
Lutton Devon 5 J5
Lutton Devon 5 L4
Lutton Lincs 68 H7
Lutton Nhants 56 C3
Luxborough Somset 20 F6
Luxulyan Cnwll 3 P3
Luxulyan Valley Cnwll 3 P3
Luzley Tamesd 76 H3
Lybster Highld 151 N9
Lydbury North Shrops 51 K3
Lydcott Devon 19 N6
Lydd Kent 17 J6
Lydd Airport Kent 17 J6
Lydden Kent 17 N2
Lydden Kent 35 P9
Lyddington Rutlnd 55 L1
Lydd-on-Sea Kent 17 K7
Lydeard St Lawrence Somset 20 H7
Lyde Green Hants 31 P11
Lydford Devon 7 P8
Lydford on Fosse Somset 22 D7
Lydgate Calder 84 D10
Lydgate Rochdl 84 E12
Lydham Shrops 51 K2
Lydiard Green Wilts 30 C5
Lydiard Millicent Wilts 30 C5
Lydiard Tregoze Swindn 30 C5
Lydiate Sefton 75 L3
Lydiate Ash Worcs 52 H5
Lydlinch Dorset 22 G10
Lydney Gloucs 41 K11
Lydstep Pembks 37 L11
Lye Dudley 52 G4
Lye Cross N Som 28 G10
Lye Green Bucks 44 D11
Lye Green E Susx 15 P4
Lye Green Warwks 53 M7
Lye Head Worcs 52 D6
Lye's Green Wilts 22 H4
Lyford Oxon 30 H3
Lymbridge Green Kent 17 K2
Lyme Regis Dorset 9 Q6
Lyminge Kent 17 L3
Lymington Hants 12 E5
Lyminster W Susx 14 E10
Lymm Warrtn 76 C6
Lymm Services Warrtn 76 C7
Lympne Kent 17 K4
Lympsham Somset 21 M2
Lympstone Devon 9 J8
Lynbridge Devon 19 N4
Lynchat Highld 130 E4
Lynch Green Norfk 70 H11
Lyndhurst Hants 12 E3
Lyndon Rutlnd 67 M11
Lyndon Green Birm 53 L4
Lyne Border 106 G2
Lyne Surrey 32 E9
Lyneal Shrops 63 M5
Lyne Down Herefs 41 K5
Lyneham Devon 8 F9
Lyneham Oxon 42 F7
Lyneham Wilts 30 B6
Lyneholmford Cumb 98 G4
Lynemouth Nthumb 109 M11
Lyne of Skene Abers 133 J2
Lynesack Dur 90 H2
Lyness Ork 147 b6
Lyng Norfk 70 F8
Lyng Somset 21 M7
Lynmouth Devon 19 P3
Lynn Staffs 65 K11
Lynn Wrekin 64 E9
Lynsted Kent 34 G10
Lynstone Cnwll 7 J4
Lynton Devon 19 N3
Lynton Cross Devon 19 K5
Lyon's Gate Dorset 10 G4
Lyonshall Herefs 51 K9
Lytchett Matravers Dorset 11 M6
Lytchett Minster Dorset 11 M6
Lyth Highld 151 N4
Lytham Lancs 83 J9
Lytham St Annes Lancs 82 H9
Lythbank Shrops 63 M10
Lythe N York 92 G4
Lythmore Highld 151 J3

M

Mabe Burnthouse Cnwll 3 J7
Mablethorpe Lincs 81 K7
Macclesfield Ches E 76 G9
Macduff Abers 140 H3
Macharioch Ag & B 103 K8
Machen Caerph 28 B4
Machrie N Ayrs 103 N3
Machrihanish Ag & B 102 H5
Machrins Ag & B 111 J3
Machynlleth Powys 61 N12
Machynys Carmth 26 D3
Mackworth Derbys 65 P5
Macmerry E Loth 116 B7
Maddaford Devon 7 Q6
Madderty P & K 123 N8
Maddington Wilts 23 N4
Maddiston Falk 114 G6
Madehurst W Susx 14 E8
Madeley Staffs 64 E3
Madeley Wrekin 64 C11
Madeley Heath Staffs 64 E3
Madford Devon 9 M3
Madingley Cambs 56 H8
Madley Herefs 40 F4
Madresfield Worcs 52 E11
Madron Cnwll 2 D8
Maenaddwyn IoA 72 G7
Maenan Conwy 73 N10
Maenclochog Pembks 37 L5
Maendy V Glam 27 N7
Maenporth Cnwll 3 K8
Maentwrog Gwynd 61 L4
Maen-y-groes Cerdgn 48 F9
Maer Cnwll 7 J3
Maer Staffs 64 E4
Maerdy Carmth 38 G6
Maerdy Conwy 62 D3
Maerdy Rhondd 27 M3
Maesbrook Shrops 63 J8
Maesbury Shrops 63 J7
Maesbury Marsh Shrops 63 K7
Maes-glas Newpt 28 D5
Maesgwynne Carmth 37 N6
Maeshafn Denbgs 74 H11

180 Maesllyn – Mobberley

Maesllyn Cerdgn 38 A3
Maesmynis Powys 39 N2
Maesmynis Powys 50 E10
Maesteg Brdgnd 27 K4
Maesybont Carmth 38 E8
Maesycwmmer Caerph 27 R3
Magdalen Laver Essex 45 P10
Maggieknockater Moray 139 P7
Maggots End Essex 45 N6
Magham Down E Susx 15 R8
Maghull Sefton 75 L3
Magna Park Leics 54 E4
Magor Mons 28 F5
Magor Services Mons 28 F5
Maidenbower W Susx 15 K4
Maiden Bradley Wilts 22 H5
Maidencombe Torbay 5 Q3
Maidenhayne Devon 9 P6
Maiden Head N Som 28 H9
Maidenhead W & M 32 C6
Maiden Law Dur 100 F8
Maiden Newton Dorset 10 F5
Maidens S Ayrs 104 D8
Maiden's Green Br For 32 C8
Maidenwell Lincs 80 F8
Maiden Wells Pembks 37 J10
Maidford Nhants 54 G10
Maids Moreton Bucks 43 P4
Maidstone Kent 34 D11
Maidstone Services Kent 34 E11
Maidwell Nhants 55 J5
Mail Shet 147 j7
Maindee Newpt 28 D5
Mainland Ork 147 c4
Mainland Shet 147 i6
Mainsforth Dur 101 J12
Mains of Balhall Angus 132 D11
Mains of Balnakettle Abers 132 F9
Mains of Dalvey Highld 139 L9
Mains of Haulkerton Abers 132 H9
Mains of Lesmoir Abers 140 D10
Mains of Melgunds Angus 125 L2
Mainsriddle D & G 97 J7
Mainstone Shrops 51 J3
Maisemore Gloucs 41 N7
Major's Green Worcs 53 L5
Makeney Derbys 66 B3
Malborough Devon 5 L8
Malcoff Derbys 77 K7
Malden Rushett Gt Lon 32 H10
Maldon Essex 46 E10
Malham N York 84 D3
Maligar Highld 134 H3
Mallaig Highld 127 M5
Mallaigvaig Highld 127 M5
Malleny Mills C Edin 115 L8
Mallows Green Essex 45 N6
Malltraeth IoA 72 G10
Mallwyd Gwynd 61 Q9
Malmesbury Wilts 29 Q5
Malmsmead Devon 20 B4
Malpas Ches W 63 N3
Malpas Cnwll 3 K6
Malpas Newpt 28 D4
Malshanger Hants 25 J3
Malswick Gloucs 41 L7
Maltby Lincs 80 F7
Maltby Rothm 78 E5
Maltby S on T 91 Q4
Maltby le Marsh Lincs 81 J7
Malting Green Essex 46 H7
Maltman's Hill Kent 16 F2
Malton N York 92 F12
Malvern Worcs 41 M2
Malvern Hills 41 M3
Malvern Link Worcs 52 E11
Malvern Wells Worcs 41 M3
Mamble Worcs 52 C6
Mamhilad Mons 40 D11
Manaccan Cnwll 3 J9
Manafon Powys 62 F11
Manais W Isls 152 e6
Manaton Devon 8 E8
Manby Lincs 80 H6
Mancetter Warwks 53 Q1
Manchester Manch 76 F4
Manchester Airport Manch 76 F7
Mancot Flints 75 K10
Mandally Highld 129 K4
Manea Cambs 57 J3
Maney Birm 53 L2
Manfield N York 91 L4
Mangersta W Isls 152 d3
Mangerton Dorset 10 D5
Mangotsfield S Glos 29 K7
Mangrove Green Herts 44 G7
Mangurstadh W Isls 152 d3
Manhay Cnwll 2 H8
Manish W Isls 152 e6
Mankinholes Calder 84 E10
Manley Ches W 75 N9
Manmoel Caerph 40 A11
Mannal Ag & B 118 D5
Manningford Bohune Wilts 30 D10
Manningford Bruce Wilts 30 D10
Manningham C Brad 84 H8
Mannings Heath W Susx 14 H5
Mannington Dorset 11 P4
Manningtree Essex 47 K5
Mannofield C Aber 133 M3
Manorbier Pembks 37 L11
Manorbier Newton Pembks 37 K10
Manordeilo Carmth 38 G6
Manorhill Border 107 Q3
Manorowen Pembks 36 H3
Manor Park Gt Lon 33 M5
Mansell Gamage Herefs 40 E3
Mansell Lacy Herefs 40 F3
Mansergh Cumb 89 P10
Mansfield E Ayrs 105 L7
Mansfield Notts 78 E11
Mansfield Woodhouse Notts 78 E11
Mansriggs Cumb 89 J10
Manston Dorset 22 H10
Manston Kent 35 P9
Manston Leeds 85 M8
Manswood Dorset 11 N3
Manthorpe Lincs 67 M5
Manthorpe Lincs 67 Q9
Manton N Linc 79 M3
Manton Notts 78 G8
Manton Rutlnd 67 L11
Manton Wilts 30 E8
Manuden Essex 45 P6
Manwood Green Essex 45 Q9
Maperton Somset 22 F8
Maplebeck Notts 78 H11
Maple Cross Herts 32 E4
Mapledurham Oxon 31 N7
Mapledurwell Hants 25 M3
Maplehurst W Susx 14 H6
Maplescombe Kent 33 Q9
Mapleton Derbys 65 M3
Mapleton Kent 15 N1
Mapperley Derbys 66 C4
Mapperley Park C Nott 66 F4
Mapperton Dorset 10 D5
Mappleborough Green Warwks 53 K7
Mappleton E R Yk 87 N6
Mapplewell Barns 77 Q2
Mappowder Dorset 10 H3
Marazanvose Cnwll 3 K4
Marazion Cnwll 2 E8
Marbhig W Isls 152 g4
Marbury Ches E 63 P3
March Cambs 56 H1
March S Lans 106 C7
Marcham Oxon 31 K3
Marchamley Shrops 63 Q6
Marchamley Wood Shrops 63 Q6
Marchington Staffs 65 L6
Marchington Woodlands Staffs 65 L6
Marchros Gwynd 60 E7
Marchwiel Wrexhm 63 K3
Marchwood Hants 12 F3
Marcross V Glam 27 L8
Marden Herefs 40 H2
Marden Kent 16 D2
Marden Wilts 30 C10
Marden Ash Essex 45 Q11
Marden Beech Kent 16 C2
Marden's Hill E Susx 15 P4
Marden Thorn Kent 16 D2
Mardlebury Herts 45 K8
Mardy Mons 40 D8
Marefield Leics 67 J10
Mareham le Fen Lincs 80 E11
Mareham on the Hill Lincs 80 F10
Marehay Derbys 66 C3
Marehill W Susx 14 F7
Maresfield E Susx 15 N6
Marfleet C KuH 87 L9
Marford Wrexhm 75 K12
Margam Neath 27 J5
Margaret Marsh Dorset 22 H9
Margaret Roding Essex 45 Q9
Margaretting Essex 34 B2
Margaretting Tye Essex 34 B2
Margate Kent 35 P8
Margnaheglish N Ayrs 103 Q3
Margrie D & G 96 C8
Margrove Park R & Cl 92 D4
Marham Norfk 69 N10
Marhamchurch Cnwll 7 J4
Marholm C Pete 68 C11
Marian-glas IoA 72 H7
Mariansleigh Devon 19 P9
Marine Town Kent 34 G7
Marionburgh Abers 132 H3
Marishader Highld 135 J3
Maristow Devon 4 G4
Marjoriebanks D & G 97 M2
Mark Somset 21 N4
Markbeech Kent 15 N2
Markby Lincs 81 J8
Mark Causeway Somset 21 N4
Mark Cross E Susx 15 Q4
Markeaton C Derb 65 Q5
Market Bosworth Leics 66 C11
Market Deeping Lincs 68 C10
Market Drayton Shrops 64 C5
Market Harborough Leics 55 J3
Market Lavington Wilts 23 M3
Market Overton Rutlnd 67 M9
Market Rasen Lincs 80 B6
Market Stainton Lincs 80 E7
Market Warsop Notts 78 F10
Market Weighton E R Yk 86 G7
Market Weston Suffk 58 E5
Markfield Leics 66 D10
Markham Caerph 28 A2
Markham Moor Notts 79 J9
Markinch Fife 115 P1
Markington N York 85 L2
Markle E Loth 116 D6
Marksbury BaNES 29 K10
Mark's Corner IoW 12 H6
Marks Tey Essex 46 F7
Markwell Cnwll 4 E5
Markyate Herts 44 F8
Marlborough Wilts 30 E8
Marlbrook Herefs 51 N9
Marlbrook Worcs 52 H6
Marlcliff Warwks 53 L10
Marldon Devon 5 P4
Marle Green E Susx 15 Q7
Marlesford Suffk 59 L9
Marley Kent 35 L12
Marley Kent 35 P11
Marley Green Ches E 63 P3
Marley Hill Gatesd 100 G6
Marlingford Norfk 70 H10
Marloes Pembks 36 F9
Marlow Bucks 32 B5
Marlow Herefs 51 L5
Marlow Bottom Bucks 32 B5
Marlpit Hill Kent 15 N1
Marlpits E Susx 15 N5
Marlpits E Susx 16 C8
Marlpool Derbys 66 D3
Marnhull Dorset 22 H9
Marple Stockp 76 H6
Marple Bridge Stockp 76 H6
Marr Donc 78 E3
Marrick N York 90 H7
Marros Carmth 37 N9
Marsden Kirk 77 K1
Marsden S Tyne 101 K5
Marsden Height Lancs 84 C8
Marsett N York 90 E9
Marsh Bucks 44 A10
Marsh C Brad 84 F8
Marsh Devon 9 P3
Marshall's Heath Herts 44 H8
Marshalswick Herts 44 H10
Marsham Norfk 71 J7
Marsh Baldon Oxon 31 M3
Marsh Benham W Berk 31 J9
Marshborough Kent 35 P11
Marshbrook Shrops 51 M3
Marshchapel Lincs 80 G4
Marsh Farm Luton 44 F6
Marshfield Newpt 28 C6
Marshfield S Glos 29 M7
Marshgate Cnwll 6 H6
Marsh Gibbon Bucks 43 N7
Marsh Green Devon 9 K6
Marsh Green Kent 15 N2
Marsh Green Wrekin 63 Q9
Marshland St James Norfk 69 K10
Marsh Lane Derbys 78 C8
Marsh Lane Gloucs 41 J10
Marshside Sefton 83 J11
Marsh Street Somset 20 F4
Marshwood Dorset 10 B5
Marske N York 91 J6
Marske-by-the-Sea R & Cl 92 D2
Marsland Green Wigan 76 C4
Marston Ches W 76 C8
Marston Herefs 51 L9
Marston Lincs 67 M3
Marston Oxon 43 L10
Marston Staffs 64 F9
Marston Staffs 64 G7
Marston Warwks 53 N2
Marston Wilts 29 Q11
Marston Green Solhll 53 M4
Marston Jabbet Warwks 54 B3
Marston Magna Somset 22 D9
Marston Meysey Wilts 30 D3
Marston Montgomery Derbys 65 L5
Marston Moretaine C Beds 44 E3
Marston on Dove Derbys 65 N6
Marston St Lawrence Nhants 43 L3
Marston Stannett Herefs 51 P9
Marston Trussell Nhants 54 H3
Marstow Herefs 40 H8
Marsworth Bucks 44 C8
Marten Wilts 30 G10
Marthall Ches E 76 E8
Martham Norfk 71 N8
Martin Hants 23 N9
Martin Kent 17 P1
Martin Lincs 80 C11
Martin Lincs 80 E10
Martindale Cumb 89 L3
Martin Dales Lincs 80 D11
Martin Drove End Hants 23 N9
Martinhoe Devon 19 N4
Martin Hussingtree Worcs 52 G8
Martinscroft Warrtn 76 C6
Martinstown Dorset 10 G7
Martlesham Suffk 47 N2
Martlesham Heath Suffk 47 M3
Martletwy Pembks 37 K8
Martley Worcs 52 D8
Martock Somset 21 P9
Marton Ches E 76 F10
Marton Ches W 76 B10
Marton Cumb 88 H11
Marton E R Yk 87 M1
Marton E R Yk 87 M7
Marton Lincs 79 L7
Marton Middsb 92 B3
Marton N York 85 N3
Marton N York 92 E10
Marton Shrops 63 J11
Marton Warwks 54 C7
Marton-le-Moor N York 85 M1
Martyr's Green Surrey 32 F11
Martyr Worthy Hants 24 H7
Marvig W Isls 152 g4
Marwell Wildlife Hants 24 H9
Marwick Ork 147 b3
Marwood Devon 19 K6
Marybank Highld 137 N5
Maryburgh Highld 137 P4
Marygold Border 116 H9
Maryhill C Glas 113 Q7
Marykirk Abers 132 G11
Maryland Mons 40 G10
Marylebone Gt Lon 33 K6
Marylebone Wigan 75 P2
Marypark Moray 139 M8
Maryport Cumb 97 L11
Maryport D & G 94 G11
Marystow Devon 7 N8
Mary Tavy Devon 7 P9
Maryton Angus 125 N2
Marywell Abers 132 F5
Marywell Abers 133 M4
Marywell Angus 125 M4
Masham N York 91 L10
Mashbury Essex 46 B9
Mason N u Ty 100 G3
Masongill N York 89 Q11
Mastin Moor Derbys 78 D8
Matching Essex 45 P9
Matching Green Essex 45 P9
Matching Tye Essex 45 P9
Matfen Nthumb 100 D4
Matfield Kent 16 B2
Mathern Mons 28 H4
Mathon Herefs 41 L2
Mathry Pembks 36 G4
Matlask Norfk 70 H5
Matlock Derbys 77 P11
Matlock Bank Derbys 77 P11
Matlock Bath Derbys 77 P12
Matlock Dale Derbys 77 P12
Matson Gloucs 41 N8
Matterdale End Cumb 89 L2
Mattersey Notts 78 H6
Mattersey Thorpe Notts 78 H6
Mattingley Hants 31 Q10
Mattishall Norfk 70 F10
Mattishall Burgh Norfk 70 F9
Mauchline E Ayrs 105 J4
Maud Abers 141 M6
Maufant Jersey 13 d2
Maugersbury Gloucs 42 E7
Maughold IoM 102 g4
Mauld Highld 137 L8
Maulden C Beds 44 F4
Maulds Meaburn Cumb 89 Q3
Maunby N York 91 N9
Maund Bryan Herefs 51 P10
Maundown Somset 20 G7
Mautby Norfk 71 P9
Mavesyn Ridware Staffs 65 K9
Mavis Enderby Lincs 80 G10
Mawbray Cumb 97 M9
Mawdesley Lancs 83 L12
Mawdlam Brdgnd 27 J6
Mawgan Cnwll 2 H9
Mawgan Porth Cnwll 6 B11
Maw Green Ches E 76 D12
Mawla Cnwll 2 H5
Mawnan Cnwll 3 K9
Mawnan Smith Cnwll 3 J9
Mawsley Nhants 55 K5
Mawthorpe Lincs 81 J9
Maxey C Pete 68 C10
Maxstoke Warwks 53 N3
Maxted Street Kent 17 K2
Maxton Border 107 P4
Maxton Kent 17 N3
Maxwelltown D & G 97 J3
Maxworthy Cnwll 7 J6
Mayals Swans 26 F4
May Bank Staffs 64 F3
Maybole S Ayrs 104 E8
Maybury Surrey 32 E10
Mayes Green Surrey 14 G3
Mayfield E Susx 15 Q5
Mayfield Mdloth 115 Q8
Mayfield Staffs 65 M3
Mayford Surrey 32 E11
May Hill Gloucs 41 L7
Mayland Essex 46 G11
Maylandsea Essex 46 F11
Maynard's Green E Susx 15 Q7
Maypole Birm 53 K5
Maypole Kent 35 M9
Maypole Mons 40 G8
Maypole Green Norfk 59 N2
Maypole Green Suffk 58 D9
Maypole Green Suffk 59 K7
May's Green Oxon 31 Q6
May's Green Surrey 32 F11
Mead Devon 18 E9
Meadgate BaNES 29 K10
Meadle Bucks 44 A10
Meadowfield Dur 100 G10
Meadowtown Shrops 63 K12
Meadwell Devon 7 M8
Meaford Staffs 64 G5
Mealabost W Isls 152 g3
Meal Bank Cumb 89 N7
Mealrigg Cumb 97 N9
Mealsgate Cumb 97 P10
Meanwood Leeds 85 L8
Mearbeck N York 84 B3
Meare Somset 21 P5
Meare Green Somset 21 L9
Meare Green Somset 21 M8
Mearns E Rens 113 Q10
Mears Ashby Nhants 55 L7
Measham Leics 65 Q9
Meath Green Surrey 15 K2
Meathop Cumb 89 L10
Meaux E R Yk 87 L7
Meavaig W Isls 152 e3
Meavy Devon 4 H3
Medbourne Leics 55 K2
Medburn Nthumb 100 E4
Meddon Devon 18 F10
Meden Vale Notts 78 F9
Medlam Lincs 68 F1
Medlar Lancs 83 K8
Medmenham Bucks 32 A5
Medomsley Dur 100 E7
Medstead Hants 25 L6
Medway Services Medway 34 E9
Meerbrook Staffs 77 J11
Meer Common Herefs 51 K10
Meesden Herts 45 M5
Meeson Wrekin 64 C8
Meeth Devon 7 Q3
Meeting Green Suffk 57 P9
Meeting House Hill Norfk 71 L6
Meidrim Carmth 37 Q6
Meifod Powys 62 G9
Meigle P & K 124 F4
Meikle Carco D & G 105 P7
Meikle Earnock S Lans 114 C10
Meikle Kilmory Ag & B 112 F9
Meikle Obney P & K 123 Q5
Meikleour P & K 124 D5
Meikle Wartle Abers 140 H9
Meinciau Carmth 38 C9
Meir C Stke 64 H4
Meir Heath Staffs 64 H4
Melbost W Isls 152 g3
Melbourn Cambs 45 M3
Melbourne Derbys 66 C7
Melbourne E R Yk 86 D6
Melbur Cnwll 3 M3
Melbury Devon 18 G9
Melbury Abbas Dorset 23 K9
Melbury Bubb Dorset 10 F3
Melbury Osmond Dorset 10 E3
Melbury Sampford Dorset 10 E4
Melchbourne Bed 55 P7
Melcombe Bingham Dorset 11 J4
Meldon Devon 7 Q6
Meldon Nthumb 100 E1
Meldon Park Nthumb 100 E1
Meldreth Cambs 45 M2
Meldrum Stirlg 114 C1
Melfort Ag & B 120 F10
Meliden Denbgs 74 E7
Melinau Pembks 37 N8
Melin-byrhedyn Powys 61 P12
Melincourt Neath 39 K11
Melin-y-coed Conwy 73 P11
Melin-y-ddol Powys 62 F10
Melin-y-wîg Denbgs 62 E2
Melkinthorpe Cumb 89 P2
Melkridge Nthumb 99 L5
Melksham Wilts 29 P9
Mellangoose Cnwll 2 H9
Mell Green W Berk 31 K7
Mellguards Cumb 98 F9
Melling Lancs 83 N1
Melling Sefton 75 L4
Melling Mount Sefton 75 L3
Mellis Suffk 58 G6
Mellon Charles Highld 143 M7
Mellon Udrigle Highld 143 N6
Mellor Lancs 83 P9
Mellor Stockp 77 J6
Mellor Brook Lancs 83 P9
Mells Somset 22 G4
Mells Suffk 59 M5
Melmerby Cumb 99 J10
Melmerby N York 90 H9
Melmerby N York 91 N11
Melness Highld 149 M4
Melon Green Suffk 58 C9
Melplash Dorset 10 D5
Melrose Border 107 N3
Melsetter Ork 147 b6
Melsonby N York 91 K5
Meltham Kirk 77 L2
Meltham Mills Kirk 77 L2
Melton E R Yk 86 H10
Melton Suffk 59 K10
Meltonby E R Yk 86 E5
Melton Constable Norfk 70 F5
Melton Mowbray Leics 67 J8
Melton Ross N Linc 79 Q2
Melvaig Highld 143 K8
Melverley Shrops 63 K9
Melverley Green Shrops 63 K8
Melvich Highld 150 F4
Membury Devon 9 P4
Membury Services W Berk 30 G7
Memsie Abers 141 N3
Memus Angus 124 H1
Menabilly Cnwll 3 Q4
Menagissey Cnwll 2 H5
Menai Bridge IoA 73 J9
Mendham Suffk 59 K4
Mendip Hills 22 C3
Mendlesham Suffk 58 G7
Mendlesham Green Suffk 58 G8
Menheniot Cnwll 4 D4
Menithwood Worcs 52 D7
Menna Cnwll 3 M4
Mennock D & G 105 Q8
Menston C Brad 85 J6
Menstrie Clacks 114 F2
Menthorpe N York 86 C8
Mentmore Bucks 44 C8
Meoble Highld 127 P7
Meole Brace Shrops 63 N10
Meonstoke Hants 25 K9
Meopham Kent 34 B9
Meopham Green Kent 34 B9
Meopham Station Kent 34 B9
Mepal Cambs 56 H4
Meppershall C Beds 44 G4
Merbach Herefs 40 D3
Mere Ches E 76 D7
Mere Wilts 22 H7
Mere Brow Lancs 83 K11
Mereclough Lancs 84 C9
Mere Green Birm 65 L12
Mere Green Worcs 52 H8
Mere Heath Ches W 76 C9
Meresborough Medway 34 E9
Mereworth Kent 34 B11
Meriden Solhll 53 N4
Merkadale Highld 134 G9
Merley BCP 11 N5
Merlin's Bridge Pembks 37 J7
Merrington Shrops 63 M8
Merrion Pembks 36 H11
Merriott Somset 21 P11
Merrivale Devon 7 Q9
Merrow Surrey 32 E12
Merry Field Hill Dorset 11 N4
Merry Hill Herts 32 G3
Merryhill Wolves 52 G1
Merry Lees Leics 66 D11
Merrymeet Cnwll 4 D3
Mersea Island Essex 47 J8
Mersey Crossing Halton 75 N7
Mersham Kent 17 J3
Merstham Surrey 33 K11
Merston W Susx 14 C10
Merstone IoW 13 J8
Merther Cnwll 3 L5
Merthyr Carmth 38 A7
Merthyr Cynog Powys 39 N4
Merthyr Dyfan V Glam 27 Q8
Merthyr Mawr Brdgnd 27 L7
Merthyr Tydfil Myr Td 39 P10
Merthyr Vale Myr Td 27 P2
Merton Devon 19 K11
Merton Gt Lon 33 J8
Merton Norfk 70 D12
Merton Oxon 43 M8
Meshaw Devon 19 P9
Messing Essex 46 F8
Messingham N Linc 79 M3
Metfield Suffk 59 L4
Metherell Cnwll 4 F3
Metheringham Lincs 79 Q11
Methil Fife 115 Q1
Methilhill Fife 115 Q1
Methley Leeds 85 N10
Methley Junction Leeds 85 N10
Methlick Abers 141 K8
Methven P & K 123 P7
Methwold Norfk 57 P2
Methwold Hythe Norfk 57 N2
Mettingham Suffk 59 M3
Metton Norfk 71 J5
Mevagissey Cnwll 3 P5
Mexborough Donc 78 D4
Mey Highld 151 N2
Meysey Hampton Gloucs 30 D2
Miabhaig W Isls 152 e3
Michaelchurch Herefs 40 H6
Michaelchurch Escley Herefs 40 D5
Michaelchurch-on-Arrow Powys 50 H10
Michaelstone-y-Fedw Newpt 28 C5
Michaelston-le-Pit V Glam 27 Q8
Michaelstow Cnwll 6 F9
Michaelwood Services Gloucs 29 L3
Michelcombe Devon 5 L3
Micheldever Hants 24 H5
Micheldever Station Hants 24 H5
Michelmersh Hants 24 F8
Mickfield Suffk 58 H8
Micklebring Donc 78 E5
Mickleby N York 92 G4
Micklefield Leeds 85 N8
Micklefield Green Herts 32 F3
Mickleham Surrey 32 H11
Mickleover C Derb 65 P5
Micklethwaite C Brad 84 G7
Micklethwaite Cumb 98 C8
Mickleton Dur 90 F2
Mickleton Gloucs 42 D3
Mickletown Leeds 85 N9
Mickle Trafford Ches W 75 M9
Mickley Derbys 77 Q8
Mickley N York 91 L11
Mickley Green Suffk 58 B9
Mickley Square Nthumb 100 D6
Mid Ardlaw Abers 141 M3
Midbea Ork 147 c2
Mid Beltie Abers 132 F4
Mid Bockhampton BCP 12 B5
Mid Calder W Loth 115 K8
Mid Clyth Highld 151 P9
Mid Culbeuchly Abers 140 G3
Middle Assendon Oxon 31 Q5
Middle Aston Oxon 43 K6
Middle Barton Oxon 43 J6
Middlebie D & G 97 P3
Middlebridge P & K 130 G11
Middle Chinnock Somset 21 Q10
Middle Claydon Bucks 43 P6
Middlecliffe Barns 78 C3
Middlecott Devon 8 D7
Middle Duntisbourne Gloucs 41 R10
Middleham N York 91 J9
Middle Handley Derbys 78 C8
Middle Harling Norfk 58 E3
Middlehill Cnwll 4 D3
Middlehill Wilts 29 N8
Middlehope Shrops 51 N3
Middle Kames Ag & B 112 D3
Middle Littleton Worcs 42 C2
Middle Madeley Staffs 64 E3
Middle Maes-coed Herefs 40 D5
Middlemarsh Dorset 10 G3
Middle Mayfield Staffs 65 L3
Middle Mill Pembks 36 F5
Middlemoor Devon 7 P10
Middle Quarter Kent 16 F3
Middle Rasen Lincs 80 B6
Middle Rocombe Devon 5 Q3
Middle Salter Lancs 83 N3
Middlesbrough Middsb 92 A3
Middlesceugh Cumb 98 E10
Middleshaw Cumb 89 N9
Middlesmoor N York 91 J12
Middle Stoford Somset 21 J9
Middle Stoke Medway 34 E7
Middlestone Dur 100 H12
Middlestone Moor Dur 100 G11
Middle Stoughton Somset 21 P3
Middlestown Wakefd 85 K11
Middle Street Gloucs 41 M10
Middle Taphouse Cnwll 4 B4
Middlethird Border 107 R1
Middleton Ag & B 118 C4
Middleton Cumb 89 Q9
Middleton Derbys 65 P1
Middleton Derbys 77 M11
Middleton Essex 46 F4
Middleton Hants 24 G4
Middleton Herefs 51 P7
Middleton Lancs 83 K3
Middleton Leeds 85 L9
Middleton N York 84 H5
Middleton N York 92 F9
Middleton Nhants 55 L3
Middleton Norfk 69 M9
Middleton Nthumb 100 D1
Middleton Nthumb 108 H3
Middleton P & K 124 C11
Middleton Rochdl 76 F3
Middleton Shrops 51 P5
Middleton Shrops 63 K6
Middleton Suffk 59 N7
Middleton Swans 26 B5
Middleton Warwks 65 M12
Middleton Cheney Nhants 43 K3
Middleton Green Staffs 65 J5
Middleton Hall Nthumb 108 F5
Middleton-in-Teesdale Dur 90 F2
Middleton Moor Suffk 59 N7
Middleton One Row Darltn 91 N4
Middleton-on-Leven N York 91 Q5
Middleton-on-Sea W Susx 14 D10
Middleton on the Hill Herefs 51 P7
Middleton on the Wolds E R Yk 86 H5
Middleton Park C Aber 133 M2
Middleton Priors Shrops 52 B3
Middleton Quernhow N York 91 N11
Middleton St George Darltn 91 N4
Middleton Scriven Shrops 52 C3
Middleton Stoney Oxon 43 L7
Middleton Tyas N York 91 L5
Middletown Cumb 88 C5
Middle Town IoS 2 b3
Middletown N Som 28 F8
Middletown Powys 63 K9
Middle Tysoe Warwks 42 H3
Middle Wallop Hants 24 E6
Middlewich Ches E 76 C10
Middle Winterslow Wilts 24 D7
Middlewood Cnwll 7 K9
Middlewood Herefs 40 C3
Middle Woodford Wilts 23 P6
Middlewood Green Suffk 58 G8
Middle Yard Gloucs 41 N11
Middlezoy Somset 21 N7
Middridge Dur 91 L2
Midford BaNES 29 M10
Midge Hall Lancs 83 L10
Midgeholme Cumb 99 J6
Midgham W Berk 31 L9
Midgley Calder 84 F10
Midgley Wakefd 85 K12
Mid Holmwood Surrey 14 H2
Midhopestones Sheff 77 N4
Midhurst W Susx 14 C6
Mid Lavant W Susx 13 Q3
Midlem Border 107 N4
Mid Mains Highld 137 M8
Midney Somset 22 C8
Midpark Ag & B 112 F9
Midsomer Norton BaNES 22 F3
Midtown Highld 149 M4
Midville Lincs 80 G12
Midway Ches E 76 G7
Mid Yell Shet 147 j3
Migdale Highld 145 P7
Migvie Abers 132 C3
Milborne Port Somset 22 F9
Milborne St Andrew Dorset 11 K5
Milborne Wick Somset 22 F9
Milbourne Nthumb 100 E3
Milbourne Wilts 29 Q5
Milburn Cumb 99 J12
Milbury Heath S Glos 29 K4
Milby N York 85 N2
Milcombe Oxon 43 J5
Milden Suffk 46 G2
Mildenhall Suffk 57 N6
Mildenhall Wilts 30 E8
Milebrook Powys 51 K6
Milebush Kent 16 D2
Mile Elm Wilts 30 A8
Mile End Essex 46 H6
Mile End Gloucs 41 J9
Mile End Suffk 59 L3
Mileham Norfk 70 D8
Mile Oak Br & H 15 J9
Mile Oak Kent 16 B2
Mile Oak Staffs 65 M11
Miles Hope Herefs 51 P7
Milesmark Fife 115 K4
Miles Platting Manch 76 F4
Mile Town Kent 34 G7
Milfield Nthumb 108 E3
Milford Derbys 66 B3
Milford Devon 18 E9
Milford Powys 50 F2
Milford Staffs 64 H8
Milford Surrey 14 D2
Milford Haven Pembks 36 H9
Milford on Sea Hants 12 D6
Milkwall Gloucs 41 J10
Millais Jersey 13 a1
Milland W Susx 25 P8
Milland Marsh W Susx 25 P8
Mill Bank Calder 84 F11
Millbeck Cumb 88 H2
Millbreck Abers 141 N7
Millbridge Surrey 25 P5
Millbrook C Beds 44 E4
Millbrook C Sotn 24 F10
Millbrook Cnwll 4 F6
Millbrook Jersey 13 b2
Millbrook Tamesd 76 H4
Mill Brow Stockp 76 H6
Millbuie Abers 133 J2
Millbuie Highld 137 P5
Millcombe Devon 5 N7
Mill Common Norfk 71 L11
Mill Common Suffk 59 N4
Millcorner E Susx 16 E6
Millcraig Highld 145 P11
Mill Cross Devon 5 M4
Milldale Staffs 65 L1
Mill End Bucks 31 R5
Millend Gloucs 29 M3
Mill End Herts 45 L5
Millerhill Mdloth 115 P7
Miller's Dale Derbys 77 L9
Millers Green Derbys 65 P2
Miller's Green Essex 45 Q10
Millerston C Glas 114 B8
Millgate Lancs 84 D11
Mill Green Cambs 46 A3
Mill Green Essex 34 B2
Mill Green Herts 45 J9
Mill Green Lincs 68 E7
Mill Green Norfk 58 H4
Millgreen Shrops 64 C6
Mill Green Staffs 65 K12
Mill Green Staffs 65 K8
Mill Green Suffk 46 G3
Mill Green Suffk 58 E9
Mill Green Suffk 58 H8
Mill Green Suffk 59 L8
Millhalf Herefs 51 J11
Millhayes Devon 9 N4
Millhead Lancs 83 L1
Millheugh S Lans 114 D11
Mill Hill E Susx 16 A9
Mill Hill Gt Lon 33 J4
Millhouse Ag & B 112 D7
Millhouse Cumb 98 D10
Millhousebridge D & G 97 M1
Millhouse Green Barns 77 N3
Millhouses Barns 78 C3
Millhouses Sheff 77 Q7
Milliken Park Rens 113 N9
Millin Cross Pembks 37 J7
Millington E R Yk 86 F5
Mill Lane Hants 25 N3
Millmeece Staffs 64 F5
Millness Cumb 89 N10
Mill of Drummond P & K 123 L9
Mill of Haldane W Duns 113 M5
Millom Cumb 88 G10
Millook Cnwll 6 H5
Millpool Cnwll 2 F8
Millpool Cnwll 6 G10
Millport N Ayrs 112 H10
Mill Side Cumb 89 M10
Mill Street Kent 34 C11
Mill Street Norfk 70 F8
Mill Street Suffk 58 F6
Millthorpe Derbys 77 P8
Millthrop Cumb 89 Q8
Milltimber C Aber 133 L4
Milltown Abers 131 N2
Milltown Abers 132 D1
Milltown Cnwll 3 Q3
Milltown D & G 98 D3
Milltown Derbys 78 B11
Milltown Devon 19 L5
Milltown Highld 135 N7
Milltown of Auchindoun Moray 139 Q8
Milltown of Campfield Abers 132 G4
Milltown of Edinvillie Moray 139 N8
Milltown of Learney Abers 132 F4
Milltown of Rothiemay Moray 140 E6
Milnathort P & K 124 C11
Milngavie E Duns 113 Q6
Milnrow Rochdl 76 G1
Milnthorpe Cumb 89 M10
Milnthorpe Wakefd 85 M11
Milovaig Highld 134 C6
Milson Shrops 52 B6
Milstead Kent 34 F10
Milston Wilts 23 Q4
Milthorpe Lincs 68 C6
Milthorpe Nhants 43 M2
Milton C Stke 64 G2
Milton Cambs 57 J8
Milton Cumb 98 H6
Milton D & G 95 J7
Milton D & G 96 G4
Milton Derbys 65 P7
Milton Highld 137 N9
Milton Highld 137 Q6
Milton Highld 146 D10
Milton Highld 151 P6
Milton Inver 113 L7
Milton Kent 34 B7
Milton Moray 139 M12
Milton Moray 140 D3
Milton N Som 28 D10
Milton Newpt 28 E5
Milton Notts 78 H9
Milton Oxon 31 K4
Milton Oxon 43 K5
Milton P & K 131 K12
Milton Pembks 37 K10
Milton Somset 21 P9
Milton Stirlg 113 P1
Milton W Duns 113 N6
Milton Abbas Dorset 11 K4
Milton Abbot Devon 7 M9
Milton Bridge Mdloth 115 N8
Milton Bryan C Beds 44 D6
Milton Clevedon Somset 22 F6
Milton Combe Devon 4 G3
Milton Common Oxon 43 N11
Milton Damerel Devon 7 M3
Milton End Gloucs 30 D2
Milton End Gloucs 41 L9
Milton Ernest Bed 55 P9
Milton Green Ches W 75 M12
Milton Hill Oxon 31 K4
Milton Keynes M Keyn 44 B4
Milton Lilbourne Wilts 30 E10
Milton Malsor Nhants 55 J9
Milton Morenish P & K 122 G5
Milton of Auchinhove Abers 132 E4
Milton of Balgonie Fife 115 P1
Milton of Buchanan Stirlg 113 N3
Milton of Campsie E Duns 114 B6
Milton of Finavon Angus 125 K1
Milton of Leys Highld 138 C7
Milton of Murtle C Aber 133 L4
Milton on Stour Dorset 22 H7
Milton Regis Kent 34 F9
Milton Street E Susx 15 P10
Milton-under-Wychwood Oxon 42 F8
Milverton Somset 20 H8
Milverton Warwks 53 P7
Milwich Staffs 64 H6
Milwr Flints 74 G8
Minard Ag & B 112 E2
Minchington Dorset 23 L10
Minchinhampton Gloucs 29 P2
Mindrum Nthumb 108 D3
Minehead Somset 20 F4
Minera Wrexhm 63 J2
Minety Wilts 30 B4
Minffordd Gwynd 61 K4
Mingarrypark Highld 127 M10
Miningsby Lincs 80 F11
Minions Cnwll 7 K10
Minishant S Ayrs 104 F7
Minllyn Gwynd 61 Q9
Minnigaff D & G 95 M5
Minnonie Abers 141 J4
Minshull Vernon Ches E 76 C11
Minskip N York 85 M2
Minstead Hants 12 D3
Minsted W Susx 25 Q9
Minster Kent 35 P9
Minsterley Shrops 63 L11
Minster Lovell Oxon 42 G9
Minster-on-Sea Kent 34 G8
Minsterworth Gloucs 41 M8
Minterne Magna Dorset 10 G4
Minterne Parva Dorset 10 G4
Minting Lincs 80 D9
Mintlaw Abers 141 N6
Minto Border 107 N6
Minton Shrops 51 M2
Minwear Pembks 37 K8
Minworth Birm 53 M2
Mirehouse Cumb 88 C4
Mireland Highld 151 P4
Mirfield Kirk 85 J11
Miserden Gloucs 41 Q10
Miskin Rhondd 27 P3
Miskin Rhondd 27 P6
Misson Notts 78 H5
Misterton Leics 54 F4
Misterton Notts 79 J5
Misterton Somset 10 C3
Mistley Essex 47 K5
Mistley Heath Essex 47 K5
Mitcham Gt Lon 33 K8
Mitcheldean Gloucs 41 K8
Mitchell Cnwll 3 L4
Mitchellslacks D & G 106 C10
Mitchel Troy Mons 40 G9
Mitford Nthumb 100 F1
Mithian Cnwll 3 J4
Mitton Staffs 64 G9
Mixbury Oxon 43 M5
Mixenden Calder 84 G9
Moats Tye Suffk 58 F9
Mobberley Ches E 76 E8
Mobberley Staffs 65 J4

Moccas – Newton 181

Moccas Herefs 40 E3
Mochdre Conwy 73 P8
Mochdre Powys 50 E3
Mochrum D & G 95 L9
Mockbeggar Hants 12 B3
Mockbeggar Kent 16 C2
Mockerkin Cumb 88 E2
Modbury Devon 5 L6
Moddershall Staffs 64 G5
Moelfre IoA 72 H6
Moelfre Powys 62 G6
Moel Tryfan Gwynd 60 H1
Moffat D & G 106 E8
Mogador Surrey 33 J11
Moggerhanger C Beds 56 C10
Moira Leics 65 P9
Molash Kent 35 J12
Mol-chlach Highld 126 H2
Mold Flints 74 H11
Moldgreen Kirk 84 H12
Molehill Green Essex 45 Q5
Molehill Green Essex 46 C7
Molescroft E R Yk 87 J7
Molesden Nthumb 100 F1
Molesworth Cambs 55 Q5
Moll Highld 135 K9
Molland Devon 20 C7
Mollington Ches W 75 L9
Mollington Oxon 54 D11
Mollinsburn N Lans 114 C7
Monachty Cerdgn 48 H8
Mondynes Abers 133 J8
Monewden Suffk 59 K9
Moneydie P & K 123 Q7
Moneyrow Green W & M 32 C7
Moniaive D & G 105 P11
Monifieth Angus 125 K6
Monikie Angus 125 K5
Monimail Fife 124 F10
Monington Pembks 37 M2
Monk Bretton Barns 78 B2
Monken Hadley Gt Lon 33 J3
Monk Fryston N York 85 Q9
Monkhide Herefs 41 J3
Monkhill Cumb 98 D6
Monkhopton Shrops 52 B2
Monkland Herefs 51 M9
Monkleigh Devon 19 J9
Monknash V Glam 27 L8
Monkokehampton Devon 7 J4
Monkseaton N Tyne 101 J4
Monks Eleigh Suffk 58 E11
Monk's Gate W Susx 14 H5
Monks Heath Ches E 76 F9
Monk Sherborne Hants 31 N10
Monks Horton Kent 17 K3
Monksilver Somset 20 G6
Monks Kirby Warwks 54 D4
Monk Soham Suffk 59 J7
Monkspath Solhll 53 L5
Monks Risborough Bucks 44 A10
Monksthorpe Lincs 80 H10
Monk Street Essex 45 R6
Monkswood Mons 40 D11
Monkton Devon 9 M4
Monkton Kent 35 N9
Monkton S Ayrs 104 F4
Monkton S Tyne 101 J5
Monkton V Glam 27 M8
Monkton Combe BaNES 29 M10
Monkton Deverill Wilts 23 J6
Monkton Farleigh Wilts 29 N9
Monkton Heathfield
Somset 21 L8
Monkton Up Wimborne
Dorset 23 M10
Monkton Wyld Dorset 9 Q5
Monkwearmouth Sundld 101 K6
Monkwood Hants 25 L7
Monmore Green Wolves 52 H1
Monmouth Mons 40 G9
Monnington on Wye
Herefs 40 E3
Monreith D & G 95 L10
Montacute Somset 22 C10
Montcliffe Bolton 76 C1
Montford Shrops 63 L9
Montford Bridge Shrops 63 M9
Montgarrie Abers 140 E12
Montgomery Powys 50 H1
Monton Salfd 76 E4
Montrose Angus 125 P1
Mont Saint Guern 12 b2
Monxton Hants 24 E4
Monyash Derbys 77 L10
Monymusk Abers 132 G1
Monzie P & K 123 M8
Moodiesburn N Lans 114 C7
Moonzie Fife 124 G9
Moor Allerton Leeds 85 L7
Moorbath Dorset 10 C6
Moorby Lincs 80 F11
Moorcot Herefs 51 K9
Moor Crichel Dorset 11 N3
Moordown BCP 11 Q6
Moore Halton 75 P7
Moor End C Beds 44 D7
Moor End Calder 84 F9
Moor End Devon 8 C3
Moorend Gloucs 41 L11
Moor End Lancs 83 J6
Moor End N York 86 B7
Moorends Donc 86 C12
Moorgreen Hants 24 G10
Moor Green Herts 45 L6
Moorgreen Notts 66 D3
Moorhall Derbys 77 P8
Moorhampton Herefs 40 E4
Moorhead C Brad 84 H8
Moor Head Leeds 85 K9
Moorhouse Cumb 98 B8
Moorhouse Cumb 98 D7
Moorhouse Donc 78 D2
Moorhouse Notts 79 K9
Moorhouse Bank Surrey 33 M11
Moorland Somset 21 M7
Moorlinch Somset 21 N6
Moor Monkton N York 85 Q4
Moor Row Cumb 88 D4
Moor Row Cumb 97 P8
Moorsholm R & Cl 92 E4
Moorside Dorset 22 H9
Moorside Dur 100 E8
Moor Side Lancs 83 K8
Moor Side Lancs 83 L8
Moorside Leeds 85 K7
Moor Side Lincs 80 E12
Moorside Oldham 76 H2
Moorstock Kent 17 K3
Moor Street Birm 53 J4
Moor Street Medway 34 E9
Moorswater Cnwll 4 C4
Moorthorpe Wakefd 78 D2
Moortown Devon 7 P10
Moortown Hants 12 B4
Moortown IoW 12 G8
Moortown Leeds 85 L7
Moortown Lincs 79 Q4
Moortown Wrekin 63 Q8
Morangie Highld 146 D8
Morar Highld 127 M6
Morborne Cambs 56 C2
Morchard Bishop Devon 8 E3
Morchard Road Devon 8 E4
Morcombelake Dorset 10 B6
Morcott Rutlnd 67 M12
Morda Shrops 63 J6
Morden Dorset 11 M5
Morden Gt Lon 33 J8
Mordiford Herefs 40 H4
Mordon Dur 91 N1
More Shrops 51 K2
Morebath Devon 20 E8
Morebattle Border 108 C5
Morecambe Lancs 83 K2
Moredon Swindn 30 D5
Morefield Highld 144 E6
Morehall Kent 17 M3
Moreleigh Devon 5 M6
Morenish P & K 122 G6
Moresby Parks Cumb 88 D3
Morestead Hants 24 H8
Moreton Dorset 11 K7
Moreton Essex 45 P10
Moreton Herefs 51 N8
Moreton Oxon 43 P10
Moreton Staffs 64 E8
Moreton Staffs 65 L6
Moreton Wirral 75 J6
Moreton Corbet Shrops 63 P7
Moretonhampstead
Devon 8 E7
Moreton-in-Marsh
Gloucs 42 E5
Moreton Jeffries Herefs 51 Q11
Moretonmill Shrops 63 P7
Moreton Morrell Warwks 53 P9
Moreton on Lugg Herefs 40 G3
Moreton Paddox Warwks 53 P9
Moreton Pinkney Nhants 54 F11
Moreton Say Shrops 64 B5
Moreton Valence Gloucs 41 M9
Morfa Cerdgn 48 E10
Morfa Bychan Gwynd 61 J5
Morfa Dinlle Gwynd 72 G12
Morfa Glas Neath 39 K10
Morfa Nefyn Gwynd 60 D4
Morganstown Cardif 27 Q6
Morgan's Vale Wilts 24 C9
Morham E Loth 116 D7
Moriah Cerdgn 49 K5
Morland Cumb 89 P2
Morley Ches E 76 F7
Morley Derbys 66 C4
Morley Dur 91 J1
Morley Leeds 85 K9
Morley Green Ches E 76 F7
Morley St Botolph Norfk 70 G12
Mornick Cnwll 7 L10
Morningside C Edin 115 N7
Morningside N Lans 114 E10
Morningthorpe Norfk 59 J2
Morpeth Nthumb 100 G1
Morphie Abers 132 H11
Morrey Staffs 65 L8
Morridge Side Staffs 65 J1
Morriston Swans 26 G3
Morston Norfk 70 E3
Mortehoe Devon 19 J4
Morthen Rothm 78 D6
Mortimer W Berk 31 N9
Mortimer Common
W Berk 31 N9
Mortimer's Cross Herefs 51 M8
Mortimer West End
Hants 31 N9
Mortlake Gt Lon 32 H7
Morton Cumb 98 E7
Morton Cumb 98 F10
Morton Derbys 78 C11
Morton IoW 13 K7
Morton Lincs 68 B7
Morton Lincs 79 K5
Morton Lincs 79 M11
Morton Notts 67 J2
Morton Shrops 63 J7
Morton-on-Swale N York 91 N8
Morton on the Hill Norfk 70 G9
Morton Tinmouth Dur 91 K2
Morvah Cnwll 2 C7
Morval Cnwll 4 C5
Morvich Highld 136 D11
Morville Shrops 52 C2
Morville Heath Shrops 52 C2
Morwenstow Cnwll 18 D10
Mosborough Sheff 78 C7
Moscow E Ayrs 105 J2
Mose Shrops 52 D3
Mosedale Cumb 98 D11
Moseley Birm 53 K4
Moseley Wolves 52 H1
Moseley Worcs 52 E8
Moses Gate Bolton 76 D2
Moss Ag & B 118 C4
Moss Donc 86 B12
Moss Wrexhm 63 J2
Mossat Abers 140 D12
Mossbank Shet 147 j5
Moss Bank St Hel 75 N4
Mossbay Cumb 88 C1
Mossblown S Ayrs 104 G5
Mossbrow Traffd 76 D6
Mossburnford Border 107 Q6
Mossdale D & G 96 D4
Mossdale E Ayrs 105 J9
Moss Edge Lancs 83 K6
Moss End Ches E 76 C8
Mossend N Lans 114 D9
Mosser Mains Cumb 88 F2
Mossley Ches E 76 G11
Mossley Tamesd 76 H3
Mosspaul Hotel Border 107 L10
Moss Side Cumb 97 P8
Moss-side Highld 138 F5
Moss Side Lancs 83 J9
Moss Side Sefton 75 L3
Mosstodloch Moray 139 Q4
Mossyard D & G 95 Q8
Mossy Lea Lancs 75 P1
Mosterton Dorset 10 C4
Moston Manch 76 G3
Moston Shrops 63 P7
Moston Green Ches E 76 D11
Mostyn Flints 74 G7
Motcombe Dorset 23 J8
Mothecombe Devon 5 K7
Motherby Cumb 98 E12
Motherwell N Lans 114 D10
Motspur Park Gt Lon 33 J9
Mottingham Gt Lon 33 M8
Mottisfont Hants 24 E8
Mottistone IoW 12 G8
Mottram in
Longdendale Tamesd 77 J5
Mottram St Andrew
Ches E 76 G8
Mouilpied Guern 12 c3
Mouldsworth Ches W 75 N9
Moulin P & K 123 N1
Moulsecoomb Br & H 15 L9
Moulsford Oxon 31 M5
Moulsoe M Keyn 44 C3
Moultavie Highld 145 P11
Moulton Ches W 76 C9
Moulton Lincs 68 F7
Moulton N York 91 L6
Moulton Nhants 55 K7
Moulton Suffk 57 N8
Moulton V Glam 27 P8
Moulton Chapel Lincs 68 F8
Moulton St Mary Norfk 71 M10
Moulton Seas End Lincs 68 F6
Mount Cnwll 3 J3
Mount Cnwll 4 A3
Mount Kirk 84 G11
Mountain C Brad 84 G9
Mountain Ash Rhondd 27 P3
Mountain Cross Border 115 L12
Mountain Street Kent 35 J11
Mount Ambrose Cnwll 2 H6
Mount Bures Essex 46 F5
Mountfield E Susx 16 C7
Mountgerald Highld 137 P3
Mount Hawke Cnwll 2 H5
Mount Hermon Cnwll 2 H11
Mountjoy Cnwll 3 L2
Mount Lothian Mdloth 115 N10
Mountnessing Essex 34 A3
Mounton Mons 28 G4
Mount Pleasant Ches E 76 F12
Mount Pleasant Derbys 65 P8
Mount Pleasant Derbys 65 Q2
Mount Pleasant Dur 100 H11
Mount Pleasant E R Yk 87 N7
Mount Pleasant E Susx 15 M7
Mount Pleasant Norfk 58 E2
Mount Pleasant Suffk 57 P11
Mount Pleasant Worcs 53 J7
Mountsorrel Leics 66 F9
Mount Sorrel Wilts 23 M8
Mount Tabor Calder 84 G9
Mousehole Cnwll 2 D9
Mouswald D & G 97 L4
Mow Cop Ches E 76 F12
Mowhaugh Border 108 C5
Mowmacre Hill C Leic 66 F10
Mowsley Leics 54 G3
Moy Highld 129 M8
Moy Highld 138 E9
Moyle Highld 136 B12
Moylegrove Pembks 48 A11
Muasdale Ag & B 103 J2
Muchalls Abers 133 L6
Much Birch Herefs 40 G5
Much Cowarne Herefs 41 J2
Much Dewchurch Herefs 40 G5
Muchelney Somset 21 P8
Muchelney Ham Somset 21 P8
Much Hadham Herts 45 M8
Much Hoole Lancs 83 L10
Much Hoole Town Lancs 83 L10
Muchlarnick Cnwll 4 C5
Much Marcle Herefs 41 K5
Much Wenlock Shrops 64 B12
Muck Highld 126 G8
Mucking Thurr 34 B6
Muckleburgh Collection
Norfk 70 G3
Muckleford Dorset 10 G6
Mucklestone Staffs 64 D5
Muckley Shrops 52 B2
Muckton Lincs 80 G7
Muddiford Devon 19 L6
Muddles Green E Susx 15 Q8
Mudeford BCP 12 C6
Mudford Somset 22 D9
Mudford Sock Somset 22 D9
Mudgley Somset 21 P4
Mud Row Kent 34 H8
Mugdock Stirlg 113 Q6
Mugeary Highld 134 H8
Mugginton Derbys 65 P4
Muggintonlane End
Derbys 65 P3
Muggleswick Dur 100 D8
Muirden Abers 140 H5
Muirdrum Angus 125 L5
Muiresk Abers 140 H6
Muirhead Angus 124 G6
Muirhead Fife 124 F11
Muirhead N Lans 114 C7
Muirhouses Falk 115 J5
Muirkirk E Ayrs 105 N4
Muirmill Stirlg 114 D4
Muir of Fowlis Abers 132 E2
Muir of Miltonduff Moray 139 M4
Muir of Ord Highld 137 P6
Muirshearlich Highld 128 G8
Muirtack Abers 141 N8
Muirton P & K 123 N10
Muirton Mains Highld 137 M5
Muirton of Ardblair P & K 124 D4
Muker N York 90 E7
Mulbarton Norfk 71 J12
Mulben Moray 139 Q6
Mulfra Cnwll 2 D7
Mull Ag & B 119 Q6
Mullacott Cross Devon 19 K4
Mullion Cnwll 2 H10
Mullion Cove Cnwll 2 G11
Mumby Lincs 81 K9
Munderfield Row Herefs 52 C10
Munderfield Stocks
Herefs 52 C10
Mundesley Norfk 71 L5
Mundford Norfk 57 Q2
Mundham Norfk 59 L1
Mundon Hill Essex 46 F11
Mundy Bois Kent 16 F2
Mungrisdale Cumb 98 D12
Munlochy Highld 138 B5
Munnoch N Ayrs 113 K11
Munsley Herefs 41 K3
Munslow Shrops 51 N3
Murchington Devon 8 C7
Murcot Worcs 42 C4
Murcott Oxon 43 M8
Murcott Wilts 29 Q4
Murkle Highld 151 L3
Murlaggan Highld 128 D6
Murrell Green Hants 25 N2
Murroes Angus 125 J6
Murrow Cambs 68 G10
Mursley Bucks 44 B6
Murston Kent 34 G9
Murthill Angus 125 J1
Murthly P & K 124 C5
Murton C York 86 C5
Murton Cumb 90 B2
Murton Dur 101 K9
Murton N Tyne 101 J4
Murton Nthumb 117 L11
Murton Swans 26 E4
Musbury Devon 9 P6
Muscoates N York 92 E10
Musselburgh E Loth 115 Q7
Muston Leics 67 K5
Muston N York 93 M10
Mustow Green Worcs 52 F6
Muswell Hill Gt Lon 33 K4
Mutehill D & G 96 E8
Mutford Suffk 59 P3
Muthill P & K 123 M9
Mutterton Devon 9 J4
Muxton Wrekin 64 D9
Mybster Highld 151 L6
Myddfai Carmth 39 J5
Myddle Shrops 63 M7
Mydroilyn Cerdgn 48 G9
Myerscough Lancs 83 L7
Mylor Cnwll 3 K7
Mylor Bridge Cnwll 3 K7
Mynachlog ddu Pembks 37 M4
Myndd-llan Flints 74 G9
Myndtown Shrops 51 L3
Mynydd Bach Cerdgn 49 M5
Mynydd-bach Mons 28 G3
Mynydd-Bach Swans 26 G3
Mynyddgarreg Carmth 38 C10
Mynydd Isa Flints 75 J11
Mynydd Llandygai Gwynd 73 K10
Mynytho Gwynd 60 E6
Myrebird Abers 132 H4
Myredykes Border 107 P10
Mytchett Surrey 32 C11
Mytholm Calder 84 E9
Mytholmroyd Calder 84 F10
Mythop Lancs 83 J8
Myton-on-Swale N York 85 N2

N

Naast Highld 143 M8
Nab's Head Lancs 83 N9
Na Buirgh W Isls 152 d6
Naburn C York 86 B6
Naccolt Kent 17 J2
Nackington Kent 35 L11
Nacton Suffk 47 M4
Nafferton E R Yk 87 K3
Nag's Head Gloucs 29 P3
Nailbridge Gloucs 41 K8
Nailsbourne Somset 21 K7
Nailsea N Som 28 G8
Nailstone Leics 66 C10
Nailsworth Gloucs 29 N2
Nairn Highld 138 G5
Nalderswood Surrey 15 J2
Nancegollan Cnwll 2 G8
Nancledra Cnwll 2 D7
Nanhoron Gwynd 60 D6
Nannerch Flints 74 G9
Nanpantan Leics 66 E8
Nanpean Cnwll 3 N3
Nanquidno Cnwll 2 B8
Nanstallon Cnwll 6 F11
Nant-ddu Powys 39 N8
Nanternis Cerdgn 48 F9
Nantgaredig Carmth 38 D7
Nantgarw Rhondd 27 Q5
Nant-glas Powys 50 D7
Nantglyn Denbgs 74 D11
Nantgwyn Powys 50 D5
Nant Gwynant Gwynd 61 L2
Nantlle Gwynd 60 H2
Nantmawr Shrops 63 J7
Nantmel Powys 50 E7
Nantmor Gwynd 61 K3
Nant Peris Gwynd 73 K12
Nantwich Ches E 64 C2
Nant-y-Bwch Blae G 39 Q9
Nantycaws Carmth 38 C8
Nant-y-derry Mons 40 D10
Nantyffyllon Brdgnd 27 K4
Nantyglo Blae G 40 B9
Nant-y-gollen Shrops 62 H6
Nant-y-moel Brdgnd 27 M4
Nant-y-pandy Conwy 73 M9
Naphill Bucks 32 B3
Napleton Worcs 52 F11
Nappa N York 84 C4
Napton on the Hill
Warwks 54 D8
Narberth Pembks 37 L7
Narborough Leics 54 E1
Narborough Norfk 69 P9
Narkurs Cnwll 4 E6
Nasareth Gwynd 60 H2
Naseby Nhants 54 H5
Nash Bucks 43 Q5
Nash Gt Lon 33 M9
Nash Herefs 51 K8
Nash Newpt 28 D5
Nash Shrops 51 Q6
Nash End Worcs 52 E4
Nashes Green Hants 25 L4
Nash Lee Bucks 44 B10
Nash Street Kent 34 B8
Nassington Nhants 55 Q1
Nastend Gloucs 41 M10
Nasty Herts 45 L7
Nateby Cumb 90 C5
Nateby Lancs 83 L6
National Memorial
Arboretum Staffs 65 M9
National Motor Museum
(Beaulieu) Hants 12 F4
National Space Centre
C Leic 66 F10
Natland Cumb 89 N9
Naughton Suffk 58 F10
Naunton Gloucs 42 D7
Naunton Worcs 41 P4
Naunton Beauchamp
Worcs 52 H10
Navenby Lincs 79 N12
Navestock Essex 33 P3
Navestock Side Essex 33 Q3
Navidale Highld 147 J2
Navity Highld 138 E3
Nawton N York 92 D9
Nayland Suffk 46 H5
Nazeing Essex 45 M10
Nazeing Gate Essex 45 M10
Neacroft Hants 12 C5
Neal's Green Warwks 53 Q4
Neap Shet 147 j6
Near Cotton Staffs 65 K3
Near Sawrey Cumb 89 K7
Neasden Gt Lon 33 J5
Neasham Darltn 91 N5
Neath Neath 26 H3
Neatham Hants 25 M5
Neatishead Norfk 71 L8
Nebo Cerdgn 49 J7
Nebo Conwy 61 P1
Nebo Gwynd 60 H2
Nebo IoA 72 H5
Necton Norfk 70 C10
Nedd Highld 148 D10
Nedderton Nthumb 100 G2
Nedging Suffk 58 E11
Nedging Tye Suffk 58 F10
Needham Norfk 59 J4
Needham Market Suffk 58 G9
Needham Street Suffk 57 N7
Needingworth Cambs 56 G6
Neen Savage Shrops 52 C6
Neen Sollars Shrops 52 C6
Neenton Shrops 52 B3
Nefyn Gwynd 60 E4
Neilston E Rens 113 P10
Nelson Caerph 27 Q3
Nelson Lancs 84 C7
Nemphlar S Lans 105 Q1
Nempnett Thrubwell
BaNES 28 H10
Nenthall Cumb 99 L9
Nenthead Cumb 99 M9
Nenthorn Border 107 R2
Neopardy Devon 8 E5
Nep Town W Susx 15 J8
Nerabus Ag & B 110 F10
Nercwys Flints 74 H11
Nerston S Lans 114 B10
Nesbit Nthumb 108 F3
Nesfield N York 84 G5
Ness Ches W 75 J8
Nesscliffe Shrops 63 L8
Neston Ches W 75 J8
Neston Wilts 29 P8
Netchwood Shrops 52 B2
Nether Abington S Lans 106 B5
Nether Alderley Ches E 76 F8
Netheravon Wilts 23 P4
Nether Blainslie Border 107 N1
Netherbrae Abers 141 J4
Nether Broughton Leics 66 H7
Netherburn S Lans 114 E11
Netherbury Dorset 10 D5
Netherby Cumb 98 D3
Netherby N York 85 M6
Nether Cerne Dorset 10 G5
Nethercleuch D & G 97 M1
Nether Compton Dorset 22 D10
Nethercote Warwks 54 E8
Nethercott Devon 7 L5
Nethercott Devon 19 J5
Nether Crimond Abers 141 K11
Nether Dallachy Moray 139 Q3
Netherend Gloucs 29 J2
Nether Exe Devon 8 H5
Netherfield E Susx 16 C7
Netherfield Leics 66 F9
Netherfield Notts 66 G4
Nether Fingland S Lans 106 B7
Nethergate N Linc 79 K4
Nethergate Norfk 70 F6
Netherhampton Wilts 23 P7
Nether Handley Derbys 78 C8
Nether Handwick Angus 124 G4
Nether Haugh Rothm 78 C4
Netherhay Dorset 10 C4
Nether Headon Notts 79 J8
Nether Heage Derbys 66 B2
Nether Heyford Nhants 54 H9
Nether Kellet Lancs 83 L2
Nether Kinmundy Abers 141 P7
Netherland Green Staffs 65 L6
Nether Langwith Notts 78 E9
Netherlaw D & G 96 F9
Netherley Abers 133 K6
Nethermill D & G 106 D12
Nethermuir Abers 141 L7
Netherne-on-the-Hill
Surrey 33 K11
Netheroyd Hill Kirk 84 H11
Nether Padley Derbys 77 N8
Nether Poppleton C York 85 R4
Nether Row Cumb 98 C10
Netherseal Derbys 65 P9
Nether Silton N York 91 Q8
Nether Skyborry Shrops 51 J6
Nether Stowey Somset 21 K5
Nether Street Essex 45 Q9
Netherstreet Wilts 29 R9
Netherthong Kirk 77 L2
Netherthorpe Derbys 78 D9
Netherton Angus 125 L1
Netherton Devon 8 G10
Netherton Dudley 52 H3
Netherton Hants 30 H10
Netherton Herefs 40 H6
Netherton Kirk 77 L1
Netherton N Lans 114 E10
Netherton Nthumb 108 F8
Netherton Oxon 31 J2
Netherton P & K 124 C2
Netherton Sefton 75 K4
Netherton Shrops 52 D4
Netherton Stirlg 113 Q5
Netherton Wakefd 85 L11
Netherton Worcs 42 A3
Nethertown Cumb 88 C5
Nethertown Highld 151 Q1
Nethertown Lancs 83 Q8
Nethertown Staffs 65 L8
Netherurd Border 115 K12
Nether Wallop Hants 24 E6
Nether Wasdale Cumb 88 F6
Nether Welton Cumb 98 D8
Nether Westcote Gloucs 42 E7
Nether Whitacre Warwks 53 N2
Nether Whitecleuch
S Lans 105 Q6
Nether Winchendon
Bucks 43 Q9
Netherwitton Nthumb 108 H11
Nethy Bridge Highld 139 J11
Netley Hants 12 G3
Netley Marsh Hants 24 E10
Nettlebed Oxon 31 P5
Nettlebridge Somset 22 F4
Nettlecombe Dorset 10 E5
Nettlecombe IoW 13 J9
Nettleden Herts 44 E9
Nettleham Lincs 79 P8
Nettlestead Kent 34 B12
Nettlestead Green Kent 34 B12
Nettlestone IoW 13 K6
Nettlesworth Dur 100 H8
Nettleton Lincs 80 B4
Nettleton Wilts 29 N7
Nettleton Shrub Wilts 29 N7
Netton Devon 5 J7
Netton Wilts 23 P6
Neuadd Carmth 38 G7
Neuadd-ddu Powys 50 C6
Nevendon Essex 34 D4
Nevern Pembks 37 L3
Nevill Holt Leics 55 K2
New Abbey D & G 97 K5
New Aberdour Abers 141 L3
New Addington Gt Lon 33 M9
Newall Leeds 85 J6
New Alresford Hants 25 K7
New Alyth P & K 124 E3
Newark C Pete 68 D12
Newark Ork 147 e2
Newark-on-Trent Notts 67 K2
New Arram E R Yk 87 J6
Newarthill N Lans 114 E9
New Ash Green Kent 33 R9
New Balderton Notts 67 K2
Newbarn Kent 17 L3
New Barn Kent 34 A8
New Barnet Gt Lon 33 K3
New Barton Nhants 55 L8
Newbattle Mdloth 115 P8
New Bewick Nthumb 108 H6
Newbie D & G 97 N5
Newbiggin Cumb 82 G1
Newbiggin Cumb 88 E8
Newbiggin Cumb 89 Q1
Newbiggin Cumb 98 F12
Newbiggin Cumb 98 H8
Newbiggin Dur 90 E1
Newbiggin Dur 100 F8
Newbiggin N York 90 F8
Newbiggin N York 90 G9
Newbiggin-by-the-Sea
Nthumb 109 M12
Newbigging Angus 124 F4
Newbigging Angus 124 H5
Newbigging Angus 125 K5
Newbigging S Lans 115 J12
Newbiggin-on-Lune
Cumb 90 B6
New Bilton Warwks 54 D5
Newbold Derbys 78 B9
Newbold Leics 66 C8
Newbold on Avon
Warwks 54 D5
Newbold on Stour
Warwks 42 F2
Newbold Pacey Warwks 53 P9
Newbold Revel Warwks 54 D4
Newbold Verdon Leics 66 D11
New Bolingbroke Lincs 80 F12
Newborough C Pete 68 D11
Newborough IoA 72 G10
Newborough Staffs 65 L7
Newbottle Nhants 43 L4
Newbottle Sundld 101 J8
New Boultham Lincs 79 N9
Newbourne Suffk 47 N3
New Bradwell M Keyn 44 B3
New Brampton Derbys 78 B9
New Brancepeth Dur 100 G10
Newbridge C Edin 115 L7
Newbridge Caerph 28 B3
Newbridge Cerdgn 48 H9
Newbridge Cnwll 2 C8
Newbridge Cnwll 3 K6
Newbridge D & G 97 J2
Newbridge Hants 24 E10
Newbridge IoW 12 G7
New Bridge N York 92 G9
Newbridge Oxon 31 J2
Newbridge Wrexhm 63 J4
Newbridge Green Worcs 41 N4
Newbridge-on-Usk Mons 28 E3
Newbridge-on-Wye
Powys 50 D9
New Brighton Flints 75 J10
New Brighton Wirral 75 K5
New Brinsley Notts 66 D2
New Brotton R & Cl 92 E3
Newbrough Nthumb 99 N5
New Broughton Wrexhm 63 K2
New Buckenham Norfk 58 G3
Newbuildings Devon 8 E4
Newburgh Abers 141 M4
Newburgh Abers 141 N10
Newburgh Fife 124 F9
Newburgh Lancs 75 N2
Newburn N u Ty 100 F5
New Bury Bolton 76 D3
Newbury Somset 22 F3
Newbury W Berk 31 K9
Newbury Wilts 22 H5
Newbury Park Gt Lon 33 N5
Newby Cumb 89 P2
Newby Lancs 84 B6
Newby N York 83 Q1
Newby N York 92 A4
Newby N York 93 L9
Newby Bridge Cumb 89 K9
Newby Cross Cumb 98 F6
Newby East Cumb 98 F6
Newby Head Cumb 89 P2
New Byth Abers 141 K5
Newby West Cumb 98 D7
Newby Wiske N York 91 N9
Newcastle Mons 40 F8
Newcastle Shrops 50 H4
Newcastle Airport
Nthumb 100 F4
Newcastle Emlyn Carmth 37 Q2
Newcastleton Border 107 M12
Newcastle-under-Lyme
Staffs 64 F3
Newcastle upon Tyne
N u Ty 100 G5
Newchapel Pembks 37 P3
Newchapel Staffs 64 F1
Newchapel Surrey 15 L2
Newchurch Blae G 40 A9
Newchurch Herefs 51 K10
Newchurch IoW 13 J7
Newchurch Kent 17 J4
Newchurch Mons 28 F3
Newchurch Powys 50 H10
Newchurch Staffs 65 L7
Newchurch in Pendle
Lancs 84 B7
New Costessey Norfk 71 J10
New Cowper Cumb 97 M9
Newcraighall C Edin 115 P7
New Crofton Wakefd 85 M11
New Cross Cerdgn 49 L5
New Cross Gt Lon 33 L7
New Cross Somset 21 P9
New Cumnock E Ayrs 105 L7
New Cut E Susx 16 E7
New Deer Abers 141 L6
New Delaval Nthumb 100 H2
New Delph Oldham 77 J2
New Denham Bucks 32 F5
Newdigate Surrey 14 H3
New Duston Nhants 54 H8
New Earswick C York 86 B4
New Eastwood Notts 66 D3
New Edlington Donc 78 E4
New Elgin Moray 139 N3
New Ellerby E R Yk 87 M7
Newell Green Br For 32 C8
New Eltham Gt Lon 33 N8
New End Worcs 53 K8
Newenden Kent 16 E5
New England C Pete 68 D12
New England Essex 46 C3
Newent Gloucs 41 L6
New Farnley Leeds 85 K9
New Ferry Wirral 75 K6
Newfield Dur 100 G11
Newfield Dur 100 G8
Newfield Highld 146 D9
New Fletton C Pete 56 D1
New Forest National
Park 12 D3
Newfound Hants 25 K3
New Fryston Wakefd 85 P10
Newgale Pembks 36 G6
New Galloway D & G 96 D3
Newgate Norfk 70 F4
Newgate Street Herts 45 K10
New Gilston Fife 125 J11
New Grimsby IoS 2 b1
Newhall Ches E 63 Q3
Newhall Derbys 65 P8
Newham Nthumb 109 K4
New Hartley Nthumb 100 H3
Newhaven C Edin 115 N6
Newhaven Derbys 77 M11
Newhaven E Susx 15 N10
New Haw Surrey 32 F9
New Hedges Pembks 37 M10
New Herrington Sundld 101 J7
Newhey Rochdl 76 H1
New Holkham Norfk 70 C4
New Holland N Linc 87 K10
Newholm N York 92 H5
New Houghton Derbys 78 D10
New Houghton Norfk 69 Q6
Newhouse N Lans 114 E9
New Houses N York 90 C12
New Houses Wigan 75 P3
New Hutton Cumb 89 P8
New Hythe Kent 34 C10
Newick E Susx 15 M6
Newingreen Kent 17 K4
Newington Kent 17 L3
Newington Kent 34 F9
Newington Oxon 31 M3
Newington Shrops 51 M4
Newington Bagpath
Gloucs 29 N3
New Inn Carmth 38 C4
New Inn Torfn 28 D2
New Invention Shrops 51 J5
New Lakenham Norfk 71 J10
New Lanark S Lans 106 A1
New Lanark Village
S Lans 106 A1
Newland C KuH 87 K9
Newland Cumb 89 J10
Newland E R Yk 86 E9
Newland Gloucs 40 H9
Newland N York 86 C10
Newland Oxon 42 H9
Newland Somset 20 C6
Newland Worcs 52 E11
Newlandrig Mdloth 115 Q9
Newlands Border 107 M11
Newlands Cumb 98 D10
Newlands Nthumb 100 E7
Newlands of Dundurcas
Moray 139 P6
New Lane Lancs 75 M1
New Lane End Warrtn 76 B5
New Langholm D & G 98 D1
New Leake Lincs 80 H12
New Leeds Abers 141 N5
New Lodge Barns 78 B2
New Longton Lancs 83 L10
New Luce D & G 94 H5
Newlyn Cnwll 2 D9
Newmachar Abers 141 L12
Newmains N Lans 114 E10
New Malden Gt Lon 33 J8
Newman's End Essex 45 P9
Newman's Green Suffk 46 F3
Newmarket Suffk 57 M8
Newmarket W Isls 152 g3
New Marske R & Cl 92 C2
New Marston Oxon 43 L10
New Marton Shrops 63 K5
New Mill Abers 133 J7
Newmill Border 107 L7
New Mill Cnwll 2 D7
New Mill Herts 44 C9
New Mill Kirk 77 M2
Newmill Moray 140 C5
Newmillerdam Wakefd 85 L12
Newmill of Inshewan
Angus 132 C12
Newmills C Edin 115 L8
New Mills Cnwll 3 L4
New Mills Derbys 77 J6
Newmills Fife 115 J4
Newmills Mons 40 G10
New Mills Powys 62 F12
Newmiln P & K 124 C7
Newmilns E Ayrs 105 K2
New Milton Hants 12 D6
New Mistley Essex 47 K5
New Moat Pembks 37 L5
Newnes Shrops 63 L5
Newney Green Essex 46 B10
Newnham Hants 25 M3
Newnham Herts 45 J4
Newnham Kent 34 G11
Newnham Nhants 54 F9
Newnham Bridge Worcs 52 B7
Newnham on Severn
Gloucs 41 L9
New Ollerton Notts 78 H10
New Oscott Birm 53 L2
New Pitsligo Abers 141 L5
New Polzeath Cnwll 6 D9
Newport Cnwll 7 L7
Newport Dorset 11 L6
Newport E R Yk 86 F9
Newport Essex 45 P5
Newport Gloucs 29 L3
Newport Highld 151 L11
Newport IoW 12 H7
Newport Newpt 28 D5
Newport Norfk 71 P8
Newport Pembks 37 L3
Newport Wrekin 64 D8
Newport-on-Tay Fife 124 H7
Newport Pagnell M Keyn 44 B3
Newport Pagnell
Services M Keyn 44 B3
Newpound Common
W Susx 14 F5
New Prestwick S Ayrs 104 F5
New Quay Cerdgn 48 F8
Newquay Cnwll 3 K2
New Quay Essex 46 H7
Newquay Zoo Cnwll 3 K2
New Rackheath Norfk 71 K9
New Radnor Powys 50 H8
New Rent Cumb 98 F11
New Ridley Nthumb 100 D6
New Road Side N York 84 E6
New Romney Kent 17 J6
New Rossington Donc 78 G4
New Row Cerdgn 49 M6
New Row Lancs 83 P7
New Sauchie Clacks 114 G2
Newsbank Ches E 76 F10
Newseat Abers 140 H9
Newsham Lancs 83 L8
Newsham N York 91 J5
Newsham N York 91 P10
Newsham Nthumb 100 H2
New Sharlston Wakefd 85 M11
Newsholme E R Yk 86 D9
Newsholme Lancs 84 C4
New Shoreston Nthumb 109 K3
New Silksworth Sundld 101 K7
New Skelton R & Cl 92 D3
Newsome Kirk 84 H12
New Somerby Lincs 67 M5
New Springs Wigan 75 Q2
Newstead Border 107 N3
Newstead Notts 66 E2
Newstead Nthumb 109 J4
New Stevenston N Lans 114 D9
New Street Herefs 51 K9
New Swanington Leics 66 C9
Newthorpe N York 85 P8
Newthorpe Notts 66 D3
New Thundersley Essex 34 D4
Newtimber W Susx 15 K8
Newtoft Lincs 79 P6
Newton Ag & B 112 F2
Newton Border 107 P5
Newton Brdgnd 27 K7
Newton C Beds 45 J3
Newton Cambs 56 H10
Newton Cambs 68 H9
Newton Cardif 28 B7
Newton Ches W 75 L10
Newton Ches W 75 N11
Newton Ches W 75 N8
Newton Cumb 88 H12
Newton Derbys 78 D11
Newton Herefs 40 D5
Newton Herefs 51 L7
Newton Herefs 51 N10
Newton Highld 137 Q6
Newton Highld 138 D6
Newton Highld 138 E3
Newton Highld 151 Q6
Newton Lancs 82 H8
Newton Lancs 89 P11
Newton Lincs 67 P5
Newton Mdloth 115 P7
Newton Moray 139 M3
Newton Moray 139 Q3
Newton N York 92 H12
Newton Nhants 55 L4
Newton Norfk 70 B9
Newton Notts 66 H4
Newton Nthumb 100 D5

182 Newton – Out Newton

Newton Nthumb 108 F8
Newton S Lans 106 B3
Newton S Lans 114 C9
Newton Sandw 53 J2
Newton Shrops 63 M5
Newton Somset 20 H6
Newton Staffs 65 J7
Newton Suffk 46 G3
Newton W Loth 115 K6
Newton Warwks 54 E5
Newton Wilts 24 C9
Newton Abbot Devon 8 F10
Newton Arlosh Cumb 97 P7
Newton Aycliffe Dur 91 M2
Newton Bewley Hartpl 91 Q1
Newton Blossomville M Keyn 55 M10
Newton Bromswold Nhants 55 P7
Newton Burgoland Leics 66 B10
Newton-by-the-Sea Nthumb 109 L5
Newton by Toft Lincs 79 P6
Newton Ferrers Devon 5 J7
Newton Ferry W Isls 152 c7
Newton Flotman Norfk 59 J1
Newtongrange Mdloth 115 P8
Newton Green Mons 28 G4
Newton Harcourt Leics 54 G1
Newton Heath Manch 76 G4
Newtonhill Abers 133 L5
Newton Hill Wakefd 85 L10
Newton-in-Bowland Lancs 83 Q5
Newton Kyme N York 85 P6
Newton-le-Willows N York 91 L9
Newton-le-Willows St Hel 75 Q4
Newtonloan Mdloth 115 P8
Newton Longville Bucks 44 B5
Newton Mearns E Rens 113 Q10
Newtonmill Angus 132 F11
Newtonmore Highld 130 C4
Newton Morrell N York 91 L5
Newton Mountain Pembks 37 J9
Newton Mulgrave N York 92 F4
Newton of Balcanquhal P & K 124 D10
Newton of Balcormo Fife 125 K12
Newton-on-Ouse N York 85 Q3
Newton-on-Rawcliffe N York 92 G8
Newton on the Hill Shrops 63 N7
Newton-on-the-Moor Nthumb 109 K8
Newton on Trent Lincs 79 L9
Newton Poppleford Devon 9 L7
Newton Purcell Oxon 43 N5
Newton Regis Warwks 65 P10
Newton Reigny Cumb 98 F12
Newton St Cyres Devon 8 G5
Newton St Faith Norfk 71 J8
Newton St Loe BaNES 29 L9
Newton St Petrock Devon 18 H11
Newton Solney Derbys 65 P7
Newton Stacey Hants 24 G5
Newton Stewart D & G 95 M5
Newton Tony Wilts 24 C5
Newton Tracey Devon 19 K8
Newton under Roseberry R & Cl 92 B4
Newton Underwood Nthumb 100 F1
Newton upon Derwent E R Yk 86 D5
Newton Valence Hants 25 M7
Newton Wamphray D & G 106 E10
Newton with Scales Lancs 83 K9
Newtown BCP 11 P6
Newtown Blae G 40 A9
Newtown Ches W 75 N8
Newtown Cnwll 2 F8
Newtown Cnwll 7 K9
Newtown Cumb 89 N2
Newtown Cumb 97 M8
Newtown Cumb 98 E6
Newtown Cumb 99 G6
Newtown D & G 105 P8
Newtown Derbys 77 J7
Newtown Devon 9 K5
Newtown Devon 19 P8
Newtown Dorset 10 D4
New Town Dorset 11 N3
New Town Dorset 23 L10
New Town Dorset 23 L9
New Town E Susx 15 N7
Newtown Gloucs 41 K11
Newtown Hants 12 D3
Newtown Hants 25 K10
Newtown Hants 31 K9
Newtown Herefs 40 H5
Newtown Herefs 41 J3
Newtown Herefs 51 N9
Newtown Highld 129 L3
Newtown IoW 12 G6
New Town Nhants 55 N5
Newtown Nthumb 108 F3
Newtown Nthumb 108 G5
Newtown Nthumb 108 G9
Newtown Powys 50 F2
Newtown Rhondd 27 P3
Newtown Shrops 63 M7
Newtown Shrops 63 N6
Newtown Somset 21 L10
Newtown Staffs 65 J11
Newtown Staffs 76 G11
Newtown Wigan 75 P3
Newtown Wilts 23 K7
New Town Wilts 30 G8
Newtown Wilts 30 G9
Newtown Worcs 52 G9
Newtown Worcs 52 H5
Newtown-in-St Martin Cnwll 3 J10
Newtown Linford Leics 66 E10
Newtown of Beltrees Rens 113 M9
Newtown St Boswells Border 107 P3
Newtown Unthank Leics 66 E11
New Tredegar Caerph 39 Q11
New Trows S Lans 105 Q2
New Tupton Derbys 78 C10
Newtyle Angus 124 F5
New Walsoken Cambs 69 J10
New Waltham NE Lin 80 F3
New Whittington Derbys 78 C8
New Winton E Loth 116 B7
New Yatt Oxon 42 H9
Newyears Green Gt Lon 32 F5
Newyork Ag & B 120 H10
New York Lincs 68 E1
New York N Tyne 101 J4
New York N York 85 J3
Nextend Herefs 51 K9
Neyland Pembks 37 J9
Niarbyl IoM 102 b6
Nibley Gloucs 41 K10
Nibley S Glos 29 L6
Nibley Green Gloucs 29 L3
Nicholashayne Devon 20 H10
Nicholaston Swans 26 D5
Nickies Hill Cumb 98 G5
Nidd N York 85 L3
Nigg C Aber 133 M4
Nigg Highld 146 E10
Nigg Ferry Highld 146 E11
Nimlet BaNES 29 M8
Ninebanks Nthumb 99 M7
Nine Elms Swindn 30 C5
Nine Wells Pembks 36 F5
Ninfield E Susx 16 C8
Ningwood IoW 12 F7
Nisbet Border 107 Q5
Nisbet Hill Border 116 H11
Niton IoW 12 H9
Nitshill C Glas 113 P9
Noah's Ark Kent 33 Q10
Noak Bridge Essex 34 C4
Noak Hill Gt Lon 33 P3
Noblethorpe Barns 77 P3
Nobold Shrops 63 M10
Nobottle Nhants 54 H8
Nocton Lincs 79 Q11
Nogdam End Norfk 71 M12
Noke Oxon 43 L9
Nolton Pembks 36 G7
Nolton Haven Pembks 36 G7
No Man's Heath Ches W 63 N3
No Man's Heath Warwks 65 P10
No Man's Land Cnwll 4 D5
Nomansland Devon 20 C10
Nomansland Wilts 24 D10
Noneley Shrops 63 N6
Nonington Kent 35 N11
Nook Cumb 89 N10
Nook Cumb 98 F2
Norbiton Gt Lon 32 H8
Norbreck Bpool 82 H7
Norbridge Herefs 41 L3
Norbury Ches E 63 P3
Norbury Derbys 65 L4
Norbury Gt Lon 33 K8
Norbury Shrops 51 L2
Norbury Staffs 64 E7
Norbury Common Ches E 63 P2
Norbury Junction Staffs 64 E7
Norchard Worcs 52 F7
Norcott Brook Ches W 75 Q7
Norcross Lancs 82 H7
Nordelph Norfk 69 K12
Norden Rochdl 84 C12
Nordley Shrops 52 C1
Norfolk Broads Norfk 71 P10
Norham Nthumb 117 K11
Norland Town Calder 84 G10
Norley Ches W 75 P9
Norleywood Hants 12 F5
Norlington E Susx 15 N8
Normanby Lincs 79 P6
Normanby N Linc 86 G12
Normanby N York 92 E10
Normanby R & Cl 92 B3
Normanby le Wold Lincs 80 C5
Norman Cross Cambs 56 C2
Normandy Surrey 32 D12
Normans Bay E Susx 16 B9
Norman's Green Devon 9 K4
Normanton C Derb 65 Q5
Normanton Leics 67 K4
Normanton Notts 66 H1
Normanton RutInd 67 M11
Normanton Wakefd 85 M10
Normanton Wilts 23 P5
Normanton le Heath Leics 66 B9
Normanton on Cliffe Lincs 67 N3
Normanton on Soar Notts 66 E7
Normanton on the Wolds Notts 66 G5
Normanton on Trent Notts 79 K10
Normoss Lancs 82 H7
Norney Surrey 14 D2
Norrington Common Wilts 29 P9
Norris Green Cnwll 4 F3
Norris Green Lpool 75 L5
Norris Hill Leics 65 Q9
Norristhorpe Kirk 85 J10
Northacre Norfk 58 E1
Northall Bucks 44 D7
Northallerton N York 91 N8
Northall Green Norfk 70 E9
Northam C Sotn 24 G11
Northam Devon 19 J7
Northampton Nhants 55 J8
Northampton Worcs 52 F7
Northampton Services Nhants 55 J9
North Anston Rothm 78 F7
North Ascot Br For 32 C8
North Aston Oxon 43 K6
Northaw Herts 45 K11
Northay Somset 9 P3
North Baddesley Hants 24 F9
North Ballachulish Highld 128 E12
North Barrow Somset 22 E7
North Barsham Norfk 70 D5
Northbay W Isls 152 b13
North Benfleet Essex 34 D4
North Berwick E Loth 116 D4
North Bitchburn Dur 100 F11
North Blyth Nthumb 101 J2
North Boarhunt Hants 13 K3
North Bockhampton BCP 12 B5
Northborough C Pete 68 C10
Northbourne Kent 35 P12
North Bovey Devon 8 D8
North Bradley Wilts 23 J2
North Brentor Devon 7 P8
North Brewham Somset 22 G6
North Bridge Surrey 14 D3
Northbridge Street E Susx 16 C6
Northbrook Hants 24 H5
Northbrook Oxon 43 K7
North Brook End Cambs 45 K3
North Buckland Devon 19 J5
North Burlingham Norfk 71 M10
North Cadbury Somset 22 E8
North Carlton Lincs 79 N8
North Carlton Notts 78 F7
North Cave E R Yk 86 G8
North Cerney Gloucs 42 B10
North Chailey E Susx 15 M6
Northchapel W Susx 14 D5
North Charford Hants 24 C9
North Charlton Nthumb 109 K5
North Cheam Gt Lon 33 J9
North Cheriton Somset 22 F8
North Chideock Dorset 10 C6
Northchurch Herts 44 D10
North Cliffe E R Yk 86 G8
North Clifton Notts 79 K9
North Close Dur 100 H11
North Cockerington Lincs 80 G5
North Connel Ag & B 120 G6
North Cornelly Brdgnd 27 K6
North Corner Cnwll 3 K10
North Cotes Lincs 80 G4
Northcott Devon 7 L6
Northcott Devon 9 L3
Northcott Devon 20 H11
North Country Cnwll 2 H6
Northcourt Oxon 31 K3
North Cove Suffk 59 P3
North Cowton N York 91 M6
North Crawley M Keyn 44 C3
North Cray Gt Lon 33 N8
North Creake Norfk 70 C4
North Curry Somset 21 M8
North Dalton E R Yk 86 H5
North Deighton N York 85 N5
Northdown Kent 35 Q8
North Downs 34 G11
North Duffield N York 86 C8
Northedge Derbys 78 B10
North Elham Kent 17 L2
North Elkington Lincs 80 F5
North Elmham Norfk 70 E8
North Elmsall Wakefd 78 D1
Northend Bucks 31 Q4
North End C Port 13 L4
North End Cumb 98 C6
North End Dorset 23 J8
North End E R Yk 87 M7
North End E R Yk 87 P9
North End Essex 46 B8
North End Hants 23 N10
North End Hants 25 K7
North End Leics 66 F9
North End Lincs 68 E4
North End Lincs 79 P10
North End Lincs 80 F3
North End Lincs 80 H6
North End N Linc 87 L10
North End N Som 28 F9
North End Nhants 55 N7
North End Norfk 58 E2
North End Nthumb 109 J9
North End Sefton 75 J3
North End W Susx 14 D10
North End W Susx 14 G9
Northend Warwks 54 C10
Northenden Manch 76 F6
Northend Woods Bucks 32 C4
North Erradale Highld 143 K9
North Evington C Leic 66 G11
North Fambridge Essex 34 E3
North Featherstone Wakefd 85 N11
North Ferriby E R Yk 87 J10
Northfield Birm 53 J5
Northfield C Aber 133 L3
Northfield E R Yk 87 J10
Northfields Lincs 67 P10
Northfleet Kent 34 B7
North Frodingham E R Yk 87 L5
North Gorley Hants 12 B2
North Green Norfk 59 J3
North Green Suffk 59 L8
North Green Suffk 59 M7
North Greetwell Lincs 79 P9
North Grimston N York 86 F2
North Halling Medway 34 C9
North Haven Shet 147 h10
North Hayling Hants 13 M4
North Hazelrigg Nthumb 108 H3
North Heasley Devon 19 P7
North Heath W Susx 14 F6
North Hele Devon 20 G8
North Hill Cnwll 7 K9
North Hillingdon Gt Lon 32 F5
North Hinksey Village Oxon 43 K10
North Holmwood Surrey 14 H1
North Huish Devon 5 L5
North Hykeham Lincs 79 N10
Northiam E Susx 16 E6
Northill C Beds 44 G2
Northington Gloucs 41 L10
Northington Hants 25 J6
North Kelsey Lincs 79 P3
North Kessock Highld 138 B6
North Killingholme N Linc 87 L11
North Kilvington N York 91 P9
North Kilworth Leics 54 G4
North Kingston Hants 12 B4
North Kyme Lincs 68 C2
North Lancing W Susx 14 H9
North Landing E R Yk 93 P12
Northlands Lincs 68 G2
Northleach Gloucs 42 D9
North Lee Bucks 44 B10
North Lees N York 91 M12
Northleigh Devon 9 M5
Northleigh Devon 19 L6
North Leigh Kent 17 K1
North Leigh Oxon 42 H9
North Leverton with Habblesthorpe Notts 79 K7
Northlew Devon 7 P5
North Littleton Worcs 53 K11
Northload Bridge Somset 22 C5
North Lopham Norfk 58 F4
North Luffenham RutInd 67 M11
North Marden W Susx 25 P9
North Marston Bucks 43 Q7
North Middleton Mdloth 115 Q9
North Middleton Nthumb 108 G5
North Millbrex Abers 141 K7
North Milmain D & G 94 F7
North Molton Devon 19 P7
Northmoor Oxon 43 J11
North Moreton Oxon 31 M4
Northmuir Angus 124 H2
North Mundham W Susx 14 C10
North Muskham Notts 79 K12
North Newbald E R Yk 86 G8
North Newington Oxon 43 J4
North Newnton Wilts 30 D11
North Newton Somset 21 L7
Northney Hants 13 M4
North Nibley Gloucs 29 L3
North Oakley Hants 25 J3
North Ockendon Gt Lon 33 Q5
Northolt Gt Lon 32 G5
Northolt Airport Gt Lon 32 G5
Northop Flints 74 H10
Northop Hall Flints 75 J10
North Ormesby Middsb 92 A3
North Ormsby Lincs 80 F5
Northorpe Kirk 85 J11
Northorpe Lincs 68 B8
Northorpe Lincs 68 D5
Northorpe Lincs 79 M4
North Otterington N York 91 N9
Northover Somset 22 B6
Northover Somset 22 C8
North Owersby Lincs 79 Q5
Northowram Calder 84 H10
North Perrott Somset 10 D3
North Petherton Somset 21 L7
North Petherwin Cnwll 7 K7
North Pickenham Norfk 70 C10
North Piddle Worcs 53 J10
North Poorton Dorset 10 D5
Northport Dorset 11 M7
North Poulner Hants 12 B3
North Queensferry Fife 115 L5
North Radworthy Devon 19 P6
North Rauceby Lincs 67 P3
Northrepps Norfk 71 K4
North Reston Lincs 80 G7
North Rigton N York 85 L5
North Ripley Hants 12 B5
North Rode Ches E 76 G10
North Ronaldsay Ork 147 f1
North Ronaldsay Airport Ork 147 f1
North Row Cumb 97 P11
North Runcton Norfk 69 M9
North Scale Cumb 82 F1
North Scarle Lincs 79 L10
North Seaton Nthumb 100 H1
North Seaton Colliery Nthumb 100 H1
North Shian Ag & B 120 G4
North Shields N Tyne 101 J4
North Shoebury Sthend 34 G5
North Shore Bpool 82 H8
North Side C Pete 68 E12
North Side Cumb 97 K10
North Skelton R & Cl 92 D3
North Somercotes Lincs 80 H4
North Stainley N York 91 M11
North Stainmore Cumb 90 D4
North Stifford Thurr 33 R6
North Stoke BaNES 29 L8
North Stoke Oxon 31 M5
North Stoke W Susx 14 E8
Northstowe Cambs 56 H7
North Street Cambs 57 L7
North Street Hants 23 P9
North Street Hants 25 L6
North Street Kent 34 H10
North Street Medway 34 E7
North Street W Berk 31 N8
North Sunderland Nthumb 109 K3
North Tamerton Cnwll 7 K5
North Tawton Devon 8 C4
North Third Stirlg 114 D3
North Thoresby Lincs 80 F4
North Togston Nthumb 109 L9
North Tolsta W Isls 152 h2
Northton W Isls 152 d6
North Town Devon 7 P3
North Town Somset 22 D5
North Town W & M 32 C6
North Tuddenham Norfk 70 F9
North Uist W Isls 152 b8
Northumberland National Park Nthumb 99 M2
North Walbottle N u Ty 100 F5
North Walsham Norfk 71 K6
North Waltham Hants 25 J4
North Warnborough Hants 25 M3
Northway Somset 21 J7
North Weald Bassett Essex 45 P11
North Wheatley Notts 79 J6
North Whilborough Devon 5 P3
Northwich Ches W 76 C9
North Wick BaNES 29 J9
Northwick S Glos 28 H5
Northwick Somset 21 M4
Northwick Worcs 52 F9
North Widcombe BaNES 28 H10
North Willingham Lincs 80 C6
North Wingfield Derbys 78 C10
North Witham Lincs 67 M8
Northwold Norfk 57 P1
Northwood C Stke 64 G2
Northwood Derbys 77 P10
Northwood Gt Lon 32 F4
Northwood IoW 12 H6
Northwood Shrops 63 M5
Northwood Green Gloucs 41 L8
North Wootton Dorset 22 E10
North Wootton Norfk 69 M7
North Wootton Somset 22 D5
North Wraxall Wilts 29 N7
North Wroughton Swindn 30 D6
North York Moors National Park 92 F6
Norton Donc 85 Q12
Norton E Susx 15 N10
Norton Gloucs 41 P7
Norton Halton 75 P7
Norton Hants 24 H5
Norton Herts 45 J5
Norton IoW 12 E7
Norton Mons 40 G7
Norton N Som 28 D9
Norton Nhants 54 F8
Norton Notts 78 F9
Norton Powys 51 J7
Norton S on T 91 Q2
Norton Sheff 78 B7
Norton Shrops 51 M4
Norton Shrops 52 B4
Norton Shrops 63 P11
Norton Shrops 64 D12
Norton Suffk 58 D7
Norton Swans 26 F5
Norton W Susx 14 C9
Norton Wilts 29 P5
Norton Worcs 52 G10
Norton Worcs 53 K11
Norton Bavant Wilts 23 K5
Norton Bridge Staffs 64 F6
Norton Canes Staffs 65 J10
Norton Canes Services Staffs 65 J10
Norton Canon Herefs 40 E2
Norton Corner Norfk 70 G6
Norton Disney Lincs 79 M11
Norton Ferris Wilts 22 H6
Norton Fitzwarren Somset 21 K8
Norton Green IoW 12 E7
Norton Hawkfield BaNES 29 J9
Norton Heath Essex 45 R10
Norton in Hales Shrops 64 D4
Norton-Juxta-Twycross Leics 65 Q10
Norton-le-Clay N York 85 N1
Norton-le-Moors C Stke 64 G2
Norton Lindsey Warwks 53 N8
Norton Little Green Suffk 58 E7
Norton Malreward BaNES 29 J9
Norton Mandeville Essex 45 Q10
Norton-on-Derwent N York 86 E1
Norton St Philip Somset 22 H2
Norton Subcourse Norfk 59 N1
Norton sub Hamdon Somset 21 P10
Norton Wood Herefs 51 L11
Norwell Notts 79 K11
Norwell Woodhouse Notts 79 J11
Norwich Norfk 71 J10
Norwich Airport Norfk 71 J9
Norwick Shet 147 k2
Norwood Clacks 114 F3
Norwood Derbys 78 D7
Norwood Kent 17 J5
Norwood End Essex 45 Q10
Norwood Green Calder 84 H10
Norwood Green Gt Lon 32 G6
Norwood Hill Surrey 15 J2
Norwoodside Cambs 56 H1
Noseley Leics 55 J1
Noss Mayo Devon 5 J7
Nosterfield N York 91 M10
Nosterfield End Cambs 46 B3
Nostie Highld 135 Q10
Notgrove Gloucs 42 C7
Nottage Brdgnd 27 K7
Notter Cnwll 4 F4
Nottingham C Nott 66 F4
Nottington Dorset 10 G8
Notton Wakefd 77 Q1
Notton Wilts 29 P8
Nounsley Essex 46 D9
Noutard's Green Worcs 52 E7
Nowton Suffk 58 C8
Nox Shrops 63 L10
Nuffield Oxon 31 N5
Nunburnholme E R Yk 86 F6
Nuncargate Notts 66 E1
Nunclose Cumb 98 F9
Nuneaton Warwks 54 B2
Nuneham Courtenay Oxon 31 L2
Nunhead Gt Lon 33 L7
Nunkeeling E R Yk 87 L5
Nun Monkton N York 85 Q4
Nunney Somset 22 G4
Nunney Catch Somset 22 G4
Nunnington Herefs 40 H3
Nunnington N York 92 D11
Nunsthorpe NE Lin 80 E2
Nunthorpe C York 86 B5
Nunthorpe Middsb 92 B4
Nunthorpe Village Middsb 92 B4
Nunton Wilts 23 P8
Nunwick N York 91 N11
Nunwick Nthumb 99 N3
Nupdown S Glos 29 J3
Nup End Bucks 44 B8
Nupend Gloucs 41 M10
Nuptown Br For 32 C7
Nursling Hants 24 F10
Nursted Hants 25 N9
Nursteed Wilts 30 B10
Nurton Staffs 64 F12
Nutbourne W Susx 13 N4
Nutbourne W Susx 14 F7
Nutfield Surrey 33 K12
Nuthall Notts 66 E3
Nuthampstead Herts 45 M5
Nuthurst W Susx 14 H6
Nutley E Susx 15 N5
Nutley Hants 25 K4
Nuttall Bury 84 B12
Nutwell Donc 78 G3
Nybster Highld 151 Q4
Nyetimber W Susx 14 C11
Nyewood W Susx 25 P9
Nymans W Susx 15 K5
Nymet Rowland Devon 8 D3
Nymet Tracey Devon 8 D5
Nympsfield Gloucs 29 N2
Nynehead Somset 21 J9
Nythe Somset 21 P6
Nyton W Susx 14 D9

O

Oadby Leics 66 G12
Oad Street Kent 34 F10
Oakall Green Worcs 52 E8
Oakamoor Staffs 65 K3
Oakbank W Loth 115 K8
Oak Cross Devon 7 Q5
Oakdale Caerph 28 B3
Oake Somset 21 J8
Oaken Staffs 64 F11
Oakenclough Lancs 83 M6
Oakengates Wrekin 64 C10
Oakenholt Flints 75 J9
Oakenshaw Dur 100 F10
Oakenshaw Kirk 85 J9
Oakerthorpe Derbys 66 C1
Oakford Cerdgn 48 G9
Oakford Devon 20 E9
Oakfordbridge Devon 20 E9
Oakgrove Ches E 76 G10
Oakham RutInd 67 L10
Oakhanger Ches E 64 E1
Oakhanger Hants 25 N6
Oakhill Somset 22 E4
Oakhurst Kent 33 Q12
Oakington Cambs 56 H8
Oaklands Powys 50 E10
Oakle Street Gloucs 41 M8
Oakley BCP 11 N5
Oakley Bed 55 P10
Oakley Bucks 43 N9
Oakley Fife 115 J3
Oakley Hants 25 J3
Oakley Oxon 31 Q2
Oakley Suffk 58 H5
Oakley Green W & M 32 C7
Oakley Park Powys 50 D3
Oakridge Lynch Gloucs 41 Q11
Oaks Lancs 83 P8
Oaks Shrops 63 M11
Oaksey Wilts 30 A4
Oaks Green Derbys 65 M5
Oakshaw Ford Cumb 98 G3
Oakshott Hants 25 N8
Oakthorpe Leics 65 Q9
Oak Tree Darltn 91 N4
Oakwood C Derb 66 B4
Oakwood Nthumb 99 P5
Oakworth C Brad 84 F7
Oare Kent 34 H9
Oare Somset 20 C4
Oare Wilts 30 D9
Oasby Lincs 67 P4
Oath Somset 21 N8
Oathlaw Angus 125 J2
Oatlands Park Surrey 32 F9
Oban Ag & B 120 F7
Oban Airport Ag & B 120 G6
Obley Shrops 51 K5
Obney P & K 123 P5
Oborne Dorset 22 E9
Obthorpe Lincs 68 B9
Occold Suffk 58 H6
Occumster Highld 151 N9
Ochiltree E Ayrs 105 J5
Ockbrook Derbys 66 C5
Ocker Hill Sandw 52 H2
Ockeridge Worcs 52 E8
Ockham Surrey 32 F11
Ockle Highld 127 K10
Ockley Surrey 14 G3
Ocle Pychard Herefs 41 J2
Octon E R Yk 87 J1
Odcombe Somset 22 C10
Odd Down BaNES 29 M10
Oddendale Cumb 89 P4
Oddingley Worcs 52 G9
Oddington Gloucs 42 E6
Oddington Oxon 43 L8
Odell Bed 55 N9
Odham Devon 7 N4
Odiham Hants 25 N3
Odsal C Brad 84 H9
Odsey Cambs 45 K4
Odstock Wilts 23 P8
Odstone Leics 66 C10
Offchurch Warwks 54 B7
Offenham Worcs 42 B2
Offerton Stockp 76 G6
Offerton Sundld 101 J7
Offham E Susx 15 M8
Offham Kent 34 B11
Offham W Susx 14 E9
Offleymarsh Staffs 64 E6
Offord Cluny Cambs 56 D7
Offord D'Arcy Cambs 56 D7
Offton Suffk 58 F10
Offwell Devon 9 M5
Ogbourne Maizey Wilts 30 E8
Ogbourne St Andrew Wilts 30 E8
Ogbourne St George Wilts 30 E7
Ogden Calder 84 G9
Ogle Nthumb 100 E2
Oglet Lpool 75 M7
Ogmore V Glam 27 L7
Ogmore-by-Sea V Glam 27 K7
Ogmore Vale Brdgnd 27 M4
Ogwen Bank Gwynd 73 K10
Okeford Fitzpaine Dorset 11 K3
Okehampton Devon 8 B6
Oker Side Derbys 77 P11
Okewood Hill Surrey 14 G3
Olchard Devon 8 G9
Old Nhants 55 K6
Old Aberdeen C Aber 133 M3
Old Alresford Hants 25 K6
Oldany Highld 148 D10
Old Auchenbrack D & G 105 P10
Old Basford C Nott 66 F3
Old Basing Hants 25 L3
Old Beetley Norfk 70 E8
Oldberrow Warwks 53 L7
Old Bewick Nthumb 108 H5
Old Bolingbroke Lincs 80 G10
Old Bramhope Leeds 85 K6
Old Brampton Derbys 77 Q9
Old Bridge of Urr D & G 96 F5
Old Buckenham Norfk 58 F2
Old Burghclere Hants 31 K10
Oldbury Kent 33 Q11
Oldbury Sandw 53 J3
Oldbury Shrops 52 D2
Oldbury Warwks 53 P2
Oldbury Naite S Glos 29 J4
Oldbury-on-Severn S Glos 29 J4
Oldbury on the Hill Gloucs 29 N5
Old Byland N York 92 B9
Old Cantley Donc 78 G3
Old Cassop Dur 101 J10
Oldcastle Mons 40 D7
Oldcastle Heath Ches W 63 N3
Old Catton Norfk 71 J9
Old Churchstoke Powys 51 J2
Old Clee NE Lin 80 F2
Old Cleeve Somset 20 G5
Old Colwyn Conwy 73 Q8
Oldcotes Notts 78 F6
Old Coulsdon Gt Lon 33 K10
Old Dailly S Ayrs 104 D10
Old Dalby Leics 66 H7
Old Dam Derbys 77 L8
Old Deer Abers 141 N6
Old Ditch Somset 22 C3
Old Edlington Donc 78 E4
Old Eldon Dur 91 L1
Old Ellerby E R Yk 87 M7
Old Felixstowe Suffk 47 P4
Oldfield C Brad 84 F7
Oldfield Worcs 52 F7
Old Fletton C Pete 56 D1
Oldford Somset 22 H3
Old Forge Herefs 40 H8
Old Furnace Herefs 40 G7
Old Glossop Derbys 77 K5
Old Goole E R Yk 86 D10
Old Grimsby IoS 2 b1
Old Hall Green Herts 45 L7
Oldhall Green Suffk 58 C9
Old Hall Street Norfk 71 L5
Oldham Oldham 76 G3
Oldhamstocks E Loth 116 G7
Old Harlow Essex 45 N9
Old Heath Essex 46 H7
Old Hunstanton Norfk 69 N4
Old Hurst Cambs 56 F5
Old Hutton Cumb 89 P9
Old Inns Services N Lans 114 D6
Old Kea Cnwll 3 L6
Old Kilpatrick W Duns 113 N7
Old Knebworth Herts 45 J7
Old Lakenham Norfk 71 J11
Oldland S Glos 29 K8
Old Langho Lancs 83 Q8
Old Laxey IoM 102 f5
Old Leake Lincs 68 H2
Old Malton N York 92 G12
Oldmeldrum Abers 141 K10
Oldmill Cnwll 7 L10
Old Milverton Warwks 53 P7
Oldmixon N Som 28 D10
Old Newton Suffk 58 F8
Old Oxted Surrey 33 M12
Old Portlethen Abers 133 M5
Old Quarrington Dur 101 J10
Old Radford C Nott 66 F4
Old Radnor Powys 50 H9
Old Rayne Abers 140 G10
Old Romney Kent 17 J6
Old Shoreham W Susx 15 J9
Oldshoremore Highld 148 E5
Old Soar Kent 34 A11
Old Sodbury S Glos 29 M6
Old Somerby Lincs 67 N5
Oldstead N York 92 B10
Old Stratford Nhants 43 Q3
Old Struan P & K 130 E11
Old Swarland Nthumb 109 K9
Old Swinford Dudley 52 G4
Old Tebay Cumb 89 Q6
Old Thirsk N York 91 Q10
Old Town Calder 84 F9
Old Town Cumb 89 P10
Old Town Cumb 98 F9
Old Town E Susx 15 Q11
Old Town IoS 2 b2
Old Trafford Traffd 76 F4
Old Tupton Derbys 78 C10
Oldwall Cumb 98 F6
Oldwalls Swans 26 D4
Old Warden C Beds 44 G3
Oldways End Somset 20 D8
Old Weston Cambs 56 B5
Old Wick Highld 151 Q7
Old Windsor W & M 32 D7
Old Wives Lees Kent 35 J11
Old Woking Surrey 32 E11
Old Wolverton M Keyn 44 A3
Old Woodhall Lincs 80 D10
Old Woods Shrops 63 M8
Olgrinmore Highld 151 K6
Olive Green Staffs 65 L8
Oliver's Battery Hants 24 G8
Ollaberry Shet 147 i4
Ollach Highld 135 J8
Ollerton Ches E 76 E8
Ollerton Notts 78 G10
Ollerton Shrops 64 C7
Olmarch Cerdgn 49 K9
Olmstead Green Cambs 46 A3
Olney M Keyn 55 M10
Olrig House Highld 151 M3
Olton Solhll 53 L4
Olveston S Glos 29 J5
Ombersley Worcs 52 F8
Ompton Notts 78 H10
Once Brewed Nthumb 99 L5
Onchan IoM 102 e5
Onecote Staffs 65 K1
Onehouse Suffk 58 F9
Onen Mons 40 F9
Ongar Street Herefs 51 L7
Onibury Shrops 51 M5
Onich Highld 128 E12
Onllwyn Neath 39 K9
Onneley Staffs 64 D4
Onslow Green Essex 46 B8
Onslow Village Surrey 14 D1
Onston Ches W 75 Q9
Openwoodgate Derbys 66 B3
Opinan Highld 143 K10
Orbliston Moray 139 P4
Orbost Highld 134 D7
Orby Lincs 81 J10
Orchard Portman Somset 21 K9
Orcheston Wilts 23 N4
Orcop Herefs 40 G6
Orcop Hill Herefs 40 G6
Ord Abers 140 F4
Ordhead Abers 132 G2
Ordie Abers 132 C4
Ordiequish Moray 139 Q4
Ordley Nthumb 99 Q6
Ordsall Notts 78 H8
Ore E Susx 16 E8
Oreleton Common Herefs 51 N7
Oreton Shrops 52 C4
Orford Suffk 59 N10
Orford Warrtn 75 Q5
Organford Dorset 11 M6
Orgreave Staffs 65 L9
Orkney Islands Ork 147 c4
Orkney Neolithic Ork 147 b4
Orlestone Kent 16 H4
Orleton Herefs 51 N7
Orleton Worcs 52 C7
Orlingbury Nhants 55 L6
Ormathwaite Cumb 88 H2
Ormesby R & Cl 92 B3
Ormesby St Margaret Norfk 71 P9
Ormesby St Michael Norfk 71 P9
Ormiscaig Highld 143 M7
Ormiston E Loth 116 A7
Ormsaigmore Highld 126 H11
Ormsary Ag & B 111 Q7
Ormskirk Lancs 75 L2
Ornsby Hill Dur 100 F8
Oronsay Ag & B 110 H3
Orphir Ork 147 b5
Orpington Gt Lon 33 N9
Orrell Sefton 75 K4
Orrell Wigan 75 P3
Orrell Post Wigan 75 P3
Orrisdale IoM 102 d3
Orroland D & G 96 F9
Orsett Thurr 34 B6
Orsett Heath Thurr 34 B6
Orslow Staffs 64 E9
Orston Notts 67 J4
Orthwaite Cumb 97 Q11
Ortner Lancs 83 M4
Orton Cumb 89 Q5
Orton Nhants 55 K5
Orton Staffs 52 F2
Orton Longueville C Pete 56 D1
Orton-on-the-Hill Leics 65 P11
Orton Rigg Cumb 98 D8
Orton Waterville C Pete 56 C1
Orwell Cambs 56 G10
Osbaldeston Lancs 83 P9
Osbaldeston Green Lancs 83 P8
Osbaldwick C York 86 B5
Osbaston Leics 66 C11
Osbaston Shrops 63 K7
Osborne IoW 12 H6
Osborne House IoW 13 J6
Osbournby Lincs 67 Q4
Oscroft Ches W 75 N10
Ose Highld 134 F7
Osgathorpe Leics 66 C8
Osgodby Lincs 79 Q5
Osgodby N York 86 B8
Osgodby N York 93 L10
Oskaig Highld 135 K8
Oskamull Ag & B 119 M5
Osmaston Derbys 65 M3
Osmington Dorset 10 H8
Osmington Mills Dorset 10 H8
Osmondthorpe Leeds 85 L8
Osmotherley N York 91 Q7
Osney Oxon 43 K10
Ospringe Kent 34 H10
Ossett Wakefd 85 K11
Ossington Notts 79 J10
Ostend Essex 34 G3
Osterley Gt Lon 32 H7
Oswaldkirk N York 92 C11
Oswaldtwistle Lancs 83 Q9
Oswestry Shrops 63 J6
Otford Kent 33 P10
Otham Kent 34 D11
Otham Hole Kent 34 E11
Othery Somset 21 N7
Otley Leeds 85 J6
Otley Suffk 59 J9
Otley Green Suffk 59 J9
Otterbourne Hants 24 G9
Otterburn N York 84 C4
Otterburn Nthumb 108 E11
Otter Ferry Ag & B 112 D4
Otterham Cnwll 6 H6
Otterhampton Somset 21 L5
Otterham Quay Kent 34 E9
Otterham Station Cnwll 6 H7
Otternish W Isls 152 c7
Ottershaw Surrey 32 E9
Otterswick Shet 147 j4
Otterton Devon 9 K7
Otterwood Hants 12 G4
Ottery St Mary Devon 9 L5
Ottinge Kent 17 L2
Ottringham E R Yk 87 P10
Oughterby Cumb 98 C7
Oughtershaw N York 90 E10
Oughterside Cumb 97 M10
Oughtibridge Sheff 77 P5
Oughtrington Warrtn 76 C6
Oulston N York 92 B12
Oulton Cumb 97 Q8
Oulton Leeds 85 M9
Oulton Norfk 70 H6
Oulton Staffs 64 E7
Oulton Staffs 64 H4
Oulton Suffk 59 Q2
Oulton Broad Suffk 59 Q2
Oulton Street Norfk 70 H7
Oundle Nhants 55 P3
Ounsdale Staffs 52 F2
Our Dynamic Earth C Edin 115 N6
Ousby Cumb 99 J11
Ousden Suffk 57 P8
Ousefleet E R Yk 86 F10
Ouston Dur 100 H7
Outchester Nthumb 109 J3
Out Elmstead Kent 35 M12
Outgate Cumb 89 K7
Outhgill Cumb 90 C6
Outhill Warwks 53 L7
Outlands Staffs 64 E6
Outlane Kirk 84 G11
Out Newton E R Yk 87 R11

Place	Region	Page	Grid
Stoney Stretton	Shrops	63	L10
Stoneywood	C Aber	133	L2
Stoneywood	Falk	114	E5
Stonham Aspal	Suffk	58	H8
Stonnall	Staffs	65	K11
Stonor	Oxon	31	Q5
Stonton Wyville	Leics	54	F3
Stony Cross	Herefs	51	P7
Stony Cross	Herefs	52	D11
Stonyford	Hants	24	E10
Stony Houghton	Derbys	78	E10
Stony Stratford	M Keyn	43	R4
Stonywell	Staffs	65	K9
Stoodleigh	Devon	19	M7
Stoodleigh	Devon	20	E9
Stop 24 Services	Kent	17	K3
Stopham	W Susx	14	E7
Stopsley	Luton	44	E7
Stoptide	Cnwll	6	D9
Storeton	Wirral	75	J7
Storeyard Green	Herefs	41	M7
Storey Arms	Powys	39	M7
Stornoway	W Isls	152	g3
Stornoway Airport	W Isls	152	g3
Storridge	Herefs	52	D11
Storrington	W Susx	14	F8
Storth	Cumb	89	M10
Storwood	E R Yk	86	D6
Stotfield	Moray	147	M11
Stotfold	C Beds	45	J4
Stottesdon	Shrops	52	C4
Stoughton	Leics	66	G11
Stoughton	Surrey	32	D12
Stoughton	W Susx	13	P2
Stoulton	Worcs	52	H11
Stourbridge	Dudley	52	G4
Stourhead	Wilts	22	H6
Stourpaine	Dorset	11	L3
Stourport-on-Severn	Worcs	52	E6
Stour Provost	Dorset	22	H9
Stour Row	Dorset	22	H9
Stourton	Leeds	85	L9
Stourton	Staffs	52	F4
Stourton	Warwks	42	G4
Stourton	Wilts	22	H6
Stourton Caundle	Dorset	22	G10
Stout	Somset	21	P7
Stove	Shet	147	i9
Stoven	Suffk	59	N4
Stow	Border	116	B12
Stow	Lincs	79	L7
Stow Bardolph	Norfk	69	M11
Stow Bedon	Norfk	58	E1
Stowbridge	Norfk	69	L10
Stow-cum-Quy	Cambs	57	K8
Stowe	Gloucs	40	H10
Stowe	Shrops	51	K6
Stowe by Chartley	Staffs	65	J7
Stowehill	Nhants	54	G9
Stowell	Somset	22	E9
Stowey	BaNES	29	J10
Stowford	Devon	7	N5
Stowford	Devon	7	N7
Stowford	Devon	9	L7
Stowford	Devon	19	M5
Stowlangtoft	Suffk	58	E7
Stow Longa	Cambs	56	B6
Stow Maries	Essex	34	E2
Stowmarket	Suffk	58	F9
Stow-on-the-Wold	Gloucs	42	E9
Stowting	Kent	17	K2
Stowting Common	Kent	17	K2
Stowupland	Suffk	58	G8
Straanruie	Highld	131	J1
Strachan	Abers	132	G6
Strachur	Ag & B	112	D1
Stradbroke	Suffk	59	J6
Stradbrook	Wilts	23	K3
Stradishall	Suffk	57	P10
Stradsett	Norfk	69	M11
Stragglethorpe	Lincs	67	M2
Stragglethorpe	Notts	66	G5
Straight Soley	Wilts	30	G8
Straiton	Mdloth	115	M8
Straiton	S Ayrs	104	G9
Straloch	Abers	141	L11
Straloch	P & K	131	J11
Stramshall	Staffs	65	K5
Strang	IoM	102	e5
Strangeways	Salfd	76	F4
Strangford	Herefs	41	M3
Stranraer	D & G	94	F6
Strata Florida	Cerdgn	49	N7
Stratfield Mortimer	W Berk	31	N9
Stratfield Saye	Hants	31	P10
Stratfield Turgis	Hants	31	P10
Stratford	C Beds	56	E11
Stratford	Gt Lon	33	M5
Stratford St Andrew	Suffk	59	M8
Stratford St Mary	Suffk	47	J5
Stratford sub Castle	Wilts	23	P7
Stratford Tony	Wilts	23	N8
Stratford-upon-Avon	Warwks	53	M9
Strath	Highld	143	L9
Strathan	Highld	144	D1
Strathan	Highld	149	M4
Strathaven	S Lans	114	C12
Strathblane	Stirlg	113	Q5
Strathcanaird	Highld	144	E5
Strathcarron	Highld	136	C7
Strathcoil	Ag & B	120	C7
Strathdon	Abers	131	Q2
Strathkinness	Fife	125	J3
Strathloanhead	W Loth	114	G7
Strathmashie House	Highld	129	Q6
Strathmiglo	Fife	124	E11
Strathpeffer	Highld	137	N4
Strathtay	P & K	123	Q2
Strathwhillan	N Ayrs	103	Q3
Strathy	Highld	150	E3
Strathy Inn	Highld	150	E3
Strathyre	Stirlg	122	F9
Stratton	Cnwll	7	J3
Stratton	Dorset	10	G6
Stratton	Gloucs	42	B11
Stratton Audley	Oxon	43	M6
Stratton-on-the-Fosse	Somset	22	F3
Stratton St Margaret	Swindn	30	D4
Stratton St Michael	Norfk	59	J2
Stratton Strawless	Norfk	71	J8
Stream	Somset	20	G5
Streat	E Susx	15	L8
Streatham	Gt Lon	33	K8
Streatley	C Beds	44	E7
Streatley	W Berk	31	M6
Street	Devon	9	N7
Street	Lancs	83	M5
Street	N York	92	E6
Street	Somset	21	N6
Street Ashton	Warwks	54	D4
Street Dinas	Shrops	63	K4
Street End	E Susx	15	R6
Street End	Kent	35	L11
Street End	W Susx	13	N6
Street Gate	Gatesd	100	G6
Streethay	Staffs	65	L10
Street Houses	N York	85	Q6
Streetlam	N York	91	M7
Street Lane	Derbys	66	C3
Streetly	Wsall	53	K1
Streetly End	Cambs	57	L11
Street on the Fosse	Somset	22	E5
Strefford	Shrops	51	M3
Strelitz	P & K	124	D5
Strelley	Notts	66	E4
Strensall	C York	86	B3
Strensham Services (northbound)	Worcs	41	P3
Strensham Services (southbound)	Worcs	41	P3
Stretcholt	Somset	21	L4
Strete	Devon	5	P7
Stretford	Herefs	51	M9
Stretford	Herefs	51	N9
Stretford	Traffd	76	E5
Strethall	Essex	45	N4
Stretham	Cambs	57	J6
Strettington	W Susx	14	C9
Stretton	Ches W	75	M9
Stretton	Derbys	78	C11
Stretton	Rutlnd	67	N9
Stretton	Staffs	64	G10
Stretton	Staffs	65	N11
Stretton	Warrtn	76	B7
Stretton en le Field	Leics	65	P10
Stretton Grandison	Herefs	41	K3
Stretton-on-Dunsmore	Warwks	54	C6
Stretton on Fosse	Warwks	42	E4
Stretton Sugwas	Herefs	40	G3
Stretton under Fosse	Warwks	54	D4
Stretton Westwood	Shrops	51	Q1
Strichen	Abers	141	M5
Strines	Stockp	76	H6
Stringston	Somset	21	J5
Strixton	Nhants	55	M8
Stroat	Gloucs	28	H3
Strollamus	Highld	135	K10
Stroma	Highld	151	Q1
Stromeferry	Highld	136	B9
Stromness	Ork	147	b4
Stronaba	Highld	128	H7
Stronachlachar	Stirlg	122	C10
Stronafian	Ag & B	112	F5
Stronchrubie	Highld	144	J5
Strone	Ag & B	113	J5
Strone	Highld	128	G8
Strone	Highld	137	P10
Stronmilchan	Ag & B	121	M7
Stronsay	Ork	147	e3
Stronsay Airport	Ork	147	e3
Strontian	Highld	127	P12
Strood	Kent	16	E4
Strood	Medway	34	C8
Strood Green	Surrey	14	H1
Strood Green	W Susx	14	E6
Stroud	Gloucs	41	N10
Stroud	Hants	25	M8
Stroude	Surrey	32	E8
Stroud Green	Essex	34	F3
Stroud Green	Gloucs	41	N10
Stroxton	Lincs	67	M5
Struan	Highld	134	F8
Struan	P & K	130	E11
Strubby	Lincs	81	J7
Strumpshaw	Norfk	71	M10
Strutherhill	S Lans	114	D11
Struthers	Fife	124	H11
Struy	Highld	137	L8
Stryd-y-Facsen	IoA	72	E7
Stryt-issa	Wrexhm	63	J3
Stuartfield	Abers	141	N7
Stubbers Green	Wsall	65	K11
Stubbington	Hants	13	J4
Stubbins	Lancs	84	B11
Stubbs Green	Norfk	59	K1
Stubhampton	Dorset	23	K10
Stubley	Derbys	77	Q8
Stubshaw Cross	Wigan	75	N3
Stubton	Lincs	67	L2
Stuckton	Hants	23	Q10
Studfold	N York	84	B1
Stud Green	W & M	32	C7
Studham	C Beds	44	E8
Studholme	Cumb	98	D7
Studland	Dorset	11	P8
Studley	Warwks	53	K8
Studley	Wilts	29	Q8
Studley Common	Warwks	53	K8
Studley Roger	N York	85	L1
Studley Royal	N York	85	L1
Studley Royal Park & Fountains Abbey	N York	85	K2
Stuntney	Cambs	57	K5
Stunts Green	E Susx	16	A8
Sturbridge	Staffs	64	F6
Sturgate	Lincs	79	L6
Sturmer	Essex	46	C3
Sturminster Common	Dorset	22	H11
Sturminster Marshall	Dorset	11	M5
Sturminster Newton	Dorset	22	G11
Sturry	Kent	35	L10
Sturton	N York	79	N3
Sturton by Stow	Lincs	79	M7
Sturton le Steeple	Notts	79	K6
Stuston	Suffk	58	H5
Stutton	N York	85	L5
Stutton	Suffk	47	L5
Styal	Ches E	76	F7
Stydd	Lancs	83	P8
Stynie	Moray	139	Q4
Styrrup	Notts	78	G5
Succoth	Ag & B	121	P11
Suckley	Worcs	52	D10
Suckley Green	Worcs	52	D10
Sudborough	Nhants	55	N4
Sudbourne	Suffk	59	N10
Sudbrook	Lincs	67	N3
Sudbrook	Mons	28	G5
Sudbrooke	Lincs	79	P9
Sudbury	Derbys	65	M6
Sudbury	Gt Lon	32	H4
Sudbury	Suffk	46	F3
Sudden	Rochdl	76	G1
Sudgrove	Gloucs	41	Q10
Suffield	Norfk	71	K6
Suffield	N York	93	K8
Sugdon	Wrekin	64	C9
Sugnall	Staffs	64	E6
Sugwas Pool	Herefs	40	F3
Suisnish	Highld	135	K11
Sulby	IoM	102	d3
Sulgrave	Nhants	43	M3
Sulham	W Berk	31	N7
Sulhamstead	W Berk	31	N8
Sulhamstead Abbots	W Berk	31	N9
Sulhamstead Bannister	W Berk	31	N9
Sullington	W Susx	14	F8
Sullom	Shet	147	i5
Sullom Voe	Shet	147	i5
Sully	V Glam	27	N8
Sumburgh Airport	Shet	147	i10
Summerbridge	N York	85	L3
Summercourt	Cnwll	3	L3
Summerfield	Norfk	69	P4
Summerfield	Worcs	52	F6
Summerhill	Pembks	37	M9
Summerhill	Staffs	65	K11
Summer Hill	Wrexhm	63	K3
Summerhouse	Darltn	91	K3
Summerlands	Cumb	89	N9
Summerley	Derbys	78	B8
Summersdale	W Susx	14	B9
Summerseat	Bury	84	B12
Summertown	Oxon	43	L10
Summit	Oldham	76	G2
Summit	Rochdl	84	D11
Sunbiggin	Cumb	89	Q5
Sunbury-on-Thames	Surrey	32	G8
Sundaywell	D & G	96	G11
Sunderland	Cumb	97	N11
Sunderland	Lancs	83	K4
Sunderland	Sundld	101	K7
Sunderland Bridge	Dur	100	H10
Sundhope	Border	107	J5
Sundon Park	Luton	44	F6
Sundridge	Kent	33	N11
Sunk Island	E R Yk	87	P11
Sunningdale	W & M	32	D9
Sunninghill	W & M	32	D9
Sunningwell	Oxon	31	K2
Sunniside	Dur	100	F10
Sunniside	Gatesd	100	G6
Sunny Brow	Dur	100	F11
Sunnyhill	C Derb	66	A5
Sunnyhurst	Bl w D	83	P10
Sunnylaw	Stirlg	114	E2
Sunnymead	Oxon	43	L9
Sunton	Wilts	24	D2
Surbiton	Gt Lon	32	H9
Surfleet	Lincs	68	E6
Surfleet Seas End	Lincs	68	E6
Surlingham	Norfk	71	L11
Surrex	Essex	46	F7
Sustead	Norfk	71	J5
Susworth	Lincs	79	L3
Sutcombe	Devon	7	L3
Sutcombemill	Devon	7	L3
Suton	Norfk	70	G12
Sutterby	Lincs	80	H7
Sutterton	Lincs	68	F5
Sutton	C Beds	45	J2
Sutton	C Pete	68	B12
Sutton	Cambs	56	H5
Sutton	Devon	5	L8
Sutton	Donc	78	F1
Sutton	E Susx	15	J11
Sutton	Gt Lon	33	J9
Sutton	Kent	35	P12
Sutton	N York	85	P10
Sutton	Norfk	71	M7
Sutton	Notts	67	J5
Sutton	Oxon	43	J10
Sutton	Pembks	36	H7
Sutton	Shrops	52	D3
Sutton	Shrops	52	C4
Sutton	Shrops	63	N10
Sutton	Shrops	64	C8
Sutton	St Hel	75	P5
Sutton	Suffk	59	M11
Sutton	Suffk	47	P2
Sutton	W Susx	14	D8
Sutton Abinger	Surrey	14	G1
Sutton-at-Hone	Kent	33	Q8
Sutton Bassett	Nhants	55	J3
Sutton Benger	Wilts	29	Q6
Sutton Bingham	Somset	10	E3
Sutton Bonington	Notts	66	C7
Sutton Bridge	Lincs	69	J8
Sutton Cheney	Leics	66	C12
Sutton Coldfield	Birm	53	L1
Sutton Courtenay	Oxon	31	L3
Sutton Crosses	Lincs	68	H7
Sutton cum Lound	Notts	78	H7
Sutton Fields	Notts	66	C7
Sutton Green	Surrey	32	E11
Sutton Green	Wrexhm	63	L3
Sutton Howgrave	N York	91	M11
Sutton-in-Ashfield	Notts	78	D10
Sutton-in-Craven	N York	84	F6
Sutton in the Elms	Leics	54	E2
Sutton Lane Ends	Ches E	76	H9
Sutton Maddock	Shrops	64	D12
Sutton Mallet	Somset	21	N6
Sutton Mandeville	Wilts	23	L7
Sutton Manor	St Hel	75	N5
Sutton Marsh	Herefs	40	H3
Sutton Montis	Somset	22	E8
Sutton-on-Hull	C KuH	87	L8
Sutton on Sea	Lincs	81	K8
Sutton-on-the-Forest	N York	86	A2
Sutton on the Hill	Derbys	65	N5
Sutton on Trent	Notts	79	K10
Sutton Poyntz	Dorset	10	H8
Sutton St Edmund	Lincs	68	H10
Sutton St James	Lincs	68	H9
Sutton St Nicholas	Herefs	40	H3
Sutton Scotney	Hants	24	H5
Sutton Street	Kent	34	E11
Sutton-under-Brailes	Warwks	42	G4
Sutton-under-Whitestonecliffe	N York	91	Q10
Sutton upon Derwent	E R Yk	86	D6
Sutton Valence	Kent	16	E1
Sutton Veny	Wilts	23	K5
Sutton Waldron	Dorset	23	J10
Sutton Weaver	Ches W	75	N9
Sutton Wick	BaNES	29	J10
Sutton Wick	Oxon	31	K3
Swaby	Lincs	80	H6
Swadlincote	Derbys	65	P9
Swaffham	Norfk	70	B10
Swaffham Bulbeck	Cambs	57	K8
Swaffham Prior	Cambs	57	K8
Swafield	Norfk	71	K6
Swainby	N York	91	Q6
Swainshill	Herefs	40	G3
Swainsthorpe	Norfk	71	J11
Swainswick	BaNES	29	M8
Swalcliffe	Oxon	42	H4
Swalecliffe	Kent	35	J9
Swallow	Lincs	80	D3
Swallow Beck	Lincs	79	N10
Swallowcliffe	Wilts	23	L8
Swallowfield	Wokham	31	P9
Swallownest	Rothm	78	D6
Swallows Cross	Essex	33	R3
Swampton	Hants	24	H3
Swanage	Dorset	11	P9
Swanbourne	Bucks	44	A6
Swanbridge	V Glam	27	N8
Swan Green	Ches W	76	D9
Swanland	E R Yk	87	J9
Swanley	Kent	33	P9
Swanley Village	Kent	33	P9
Swanmore	Hants	25	J10
Swannington	Leics	66	C9
Swannington	Norfk	70	H8
Swanpool	Lincs	79	N10
Swanscombe	Kent	33	R7
Swansea	Swans	26	G4
Swansea Airport	Swans	26	E4
Swansea West Services	Swans	26	F2
Swan Street	Essex	46	F7
Swanton Abbot	Norfk	71	K7
Swanton Morley	Norfk	70	F8
Swanton Novers	Norfk	70	F5
Swanton Street	Kent	34	F10
Swan Valley	Nhants	55	J9
Swan Village	Sandw	52	J2
Swanwick	Derbys	66	C2
Swanwick	Hants	13	H3
Swarby	Lincs	67	P4
Swardeston	Norfk	71	J11
Swarkestone	Derbys	66	B6
Swarland	Nthumb	109	K9
Swarraton	Hants	25	J6
Swartha	C Brad	84	F6
Swarthmoor	Cumb	88	H11
Swaton	Lincs	67	Q4
Swavesey	Cambs	56	G7
Sway	Hants	12	F5
Swayfield	Lincs	67	N7
Swaythling	C Sotn	24	G10
Sweet Green	Worcs	52	C8
Sweetham	Devon	8	H5
Sweethaws	E Susx	15	P5
Sweetlands Corner	Kent	16	E2
Sweets	Cnwll	6	H5
Sweetshouse	Cnwll	3	Q2
Swefling	Suffk	59	L8
Swepstone	Leics	66	B10
Swerford	Oxon	42	H5
Swettenham	Ches E	76	E10
Swffryd	Blae G	28	B3
Swift's Green	Kent	16	F2
Swilland	Suffk	59	J10
Swillbrook	Lancs	83	L8
Swillington	Leeds	85	M9
Swimbridge	Devon	19	M7
Swimbridge Newland	Devon	19	L7
Swinbrook	Oxon	42	G9
Swincliffe	N York	85	K4
Swincombe	Devon	19	N5
Swindale	Cumb	89	N4
Swinden	N York	84	C4
Swinderby	Lincs	79	L11
Swindon	Gloucs	41	Q7
Swindon	Staffs	52	F2
Swindon	Swindn	30	D5
Swine	E R Yk	87	L8
Swinefleet	E R Yk	86	E10
Swineford	S Glos	29	L8
Swineshead	Bed	55	Q7
Swineshead	Lincs	68	C4
Swineshead Bridge	Lincs	68	D4
Swiney	Highld	151	M9
Swinford	Leics	54	F5
Swinford	Oxon	43	J10
Swingfield Minnis	Kent	17	M2
Swingfield Street	Kent	17	M2
Swingleton Green	Suffk	46	H2
Swinhoe	Nthumb	109	K4
Swinhope	Lincs	80	D4
Swinithwaite	N York	90	H8
Swinmore Common	Herefs	41	K3
Swinscoe	Staffs	65	L3
Swinside	Cumb	88	F7
Swinstead	Lincs	67	P7
Swinthorpe	Lincs	79	P8
Swinton	Border	117	J11
Swinton	N York	91	K11
Swinton	N York	92	F12
Swinton	Rothm	78	D4
Swinton	Salfd	76	E3
Swithland	Leics	66	F9
Swordale	Highld	137	N3
Swordland	Highld	127	P6
Swordly	Highld	150	F3
Sworton Heath	Ches E	76	C7
Swyddffynnon	Cerdgn	49	M7
Swyncombe	Oxon	31	P4
Swynnerton	Staffs	64	F5
Swyre	Dorset	10	E7
Sycharth	Powys	63	J7
Sychnant	Powys	50	D5
Sychtyn	Powys	62	D10
Syde	Gloucs	41	Q9
Sydenham	Gt Lon	33	L8
Sydenham	Oxon	43	Q11
Sydenham Damerel	Devon	7	M9
Sydenhurst	Surrey	14	D4
Syderstone	Norfk	70	B6
Sydling St Nicholas	Dorset	10	F5
Sydmonton	Hants	31	K10
Sydnal Lane	Shrops	64	E11
Syerston	Notts	67	K3
Syke	Rochdl	84	D12
Sykehouse	Donc	86	B11
Sykeham	Lincs	59	J5
Sylen	Carmth	38	D10
Symbister	Shet	147	j6
Symington	S Ayrs	104	G3
Symington	S Lans	106	C3
Symondsbury	Dorset	10	C6
Symonds Yat (East)	Herefs	40	H8
Symonds Yat (West)	Herefs	40	H8
Sympson Green	C Brad	85	J7
Synderford	Dorset	10	B4
Synod Inn	Cerdgn	48	H5
Syre	Highld	149	P8
Syreford	Gloucs	42	B8
Syresham	Nhants	43	N3
Syston	Leics	66	G9
Syston	Lincs	67	M3
Sytchampton	Worcs	52	F7
Sywell	Nhants	55	K7
Tabley Hill	Ches E	76	D8
Tackley	Oxon	43	K7
Tacolneston	Norfk	58	H2
Tadcaster	N York	85	P6
Taddington	Derbys	77	L9
Taddiport	Devon	19	J9
Tadley	Hants	31	M10
Tadlow	Cambs	56	F11
Tadmarton	Oxon	43	J4
Tadwick	BaNES	29	L8
Tadworth	Surrey	33	J11
Tafarnaubach	Blae G	39	Q9
Tafarn-y-bwlch	Pembks	37	L4
Tafarn-y-Gelyn	Denbgs	74	G11
Taff's Well	Rhondd	27	N6
Tafolwern	Powys	62	B11
Taibach	Neath	27	J4
Tain	Highld	146	D8
Tain	Highld	151	M3
Tai'n Lôn	Gwynd	60	G2
Tairbeart	W Isls	152	f4
Tai'r Bull	Powys	39	N6
Takeley	Essex	45	Q7
Takeley Street	Essex	45	Q7
Talachddu	Powys	39	P5
Talacre	Flints	74	G8
Talaton	Devon	9	K5
Talbenny	Pembks	36	G8
Talbot Green	Rhondd	27	N6
Talbot Village	BCP	11	P6
Taleford	Devon	9	L5
Talerddig	Powys	62	C12
Talgarreg	Cerdgn	48	G10
Talgarth	Powys	39	R5
Talisker	Highld	134	F10
Talke	Staffs	64	F2
Talke Pits	Staffs	64	F2
Talkin	Cumb	98	G7
Talla Linnfoots	Border	106	F6
Tallaminnock	S Ayrs	104	G10
Tallarn Green	Wrexhm	63	M3
Tallentire	Cumb	97	M11
Talley	Carmth	38	F5
Tallington	Lincs	68	B10
Talmine	Highld	149	M4
Talog	Carmth	37	Q5
Talsarn	Cerdgn	49	J9
Talsarnau	Gwynd	61	L3
Talskiddy	Cnwll	6	C11
Talwrn	IoA	72	H8
Talwrn	Wrexhm	63	L3
Tal-y-bont	Cerdgn	49	N3
Tal-y-Bont	Conwy	73	N10
Tal-y-bont	Gwynd	61	K9
Tal-y-bont	Gwynd	73	K9
Talybont-on-Usk	Powys	39	Q7
Tal-y-Cafn	Conwy	73	N9
Tal-y-coed	Mons	40	F8
Tal-y-garn	Rhondd	27	N6
Talysarn	Gwynd	60	H2
Tal-y-Waun	Torfn	40	C10
Talywern	Powys	61	P12
Tamar Valley Mining District	Cnwll	4	D4
Tamer Lane End	Wigan	76	B3
Tamerton Foliot	C Plym	4	G4
Tamworth	Staffs	65	N11
Tamworth Green	Lincs	68	G4
Tamworth Services	Warwks	65	N12
Tancred	N York	85	P3
Tancredston	Pembks	36	G5
Tandridge	Surrey	33	L12
Tanfield	Dur	100	F7
Tanfield Lea	Dur	100	F7
Tangasdale	W Isls	152	b13
Tangiers	Pembks	37	J6
Tangley	Hants	24	E3
Tangmere	W Susx	14	C9
Tan Hill	N York	90	E5
Tankerness	Ork	147	d4
Tankersley	Barns	77	Q4
Tankerton	Kent	35	J9
Tannach	Highld	151	P7
Tannachie	Abers	133	J7
Tannadice	Angus	125	J1
Tanner's Green	Worcs	53	K6
Tannington	Suffk	59	K7
Tannochside	N Lans	114	C9
Tansley	Derbys	77	Q11
Tansor	Nhants	55	Q2
Tantobie	Dur	100	F7
Tanton	N York	92	B5
Tanwood	Worcs	52	G6
Tanworth in Arden	Warwks	53	L6
Tan-y-Bwlch	Gwynd	61	L4
Tan-y-fron	Conwy	74	C11
Tan-y-fron	Wrexhm	63	J3
Tan-y-grisiau	Gwynd	61	M3
Tan-y-groes	Cerdgn	48	D10
Taobh Tuath	W Isls	152	d6
Taplow	Bucks	32	C6
Tarbert	Ag & B	111	Q6
Tarbert	Ag & B	112	C7
Tarbert	W Isls	152	e5
Tarbet	Ag & B	121	Q12
Tarbet	Highld	127	P6
Tarbet	Highld	148	D7
Tarbock Green	Knows	75	M6
Tarbolton	S Ayrs	104	H4
Tarbrax	S Lans	115	J10
Tardebigge	Worcs	53	J7
Tarfside	Angus	132	D8
Tarland	Abers	132	D3
Tarleton	Lancs	83	K11
Tarlscough	Lancs	83	K12
Tarlton	Gloucs	29	Q2
Tarnock	Somset	21	L3
Tarns	Cumb	97	M8
Tarporley	Ches W	75	P11
Tarr	Somset	21	J7
Tarrant Crawford	Dorset	11	M4
Tarrant Gunville	Dorset	23	K10
Tarrant Hinton	Dorset	11	M2
Tarrant Keyneston	Dorset	11	M4
Tarrant Launceston	Dorset	11	M3
Tarrant Monkton	Dorset	11	M3
Tarrant Rawston	Dorset	11	M4
Tarrant Rushton	Dorset	11	M4
Tarring Neville	E Susx	15	N10
Tarrington	Herefs	41	J4
Tarskavaig	Highld	127	K2
Tarves	Abers	141	L9
Tarvin	Ches W	75	N10
Tarvin Sands	Ches W	75	N10
Tasburgh	Norfk	59	J2
Tasley	Shrops	52	C2
Taston	Oxon	42	H7
Tatenhill	Staffs	65	M8
Tathall End	M Keyn	44	B2
Tatham	Lancs	83	N1
Tathwell	Lincs	80	G6
Tatsfield	Surrey	33	M11
Tatterford	Norfk	70	C6
Tattersett	Norfk	70	C6
Tattershall	Lincs	80	D12
Tattershall Bridge	Lincs	80	D11
Tattershall Thorpe	Lincs	80	D11
Tattingstone	Suffk	47	K4
Tattingstone White Horse	Suffk	47	K4
Tatton Park	Ches E	76	D7
Tatworth	Somset	9	Q4
Tauchers	Moray	140	B6
Taunton	Somset	21	K9
Taunton Deane Services	Somset	21	K9
Taverham	Norfk	70	H9
Taverners Green	Essex	45	Q8
Tavernspite	Pembks	37	N7
Tavistock	Devon	7	N10
Taw Green	Devon	8	C5
Tawstock	Devon	19	K8
Taxal	Derbys	77	J8
Tay Bridge	C Dund	124	H7
Taychreggan Hotel	Ag & B	121	K8
Tay Forest Park	P & K	130	C12
Tayinloan	Ag & B	111	P12
Taynton	Gloucs	41	L7
Taynton	Oxon	42	F9
Taynuilt	Ag & B	121	K6
Tayport	Fife	125	J7
Tayvallich	Ag & B	111	Q4
Tealby	Lincs	80	C5
Tealing	Angus	124	H5
Team Valley	Gatesd	100	G6
Teangue	Highld	127	K4
Teanord	Highld	137	M3
Tebay	Cumb	89	Q6
Tebay Services	Cumb	89	P5
Tebworth	C Beds	44	E6
Tedburn St Mary	Devon	8	F6
Teddington	Gloucs	41	Q5
Teddington	Gt Lon	32	H8
Tedstone Delamere	Herefs	52	C9
Tedstone Wafer	Herefs	52	C9
Teesport	R & C	92	B2
Teesside Park	S on T	91	P3
Teeton	Nhants	54	H6
Teffont Evias	Wilts	23	L7
Teffont Magna	Wilts	23	L7
Tegryn	Pembks	37	P4
Teigh	Rutlnd	67	L9
Teigncombe	Devon	8	C7
Teigngrace	Devon	8	F10
Teignmouth	Devon	8	H10
Teindside	Border	107	L8
Telford	Wrekin	64	C10
Telford Services	Shrops	64	D10
Tellisford	Somset	22	H2
Telscombe	E Susx	15	M10
Telscombe Cliffs	E Susx	15	M10
Tempar	P & K	122	H1
Templand	D & G	97	M1
Temple	Cnwll	6	H10
Temple	Mdloth	115	P9
Temple Balsall	Solhll	53	N5
Temple Bar	Cerdgn	49	J9
Temple Cloud	BaNES	29	K11
Temple End	Suffk	57	M10
Temple Ewell	Kent	17	N2
Temple Grafton	Warwks	53	L9
Temple Guiting	Gloucs	42	C6
Temple Herdewyke	Warwks	54	C10
Temple Hirst	N York	86	B10
Temple Normanton	Derbys	78	C10
Temple of Fiddes	Abers	133	K8
Temple Sowerby	Cumb	89	Q1
Templeton	Devon	20	D10
Templeton	Pembks	37	M8
Templetown	Dur	100	E8
Tempsford	C Beds	56	C10
Tenbury Wells	Worcs	51	Q7
Tenby	Pembks	37	M10
Tendring	Essex	47	L7
Tendring Green	Essex	47	L6
Tendring Heath	Essex	47	L6
Ten Mile Bank	Norfk	57	L1
Tenpenny Heath	Essex	47	K7
Tenterden	Kent	16	F4
Terling	Essex	46	D8
Tern	Wrekin	64	C9
Ternhill	Shrops	64	C6
Terregles	D & G	97	J3
Terrington	N York	92	E12
Terrington St Clement	Norfk	69	K8
Terrington St John	Norfk	69	K9
Terry's Green	Warwks	53	L6
Teston	Kent	34	C11
Testwood	Hants	24	F10
Tetbury	Gloucs	29	P3
Tetbury Upton	Gloucs	29	P3
Tetchill	Shrops	63	L5
Tetcott	Devon	7	L5
Tetford	Lincs	80	G8
Tetney	Lincs	80	G3
Tetney Lock	Lincs	80	H3
Tetsworth	Oxon	43	P11
Tettenhall	Wolves	64	G12
Tettenhall Wood	Wolves	64	G12
Teversal	Notts	78	D11
Teversham	Cambs	57	J9
Teviothead	Border	107	L8
Tewin	Herts	45	K8
Tewin Wood	Herts	45	K8
Tewkesbury	Gloucs	41	Q4
Teynham	Kent	34	G9
Thackley	C Brad	85	J7
Thackthwaite	Cumb	88	F2
Thackthwaite	Cumb	89	L2
Thainstone	Abers	141	J12
Thakeham	W Susx	14	G7
Thame	Oxon	43	P10
Thames Ditton	Surrey	32	H9
Thamesmead	Gt Lon	33	N6
Thamesport	Medway	34	F7
Thanington	Kent	34	L11
Thankerton	S Lans	106	C2
Tharston	Norfk	59	J2
Thatcham	W Berk	31	L9
Thatto Heath	St Hel	75	N5
Thaxted	Essex	45	R5
Theakston	N York	91	M10
Thealby	N Linc	86	G11
Theale	Somset	21	N4
Theale	W Berk	31	N8
Thearne	E R Yk	87	K8
The Bank	Ches E	76	F12
The Beeches	Gloucs	42	B11
Theberton	Suffk	59	N7
The Blythe	Staffs	65	K6
The Bog	Shrops	51	K1
The Bourne	Worcs	52	H7
The Braes	Highld	135	J9
The Bratch	Staffs	52	F2
The Broad	Herefs	51	N8
The Broads	—	71	P10
The Brunt	E Loth	116	H7
The Bryn	Mons	40	C9
The Bungalow	IoM	102	e4
The Burf	Worcs	52	E7
The Camp	Gloucs	41	Q10
The Chequer	Wrexhm	63	N4
The City	Bed	56	B9
The City	Bucks	31	R3
The Common	Oxon	43	K9
The Common	Wilts	24	D7
The Common	Wilts	30	C3
The Corner	Kent	16	C2
The Cronk	IoM	102	d3
Theddingworth	Leics	54	H3
Theddlethorpe All Saints	Lincs	81	J6
Theddlethorpe St Helen	Lincs	81	J6
The Deep	C KuH	—	—
The Den	N Ayrs	113	L11
The Forge	Herefs	51	K11
The Forstal	Kent	17	J3
The Fouralls	Shrops	64	C6
The Green	Cumb	88	E8
The Green	Cumb	89	Q4
The Green	Essex	46	D7
The Green	N York	92	F6
The Green	Wilts	23	J6
The Grove	Worcs	41	P2
The Haven	W Susx	14	F5
The Haw	Gloucs	41	N6
The Headland	Hartpl	101	M11
The Hendre	Mons	40	F9
The Hill	Cumb	88	G10
The Holt	Wokham	32	A7
The Hundred	Herefs	51	N8
The Leacon	Kent	16	H4
The Lee	Bucks	44	C11
The Lhen	IoM	102	e2
Thelnetham	Suffk	58	F5
The Lochs	Moray	139	P3
Thelveton	Norfk	58	H4
Thelwall	Warrtn	76	C6
The Marsh	Powys	51	K1
Themelthorpe	Norfk	70	F7
The Middles	Dur	100	G8
The Moor	Kent	16	D5
The Mumbles	Swans	26	F5
The Murray	S Lans	114	B10
The Mythe	Gloucs	41	P5
The Narth	Mons	40	H10
The Neuk	Abers	132	H5
Thenford	Nhants	43	L3
Theobald's Green	Wilts	30	B8
The Quarter	Gloucs	16	F2
The Quarter	Kent	16	F2
The Reddings	Gloucs	41	P7
Therfield	Herts	45	L4
The Rhôs	Powys	40	A5
The Ross	P & K	123	K8
The Sands	Surrey	14	C7
The Shoe	Wilts	29	N7
The Smithies	Shrops	52	C1
The Spring	Warwks	53	P6
The Square	Torfn	28	C3
The Stair	Kent	15	R1
The Stocks	Kent	16	G5
The Straits	Hants	25	N5
The Strand	Wilts	29	Q10
Thetford	Lincs	68	C10
Thetford	Norfk	57	Q3
Thetford Forest Park	—	57	Q3
Thethwaite	Cumb	98	D9
The Towans	Cnwll	2	E7
The Vauld	Herefs	51	P10
The Wyke	Shrops	64	D10
Theydon Bois	Essex	33	N2
Theydon Mount	Essex	33	P2
Thicket Priory	N York	86	C6
Thickwood	Wilts	29	N8
Thimbleby	Lincs	80	E9
Thimbleby	N York	91	Q11
Thingwall	Wirral	75	J7
Thirkleby	N York	91	Q11
Thirn	N York	91	L9
Thirsk	N York	91	Q10
Thirtleby	E R Yk	87	M8
Thirlestane	Border	116	D11
Thirlspot	Cumb	89	J3
Thistleton	Lancs	83	K7
Thistleton	Rutlnd	67	M8
Thistley Green	Suffk	57	M5
Thixendale	N York	86	F3
Thockrington	Nthumb	99	Q2
Tholomas Drove	Cambs	68	H11
Tholthorpe	N York	85	P2
Thomas Chapel	Pembks	37	L8
Thomas Close	Cumb	98	E10
Thomastown	Abers	140	E8
Thompson	Norfk	58	D1
Thong	Kent	34	B8
Thongsbridge	Kirk	77	M2
Thoralby	N York	90	G9
Thoresby	Notts	78	G9
Thoresthorpe	Lincs	81	J8
Thoresway	Lincs	80	D4
Thorganby	Lincs	80	D4
Thorganby	N York	86	C6
Thorgill	N York	92	E7
Thorington	Suffk	59	N6
Thorington Street	Suffk	46	H4
Thorlby	N York	84	E5
Thorley	Herts	45	N8
Thorley	IoW	12	F7
Thorley Houses	Herts	45	N7
Thorley Street	IoW	12	F7
Thornaby-on-Tees	S on T	91	P3
Thornage	Norfk	70	F5
Thornborough	Bucks	43	P5
Thornborough	N York	91	M10
Thornbury	C Brad	85	J8
Thornbury	Devon	7	M3
Thornbury	Herefs	52	C9
Thornbury	S Glos	29	K4
Thornby	Cumb	98	B7
Thornby	Nhants	54	H5
Thorncliff	Staffs	77	J12
Thorncombe	Dorset	10	B4
Thorncombe Street	Surrey	14	E2
Thorncott Green	C Beds	56	C11
Thorncross	IoW	12	G8
Thorndon	Suffk	58	H7
Thorndon Cross	Devon	7	P6
Thorne	Donc	78	H1
Thorne Coffin	Somset	22	C10
Thornecroft	Devon	5	N3
Thornehillhead	Devon	18	H10
Thorner	Leeds	85	M7
Thornes	Staffs	65	K11
Thornes	Wakefd	85	L11
Thorne St Margaret	Somset	20	H9
Thorney	Bucks	32	F6
Thorney	C Pete	68	F11
Thorney	Notts	79	L9
Thorney	Somset	21	M9
Thorney Hill	Hants	12	C5
Thorney Island	W Susx	13	N4
Thorney Toll	Cambs	68	G11
Thornfalcon	Somset	21	K9
Thornford	Dorset	22	D11
Thorngrafton	Nthumb	99	M5
Thorngrove	Somset	21	N7
Thorngumbald	E R Yk	87	N10
Thornham	Norfk	69	R3
Thornham Magna	Suffk	58	G6
Thornham Parva	Suffk	58	G6
Thornhaugh	C Pete	67	Q12
Thornhill	C Sotn	24	H10
Thornhill	Caerph	27	R5
Thornhill	Cumb	88	D5
Thornhill	D & G	105	P10
Thornhill	Derbys	77	M7
Thornhill	Kirk	85	K11
Thornhill	Stirlg	114	A1
Thornhill	Wilts	30	D4
Thornhill Lees	Kirk	85	K10
Thornholme	E R Yk	87	L2
Thornicombe	Dorset	11	L5
Thornington	Nthumb	108	E3
Thornley	Dur	100	E10
Thornley	Dur	101	M10
Thornley Gate	Nthumb	99	M7
Thornliebank	E Rens	113	P9
Thorns	Suffk	57	P9
Thorns Green	Ches E	76	E7
Thornthwaite	Cumb	88	H2
Thornthwaite	N York	85	J3
Thornton	Angus	124	H3
Thornton	Bucks	43	Q4
Thornton	C Brad	84	G8
Thornton	E R Yk	86	E6

Thornton – Twycross Zoo 189

Thornton Fife 115 P2
Thornton Lancs 82 H7
Thornton Leics 66 D10
Thornton Lincs 80 E10
Thornton Middsb 91 Q4
Thornton Nthumb 117 L11
Thornton Pembks 36 H9
Thornton Sefton 75 K3
Thornton Curtis N Linc 87 K11
Thorntonhall S Lans 113 R10
Thornton Heath Gt Lon 33 K8
Thornton Hough Wirral 75 J7
Thornton-in-Craven N York 84 D5
Thornton in Lonsdale N York 89 R12
Thornton-le-Beans N York 91 P8
Thornton-le-Clay N York 86 C2
Thornton-le-Dale N York 92 G10
Thornton le Moor Lincs 79 P4
Thornton-le-Moor N York 91 P9
Thornton-le-Moors Ches W 75 M9
Thornton-le-Street N York 91 P9
Thorntonloch E Loth 116 G6
Thornton Rust N York 90 F9
Thornton Steward N York 91 K9
Thornton Watlass N York 91 L9
Thornwood Common Essex 45 N10
Thornydykes Border 116 E11
Thornythwaite Cumb 89 L2
Thoroton Notts 67 J4
Thorp Arch Leeds 85 N6
Thorpe Derbys 65 M2
Thorpe E R Yk 87 J6
Thorpe Lincs 81 J7
Thorpe N York 84 F3
Thorpe Norfk 59 N1
Thorpe Notts 67 J2
Thorpe Surrey 32 E8
Thorpe Abbotts Norfk 59 J5
Thorpe Acre Leics 66 E8
Thorpe Arnold Leics 67 K8
Thorpe Audlin Wakefd 85 P12
Thorpe Bassett N York 92 H12
Thorpe Bay Sthend 34 G5
Thorpe by Water Rutlnd 55 M1
Thorpe Common Rothm 78 C5
Thorpe Constantine Staffs 65 N10
Thorpe End Norfk 71 K10
Thorpe Green Essex 47 L7
Thorpe Green Lancs 83 N10
Thorpe Green Suffk 58 D9
Thorpe Hesley Rothm 78 B4
Thorpe in Balne Donc 78 F2
Thorpe Langton Leics 55 J2
Thorpe Larches Dur 91 P2
Thorpe Lea Surrey 32 E8
Thorpe le Fallows Lincs 79 M7
Thorpe-le-Soken Essex 47 L7
Thorpe le Street E R Yk 86 F6
Thorpe Malsor Nhants 55 L5
Thorpe Mandeville Nhants 43 L3
Thorpe Market Norfk 71 K5
Thorpe Marriot Norfk 70 H9
Thorpe Morieux Suffk 58 D10
Thorpeness Suffk 59 P8
Thorpe on the Hill Leeds 85 L10
Thorpe on the Hill Lincs 79 M10
Thorpe Park Surrey 32 E8
Thorpe St Andrew Norfk 71 K10
Thorpe St Peter Lincs 81 J11
Thorpe Salvin Rothm 78 E7
Thorpe Satchville Leics 67 J10
Thorpe Thewles S on T 91 P2
Thorpe Tilney Lincs 80 C12
Thorpe Underwood N York 85 P3
Thorpe Underwood Nhants 55 K4
Thorpe Waterville Nhants 55 P4
Thorpe Willoughby N York 86 A9
Thorpland Norfk 69 M10
Thorrington Essex 47 K7
Thorverton Devon 8 H4
Thrales End C Beds 44 G8
Thrandeston Suffk 58 G5
Thrapston Nhants 55 P5
Threapland Cumb 97 N10
Threapland N York 84 E3
Threapwood Ches W 63 M3
Threapwood Staffs 65 J4
Threapwood Head Staffs 65 J4
Threave S Ayrs 104 F8
Three Ashes Herefs 40 G7
Three Bridges W Susx 15 K3
Three Burrows Cnwll 3 J5
Three Chimneys Kent 16 E3
Three Cocks Powys 40 A4
Three Crosses Swans 26 E3
Three Cups Corner E Susx 16 B7
Three Gates Worcs 52 C8
Threehammer Common Norfk 71 L8
Three Hammers Cnwll 7 J7
Three Holes Norfk 69 K12
Threekingham Lincs 68 B5
Three Leg Cross E Susx 16 B4
Three Legged Cross Dorset 11 Q4
Three Mile Cross Wokham 31 P9
Threemilestone Cnwll 3 J5
Threemiletown W Loth 115 K6
Three Oaks E Susx 16 E8
Threlkeld Cumb 89 J2
Threshers Bush Essex 45 P10
Threshfield N York 84 E2
Thrigby Norfk 71 P9
Thringarth Dur 90 F2
Thringstone Leics 66 C8
Thrintoft N York 91 N8
Thriplow Cambs 45 N2
Throapham Rothm 78 E6
Throckenhalt Lincs 68 G10
Throcking Herts 45 L6
Throckley N u Ty 100 F5
Throckmorton Worcs 52 H10
Throop BCP 11 Q6
Throop Dorset 11 K6
Throphill Nthumb 100 E1
Thropton Nthumb 108 G9
Throsk Stirlg 114 F3
Througham Gloucs 41 Q10
Throughgate D & G 96 H1
Throwleigh Devon 8 C6
Throwley Kent 34 H11
Throwley Forstal Kent 34 H11
Thrumpton Notts 66 E6
Thrumpton Notts 78 H7
Thrumster Highld 151 P7
Thrunscoe NE Lin 80 F2
Thrunton Nthumb 108 H7
Thrup Oxon 30 G3
Thrupp Gloucs 41 P11
Thrupp Oxon 43 K8
Thrushelton Devon 7 N7
Thrussington Leics 66 G9
Thruxton Hants 24 D4
Thruxton Herefs 40 F5
Thrybergh Rothm 78 D5
Thulston Derbys 66 C6
Thundersley Essex 34 D5
Thurcaston Leics 66 F10
Thurcroft Rothm 78 E6
Thurdon Cnwll 7 K3
Thurgarton Norfk 71 J5
Thurgarton Notts 66 H2
Thurgoland Barns 77 P3
Thurlaston Leics 66 E12
Thurlaston Warwks 54 D6
Thurlbear Somset 21 L9
Thurlby Lincs 68 B9
Thurlby Lincs 79 M11
Thurlby Lincs 81 J8
Thurleigh Bed 55 Q9
Thurlestone Devon 5 L8
Thurloxton Somset 21 L7
Thurlstone Barns 77 N3
Thurlton Norfk 59 N1
Thurlwood Ches E 76 E12
Thurmaston Leics 66 G10
Thurnby Leics 66 G11
Thurne Norfk 71 M9
Thurnham Kent 34 E10
Thurning Nhants 56 B4
Thurning Norfk 70 G6
Thurnscoe Barns 78 D3
Thurrock Services Thurr 33 Q6
Thursby Cumb 98 C8
Thursden Lancs 84 D8
Thursford Norfk 70 E5
Thursley Surrey 14 C3
Thurso Highld 151 K3
Thurstaston Wirral 74 H7
Thurston Suffk 58 D7
Thurston Clough Oldham 76 H2
Thurstonfield Cumb 98 C7
Thurstonland Kirk 77 M2
Thurston Planch Suffk 58 D8
Thurton Norfk 71 L12
Thurvaston Derbys 65 N5
Thuxton Norfk 70 F10
Thwaite N York 90 E7
Thwaite Suffk 58 G7
Thwaite Head Cumb 89 K8
Thwaites C Brad 84 G7
Thwaite St Mary Norfk 59 L2
Thwaites Brow C Brad 84 G7
Thwing E R Yk 87 K1
Tibbermore P & K 123 Q8
Tibbers D & G 105 Q10
Tibberton Gloucs 41 M7
Tibberton Worcs 52 G9
Tibberton Wrekin 64 C8
Tibenham Norfk 58 H3
Tibshelf Derbys 78 D11
Tibshelf Services Derbys 78 D11
Tibthorpe E R Yk 86 H4
Ticehurst E Susx 16 C5
Tichborne Hants 25 J7
Tickencote Rutlnd 67 N10
Tickenham N Som 28 F8
Tickford End M Keyn 44 C3
Tickhill Donc 78 F5
Ticklerton Shrops 51 N2
Ticknall Derbys 66 B7
Tickton E R Yk 87 K7
Tidbury Green Solhll 53 L5
Tidcombe Wilts 30 G10
Tiddington Oxon 43 N10
Tiddington Warwks 53 N9
Tiddleywink Wilts 29 P7
Tidebrook E Susx 15 R5
Tideford Cnwll 4 E5
Tideford Cross Cnwll 4 E4
Tidenham Gloucs 28 H3
Tideswell Derbys 77 M8
Tidmarsh W Berk 31 N7
Tidmington Warwks 42 F4
Tidpit Hants 23 N9
Tidworth Wilts 24 D4
Tiers Cross Pembks 36 H8
Tiffield Nhants 54 H10
Tigerton Angus 132 E11
Tigh a' Ghearraidh W Isls 152 b8
Tigharry W Isls 152 b8
Tighnabruaich Ag & B 112 E7
Tigley Devon 5 M4
Tilbrook Cambs 55 Q7
Tilbury Thurr 34 B7
Tilbury Dock Thurr 34 B7
Tilbury Green Essex 46 D3
Tilbury Juxta Clare Essex 46 D4
Tile Cross Birm 53 M3
Tile Hill Covtry 53 P5
Tilehouse Green Solhll 53 M5
Tilehurst Readg 31 N7
Tilford Surrey 14 B2
Tilgate W Susx 15 K4
Tilgate Forest Row W Susx 15 J4
Tilham Street Somset 22 D6
Tillers Green Gloucs 41 L5
Tillicoultry Clacks 114 G2
Tillietudlem S Lans 114 E12
Tillingham Essex 46 H11
Tillington Herefs 40 G3
Tillington W Susx 14 D6
Tillington Common Herefs 40 F3
Tillybirloch Abers 132 G3
Tillyfourie Abers 132 G2
Tillygreig Abers 141 L11
Tillyrie P & K 124 C11
Tilmanstone Kent 35 N12
Tilney All Saints Norfk 69 L8
Tilney High End Norfk 69 L8
Tilney St Lawrence Norfk 69 K9
Tilshead Wilts 23 M4
Tilstock Shrops 63 P5
Tilston Ches W 63 M2
Tilstone Bank Ches W 75 P11
Tilstone Fearnall Ches W 75 P11
Tilsworth C Beds 44 D7
Tilton on the Hill Leics 67 J11
Tiltups End Gloucs 29 N3
Tilty Essex 45 Q6
Timberland Lincs 80 C12
Timbersbrook Ches E 76 G11
Timberscombe Somset 20 E5
Timble N York 85 J4
Timewell Devon 20 E8
Timpanheck D & G 98 C3
Timperley Traffd 76 E6
Timsbury BaNES 29 K10
Timsbury Hants 24 E8
Timsgarry W Isls 152 d3
Timsgearraidh W Isls 152 d3
Timworth Suffk 58 C7
Timworth Green Suffk 58 C7
Tincleton Dorset 11 J6
Tindale Cumb 99 J6
Tingewick Bucks 43 N5
Tingley Leeds 85 L10
Tingrith C Beds 44 E5
Tingwall Airport Shet 147 i7
Tingwell Ork 147 c3
Tinhay Devon 7 M7
Tinker's Hill Hants 24 F4
Tinkersley Derbys 77 P10
Tinsley Sheff 78 C5
Tinsley Green W Susx 15 K3
Tintagel Cnwll 6 F7
Tintern Mons 28 H2
Tintinhull Somset 22 C9
Tintwistle Derbys 77 J4
Tinwald D & G 97 K2
Tinwell Rutlnd 67 P11
Tippacott Devon 19 P4
Tipp's End Norfk 57 K2
Tiptoe Hants 12 D5
Tipton Sandw 52 H2
Tipton Green Sandw 52 H2
Tipton St John Devon 9 L6
Tiptree Essex 46 F8
Tiptree Heath Essex 46 F8
Tirabad Powys 39 L3
Tircoed Swans 26 F2
Tiree Ag & B 118 E4
Tiree Airport Ag & B 118 D4
Tiretigan Ag & B 111 Q9
Tirley Gloucs 41 N6
Tiroran Ag & B 119 N7
Tirphil Caerph 39 Q11
Tirril Cumb 89 N1
Tir-y-fron Flints 75 J11
Tisbury Wilts 23 L7
Tisman's Common W Susx 14 F4
Tissington Derbys 65 M2
Titchberry Devon 18 E8
Titchfield Hants 13 J4
Titchfield Common Hants 13 J3
Titchmarsh Nhants 55 P5
Titchwell Norfk 69 P3
Tithby Notts 66 H5
Titley Herefs 51 K8
Titmore Green Herts 45 J6
Titsey Surrey 33 M11
Titson Cnwll 7 J4
Tittensor Staffs 64 G4
Tittleshall Norfk 70 C8
Titton Worcs 52 F6
Tiverton Ches W 75 P11
Tiverton Devon 20 E10
Tivetshall St Margaret Norfk 58 H3
Tivetshall St Mary Norfk 58 H3
Tivington Somset 20 E4
Tivy Dale Barns 77 P2
Tixall Staffs 64 H7
Tixover Rutlnd 67 N12
Toab Shet 147 i10
Toadhole Derbys 78 C12
Toadmoor Derbys 65 Q2
Tobermory Ag & B 119 N2
Toberonochy Ag & B 120 D11
Tobha Mòr W Isls 152 b10
Tocher Abers 140 H9
Tochieneal Moray 140 D3
Tockenham Wilts 30 B6
Tockenham Wick Wilts 30 B6
Tocketts R & Cl 92 C3
Tockholes Bl w D 83 P10
Tockington S Glos 29 J5
Tockwith N York 85 P5
Todber Dorset 22 H9
Todburn Nthumb 109 J10
Toddington C Beds 44 E6
Toddington Gloucs 42 B5
Toddington Services C Beds 44 E6
Todds Green Herts 45 J6
Todenham Gloucs 42 F4
Todhills Angus 124 H5
Todhills Cumb 98 D6
Todhills Dur 100 G11
Todhills Rest Area Cumb 98 D6
Todmorden Calder 84 D10
Todwick Rothm 78 E7
Toft Cambs 56 G9
Toft Ches E 76 E8
Toft Lincs 67 Q8
Toft Shet 147 i5
Toft Warwks 54 D6
Toft Hill Dur 91 K1
Toft Hill Lincs 80 E11
Toft Monks Norfk 59 N2
Toft next Newton Lincs 79 P6
Toftrees Norfk 70 C6
Toftwood Norfk 70 E10
Togston Nthumb 109 L9
Tokavaig Highld 127 L2
Tokers Green Oxon 31 P7
Tolastadh bho Thuath W Isls 152 h2
Toldish Cnwll 3 M3
Tolland Somset 20 H7
Tollard Farnham Dorset 23 L10
Tollard Royal Wilts 23 L10
Toll Bar Donc 78 F2
Tollbar End Covtry 54 B5
Toller Fratrum Dorset 10 F5
Toller Porcorum Dorset 10 E5
Tollerton N York 85 Q2
Tollerton Notts 66 G5
Toller Whelme Dorset 10 D4
Tollesbury Essex 46 G9
Tolleshunt D'Arcy Essex 46 G9
Tolleshunt Knights Essex 46 G8
Tolleshunt Major Essex 46 F9
Tollingham E R Yk 86 F8
Toll of Birness Abers 141 N9
Tolpuddle Dorset 11 J6
Tolworth Gt Lon 32 H9
Tomatin Highld 138 E10
Tomchrasky Highld 129 J2
Tomdoun Highld 128 G4
Tomich Highld 137 K10
Tomich Highld 137 P6
Tomich Highld 145 N4
Tomich Highld 146 C11
Tomintoul Moray 139 M12
Tomlow Warwks 54 D8
Tomnacross Highld 137 N7
Tomnavoulin Moray 139 M10
Tompkin Staffs 64 H2
Ton Mons 28 D2
Ton Mons 28 E3
Tonbridge Kent 15 Q2
Tondu Brdgnd 27 L5
Tonedale Somset 20 H9
Tonfanau Gwynd 61 J11
Tong C Brad 85 J9
Tong Kent 34 G11
Tong Shrops 64 E10
Tong W Isls 152 g3
Tonge Leics 66 C7
Tong Green Kent 34 H11
Tongham Surrey 14 C1
Tongland D & G 96 E7
Tong Norton Shrops 64 E10
Tongue Highld 149 M5
Tongue End Lincs 68 C8
Tongwynlais Cardif 27 Q6
Tonmawr Neath 27 J3
Tonna Neath 27 J3
Ton-teg Rhondd 27 P5
Tonwell Herts 45 L8
Tonypandy Rhondd 27 N4
Tonyrefail Rhondd 27 N5
Toot Baldon Oxon 31 M2
Toot Hill Essex 45 P11
Toothill Hants 24 F9
Toothill Swindn 30 D6
Tooting Gt Lon 33 K8
Tooting Bec Gt Lon 33 K8
Topcliffe N York 91 P11
Topcroft Norfk 59 K2
Topcroft Street Norfk 59 K2
Top End Bed 55 P8
Topham Donc 86 B11
Top of Hebers Rochdl 76 F2
Toppesfield Essex 46 C4
Toprow Norfk 58 H1
Topsham Devon 8 H7
Top-y-rhos Flints 75 J12
Torbeg N Ayrs 103 N4
Torboll Highld 146 D5
Torbreck Highld 138 B7
Torbryan Devon 5 N3
Torcastle Highld 128 G8
Torcross Devon 5 N8
Tore Highld 137 Q5
Torfrey Cnwll 3 Q4
Torinturk Ag & B 112 B8
Torksey Lincs 79 L8
Torlundy Highld 128 G9
Tormarton S Glos 29 M6
Tormore N Ayrs 103 N3
Tornagrain Highld 138 E6
Tornaveen Abers 132 F3
Torness Highld 137 Q10
Toronto Dur 100 G12
Torpenhow Cumb 97 P10
Torphichen W Loth 114 H7
Torphins Abers 132 F4
Torpoint Cnwll 4 G6
Torquay Torbay 5 Q4
Torquhan Border 116 B11
Torr Devon 5 J6
Torran Highld 135 K6
Torrance E Duns 114 B6
Torranyard N Ayrs 104 F1
Torre Somset 20 G5
Torridon Highld 136 C5
Torridon House Highld 136 B4
Torrin Highld 135 K11
Torrisdale Ag & B 103 L3
Torrisdale Highld 149 P4
Torrish Highld 146 H1
Torrisholme Lancs 83 K2
Torrobull Highld 145 N4
Torry C Aber 133 M3
Torryburn Fife 115 J4
Torteval Guern 12 b3
Torthorwald D & G 97 L3
Tortington W Susx 14 E10
Torton Worcs 52 F6
Tortworth S Glos 29 L4
Torvaig Highld 135 J7
Torver Cumb 89 J8
Torwood Falk 114 F4
Torwoodlee Border 107 M2
Torworth Notts 78 G6
Tosberry Devon 18 E9
Toscaig Highld 135 N8
Toseland Cambs 56 E8
Tosside Lancs 84 A4
Tostock Suffk 58 D8
Totaig Highld 134 C6
Tote Highld 134 G6
Tote Highld 135 J4
Tote Hill W Susx 14 B6
Totford Hants 25 J6
Tothill Lincs 80 H7
Totland IoW 12 E7
Totley Sheff 77 P8
Totley Brook Sheff 77 P7
Totnes Devon 5 N5
Toton Notts 66 E5
Totronald Ag & B 118 G2
Totscore Highld 134 G3
Tottenham Gt Lon 33 L4
Tottenhill Norfk 69 M10
Totteridge Gt Lon 33 J3
Totternhoe C Beds 44 D7
Tottington Bury 76 E1
Tottleworth Lancs 83 Q9
Totton Hants 24 F10
Touchen End W & M 32 C7
Toulston N York 85 P6
Toulton Somset 21 K7
Toulvaddie Highld 146 F9
Tovil Kent 34 D11
Towan Cnwll 3 P5
Towan Cnwll 6 C10
Toward Ag & B 112 H7
Toward Quay Ag & B 112 G7
Towcester Nhants 54 H11
Towednack Cnwll 2 D7
Tower of London Gt Lon 33 L6
Towersey Oxon 43 Q10
Towie Abers 132 C2
Tow Law Dur 100 E10
Town End Cambs 56 H2
Town End Cumb 89 K5
Town End Cumb 89 L10
Town End Cumb 89 Q2
Townend W Duns 113 M6
Towngate Cumb 98 G9
Towngate Lincs 68 C10
Town Green Lancs 75 L3
Town Green Norfk 71 M9
Townhead Barns 77 M3
Town Head Cumb 89 L6
Townhead Cumb 97 M11
Townhead Cumb 99 J11
Townhead D & G 106 C12
Town Head N York 84 B3
Townhead of Greenlaw D & G 96 F5
Townhill Fife 115 K3
Town Kelloe Dur 101 J11
Townlake Devon 7 M9
Town Lane Wigan 76 C4
Town Littleworth E Susx 15 M7
Town of Lowton Wigan 75 Q4
Town Row E Susx 15 Q5
Towns End Hants 31 M10
Townsend Somset 21 N10
Townshend Cnwll 2 F8
Town Street Suffk 57 P3
Townwell S Glos 29 L4
Town Yetholm Border 108 C4
Towthorpe C York 86 B3
Towthorpe E R Yk 86 G3
Towton N York 85 P7
Towyn Conwy 74 D8
Toxteth Lpool 75 K6
Toynton All Saints Lincs 80 H11
Toynton Fen Side Lincs 80 H11
Toynton St Peter Lincs 80 H11
Toy's Hill Kent 33 N12
Trabboch E Ayrs 104 H5
Trabbochburn E Ayrs 104 H5
Traboe Cnwll 3 J10
Tracebridge Somset 20 G9
Tradespark Highld 138 F5
Trafford Park Traffd 76 E4
Trallong Powys 39 M6
Tranent E Loth 115 R7
Tranmere Wirral 75 K6
Trantelbeg Highld 150 F6
Trantlemore Highld 150 F6
Tranwell Nthumb 100 F2
Trap Carmth 38 G8
Traprain E Loth 116 D6
Trap's Green Warwks 53 L7
Trapshill W Berk 30 H9
Traquair Border 107 J3
Trash Green W Berk 31 N8
Trawden Lancs 84 D7
Trawscoed Cerdgn 49 L6
Trawsfynydd Gwynd 61 M5
Trealaw Rhondd 27 N4
Treales Lancs 83 K8
Trearddur Bay IoA 72 D8
Treator Cnwll 6 C9
Tre Aubrey V Glam 27 N8
Trebanog Rhondd 27 N4
Trebanos Neath 38 H11
Trebartha Cnwll 7 K9
Trebarwith Cnwll 6 F7
Trebeath Cnwll 7 J7
Trebetherick Cnwll 6 D9
Treborough Somset 20 F6
Trebudannon Cnwll 3 L2
Trebullett Cnwll 7 L9
Treburgett Cnwll 6 F9
Treburley Cnwll 7 L9
Treburrick Cnwll 6 B10
Trebyan Cnwll 3 Q2
Trecastle Powys 39 L6
Trecogo Cnwll 7 K8
Trecott Devon 8 C5
Trecwn Pembks 37 J4
Trecynon Rhondd 39 N11
Tredaule Cnwll 7 J8
Tredavoe Cnwll 2 D9
Tredegar Blae G 39 Q10
Tredethy Cnwll 6 F10
Tredington Gloucs 41 P6
Tredington Warwks 42 F3
Tredinnick Cnwll 3 P3
Tredinnick Cnwll 4 B3
Tredinnick Cnwll 4 C5
Tredinnick Cnwll 4 D5
Tredinnick Cnwll 6 D10
Tredomen Powys 39 Q5
Tredrissi Pembks 37 L2
Tredrizzick Cnwll 6 D9
Tredunnock Mons 28 E3
Tredustan Powys 39 Q5
Treen Cnwll 2 B10
Treen Cnwll 2 C7
Treesmill Cnwll 3 Q3
Treeton Rothm 78 C6
Trefasser Pembks 36 H3
Trefdraeth IoA 72 G9
Trefecca Powys 39 Q5
Trefeglwys Powys 50 C3
Trefenter Cerdgn 49 K7
Treffgarne Pembks 37 J6
Treffgarne Owen Pembks 36 G5
Treffynnon Pembks 36 G5
Trefil Blae G 39 Q9
Trefilan Cerdgn 49 J9
Trefin Pembks 36 G4
Treflach Wood Shrops 63 J7
Trefnannau Powys 62 H9
Trefnant Denbgs 74 E9
Trefonen Shrops 63 J7
Trefor Gwynd 60 F3
Trefor IoA 72 F7
Treforest Rhondd 27 P4
Trefrew Cnwll 6 G8
Trefriw Conwy 73 N11
Tregadillett Cnwll 7 K8
Tre-gagle Mons 40 H10
Tregaian IoA 72 G7
Tregare Mons 40 F9
Tregarne Cnwll 3 J10
Tregaron Cerdgn 49 L8
Tregarth Gwynd 73 K10
Tregaswith Cnwll 3 L2
Tregatta Cnwll 6 F7
Tregawne Cnwll 6 E11
Tregeare Cnwll 7 J7
Tregeiriog Wrexhm 62 G5
Tregele IoA 72 F5
Tregellist Cnwll 6 E9
Tregenna Cnwll 3 L6
Tregeseal Cnwll 2 B8
Tregew Cnwll 3 K7
Tre-Gibbon Rhondd 39 N10
Tregidden Cnwll 3 J10
Tregiskey Cnwll 3 P5
Treglemais Pembks 36 F5
Tregole Cnwll 6 H5
Tregolls Cnwll 3 J7
Tregonce Cnwll 6 D10
Tregonetha Cnwll 3 N2
Tregonning & Gwinear Mining District Cnwll 2 F8
Tregony Cnwll 3 M5
Tregoodwell Cnwll 6 G8
Tregorrick Cnwll 3 P4
Tregoss Cnwll 3 N2
Tregoyd Powys 40 B4
Tregrehan Mills Cnwll 3 P4
Tre-groes Cerdgn 38 B3
Tregullon Cnwll 3 P2
Tregunna Cnwll 6 D10
Tregunnon Cnwll 7 J8
Tregurrian Cnwll 6 B11
Tregynon Powys 50 F1
Tre-gynwr Carmth 38 B8
Trehafod Rhondd 27 P4
Trehan Cnwll 4 F5
Treharris Myr Td 27 P3
Treharrock Cnwll 6 E9
Trehemborne Cnwll 6 C10
Treherbert Carmth 38 E2
Treherbert Rhondd 27 M3
Trehunist Cnwll 4 D4
Trekenner Cnwll 7 L9
Treknow Cnwll 6 F7
Trelan Cnwll 3 J10
Trelash Cnwll 6 H7
Trelassick Cnwll 3 L4
Trelawne Cnwll 4 C6
Trelawnyd Flints 74 F8
Treleague Cnwll 3 K10
Treleaver Cnwll 3 J11
Trelech Carmth 37 Q4
Trelech a'r Betws Carmth 37 Q5
Treleddyd-fawr Pembks 36 E5
Trelew Cnwll 3 K7
Trelewis Myr Td 27 Q3
Treligga Cnwll 6 F8
Trelights Cnwll 6 E9
Trelill Cnwll 6 F9
Trelinnoe Cnwll 7 K8
Trelion Cnwll 3 M4
Trelissick Cnwll 3 K6
Trellech Mons 40 G10
Trelleck Grange Mons 28 G2
Trelogan Flints 74 F7
Trelow Cnwll 6 D10
Trelowarren Cnwll 2 H9
Trelowia Cnwll 4 D5
Treluggan Cnwll 3 L7
Trelystan Powys 63 J11
Tremadog Gwynd 61 J4
Tremail Cnwll 6 H7
Tremain Cerdgn 48 C11
Tremaine Cnwll 7 J7
Tremar Cnwll 4 C3
Trematon Cnwll 4 F5
Trembraze Cnwll 4 C4
Tremeirchion Denbgs 74 F9
Tremethick Cross Cnwll 2 C8
Tremore Cnwll 6 E11
Tre-Mostyn Flints 74 G8
Trenance Cnwll 3 K10
Trenance Cnwll 6 B11
Trenance Cnwll 6 D10
Trenarren Cnwll 3 P5
Trench Wrekin 64 C9
Trench Green Oxon 31 P7
Trendeal Cnwll 3 L4
Trendrine Cnwll 2 D6
Treneague Cnwll 6 E10
Trenear Cnwll 2 H8
Treneglos Cnwll 7 J7
Trenerth Cnwll 2 F7
Trenewan Cnwll 4 B6
Trenewth Cnwll 6 F9
Trengune Cnwll 6 H6
Treninnick Cnwll 3 K2
Trenowah Cnwll 3 K3
Trenoweth Cnwll 3 J8
Trent Dorset 22 D9
Trentham C Stke 64 G4
Trentishoe Devon 19 M4
Trentlock Derbys 66 D6
Trent Port Lincs 79 L7
Trent Vale C Stke 64 F3
Trenwheal Cnwll 2 G8
Treoes V Glam 27 M7
Treorchy Rhondd 27 M3
Trequite Cnwll 6 E9
Tre'r-ddol Cerdgn 49 L2
Trerhyngyll V Glam 27 N7
Trerulefoot Cnwll 4 E5
Tresaith Cerdgn 48 D10
Tresawle Cnwll 3 L5
Tresco IoS 2 b1
Trescott Staffs 52 F1
Trescowe Cnwll 2 F8
Tresean Cnwll 3 J3
Tresham Gloucs 29 M4
Treshnish Isles Ag & B 118 H5
Tresillian Cnwll 3 L5
Tresinney Cnwll 6 G8
Treskinnick Cross Cnwll 7 J5
Tresmeer Cnwll 7 J7
Tresparrett Cnwll 6 G6
Tressait P & K 130 E12
Tresta Shet 147 i6
Tresta Shet 147 k3
Treswell Notts 79 K8
Treswithian Cnwll 2 G6
Tre Taliesin Cerdgn 49 L2
Trethevey Cnwll 6 F7
Trethewey Cnwll 2 B9
Trethomas Caerph 28 A4
Trethosa Cnwll 3 M4
Trethurgy Cnwll 3 P3
Tretio Pembks 36 F5
Tretire Herefs 40 G7
Tretower Powys 40 B7
Treuddyn Flints 75 J12
Trevadlock Cnwll 7 K9
Trevalga Cnwll 6 F7
Trevalyn Wrexhm 75 L12
Trevanger Cnwll 6 D9
Trevanson Cnwll 6 E10
Trevarrack Cnwll 2 D8
Trevarren Cnwll 3 M2
Trevarrian Cnwll 6 B11
Trevarrick Cnwll 3 N6
Trevarth Cnwll 2 H6
Trevaughan Carmth 37 N7
Tre-vaughan Carmth 38 B7
Treveal Cnwll 2 D6
Treveal Cnwll 3 J3
Treveighan Cnwll 6 F9
Trevellas Downs Cnwll 3 J4
Trevelmond Cnwll 4 B4
Trevemper Cnwll 3 K3
Treveor Cnwll 3 N6
Treverbyn Cnwll 3 L5
Treverbyn Cnwll 3 P3
Treverva Cnwll 3 J8
Trevescan Cnwll 2 B9
Trevethin Torfn 40 C11
Trevia Cnwll 6 G8
Trevigro Cnwll 4 E3
Trevilla Cnwll 3 K7
Trevilson Cnwll 3 L3
Treviscoe Cnwll 3 M3
Treviskey Cnwll 3 M6
Trevithick Cnwll 3 L2
Trevithick Cnwll 3 N5
Trevoll Cnwll 3 K3
Trevone Cnwll 6 C9
Trevor Wrexhm 63 J4
Trevorgans Cnwll 2 C9
Trevorrick Cnwll 6 D10
Trevose Cnwll 6 B9
Trew Cnwll 2 F8
Trewalder Cnwll 6 F8
Trewalkin Powys 39 R5
Trewarmett Cnwll 6 F7
Trewassa Cnwll 6 H7
Trewavas Cnwll 2 F9
Trewavas Mining District Cnwll 2 F9
Treween Cnwll 7 J8
Trewellard Cnwll 2 B8
Trewen Cnwll 7 J8
Trewennack Cnwll 2 H9
Trewent Pembks 37 K11
Trewern Powys 63 J10
Trewetha Cnwll 6 E8
Trewethern Cnwll 6 E9
Trewidland Cnwll 4 C5
Trewillis Cnwll 3 J11
Trewint Cnwll 4 D4
Trewint Cnwll 7 J8
Trewithian Cnwll 3 L7
Trewoodloe Cnwll 7 L10
Trewoon Cnwll 2 H10
Trewoon Cnwll 3 N4
Treworga Cnwll 3 L6
Treworgan Cnwll 3 K4
Treworlas Cnwll 3 L7
Treworld Cnwll 6 G6
Treworthal Cnwll 3 L7
Tre-wyn Mons 40 D7
Treyarnon Cnwll 6 B10
Treyford W Susx 25 P9
Trickett's Cross Dorset 11 Q4
Triermain Cumb 98 H5
Triffleton Pembks 37 J6
Trillacott Cnwll 7 K7
Trimdon Dur 101 K11
Trimdon Colliery Dur 101 K11
Trimdon Grange Dur 101 K11
Trimingham Norfk 71 K4
Trimley Lower Street Suffk 47 N4
Trimley St Martin Suffk 47 N4
Trimley St Mary Suffk 47 N4
Trimpley Worcs 52 E5
Trimsaran Carmth 38 C10
Trims Green Herts 45 N8
Trimstone Devon 19 K5
Trinafour P & K 130 D11
Trinant Caerph 28 B2
Tring Herts 44 C9
Tringford Herts 44 C9
Tring Wharf Herts 44 C9
Trinity Angus 132 F12
Trinity Jersey 13 c1
Trinity Gask P & K 123 N9
Triscombe Somset 21 J6
Trislaig Highld 128 F9
Trispen Cnwll 3 K4
Tritlington Nthumb 109 K11
Troan Cnwll 3 L3
Trochry P & K 123 P5
Troedrhiwfuwch Caerph 39 Q10
Troedyraur Cerdgn 48 E11
Troedyrhiw Myr Td 39 P11
Trofarth Conwy 73 Q9
Trois Bois Jersey 13 b2
Troon Cnwll 2 G7
Troon S Ayrs 104 F4
Tropical World Roundhay Park Leeds 85 L7
Trossachs Stirlg 122 E11
Trossachs Pier Stirlg 122 E11
Troston Suffk 58 C6
Troswell Cnwll 7 J6
Trotshill Worcs 52 G9
Trottiscliffe Kent 34 B10
Trotton W Susx 25 P9
Troughend Nthumb 108 D11
Trough Gate Lancs 84 D11
Troutbeck Cumb 89 L1
Troutbeck Cumb 89 L6
Troutbeck Bridge Cumb 89 L7
Troway Derbys 78 C8
Trowbridge Wilts 29 P10
Trowell Notts 66 D4
Trowell Services Notts 66 E4
Trowle Common Wilts 29 N10
Trowley Bottom Herts 44 F9
Trowse Newton Norfk 71 K10
Troy Leeds 85 K7
Trudoxhill Somset 22 G5
Trull Somset 21 K9
Trumfleet Donc 78 F1
Trumpan Highld 134 D4
Trumpet Herefs 41 K4
Trumpington Cambs 56 H9
Trumpsgreen Surrey 32 E9
Trunch Norfk 71 K5
Trunnah Lancs 82 H6
Truro Cnwll 3 K5
Truscott Cnwll 7 K7
Trusham Devon 8 F8
Trusley Derbys 65 N5
Trusthorpe Lincs 81 K7
Trysull Staffs 52 F2
Tubney Oxon 31 J3
Tuckenhay Devon 5 N5
Tuckhill Shrops 52 E3
Tuckingmill Cnwll 2 G6
Tuckingmill Wilts 23 L7
Tuckton BCP 12 B6
Tucoyse Cnwll 3 N5
Tuddenham Suffk 57 P6
Tuddenham Suffk 59 J11
Tudeley Kent 16 A2
Tudhoe Dur 100 H11
Tudorville Herefs 41 J7
Tudweiliog Gwynd 60 D5
Tuesley Surrey 14 D2
Tuffley Gloucs 41 N8
Tufton Hants 24 G4
Tufton Pembks 37 K5
Tugby Leics 67 J12
Tugford Shrops 51 P3
Tughall Nthumb 109 K4
Tullibody Clacks 114 F2
Tullich Abers 132 B5
Tullich Highld 138 B10
Tullich Highld 146 F10
Tulliemet P & K 123 P2
Tulloch Abers 141 J9
Tullochgorm Ag & B 112 E2
Tulloch Station Highld 129 L8
Tullymurdoch P & K 124 D2
Tullynessle Abers 140 E12
Tulse Hill Gt Lon 33 K8
Tumble Carmth 38 E9
Tumbler's Green Essex 46 E6
Tumby Lincs 80 E11
Tumby Woodside Lincs 80 E12
Tummel Bridge P & K 123 K1
Tunbridge Wells Kent 15 Q3
Tundergarth D & G 97 N2
Tunga W Isls 152 g3
Tungate Norfk 71 K6
Tunley BaNES 29 L10
Tunstall C Stke 64 F2
Tunstall E R Yk 87 P9
Tunstall Kent 34 F10
Tunstall Lancs 89 P12
Tunstall N York 91 L7
Tunstall Norfk 71 N10
Tunstall Staffs 64 E6
Tunstall Suffk 59 M9
Tunstall Sundld 101 K7
Tunstead Derbys 77 L8
Tunstead Norfk 71 L8
Tunstead Milton Derbys 77 J7
Tunworth Hants 25 L4
Tupsley Herefs 40 H4
Turgis Green Hants 31 P10
Turkdean Gloucs 42 C8
Tur Langton Leics 54 H2
Turleigh Wilts 29 N10
Turleygreen Shrops 52 E4
Turn Lancs 84 B11
Turnastone Herefs 40 E4
Turnberry S Ayrs 104 D8
Turnchapel C Plym 4 H6
Turnditch Derbys 65 P3
Turner Green Lancs 83 N9
Turner's Green E Susx 16 B7
Turner's Green Warwks 53 M7
Turners Hill W Susx 15 L4
Turners Puddle Dorset 11 K6
Turnford Herts 45 L10
Turnhouse C Edin 115 L6
Turnworth Dorset 11 K3
Turriff Abers 140 H6
Turton Bottoms Bl w D 83 Q12
Turves Cambs 56 G1
Turvey Bed 55 N10
Turville Bucks 31 Q4
Turville Heath Bucks 31 Q4
Turweston Bucks 43 M4
Tushielaw Inn Border 107 J6
Tutbury Staffs 65 N6
Tutnall Worcs 53 J6
Tutshill Gloucs 28 H3
Tuttington Norfk 71 J7
Tutwell Cnwll 7 M9
Tuxford Notts 79 J9
Twatt Ork 147 b3
Twatt Shet 147 i6
Twechar E Duns 114 C6
Tweedbank Border 107 N3
Tweedmouth Nthumb 117 M10
Tweedsmuir Border 106 E5
Twelveheads Cnwll 3 J6
Twelve Oaks E Susx 16 C7
Twemlow Green Ches E 76 E10
Twenty Lincs 68 C8
Twerton BaNES 29 L9
Twickenham Gt Lon 32 H7
Twigworth Gloucs 41 N7
Twineham W Susx 15 J7
Twineham Green W Susx 15 J7
Twinhoe BaNES 29 M10
Twinstead Essex 46 F4
Twitchen Devon 20 B7
Twitchen Shrops 51 L5
Twitham Kent 35 N11
Two Bridges Devon 8 B9
Two Dales Derbys 77 P11
Two Gates Staffs 65 N12
Two Mile Ash W Susx 14 G5
Two Mile Oak Cross Devon 5 P3
Two Pots Devon 19 K4
Two Waters Herts 44 F10
Twycross Leics 65 Q11
Twycross Zoo Leics 65 P11

Well – Willenhall 191

Well N York 91 M10
Welland Worcs 41 M4
Wellbank Angus 125 J5
Well End Bucks 32 C5
Well End Herts 32 H3
Wellesbourne Warwks 53 P9
Wellesbourne Mountford Warwks 53 P9
Well Head Herts 44 H6
Well Hill Kent 33 P9
Wellhouse W Berk 31 L8
Welling Gt Lon 33 N7
Wellingborough Nhants 55 M7
Wellingham Norfk 70 C8
Wellingore Lincs 79 N12
Wellington Cumb 88 E6
Wellington Herefs 51 N11
Wellington Somset 21 J9
Wellington Wrekin 64 C10
Wellington Heath Herefs 41 L4
Wellington Marsh Herefs 40 G2
Wellow BaNES 29 L10
Wellow IoW 12 F7
Wellow Notts 78 H10
Wellpond Green Herts 45 M7
Wells Somset 22 D4
Wellsborough Leics 66 B11
Wells Green Ches E 64 C1
Wells Head C Brad 84 G8
Wells-next-the-Sea Norfk 70 D3
Wellstye Green Essex 46 B8
Well Town Devon 8 G3
Welltree P & K 123 N8
Wellwood Fife 115 K3
Welney Norfk 57 K2
Welshampton Shrops 63 M5
Welsh Bicknor Herefs 41 J8
Welsh End Shrops 63 N5
Welsh Frankton Shrops 63 K5
Welsh Hook Pembks 36 H5
Welsh Newton Herefs 40 G8
Welshpool Powys 62 H10
Welsh St Donats V Glam 27 N7
Welton Cumb 98 D9
Welton E R Yk 86 H9
Welton Lincs 79 P8
Welton Nhants 54 F7
Welton le Marsh Lincs 81 J10
Welton le Wold Lincs 80 E6
Welwick E R Yk 87 Q11
Welwyn Herts 45 J8
Welwyn Garden City Herts 45 J9
Wem Shrops 63 N6
Wembdon Somset 21 L6
Wembley Gt Lon 32 H5
Wembury Devon 4 H7
Wembworthy Devon 8 C3
Wemyss Bay Inver 113 J7
Wenallt Cerdgn 49 L6
Wendens Ambo Essex 45 P4
Wendlebury Oxon 43 M8
Wendling Norfk 70 D9
Wendover Bucks 44 B10
Wendron Cnwll 2 H8
Wendron Mining District Cnwll 2 H8
Wendy Cambs 56 F11
Wenfordbridge Cnwll 6 F9
Wenhaston Suffk 59 N5
Wennington Cambs 56 E5
Wennington Gt Lon 33 P6
Wennington Lancs 83 N1
Wensley Derbys 77 N11
Wensley N York 90 H9
Wentbridge Wakefd 85 P11
Wentnor Shrops 51 L2
Wentworth Cambs 57 J5
Wentworth Rothm 78 C4
Wentworth Castle Barns 77 Q3
Wenvoe V Glam 27 Q8
Weobley Herefs 51 L10
Weobley Marsh Herefs 51 L10
Wepham W Susx 14 F9
Wereham Norfk 69 N11
Wergs Wolves 64 F12
Wern Gwynd 61 J4
Wern Powys 39 Q8
Wern Powys 63 J9
Wern Shrops 63 J5
Werneth Low Tamesd 76 H5
Wernffrwd Swans 26 D3
Wern-y-gaer Flints 74 H10
Werrington C Pete 68 C11
Werrington Cnwll 7 L7
Werrington Staffs 64 H3
Wervin Ches W 75 M9
Wesham Lancs 83 K8
Wessington Derbys 78 B12
West Aberthaw V Glam 27 N9
West Acre Norfk 69 P9
West Allerdean Nthumb 117 L12
West Alvington Devon 5 M8
West Amesbury Wilts 23 P5
West Anstey Devon 20 C8
West Appleton N York 91 L8
West Ashby Lincs 80 E9
West Ashling W Susx 13 P3
West Ashton Wilts 23 J2
West Auckland Dur 91 K2
West Ayton N York 93 K9
West Bagborough Somset 21 J6
West Bank Blae G 40 B10
West Bank Halton 75 N7
West Barkwith Lincs 80 C7
West Barnby N York 92 G4
West Barns E Loth 116 F6
West Barsham Norfk 70 D5
West Bay Dorset 10 C6
West Beckham Norfk 70 H4
West Bedfont Surrey 32 F7
Westbere Kent 35 M10
West Bergholt Essex 46 G6
West Bexington Dorset 10 E7
West Bilney Norfk 69 N9
West Blatchington Br & H 15 K9
West Boldon S Tyne 101 J6
Westborough Lincs 67 L3
Westbourne BCP 11 P6
Westbourne W Susx 13 N3
West Bourton Dorset 22 G7
West Bowling C Brad 85 J9
West Brabourne Kent 17 K2
West Bradenham Norfk 70 D10
West Bradford Lancs 83 R6
West Bradley Somset 22 D6
West Bretton Wakefd 77 P1
West Bridgford Notts 66 F5
West Briscoe Dur 90 F3
West Bromwich Sandw 53 J2
Westbrook Kent 35 P8
Westbrook W Berk 31 J8
Westbrook Wilts 29 Q9
West Buckland Devon 19 M7
West Buckland Somset 21 J9
West Burrafirth Shet 147 h6
West Burton N York 90 G9
West Burton W Susx 14 E8
Westbury Bucks 43 N4
Westbury Shrops 63 K10
Westbury Wilts 23 J3
Westbury Leigh Wilts 23 J3
Westbury-on-Severn Gloucs 41 L9
Westbury-on-Trym Bristl 28 H7
Westbury-sub-Mendip Somset 22 C3
West Butsfield Dur 100 E9
West Butterwick N Linc 79 L3
Westby Lancs 83 J9
West Byfleet Surrey 32 F10
West Cairngaan D & G 94 G12
West Caister Norfk 71 P10
West Calder W Loth 115 J8
West Camel Somset 22 D8
West Chaldon Dorset 11 J8
West Challow Oxon 30 H5
West Charleton Devon 5 M8
West Chelborough Dorset 10 E4
West Chevington Nthumb 109 L10
West Chiltington W Susx 14 F7
West Chinnock Somset 21 P10
West Chisenbury Wilts 23 P3
West Clandon Surrey 32 F11
West Cliffe Kent 17 P2
Westcliff-on-Sea Sthend 34 F5
West Coker Somset 22 C10
West Combe Devon 5 M4
Westcombe Somset 22 F5
West Compton Somset 22 D5
West Compton Abbas Dorset 10 E6
Westcote Gloucs 42 E7
Westcote Barton Oxon 43 J6
Westcott Bucks 43 P8
Westcott Devon 9 J4
Westcott Surrey 14 G1
West Cottingwith N York 86 C7
Westcourt Wilts 30 E10
West Cowick E R Yk 86 C11
West Cross Swans 26 F4
West Curry Cnwll 7 K6
West Curthwaite Cumb 98 C8
Westdean E Susx 15 P11
West Dean W Susx 14 B8
West Dean Wilts 24 D8
West Deeping Lincs 68 B10
West Derby Lpool 75 L5
West Dereham Norfk 69 M12
West Ditchburn Nthumb 109 J5
West Down Devon 19 K5
Westdown Camp Wilts 23 M4
Westdowns Cnwll 6 F8
West Drayton Gt Lon 32 F6
West Drayton Notts 78 H8
West Dunnet Highld 151 M2
Wested Kent 33 P9
West Ella E R Yk 87 J9
West End Bed 55 N10
West End Br For 32 B8
West End Caerph 28 B3
West End Cambs 56 F7
West End Cumb 98 C6
West End E R Yk 86 G9
West End E R Yk 87 M9
West End E R Yk 87 P9
Westend Gloucs 41 M10
West End Hants 24 H10
West End Hants 25 L6
West End Herts 45 J10
West End Herts 45 L10
West End Lancs 83 Q9
West End Leeds 85 K7
West End Lincs 80 G4
West End N Som 28 F8
West End N York 85 Q7
West End Norfk 70 D10
West End Norfk 71 P10
West End Oxon 31 M5
West End S Glos 29 L5
West End Somset 22 F6
West End Surrey 32 D10
West End Surrey 32 G9
West End W & M 32 B7
West End W Susx 14 H7
West End Wilts 23 K8
West End Wilts 23 L8
West End Wilts 29 R7
West End Green Hants 31 N10
Westend Town Nthumb 99 M5
Westenhanger Kent 17 K3
Wester Aberchalder Highld 137 P11
Westerdale Highld 151 L6
Westerdale N York 92 D5
Westerfield Suffk 58 H11
Westergate W Susx 14 D10
Westerham Kent 33 N11
Westerhope N u Ty 100 F5
Westerland Devon 5 P4
Westerleigh S Glos 29 L6
Western Isles W Isls 152 e6
Wester Ochiltree W Loth 115 J6
Wester Pitkierie Fife 125 L11
Wester Ross Highld 143 P9
Westerton W Susx 14 C9
Westerton of Rossie Angus 125 N2
Westerwick Shet 147 h7
West Ewell Surrey 32 H9
West Farleigh Kent 34 C11
West Farndon Nhants 54 E10
West Felton Shrops 63 K7
Westfield BaNES 22 F3
Westfield Cumb 88 C1
Westfield E Susx 16 E8
Westfield Highld 151 J4
Westfield N Lans 114 D6
Westfield Norfk 70 E10
Westfield W Loth 114 G7
Westfields Dorset 10 H3
Westfields Herefs 40 G3
Westfields of Rattray P & K 124 D3
Westfield Sole Kent 34 D10
West Flotmanby N York 93 M11
Westford Somset 20 H9
Westgate Dur 99 P10
Westgate N Linc 79 K2
Westgate Norfk 70 E4
Westgate Hill C Brad 85 J9
Westgate-on-Sea Kent 35 P8
Westgate Street Norfk 71 J8
West Ginge Oxon 31 J5
West Grafton Wilts 30 F10
West Green Hants 31 Q11
West Grimstead Wilts 24 C8
West Grinstead W Susx 14 H6
West Haddlesey N York 85 R10
West Haddon Nhants 54 G6
West Hagbourne Oxon 31 L5
West Hagley Worcs 52 G4
Westhall Suffk 59 N4
West Hallam Derbys 66 C4
West Hallam Common Derbys 66 C4
West Halton N Linc 86 G11
Westham Dorset 10 G9
Westham E Susx 16 B10
West Ham Gt Lon 33 M5
Westham Somset 21 N4
Westhampnett W Susx 14 C9
West Handley Derbys 78 C8
West Hanney Oxon 31 J4
West Hanningfield Essex 34 C2
West Harnham Wilts 23 P7
West Harptree BaNES 28 H11
West Harting W Susx 25 N9
West Hatch Somset 21 L9
West Hatch Wilts 23 K8
West Haven Angus 125 L6
Westhay Somset 21 P5
Westhead Lancs 75 M2
West Head Norfk 69 L11
West Heath Birm 53 J5
West Heath Hants 31 M10
West Helmsdale Highld 147 J2
West Hendred Oxon 31 J5
West Heslerton N York 93 J11
West Hewish N Som 28 E9
Westhide Herefs 41 J3
Westhill Abers 133 K3
West Hill Devon 9 K6
Westhill Highld 138 D7
West Hoathly W Susx 15 L4
West Holme Dorset 11 L7
Westholme Somset 22 D5
Westhope Herefs 51 M10
Westhope Shrops 51 M3
West Horndon Essex 34 A5
Westhorp Nhants 54 E10
Westhorpe Lincs 68 D6
Westhorpe Suffk 58 F7
West Horrington Somset 22 D4
West Horsley Surrey 32 F11
West Horton Nthumb 108 G4
West Hougham Kent 17 N3
Westhoughton Bolton 76 C2
Westhouse N York 89 R12
Westhouses Derbys 78 C12
West Howe BCP 11 P5
West Howetown Somset 20 E6
Westhumble Surrey 32 H12
West Huntingtower P & K 124 B8
West Huntspill Somset 21 M4
West Hyde C Beds 44 G8
West Hyde Herts 32 E4
West Hythe Kent 17 K4
West Ilkerton Devon 19 N4
West Ilsley W Berk 31 K6
West Itchenor W Susx 13 P4
West Keal Lincs 80 G11
West Kennett Wilts 30 C8
West Kilbride N Ayrs 113 J11
West Kingsdown Kent 33 Q9
West Kington Wilts 29 N7
West Kirby Wirral 74 H6
West Knapton N York 92 H11
West Knighton Dorset 10 H7
West Knoyle Wilts 23 J7
West Kyloe Nthumb 108 H2
Westlake Devon 5 K6
West Lambrook Somset 21 P9
Westland Green Herts 45 M7
West Langdon Kent 17 P1
West Lavington W Susx 14 C7
West Lavington Wilts 23 M3
West Layton N York 91 J5
West Leake Notts 66 E7
West Learmouth Nthumb 108 D2
West Lees N York 91 Q6
West Leigh Devon 8 C4
Westleigh Devon 19 J7
Westleigh Devon 20 G10
West Leigh Somset 20 H7
Westleton Suffk 59 N7
West Lexham Norfk 70 B8
Westley Shrops 63 K10
Westley Suffk 58 B8
Westley Waterless Cambs 57 M9
West Lilling N York 86 C2
Westlington Bucks 43 Q9
West Linton Border 115 L11
Westlinton Cumb 98 E5
West Littleton S Glos 29 M7
West Lockinge Oxon 31 J5
West Lulworth Dorset 11 K8
West Lutton N York 86 H1
West Lydford Somset 22 D7
West Lyn Devon 19 P4
West Lyng Somset 21 M7
West Lynn Norfk 69 L8
West Malling Kent 34 B10
West Malvern Worcs 41 M2
West Marden W Susx 25 N10
West Markham Notts 79 J9
Westmarsh Kent 35 N10
West Marsh NE Lin 80 E2
West Marton N York 84 D5
West Melbury Dorset 23 J9
West Melton Rothm 78 C3
West Meon Hants 25 L8
West Meon Hut Hants 25 L8
West Meon Woodlands Hants 25 L8
West Mersea Essex 46 H9
Westmeston E Susx 15 L8
West Mickley Nthumb 100 D6
West Midland Safari Park Worcs 52 E5
Westmill Herts 45 L6
Westmill Herts 45 L8
West Milton Dorset 10 D5
Westminster Gt Lon 33 K6
Westminster Abbey & Palace Gt Lon 33 K6
West Molesey Surrey 32 G8
West Monkton Somset 21 L7
West Moors Dorset 11 P4
West Morden Dorset 11 L6
West Morriston Border 107 P2
West Morton C Brad 84 G6
West Mudford Somset 22 D9
Westmuir Angus 124 G2
West Ness N York 92 E11
West Newbiggin Darltn 91 N3
Westnewton Cumb 97 N9
West Newton E R Yk 87 M7
West Newton Norfk 69 N6
West Newton Somset 21 L7
West Norwood Gt Lon 33 K8
Westoe S Tyne 101 K5
West Ogwell Devon 5 N3
Weston BaNES 29 L9
Weston Ches E 64 D2
Weston Devon 9 M5
Weston Devon 9 M7
Weston Dorset 10 G10
Weston Halton 75 N7
Weston Hants 25 M9
Weston Herefs 51 L9
Weston Herts 45 J5
Weston Lincs 68 F7
Weston N York 85 J6
Weston Nhants 43 M2
Weston Notts 79 K10
Weston Shrops 51 K6
Weston Shrops 51 Q2
Weston Shrops 63 J6
Weston Staffs 64 H7
Weston Suffk 59 N3
Weston W Berk 31 J7
Weston Beggard Herefs 41 J3
Westonbirt Gloucs 29 P4
Weston by Welland Nhants 55 K2
Weston Colley Hants 24 H5
Weston Colville Cambs 57 L10
Weston Corbett Hants 25 M4
Weston Coyney C Stke 64 H3
Weston Favell Nhants 55 K8
Weston Green Cambs 57 M10
Weston Heath Shrops 64 E9
Weston Hills Lincs 68 E8
Weston in Arden Warwks 54 C3
Westoning C Beds 44 E5
Weston-in-Gordano N Som 28 F7
Westoning Woodend C Beds 44 E5
Weston Jones Staffs 64 E7
Weston Longville Norfk 70 G9
Weston Lullingfields Shrops 63 M7
Weston-on-Avon Warwks 53 M10
Weston-on-the-Green Oxon 43 L8
Weston Park Staffs 64 E10
Weston Patrick Hants 25 M4
Weston Rhyn Shrops 63 J5
Weston-sub-Edge Gloucs 42 D3
Weston-super-Mare N Som 28 D10
Weston Turville Bucks 44 B9
Weston-under-Lizard Staffs 64 E10
Weston under Penyard Herefs 41 K7
Weston-under-Redcastle Shrops 63 P6
Weston under Wetherley Warwks 54 B7
Weston Underwood Derbys 65 P4
Weston Underwood M Keyn 55 L10
Weston-upon-Trent Derbys 66 C6
Westonzoyland Somset 21 M6
West Orchard Dorset 22 H10
West Overton Wilts 30 D9
Westow N York 86 D2
West Panson Devon 7 L6
West Park Abers 133 J5
West Parley Dorset 11 Q5
West Peckham Kent 34 B11
West Peeke Devon 7 L6
West Pelton Dur 100 G7
West Pennard Somset 22 D5
West Pentire Cnwll 3 J2
West Perry Cambs 56 C7
West Pinchbeck Lincs 68 D7
West Porlock Somset 20 D4
Westport Somset 21 N9
West Pulham Dorset 10 H3
West Putford Devon 18 G10
West Quantoxhead Somset 20 H5
Westquarter Falk 114 G5
Westra V Glam 27 Q8
West Raddon Devon 8 G4
West Rainton Dur 101 J9
West Rasen Lincs 79 Q6
West Ravendale NE Lin 80 E4
Westray Ork 147 c2
Westray Airport Ork 147 c1
West Raynham Norfk 70 C7
West Retford Notts 78 H7
Westridge Green W Berk 31 M6
Westrigg W Loth 114 G8
Westrop Swindn 30 E4
West Rounton N York 91 P6
West Row Suffk 57 N5
West Rudham Norfk 70 B6
West Runton Norfk 71 J4
Westruther Border 116 E11
Westry Cambs 56 H1
West Saltoun E Loth 116 B8
West Sandford Devon 8 F4
West Sandwick Shet 147 j4
West Scrafton N York 90 H10
West Sleekburn Nthumb 100 H1
West Somerton Norfk 71 P8
West Stafford Dorset 10 H7
West Stockwith Notts 79 K5
West Stoke W Susx 13 P3
West Stonesdale N York 90 E6
West Stoughton Somset 21 P4
West Stour Dorset 22 H9
West Stourmouth Kent 35 N9
West Stow Suffk 57 Q6
West Stowell Wilts 30 D10
West Stratton Hants 25 J5
West Street Kent 34 F11
West Street Kent 35 P11
West Street Medway 34 C7
West Street Suffk 58 E6
West Tanfield N York 91 M11
West Taphouse Cnwll 4 A4
West Tarbert Ag & B 112 C8
West Tarring W Susx 14 G10
West Thirston Nthumb 109 K10
West Thorney W Susx 13 N4
Westthorpe Derbys 78 D8
West Thorpe Notts 66 G7
West Thurrock Thurr 33 Q7
West Tilbury Thurr 34 B7
West Tisted Hants 25 L7
West Torrington Lincs 80 C7
West Town BaNES 28 G10
West Town Hants 13 M5
West Town Herefs 51 M8
West Town N Som 28 G8
West Town Somset 22 C6
West Town Somset 22 F5
West Tytherley Hants 24 D7
West Walton Norfk 69 J9
Westward Cumb 98 C9
Westward Ho! Devon 18 H7
Westwell Kent 16 H1
Westwell Oxon 42 E9
Westwell Leacon Kent 16 G1
West Wellow Hants 24 D9
West Wembury Devon 4 H7
West Wemyss Fife 115 P2
Westwick Cambs 56 H7
Westwick Dur 90 H4
West Wick N Som 28 E10
Westwick Norfk 71 K7
West Wickham Cambs 57 L10
West Wickham Gt Lon 33 M9
West Williamston Pembks 37 K9
West Winch Norfk 69 M9
West Winterslow Wilts 24 C7
West Wittering W Susx 13 N5
West Witton N York 90 H9
Westwood Devon 9 J5
Westwood Kent 33 R8
Westwood Kent 35 Q9
Westwood Notts 66 D2
Westwood Nthumb 99 L5
Westwood Wilts 29 N10
West Woodburn Nthumb 108 E12
West Woodhay W Berk 31 J9
Westwood Heath Covtry 53 P5
West Woodlands Somset 22 H4
Westwoodside N Linc 79 J4
West Worldham Hants 25 M6
West Worthing W Susx 14 G10
West Wratting Cambs 57 L10
West Wycombe Bucks 32 B3
West Wylam Nthumb 100 E5
West Yatton Wilts 29 P7
West Yoke Kent 33 Q9
West Youlstone Cnwll 18 E10
Wetham Green Kent 34 E8
Wetheral Cumb 98 F7
Wetherby Leeds 85 N5
Wetherby Services N York 85 N5
Wetherden Suffk 58 E8
Wetheringsett Suffk 58 H7
Wethersfield Essex 46 C5
Wetherup Street Suffk 58 H8
Wetley Rocks Staffs 64 H2
Wettenhall Ches E 76 B11
Wetton Staffs 65 L1
Wetwang E R Yk 86 H3
Wetwood Staffs 64 E5
Wexcombe Wilts 30 F10
Wexham Slough 32 E6
Wexham Street Bucks 32 E6
Weybourne Norfk 70 G4
Weybourne Surrey 25 P3
Weybread Suffk 59 K4
Weybread Street Suffk 59 K5
Weybridge Surrey 32 F9
Weycroft Devon 9 P5
Weydale Highld 151 L4
Weyhill Hants 24 E4
Weymouth Dorset 10 G9
Whaddon Bucks 44 A5
Whaddon Cambs 45 L2
Whaddon Gloucs 41 N9
Whaddon Wilts 24 C8
Whaddon Wilts 29 P10
Whale Cumb 89 N2
Whaley Derbys 78 E9
Whaley Bridge Derbys 77 J7
Whaley Thorns Derbys 78 E9
Whaligoe Highld 151 P8
Whalley Lancs 83 Q8
Whalley Banks Lancs 83 Q8
Whalsay Shet 147 k5
Whalton Nthumb 100 E2
Whaplode Lincs 68 F7
Whaplode Drove Lincs 68 F9
Wharf Warwks 54 C10
Wharfe N York 84 B1
Wharles Lancs 83 K8
Wharley End C Beds 44 D3
Wharncliffe Side Sheff 77 P5
Wharram-le-Street N York 86 F2
Wharton Ches W 76 C10
Wharton Herefs 51 N9
Whashton N York 91 K5
Whasset Cumb 89 N10
Whatcote Warwks 42 G3
Whateley Warwks 65 N12
Whatfield Suffk 47 J2
Whatley Somset 10 B3
Whatley Somset 22 G4
Whatley's End S Glos 29 K6
Whatlington E Susx 16 D7
Whatsole Street Kent 17 K2
Whatstandwell Derbys 65 Q1
Whatton-in-the-Vale Notts 67 J4
Whauphill D & G 95 M8
Whaw N York 90 G6
Wheal Peevor Cnwll 2 H5
Wheal Rose Cnwll 2 H5
Wheatacre Norfk 59 P2
Wheatfield Oxon 31 P2
Wheathampstead Herts 44 H9
Wheathill Shrops 52 B4
Wheathill Somset 22 D7
Wheatley Calder 84 G10
Wheatley Hants 25 N5
Wheatley Oxon 43 M10
Wheatley Hill Dur 101 K10
Wheatley Hills Donc 78 F3
Wheatley Lane Lancs 84 C7
Wheaton Aston Staffs 64 F9
Wheddon Cross Somset 20 E5
Wheelbarrow Town Kent 17 L2
Wheeler End Bucks 32 A4
Wheeler's Green Wokham 31 Q8
Wheelerstreet Surrey 14 D3
Wheelock Ches E 76 D12
Wheelock Heath Ches E 76 D12
Wheelton Lancs 83 N11
Wheldale Wakefd 85 P10
Wheldrake C York 86 C6
Whelford Gloucs 30 D3
Whelpley Hill Bucks 44 E10
Whelpo Cumb 98 C10
Whelston Flints 74 H8
Whempstead Herts 45 K7
Whenby N York 86 B1
Whepstead Suffk 58 B9
Wherstead Suffk 47 L3
Wherwell Hants 24 F5
Wheston Derbys 77 L8
Whetsted Kent 16 B2
Whetstone Gt Lon 33 J4
Whetstone Leics 54 F1
Wheyrigg Cumb 97 P8
Whicham Cumb 88 F10
Whichford Warwks 42 G5
Whickham Gatesd 100 G6
Whiddon Devon 7 N5
Whiddon Down Devon 8 C6
Whigstreet Angus 125 J4
Whilton Nhants 54 G7
Whimble Devon 7 L4
Whimple Devon 9 K5
Whimpwell Green Norfk 71 M6
Whinburgh Norfk 70 E10
Whin Lane End Lancs 83 J7
Whinnieliggate D & G 96 E8
Whinnow Cumb 98 C8
Whinnyfold Abers 141 P9
Whinny Hill S on T 91 P3
Whippingham IoW 12 H6
Whipsnade C Beds 44 E8
Whipsnade Zoo ZSL C Beds 44 E8
Whipton Devon 8 H6
Whirlow Sheff 77 P7
Whisby Lincs 79 M10
Whissendine Rutlnd 67 K9
Whissonsett Norfk 70 D7
Whistlefield Ag & B 113 J3
Whistlefield Inn Ag & B 112 H3
Whistley Green Wokham 31 R7
Whiston Knows 75 N5
Whiston Nhants 55 L8
Whiston Rothm 78 D6
Whiston Staffs 64 G9
Whiston Staffs 65 J3
Whiston Cross Shrops 64 E11
Whiston Eaves Staffs 65 K3
Whitacre Fields Warwks 53 N2
Whitbeck Cumb 88 F10
Whitbourne Herefs 52 D9
Whitburn S Tyne 101 K6
Whitburn W Loth 114 H8
Whitby Ches W 75 L8
Whitby N York 92 H4
Whitbyheath Ches W 75 L9
Whitchester Border 116 G9
Whitchurch BaNES 29 J9
Whitchurch Bucks 44 A7
Whitchurch Cardif 27 R6
Whitchurch Devon 7 P10
Whitchurch Hants 24 H4
Whitchurch Herefs 40 H8
Whitchurch Oxon 31 N7
Whitchurch Pembks 36 F5
Whitchurch Shrops 63 P4
Whitchurch Canonicorum Dorset 10 B6
Whitchurch Hill Oxon 31 N6
Whitcombe Dorset 10 H7
Whitcot Shrops 51 L2
Whitcott Keysett Shrops 51 J4
Whiteacre Kent 17 K1
Whiteacre Heath Warwks 53 N2
Whiteash Green Essex 46 D5
White Ball Somset 20 H9
Whitebridge Highld 129 N1
Whitebrook Mons 40 H10
Whitebushes Surrey 15 K1
Whitecairns Abers 141 M12
Whitechapel Gt Lon 33 L6
White Chapel Lancs 83 M7
Whitechurch Pembks 37 M3
Whitecliff Gloucs 40 H9
White Colne Essex 46 F6
White Coppice Lancs 83 N11
Whitecraig E Loth 115 Q7
Whitecroft Gloucs 41 J10
Whitecrook D & G 94 H7
Whitecross Cnwll 2 E7
White Cross Cnwll 2 H10
Whitecross Cnwll 6 D10
Whitecross Falk 114 H6
White End Worcs 41 M5
Whiteface Highld 146 C7
Whitefarland N Ayrs 103 M1
Whitefaulds S Ayrs 104 E8
Whitefield Bury 76 E2
Whitefield Devon 19 N6
Whitefield Somset 20 G7
Whitefield Lane End Knows 75 M6
Whiteford Abers 140 H10
Whitegate Ches W 76 B10
Whitehall Hants 25 N3
Whitehall Ork 147 e3
Whitehall W Susx 14 G6
Whitehaven Cumb 88 C3
Whitehill Kent 34 H10
Whitehill Leics 66 C10
Whitehill and Bordon Hants 25 N6
Whitehills Abers 140 G3
Whitehouse Abers 132 F1
Whitehouse Ag & B 112 B9
Whitehouse Common Birm 53 L1
Whitekirk E Loth 116 E5
White Kirkley Dur 100 C11
White Lackington Dorset 10 H5
Whitelackington Somset 21 N10
White Ladies Aston Worcs 52 G10
Whiteleaf Bucks 44 B10
White-le-Head Dur 100 F7
Whiteley Hants 13 J3
Whiteley Bank IoW 13 J8
Whiteley Green Ches E 76 G8
Whiteley Village Surrey 32 F10
Whitemans Green W Susx 15 K6
White Mill Carmth 38 C7
Whitemire Moray 138 H5
Whitemoor C Nott 66 E4
Whitemoor Cnwll 3 N3
Whitemoor Derbys 66 B3
Whitemoor Staffs 76 G11
Whiteness Shet 147 i7
White Notley Essex 46 D8
Whiteoak Green Oxon 42 H9
White Ox Mead BaNES 29 L10
Whiteparish Wilts 24 D8
White Pit Lincs 80 G8
Whiterashes Abers 141 K11
White Roding Essex 45 Q9
Whiterow Highld 151 Q7
Whiterow Moray 139 J4
Whiteshill Gloucs 41 N10
Whitesmith E Susx 15 P8
White Stake Lancs 83 M10
Whitestaunton Somset 9 P3
Whitestone Devon 8 G6
White Stone Herefs 40 H3
Whitestone Cross Devon 8 G6
Whitestreet Green Suffk 46 H4
Whitewall Corner N York 86 E1
White Waltham W & M 32 B7
Whiteway BaNES 29 L9
Whiteway Gloucs 41 Q9
Whitewell Lancs 83 P6
Whiteworks Devon 8 B10
Whitfield C Dund 125 J6
Whitfield Kent 17 N2
Whitfield Nhants 43 M4
Whitfield Nthumb 99 M7
Whitfield S Glos 29 K4
Whitfield Hall Nthumb 99 M7
Whitford Devon 9 P5
Whitford Flints 74 G8
Whitgift E R Yk 86 E10
Whitgreave Staffs 64 G6
Whithorn D & G 95 N10
Whiting Bay N Ayrs 103 Q4
Whitkirk Leeds 85 M8
Whitland Carmth 37 N7
Whitlaw Border 107 M7
Whitletts S Ayrs 104 G5
Whitley N York 85 R11
Whitley Readg 31 P8
Whitley Sheff 77 Q5
Whitley Wilts 29 P9
Whitley Bay N Tyne 101 J4
Whitley Chapel Nthumb 99 P7
Whitley Heath Staffs 64 F7
Whitley Lower Kirk 85 J11
Whitley Row Kent 33 P11
Whitlock's End Solhll 53 L5
Whitminster Gloucs 41 M10
Whitmore Dorset 11 P3
Whitmore Staffs 64 E4
Whitnage Devon 20 G10
Whitnash Warwks 53 Q8
Whitney-on-Wye Herefs 40 C2
Whitrigg Cumb 97 P10
Whitrigg Cumb 97 P6
Whitrigglees Cumb 97 P7
Whitsbury Hants 23 P9
Whitsome Border 117 J11
Whitson Newpt 28 E6
Whitstable Kent 35 K9
Whitstone Cnwll 7 K5
Whittingham Nthumb 108 H7
Whittingslow Shrops 51 M3
Whittington Derbys 78 C8
Whittington Gloucs 42 B7
Whittington Lancs 89 P11
Whittington Norfk 69 N12
Whittington Shrops 63 K6
Whittington Staffs 52 F4
Whittington Staffs 65 M10
Whittington Warwks 65 P12
Whittington Worcs 52 G10
Whittington Moor Derbys 78 B9
Whittlebury Nhants 43 P3
Whittle-le-Woods Lancs 83 N11
Whittlesey Cambs 56 E1
Whittlesford Cambs 57 J11
Whittlestone Head Bl w D 83 Q11
Whitton N Linc 86 G10
Whitton Nthumb 108 H9
Whitton Powys 51 J7
Whitton S on T 91 P2
Whitton Shrops 51 P6
Whitton Suffk 58 H11
Whittonditch Wilts 30 G8
Whittonstall Nthumb 100 D7
Whitway Hants 31 K10
Whitwell Derbys 78 E8
Whitwell Herts 44 H7
Whitwell IoW 13 J9
Whitwell N York 91 M7
Whitwell Rutlnd 67 M10
Whitwell-on-the-Hill N York 86 D2
Whitwell Street Norfk 70 G8
Whitwick Leics 66 D9
Whitwood Wakefd 85 N10
Whitworth Lancs 84 D11
Whixall Shrops 63 N5
Whixley N York 85 N4
Whorlton Dur 91 J4
Whorlton N York 91 Q6
Whyle Herefs 51 P8
Whyteleafe Surrey 33 L10
Wibdon Gloucs 28 H3
Wibsey C Brad 84 H9
Wibtoft Warwks 54 D3
Wichenford Worcs 52 E8
Wichling Kent 34 G11
Wick BCP 12 B6
Wick Devon 9 M4
Wick Highld 151 Q6
Wick S Glos 29 L8
Wick Somset 21 K4
Wick Somset 21 N8
Wick V Glam 27 L8
Wick W Susx 14 E10
Wick Wilts 23 Q9
Wick Worcs 41 Q3
Wicken Cambs 57 L6
Wicken Nhants 43 Q4
Wicken Bonhunt Essex 45 P5
Wickenby Lincs 80 B7
Wick End Bed 55 N10
Wicken Green Village Norfk 70 B6
Wickersley Rothm 78 D5
Wicker Street Green Suffk 46 H3
Wickford Essex 34 D4
Wickham Hants 13 K2
Wickham W Berk 31 J8
Wickham Bishops Essex 46 E9
Wickhambreaux Kent 35 M10
Wickhambrook Suffk 57 P9
Wickhamford Worcs 42 C3
Wickham Green Suffk 58 G7
Wickham Green W Berk 31 J8
Wickham Heath W Berk 31 J8
Wickham Market Suffk 59 L9
Wickhampton Norfk 71 N11
Wickham St Paul Essex 46 E4
Wickham Skeith Suffk 58 G7
Wickham Street Suffk 57 P10
Wickham Street Suffk 58 G7
Wickhurst Green W Susx 14 G5
Wick John o' Groats Airport Highld 151 Q6
Wicklewood Norfk 70 G11
Wickmere Norfk 70 H5
Wick St Lawrence N Som 28 E9
Wicksteed Park Nhants 55 L5
Wickstreet E Susx 15 P9
Wickwar S Glos 29 L5
Widdington Essex 45 P5
Widdop Calder 84 D8
Widdrington Nthumb 109 L10
Widdrington Station Nthumb 109 L11
Widecombe in the Moor Devon 8 D9
Widegates Cnwll 4 D5
Widemouth Bay Cnwll 7 J4
Wide Open N Tyne 100 G4
Widford Essex 46 C10
Widford Herts 45 M8
Widham Wilts 30 C5
Widley Hants 13 L3
Widmer End Bucks 32 C3
Widmerpool Notts 66 G6
Widmore Gt Lon 33 M8
Widnes Halton 75 N6
Widworthy Devon 9 N5
Wigan Wigan 75 P3
Wigborough Somset 21 P10
Wiggaton Devon 9 L6
Wiggenhall St Germans Norfk 69 L9
Wiggenhall St Mary Magdalen Norfk 69 L10
Wiggenhall St Mary the Virgin Norfk 69 L9
Wiggenhall St Peter Norfk 69 L9
Wiggens Green Essex 46 B3
Wiggenstall Staffs 77 K11
Wiggington Shrops 63 K5
Wigginton C York 86 B3
Wigginton Herts 44 D9
Wigginton Oxon 42 H5
Wigginton Staffs 65 N11
Wigginton Bottom Herts 44 D10
Wigglesworth N York 84 B4
Wiggonby Cumb 98 C7
Wiggonholt W Susx 14 F7
Wighill N York 85 P6
Wighton Norfk 70 D4
Wightwick Wolves 52 F1
Wigley Derbys 77 P9
Wigley Hants 24 E10
Wigmore Herefs 51 L7
Wigmore Medway 34 D9
Wigsley Notts 79 L9
Wigsthorpe Nhants 55 P4
Wigston Leics 54 G1
Wigston Fields Leics 66 F12
Wigston Parva Leics 54 D3
Wigthorpe Notts 78 F7
Wigtoft Lincs 68 E5
Wigton Cumb 97 Q8
Wigtown D & G 95 N7
Wigtwizzle Sheff 77 N4
Wike Leeds 85 M7
Wilbarston Nhants 55 K3
Wilberfoss E R Yk 86 D5
Wilburton Cambs 57 J6
Wilby Nhants 55 L7
Wilby Norfk 58 F3
Wilby Suffk 59 K6
Wilcot Wilts 30 D10
Wilcott Shrops 63 L8
Wilcrick Newpt 28 F5
Wilday Green Derbys 77 Q9
Wildboarclough Ches E 76 H10
Wilden Bed 56 B9
Wilden Worcs 52 F6
Wilde Street Suffk 57 N5
Wildhern Hants 24 F3
Wildhill Herts 45 J10
Wildmanbridge S Lans 114 E10
Wildmill Brdgnd 27 L6
Wildmoor Hants 25 L2
Wildmoor Worcs 52 H5
Wildsworth Lincs 79 K4
Wilford C Nott 66 F5
Wilkesley Ches E 64 B4
Wilkhaven Highld 146 G8
Wilkieston W Loth 115 L7
Wilkin's Green Herts 44 H10
Wilksby Lincs 80 F11
Willand Devon 9 K3
Willards Hill E Susx 16 C6
Willaston Ches E 64 C2
Willaston Ches W 75 K8
Willen M Keyn 44 C3
Willenhall Covtry 54 B5
